MW00784863

Toyota Corolla, Matrix & Pontiac Vibe Automotive Repair Manual

by Jeff Killingsworth

Models covered:

Toyota Corolla - 2003 through 2019
Toyota Matrix - 2003 through 2014
Pontiac Vibe - 2003 through 2010
Does not include information specific to Corolla XRS, Corolla Hatchback, Corolla IM, Matrix XRS, Vibe GT or all-wheel drive models.

Haynes UK *(92037-11Y11)*
Sparkford Nr Yeovil   AB
Somerset BA22 7JJ England

Haynes North America, Inc
859 Lawrence Drive
Newbury Park, CA 91320 USA
www.haynes.com

Acknowledgements

Wiring diagrams provided exclusively for Haynes North America, Inc. by Solution Builders and HaynesPro BV. Technical writers who contributed to this project iclude Jay Storer and Ralph Rendina, Demain Hurst and Scott "Gonzo" Weaver.

© Haynes North America, Inc. 2006, 2010, 2012, 2016, 2019

With permission from J.H. Haynes & Co. Ltd.

A book in the Haynes Automotive Repair Manual Series

Printed in India

ISBN-10: 1-62092-363-7
ISBN-13: 978-1-62092-363-4

Library of Congress Control Number: 2019947128

19-368

Contents

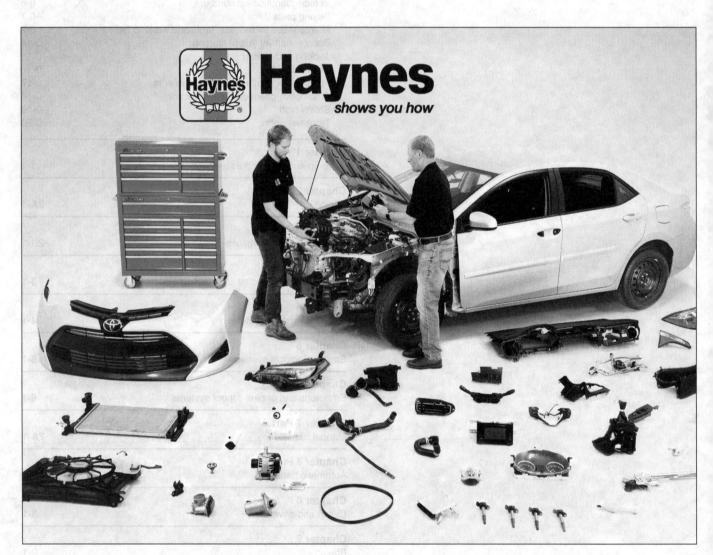

Haynes mechanic and photographer with a 2018 Toyota Corolla

About this manual

Its purpose

The purpose of this manual is to help you get the best value from your vehicle. It can do so in several ways. It can help you decide what work must be done, even if you choose to have it done by a dealer service department or a repair shop; it provides information and procedures for routine maintenance and servicing; and it offers diagnostic and repair procedures to follow when trouble occurs.

We hope you use the manual to tackle the work yourself. For many simpler jobs, doing it yourself may be quicker than arranging an appointment to get the vehicle into a shop and making the trips to leave it and pick it up. More importantly, a lot of money can be saved by avoiding the expense the shop must

pass on to you to cover its labor and overhead costs. An added benefit is the sense of satisfaction and accomplishment that you feel after doing the job yourself.

Using the manual

The manual is divided into Chapters. Each Chapter is divided into numbered Sections, which are headed in bold type between horizontal lines. Each Section consists of consecutively numbered paragraphs.

The reference numbers used in illustration captions pinpoint the pertinent Section and the Step within that Section. That is, illustration 3.2 means the illustration refers to Section 3 and Step (or paragraph) 2 within that Section.

Procedures, once described in the text, are not normally repeated. When it's necessary to refer to another Chapter, the reference will be given as Chapter and Section number. Cross references given without use of the word "Chapter" apply to Sections and/or paragraphs in the same Chapter. For example, "see Section 8" means in the same Chapter.

References to the left or right side of the vehicle assume you are sitting in the driver's seat, facing forward.

Even though we have prepared this manual with extreme care, neither the publisher nor the author can accept responsibility for any errors in, or omissions from, the information given.

NOTE

A **Note** provides information necessary to properly complete a procedure or information which will make the procedure easier to understand.

CAUTION

A **Caution** provides a special procedure or special steps which must be taken while completing the procedure where the Caution is found. Not heeding a Caution can result in damage to the assembly being worked on.

WARNING

A **Warning** provides a special procedure or special steps which must be taken while completing the procedure where the Warning is found. Not heeding a Warning can result in personal injury.

Introduction to the Toyota Corolla, Matrix and Pontiac Vibe

The Toyota Corolla, Matrix and Pontiac Vibe models covered by this manual are four-door sedans and station-wagon designs.

The transversely-mounted inline four-cylinder engine used in these vehicles is equipped with electronic fuel injection.

The engine drives the front wheels through either a five- or six-speed manual

transaxle, a four-speed automatic transaxle or a Continuously Variable Transaxle (CVT), via independent driveaxles.

Independent suspension, featuring coil spring/strut damper units, is used on the front of the vehicle. The rack-and-pinion steering unit is mounted behind the engine with power-assist on most models. The rear suspension

uses coil-over shock absorber assemblies, connected to a beam-type axle.

The brakes are disc at the front and either disc or drum-type at the rear, with power-assist standard. An Anti-lock Brake System (ABS) is available on all models, with optional Electronic Brake Distribution (EBD) for better traction and handling.

Vehicle identification numbers

Modifications are a continuing and unpublicized process in vehicle manufacturing. Since spare parts manuals and lists are compiled on a numerical basis, the individual vehicle numbers are essential to correctly identify the component required.

Vehicle Identification Number (VIN)

This very important identification number is stamped on the firewall in the engine compartment, on a plate attached to the dashboard inside the windshield on the driver's side of the vehicle and, on some models, on the Vehicle Safety Certification label in the driver's door opening (see illustration). The VIN also appears on the Vehicle Certificate of Title and Registration. It contains information such as where and when the vehicle was manufactured, the model year and the body style.

Manufacturer's Certification Regulation label

The manufacturer's Certification Regula-

tion label is attached to the driver's side door end or post. The plate contains the name of the manufacturer, the month and year of production, the Gross Vehicle Weight Rating (GVWR), the Gross Axle Weight Rating (GAWR) and the certification statement (see illustration).

Engine and transaxle identification numbers

The engine code number can be found on a pad on the rear side of the block (see illustration) on early models or the front side of the engine block on later models (see illustration). The transaxle identification number is located on a plate attached to the top of the transaxle case (see illustration), or stamped on the transaxle housing.

VIN model year codes

One particularly important piece of information found within the VIN is the model year code. Counting from the left, the model year code designation is the 10th character in the VIN.

On all models covered by this manual, the model year codes are:

3	2003
4	2004
5	2005
6	2006
7	2007
8	2008
9	2009
A	2010
B	2011
C	2012
D	2013
E	2014
F	2015
G	2016
H	2017
J	2018
K	2019

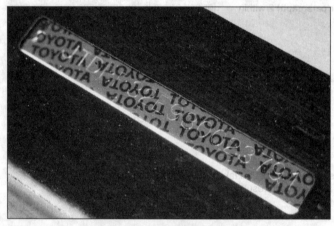

The Vehicle Identification Number (VIN) is visible through the driver's side of the windshield

Manufacturer's Certification Regulation label

Location of the engine identification number early models (1ZZ-FE shown)

Location of the engine identification number later models (2ZR-FE shown, alternator removed for clarity)

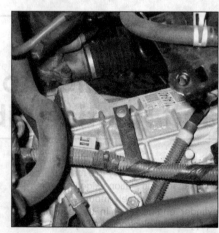

Location of the transaxle identification number

Buying parts

Replacement parts are available from many sources. Our advice concerning them is as follows::

Retail auto parts stores: Good auto parts stores will stock frequently needed components which wear out relatively fast, such as clutch components, exhaust systems, brake parts, tune-up parts, etc. These stores often supply new or reconditioned parts on an exchange basis, which can save a considerable amount of money. Discount auto parts stores are often very good places to buy materials and parts needed for general vehicle maintenance such as oil, grease, filters, spark plugs, belts, touch-up paint, bulbs, etc. They also usually sell tools and general accessories, have convenient hours, charge lower prices and can give you knowledgeable answers to your questions. To be sure of obtaining the correct parts, have engine and chassis numbers available and, if possible, take the old parts along for positive identification.

Authorized dealer parts department: This is the best source for parts which are unique to the vehicle and not generally available elsewhere. Prices for most parts tend to be higher than at retail auto parts stores.

Auto recyclers or salvage yards: Auto recyclers and salvage yards are good sources for components that are specific to the vehicle and not subject to wear, such as fenders, bumpers, trim pieces, etc. You can expect substantial savings by going this route, and self-service salvage yards offer still more savings if you're willing to bring your own tools and pull the part(s) yourself.

Warranty information: If the vehicle is still covered under warranty, be sure that any replacement parts purchased - regardless of the source - do not invalidate the warranty! In most cases, replacement parts, even from aftermarket suppliers, are designed to meet manufacturer specifications. If in doubt, check with the parts supplier.

Because of a Federally mandated extended warranty that covers the emissions control system components, check with your dealer about warranty coverage before working on any emissions-related systems.

To be sure of obtaining the correct parts, have engine and chassis numbers available and, if possible, take the old parts along for positive identification.

Maintenance techniques, tools and working facilities

Maintenance techniques

There are a number of techniques involved in maintenance and repair that will be referred to throughout this manual. Application of these techniques will enable the home mechanic to be more efficient, better organized and capable of performing the various tasks properly, which will ensure that the repair job is thorough and complete.

Fasteners

Fasteners are nuts, bolts, studs and screws used to hold two or more parts together. There are a few things to keep in mind when working with fasteners. Almost all of them use a locking device of some type, either a lockwasher, locknut, locking tab or thread adhesive. All threaded fasteners should be clean and straight, with undamaged threads and undamaged corners on the hex head where the wrench fits. Develop the habit of replacing all damaged nuts and bolts with new ones. Special locknuts with nylon or fiber inserts can only be used once. If they are removed, they lose their locking ability and must be replaced with new ones.

Rusted nuts and bolts should be treated with a penetrating fluid to ease removal and prevent breakage. Some mechanics use turpentine in a spout-type oil can, which works quite well. After applying the rust penetrant, let it work for a few minutes before trying to loosen the nut or bolt. Badly rusted fasteners may have to be chiseled or sawed off or removed with a special nut breaker, available at tool stores.

If a bolt or stud breaks off in an assembly, it can be drilled and removed with a special tool commonly available for this purpose. Most automotive machine shops can perform this task, as well as other repair procedures, such as the repair of threaded holes that have been stripped out.

Flat washers and lockwashers, when removed from an assembly, should always be replaced exactly as removed. Replace any damaged washers with new ones. Never use a lockwasher on any soft metal surface (such as aluminum), thin sheet metal or plastic.

Fastener sizes

For a number of reasons, automobile manufacturers are making wider and wider use of metric fasteners. Therefore, it is important to be able to tell the difference between standard (sometimes called U.S. or SAE) and metric hardware, since they cannot be interchanged.

All bolts, whether standard or metric, are sized according to diameter, thread pitch and length. For example, a standard 1/2 - 13 x 1 bolt is 1/2 inch in diameter, has 13 threads per inch and is 1 inch long. An M12 - 1.75 x 25 metric bolt is 12 mm in diameter, has a thread pitch of 1.75 mm (the distance between threads) and is 25 mm long. The two bolts are nearly identical, and easily confused, but they are not interchangeable.

In addition to the differences in diameter, thread pitch and length, metric and standard bolts can also be distinguished by examining the bolt heads. To begin with, the distance across the flats on a standard bolt head is measured in inches, while the same dimension on a metric bolt is sized in millimeters (the same is true for nuts). As a result, a standard wrench should not be used on a metric bolt and a metric wrench should not be used on a standard bolt. Also, most standard bolts have slashes radiating out from the center of the head to denote the grade or strength of the bolt, which is an indication of the amount of torque that can be applied to it. The greater the number of slashes, the greater the strength of the bolt. Grades 0 through 5 are commonly used on automobiles. Metric bolts have a property class (grade) number, rather than a slash, molded into their heads to indicate bolt strength. In this case, the higher the number, the stronger the bolt. Property class numbers 8.8, 9.8 and 10.9 are commonly used on automobiles.

Strength markings can also be used to distinguish standard hex nuts from metric hex nuts. Many standard nuts have dots stamped into one side, while metric nuts are marked with a number. The greater the number of dots, or the higher the number, the greater the strength of the nut.

Metric studs are also marked on their ends according to property class (grade). Larger studs are numbered (the same as metric bolts), while smaller studs carry a geometric code to denote grade.

It should be noted that many fasteners, especially Grades 0 through 2, have no distinguishing marks on them. When such is the case, the only way to determine whether it is standard or metric is to measure the thread pitch or compare it to a known fastener of the same size.

Standard fasteners are often referred to as SAE, as opposed to metric. However, it should be noted that SAE technically refers to a non-metric fine thread fastener only. Coarse thread non-metric fasteners are referred to as USS sizes.

Since fasteners of the same size (both standard and metric) may have different strength ratings, be sure to reinstall any bolts, studs or nuts removed from your vehicle in their original locations. Also, when replacing a fastener with a new one, make sure that the new one has a strength rating equal to or greater than the original.

Tightening sequences and procedures

Most threaded fasteners should be tightened to a specific torque value (torque is the twisting force applied to a threaded component such as a nut or bolt). Overtightening the fastener can weaken it and cause it to break, while undertightening can cause it to eventually come loose. Bolts, screws and studs, depending on the material they are made of and their

thread diameters, have specific torque values, many of which are noted in the Specifications at the beginning of each Chapter. Be sure to follow the torque recommendations closely. For fasteners not assigned a specific torque, a general torque value chart is presented here as a guide. These torque values are for dry (unlubricated) fasteners threaded into steel or cast iron (not aluminum). As was previously mentioned, the size and grade of a fastener determine the amount of torque that can safely be applied to it. The figures listed here are approximate for Grade 2 and Grade 3 fasteners. Higher grades can tolerate higher torque values.

Fasteners laid out in a pattern, such as cylinder head bolts, oil pan bolts, differential cover bolts, etc., must be loosened or tightened in sequence to avoid warping the component. This sequence will normally be shown in the appropriate Chapter. If a specific pattern is not given, the following procedures can be used to prevent warping.

Initially, the bolts or nuts should be assembled finger-tight only. Next, they should be tightened one full turn each, in a criss-cross or diagonal pattern. After each one has been tightened one full turn, return to the first one and tighten them all one-half turn, following the same pattern. Finally, tighten each of them one-quarter turn at a time until each fastener has been tightened to the proper torque. To loosen and remove the fasteners, the procedure would be reversed.

Component disassembly

Component disassembly should be done with care and purpose to help ensure that the parts go back together properly. Always keep track of the sequence in which parts are removed. Make note of special characteristics or marks on parts that can be installed more than one way, such as a grooved thrust washer on a shaft. It is a good idea to lay the disassembled parts out on a clean surface in

Grade 1 or 2   Grade 5   Grade 8

Bolt strength marking (standard/SAE/USS; bottom - metric)

Grade	Identification
Hex Nut Grade 5	3 Dots
Hex Nut Grade 8	6 Dots

Standard hex nut strength markings

Grade	Identification
Hex Nut Property Class 9	Arabic 9
Hex Nut Property Class 10	Arabic 10

Metric hex nut strength markings

Class 10.9   Class 9.8   Class 8.8

Metric stud strength markings

the order that they were removed. It may also be helpful to make sketches or take instant photos of components before removal.

When removing fasteners from a component, keep track of their locations. Sometimes threading a bolt back in a part, or putting the washers and nut back on a stud, can prevent mix-ups later. If nuts and bolts cannot be returned to their original locations, they should be kept in a compartmented box or a series of small boxes. A cupcake or muffin tin is ideal for this purpose, since each cavity can hold the bolts and nuts from a particular area (i.e. oil pan bolts, valve cover bolts, engine mount bolts, etc.). A pan of this type is especially helpful when working on assemblies with very small parts, such as the carburetor, alternator, valve train or interior dash and trim pieces. The cavities can be marked with paint or tape to identify the contents.

Whenever wiring looms, harnesses or connectors are separated, it is a good idea to identify the two halves with numbered pieces of masking tape so they can be easily reconnected.

Gasket sealing surfaces

Throughout any vehicle, gaskets are used to seal the mating surfaces between two parts and keep lubricants, fluids, vacuum or pressure contained in an assembly.

Metric thread sizes	Ft-lbs	Nm
M-6	6 to 9	9 to 12
M-8	14 to 21	19 to 28
M-10	28 to 40	38 to 54
M-12	50 to 71	68 to 96
M-14	80 to 140	109 to 154

Pipe thread sizes		
1/8	5 to 8	7 to 10
1/4	12 to 18	17 to 24
3/8	22 to 33	30 to 44
1/2	25 to 35	34 to 47

U.S. thread sizes		
1/4 - 20	6 to 9	9 to 12
5/16 - 18	12 to 18	17 to 24
5/16 - 24	14 to 20	19 to 27
3/8 - 16	22 to 32	30 to 43
3/8 - 24	27 to 38	37 to 51
7/16 - 14	40 to 55	55 to 74
7/16 - 20	40 to 60	55 to 81
1/2 - 13	55 to 80	75 to 108

Standard (SAE and USS) bolt dimensions/grade marks

G   Grade marks (bolt strength)
L   Length (in inches)
T   Thread pitch (number of threads per inch)
D   Nominal diameter (in inches)

Metric bolt dimensions/grade marks

P   Property class (bolt strength)
L   Length (in millimeters)
T   Thread pitch (distance between threads in millimeters)
D   Diameter

Micrometer set

Dial indicator set

Many times these gaskets are coated with a liquid or paste-type gasket sealing compound before assembly. Age, heat and pressure can sometimes cause the two parts to stick together so tightly that they are very difficult to separate. Often, the assembly can be loosened by striking it with a soft-face hammer near the mating surfaces. A regular hammer can be used if a block of wood is placed between the hammer and the part. Do not hammer on cast parts or parts that could be easily damaged. With any particularly stubborn part, always recheck to make sure that every fastener has been removed.

Avoid using a screwdriver or bar to pry apart an assembly, as they can easily mar the gasket sealing surfaces of the parts, which must remain smooth. If prying is absolutely necessary, use an old broom handle, but keep in mind that extra clean up will be necessary if the wood splinters.

After the parts are separated, the old gasket must be carefully scraped off and the gasket surfaces cleaned. Stubborn gasket material can be soaked with rust penetrant or treated with a special chemical to soften it so it can be easily scraped off. **Caution:** *Never use gasket removal solutions or caustic chemicals on plastic or other composite components.* A scraper can be fashioned from a piece of copper tubing by flattening and sharpening one end. Copper is recommended because it is usually softer than the surfaces to be scraped, which reduces the chance of gouging the part. Some gaskets can be removed with a wire brush, but regardless of the method used, the mating surfaces must be left clean and smooth. If for some reason the gasket surface is gouged, then a gasket sealer thick enough to fill scratches will have to be used during reassembly of the components. For most applications, a non-drying (or semi-drying) gasket sealer should be used.

Hose removal tips

Warning: *If the vehicle is equipped with air conditioning, do not disconnect any of the A/C*

hoses without first having the system depressurized by a dealer service department or a service station.

Hose removal precautions closely parallel gasket removal precautions. Avoid scratching or gouging the surface that the hose mates against or the connection may leak. This is especially true for radiator hoses. Because of various chemical reactions, the rubber in hoses can bond itself to the metal spigot that the hose fits over. To remove a hose, first loosen the hose clamps that secure it to the spigot. Then, with slip-joint pliers, grab the hose at the clamp and rotate it around the spigot. Work it back and forth until it is completely free, then pull it off. Silicone or other lubricants will ease removal if they can be applied between the hose and the outside of the spigot. Apply the same lubricant to the inside of the hose and the outside of the spigot to simplify installation.

As a last resort (and if the hose is to be replaced with a new one anyway), the rubber can be slit with a knife and the hose peeled from the spigot. If this must be done, be careful that the metal connection is not damaged.

If a hose clamp is broken or damaged, do not reuse it. Wire-type clamps usually weaken with age, so it is a good idea to replace them with screw-type clamps whenever a hose is removed.

Tools

A selection of good tools is a basic requirement for anyone who plans to maintain and repair his or her own vehicle. For the owner who has few tools, the initial investment might seem high, but when compared to the spiraling costs of professional auto maintenance and repair, it is a wise one.

To help the owner decide which tools are needed to perform the tasks detailed in this manual, the following tool lists are offered: *Maintenance and minor repair, Repair/overhaul* and *Special.*

The newcomer to practical mechanics should start off with the *maintenance and minor repair* tool kit, which is adequate for the simpler jobs performed on a vehicle. Then, as

confidence and experience grow, the owner can tackle more difficult tasks, buying additional tools as they are needed. Eventually the basic kit will be expanded into the *repair and overhaul* tool set. Over a period of time, the experienced do-it-yourselfer will assemble a tool set complete enough for most repair and overhaul procedures and will add tools from the special category when it is felt that the expense is justified by the frequency of use.

Maintenance and minor repair tool kit

The tools in this list should be considered the minimum required for performance of routine maintenance, servicing and minor repair work. We recommend the purchase of combination wrenches (box-end and open-end combined in one wrench). While more expensive than open end wrenches, they offer the advantages of both types of wrench.

*Combination wrench set
    (1/4-inch to 1 inch or 6 mm to 19 mm)
Adjustable wrench, 8 inch
Spark plug wrench with rubber insert
Spark plug gap adjusting tool
Feeler gauge set
Brake bleeder wrench
Standard screwdriver
    (5/16-inch x 6 inch)
Phillips screwdriver (No. 2 x 6 inch)
Combination pliers - 6 inch
Hacksaw and assortment of blades
Tire pressure gauge
Grease gun
Oil can
Fine emery cloth
Wire brush
Battery post and cable cleaning tool
Oil filter wrench
Funnel (medium size)
Safety goggles
Jackstands (2)
Drain pan*

Note: *If basic tune-ups are going to be part of routine maintenance, it will be necessary to purchase a good quality stroboscopic timing light and combination tachometer/dwell*

Dial caliper

Hand-operated vacuum pump

Fuel pressure gauge set

Trouble code reader

**Compression gauge with
spark plug hole adapter**

Cooling system pressure tester

Damper/steering wheel puller

Balljoint separator

General purpose puller

Hydraulic lifter removal tool

Valve spring compressor

Valve spring compressor

Ridge reamer

Piston ring groove cleaning tool

Ring removal/installation tool

Ring compressor

Cylinder hone

Brake hold-down spring tool

Torque angle gauge

Clutch plate alignment tool

Tap and die set

meter. Although they are included in the list of special tools, it is mentioned here because they are absolutely necessary for tuning most vehicles properly.

Repair and overhaul tool set

These tools are essential for anyone who plans to perform major repairs and are in addition to those in the maintenance and minor repair tool kit. Included is a comprehensive set of sockets which, though expensive, are invaluable because of their versatility, especially when various extensions and drives are available. We recommend the 1/2-inch drive over the 3/8-inch drive. Although the larger drive is bulky and more expensive, it has the capacity

of accepting a very wide range of large sockets. Ideally, however, the mechanic should have a 3/8-inch drive set and a 1/2-inch drive set.

> *Socket set(s)*
> *Reversible ratchet*
> *Extension - 10 inch*
> *Universal joint*
> *Torque wrench*
>   *(same size drive as sockets)*
> *Ball peen hammer - 8 ounce*
> *Soft-face hammer (plastic/rubber)*
> *Standard screwdriver (1/4-inch x 6 inch)*
> *Standard screwdriver*
>   *(stubby - 5/16-inch)*
> *Phillips screwdriver (No. 3 x 8 inch)*

> *Phillips screwdriver (stubby - No. 2)*
> *Pliers - vise grip*
> *Pliers - lineman's*
> *Pliers - needle nose*
> *Pliers - snap-ring (internal and external)*
> *Cold chisel - 1/2-inch*
> *Scribe*
> *Scraper (made from flattened*
>   *copper tubing)*
> *Centerpunch*
> *Pin punches (1/16, 1/8, 3/16-inch)*
> *Steel rule/straightedge - 12 inch*
> *Allen wrench set (1/8 to 3/8-inch or*
>   *4 mm to 10 mm)*
> *A selection of files*

Wire brush (large)
Jackstands (second set)
Jack (scissor or hydraulic type)

Note: *Another tool which is often useful is an electric drill with a chuck capacity of 3/8-inch and a set of good quality drill bits.*

Special tools

The tools in this list include those which are not used regularly, are expensive to buy, or which need to be used in accordance with their manufacturer's instructions. Unless these tools will be used frequently, it is not very economical to purchase many of them. A consideration would be to split the cost and use between yourself and a friend or friends. In addition, most of these tools can be obtained from a tool rental shop on a temporary basis.

This list primarily contains only those tools and instruments widely available to the public, and not those special tools produced by the vehicle manufacturer for distribution to dealer service departments. Occasionally, references to the manufacturer's special tools are included in the text of this manual. Generally, an alternative method of doing the job without the special tool is offered. However, sometimes there is no alternative to their use. Where this is the case, and the tool cannot be purchased or borrowed, the work should be turned over to the dealer service department or an automotive repair shop.

Valve spring compressor
Piston ring groove cleaning tool
Piston ring compressor
Piston ring installation tool
Cylinder compression gauge
Cylinder ridge reamer
Cylinder surfacing hone
Cylinder bore gauge
Micrometers and/or dial calipers
Hydraulic lifter removal tool
Balljoint separator
Universal-type puller
Impact screwdriver
Dial indicator set
Stroboscopic timing light
    (inductive pick-up)
Hand operated vacuum/pressure pump
Tachometer/dwell meter
Universal electrical multimeter
Cable hoist
Brake spring removal and
    installation tools
Floor jack

Buying tools

For the do-it-yourselfer who is just starting to get involved in vehicle maintenance and repair, there are a number of options available when purchasing tools. If maintenance and minor repair is the extent of the work to be done, the purchase of individual tools is satisfactory. If, on the other hand, extensive work is planned, it would be a good idea to purchase a modest tool set from one of the large retail chain stores. A set can usually be bought at

a substantial savings over the individual tool prices, and they often come with a tool box. As additional tools are needed, add-on sets, individual tools and a larger tool box can be purchased to expand the tool selection. Building a tool set gradually allows the cost of the tools to be spread over a longer period of time and gives the mechanic the freedom to choose only those tools that will actually be used.

Tool stores will often be the only source of some of the special tools that are needed, but regardless of where tools are bought, try to avoid cheap ones, especially when buying screwdrivers and sockets, because they won't last very long. The expense involved in replacing cheap tools will eventually be greater than the initial cost of quality tools.

Care and maintenance of tools

Good tools are expensive, so it makes sense to treat them with respect. Keep them clean and in usable condition and store them properly when not in use. Always wipe off any dirt, grease or metal chips before putting them away. Never leave tools lying around in the work area. Upon completion of a job, always check closely under the hood for tools that may have been left there so they won't get lost during a test drive.

Some tools, such as screwdrivers, pliers, wrenches and sockets, can be hung on a panel mounted on the garage or workshop wall, while others should be kept in a tool box or tray. Measuring instruments, gauges, meters, etc. must be carefully stored where they cannot be damaged by weather or impact from other tools.

When tools are used with care and stored properly, they will last a very long time. Even with the best of care, though, tools will wear out if used frequently. When a tool is damaged or worn out, replace it. Subsequent jobs will be safer and more enjoyable if you do.

How to repair damaged threads

Sometimes, the internal threads of a nut or bolt hole can become stripped, usually from overtightening. Stripping threads is an all-too-common occurrence, especially when working with aluminum parts, because aluminum is so soft that it easily strips out.

Usually, external or internal threads are only partially stripped. After they've been cleaned up with a tap or die, they'll still work. Sometimes, however, threads are badly damaged. When this happens, you've got three choices:

1) *Drill and tap the hole to the next suitable oversize and install a larger diameter bolt, screw or stud.*
2) *Drill and tap the hole to accept a threaded plug, then drill and tap the plug to the original screw size. You can also buy a plug already threaded to the original size. Then you simply drill a hole to the specified size, then run the threaded*

plug into the hole with a bolt and jam nut. Once the plug is fully seated, remove the jam nut and bolt.
3) *The third method uses a patented thread repair kit like Heli-Coil or Slimsert. These easy-to-use kits are designed to repair damaged threads in straight-through holes and blind holes. Both are available as kits which can handle a variety of sizes and thread patterns. Drill the hole, then tap it with the special included tap. Install the Heli-Coil and the hole is back to its original diameter and thread pitch.*

Regardless of which method you use, be sure to proceed calmly and carefully. A little impatience or carelessness during one of these relatively simple procedures can ruin your whole day's work and cost you a bundle if you wreck an expensive part.

Working facilities

Not to be overlooked when discussing tools is the workshop. If anything more than routine maintenance is to be carried out, some sort of suitable work area is essential.

It is understood, and appreciated, that many home mechanics do not have a good workshop or garage available, and end up removing an engine or doing major repairs outside. It is recommended, however, that the overhaul or repair be completed under the cover of a roof.

A clean, flat workbench or table of comfortable working height is an absolute necessity. The workbench should be equipped with a vise that has a jaw opening of at least four inches.

As mentioned previously, some clean, dry storage space is also required for tools, as well as the lubricants, fluids, cleaning solvents, etc. which soon become necessary.

Sometimes waste oil and fluids, drained from the engine or cooling system during normal maintenance or repairs, present a disposal problem. To avoid pouring them on the ground or into a sewage system, pour the used fluids into large containers, seal them with caps and take them to an authorized disposal site or recycling center. Plastic jugs, such as old antifreeze containers, are ideal for this purpose.

Always keep a supply of old newspapers and clean rags available. Old towels are excellent for mopping up spills. Many mechanics use rolls of paper towels for most work because they are readily available and disposable. To help keep the area under the vehicle clean, a large cardboard box can be cut open and flattened to protect the garage or shop floor.

Whenever working over a painted surface, such as when leaning over a fender to service something under the hood, always cover it with an old blanket or bedspread to protect the finish. Vinyl covered pads, made especially for this purpose, are available at auto parts stores.

Booster battery (jump) starting

Observe these precautions when using a booster battery to start a vehicle:

a) *Before connecting the booster battery, make sure the ignition switch is in the Off position.*
b) *Turn off the lights, heater and other electrical loads.*
c) *Your eyes should be shielded. Safety goggles are a good idea.*
d) *Make sure the booster battery is the same voltage as the dead one in the vehicle.*
e) *The two vehicles MUST NOT TOUCH each other!*
f) *Make sure the transaxle is in Neutral (manual) or Park (automatic).*
g) *If the booster battery is not a maintenance-free type, remove the vent caps and lay a cloth over the vent holes.*

Connect the red jumper cable to the positive (+) terminals of each battery **(see illustration)**.

Connect one end of the black jumper cable to the negative (-) terminal of the booster battery. The other end of this cable should be connected to a good ground on the vehicle to be started, such as a bolt or bracket on the body.

Start the engine using the booster battery, then, with the engine running at idle speed, disconnect the jumper cables in the reverse order of connection.

Make the booster battery cable connections in the numerical order shown (note that the negative cable of the booster battery is NOT attached to the negative terminal of the dead battery)

Jacking and towing

Jacking

Warning: *The jack supplied with the vehicle should only be used for changing a tire or placing jackstands under the frame. Never work under the vehicle or start the engine while this jack is being used as the only means of support.*

The vehicle should be on level ground. Place the shift lever in Park, if you have an automatic, or Reverse if you have a manual transaxle. Block the wheel diagonally opposite the wheel being changed. Set the parking brake.

Remove the spare tire and jack from stowage. Remove the wheel cover and trim ring (if so equipped) with the tapered end of the lug nut wrench by inserting and twisting the handle and then prying against the back of the wheel cover. Loosen, but do not remove, the lug nuts (one-half turn is sufficient).

Place the scissors-type jack under the side of the vehicle and adjust the jack height until it fits between the notches in the vertical rocker panel flange nearest the wheel to be changed. There is a front and rear jacking point on each side of the vehicle **(see illustration)**.

Turn the jack handle clockwise until the tire clears the ground. Remove the lug nuts and pull the wheel off. Replace it with the spare.

Install the lug nuts with the beveled edges facing in. Tighten them snugly. Don't attempt to tighten them completely until the vehicle is lowered or it could slip off the jack. Turn the jack handle counterclockwise to lower the vehicle. Remove the jack and tighten the lug nuts in a diagonal pattern.

Install the cover (and trim ring, if used) and be sure it's snapped into place all the way around.

Stow the tire, jack and wrench. Unblock the wheels.

Towing

The manufacturer does not recommend towing except with a towing dolly under the front wheels. In an emergency the vehicle can be towed a short distance with a cable or chain attached to one of the towing eyelets located under the front or rear bumpers following the precautions above. The driver must remain in the vehicle to operate the steering and brakes (remember that power steering and power brakes will not work with the engine off).

The jack fits over the rocker panel flange, between the two notches (there are two jacking points on each side of the vehicle)

Conversion factors

Length (distance)

Inches (in)	X	25.4	= Millimeters (mm)	X 0.0394	= Inches (in)
Feet (ft)	X	0.305	= Meters (m)	X 3.281	= Feet (ft)
Miles	X	1.609	= Kilometers (km)	X 0.621	= Miles

Volume (capacity)

Cubic inches (cu in; in^3)	X	16.387	= Cubic centimeters (cc; cm^3)	X 0.061	= Cubic inches (cu in; in^3)
Imperial pints (Imp pt)	X	0.568	= Liters (l)	X 1.76	= Imperial pints (Imp pt)
Imperial quarts (Imp qt)	X	1.137	= Liters (l)	X 0.88	= Imperial quarts (Imp qt)
Imperial quarts (Imp qt)	X	1.201	= US quarts (US qt)	X 0.833	= Imperial quarts (Imp qt)
US quarts (US qt)	X	0.946	= Liters (l)	X 1.057	= US quarts (US qt)
Imperial gallons (Imp gal)	X	4.546	= Liters (l)	X 0.22	= Imperial gallons (Imp gal)
Imperial gallons (Imp gal)	X	1.201	= US gallons (US gal)	X 0.833	= Imperial gallons (Imp gal)
US gallons (US gal)	X	3.785	= Liters (l)	X 0.264	= US gallons (US gal)

Mass (weight)

Ounces (oz)	X	28.35	= Grams (g)	X 0.035	= Ounces (oz)
Pounds (lb)	X	0.454	= Kilograms (kg)	X 2.205	= Pounds (lb)

Force

Ounces-force (ozf; oz)	X	0.278	= Newtons (N)	X 3.6	= Ounces-force (ozf; oz)
Pounds-force (lbf; lb)	X	4.448	= Newtons (N)	X 0.225	= Pounds-force (lbf; lb)
Newtons (N)	X	0.1	= Kilograms-force (kgf; kg)	X 9.81	= Newtons (N)

Pressure

Pounds-force per square inch (psi; lbf/in^2; lb/in^2)	X	0.070	= Kilograms-force per square centimeter (kgf/cm^2; kg/cm^2)	X 14.223	= Pounds-force per square inch (psi; lbf/in^2; lb/in^2)
Pounds-force per square inch (psi; lbf/in^2; lb/in^2)	X	0.068	= Atmospheres (atm)	X 14.696	= Pounds-force per square inch (psi; lbf/in^2; lb/in^2)
Pounds-force per square inch (psi; lbf/in^2; lb/in^2)	X	0.069	= Bars	X 14.5	= Pounds-force per square inch (psi; lbf/in^2; lb/in^2)
Pounds-force per square inch (psi; lbf/in^2; lb/in^2)	X	6.895	= Kilopascals (kPa)	X 0.145	= Pounds-force per square inch (psi; lbf/in^2; lb/in^2)
Kilopascals (kPa)	X	0.01	= Kilograms-force per square centimeter (kgf/cm^2; kg/cm^2)	X 98.1	= Kilopascals (kPa)

Torque (moment of force)

Pounds-force inches (lbf in; lb in)	X	1.152	= Kilograms-force centimeter (kgf cm; kg cm)	X 0.868	= Pounds-force inches (lbf in; lb in)
Pounds-force inches (lbf in; lb in)	X	0.113	= Newton meters (Nm)	X 8.85	= Pounds-force inches (lbf in; lb in)
Pounds-force inches (lbf in; lb in)	X	0.083	= Pounds-force feet (lbf ft; lb ft)	X 12	= Pounds-force inches (lbf in; lb in)
Pounds-force feet (lbf ft; lb ft)	X	0.138	= Kilograms-force meters (kgf m; kg m)	X 7.233	= Pounds-force feet (lbf ft; lb ft)
Pounds-force feet (lbf ft; lb ft)	X	1.356	= Newton meters (Nm)	X 0.738	= Pounds-force feet (lbf ft; lb ft)
Newton meters (Nm)	X	0.102	= Kilograms-force meters (kgf m; kg m)	X 9.804	= Newton meters (Nm)

Vacuum

Inches mercury (in. Hg)	X	3.377	= Kilopascals (kPa)	X 0.2961	= Inches mercury
Inches mercury (in. Hg)	X	25.4	= Millimeters mercury (mm Hg)	X 0.0394	= Inches mercury

Power

Horsepower (hp)	X	745.7	= Watts (W)	X 0.0013	= Horsepower (hp)

Velocity (speed)

Miles per hour (miles/hr; mph)	X	1.609	= Kilometers per hour (km/hr; kph)	X 0.621	= Miles per hour (miles/hr; mph)

Fuel consumption*

Miles per gallon, Imperial (mpg)	X	0.354	= Kilometers per liter (km/l)	X 2.825	= Miles per gallon, Imperial (mpg)
Miles per gallon, US (mpg)	X	0.425	= Kilometers per liter (km/l)	X 2.352	= Miles per gallon, US (mpg)

Temperature

Degrees Fahrenheit = (°C x 1.8) + 32   Degrees Celsius (Degrees Centigrade; °C) = (°F - 32) x 0.56

It is common practice to convert from miles per gallon (mpg) to liters/100 kilometers (l/100km), where mpg (Imperial) x l/100 km = 282 and mpg (US) x l/100 km = 235

DECIMALS to MILLIMETERS

Decimal	mm	Decimal	mm
0.001	0.0254	0.500	12.7000
0.002	0.0508	0.510	12.9540
0.003	0.0762	0.520	13.2080
0.004	0.1016	0.530	13.4620
0.005	0.1270	0.540	13.7160
0.006	0.1524	0.550	13.9700
0.007	0.1778	0.560	14.2240
0.008	0.2032	0.570	14.4780
0.009	0.2286	0.580	14.7320
		0.590	14.9860
0.010	0.2540		
0.020	0.5080		
0.030	0.7620		
0.040	1.0160	0.600	15.2400
0.050	1.2700	0.610	15.4940
0.060	1.5240	0.620	15.7480
0.070	1.7780	0.630	16.0020
0.080	2.0320	0.640	16.2560
0.090	2.2860	0.650	16.5100
		0.660	16.7640
0.100	2.5400	0.670	17.0180
0.110	2.7940	0.680	17.2720
0.120	3.0480	0.690	17.5260
0.130	3.3020		
0.140	3.5560		
0.150	3.8100		
0.160	4.0640	0.700	17.7800
0.170	4.3180	0.710	18.0340
0.180	4.5720	0.720	18.2880
0.190	4.8260	0.730	18.5420
		0.740	18.7960
0.200	5.0800	0.750	19.0500
0.210	5.3340	0.760	19.3040
0.220	5.5880	0.770	19.5580
0.230	5.8420	0.780	19.8120
0.240	6.0960	0.790	20.0660
0.250	6.3500		
0.260	6.6040		
0.270	6.8580	0.800	20.3200
0.280	7.1120	0.810	20.5740
0.290	7.3660	0.820	21.8280
		0.830	21.0820
0.300	7.6200	0.840	21.3360
0.310	7.8740	0.850	21.5900
0.320	8.1280	0.860	21.8440
0.330	8.3820	0.870	22.0980
0.340	8.6360	0.880	22.3520
0.350	8.8900	0.890	22.6060
0.360	9.1440		
0.370	9.3980		
0.380	9.6520		
0.390	9.9060		
0.400	10.1600	0.900	22.8600
0.410	10.4140	0.910	23.1140
0.420	10.6680	0.920	23.3680
0.430	10.9220	0.930	23.6220
0.440	11.1760	0.940	23.8760
0.450	11.4300	0.950	24.1300
0.460	11.6840	0.960	24.3840
0.470	11.9380	0.970	24.6380
0.480	12.1920	0.980	24.8920
0.490	12.4460	0.990	25.1460
		1.000	25.4000

FRACTIONS to DECIMALS to MILLIMETERS

Fraction	Decimal	mm	Fraction	Decimal	mm
1/64	0.0156	0.3969	33/64	0.5156	13.0969
1/32	0.0312	0.7938	17/32	0.5312	13.4938
3/64	0.0469	1.1906	35/64	0.5469	13.8906
1/16	0.0625	1.5875	9/16	0.5625	14.2875
5/64	0.0781	1.9844	37/64	0.5781	14.6844
3/32	0.0938	2.3812	19/32	0.5938	15.0812
7/64	0.1094	2.7781	39/64	0.6094	15.4781
1/8	0.1250	3.1750	5/8	0.6250	15.8750
9/64	0.1406	3.5719	41/64	0.6406	16.2719
5/32	0.1562	3.9688	21/32	0.6562	16.6688
11/64	0.1719	4.3656	43/64	0.6719	17.0656
3/16	0.1875	4.7625	11/16	0.6875	17.4625
13/64	0.2031	5.1594	45/64	0.7031	17.8594
7/32	0.2188	5.5562	23/32	0.7188	18.2562
15/64	0.2344	5.9531	47/64	0.7344	18.6531
1/4	0.2500	6.3500	3/4	0.7500	19.0500
17/64	0.2656	6.7469	49/64	0.7656	19.4469
9/32	0.2812	7.1438	25/32	0.7812	19.8438
19/64	0.2969	7.5406	51/64	0.7969	20.2406
5/16	0.3125	7.9375	13/16	0.8125	20.6375
21/64	0.3281	8.3344	53/64	0.8281	21.0344
11/32	0.3438	8.7312	27/32	0.8438	21.4312
23/64	0.3594	9.1281	55/64	0.8594	21.8281
3/8	0.3750	9.5250	7/8	0.8750	22.2250
25/64	0.3906	9.9219	57/64	0.8906	22.6219
13/32	0.4062	10.3188	29/32	0.9062	23.0188
27/64	0.4219	10.7156	59/64	0.9219	23.4156
7/16	0.4375	11.1125	15/16	0.9375	23.8125
29/64	0.4531	11.5094	61/64	0.9531	24.2094
15/32	0.4688	11.9062	31/32	0.9688	24.6062
31/64	0.4844	12.3031	63/64	0.9844	25.0031
1/2	0.5000	12.7000	1	1.0000	25.4000

Automotive chemicals and lubricants

A number of automotive chemicals and lubricants are available for use during vehicle maintenance and repair. They include a wide variety of products ranging from cleaning solvents and degreasers to lubricants and protective sprays for rubber, plastic and vinyl.

Cleaners

Carburetor cleaner and choke cleaner is a strong solvent for gum, varnish and carbon. Most carburetor cleaners leave a dry-type lubricant film which will not harden or gum up. Because of this film it is not recommended for use on electrical components.

Brake system cleaner is used to remove brake dust, grease and brake fluid from the brake system, where clean surfaces are absolutely necessary. It leaves no residue and often eliminates brake squeal caused by contaminants.

Electrical cleaner removes oxidation, corrosion and carbon deposits from electrical contacts, restoring full current flow. It can also be used to clean spark plugs, carburetor jets, voltage regulators and other parts where an oil-free surface is desired.

Demoisturants remove water and moisture from electrical components such as alternators, voltage regulators, electrical connectors and fuse blocks. They are non-conductive and non-corrosive.

Degreasers are heavy-duty solvents used to remove grease from the outside of the engine and from chassis components. They can be sprayed or brushed on and, depending on the type, are rinsed off either with water or solvent.

Lubricants

Motor oil is the lubricant formulated for use in engines. It normally contains a wide variety of additives to prevent corrosion and reduce foaming and wear. Motor oil comes in various weights (viscosity ratings) from 0 to 50. The recommended weight of the oil depends on the season, temperature and the demands on the engine. Light oil is used in cold climates and under light load conditions. Heavy oil is used in hot climates and where high loads are encountered. Multi-viscosity oils are designed to have characteristics of both light and heavy oils and are available in a number of weights from 0W-20 to 20W-50.

Gear oil is designed to be used in differentials, manual transmissions and other areas where high-temperature lubrication is required.

Chassis and wheel bearing grease is a heavy grease used where increased loads and friction are encountered, such as for wheel bearings, balljoints, tie-rod ends and universal joints.

High-temperature wheel bearing grease is designed to withstand the extreme temperatures encountered by wheel bearings in disc brake equipped vehicles. It usually contains molybdenum disulfide (moly), which is a dry-type lubricant.

White grease is a heavy grease for metal-to-metal applications where water is a problem. White grease stays soft under both low and high temperatures (usually from -100 to +190-degrees F), and will not wash off or dilute in the presence of water.

Assembly lube is a special extreme pressure lubricant, usually containing moly, used to lubricate high-load parts (such as main and rod bearings and cam lobes) for initial start-up of a new engine. The assembly lube lubricates the parts without being squeezed out or washed away until the engine oiling system begins to function.

Silicone lubricants are used to protect rubber, plastic, vinyl and nylon parts.

Graphite lubricants are used where oils cannot be used due to contamination problems, such as in locks. The dry graphite will lubricate metal parts while remaining uncontaminated by dirt, water, oil or acids. It is electrically conductive and will not foul electrical contacts in locks such as the ignition switch.

Moly penetrants loosen and lubricate frozen, rusted and corroded fasteners and prevent future rusting or freezing.

Heat-sink grease is a special electrically non-conductive grease that is used for mounting electronic ignition modules where it is essential that heat is transferred away from the module.

Sealants

RTV sealant is one of the most widely used gasket compounds. Made from silicone, RTV is air curing, it seals, bonds, waterproofs, fills surface irregularities, remains flexible, doesn't shrink, is relatively easy to remove, and is used as a supplementary sealer with almost all low and medium temperature gaskets.

Anaerobic sealant is much like RTV in that it can be used either to seal gaskets or to form gaskets by itself. It remains flexible, is solvent resistant and fills surface imperfections. The difference between an anaerobic sealant and an RTV-type sealant is in the curing. RTV cures when exposed to air, while an anaerobic sealant cures only in the absence of air. This means that an anaerobic sealant cures only after the assembly of parts, sealing them together.

Thread and pipe sealant is used for sealing hydraulic and pneumatic fittings and vacuum lines. It is usually made from a Teflon compound, and comes in a spray, a paint-on liquid and as a wrap-around tape.

Chemicals

Anti-seize compound prevents seizing, galling, cold welding, rust and corrosion in fasteners. High-temperature anti-seize, usually made with copper and graphite lubricants, is used for exhaust system and exhaust manifold bolts.

Anaerobic locking compounds are used to keep fasteners from vibrating or working loose and cure only after installation, in the absence of air. Medium strength locking compound is used for small nuts, bolts and screws that may be removed later. High-strength locking compound is for large nuts, bolts and studs which aren't removed on a regular basis.

Oil additives range from viscosity index improvers to chemical treatments that claim to reduce internal engine friction. It should be noted that most oil manufacturers caution against using additives with their oils.

Gas additives perform several functions, depending on their chemical makeup. They usually contain solvents that help dissolve gum and varnish that build up on carburetor, fuel injection and intake parts. They also serve to break down carbon deposits that form on the inside surfaces of the combustion chambers. Some additives contain upper cylinder lubricants for valves and piston rings, and others contain chemicals to remove condensation from the gas tank.

Miscellaneous

Brake fluid is specially formulated hydraulic fluid that can withstand the heat and pressure encountered in brake systems. Care must be taken so this fluid does not come in contact with painted surfaces or plastics. An opened container should always be resealed to prevent contamination by water or dirt.

Weatherstrip adhesive is used to bond weatherstripping around doors, windows and trunk lids. It is sometimes used to attach trim pieces.

Undercoating is a petroleum-based, tar-like substance that is designed to protect metal surfaces on the underside of the vehicle from corrosion. It also acts as a sound-deadening agent by insulating the bottom of the vehicle.

Waxes and polishes are used to help protect painted and plated surfaces from the weather. Different types of paint may require the use of different types of wax and polish. Some polishes utilize a chemical or abrasive cleaner to help remove the top layer of oxidized (dull) paint on older vehicles. In recent years many non-wax polishes that contain a wide variety of chemicals such as polymers and silicones have been introduced. These non-wax polishes are usually easier to apply and last longer than conventional waxes and polishes.

Safety first!

Regardless of how enthusiastic you may be about getting on with the job at hand, take the time to ensure that your safety is not jeopardized. A moment's lack of attention can result in an accident, as can failure to observe certain simple safety precautions. The possibility of an accident will always exist, and the following points should not be considered a comprehensive list of all dangers. Rather, they are intended to make you aware of the risks and to encourage a safety conscious approach to all work you carry out on your vehicle.

Essential DOs and DON'Ts

DON'T rely on a jack when working under the vehicle. Always use approved jackstands to support the weight of the vehicle and place them under the recommended lift or support points.

DON'T attempt to loosen extremely tight fasteners (i.e. wheel lug nuts) while the vehicle is on a jack - it may fall.

DON'T start the engine without first making sure that the transmission is in Neutral (or Park where applicable) and the parking brake is set.

DON'T remove the radiator cap from a hot cooling system - let it cool or cover it with a cloth and release the pressure gradually.

DON'T attempt to drain the engine oil until you are sure it has cooled to the point that it will not burn you.

DON'T touch any part of the engine or exhaust system until it has cooled sufficiently to avoid burns.

DON'T siphon toxic liquids such as gasoline, antifreeze and brake fluid by mouth, or allow them to remain on your skin.

DON'T inhale brake lining dust - it is potentially hazardous (see *Asbestos* below).

DON'T allow spilled oil or grease to remain on the floor - wipe it up before someone slips on it.

DON'T use loose fitting wrenches or other tools which may slip and cause injury.

DON'T push on wrenches when loosening or tightening nuts or bolts. Always try to pull the wrench toward you. If the situation calls for pushing the wrench away, push with an open hand to avoid scraped knuckles if the wrench should slip.

DON'T attempt to lift a heavy component alone - get someone to help you.

DON'T rush or take unsafe shortcuts to finish a job.

DON'T allow children or animals in or around the vehicle while you are working on it.

DO wear eye protection when using power tools such as a drill, sander, bench grinder, etc. and when working under a vehicle.

DO keep loose clothing and long hair well out of the way of moving parts.

DO make sure that any hoist used has a safe working load rating adequate for the job.

DO get someone to check on you periodically when working alone on a vehicle.

DO carry out work in a logical sequence and make sure that everything is correctly assembled and tightened.

DO keep chemicals and fluids tightly capped and out of the reach of children and pets.

DO remember that your vehicle's safety affects that of yourself and others. If in doubt on any point, get professional advice.

Steering, suspension and brakes

These systems are essential to driving safety, so make sure you have a qualified shop or individual check your work. Also, compressed suspension springs can cause injury if released suddenly - be sure to use a spring compressor.

Airbags

Airbags are explosive devices that can **CAUSE** injury if they deploy while you're working on the vehicle. Follow the manufacturer's instructions to disable the airbag whenever you're working in the vicinity of airbag components.

Asbestos

Certain friction, insulating, sealing, and other products - such as brake linings, brake bands, clutch linings, torque converters, gaskets, etc. - may contain asbestos or other hazardous friction material. Extreme care must be taken to avoid inhalation of dust from such products, since it is hazardous to health. If in doubt, assume that they do contain asbestos.

Fire

Remember at all times that gasoline is highly flammable. Never smoke or have any kind of open flame around when working on a vehicle. But the risk does not end there. A spark caused by an electrical short circuit, by two metal surfaces contacting each other, or even by static electricity built up in your body under certain conditions, can ignite gasoline vapors, which in a confined space are highly explosive. Do not, under any circumstances, use gasoline for cleaning parts. Use an approved safety solvent.

Always disconnect the battery ground (-) cable at the battery before working on any part of the fuel system or electrical system. Never risk spilling fuel on a hot engine or exhaust component. It is strongly recommended that a fire extinguisher suitable for use on fuel and electrical fires be kept handy in the garage or workshop at all times. Never try to extinguish a fuel or electrical fire with water.

Fumes

Certain fumes are highly toxic and can quickly cause unconsciousness and even death if inhaled to any extent. Gasoline vapor falls into this category, as do the vapors from some cleaning solvents. Any draining or pouring of such volatile fluids should be done in a well ventilated area.

When using cleaning fluids and solvents, read the instructions on the container carefully. Never use materials from unmarked containers. Never run the engine in an enclosed space, such as a garage. Exhaust fumes contain carbon monoxide, which is extremely poisonous. If you need to run the engine, always do so in the open air, or at least have the rear of the vehicle outside the work area.

The battery

Never create a spark or allow a bare light bulb near a battery. They normally give off a certain amount of hydrogen gas, which is highly explosive.

Always disconnect the battery ground (-) cable at the battery before working on the fuel or electrical systems.

If possible, loosen the filler caps or cover when charging the battery from an external source (this does not apply to sealed or maintenance-free batteries). Do not charge at an excessive rate or the battery may burst.

Take care when adding water to a non maintenance-free battery and when carrying a battery. The electrolyte, even when diluted, is very corrosive and should not be allowed to contact clothing or skin.

Always wear eye protection when cleaning the battery to prevent the caustic deposits from entering your eyes.

Household current

When using an electric power tool, inspection light, etc., which operates on household current, always make sure that the tool is correctly connected to its plug and that, where necessary, it is properly grounded. Do not use such items in damp conditions and, again, do not create a spark or apply excessive heat in the vicinity of fuel or fuel vapor.

Secondary ignition system voltage

A severe electric shock can result from touching certain parts of the ignition system (such as the spark plug wires) when the engine is running or being cranked, particularly if components are damp or the insulation is defective. In the case of an electronic ignition system, the secondary system voltage is much higher and could prove fatal.

Hydrofluoric acid

This extremely corrosive acid is formed when certain types of synthetic rubber, found in some O-rings, oil seals, fuel hoses, etc. are exposed to temperatures above 750-degrees F (400-degrees C). The rubber changes into a charred or sticky substance containing the acid. *Once formed, the acid remains dangerous for years. If it gets onto the skin, it may be necessary to amputate the limb concerned.*

When dealing with a vehicle which has suffered a fire, or with components salvaged from such a vehicle, wear protective gloves and discard them after use.

Troubleshooting

Contents

1   This section provides an easy reference guide to the more common problems which may occur during the operation of your vehicle. These problems and their possible causes are grouped under headings denoting various components or systems, such as Engine, Cooling system, etc. They also refer you to the chapter and/or section which deals with the problem.

2   Remember that successful troubleshooting is not a mysterious art practiced only by professional mechanics. It is simply the result of the right knowledge combined with an intelligent, systematic approach to the problem. Always work by a process of elimination, starting with the simplest solution and working through to the most complex - and never overlook the obvious. Anyone can run the gas tank dry or leave the lights on overnight, so don't assume that you are exempt from such oversights.

3   Finally, always establish a clear idea of why a problem has occurred and take steps to ensure that it doesn't happen again. If the electrical system fails because of a poor connection, check the other connections in the system to make sure that they don't fail as well. If a particular fuse continues to blow, find out why - don't just replace one fuse after another. Remember, failure of a small component can often be indicative of potential failure or incorrect functioning of a more important component or system.

Engine

1   Engine will not rotate when attempting to start

1   Battery terminal connections loose or corroded (Chapter 1).
2   Battery discharged or faulty (Chapter 1).
3   Automatic transaxle not completely engaged in Park (Chapter 7B) or clutch not completely depressed (Chapter 8).
4   Broken, loose or disconnected wiring in the starting circuit.
5   Starter motor pinion jammed in flywheel ring gear (Chapter 5).
6   Starter solenoid faulty (Chapter 5).
7   Starter motor faulty (Chapter 5).
8   Ignition switch faulty (Chapter 12).
9   Starter pinion or flywheel teeth worn or broken (Chapter 5).
10 Theft Deterrent System problem.

2   Engine rotates but will not start

1   Fuel tank empty.
2   Battery discharged (engine rotates slowly) (Chapter 5).
3   Faulty fuel pump (Chapter 4).
4   Fault in engine management system (Chapter 6).
5   Worn, faulty or incorrectly gapped spark plugs (Chapter 1).
6   Broken, loose or disconnected wires at the ignition coil(s) or faulty coil(s) (Chapter 5).
7   Faulty camshaft or crankshaft position sensor (Chapter 6).
8   Theft Deterrent System problem.

3   Engine hard to start when cold

1   Battery discharged or low (Chapter 1).
2   Malfunctioning fuel system (Chapter 4).
3   Injector(s) leaking (Chapter 4).
4   Faulty coolant temperature sensor (Chapter 6).

4   Engine hard to start when hot

1   Air filter clogged (Chapter 1).
2   Fuel not reaching the fuel injection system (Chapter 4).
3   Corroded battery connections, especially ground (Chapter 1).

5   Starter motor noisy or excessively rough in engagement

1   Pinion or flywheel gear teeth worn or broken (Chapter 5).
2   Starter motor mounting bolts loose or missing (Chapter 5).

6   Engine starts but stops immediately

1   Loose or faulty electrical connections at coil(s) or alternator (Chapter 5).
2   Faulty fuel pump (Chapter 4).
3   Vacuum leak at the gasket between the intake manifold/plenum and throttle body (Chapters 1 and 4).

7   Oil puddle under engine

1   Oil pan gasket and/or oil pan drain bolt washer leaking (Chapter 2A).
2   Oil pressure sending unit leaking (Chapter 2B).
3   Valve cover leaking (Chapter 2A).
4   Engine oil seals leaking (Chapter 2A).
5   Timing chain cover leaking (Chapter 2A).

8   Engine lopes while idling or idles erratically

1   Vacuum leakage (Chapters 2A and 4).
2   Air filter clogged (Chapter 1).
3   Fuel pump not delivering sufficient fuel to the fuel injection system (Chapter 4).
4   Leaking head gasket (Chapter 2A).

5   Timing chain and/or sprockets worn (Chapter 2A).
6   Camshaft lobes worn (Chapter 2A).

9   Engine misses at idle speed

1   Spark plugs worn or not gapped properly (Chapter 1).
2   Faulty ignition coil (Chapter 5).
3   Vacuum leaks (Chapter 1).
4   Fault in engine management system (Chapter 6).
5   Uneven or low compression (Chapter 2B).

10 Engine misses throughout driving speed range

1   Fuel filter clogged and/or impurities in the fuel system (Chapter 4).
2   Low fuel output at the injector(s) (Chapter 4).
3   Faulty or incorrectly gapped spark plugs (Chapter 1).
4   Fault in engine management system (Chapter 6).
5   Faulty emission system components (Chapter 6).
6   Low or uneven cylinder compression pressures (Chapter 2B).
7   Weak or faulty ignition system (Chapter 5).
8   Vacuum leak in fuel injection system, intake manifold/plenum, air control valve or vacuum hoses (Chapter 4).

11 Engine stumbles on acceleration

1   Spark plugs fouled (Chapter 1).
2   Fuel injection system faulty (Chapter 4).
3   Fuel filter clogged (Chapter 4).
4   Fault in engine management system (Chapter 6).
5   Intake manifold or plenum air leak (Chapters 2A and 4).

12 Engine surges while holding accelerator steady

1 Intake air leak (Chapter 4).
2 Fuel pump faulty (Chapter 4).
3 Loose fuel injector wire harness connectors (Chapter 4).
4 Defective PCM or information sensor (Chapter 6).

13 Engine stalls

1 Fuel filter clogged and/or water and impurities in the fuel system (Chapter 4).
2 Faulty emissions system components (Chapter 6).
3 Faulty or incorrectly gapped spark plugs (Chapter 1).
4 Vacuum leak in the fuel injection system, intake manifold or vacuum hoses (Chapters 2A and 4).
5 Valve clearances incorrectly set (Chapter 1).

14 Engine lacks power

1 Air filter clogged (Chapter 1).
2 Fault in engine management system (Chapter 6).
3 Fuel injection system malfunction (Chapter 4).
4 Faulty coil(s) (Chapter 5).
5 Brakes binding (Chapter 9).
6 Automatic transaxle fluid level incorrect (Chapter 7B).
7 Clutch slipping (Chapter 8).
8 Fuel filter clogged and/or impurities in the fuel system (Chapter 4).
9 Low or uneven cylinder compression pressures (Chapter 2B).
10 Obstructed exhaust system (Chapter 4).

15 Engine backfires

1 Emission control system not functioning properly (Chapter 6).
2 Fault in engine management system (Chapter 6).
3 Faulty secondary ignition system (cracked spark plug insulator, faulty ignition coil) (Chapters 1 and 5).
4 Fuel injection system malfunction (Chapter 4).
5 Vacuum leak at fuel injector(s), intake manifold, air control valve or vacuum hoses (Chapters 2A and 4).
6 Valve clearances incorrectly set and/or valves sticking (Chapter 1).

16 Pinging or knocking engine sounds during acceleration or uphill

1 Incorrect grade of fuel.
2 Fault in engine management system (Chapter 6).
3 Fuel injection system faulty (Chapter 4).
4 Improper or damaged spark plugs (Chapter 1).
5 Vacuum leak (Chapters 2A and 4).
6 Defective knock sensor (Chapter 6).

17 Engine runs with oil pressure light on

1 Low oil level (Chapter 1).
2 Idle rpm below specification (Chapter 4).
3 Short in wiring circuit (Chapter 12).
4 Faulty oil pressure sender (Chapter 2B).
5 Worn engine bearings and/or oil pump (Chapter 2A).

18 Engine diesels (continues to run) after switching off

1 Excessive engine operating temperature (Chapter 3).
2 Faulty ignition switch (Chapter 12).
3 Fault in engine management system (Chapter 12).

Engine electrical system

19 Battery will not hold a charge

1 Drivebelt or tensioner defective (Chapter 1).
2 Battery electrolyte level low (Chapter 1).
3 Battery terminals loose or corroded (Chapter 1).
4 Alternator not charging properly (Chapter 5).
5 Loose, broken or faulty wiring in the charging circuit (Chapter 5).
6 Short in vehicle wiring (Chapter 12).
7 Internally defective battery (Chapters 1 and 5).

20 Alternator light fails to go out

1 Faulty alternator or charging circuit (Chapter 5).
2 Alternator drivebelt defective or out of adjustment (Chapter 1).
3 Alternator voltage regulator inoperative (Chapter 5).

21 Alternator light fails to come on when key is turned on

1 Warning light defective.
2 Fault in the instrument cluster or wiring harness (Chapter 12).

Fuel system

22 Excessive fuel consumption

1 Dirty or clogged air filter element (Chapter 1).
2 Fault in engine management system (Chapter 6).
3 Emissions systems not functioning properly (Chapter 6).
4 Fuel injection system not functioning properly (Chapter 4).
5 Low tire pressure or incorrect tire size (Chapter 1).

23 Fuel leakage and/or fuel odor

1 Leaking fuel feed line (Chapters 1 and 4).
2 Tank overfilled.
3 Evaporative emissions canister clogged or other EVAP system problem (Chapter 6).
4 Fuel injection system not functioning properly (Chapter 4).

Cooling system

24 Overheating

1 Insufficient coolant in system (Chapter 1).
2 Water pump defective (Chapter 3).
3 Radiator core blocked or grille restricted (Chapter 3).
4 Thermostat faulty (Chapter 3).
5 Electric coolant fan blades broken or cracked (Chapter 3).
6 Radiator cap not maintaining proper pressure (Chapter 3).
7 Fault in engine management system (Chapter 6).

25 Overcooling

1 Faulty thermostat (Chapter 3).
2 Inaccurate temperature gauge sending unit (Chapter 3).

26 External coolant leakage

1   Deteriorated/damaged hoses; loose clamps.
2   Water pump defective (Chapter 3).
3   Leakage from radiator core or coolant reservoir bottle (Chapter 3).
4   Engine drain or water jacket core plugs leaking (Chapter 2A).

27 Internal coolant leakage

1   Leaking cylinder head gasket (Chapter 2A).
2   Cracked cylinder bore or cylinder head (Chapter 2A).

28 Coolant loss

1   Too much coolant in system (Chapter 1).
2   Coolant boiling away because of overheating (Chapter 3).
3   Internal or external leakage (Chapter 3).
4   Faulty radiator cap (Chapter 3).

29 Poor coolant circulation

1   Inoperative water pump (Chapter 3).
2   Restriction in cooling system (Chapters 1 and 3).
3   Drivebelt or tensioner defective (Chapter 1).
4   Thermostat sticking (Chapter 3).

Clutch

30 Pedal travels to floor - no pressure or very little resistance

1   Master or release cylinder faulty (Chapter 8).
2   Hose/pipe burst or leaking (Chapter 8).
3   Connections leaking (Chapter 8).
4   No fluid in reservoir (Chapter 8).
5   If fluid level in reservoir rises as pedal is depressed, master cylinder center valve seal is faulty (Chapter 8).
6   If there is fluid on dust seal at master cylinder, piston primary seal is leaking (Chapter 8).
7   Broken release bearing or fork (Chapter 8).

31 Fluid in area of master cylinder dust cover and on pedal

Rear seal failure in master cylinder (Chapter 8).

32 Fluid on release cylinder

Release cylinder plunger seal faulty (Chapter 8).

33 Pedal feels spongy when depressed

Air in system (Chapter 8).

34 Unable to select gears

1   Faulty transaxle (Chapter 7A).
2   Faulty clutch disc (Chapter 8).
3   Release lever and bearing not assembled properly (Chapter 8).
4   Faulty pressure plate (Chapter 8).
5   Pressure plate-to-flywheel bolts loose (Chapter 8).

35 Clutch slips (engine speed increases with no increase in vehicle speed)

1   Clutch plate worn (Chapter 8).
2   Clutch plate is oil soaked by leaking rear main seal (Chapter 8).
3   Clutch plate not seated. It may take 30 or 40 normal starts for a new one to seat.
4   Warped pressure plate or flywheel (Chapter 8).
5   Weak diaphragm spring (Chapter 8).
6   Clutch plate overheated. Allow to cool.

36 Grabbing (chattering) as clutch is engaged

1   Oil on clutch plate lining, burned or glazed facings (Chapter 8).
2   Worn or loose engine or transaxle mounts (Chapter 2A).
3   Worn splines on clutch plate hub (Chapter 8).
4   Warped pressure plate or flywheel (Chapter 8).
5   Burned or smeared resin on flywheel or pressure plate (Chapter 8).

37 Transaxle rattling (clicking)

1   Release lever loose (Chapter 8).
2   Clutch plate damper spring failure (Chapter 8).
3   Low engine idle speed (Chapter 1).

38 Noise in clutch area

1   Release fork improperly installed (Chapter 8).
2   Faulty bearing (Chapter 8).

39 Clutch pedal stays on floor

1   Clutch master cylinder piston binding in bore (Chapter 8).
2   Broken release bearing or fork (Chapter 8).

40 High pedal effort

1   Piston binding in bore (Chapter 8).
2   Pressure plate faulty (Chapter 8).
3   Incorrect size master or release cylinder (Chapter 8).

Manual transaxle

41 Knocking noise at low speeds

1   Worn driveaxle constant velocity (CV) joints (Chapter 8).
2   Worn side gear shaft counterbore in differential case (Chapter 7A).*

42 Noise most pronounced when turning

Differential gear noise (Chapter 7A).*

43 Clunk on acceleration or deceleration

1   Loose engine or transaxle mounts (Chapter 2A).
2   Worn differential pinion shaft in case.*
3   Worn side gear shaft counterbore in differential case (Chapter 7A).*
4   Worn or damaged driveaxle inner CV joints (Chapter 8).

44 Clicking noise in turns

Worn or damaged outer CV joint (Chapter 8).

45 Vibration

1   Rough wheel bearing (Chapters 1 and 10).
2   Damaged driveaxle (Chapter 8).
3   Out of round tires (Chapter 1).
4   Tire out of balance (Chapters 1 and 10).
5   Worn CV joint (Chapter 8).

46 Noisy in neutral with engine running

1   Damaged input gear bearing (Chapter 7A).*
2   Damaged clutch release bearing (Chapter 8).

47 Noisy in one particular gear

1   Damaged or worn constant mesh gears (Chapter 7A).*
2   Damaged or worn synchronizers (Chapter 7A).*
3   Bent reverse fork (Chapter 7A).*
4   Damaged fourth speed gear or output gear (Chapter 7A).*
5   Worn or damaged reverse idler gear or idler bushing (Chapter 7A).*

48 Noisy in all gears

1   Insufficient lubricant (Chapters 1 and 7A).
2   Damaged or worn bearings (Chapter 7A).*
3   Worn or damaged input gear shaft and/or output gear shaft (Chapter 7A).*

49 Slips out of gear

1   Worn or improperly adjusted shift linkage/cable (Chapter 7A).
2   Transaxle loose on engine (Chapters 2A and 7A).
3   Shift linkage does not work freely, binds (Chapter 7A).
4   Input gear bearing retainer broken or loose (Chapter 7A).*
5   Worn shift fork (Chapter 7A).*

50 Leaks lubricant

1   Side gear shaft seals worn (Chapter 7A).

2   Excessive amount of lubricant in transaxle (Chapters 1 and 7A).
3   Loose or broken input gear shaft bearing retainer (Chapter 7A).*
4   Input gear bearing retainer O-ring and/or lip seal damaged (Chapter 7A).*

51 Locked in gear

1   Lock pin or interlock pin missing (Chapter 7A).*

Although the corrective action necessary to remedy the symptoms described is beyond the scope of this manual, the above information should be helpful in isolating the cause of the condition so that the owner can communicate clearly with a professional mechanic.

Automatic transaxle

52 Fluid leakage

1   Automatic transaxle fluid is a deep red color. Fluid leaks should not be confused with engine oil, which can easily be blown onto the transaxle by air flow.
2   To pinpoint a leak, first remove all built-up dirt and grime from the transaxle housing with degreasing agents and/or steam cleaning. Then drive the vehicle at low speeds so air flow will not blow the leak far from its source. Raise the vehicle and determine where the leak is coming from. Common areas of leakage are:
   Pan (Chapters 1 and 7B)
   Dipstick tube (Chapters 1 and 7B)
   Transaxle oil lines (Chapters 3 and 7B)
   Speed sensor (Chapter 7B)
   Differential drain plug (Chapters 1 and 8)

53 Transaxle fluid brown or has a burned smell

Transaxle fluid overheated (Chapter 1).

54 General shift mechanism problems

1   Chapter 7, Part B, (Chapter 7B) deals with checking and adjusting the shift linkage on automatic transaxles. Common problems which may be attributed to poorly adjusted linkage are:
   a) *Engine starting in gears other than Park or Neutral.*
   b) *Indicator on shifter pointing to a gear other than the one actually being used.*

   c) *Vehicle moves when in Park.*
2   Refer to Chapter 7B for the shift linkage adjustment procedure.

55 Transaxle will not downshift with accelerator pedal pressed to the floor

Problem with the transmission electronic control system (Chapter 7B).

56 Engine will start in gears other than Park or Neutral

Transmission range sensor/neutral start switch malfunctioning (Chapter 7B).

57 Transaxle slips, shifts roughly, is noisy or has no drive in forward or reverse gears

There are many probable causes for the above problems, but the home mechanic should be concerned with only one possibility - fluid level. Before taking the vehicle to a repair shop, check the level and condition of the fluid as described in Chapter 1. Correct the fluid level as necessary or change the fluid and filter if needed. If the problem persists, have a professional diagnose the cause.

Driveaxles

58 Clicking noise in turns

Worn or damaged outboard CV joint (Chapter 8).

59 Shudder or vibration during acceleration

1   Excessive toe-in (Chapter 10).
2   Incorrect spring heights.
3   Worn or damaged inboard or outboard CV joints (Chapter 8).
4   Sticking inboard CV joint assembly (Chapter 8).

60 Vibration at highway speeds

1   Out of balance front wheels and/or tires.
2   Out of round front tires.
3   Worn CV joint(s) (Chapter 8).

Brakes

61 Vehicle pulls to one side during braking

1   Incorrect tire pressures (Chapter 1).
2   Front end out of alignment (have the front end aligned).
3   Front or rear tires not matched to one another.
4   Restricted brake lines or hoses (Chapter 9).
5   Malfunctioning drum brake or caliper assembly (Chapter 9).
6   Loose suspension parts (Chapter 10).
7   Excessive wear of brake shoe or pad material or disc/drum on one side.

62 Noise (high-pitched squeal when the brakes are applied)

Disc brake pads worn out. The noise comes from the wear sensor rubbing against the disc (does not apply to all vehicles). Replace pads with new ones immediately (Chapter 9).

63 Brake roughness or chatter (pedal pulsates)

1   Excessive lateral runout (Chapter 9).
2   Uneven pad wear (Chapter 9).
3   Defective disc (Chapter 9).
4   Out-of-round drum (Chapter 9).

64 Excessive brake pedal effort required to stop vehicle

1   Malfunctioning power brake booster (Chapter 9).
2   Partial system failure (Chapter 9).
3   Excessively worn pads or shoes (Chapter 9).
4   Piston in caliper or wheel cylinder stuck or sluggish (Chapter 9).
5   Brake pads or shoes contaminated with oil or grease (Chapter 9).
6   New pads or shoes installed and not yet seated. It will take a while for the new material to seat against the disc or drum.

65 Excessive brake pedal travel

1   Partial brake system failure (Chapter 9).
2   Insufficient fluid in master cylinder (Chapters 1 and 9).
3   Air trapped in system (Chapter 9).

66 Dragging brakes

1   Incorrect adjustment of brake light switch (Chapter 9).
2   Master cylinder pistons not returning correctly (Chapter 9).
3   Restricted brake lines or hoses (Chapters 1 and 9).
4   Incorrect parking brake adjustment (Chapter 9).

67 Grabbing or uneven braking action

1   Malfunction of proportioning valve (Chapter 9).
2   Malfunction of power brake booster unit (Chapter 9).
3   Binding brake pedal mechanism (Chapter 9).

68 Brake pedal feels spongy when depressed

1   Air in hydraulic lines (Chapter 9).
2   Master cylinder mounting bolts loose (Chapter 9).
3   Master cylinder defective (Chapter 9).

69 Brake pedal travels to the floor with little resistance

1   Little or no fluid in the master cylinder reservoir caused by leaking caliper piston(s) (Chapter 9).
2   Loose, damaged or disconnected brake lines (Chapter 9).

70 Parking brake does not hold

Parking brake improperly adjusted (Chapter 9).

Suspension and steering systems

71 Vehicle pulls to one side

1   Mismatched or uneven tires (Chapter 10).
2   Broken or sagging springs (Chapter 10).
3   Wheel alignment (Chapter 10).
4   Front brake dragging (Chapter 9).

72 Abnormal or excessive tire wear

1   Wheel alignment (Chapter 10).
2   Sagging or broken springs (Chapter 10).
3   Tire out of balance (Chapter 10).
4   Worn strut or shock absorber (Chapter 10).
5   Overloaded vehicle.
6   Tires not rotated regularly.

73 Wheel makes a thumping noise

1   Blister or bump on tire (Chapter 10).
2   Improper strut or shock absorber action (Chapter 10).

74 Shimmy, shake or vibration

1   Tire or wheel out-of-balance or out-of-round (Chapter 10).
2   Loose or worn wheel bearings (Chapters 1, 8 and 10).
3   Worn tie-rod ends (Chapter 10).
4   Worn balljoints (Chapters 1 and 10).
5   Excessive wheel runout (Chapter 10).
6   Blister or bump on tire (Chapter 10).
7   Loose wheel lug nuts.

75 Hard steering

1   Lack of lubrication at balljoints, tie-rod ends and rack and pinion assembly (Chapter 10).
2   Front wheel alignment (Chapter 10).
3   Low tire pressure(s) (Chapters 1 and 10).

76 Poor returnability of steering to center

1   Worn balljoints and/or tie-rod ends (Chapter 10).
2   Binding in balljoints (Chapter 10).
3   Binding in steering column (Chapter 10).
4   Lack of lubricant in steering gear assembly (Chapter 10).
5   Front wheel alignment (Chapter 10).

77 Abnormal noise at the front end

1   Lack of lubrication at balljoints and tie-rod ends (Chapters 1 and 10).
2   Damaged strut mounting (Chapter 10).
3   Worn control arm bushings or tie-rod ends (Chapter 10).
4   Loose stabilizer bar (Chapter 10).
5   Loose wheel nuts.
6   Loose suspension bolts (Chapter 10).

78 Wander or poor steering stability

1   Mismatched or uneven tires (Chapter 10).
2   Worn balljoints or tie-rod ends (Chapters 1 and 10).
3   Worn strut assemblies (Chapter 10).
4   Loose stabilizer bar (Chapter 10).
5   Broken or sagging springs (Chapter 10).
6   Wheels out of alignment (Chapter 10).

79 Erratic steering when braking

1   Wheel bearings worn (Chapter 10).
2   Broken or sagging springs (Chapter 10).
3   Leaking wheel cylinder or caliper (Chapter 9).
4   Warped discs or drums (Chapter 9).

80 Excessive pitching and/or rolling around corners or during braking

1   Loose stabilizer bar (Chapter 10).
2   Worn strut/shock absorber or mountings (Chapter 10).
3   Broken or sagging springs (Chapter 10).
4 Overloaded vehicle.

81 Suspension bottoms

1   Overloaded vehicle.
2   Worn struts or shock absorbers (Chapter 10).

3   Incorrect, broken or sagging springs (Chapter 10).

82 Cupped tires

1   Front wheel or rear wheel alignment (Chapter 10).
2   Worn struts or shock absorbers (Chapter 10).
3   Wheel bearings worn (Chapter 10).
4   Excessive tire or wheel runout (Chapter 10).
5   Worn balljoints (Chapter 10).

83 Excessive tire wear on outside edge

1   Inflation pressures incorrect (Chapter 1).
2   Excessive speed in turns.
3   Front end alignment incorrect (excessive toe-in). Have professionally aligned.
4   Suspension arm bent (Chapter 10).

84 Excessive tire wear on inside edge

1   Inflation pressures incorrect (Chapter 1).
2   Front end alignment incorrect (toe-out). Have professionally aligned.
3   Loose or damaged steering components (Chapter 10).

85 Tire tread worn in one place

1   Tires out of balance.
2   Damaged wheel. Inspect and replace if necessary.
3   Defective tire (Chapter 1).

86 Excessive play or looseness in steering system

1   Wheel bearing(s) worn (Chapter 10).
2   Tie-rod end loose (Chapter 10).
3   Steering gear loose or worn (Chapter 10).
4   Worn or loose steering intermediate shaft (Chapter 10).

87 Rattling or clicking noise in steering gear

1   Steering gear loose (Chapter 10).
2   Steering gear defective.

Chapter 1
Tune-up and routine maintenance

Contents

Specifications

Recommended lubricants and fluids

Note: *Listed here are manufacturer recommendations at the time this manual was written. Manufacturers occasionally upgrade their fluid and lubricant specifications, so check with your local auto parts store for current recommendations.*

Engine oil
Type .... API "Certified for gasoline engines"
Viscosity .... See accompanying charts

2008 and earlier models

2009 and later models

Recommended engine oil viscosity

Recommended lubricants and fluids (continued)

Note: *Listed here are manufacturer recommendations at the time this manual was written. Manufacturers occasionally upgrade their fluid and lubricant specifications, so check with your local auto parts store for current recommendations.*

Fuel	Unleaded gasoline, 87 octane or higher
Engine coolant	Toyota Genuine Long Life Coolant or equivalent
Automatic transaxle fluid	
MU4, MU5, U245E, U250E, and U341E transaxles (Corolla, Matrix and Vibe models)	
2008 and earlier	Toyota ATF Type T-IV automatic transmission fluid
2009 and later	Toyota ATF Type ATF-WS automatic transmission fluid
K313 and K120 CVT transaxles (Corolla models)	Toyota Genuine CVT type FE fluid
Manual transaxle lubricant	
2008 and earlier	API GL-4 or GL-5 75W-90 gear oil
2009 and later	API GL-4 75W gear oil
Brake fluid	DOT 3 brake fluid
Clutch fluid	DOT 3 brake fluid
Power steering system	
All models (except Vibe models)	DEXRON III automatic transmission fluid
2007 and earlier Vibe models	GM Dexron® VI
2008 and later Vibe models	GM Power Steering Fluid or equivalent

Capacities*

Engine oil (with filter change)	
1.8L engines	
2005 and earlier models	3.9 qts
2006 and later models	4.4 qts
2.4L engines	4.0 qts
Coolant	
1.8L engines	
2008 and earlier models	6.9 qts
2009 and later models	5.8 qts
2.4L engines	6.0 qts
Transaxle (drain and refill)	
Automatic	
MU4, MU5, U245E, U250E and U341E transaxles	3.2 qts
K313 and K120 CVT transaxles	1.3 qts
Manual	
1.8L engine	2.0 qts
2.4L engine	2.6 qts

All capacities approximate. Add as necessary to bring up to appropriate level.

Ignition system

Spark plug type	
2008 and earlier models	Denso SK16R11 or NGK IFR5A11
2009 and later 1.8L models	Denso SC20HR11
2009 and later 2.4L models	Denso SK20R11 or NGK IFR6A11
Spark plug gap	0.043 inch
Firing order	1-3-4-2

FRONT OF VEHICLE

① ② ③ ④

92036-2B SPECS HAYNES

Cylinder numbering diagram

Cooling system

Thermostat rating fully open	203-degrees F

Clutch pedal

Freeplay	3/16 to 5/8 inch
Height	5.3 to 5.7 inches

Brakes

Disc brake pad thickness (minimum)	3/32 inch
Drum brake shoe lining thickness (minimum)	1/16 inch
Parking brake adjustment	6 to 9 clicks

Suspension and steering

Steering wheel freeplay limit	1.2 inches
Balljoint allowable movement	0 inches

Valve clearance (cold)

Note: *This procedure is applicable only to 2008 and earlier Corolla models and all Matrix and Vibe models equipped with the engines listed below*

1ZZ-FE engines (2008 and earlier models)	
Intake	0.006 to 0.010 inch
Exhaust	0.010 to 0.014 inch
2AZ-FE engines (2009 to 2013 models)	
Intake	0.008 to 0.011 inch
Exhaust	0.015 to 0.018 inch

Torque specifications

Ft-lbs (unless otherwise indicated)

Note: *One foot-pound (ft-lb) of torque is equivalent to 12 inch-pounds (in-lbs) of torque. Torque values below approximately 15 ft-lbs are expressed in inch-pounds, since most foot-pound torque wrenches are not accurate at these smaller values.*

Wheel lug nuts...	76
Spark plugs	
2013 and earlier 1.8L and 2.4L engines..	18
2014 and later 1.8L engines..	15
Seat bolts/nuts..	27
Drivebelt tensioner	
2008 and earlier 1.8L (1ZZ-FE) engines	
Nut (To cylinder head)...	21
Bolt (To block)...	51
2009 through 2013 2.4L (2AZ-FE) engines..	44
2009 and later 1.8L (2ZR-FE) engines	
Tensioner mounting and lock bolt	18
Alternator lower bolt..	32
2014 and later 1.8L (2ZR-FAE) engines	15
Engine oil pan drain plug..	27
Engine oil filter cap (2009 and later models)*	
2ZR-FE (Matrix and Vibe) engines..	18
2ZR-FE and 2ZR-FAE (Corolla) engines	156 in-lbs
Automatic transaxle pan bolts	
U245E, U250E and U341E models	
2005 and earlier models...	48 in-lbs
2006 through 2008 models..	156 in-lbs
2009 and later models..	69 in-lbs
CVT transaxle	69 in-lbs
Automatic transaxle fluid pan drain plug	
U245E, U250E and U341E models	
2008 and earlier models	156 in-lbs
2009 and later models	36
CVT transaxle	
CVT leveling (check) tube...	15 in-lbs
CVT drain (check) plug	30
CVT fill plug	36

* 2009 and later models can have two different type of oil filters, either a cartridge type that has an oil filter cap or a spin on canister-type filter.

2.2a Typical engine compartment components (engine cover removed) - 2008 and earlier 1.8L (1ZZ-FE) shown

1	Engine oil dipstick	6	Ignition coils and spark plugs	11	Battery
2	Drivebelt	7	PCV valve	12	Automatic transaxle dipstick
3	Fuse/relay block	8	Engine oil filler cap	13	Coolant reservoir
4	Windshield washer fluid reservoir	9	Brake fluid reservoir	14	Radiator cap
5	Power steering fluid reservoir	10	Air filter housing	15	Upper radiator hose

2.2b Typical engine compartment components (engine cover removed) - 2009 and later 1.8L (2ZR-FE) shown

1	Brake fluid reservoir	6	Coolant reservoir	10	Engine oil dipstick
2	Air filter housing	7	Radiator cap	11	Engine oil filler cap
3	Fuse/relay block	8	Windshield washer fluid reservoir	12	Ignition coils and spark plugs
4	Battery	9	Alternator / drivebelt / drivebelt		
5	Upper radiator hose		manual tensioner		

2.2c Typical engine compartment components (engine cover removed) - 2009 and later 2.4L (2AZ-FE) shown

1　Brake fluid reservoir
2　Air filter housing
3　Fuse/relay block
4　Battery
5　Automatic transaxle dipstick

6　Engine cover (remove for access to
　　ignition coils / spark plugs)
7　Engine oil filler cap
8　Engine oil dipstick
9　Alternator

10　Radiator cap
11　Windshield washer fluid reservoir
12　Coolant expansion tank
13　Upper radiator hose

2.2d Typical early model engine compartment underside components

1 Driveaxle boot	4 Steering gear boot	7 Radiator drain fitting
2 Automatic transaxle drain plug	5 Engine oil drain plug	8 Engine oil filter
3 Catalytic converter	6 Front suspension strut unit	9 Front disc brake caliper

2.2e Typical later model engine compartment underside components

1 Exhaust pipe	4 Front disc brake caliper	7 Automatic transaxle drain plug
2 Driveaxle boot	5 Front suspension strut unit	
3 Engine oil filter	6 Engine oil drain plug	

2.2f Typical early model rear underside components

1	Gas tank filler pipe	4	Exhaust system	7	Rear axle beam
2	Muffler	5	Gas tank		
3	Shock absorber/coil spring assembly	6	Rear brake assembly		

2.2g Typical later model rear underside components

1	Gas tank filler pipe	4	Exhaust pipe	7	Rear axle beam
2	Muffler	5	Gas tank	8	Fuel tank heat shield
3	Shock absorber/coil spring assembly	6	Rear brake assembly	9	EVAP canister

1 Maintenance schedule

The maintenance intervals in this manual are provided with the assumption that you, not the dealer, will be doing the work. These are the minimum maintenance intervals recommended by the factory for vehicles that are driven daily. If you wish to keep your vehicle in peak condition at all times, you may wish to perform some of these procedures even more often. Because frequent maintenance enhances the efficiency, performance and resale value of your car, we encourage you to do so. If you drive in dusty areas, tow a trailer, idle or drive at low speeds for extended periods or drive for short distances (less than four miles) in below freezing temperatures, shorter intervals are also recommended.

When your vehicle is new, it should be serviced by a factory authorized dealer service department to protect the factory warranty. In many cases, the initial maintenance check is done at no cost to the owner.

Every 250 miles or weekly, whichever comes first

Check the engine oil level (Section 4)
Check the engine coolant level (Section 4)
Check the windshield washer fluid level (Section 4)
Check the brake fluid level (Section 4)
Check the power steering fluid level (Section 4)
Check the automatic transaxle fluid level (Section 4)
Check the tires and tire pressures (Section 5)

Every 3000 miles or 3 months, whichever comes first

All items listed above plus:
Change the engine oil and oil filter

Every 7500 miles or 6 months, whichever comes first

All items listed above plus:
Inspect (and replace, if necessary) the windshield wiper blades (Section 7)
Check the clutch pedal for proper freeplay (Section 8)
Check and service the battery (Section 9)
Check the engine drivebelt (Section 10)
Inspect (and replace if, necessary) all underhood hoses (Section 11)
Check the cooling system (Section 12)
Rotate the tires (Section 13)
Check the seat belts (Section 14)

Every 15,000 miles or 12 months, whichever comes first

All items listed above plus:
Inspect the brake system (Section 15)*
Replace the air filter (Section 16)
Inspect the fuel system (Section 17)
Check the manual transaxle lubricant level (Section 18)
Inspect the suspension and steering components (Section 19)*
Check the driveaxle boots (Section 19)
Replace the cabin air filter (Section 20)

Every 30,000 miles or 24 months, whichever comes first

All items listed above plus:
Change the brake fluid (Section 21)
Check (and replace, if necessary) the spark plugs (Section 22)
Service the cooling system (drain, flush and refill) (Section 23)
Inspect the evaporative emissions control system (Section 24)
Inspect the exhaust system (Section 25)
Change the automatic transaxle fluid and filter and differential lubricant (Section 26)**
Change the manual transaxle lubricant (Section 26)**
Check and replace if necessary the PCV valve (Section 28)

Every 60,000 miles or 48 months, whichever comes first

All items listed above plus:
Check and adjust the valve clearances (2008 and earlier models)

* This item is affected by "severe" operating conditions as described below. If your vehicle is operated under "severe" conditions, perform all maintenance indicated with an asterisk (*) at 3000 mile/3 month intervals. Severe conditions are indicated if you mainly operate your vehicle under one or more of the following conditions:

a) *Operating in dusty areas*
b) *Towing a trailer*
c) *Idling for extended periods and/or low speed operation*
d) *Operating when outside temperatures remain below freezing and when most trips are less than 4 miles*

** If operated under one or more of the following conditions, change the manual or automatic transaxle fluid and differential lubricant every 15,000 miles:

a) *In heavy city traffic where the outside temperature regularly reaches 90-degrees F (32-degrees C) or higher*
b) *In hilly or mountainous terrain*
c) *Frequent trailer pulling*

2   Introduction

1   This chapter is designed to help the home mechanic maintain the Toyota Corolla, Matrix and Pontiac Vibe for peak performance, economy, safety and long life.

2   Included is a master maintenance schedule, followed by sections dealing specifically with each item on the schedule. Visual checks, adjustments, component replacement and other helpful items are included. Refer to the **accompanying illustrations** of the engine compartment and the underside of the vehicle for the location of various components.

3   Servicing your Corolla, Matrix or Vibe in accordance with the mileage/time maintenance schedule and the following Sections will provide it with a planned maintenance program that should result in a long and reliable service life. This is a comprehensive plan, so maintaining some items but not others at the specified service intervals will not produce the same results.

4   As you service your vehicle, you will discover that many of the procedures can - and should - be grouped together because of the nature of the particular procedure you're performing or because of the close proximity of two otherwise unrelated components to one another.

5   For example, if the vehicle is raised for any reason, you should inspect the exhaust, suspension, steering and fuel systems while you're under the vehicle. When you're rotating the tires, it makes good sense to check the brakes and wheel bearings since the wheels are already removed.

6   Finally, let's suppose you have to borrow or rent a torque wrench. Even if you only need to tighten the spark plugs, you might as well check the torque of as many critical fasteners as time allows.

7   The first step of this maintenance program is to prepare yourself before the actual work begins. Read through all sections pertinent to the procedures you're planning to do, then make a list of and gather together all the parts and tools you will need to do the job. If it looks as if you might run into problems during a particular segment of some procedure, seek advice from your local parts counterperson or dealer service department.

Owner's manual and VECI label information

8   Your vehicle owner's manual was written for your year and model and contains very specific information on component locations, specifications, fuse ratings, part numbers, etc. The owner's manual is an important resource for the do-it-yourselfer to have; if one was not supplied with your vehicle, it can generally be ordered from a dealer parts department.

9   Among other important information, the Vehicle Emissions Control Information (VECI) label contains specifications and procedures for applicable tune-up adjustments and, in some instances, spark plugs (see Chapter 6 for more information on the VECI label). The information on this label is the exact maintenance data recommended by the manufacturer. This data often varies by intended operating altitude, local emissions regulations, month of manufacture, etc.

10   This Chapter contains procedural details, safety information and more ambitious maintenance intervals than you might find in manufacturer's literature. However, you may also find procedures or specifications in your owner's manual or VECI label that differ with what's printed here. In these cases, the owner's manual or VECI label can be considered correct, since it is specific to your particular vehicle.

3   Tune-up general information

1   The term *tune-up* is used in this manual to represent a combination of individual operations rather than one specific procedure.

2   If, from the time the vehicle is new, the routine maintenance schedule is followed closely and frequent checks are made of fluid levels and high wear items, as suggested throughout this manual, the engine will be kept in relatively good running condition and the need for additional work will be minimized.

3   More likely than not, however, there will be times when the engine is running poorly due to lack of regular maintenance. This is even more likely if a used vehicle, which has not received regular and frequent maintenance checks, is purchased. In such cases, an engine tune-up will be needed outside of the regular routine maintenance intervals.

4   The first step in any tune-up or engine diagnosis to help correct a poor running engine would be a cylinder compression check. A check of the engine compression (Chapter 2B) will give valuable information regarding the overall performance of many internal components and should be used as a basis for tune-up and repair procedures. If, for instance, a compression check indicates serious internal engine wear, a conventional tune-up will not help the running condition of the engine and would be a waste of time and money.

5   The following series of operations are those most often needed to bring a generally poor running engine back into a proper state of tune.

Minor tune-up

Check all engine related fluids (Section 4)
Clean, inspect and test the battery (Section 9)
Check the drivebelt (Section 10)
Check all underhood hoses (Section 11)
Check the cooling system (Section 12)
Check the air filter (Section 16)
Replace the spark plugs (Section 22)

Major tune-up

6   All items listed under Minor tune-up, plus :
Replace the air filter (Section 16)
Check the fuel system (Section 17)
Check the charging system (Chapter 5)

4   Fluid level checks (every 250 miles or weekly)

1   Fluids are an essential part of the lubrication, cooling, brake, clutch and other systems. Because these fluids gradually become depleted and/or contaminated during normal operation of the vehicle, they must be periodically replenished. See *Recommended lubricants and fluids* and *Capacities* at the beginning of this Chapter before adding fluid to any of the following components. **Note:** *The vehicle must be on level ground before fluid levels can be checked.*

Engine oil

2   The engine oil level is checked with a dipstick located at the front of the engine **(see illustration)**. The dipstick extends through a metal tube from which it protrudes down into the engine oil pan.

3   The oil level should be checked before the vehicle has been driven, or about five minutes after the engine has been shut off. If the oil is checked immediately after driving the vehicle, some of the oil will remain in the upper engine components, producing an inaccurate reading on the dipstick.

4.2 The engine oil dipstick (A) is located at the front of the engine - the oil filler cap (B) is in the valve cover (later model shown, earlier models similar)

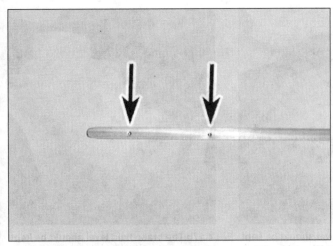

4.4 The engine oil dipstick has two dimples - keep the oil level at or near the upper dimple

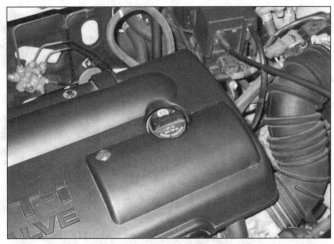

4.6 The threaded oil filler cap is located on the valve cover - always make sure the area around the opening is clean before unscrewing the cap to prevent dirt from contaminating the engine (early model shown)

4   Pull the dipstick from the tube and wipe all the oil from the end with a clean rag or paper towel. Insert the clean dipstick all the way back into its metal tube and pull it out again. Observe the oil at the end of the dipstick. At its highest point, the level should be between the two dimples **(see illustration)**.

5   It takes about one quart of oil to raise the level from the lower dimple to the upper dimple on the dipstick. Do not allow the level to drop below the lower dimple or oil starvation may cause engine damage. Conversely, overfilling the engine (adding oil above the upper dimple) may cause oil fouled spark plugs, oil leaks or oil seal failures.

6   Remove the threaded cap from the valve cover to add oil **(see illustration)**. Use a funnel to prevent spills. After adding the oil, install the filler cap hand tight. Start the engine and look carefully for any small leaks around the oil filter or drain plug. Stop the engine and check the oil level again after it has had sufficient time to drain from the upper block and cylinder head galleys.

7   Checking the oil level is an important preventive maintenance step. A continu-

ally dropping oil level indicates oil leakage through damaged seals, from loose connections, or past worn rings or valve guides. If the oil looks milky in color or has water droplets in it, a cylinder head gasket may be blown. The engine should be checked immediately. The condition of the oil should also be checked. Each time you check the oil level, slide your thumb and index finger up the dipstick before wiping off the oil. If you see small dirt or metal particles clinging to the dipstick, the oil should be changed (see Section 6).

Engine coolant

Warning: *Do not allow antifreeze to come in contact with your skin or painted surfaces of the vehicle. Flush contaminated areas immediately with plenty of water. Don't store new coolant or leave old coolant lying around where it's accessible to children or pets - they're attracted by its sweet smell and may drink it. Ingestion of even a small amount of coolant can be fatal! Wipe up garage floor and drip pan spills immediately. Keep antifreeze containers covered and repair cooling system leaks as soon as they're noticed.*

8   All vehicles covered by this manual are equipped with a pressurized coolant recovery system. A white coolant reservoir located at the right side of the radiator or at the right fender in the engine compartment and is connected by a hose to the base of the radiator filler neck **(see illustration)**. If the coolant heats up during engine operation, coolant can escape through a pressurized filler cap, then through a connecting hose into the reservoir. As the engine cools, the coolant is automatically drawn back into the cooling system to maintain the correct level.

9   The coolant level should be checked regularly. It must be between the Full and Low lines on the tank. The level will vary with the temperature of the engine. When the engine is cold, the coolant level should be at or slightly above the Low mark on the tank. Once the engine has warmed up, the level should be at or near the Full mark. If it isn't, allow the fluid in the tank to cool, then remove the cap from the reservoir and add coolant to bring the level up to the Full line. Use only the coolant listed in this Chapter's Specifications, or its equivalent. Do not use supplemental inhibitor additives. If only a small amount of coolant is required to bring the system up to the proper level, water can be used. However, repeated additions of water will dilute the recommended antifreeze and water solution. In order to maintain the proper ratio of antifreeze and water, it is advisable to top up the coolant level with the correct mixture.

10   If the coolant level drops within a short time after replenishment, there may be a leak in the system. Inspect the radiator, hoses, engine coolant filler cap, drain plugs, air bleeder plugs and water pump. If no leak is evident, have the radiator cap pressure tested by your dealer. **Warning:** *Never remove the radiator cap or the coolant recovery reservoir cap when the engine is running or has just been shut down, because the cooling system is hot. Escaping steam and scalding liquid could cause serious injury.*

4.8 The coolant reservoir is at the right side of the radiator on most models - make sure the coolant level is between the Low and Full marks on the reservoir

4.14 The windshield washer fluid reservoir is located in the right front corner of the engine compartment

4.17a The brake fluid level should be kept between the MIN and MAX marks on the translucent plastic reservoir - early model shown

4.17b The brake fluid level should be kept between the MIN and MAX marks on the translucent plastic reservoir - later model shown

11   If it is necessary to open the radiator cap, wait until the system has cooled completely, then wrap a thick cloth around the cap and turn it to the first stop. If any steam escapes, wait until the system has cooled further, then remove the cap.

12   When checking the coolant level, always note its condition. It should be relatively clear. If it is brown or rust colored, the system should be drained, flushed and refilled. Even if the coolant appears to be normal, the corrosion inhibitors wear out with use, so it must be replaced at the specified intervals.

13   Do not allow antifreeze to come in contact with your skin or painted surfaces of the vehicle. Flush contacted areas immediately with plenty of water.

Windshield washer fluid

14   Fluid for the windshield washer system is stored in a plastic reservoir which is located on the right side of the engine compartment **(see illustration)**. In milder climates, plain water can be used to top up the reservoir, but the reservoir should be kept no more than two-thirds full to allow for expansion should the water freeze. In colder climates, the use of a specially designed windshield washer fluid, available at your dealer and any auto parts store, will help lower the freezing point of the fluid. Mix the solution with water in accordance with the manufacturer's directions on the container. Do not use regular antifreeze. It will damage the vehicle's paint.

Battery electrolyte

15   On models not equipped with a sealed battery, remove the filler/vent cap and check the electrolyte level. It must be between the upper and lower levels. If the level is low, add distilled water. Install and securely retighten the cap. **Caution:** *Overfilling the cells may cause electrolyte to spill over during periods of heavy charging, causing corrosion or damage.*

Brake and clutch fluid

16   The brake master cylinder is mounted on the front of the power booster unit in the engine compartment. The clutch master cylinder on vehicles with manual transaxles is connected by a hose to the brake master cylinder.

17   To check the fluid level, simply look at the MAX and MIN marks on the reservoir **(see illustrations)**. The level should be at or near the maximum fill line.

18   If the level is low, disengage the weatherstripping and remove the reservoir cover from the cowl on 2009 and later models **(see illustration)**, then, on all models, wipe the top of the reservoir cap with a clean rag to prevent contamination of the brake or clutch system before removing the cap.

19   Add only the specified brake fluid to the reservoir (refer to *Recommended lubricants and fluids* at the front of this chapter or to your owner's manual). Mixing different types of brake fluid can damage the system.

Warning: *Use caution when filling the reservoir - brake fluid can harm your eyes and damage painted surfaces. Do not use brake fluid that has been opened for more than one year (even if the cap has been on) or has been left*

open. *Brake fluid absorbs moisture from the air. Excess moisture can cause a dangerous loss of braking.*

20   While the reservoir cap is removed, inspect the master cylinder reservoir for contamination. If deposits, dirt particles or water droplets are present, the fluid in the brake system should be changed (see Section 21 for the brake fluid replacement procedure or Chapter 9 for the clutch hydraulic system bleeding procedure).

21   After filling the reservoir to the proper level, make sure the lid is properly seated to prevent fluid leakage and/or system pressure loss.

22   The brake fluid in the master cylinder will drop slightly as the brake pads at each wheel wear down during normal operation. If the master cylinder requires repeated replenishing to keep it at the proper level, this is an indication of leakage in the brake system, which should be corrected immediately. Check all brake lines and connections, along with the calipers, wheel cylinders and booster (see Section 15 for more information).

23   If, upon checking the master cylinder fluid level, you discover the reservoir empty

4.18 To add fluid on 2009 and later models, remove the section of the cowl cover over the brake master cylinder

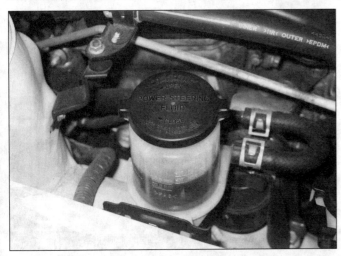

4.25 The power steering fluid reservoir is located near the right shock tower in the engine compartment

4.29 The power steering fluid level is checked by looking through the plastic reservoir

or nearly empty, the brake and clutch systems must be diagnosed immediately (see Chapter 9 and Chapter 8).

Power steering fluid

Note: *The power steering fluid level check applies to 2008 and earlier models only - 2009 and later models have electrically assisted power steering and lack a power steering fluid reservoir*

24 Unlike manual steering, the power steering system relies on fluid which may, over a period of time, require replenishing.
25 The fluid reservoir for the power steering pump is located on the passenger's side inner fender panel, just behind the windshield washer fluid reservoir **(see illustration)**.
26 For the check, the front wheels should be pointed straight ahead and the engine should be off.
27 Use a clean rag to wipe off the reservoir cap and the area around the cap. This will help prevent any foreign matter from entering the reservoir during the check.
28 Twist off the cap and check the temperature of the fluid at the end of the dipstick with your finger.
29 View the level of power steering fluid through the translucent reservoir **(see illustration)**. At no time should the fluid level drop below the upper mark for each heat range.
30 If additional fluid is required, pour the specified type directly into the reservoir, using a funnel to prevent spills.
31 If the reservoir requires frequent fluid additions, all power steering hoses, hose connections, the power steering pump and the rack and pinion assembly should be carefully checked for leaks.

Automatic transaxle fluid

32 The level of the automatic transaxle fluid should be carefully maintained. Low fluid level can lead to slipping or loss of drive, while overfilling can cause foaming, loss of fluid and transaxle damage.

U245E, U250E and U341E automatic transaxles

33 The transaxle fluid level should only be checked when the transaxle is hot (at its normal operating temperature). If the vehicle has just been driven over 10 miles (15 miles in a frigid climate), and the fluid temperature is 160 to 175-degrees F, the transaxle is hot. **Caution:** *If the vehicle has just been driven for a long time at high speed or in city traffic in hot weather, or if it has been pulling a trailer, an accurate fluid level reading cannot be obtained. Allow the fluid to cool down for about 30 minutes.*
34 If the vehicle has not just been driven, park the vehicle on level ground, set the parking brake and start the engine. While the engine is idling, depress the brake pedal and move the selector lever through all the gear ranges, beginning and ending in Park.
35 With the engine still idling, remove the dipstick from its tube **(see illustration)**. Check the level of the fluid on the dipstick **(see illustration)** and note its condition.
36 Wipe the fluid from the dipstick with a clean rag and reinsert it back into the filler tube until the cap seats.
37 Pull the dipstick out again and note the fluid level. If the transaxle is cold, the level should be in the Cold or Cool range on the dipstick. If it is hot, the fluid level should be in the Hot range. If the level is at the low side of either range, add the specified automatic transmission fluid through the dipstick tube with a funnel.
38 Add just enough of the recommended fluid to fill the transaxle to the proper level. It takes about one pint to raise the level from the low mark to the high mark when the fluid is hot, so add the fluid a little at a time and keep checking the level until it is correct.

4.35a The automatic transaxle dipstick is located in a tube which extends forward from the transaxle

4.35b If the automatic transaxle fluid is cold, the level should be between the two lower notches; if it's at operating temperature, the level should be between the two upper notches

4.41 Remove the driver's side under-vehicle splash shield

a) *Remove the screws*
b) *Remove the pushpin fasteners*
c) *Disengage the hook and remove the splash shield*

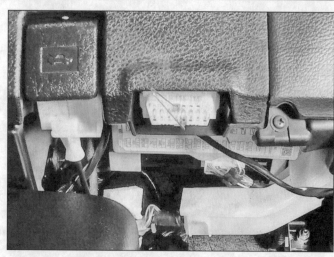

4.42 Using a paper clip, connect these terminals of the diagnostic port with the ignition switch turned off

39   The condition of the fluid should also be checked along with the level. If the fluid at the end of the dipstick is black or a dark reddish brown color, or if it emits a burned smell, the fluid should be changed (see Section 26). If you are in doubt about the condition of the fluid, purchase some new fluid and compare the two for color and smell.

CVT transaxles

Note: *It isn't necessary to check this fluid weekly - every 15,000 miles (24,000 km) or 12 months will be adequate (unless a fluid leak is noticed).*
Note: *This CVT transaxle does not have an oil filler tube or transaxle fluid dipstick - fluid is added through the refill hole in the CVT transaxle assembly*
Note: *Greater access to the transaxle is obtained with the driver's side front wheel removed*
40   Raise the vehicle and support it securely on jackstands. **Note:** *Both ends of the vehicle should be raised and evenly supported on jackstands for an accurate check.*
41   Remove the driver's side under-vehicle splash shield **(see illustration)**.
42   To properly check the fluid level on CVT transaxles, the transaxle must be placed in fluid temperature adjustment mode as follows:

a) *Using a paper clip or jumper wire, connect terminals 13 and 4 of the OBDII diagnostic port with the ignition switch off* **(see illustration)**.
b) *Make sure all the accessories and lights are off, then depress the brake pedal and start the engine. You should see an array of extra lights flash on the instrument cluster that wouldn't normally illuminate.*
c) *With the engine running, slowly shift the selector from the P to the D position, then back to Park, keeping the shifter in each position along the way for three seconds.*

d) *Now, quickly move the shift lever back and forth between N and D, while paying close attention to the "D" shift indicator on the instrument cluster. Do not pause between positions for more the 1.5 seconds. While performing this shifting pattern, it should cause the D shift indicator light to illuminate solid for two seconds, overriding the N and D indicators. When the D shift indicator light comes on, the vehicle has entered the fluid temperature detection mode - you can now shift back into Park.*

43   When shifted back into Park, you must observe the following to make sure the transaxle is at the correct temperature for checking the fluid:

The "D" indicator disappears / is off
The transaxle fluid temperature is below the desired range (below 95-degrees F) - allow the transaxle to keep warming up

The "D" indicator shows up solid
The transaxle fluid temperature is within

the desired range (95 to 113-degrees F) - the fluid level must now be checked with the engine running

The "D" indicator is blinking
The transaxle fluid temperature is too hot (above 113-degrees F) - turn the engine off, allow the transaxle to cool, then repeat Sequence A through D in Step 42

Caution: *The fluid level must be checked with the vehicle level and the engine running at idle.*
44   Locate the fluid check plug on the bottom of the oil pan, then remove the fluid check plug **(see illustration)**. If the fluid level is correct, it should only drip from the hole.
45   If the transaxle needs more fluid (if the fluid doesn't trickle out of the hole), you can use a pump to add more through the fill plug at the side of the transaxle **(see illustration)**. Stop filling the transaxle when the lubricant begins to run out the check plug hole in the transaxle pan **(see illustration)**. Allow the fluid to flow from the hole until it just drips out.

4.44 Location of the CVT transaxle fluid check plug

4.45a A hose and fluid pump can be used to add fluid through the fill plug hole . . .

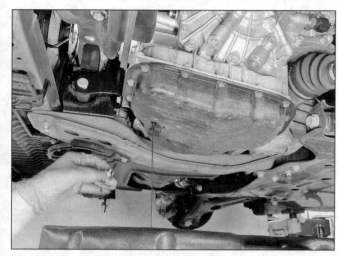

4.45b . . . allow the excess fluid to drain until just a few drops are running out of the hole

5.2 A tire tread depth indicator should be used to monitor tire wear - they are available at auto parts stores and service stations and cost very little

46   Install the plugs and tighten them to the torque listed in this Chapter's Specifications. Turn off the engine and lower the vehicle. Drive the vehicle a short distance, then check for leaks.

47   The condition of the fluid should also be checked along with the level. If the fluid is black or a dark reddish brown color, or if it emits a burned smell, the fluid should be changed (see Section 26). If you are in doubt about the condition of the fluid, purchase some new fluid and compare the two for color and smell.

5   Tire and tire pressure checks (every 250 miles or weekly)

1   Periodic inspection of the tires may spare you from the inconvenience of being stranded with a flat tire. It can also provide you with vital information regarding possible problems in the steering and suspension systems before major damage occurs.

2   Normal tread wear can be monitored with a simple, inexpensive device known as a

tread depth indicator (**see illustration**). When the tread depth reaches the specified minimum, replace the tire(s).

3   Note any abnormal tread wear (**see illustration**). Tread pattern irregularities such as cupping, flat spots and more wear on one side than the other are indications of front end alignment and/or balance problems. If any of these conditions are noted, take the vehicle to a tire shop or service station to correct the problem.

4   Look closely for cuts, punctures and

UNDERINFLATION

CUPPING

Cupping may be caused by:
- Underinflation and/or mechanical irregularities such as out-of-balance condition of wheel and/or tire, and bent or damaged wheel.
- Loose or worn steering tie-rod or steering idler arm.
- Loose, damaged or worn front suspension parts.

OVERINFLATION

INCORRECT TOE-IN OR EXTREME CAMBER

FEATHERING DUE TO MISALIGNMENT

5.3 This chart will help you determine the condition of your tires, the probable cause(s) of abnormal wear and the corrective action necessary

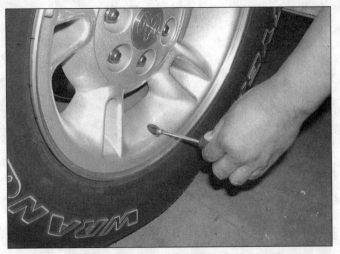

5.4a If a tire loses air on a steady basis, check the valve core first to make sure it's snug (special inexpensive wrenches are commonly available at auto parts stores)

5.4b If the valve core is tight, raise the corner of the vehicle with the low tire and spray a soapy water solution onto the tread as the tire is turned slowly - slow leaks will cause small bubbles to appear

embedded nails or tacks. Sometimes a tire will hold its air pressure for a short time or leak down very slowly even after a nail has embedded itself into the tread. If a slow leak persists, check the valve stem core to make sure it is tight **(see illustration)**. Examine the tread for an object that may have embedded itself into the tire or for a "plug" that may have begun to leak (radial tire punctures are repaired with a plug that is installed in a puncture). If a puncture is suspected, it can be easily verified by spraying a solution of soapy water onto the puncture area **(see illustration)**. The soapy solution will bubble if there is a leak. Unless the puncture is inordinately large, a tire shop or gas station can usually repair the punctured tire.

5   Carefully inspect the inner sidewall of each tire for evidence of brake fluid leakage. If you see any, inspect the brakes immediately.

6   Correct tire air pressure adds miles to the lifespan of the tires, improves mileage and enhances overall ride quality. Tire pressure cannot be accurately estimated by looking at a tire, particularly if it is a radial. A tire pressure gauge is therefore essential. Keep an accurate gauge in the glovebox. The pressure gauges fitted to the nozzles of air hoses at gas stations are often inaccurate.

7   Always check tire pressure when the tires are cold. "Cold," in this case, means the vehicle has not been driven over a mile in the three hours preceding a tire pressure check. A pressure rise of four to eight pounds is not uncommon once the tires are warm.

8   Unscrew the valve cap protruding from the wheel or hubcap and push the gauge firmly onto the valve **(see illustration)**. Note the reading on the gauge and compare this figure to the recommended tire pressure shown on the tire placard on the left door. Be sure to reinstall the valve cap to keep dirt and moisture out of the valve stem mechanism. Check all four tires and, if necessary, add enough air to bring them up to the recommended pressure levels.

5.8 To extend the life of your tires, check the air pressure at least once a week with an accurate gauge (don't forget the spare!)

9   Don't forget to keep the spare tire inflated to the specified pressure (consult your owner's manual). Note that the air pressure specified for the compact spare is significantly higher than the pressure of the regular tires.

6   Engine oil and oil filter change (every 3000 miles or 3 months)

1   Frequent oil changes are the best preventive maintenance the home mechanic can give the engine, because aging oil becomes diluted and contaminated, which leads to premature engine wear.

2   Make sure that you have all the necessary tools before you begin this procedure **(see illustration)**. You should also have plenty of rags or newspapers handy for mopping up any spills.

6.2 These tools are required when changing the engine oil and filter

1   **Drain pan** - *It should be fairly shallow in depth, but wide to prevent spills*

2   **Rubber gloves** - *When removing the drain plug and filter, you will get oil on your hands (the gloves will prevent burns)*

3   **Breaker bar** - *Sometimes the oil drain plug is tight, and a long breaker bar is needed to loosen it*

4   **Socket** – *To be used with the breaker bar or a ratchet (must be the correct size to fit the drain plug - six-point preferred)*

5   **Filter wrench** - *This is a metal band-type wrench, which requires clearance around the filter to be effective*

6   **Filter wrench** - *This type fits on the bottom of the filter and can be turned with a ratchet or breaker bar (different-size wrenches are available for different types of filters)*

3   Access to the underside of the vehicle is greatly improved if the vehicle can be lifted on a hoist, driven onto ramps or supported by jackstands.

6.7 Use a proper size box-end wrench or socket to remove the oil drain plug and avoid rounding it off

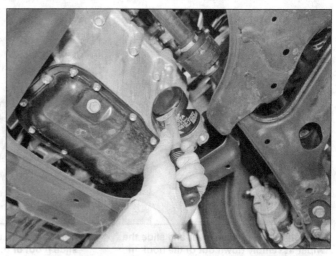

6.12 Loosen the oil filter by turning it counterclockwise with a filter wrench

6.14 Lubricate the oil filter gasket with clean engine oil before installing the filter on the engine

Warning: *Do not work under a vehicle which is supported only by a bumper, hydraulic or scissors-type jack.*

4   If this is your first oil change, get under the vehicle and familiarize yourself with the location of the oil drain plug. The engine and exhaust components will be warm during the actual work, so try to anticipate any potential problems before the engine and accessories are hot.

5   Park the vehicle on a level spot. Start the engine and allow it to reach its normal operating temperature (the needle on the temperature gauge should be at least above the bottom mark). Warm oil and sludge will flow out more easily. Turn off the engine when it's warmed up. Remove the filler cap in the valve cover.

6   Raise the vehicle and support it on jackstands.

Warning: *To avoid personal injury, never get beneath the vehicle when it is supported only by a jack. The jack provided with your vehicle is designed solely for raising the vehicle to remove and replace the wheels. Always use*

jackstands to support the vehicle when it becomes necessary to place your body underneath the vehicle.

7   Remove the under-vehicle splash shield, if necessary. Being careful not to touch the hot exhaust components, place the drain pan under the drain plug in the bottom of the pan and remove the plug (**see illustration**). You should wear gloves while unscrewing and removing the plug.

8   Allow the old oil to drain into the pan. It may be necessary to reposition the pan under the engine as the oil flow slows to a trickle. Inspect the old oil for the presence of metal shavings and chips.

9   After all the oil has drained, wipe off the drain plug with a clean rag. Even minute metal particles clinging to the plug would immediately contaminate the new oil.

10   Clean the area around the drain plug opening, reinstall the plug and tighten it to the torque listed in this Chapter's Specifications.

11   Move the drain pan into position under the oil filter.

All models except 2009 and later 1.8L engines with cartridge type filters

12   Loosen the oil filter (**see illustration**) by turning it counterclockwise with the filter wrench. Any standard filter wrench should work. Once the filter is loose, use your hands to unscrew it from the block.

13   With a clean rag, wipe off the mounting surface on the block. If a residue of old oil is allowed to remain, it will smoke when the block is heated up. It will also prevent the new filter from seating properly. Also make sure that the none of the old gasket remains stuck to the mounting surface. It can be removed with a scraper if necessary.

14   Compare the old filter with the new one to make sure they are the same type. Smear some clean engine oil on the rubber gasket of the new filter and screw it into place (**see**

illustration). Because overtightening the filter will damage the gasket, do not use a filter wrench to tighten the filter. Tighten it by hand following the directions on the canister or packing box.

15   Because over tightening the filter will damage the gasket, do not use a filter wrench to tighten the filter. Tighten it by hand until the gasket contacts the seating surface, then seat the filter by giving it an additional 3/4-turn. Lower the vehicle.

2009 and later 1.8L engines (with cartridge type filters)

16   Place a drain pan under the oil filter housing. Using a box-end wrench, loosen the oil filter element housing or cap four turns and allow the oil to drain. Remove the housing

Note: *The tabs on the filter housing should be facing vertically.*

17   Remove the filter element and the large O-ring from the housing. **Note:** *Don't use a metal tool to remove the O-ring, as this may scratch the soft housing.*

18   Carefully clean all components and the engine block sealing area. Install a new O-ring and filter, align the cutout in the filter housing with the grooves in the engine (three and nine o'clock position), then screw the assembly back onto the engine. Tighten it to the torque listed in this Chapter's Specifications.

All models

19   Add new oil to the engine through the oil filler cap in the valve cover. Use a funnel to prevent oil from spilling onto the top of the engine. Pour three quarts of fresh oil into the engine. Wait a few minutes to allow the oil to drain into the pan, then check the level on the oil dipstick (see Section 4). If the oil level is at or near the Full mark, install the filler cap hand-tight, start the engine and allow the new oil to circulate.

7.5 Push on the release lever and slide the wiper assembly down out of the hook in the end of the wiper arm

7.6 After detaching the end of the element, slide it out of the end of the frame

7.7 Slide the element into place until the cutouts seat into the locking claw

20   Allow the engine to run for about a minute. While the engine is running, look under the vehicle and check for leaks at the oil pan drain plug and around the oil filter. If either is leaking, stop the engine and tighten the plug or filter slightly.

21   Wait a few minutes to allow the oil to trickle down into the pan, then recheck the level on the dipstick and, if necessary, add enough oil to bring the level to the Full mark.

22   During the first few trips after an oil change, make it a point to check frequently for leaks and proper oil level.

23   The old oil drained from the engine cannot be reused in its present state and should be discarded. Check with your local refuse disposal company, disposal facility or environmental agency to see if they will accept the oil for recycling. Don't pour used oil into drains

92037-1-8.2 HAYNES

8.1 Clutch pedal height and freeplay measuring points and adjustments

A   Pedal freeplay adjustment point
B   Pedal height adjustment point
C   Pedal height measurement point
D   Freeplay measurement point

or onto the ground. After the oil has cooled, it can be drained into a suitable container (capped plastic jugs, topped bottles, milk cartons, etc.) for transport to one of these disposal sites.

Service reminder light resetting

Models without smart key system

24   Turn the ignition key to the On position and depress the button to the right of the speedometer until the odometer is displayed.

25   Turn the ignition key to the Off position.

26   Depress the button again and hold it, then turn the ignition key to the On position. Hold the button in the depressed position for five seconds.

27   The odometer should indicate "000000" and the MAINT REQD light should turn off.

Models with smart key system

28   With the key fob inside the vehicle, press the ignition button until it is in the "IGNITION ON " position. Push the "DISP" switch and set the trip meter on the "instrument cluster to the "A" reading, then turn the engine switch off. Do not start the engine.

29   While pressing and holding the "DISP" switch or display change button, turn the engine switch to the "IGNITION ON" position but do not start the engine, or the reset procedure will be canceled.

30   Continue to press and hold the "DISP" switch or display change button until the trip displays "000000"

---

7   Windshield wiper blade inspection and replacement (every 7500 miles or 6 months)

1   The windshield wiper and blade assembly should be inspected periodically for damage, loose components and cracked or worn blade elements.

2   Road film can build up on the wiper blades tund affect their efficiency, so they

should be washed regularly with a mild detergent solution.

3   The action of the wiping mechanism can loosen bolts, nuts and fasteners, so they should be checked and tightened, as necessary, at the same time the wiper blades are checked.

4   If the wiper blade elements are cracked, worn or warped, or no longer clean adequately, they should be replaced with new ones.

5   Remove the wiper blade assembly from the arm by pushing on the release lever, then sliding the assembly down and out of the hook in the end of the arm **(see illustration)**.

6   If you're replacing just the blade element and not the entire blade itself, squeeze the end of the wiper element and pull it out of the wiper frame **(see illustration)**.

7   Insert the new element end without the cutouts into the wiper frame. Slide the element fully into place, then seat the protrusions in the end of the frames to secure it (see illustration).

---

8   Clutch pedal freeplay check and adjustment (every 7500 miles or 6 months)

1   Peel back the carpet and check the clutch pedal height **(see illustration)**. If pedal height is incorrect, loosen the locknut and turn the stopper bolt until the height is correct. Tighten the locknut.

2   Press down lightly on the clutch pedal and measure the distance that it moves freely before the clutch resistance is felt. The freeplay should be within the specified limits. If it isn't, it must be adjusted.

3   Loosen the locknut on the pedal end of the clutch pushrod **(see illustration 8.1)**.

4   Turn the pushrod until pedal freeplay is correct.

5   Tighten the locknut.

6   After adjusting the pedal freeplay, check the pedal height again, adjusting it if necessary.

9.1 Tools and materials required for battery maintenance

1   **Face shield/safety goggles** - When removing corrosion with a brush, the acidic particles can easily fly up into your eyes

2   **Baking soda** - A solution of baking soda and water can be used to neutralize corrosion

3   **Petroleum jelly** - A layer of this on the battery posts will help prevent corrosion

4   **Battery post/cable cleaner** - This wire brush cleaning tool will remove all traces of corrosion from the battery posts and cable clamps

5   **Treated felt washers** - Placing one of these on each post, directly under the cable clamps, will help prevent corrosion

6   **Puller** - Sometimes the cable clamps are very difficult to pull off the posts, even after the nut/bolt has been completely loosened. This tool pulls the clamp straight up and off the post without damage

7   **Battery post/cable cleaner** - Here is another cleaning tool which is a slightly different version of number 4 above, but it does the same thing

8   **Rubber gloves** - Another safety item to consider when servicing the battery; remember that's acid inside the battery

---

9   Battery check, maintenance and charging (every 7500 miles or 6 months)

Warning: Certain precautions must be followed when checking and servicing the battery. Hydrogen gas, which is highly flammable, is always present in the battery cells, so keep lighted tobacco and all other open flames and sparks away from the battery. The electrolyte inside the battery is actually diluted sulfuric acid, which will cause injury if splashed on your skin or in your eyes. It will also ruin clothes and painted surfaces. When disconnecting the battery cables, always detach the negative cable first and hook it up last!

1   A routine preventive maintenance program for the battery in your vehicle is the only way to ensure quick and reliable starts. But before performing any battery maintenance, make sure that you have the proper equip-

9.6a Battery terminal corrosion usually appears as light, fluffy powder

9.7a When cleaning the cable clamps, all corrosion must be removed (the inside of the clamp is tapered to match the taper on the post, so don't remove too much material)

ment necessary to work safely around the battery **(see illustration)**.

2   There are also several precautions that should be taken whenever battery maintenance is performed. Before servicing the battery, always turn the engine and all accessories off and disconnect the cable from the negative terminal of the battery.

3   The battery produces hydrogen gas, which is both flammable and explosive. Never create a spark, smoke or light a match around the battery. Always charge the battery in a ventilated area.

4   Electrolyte contains poisonous and corrosive sulfuric acid. Do not allow it to get in your eyes, on your skin or on your clothes. Never ingest it. Wear protective safety glasses when working near the battery. Keep children away from the battery.

5   Note the external condition of the battery. If the positive terminal and cable clamp on your vehicle's battery is equipped with a rubber protector, make sure that it's not torn or damaged. It should completely cover the terminal. Look for any corroded or loose connections, cracks in the case or cover or loose hold-down clamps. Also check the entire length of each cable for cracks and frayed conductors.

9.6b Removing a cable from the battery post with a wrench - sometimes a pair of special battery pliers are required for this procedure if corrosion has caused deterioration of the nut hex (always remove the ground (-) cable first and hook it up last!)

9.7b Regardless of the type of tool used to clean the battery posts, a clean, shiny surface should be the result

6   If corrosion, which looks like white, fluffy deposits **(see illustration)** is evident, particularly around the terminals, the battery should be removed for cleaning. Loosen the cable clamp bolts with a wrench, being careful to remove the ground cable first, and slide them off the terminals **(see illustration)**. Then disconnect the hold-down clamp bolt and nut, remove the clamp and lift the battery from the engine compartment.

7   Clean the cable clamps thoroughly with a battery brush or a terminal cleaner and a solution of warm water and baking soda **(see illustration)**. Wash the terminals and the top of the battery case with the same solution but make sure that the solution doesn't get into the battery. When cleaning the cables, terminals and battery top, wear safety goggles and rubber gloves to prevent any solution from coming in contact with your eyes or hands. Wear old clothes too - even diluted, sulfuric acid splashed onto clothes will burn holes in them. If the terminals have been extensively corroded, clean them up with a terminal cleaner **(see illustration)**. Thoroughly wash all cleaned areas with plain water.

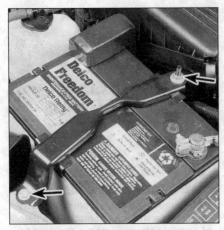

9.8 Make sure the battery clamp nut and bolt are tight

10.3 Check the multi-ribbed belt for signs of wear like these - if the belt looks worn, replace it

8   Make sure that the battery tray is in good condition and the hold-down nut and bolt are tight **(see illustration)**. If the battery is removed from the tray, make sure no parts remain in the bottom of the tray when the battery is reinstalled. When reinstalling the hold-down clamp bolt or nut, do not overtighten it.

9   Information on removing and installing the battery can be found in Chapter 5. Information on jump starting can be found at the front of this manual. For more detailed battery checking procedures, refer to the *Haynes Automotive Electrical Manual*.

Cleaning

10   Corrosion on the hold-down components, battery case and surrounding areas can be removed with a solution of water and baking soda. Thoroughly rinse all cleaned areas with plain water.

11   Any metal parts of the vehicle damaged by corrosion should be covered with a zinc-based primer, then painted.

Charging

Warning: *When batteries are being charged, hydrogen gas, which is very explosive and flammable, is produced. Do not smoke or allow open flames near a charging or a recently charged battery. Wear eye protection when near the battery during charging. Also, make sure the charger is unplugged before connecting or disconnecting the battery from the charger.*

12   Slow-rate charging is the best way to restore a battery that's discharged to the point where it will not start the engine. It's also a good way to maintain the battery charge in a vehicle that's only driven a few miles between starts. Maintaining the battery charge is particularly important in the winter when the battery must work harder to start the engine and electrical accessories that drain the battery are in greater use.

13   It's best to use a one or two-amp battery charger (sometimes called a "trickle" charger). They are the safest and put the least strain

on the battery. They are also the least expensive. For a faster charge, you can use a higher amperage charger, but don't use one rated more than 1/10th the amp/hour rating of the battery. Rapid boost charges that claim to restore the power of the battery in one to two hours are hardest on the battery and can damage batteries not in good condition. This type of charging should only be used in emergency situations.

14   The average time necessary to charge a battery should be listed in the instructions that come with the charger. As a general rule, a trickle charger will charge a battery in 12 to 16 hours.

10   Drivebelt check and replacement (every 7500 miles or 6 months)

Check

1   The alternator, power steering pump, water pump and air-conditioning compressor are all driven by one serpentine belt. Because of their composition and the stresses they are subjected to, drivebelts stretch and deteriorate as they get older. They must therefore be inspected periodically.

2   On some models, the serpentine belt has no adjustment for tension. The engine has a tensioner that automatically applies the right belt tension and compensates for belt stretch over time. On others, the tension must be adjusted manually.

3   With the engine off, open the hood and locate the drivebelt. With a flashlight, check the belt for separation of the adhesive rubber on both sides of the core, core separation from the belt side, a severed core, separation of the ribs from the adhesive rubber, cracking or separation of the ribs, and torn or worn ribs or cracks in the inner ridges of the ribs **(see illustration)**. Also check for fraying and glazing, which gives the belt a shiny appearance.

Both sides of the belt should be inspected, which means you will have to twist the belt to check the underside. Use your fingers to feel the belt where you can't see it. If any of the above conditions are evident, replace the belt (see Steps 4 through 6).

4   If necessary, remove the passenger's side under-vehicle splash shield in order to gain access to the lower portion of the drivebelt **(see illustration)**.

Replacement

1ZZ-FE, 2ZR-FAE (1.8L) engines, all 2AZ-FE (2.4L) engines - (automatic tensioner-type)

Note: *On 2014 and later 2ZR-FAE engines- There are two access points (hex fittings) that allow for the tensioner to be rotated with a wrench by working from above or below the engine. Once the tensioner has been rotated completely clockwise, a 5mm allen wrench can be inserted through the rearmost hex fitting, allowing the tensioner to hold its rotated position. Make sure the allen wrench is completely inserted and does not become dislodged when handling the belt.*

5   Rotate the belt tensioner clockwise to release the tension, then slip the belt off the pulleys **(see illustration)**. Slowly release the tensioner to its stopping point.

6   Route the new belt loosely over the pulleys **(see illustration)**, again rotating the tensioner to allow the belt to be installed, then release the belt tensioner. The drivebelt routing on 2014 and later 2ZR-FAE engines is instead similar to the 2ZR-FE engine routing shown in **illustration 10.8**.

7   Make sure the belt is properly centered in the pulley grooves.

2ZR-FE (1.8L) engines - (manual tensioner-type)

8   Loosen the alternator lower mounting bolt and tensioner lock nut, then turn the adjuster

10.4 Remove the passenger's side under-vehicle splash shield (2009 and later model shown)

A   *Remove the screws*
B   *Remove the pushpin fasteners*
C   *Disengage the hook and remove the splash shield*

10.5 To release the tension on the drivebelt, place a long wrench or socket and ratchet on the hex-shaped boss, then turn the tensioner clockwise (2008 and earlier 1.8L engines and all 2.4L engines)

bolt until there is enough slack to remove the belt from the pulley **(see illustration)**.

9   Route the new belt over the pulley **(see illustration)** and turn the adjuster bolt to set the tension. Make sure the belt is properly centered in the pulley grooves.

10 When you have obtained sufficient belt tension, tighten the alternator lower bolt and tensioner luck nut securely. The belt tension/deflection can be measured by holding a ruler perpendicular to the longest run of the belt (between the crankshaft and alternator pulleys). While holding the ruler steady, push the belt inward with your thumb as far as possible and measure how much the belt deflects. The correct measurement should be slightly more than one-quarter of an inch.

Drivebelt tensioner replacement - models with automatic tensioners

11 To replace a tensioner that can no longer apply sufficient tension to the belt, or one that exhibits binding or a worn-out bearing/pulley, remove the drivebelt (see Step 4) then unscrew the mounting bolts/nuts **(see illustration)**.

12 Installation is the reverse of the removal procedure. Tighten the fasteners to the torque values listed in this Chapter's Specifications.

13 Install the drivebelt (see Steps 5 and 6).

10.6 Drivebelt routing diagram (2008 and earlier 1.8L engines and all 2.4L engines)

10.8 Loosen the necessary bolt/nut, then turn the adjuster bolt until the belt can be removed from the pulley.

A   *Tensioner lock nut*
B   *Alternator lower bolt*
C   *Adjuster bolt*

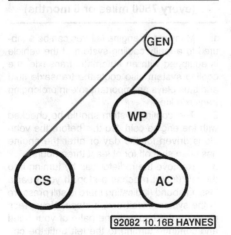

10.9 Drivebelt routing diagram (2009 and later 1.8L engines)

10.11 Drivebelt tensioner mounting fasteners (typical)

11 Underhood hose check and replacement (every 7500 miles or 6 months)

Caution: *Replacement of air conditioning hoses must be left to a dealer service department or air conditioning shop that has the equipment to depressurize the system safely. Never remove air conditioning components or hoses until the system has been depressurized.*

General

1   High temperatures in the engine compartment can cause the deterioration of the rubber and plastic hoses used for engine, accessory and emission systems operation. Periodic inspection should be made for cracks, loose clamps, material hardening and leaks.

2   Information specific to the cooling system hoses can be found in Section 12.

3   Some, but not all, hoses are secured to the fittings with clamps. Where clamps are used, check to be sure they haven't lost their tension, allowing the hose to leak. If clamps aren't used, make sure the hose has not expanded and/or hardened where it slips over the fitting, allowing it to leak.

Vacuum hoses

4   It's quite common for vacuum hoses, especially those in the emissions system, to be color coded or identified by colored stripes molded into them. Various systems require hoses with different wall thickness, collapse resistance and temperature resistance. When replacing hoses, be sure the new ones are made of the same material.

5   Often the only effective way to check a hose is to remove it completely from the vehicle. If more than one hose is removed, be sure to label the hoses and fittings to ensure correct installation.

6   When checking vacuum hoses, be sure to include any plastic T-fittings in the check. Inspect the fittings for cracks and the hose where it fits over the fitting for distortion, which could cause leakage.

7   A small piece of vacuum hose (1/4-inch inside diameter) can be used as a stethoscope to detect vacuum leaks. Hold one end of the hose to your ear and probe around vacuum hoses and fittings, listening for the "hissing" sound characteristic of a vacuum leak. **Warning:** *When probing with the vacuum hose stethoscope, be very careful not to come into contact with moving engine components such as the drivebelt, cooling fan, etc.*

Fuel hose

Warning: *Gasoline is extremely flammable, so take extra precautions when you work on any part of the fuel system. Don't smoke or allow open flames or bare light bulbs near the work area, and don't work in a garage where a gas-type appliance (such as a water heater or a clothes dryer) is present. Since gasoline is carcinogenic, wear fuel-resistant gloves when there's a possibility of being exposed to fuel, and, if you spill any fuel on your skin, rinse*

it off immediately with soap and water. Mop up any spills immediately and do not store fuel-soaked rags where they could ignite. The fuel system is under constant pressure, so, if any fuel lines are to be disconnected, the fuel pressure in the system must be relieved first. When you perform any kind of work on the fuel system, wear safety glasses and have a Class B type fire extinguisher on hand.

8   Check all rubber fuel lines for deterioration and chafing. Check especially for cracks in areas where the hose bends and just before fittings, such as where a hose attaches to the fuel filter.

9   High quality fuel line, specifically designed for fuel injection systems, must be used for fuel line replacement. **Warning:** *Never use anything other than the proper fuel line for fuel line replacement.*

10   Spring-type clamps are commonly used on fuel lines. These clamps often lose their tension over a period of time, and can be "sprung" during removal. Replace all spring-type clamps with screw clamps whenever a hose is replaced.

Metal lines

11   Sections of metal line are often used for fuel line between the fuel pump and fuel injection unit. Check carefully to be sure the line has not been bent or crimped and that cracks have not started in the line.

12   If a section of metal fuel line must be replaced, only seamless steel tubing should be used, since copper and aluminum tubing don't have the strength necessary to withstand normal engine vibration.

13   Check the metal brake lines where they enter the master cylinder and brake proportioning unit (if used) for cracks in the lines or loose fittings. Any sign of brake fluid leakage calls for an immediate thorough inspection of the brake system.

12 Cooling system check (every 7500 miles or 6 months)

1   Many major engine failures can be attributed to a faulty cooling system. If the vehicle is equipped with an automatic transaxle, the cooling system also cools the transaxle fluid and thus plays an important role in prolonging transaxle life.

2   The cooling system should be checked with the engine cold. Do this before the vehicle is driven for the day or after the engine has been shut off for at least three hours.

3   Remove the radiator cap by turning it to the left until it reaches a stop. If you hear a hissing sound (indicating there is still pressure in the system), wait until it stops. Now press down on the cap with the palm of your hand and continue turning to the left until the cap can be removed. Thoroughly clean the cap, inside and out, with clean water. Also clean the filler neck on the radiator. All traces of corrosion should be removed. The coolant inside the radiator should be relatively transparent. If

Check for a chafed area that could fail prematurely.

Check for a soft area indicating the hose has deteriorated inside.

Overtightening the clamp on a hardened hose will damage the hose and cause a leak.

Check each hose for swelling and oil-soaked ends. Cracks and breaks can be located by squeezing the hose.

12.4 Hoses, like drivebelts, have a habit of failing at the worst possible time - to prevent the inconvenience of a blown radiator or heater hose, inspect them carefully as shown here

it's rust colored, the system should be drained and refilled (see Section 23). If the coolant level isn't up to the top, add additional antifreeze/coolant mixture (see Section 4).

4   Carefully check the large upper and lower radiator hoses along with the smaller diameter heater hoses which run from the engine to the firewall. Inspect each hose along its entire length, replacing any hose which is cracked, swollen or shows signs of deterioration. Cracks may become more apparent if the hose is squeezed (**see illustration**). Regardless of condition, it's a good idea to replace hoses with new ones every two years.

5   Make sure that all hose connections are tight. A leak in the cooling system will usually show up as white or rust colored deposits on the areas adjoining the leak. If wire-type clamps are used at the ends of the hoses, it may be a good idea to replace them with more secure screw-type clamps.

6   Use compressed air or a soft brush to remove bugs, leaves, etc., from the front of the radiator or air conditioning condenser. Be careful not to damage the delicate cooling fins or cut yourself on them.

13.2 The recommended tire rotation pattern for these vehicles

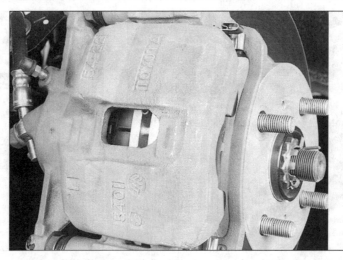

15.6 You will find an inspection hole like this in each caliper - placing a ruler across the hole should enable you to determine the thickness of remaining pad material for both inner and outer pads

7   Every other inspection, or at the first indication of cooling system problems, have the cap and system pressure tested. If you don't have a pressure tester, most gas stations and repair shops will do this for a minimal charge.

13   Tire rotation (every 7500 miles or 6 months)

1   The tires should be rotated at the specified intervals and whenever uneven wear is noticed. Since the vehicle will be raised and the tires removed anyway, check the brakes (see Section 15) at this time.
2   Radial tires must be rotated in a specific pattern **(see illustration)**.
3   Refer to the information in *Jacking and towing* at the front of this manual for the proper procedures to follow when raising the vehicle and changing a tire. If the brakes are to be checked, do not apply the parking brake as stated. Make sure the tires are blocked to prevent the vehicle from rolling.
4   Preferably, the entire vehicle should be raised at the same time. This can be done on a hoist or by jacking up each corner and then lowering the vehicle onto jackstands placed under the frame rails. Always use four jackstands and make sure the vehicle is firmly supported.
5   After rotation, check and adjust the tire pressures as necessary and be sure to check the lug nut tightness.
6   For further information on the wheels and tires, refer to Chapter 10.

14   Seat belt check (every 7500 miles or 6 months)

1   Check the seat belts, buckles, latch plates and guide loops for obvious damage and signs of wear. Seat belts that exhibit fraying along the edges should be replaced.

2   Where the seat belt receptacle bolts to the floor of the vehicle, check that the bolts are secure.
3   See if the seat belt reminder light comes on when the key is turned to the Run or Start position. A chime should also sound.

15   Brake check (every 15,000 miles or 12 months)

Warning: *Dust created by the brake system is harmful to your health. Never blow it out with compressed air and don't inhale any of it. An approved filtering mask should be worn when working on the brakes. Do not, under any circumstances, use petroleum-based solvents to clean brake parts. Use brake system cleaner only!*
Note: *For detailed photographs of the brake system, refer to Chapter 9.*
1   In addition to the specified intervals, the brakes should be inspected every time the wheels are removed or whenever a defect is suspected. Any of the following symptoms could indicate a potential brake system defect: The vehicle pulls to one side when the brake pedal is depressed; the brakes make squealing or dragging noises when applied; brake travel is excessive; the pedal pulsates; brake fluid leaks, usually onto the inside of the tire or wheel.
2   The disc brake pads have built-in wear indicators which should make a high-pitched squealing or scraping noise when they are worn to the replacement point. When you hear this noise, replace the pads immediately or expensive damage to the discs can result.
3   Loosen the wheel lug nuts.
4   Raise the vehicle and place it securely on jackstands.
5   Remove the wheels (see *Jacking and towing* at the front of this book, or your owner's manual, if necessary).

Disc brakes

6   There are two pads - an outer and an inner - in each caliper. The pads are visible through small inspection holes in each caliper **(see illustration)**.

7   Check the pad thickness by looking at each end of the caliper and through the inspection hole in the caliper body. If the lining material is less than the thickness listed in this Chapter's Specifications, replace the pads.
Note: *Keep in mind that the lining material is riveted or bonded to a metal backing plate and the metal portion is not included in this measurement.*
8   If it is difficult to determine the exact thickness of the remaining pad material by the above method, or if you are at all concerned about the condition of the pads, remove the caliper(s), then remove the pads for further inspection (refer to Chapter 9).
9   Once the pads are removed from the calipers, clean them with brake cleaner and re-measure them.
10   Measure the disc thickness with a micrometer to make sure that it still has service life remaining. If any disc is thinner than the specified minimum thickness, replace it (refer to Chapter 9). Even if the disc has service life remaining, check its condition. Look for scoring, gouging and burned spots. If these conditions exist, remove the disc and have it resurfaced (see Chapter 9).
11   Before installing the wheels, check all brake lines and hoses for damage, wear, deformation, cracks, corrosion, leakage, bends and twists, particularly in the vicinity of the rubber hoses at the calipers.
12   Check the clamps for tightness and the connections for leakage. Make sure that all hoses and lines are clear of sharp edges, moving parts and the exhaust system. If any of the above conditions are noted, repair, reroute or replace the lines and/or fittings as necessary (see Chapter 9).

Rear drum brakes

13   To check the brake shoe lining thickness without removing the brake drums, remove the rubber plug from the backing plate and use a flashlight to inspect the linings. For a more thorough brake inspection, follow the procedure below.
14   Refer to Chapter 9 and remove the rear brake drums.

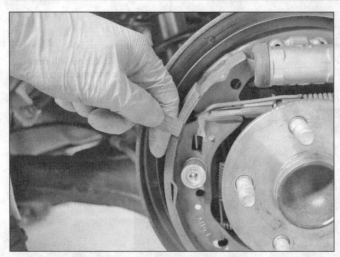

15.15 If the lining is bonded to the brake shoe, measure the lining thickness from the outer surface to the metal shoe, as shown here; if the lining is riveted to the shoe, measure from the lining outer surface to the rivet head

15.17 Carefully peel back the wheel cylinder boot and check for leaking fluid indicating that the cylinder must be replaced

15   Note the thickness of the lining material on the rear brake shoes **(see illustration)** and look for signs of contamination by brake fluid and grease. If the lining material is within 1/16-inch of the recessed rivets or metal shoes, replace the brake shoes with new ones. The shoes should also be replaced if they are cracked, glazed (shiny lining surfaces) or contaminated with brake fluid or grease. See Chapter 9 for the replacement procedure.

16   Check the shoe return and hold-down springs and the adjusting mechanism to make sure they're installed correctly and in good condition. Deteriorated or distorted springs, if not replaced, could allow the linings to drag and wear prematurely.

17   Check the wheel cylinders for leakage by carefully peeling back the rubber boots **(see illustration)**. If brake fluid is noted behind the boots, the wheel cylinders must be replaced (see Chapter 9).

18   Check the drums for cracks, score marks, deep scratches and hard spots, which will appear as small discolored areas. If imperfections cannot be removed with emery cloth, the drums must be resurfaced by an automotive machine shop (see Chapter 9 for more detailed information).

19   Install the brake drums.

20   Install the wheels and lug nuts.

21   Remove the jackstands and lower the vehicle.

22   Tighten the wheel lug nuts to the torque listed in this Chapter's Specifications.

Brake booster check

23   Sit in the driver's seat and perform the following sequence of tests.

24   With the brake fully depressed, start the engine - the pedal should move down a little when the engine starts.

25   With the engine running, depress the brake pedal several times - the travel distance should not change.

26   Depress the brake, stop the engine and hold the pedal in for about 30 seconds - the pedal should neither sink nor rise.

27   Restart the engine, run it for about a minute and turn it off. Then firmly depress the brake several times - the pedal travel should decrease with each application.

28   If your brakes do not operate as described above when the preceding tests are performed, the brake booster has failed. Refer to Chapter 9 for the replacement procedure.

Parking brake

29   Slowly pull up on the parking brake and count the number of clicks you hear until the handle is up as far as it will go. The adjustment is correct if you hear the specified number of clicks. If you hear more or fewer clicks, it's time to adjust the parking brake (refer to Chapter 9).

30   An alternative method of checking the parking brake is to park the vehicle on a

steep hill with the parking brake set and the transaxle in Neutral (be sure to stay in the vehicle for this procedure). If the parking brake cannot prevent the vehicle from rolling, it is in need of adjustment (see Chapter 9).

16   Air filter replacement (every 15,000 miles or 12 months)

1   The air filter is located inside a housing at the left (driver's) side of the engine compartment.

2   To remove the air filter, release the spring clips that keep the two halves of the air filter housing together, then lift the cover up and remove the air filter element **(see illustrations)**. On later model vehicles, you will also need to disconnect the intake tube.

3   Inspect the outer surface of the filter element. If it is dirty, replace it. If it is only moderately dusty, it can be reused by blowing it

16.2a On earlier models, detach the clips and separate the cover from the air cleaner housing . . .

16.2b . . . then hold the cover up and lift out the element

16.2c On later models, loosen the intake air tube clamp (A) and detach the tube, then unlatch the clips (B) and separate the cover from the air cleaner housing . . .

16.2d . . . hold the cover up and lift out the element

17.2 Use a small screwdriver to carefully pry out the old gasket - take care not to damage the cap

clean from the back to the front surface with compressed air. Because it is a pleated paper type filter, it cannot be washed or oiled. If it cannot be cleaned satisfactorily with compressed air, discard and replace it. While the cover is off, be careful not to drop anything down into the housing. **Caution:** *Never drive the vehicle with the air filter removed. Excessive engine wear could result and backfiring could even cause a fire under the hood.*

4   Wipe out the inside of the air filter housing.

5   Place the new filter into the air filter housing, making sure it seats properly.

6 Installation of the cover is the reverse of removal.

17   Fuel system check (every 15,000 miles or 12 months)

Warning: *Gasoline is extremely flammable, so take extra precautions when you work on any part of the fuel system. Don't smoke or allow open flames or bare light bulbs near the work area, and don't work in a garage where a gas-type appliance (such as a water heater*

or a clothes dryer) is present. Since gasoline is carcinogenic, wear latex gloves when there's a possibility of being exposed to fuel, and, if you spill any fuel on your skin, rinse it off immediately with soap and water. Mop up any spills immediately and do not store fuel-soaked rags where they could ignite. The fuel system is under constant pressure, so, if any fuel lines are to be disconnected, the fuel pressure in the system must be relieved first. When you perform any kind of work on the fuel system, wear safety glasses and have a Class B type fire extinguisher on hand.

1   If you smell gasoline while driving or after the vehicle has been sitting in the sun, inspect the fuel system immediately.

2   Remove the gas filler cap and inspect it for damage and corrosion. The gasket should have an unbroken sealing imprint. If the gasket is damaged or corroded, remove it and install a new one **(see illustration)**.

3   Inspect the fuel feed and return lines for cracks. Make sure that the threaded flare-nut type connectors which secure the metal fuel lines to the fuel injection system are tight.

4   Since some components of the fuel system - the fuel tank and part of the fuel feed

and return lines, for example - are underneath the vehicle, they can be inspected more easily with the vehicle raised on a hoist. If that's not possible, raise the vehicle and support it securely on jackstands.

5   With the vehicle raised and safely supported, inspect the gas tank and filler neck for punctures, cracks and other damage. The connection between the filler neck and the tank is particularly critical. Sometimes a rubber filler neck will leak because of loose clamps or deteriorated rubber **(see illustration)**. These are problems a home mechanic can usually rectify. **Warning:** *Do not, under any circumstances, try to repair a fuel tank (except rubber components). A welding torch or any open flame can easily cause fuel vapors inside the tank to explode.*

6   Carefully check all rubber hoses and metal lines leading away from the fuel tank. Check for loose connections, deteriorated hoses, crimped lines and other damage. Carefully inspect the lines from the tank to the fuel injection system. Repair or replace damaged sections as necessary (see Chapter 4).

18   Manual transaxle lubricant level check (every 15,000 miles or 12 months)

1   The manual transaxle does not have a dipstick. To check the fluid level, raise the vehicle and support it securely and evenly on jackstands. On 2013 and earlier models, the check/fill plug is located on the lower front side of the transaxle housing. On 2014 and later models, the check/fill plug is located on the lower, driver's end of the transaxle housing. Remove it. If the lubricant level is correct, it should be up to the lower edge of the hole.

2   If the transaxle needs more lubricant (if the level is not up to the hole), use a syringe or a gear oil pump to add more. Stop filling the transaxle when the lubricant begins to run out the hole.

17.5 Inspect the filler hose for cracks and make sure the clamps are tight

19.7 To check a balljoint for wear, try to move the control arm up and down with a prybar to make sure there is no play in the balljoint (if there is, replace it)

19.8 Push on the balljoint boot to check for damage

3   Install the plug and tighten it securely. Drive the vehicle a short distance, then check for leaks.

19   Steering, suspension and driveaxle boot check (every 15,000 miles or 12 months)

Note: *For detailed illustrations of the steering and suspension components, refer to Chapter 10.*

Steering and suspension check
With the wheels on the ground
1   With the vehicle stopped and the front wheels pointed straight ahead, rock the steering wheel gently back and forth. If freeplay is excessive- a front wheel bearing, main shaft yoke, intermediate shaft yoke, lower arm balljoint or steering system joint is worn or the steering gear is out of adjustment or broken. Refer to Chapter 10 (or Chapter 8) for the appropriate repair procedure.

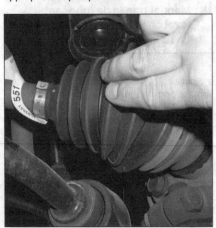

19.10 Flex the driveaxle boots by hand to check for cracks and/or leaking grease

2   Other symptoms, such as excessive vehicle body movement over rough roads, swaying (leaning) around corners and binding as the steering wheel is turned, may indicate faulty steering and/or suspension components.
3   Check the shock absorbers by pushing down and releasing the vehicle several times at each corner. If the vehicle does not come back to a level position within one or two bounces, the shocks/struts are worn and must be replaced. When bouncing the vehicle up and down, listen for squeaks and noises from the suspension components. Additional information on suspension components can be found in Chapter 10.

Under the vehicle
4   Raise the vehicle with a floor jack and support it securely on jackstands. See *Jacking and towing* at the front of this book for the proper jacking points.
5   Check the tires for irregular wear patterns and proper inflation. See Section 5 in this Chapter for information regarding tire wear and Chapter 10 for the wheel bearing replacement procedures.
6   Inspect the universal joint between the steering shaft and the steering gear housing. Check the steering gear housing for grease leakage or oozing. Make sure that the dust seals and boots are not damaged and that the boot clamps are not loose. Check the steering linkage for looseness or damage. Check the tie-rod ends for excessive play. Look for loose bolts, broken or disconnected parts and deteriorated rubber bushings on all suspension and steering components. While an assistant turns the steering wheel from side to side, check the steering components for free movement, chafing and binding. If the steering components do not seem to be reacting with the movement of the steering wheel, try to determine where the slack is located.
7   Move each control arm up and down

with a pry bar **(see illustration)** to ensure that its balljoint has no play. If any balljoint does have play, replace it. See Chapter 10 for the balljoint replacement procedure.
8   Inspect the balljoint boots for damage and leaking grease **(see illustration)**. Replace the balljoints with new ones if they are damaged (see Chapter 10).

Driveaxle boot check
9   The driveaxle boots are very important because they prevent dirt, water and foreign material from entering and damaging the constant velocity (CV) joints. Oil and grease can cause the boot material to deteriorate prematurely, so it's a good idea to wash the boots with soap and water. Because it constantly pivots back and forth following the steering action of the front hub, the outer CV boot wears out sooner and should be inspected regularly.
10   Inspect the boots for tears and cracks as well as loose clamps **(see illustration)**. If there is any evidence of cracks or leaking lubricant, they must be replaced as described in Chapter 8.

20   Cabin air filter - replacement (every 15,000 miles or 12 months)

1   The covered models are equipped with a cabin air filter in the blower housing. The filter traps dust and pollen before the air enters the passenger compartment.
2   For access to the cabin air filter, remove the glove box (see Chapter 11).
3   Release the two clips on the filter door **(see illustration)**.
4   Open the door and remove the filter **(see illustration)**.
5   Installation is the reverse of the removal procedure. Be sure to install the cabin filter correctly. For example: the arrows marked on Toyota factory-made filters may indicate that

20.3 Release the two clips on the filter door

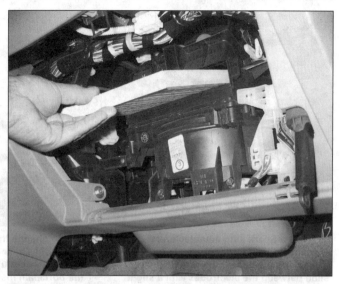

20.4 Open the cabin air filter door and slide the filter out, noting the direction it is facing

it needs to be pointing UP - however, those arrows might not indicate the directional flow of air. The arrows marked on filters made from other manufacturers may vary, and indicate the actual flow of air. If in doubt, observe the dirty side of the filter when removing it, and install the new filter with the airflow arrows placed accordingly.

21   Brake fluid change (every 30,000 miles or 24 months)

Warning: *Brake fluid can harm your eyes and damage painted surfaces, so use extreme caution when handling or pouring it. Do not use brake fluid that has been standing open or is more than one year old. Brake fluid absorbs moisture from the air. Excess moisture can cause a dangerous loss of braking effectiveness.*

1   At the specified intervals, the brake fluid should be drained and replaced. Since the brake fluid may drip or splash when pouring it, place plenty of rags around the master cylinder to protect any surrounding painted surfaces.

2   Before beginning work, purchase the specified brake fluid (see *Recommended lubricants and fluids* at the beginning of this Chapter).

3   Remove the cap from the master cylinder reservoir.

4   Using a hand suction pump or similar device, withdraw the fluid from the master cylinder reservoir.

5   Add new fluid to the master cylinder until it rises to the line indicated on the reservoir.

6   Bleed the brake system as described in Chapter 9 at all four brakes until new and uncontaminated fluid is expelled from the bleeder screw. Be sure to maintain the fluid level in the master cylinder as you per-

form the bleeding process. If you allow the master cylinder to run dry, air will enter the system.

7   Refill the master cylinder with fluid and check the operation of the brakes. The pedal should feel solid when depressed, with no sponginess.

Warning: *Do not operate the vehicle if you are in doubt about the effectiveness of the brake system.*

22   Spark plug check and replacement (every 30,000 miles or 24 months)

1   Spark plug replacement requires a spark plug socket which fits onto a ratchet wrench. This socket is lined with a rubber grommet to protect the porcelain insulator of the spark plug and to hold the plug while you insert it into the spark plug hole. You will also need a wire-type feeler gauge to check and adjust the spark plug gap and a torque wrench to tighten the new plugs to the specified torque **(see illustration)**.

2   If you are replacing the plugs, purchase the new plugs, adjust them to the proper gap and then replace each plug one at a time. **Note:** *When buying new spark plugs, it's essential that you obtain the correct plugs for your specific vehicle. This informationcan be found in this Chapter's Specifications, on the Vehicle Emissions Control Information (VECI) label located on the underside of the hood or in the owner's manual. If these sources specify different plugs, purchase the spark plug type specified on the VECI label because that information is provided specifically for your engine.*

3   Inspect each of the new plugs for defects. If there are any signs of cracks in the porcelain insulator of a plug, don't use it.

22.1 Tools required for changing spark plugs

1   *Spark plug socket - This will have special padding inside to protect the spark plug porcelain insulator*

2   *Torque wrench - Although not mandatory, use of this tool is the best way to ensure that the plugs are tightened properly*

3   *Ratchet - Standard hand tool to fit the plug socket*

4   *Extension - Depending on model and accessories, you may need special extensions and universal joints to reach one or more of the plugs*

5   *Spark plug gap gauge - This gauge for checking the gap comes in a variety of styles. Make sure the gap for your engine is included*

Caution: *Don't attempt to adjust the gap on a platinum or iridium-coated plug - the gap is preset to a certain measurement from the factory and must not be touched*

22.4a Spark plug manufacturers recommend using a wire-type gauge when checking the gap - if the wire does not slide between the electrodes with a slight drag, adjustment is required

22.4b To change the gap, bend the side electrode only, as indicated by the arrows, and be very careful not to crack or chip the porcelain insulator surrounding the center electrode

22.6a Engine cover fastener locations - typical earlier models

22.6b Lift the front of the cover up and off of the ball studs - typical later models

22.10a Apply a thin coat of anti-seize compound to the spark plug threads

22.10b A length of snug-fitting rubber hose will save time and prevent damaged threads when installing the spark plugs

4   Check the electrode gaps of the new plugs. Check the gap by inserting the wire gauge of the proper thickness between the electrodes at the tip of the plug **(see illustration)**. The gap between the electrodes should be identical to that listed in this Chapter's Specifications or on the VECI label. If the gap is incorrect, use the notched adjuster on the feeler gauge body to bend the curved side electrode slightly **(see illustration)**.
5   If the side electrode is not exactly over the center electrode, use the notched adjuster to align them. **Caution:** *If the gap of a new plug must be adjusted, bend only the base of the ground electrode - do not touch the tip.*

Removal

6   Remove the engine cover **(see illustrations)**, if equipped, then remove the ignition coils (see Chapter 5).
7   If compressed air is available, blow any dirt or foreign material away from the spark plug area before proceeding.
8   Remove the spark plug.

9   Whether you are replacing the plugs at this time or intend to reuse the old plugs, compare each old spark plug with the chart on the inside back cover of this manual to determine the overall running condition of the engine.

Installation

10   Prior to installation, it's a good idea to coat the spark plug threads with anti-seize compound **(see illustration)**. Also, it's often difficult to insert spark plugs into their holes without cross-threading them. To avoid this possibility, fit a length of snug-fitting rubber hose over the end of the spark plug **(see illustration)**. The flexible hose acts as a universal joint to help align the plug with the plug hole. Should the plug begin to cross-thread, the hose will slip on the spark plug, preventing thread damage. Tighten the plug to the torque listed in this Chapter's Specifications.
11   Follow the above procedure for the remaining spark plugs.
12   Install the ignition coils (see Chapter 5).

23   Cooling system servicing (draining, flushing and refilling) (every 30,000 miles or 24 months)

Warning: *Do not allow engine coolant (antifreeze) to come in contact with your skin or painted surfaces of the vehicle. Rinse off spills immediately with plenty of water. Antifreeze is highly toxic if ingested. Never leave antifreeze lying around in an open container or in puddles on the floor; children and pets are attracted by its sweet smell and may drink it. Check with local authorities on disposing of used antifreeze. Many communities have collection centers which will see that antifreeze is disposed of safely. Antifreeze is flammable under certain conditions - be sure to read the precautions on the container.*
Note: *Non-toxic antifreeze is available at most auto parts stores. Although the antifreeze is non-toxic when fresh, proper disposal is still required.*

1   Periodically, the cooling system should

23.4 Depending on the model vehicle, you might have to remove a cover for access to the radiator drain fitting located at the bottom of the radiator - before opening the valve, push a short section of 3/8-inch ID hose onto the plastic fitting to prevent the coolant from splashing

23.5 Attach a length of tubing to the spigot on the engine block drain, then loosen the drain bolt and allow the block to drain

be drained, flushed and refilled to replenish the antifreeze mixture and prevent formation of rust and corrosion, which can impair the performance of the cooling system and cause engine damage. When the cooling system is serviced, all hoses and the radiator cap should be checked and replaced if necessary.

Draining

2   Apply the parking brake and block the wheels. If the vehicle has just been driven, wait several hours to allow the engine to cool down before beginning this procedure.
3   Once the engine is completely cool, remove the radiator cap.
4   Move a large container under the radiator drain to catch the coolant. Attach a 3/8-inch inner diameter hose to the drain fitting to direct the coolant into the container (some models are already equipped with a hose), then open the drain fitting (a pair of pliers may be required to turn it) **(see illustration)**.
5   After the coolant stops flowing out of the radiator, move the container under the engine block drain plug **(see illustration)**. Loosen the plug and allow the coolant in the block to drain.
6   While the coolant is draining, check the condition of the radiator hoses, heater hoses and clamps (refer to Section 12 if necessary). Replace any damaged clamps or hoses.

Flushing

7   Once the system is completely drained, remove the thermostat from the engine (see Chapter 3). Then reinstall the thermostat housing without the thermostat. This will allow the system to be thoroughly flushed.
8   Tighten the radiator drain plug. Turn your heating system controls to Hot, so that the heater core will be flushed at the same time as the rest of the cooling system.

9   Disconnect the upper radiator hose from the radiator, then place a garden hose in the upper radiator inlet and flush the system until the water runs clear at the upper radiator hose **(see illustration)**.
10   In severe cases of contamination or clogging of the radiator, remove the radiator (see Chapter 3) and have a radiator repair facility clean and repair it if necessary.
11   Many deposits can be removed by the chemical action of a cleaner available at auto parts stores. Follow the procedure outlined in the manufacturer's instructions. **Note:** *When the coolant is regularly drained and the system refilled with the correct antifreeze/water mixture, there should be no need to use chemical cleaners or descalers.*
12   Remove the overflow hose from the coolant recovery reservoir. Drain the reservoir and flush it with clean water, then reconnect the hose.

Refilling

13   Close and tighten the radiator drain. Install and/or tighten the block drain plug. Reinstall the thermostat (see Chapter 4).
14   Place the heater temperature control in the maximum heat position, with the blower control on low and a/c switch turned off.
15   Slowly add new coolant (a 50/50 mixture of water and antifreeze) to the radiator until it's full. Squeeze the radiator hoses, then add more coolant, if possible. Add coolant to the reservoir up to the lower mark.
16   Install the radiator cap and run the engine in a well-ventilated area until the thermostat opens (coolant will begin flowing through the radiator and the upper radiator hose will become hot).
17   Turn the engine off and let it cool. Add more coolant mixture to bring the level back up to the lip on the radiator filler neck.

23.9 With the thermostat removed, disconnect the upper radiator hose and flush the radiator and engine block with a garden hose

18   Squeeze the upper radiator hose to expel air, then add more coolant mixture if necessary. Reinstall the radiator cap.
19   Start the engine, allow it to reach normal operating temperature and check for leaks.

24   Evaporative emissions control system check (every 30,000 miles or 24 months)

1   The function of the evaporative emissions control system is to draw fuel vapors from the gas tank and fuel system, store them in a charcoal canister and then burn them during normal engine operation.

24.2 The charcoal canister is located above the rear suspension crossmember

25.4 Be sure to check each exhaust system rubber hanger for damage

26.8a After loosening the front bolts, remove the rear transaxle pan bolts . . .

26.8b . . . and allow the remaining fluid to drain out

26.9 Remove the filter bolts and lower the filter (be careful, there will be some residual fluid) - note that here one of the pan magnets is stuck to the filter (arrow); be sure to clean any magnets and return them to the pan

26.11 Noting their locations, remove any magnets and wash them and the pan in solvent before reinstalling them

2   The most common symptom of a fault in the evaporative emissions control system is a strong fuel odor from the rear of the vehicle. If a fuel odor is detected, inspect the charcoal canister duct **(see illustration)** located under the rear of the vehicle, above the rear suspension crossmember. Check the canister and all hoses for damage and deterioration.

3   The evaporative emissions control system is explained in more detail in Chapter 6.

25 Exhaust system check (every 30,000 miles or 24 months)

1   With the engine cold (at least three hours after the vehicle has been driven), check the complete exhaust system from its starting point at the engine to the end of the tailpipe. This should be done on a hoist where unrestricted access is available.

2   Check the pipes and connections for evi-

dence of leaks, severe corrosion or damage. Make sure that all brackets and hangers are in good condition and tight.

3   At the same time, inspect the underside of the body for holes, corrosion, open seams, etc., which may allow exhaust gases to enter the passenger compartment. Seal all body openings with silicone or body putty.

4   Rattles and other noises can often be traced to the exhaust system, especially the mounts and hangers. Try to move the pipes, muffler and catalytic converter. If the components can come in contact with the body or suspension parts, secure the exhaust system with new mounts **(see illustration)**.

5   Check the running condition of the engine by inspecting inside the end of the tailpipe. The exhaust deposits here are an indication of engine state-of-tune. If the pipe is black and sooty or coated with white deposits, the engine is in need of a tune-up, including a thorough engine control system inspection.

26 Automatic transaxle fluid and filter change (every 30,000 miles or 24 months)

1   At the specified time intervals, the automatic transaxle fluid should be drained and replaced.

2   Before beginning work, purchase the specified transmission fluid (see *Recommended lubricants and fluids* at the front of this Chapter).

3   Other tools necessary for this job include jackstands to support the vehicle in a raised position, wrenches, drain pan capable of holding at least four quarts, newspapers and clean rags.

4   The fluid should be drained immediately after the vehicle has been driven. Hot fluid is more effective than cold fluid at removing built up sediment. **Warning:** *Fluid temperature can exceed 350-degrees F in a hot transaxle. Wear protective gloves.*

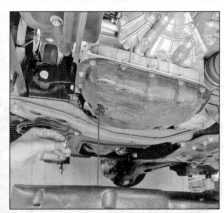

26.18a Remove the fluid check plug from the bottom of the CVT transaxle pan and allow any excess fluid to drain . . .

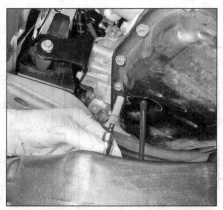

26.18b . . . Insert the 6 mm hex socket into the hole, then loosen and remove the oil leveling tube from the oil pan

28.1a The PCV valve is threaded into the valve cover (all models except 2009 and later 1.8L engines)

28.1b The PCV valve is threaded into the breather case - 2009 and later 1.8L models

U245E, U250E and U341E automatic transaxles

5   After the vehicle has been driven to warm up the fluid, raise it and support it on jackstands for access to the transaxle and differential drain plugs.
6   Move the necessary equipment under the vehicle, being careful not to touch any of the hot exhaust components.
7   Place the drain pan under the drain plug in the transaxle pan and remove the drain plug. Be sure the drain pan is in position, as fluid will come out with some force. Once the fluid is drained, reinstall the drain plug securely.
8   Remove the front transaxle pan bolts, then loosen the rear bolts and carefully pry the pan loose with a screwdriver and allow the remaining fluid to drain (see illustrations). Once the fluid has drained, remove the bolts and lower the pan.
9   Remove the filter retaining bolts, disconnect the clip (some models) and lower the filter from the transaxle (see illustration). Be careful when lowering the filter as it contains residual fluid.

10   Place the new filter in position, connect the clip (if equipped) and install the bolts. Tighten the bolts securely.
11   Carefully clean the gasket surfaces of the fluid pan, removing all traces of old gasket material. Noting their location, remove the magnets, wash the pan in clean solvent and dry it. Be sure to clean and reinstall any magnets (see illustration).
12   Install a new gasket, place the fluid pan in position and install the bolts in their original positions. Tighten the bolts to the torque listed in this Chapter's Specifications.
13   Lower the vehicle.
14   With the engine off, add new fluid to the transaxle through the dipstick tube (see this Chapter's Specifications for the recommended fluid type and capacity). Use a funnel to prevent spills. It is best to add a little fluid at a time, continually checking the level with the dipstick (see Section 4). Allow the fluid time to drain into the pan.
15   Start the engine and shift the selector into all positions from P through L, then shift into P and apply the parking brake.
16   With the engine idling, check the fluid level. Add fluid up to the Cool level on the dipstick.

CVT transaxles

Note: These CVT transaxles do not have a typical oil filler tube or transaxle fluid dipstick - fluid is added through the refill hole in the side of the CVT transaxle assembly
Note: Greater access to the transaxle is obtained with the driver's side front wheel removed
17   Raise the vehicle and support it securely and evenly on jackstands. Remove the driver's side under-vehicle splash shield (see illustration 4.41).
Note: Both ends of the vehicle should be raised and supported on jackstands for an accurate check.
18   To drain the fluid, locate the fluid check plug on the bottom of the transaxle oil pan and remove the plug with a 6 mm hex socket (see illustration). Then, using the same 6 mm hex socket, remove the oil check tube (oil leveling

tube) from the check plug hole (see illustration) and allow the fluid to drain. Note: Once the fluid has drained, measure the amount of fluid that has drained and use this as a guide for refilling.
19   Once the fluid has drained, install the oil leveling tube and the oil check plug into the oil pan. Tighten the tube and plug to the torque settings listed in this Chapter's Specifications. Using a pump (see illustration 4.45a), add the measured amount of NEW fluid to the transaxle through the fill plug hole.
20   Check the transaxle fluid level (Section 4).

27 Manual transaxle lubricant change (every 30,000 miles or 24 months)

1   Raise the vehicle and support it securely on jackstands.
2   Remove the filler plug and drain plug(s) and drain the fluid.
Note: On 2013 and earlier models the check/fill plug is located on the lower front side of the transaxle housing. On 2014 and later models, the check/fill plug is located on the lower driver's end of the transaxle housing.
3   Reinstall the drain plug(s) and tighten securely.
4   Add new fluid until it is even with the lower edge of the filler hole. See Recommended lubricants and fluids for the specified lubricant type.

28 Positive Crankcase Ventilation (PCV) valve and hose - check and replacement (every 30,000 miles or 24 months)

1   The PCV valve and hose are located in the valve cover on all models except 2009 and later 1.8L engines. It's threaded into the left (driver's) end of the valve cover (see illustration). On 2009 and later 1.8L engines, the PCV valve is located under the intake manifold, mounted into the breather case (see illustration).

29.6a When the No. 1 piston is at TDC on the compression stroke, the valve clearance for the No. 1 and No. 3 cylinder exhaust valves and the No. 1 and No. 2 intake valves can be measured (2008 and earlier 1.8L engine shown)

29.6b When the No. 1 piston is at TDC on the compression stroke, the valve clearance for the No. 1 and No. 3 cylinder exhaust valves and the No. 1 and No. 2 intake valves can be measured (2.4L engine shown)

2   On 2009 and later 1.8L engines, remove the intake manifold (see Chapter 2A).

3   Disconnect the hose, unscrew the valve from the cover or breather case, then reconnect the hose to the valve (and install the intake manifold, if necessary).

4   With the engine idling at normal operating temperature, place your finger over the end of the valve. If there's no vacuum at the valve, check for a plugged hose or valve. Replace any plugged or deteriorated hoses.

5   Turn off the engine. Remove the PCV valve from the hose. Connect a clean piece of hose and blow through the valve from the valve cover (cylinder head) end. If air will not pass through the valve in this direction, replace it with a new one.

Note: *Make sure the PCV valve rattles slightly when you shake it - if it does not, then the valve may be stuck and will need replacement*

6   When purchasing a replacement PCV valve, make sure it's for your particular vehicle and engine size. Compare the old valve with the new one to make sure they're the same.

---

29   Valve clearance check and adjustment (2008 and earlier models and all 2.4L models) (every 60,000 miles or 48 months)

Warning: *These models are equipped with airbags. Always disable the airbag system before working in the vicinity of any airbag system component to avoid the possibility of accidental deployment of the airbag(s), which could cause personal injury (see Chapter 12).*

Note: *The valve clearance check and adjustment is the same procedure for the 2.4L engine, except the intake and exhaust camshafts are on the opposite sides of the cylinder head as compared to the 2008 and earlier 1.8L en-*

gines. The 2009 and later 1.8L engines have hydraulic lash adjusters that don't require checking or adjustment.

Check

1   Disconnect the negative cable from the battery.

2   Remove the ignition coils (see Chapter 5) and remove any other components that will interfere with valve cover removal.

3   Blow out the recessed area around the spark plug openings with compressed air, if available, to remove any debris that might fall into the cylinders, then remove the spark plugs (see Section 22).

4   Remove the valve cover (see Chapter 2A).

5   Position the number 1 piston at TDC on the compression stroke (Chapter 2A).

6   Measure the clearances of the indicated valves with feeler gauges **(see illustrations)**. Record the measurements which are out of specification. They will be used later to determine the required replacement lifters.

7   Turn the crankshaft one complete revolution and realign the timing marks. Measure the remaining valves **(see illustrations)**.

Adjustment

8   If any of the valve clearances were out of adjustment, remove the camshaft(s) from over the lifter(s) that was/were out of the specified clearance range (see Chapter 2A).

9   Measure the thickness of the lifter with a micrometer **(see illustration)**. To calculate the correct thickness of a replacement shim or lifter that will place the valve clearance within the specified value, use the following formula:

10   $N = T + (A - V)$

11   T = thickness of the old shim or lifter

12   A = valve clearance measured

13   N = thickness of the new shim or lifter

14   V = desired valve clearance (see this Chapter's Specifications)

15   Select a lifter with a thickness as close as possible to the valve clearance calculated. The lifters are available in 35 sizes in increments of 0.0008-inch (0.020 mm), range in

29.6c Check the clearance for each valve with a feeler gauge of the specified thickness - if the clearance is correct, you should feel a slight drag on the gauge as you pull it out

Exhaust   2 2   4 4
← Front
Intake   3 3   4 4

29.7a When the No. 4 piston is at TDC on the compression stroke, the valve clearance for the No. 2 and No. 4 exhaust valves and the No. 3 and No. 4 intake valves can be measured (2008 and earlier 1.8L engine shown)

Intake   3 3 4 4
← Front
Exhaust   2 2   4 4

92037-1-29.07 HAYNES

92037-1-29.07b HAYNES

29.7b When the No. 4 piston is at TDC on the compression stroke, the valve clearance for the No. 2 and No. 4 exhaust valves and the No. 3 and No. 4 intake valves can be measured (2.4L engine shown)

size from 0.1992-inch (5.060 mm) to 0.2260-inch (5.740 mm) **(see illustration)**.

Note: *Through careful analysis of the lifter sizes needed to bring the out-of-specification valve clearance within specification, it is often possible to simply move a lifter that has to come out anyway to another location requiring a lifter of that particular size, thereby reducing the number of new lifters that must be purchased.*

16   Install the proper thickness lifter(s) in position, making sure to lubricate them with camshaft installation lube first.

Note: *Apply the lubricant to the underside of the lifter where it contacts the valve stem, the walls of the lifter and the face of the lifter.*

17   Install the camshaft(s) (see Chapter 2A).
18 Recheck the valve clearances.
19 Installation of the spark plugs, valve cover, spark plug wires and boots (or ignition coils), etc., is the reverse of removal.

29.9 Measure the thickness of each lifter head with a micrometer

LIFTER NO.	THICKNESS	LIFTER NO.	THICKNESS	LIFTER NO.	THICKNESS
06	0.1992 in.	30	0.2087 in.	54	0.2181 in.
08	0.2000 in.	32	0.2094 in.	56	0.2189 in.
10	0.2008 in.	34	0.2102 in.	58	0.2197 in.
12	0.2016 in.	36	0.2110 in.	60	0.2205 in.
14	0.2024 in.	38	0.2118 in.	62	0.2213 in.
16	0.2031 in.	40	0.2126 in.	64	0.2220 in.
18	0.2039 in.	42	0.2134 in.	66	0.2228 in.
20	0.2047 in.	44	0.2142 in.	68	0.2236 in.
22	0.2055 in.	46	0.2150 in.	70	0.2244 in.
24	0.2063 in.	48	0.2157 in.	72	0.2252 in.
26	0.2071 in.	50	0.2165 in.	74	0.2260 in.
28	0.2079 in.	52	0.2173 in.		

29.15 Valve lifter thickness chart

Service record

Date	Mileage/hours	Work performed

Service record

Date	Mileage/hours	Work performed

Notes

Chapter 2 Part A
Engine

Contents

Specifications

General

Engine type...	DOHC, inline four-cylinder, four valves per cylinder
Engine designation	
2008 and earlier 1.8L engines............................	1ZZ-FE
2009 and later 1.8L engines.............................	2ZR-FE and 2ZR-FAE
2009 and later 2.4L engines.............................	2AZ-FE
Cylinder numbers (drivebelt end-to-transaxle end)	1-2-3-4
Firing order..	1-3-4-2
Displacement	
1ZZ-FE...	1.8L
2ZR-FE and 2ZR-FAE	1.8L
2AZ-FE...	2.4L

FRONT OF VEHICLE ↓ ① ② ③ ④

92036-2B SPECS HAYNES

Cylinder number locations

Timing chain

Timing chain sprocket wear limit (minimum diameter)	
Camshaft sprocket(s) (w/chain)	
Toyota models	
2003 and 2004 engines............................	3.831 inches
2005 and later 1.8L engines........................	3.811 inches
2009 and later 2.4L engines........................	3.831 inches
Pontiac models	
1.8L engines.....................................	3.811 inches
2.4L engines.....................................	3.831 inches
Crankshaft sprocket (w/chain)	
Toyota models	
2003 and 2004 models.............................	2.032 inches
2005 to 2008 models..............................	2.008 inches
2009 and later 1.8L engines........................	2.012 inches
2009 and later 2.4L engines........................	2.031 inches
Pontiac models	
2003 to 2008 models..............................	2.031 inches
2009 and later models	
1.8L engines...................................	2.012 inches
2.4L engines...................................	2.031 inches
Oil pump drive sprocket (w/chain) - 2009 and later models	1.898 inches
Oil pump drive shaft sprocket (w/chain)	
2009 and later 1.8L engines..........................	1.921 inches
2009 and later 2.4L engines..........................	1.898 inches

Timing chain stretch limit
  Toyota models (1ZZ-FE engines)
    2003 and 2004 (16 pins)... 4.827 inches
    2005 through 2008 (15 pins)... 4.539 inches
  Pontiac models (2003 through 2008)..................................... 4.827 inches
  All models (2009 and later)
    No. 1 chain (15 pins)
      1.8L engines... 4.535 inches
      2.4L engines... 4.508 inches
    No. 2 - oil pump drive chain (15 pins)
      1.8L engines... 4.019 inches
      2.4L engines... 4.024 inches
    No. 1 chain vibration damper wear limit............................ 0.039 inch
Timing chain guide wear limit .... 0.039 inch

Cylinder head

Warpage limit
  Cylinder to block side.. 0.0031 inch
  Intake and exhaust manifold sides..................................... 0.0031 inch

Camshaft and lifters

Journal diameter - standard
  1.8L engines
    No. 1 journal .... 1.3563 to 1.3569 inches
    All others... 0.9035 to 0.9041 inch
  2.4L engines
    No. 1 journal .... 1.4162 to 1.4167 inches
    All others... 0.9039 to 0.9045 inch
Bearing oil clearance
  2008 and earlier
    Standard
      Toyota models .... 0.0014 to 0.0028 inch
      Pontiac models .... 0.0014 to 0.0030 inch
    Service limit (maximum) .... 0.0039 inch
  2009 and later
    Intake camshaft
      1.8L engines
        No.1 journal... 0.0012 to 0.0025 inch
        All others.. 0.0014 to 0.0028 inch
      2.4L engines
        No.1 journal (mark 1).................................. 0.000276 to 0.0015 inch
        No.1 journal (mark 2).................................. 0.000315 to 0.0015 inch
        No.1 journal (mark 3).................................. 0.000315 to 0.0015 inch
        All others.. 0.000984 to 0.00244 inch
    Exhaust camshaft
      1.8L engines
        No.1 journal... 0.0012 to 0.0025 inch
        All others.. 0.0014 to 0.0028 inch
      2.4L engines
        No.1 journal... 0.000157 to 0.00283 inch
        All others.. 0.000984 to 0.00244 inch
    Service limit (maximum)
      1.8L engines (intake and exhaust)
        No.1 journal... 0.0033 inch
        All others.. 0.0035 inch
      2.4L engines
        Intake... 0.00276 inch
        Exhaust .... 0.00394 inch
Runout limit - standard
  1.8L engines
    2008 and earlier .... 0.0012 inch
    2009 and later engines .... 0.0016 inch
  2.4L engines... 0.0012 inch
Thrust clearance (endplay)..
  Standard
    2008 and earlier Toyota models.................................... 0.0016 to 0.0037 inch
    2008 and earlier Pontiac models .... 0.0016 to 0.0055 inch
    2009 and later 1.8L engines (intake and exhaust)........... 0.0024 to 0.0061 inch
    2009 and later 2.4L engines
      Intake... 0.0016 to 0.0037 inch
      Exhaust .... 0.0035 to 0.0057 inch

Service limit (maximum)
  2008 and earlier Toyota models... 0.0043 inch
  2008 and earlier Pontiac models .... 0.0059 inch
  2009 and later 1.8L engines (intake and exhaust)..................... 0.0067 inch
  2009 and later 2.4L engines
    Intake... 0.0043 inch
    Exhaust .... 0.0059 inch
Camshaft timing sprocket-to-camshaft flange clearance........................ 0 inch
Lobe height
  Intake camshaft
    2008 and earlier Toyota models
      Standard.. 1.7454 to 1.7493 inches
      Service limit (minimum) .... 1.7394 inches
    2008 and earlier Pontiac models
      Lobe 1
        Standard.. 1.5958 to 1.5997 inches
        Service limit (minimum) .... 1.5925 inches
      Lobe 2
        Standard.. 1.5236 to 1.5275 inches
        Service limit (minimum) .... 1.5201 inches
    2009 and later 1.8L engines
      Standard.. 1.6857 to 1.6896 inches
      Service limit (minimum) .... 1.6798 inches
    2009 and later 2.4L engines
      Standard.. 1.8654 to 1.8664 inches
      Service limit (minimum) .... 1.8581 inches
  Exhaust camshaft
    2008 and earlier Toyota models
      Standard.. 1.7229 to 1.7268 inches
      Service limit (minimum) .... 1.7169 inches
    2008 and earlier Pontiac models
      Lobe 1
        Standard.. 1.5727 to 1.5766 inches
        Service limit (minimum) .... 1.5693 inches
      Lobe 2
        Standard.. 1.5273 to 1.5312 inches
        Service limit (minimum) .... 1.5240 inches
    2009 and later 1.8L engines
      Standard.. 1.7455 to 1.7494 inches
      Service limit (minimum) .... 1.7396 inches
    2009 and later 2.4L engines
      Standard.. 1.8135 to 1.8174 inches
      Service limit (minimum) .... 1.8092 inches
Valve lifter
  2008 and earlier 1.8L (1ZZ-FE) and 2009 and later .... 2.4L (2AZ-FE) engines
  Diameter .... 1.2191 to 1.2195 inches
  Bore diameter .... 1.2205 to 1.2215 inches
Lifter oil clearance
  2008 and earlier 1.8L (1ZZ-FE) and 2009 and later .... 2.4L (2AZ-FE) engines
  Standard .... 0.0013 to 0.0023 inch
  Service limit (maximum) .... 0.0031 inch

Oil pump

Rotor-to-body clearance
  Standard
    2008 and earlier 1.8L engines .... 0.0102 to 0.0128 inch
    2009 and later 1.8L engines .... 0.00472 to 0.00748 inch
    2009 and later 2.4L engines .... 0.00394 to 0.00669 inch
  Service limit (all)... 0.0128 inch
Rotor tip clearance
  Standard
    2008 and earlier engines .... 0.0016 to 0.0063 inch
    2009 and later engines .... 0.00315 to 0.00630 inch
  Service limit (all)
    2008 and earlier engines .... 0.0063 inch
    2009 and later engines .... 0.0138 inch
Rotor-to-rotor clearance
  Standard
    2008 and earlier engines .... 0.0010 to 0.0028 inch
    2009 to 2013 1.8L engines .... 0.00118 to 0.00315 inch
    2014 and later 1.8L engines .... 0.00335 to 0.00531 inch
    2009 and later 2.4L engines .... 0.00118 to 0.00315 inch
  Service limit
    2008 and earlier engines .... 0.0028 inch
    2009 and later engines .... 0.0063 inch

Torque specifications

Ft-lbs (unless otherwise indicated)

Note: One foot-pound (ft-lb) of torque is equivalent to 12 inch-pounds (in-lbs) of torque. Torque values below approximately 15 ft-lbs are expressed in inch-pounds, because most foot-pound torque wrenches are not accurate at these smaller values.

Camshaft bearing cap bolts	
2008 and earlier 1.8L engines	
Journal No.1 (intake and exhaust)	17
All others	120 in-lbs
2009 and later 1.8L (2ZR-FE) engines **(see illustration 8.42)**	
Camshaft bearing cap-to-cylinder head bolts	20
Camshaft bearing cap-to-camshaft housing bolts	144 in-lbs
2009 and later 2.4L engines	
Journal No.1 (intake and exhaust)	22
All others	80 in-lbs
Camshaft housing and large bearing cap bolts, 2009 and later 1.8L (2ZR-FE) engines	20
Camshaft housing bolts, 2014 and later 1.8L (2ZR-FAE) engines	20
Camshaft timing gear assembly center bolt or sprocket bolt(s)	
2008 and earlier 1.8L engines (intake and exhaust)	40
2009 and later 1.8L engines	
Intake camshaft	40
Exhaust camshaft	
Without special service tool (default method on 2ZR-FAE engines)	40
With special service tool	29
2009 and later 2.4L engines (intake and exhaust)	40
Crankshaft pulley/vibration damper bolt	
2008 and earlier 1.8L engines	102
2009 and later 1.8L engines	140
2009 and later 2.4L engines	133
Cylinder head bolts **(see illustration 11.32a, 11.32b or 11.32c)**	
2008 and earlier 1.8L engines	
Step 1	18
Step 2	36
Step 3	Tighten an additional 90-degrees
2009 and later 1.8L engines	
Step 1	36
Step 2	Tighten an additional 90-degrees
Step 3	Tighten an additional 45-degrees
2009 and later 2.4L engines	
Step 1	52
Step 2	Tighten an additional 90-degrees
Drivebelt tensioner	
2008 and earlier 1.8L engines	
Bolt	51
Nut	21
2009 and later 2.4L engines	44
2014 and later 1.8L (2ZR-FAE) engines	15
Engine balancer assembly, 2009 and later 2.4L engines	
Step 1	16
Step 2	Tighten an additional 90-degrees
Exhaust manifold-to-cylinder head nuts/bolts	
2008 and earlier 1.8L engines	
Toyota models	27
Pontiac models	36
2009 through 2010 1.8L engines	16
2011 through 2013 1.8L engines	27
2014 and later 1.8L engines	
17 mm nuts	19
18 mm nuts	27
2009 and later 2.4L engines	27
Exhaust manifold brace bolts	
2008 and earlier 1.8L engines	
Toyota models	36
Pontiac models	24
2009 and later 1.8L engines	32
2009 and later 2.4L engines	33
Exhaust manifold heat shield bolts	
2008 and earlier 1.8L engines	
Toyota models	156 in-lbs
Pontiac models	132 in-lbs
2009 and later engines	108 in-lbs
Exhaust pipe-to-exhaust manifold bolts	
1.8L engine models	32
2.4L engine models	46

Flywheel/driveplate bolts
  Manual transaxle
    1.8L engine models
      Step 1 36
      Step 2 .... Tighten an additional 90-degrees
    2.4L engine models 96
  Automatic transaxle
    All Toyota models with 1.8L engines.......................... 65
    2008 and earlier Pontiac models with 1.8L engines 61
    2009 and later models with 2.4L engines 72
Intake manifold nuts/bolts
  2008 and earlier 1.8L and all 2.4L engines 22
  2009 and later 1.8L engines 21
Intake manifold support bracket bolts
  2008 and earlier Toyota models 22
  2008 and earlier Pontiac models............................... 37
Lower crankcase-to-engine block bolts
  2009 and later 1.8L engines 16
  2009 and later 2.4L engines 18
Oil pump
  Oil pump bolts
    2008 and earlier 1.8L engines .... 80 in-lbs
    2009 and later 1.8L engines 16
    2009 and later 2.4L engines .... 168 in-lbs
  Oil pick-up strainer nuts/bolts .... 80 in-lbs
  Oil pump drive chain tensioner (arm)
    2009 and later 1.8L engines .... 84 in-lbs
    2009 and later 2.4L engines .... 108 in-lbs
  Oil pump drive shaft sprocket nut/bolt
    2009 and later 1.8L engines 21
    2009 and later 2.4L engines 22
Oil pan bolts
  2008 and earlier 1.8L and all 2.4L engines .... 80 in-lbs
  2009 and later 1.8L engines .... 84 in-lbs
Oil pan drain plug
  1.8L engines.. 27
  2.4L engines.. 30
Timing chain guide bolts (stationary)
  2008 and earlier 1.8L and all 2.4L engines .... 80 in-lbs
  2009 and later 1.8L engines 15
Timing chain tensioner pivot arm bolt............................. 168 in-lbs
Timing chain cover bolts/nuts
  2008 and earlier Toyota models
    10 mm bolt head .... 120 in-lbs
    12 mm bolt head .... 168 in-lbs
  2008 and earlier Pontiac models
    10 mm bolt head .... 89 in-lbs
    12 mm bolt head .... 168 in-lbs
  2009 and later 1.8L engines **(see illustration 7.70a and 7.70b)**
    (A) 35 mm bolt 19
    (B) 55 mm bolt 38
    (C) 80 mm bolt 38
    (D) 40 mm bolt .... 84 in-lbs
    (E) 35 mm bolt 19
  2009 and later 2.4L engines **(see illustration 7.86)**
    (A) 10 mm bolt .... 80 in-lbs
    (B) 12 mm bolt 18
    (C) 14 mm bolt 41
    (D) Nuts .... 96 in-lbs
Timing chain tensioner (nuts/bolt)
  2008 and earlier 1.8L engines.................................. 168 in-lbs
  2009 and later 1.8L engines .... 108 in-lbs
  2009 and later 2.4L engines .... 80 in-lbs
Valve cover
  2008 and earlier 1.8L engines
    Perimeter bolts and nuts...................................... 80 in-lbs
    Center two bolts... 96 in-lbs
  2009 and later 1.8L engines .... 84 in-lbs
  2009 and later 2.4L engines
    A bolts.. 86 in-lbs
    B bolts.. 120 in-lbs
    C nuts .... 86 in-lbs

3.4 There are two lower engine splash shields; remove the fasteners and the shield - right-side shield shown

3.5 A compression gauge can be used in the number one plug hole to assist in finding TDC

1   General information

1   This Part of Chapter 2 is devoted to in-vehicle repair procedures for the four-cylinder engine. Information concerning engine removal and overhaul or replacement can be found in Chapter 2B.

2   The following repair procedures are based on the assumption that the engine is installed in the vehicle. If the engine has been removed from the vehicle and mounted on a stand, many of the steps outlined in this Part of Chapter 2 will not apply.

3   The Specifications included in this Part of Chapter 2 apply only to the procedures contained in this Part.

4   All 2008 and earlier 1.8L engines are designated 1ZZ-FE; 2009 and later models have multiple engines - the 1.8L engines are designated 2ZR-FE and 2ZR-FAE, and the 2.4L engine is designated 2AZ-FE. The engines incorporate an aluminum cylinder block with a lower crankcase to strengthen the lower half of the block. The cylinder head utilizes dual overhead camshafts (DOHC) with four valves per cylinder. The camshafts are driven from a single timing chain off the crankshaft, and a Variable Valve Timing (VVT-i) system is incorporated on the intake camshaft on all models, and exhaust camshaft on 2ZR-FE and 2ZR-FAE engines, to increase horsepower and decrease emissions.

2   Repair operations possible with the engine in the vehicle

1   Many major repair operations can be accomplished without removing the engine from the vehicle.

2   Clean the engine compartment and the exterior of the engine with some type of degreaser before any work is done. It will make the job easier and help keep dirt out of the internal areas of the engine.

3   Depending on the components involved, it may be helpful to remove the hood to improve access to the engine as repairs are performed (refer to Chapter 11 if necessary). Cover the fenders to prevent damage to the paint. Special pads are available, but an old bedspread or blanket will also work.

4   If vacuum, exhaust, oil or coolant leaks develop, indicating a need for gasket or seal replacement, the repairs can generally be made with the engine in the vehicle. The intake and exhaust manifold gaskets, oil pan gasket, crankshaft oil seals and cylinder head gasket (all models except 2009 and later 1.8L [2ZR-FE and 2ZR-FAE] engines) are all accessible with the engine in place.

5   Exterior engine components, such as the intake and exhaust manifolds, the oil pan, the oil pump (all models except 2009 and later 1.8L [2ZR-FE and 2ZR-FAE] engines), the water pump, the starter motor, the alternator and the fuel system components can be removed for repair with the engine in place.

6   Since the cylinder head can be removed without pulling the engine (all models except 2009 and later 1.8L [2ZR-FE and 2ZR-FAE] engines), camshaft and valve component servicing can also be accomplished with the engine in the vehicle. Replacement of the timing chain and sprockets is also possible with the engine in the vehicle (all models except 2009 and later 1.8L [2ZR-FE and 2ZR-FAE] engines).

7   In extreme cases caused by a lack of necessary equipment, repair or replacement of piston rings, pistons, connecting rods and rod bearings is possible with the engine in the vehicle. However, this practice is not recommended because of the cleaning and preparation work that must be done to the components involved.

3   Top Dead Center (TDC) for number one piston - locating

1   Top Dead Center (TDC) is the highest point in the cylinder that each piston reaches as it travels up the cylinder bore. Each piston reaches TDC on the compression stroke and again on the exhaust stroke, but TDC generally refers to piston position on the compression stroke.

2   Positioning the piston(s) at TDC is an essential part of certain procedures such as valve adjustment and camshaft and timing chain/sprocket removal.

3   Before beginning this procedure, be sure to place the transaxle in Neutral and apply the parking brake or block the rear wheels. If method "C)" in the next Step will be used to rotate the engine, remove the EFI fuse from the underhood fuse/relay block, then disconnect the electrical connectors from the ignition coils (see Chapter 5).

4   In order to bring any piston to TDC, the crankshaft must be turned using one of the methods outlined below. When looking at the front of the engine, normal crankshaft rotation is clockwise.

a) *The preferred method is to turn the crankshaft with a socket and ratchet attached to the bolt threaded into the front of the crankshaft. Turn the bolt in a clockwise direction. You will have to remove the right-side engine lower splash shield* **(see illustration)**.

b) *A remote starter switch, which may save some time, can also be used. Follow the instructions included with the switch. Once the piston is close to TDC, use a socket and ratchet as described in the previous paragraph.*

c) *If an assistant is available to turn the ignition switch to the Start position in short bursts, you can get the piston close to TDC without a remote starter switch. Make sure your assistant is out of the vehicle, away from the ignition switch, then use a socket and ratchet as described in Paragraph a) to complete the procedure.*

5   Install a compression gauge in the number one spark plug hole **(see illustration)**. It should be a gauge with a screw-in fitting and a hose at least six inches long.

3.8 Align the groove in the damper with the "0" mark on the timing chain cover

4.2 Remove the engine cover - upper arrows indicate plastic retaining clips, lower arrows indicate two retaining nuts (2008 and earlier 1.8L and all 2.4L models)

6   Rotate the crankshaft using one of the methods described above while observing for pressure on the compression gauge. The moment the gauge shows pressure indicates that the number one cylinder has begun the compression stroke.

7   Once the compression stroke has begun, TDC for the compression stroke is reached by bringing the piston to the top of the cylinder.

8   Continue turning the crankshaft until the notch in the crankshaft damper is aligned with the "TDC" or the "0" mark on the timing chain cover **(see illustration)**. At this point, the number one cylinder is at TDC on the compression stroke. If the marks are aligned but there was no compression, the piston was on the exhaust stroke; continue rotating the crankshaft 360-degrees (1-turn) and realign the marks.

Note: *With the valve cover off, verify the TDC position by noting the timing marks on the camshaft sprockets. They should line up as if on a straight line that is parallel to the top of the timing chain cover.*

Note: *If a compression gauge is not available, you can simply place a blunt object over the*

spark plug hole and listen for compression as the engine is rotated. Once compression at the No.1 spark plug hole is noted, the remainder of the Step is the same.

9   After the number one piston has been positioned at TDC on the compression stroke, TDC for any of the remaining cylinders can be located by turning the crankshaft 180-degrees (clockwise) and following the firing order (refer to this Chapter's Specifications). Rotating the engine 180-degrees past TDC #1 will put the engine at TDC compression for cylinder #3.

4   Valve cover - removal and installation

Removal

1   Disconnect the cable from the negative terminal of the battery (see Chapter 5).

2   On 2008 and earlier models and all 2.4L engine models, remove the engine cover mounting fasteners and remove the cover **(see illustration)**. On 2009 and later 1.8L engines, lift the cover straight up and off of the

ballstuds to remove the cover.

3   Disconnect the electrical connectors from the ignition coils, remove the nuts securing the wiring harness to the valve cover and position the ignition coil wiring harness aside. Then remove the ignition coil from each of the spark plugs (see Chapter 5).

4   Detach the breather hoses from the valve cover and remove the ground harness bolts.

5   On 2009 and later 1.8L engines, disconnect the camshaft oil control valve and camshaft position sensor electrical connectors (see Chapter 6).

6   Remove the valve cover mounting fasteners, then detach the valve cover and gasket from the cylinder head **(see illustrations)**. If the valve cover is stuck to the cylinder head, bump the end with a wood block and a hammer to jar it loose. If that doesn't work, try to slip a flexible putty knife between the cylinder head and valve cover to break the seal.

Caution: *Don't pry at the valve cover-to-cylinder head joint or damage to the sealing surfaces may occur, leading to oil leaks after the valve cover is reinstalled.*

4.6a Valve cover fastener locations (2008 and earlier model shown, 2.4L models similar)

4.6b Valve cover fastener locations (2009 and later 1.8L model shown)

4.7 The valve cover gasket and the spark plug tube seals are incorporated into a single rubber O-ring-like seal - press the gasket evenly into the grooves around the underside of the valve cover and the spark plug openings (2008 and earlier model shown, later models similar)

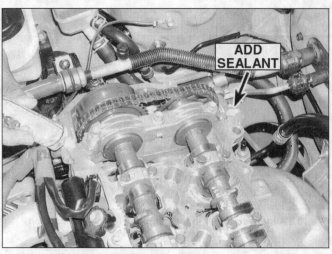

4.8 Apply sealant at the timing chain cover-to-cylinder head joints before installing the valve cover

Installation

7   Remove the valve cover gasket from the valve cover and clean the mating surfaces with brake system cleaner. On 2009 and later 1.8L engines, remove the O-rings from the No.1 camshaft bearing cap. Install a new rubber gasket (and O-rings on 2009 and later 1.8L engines), pressing it evenly into the grooves around the underside of the valve cover. Make sure the spark plug tube seals are in place on the underside of the valve cover before reinstalling it **(see illustration)**. The mating surfaces of the timing chain cover, the cylinder head and valve cover must be perfectly clean when the valve cover is installed. If there's residue or oil on the mating surfaces when the valve cover is installed, oil leaks may develop.
Note: *On 2009 and later 1.8L engines, also replace the camshaft cap seals which are located near the timing chain*
8   Apply RTV sealant at the timing chain cover-to-cylinder head joints, then install the valve cover and fasteners **(see illustration)**.
9   Tighten the nuts/bolts to the torque listed in this Chapter's Specifications in three or four equal steps.
10   Reinstall the remaining parts, run the engine and check for oil leaks.

5   Variable Valve Timing (VVT and VVT-i) system and Valvematic (Continuously Variable Valve Lift) control system - description and component replacement

VVT and VVT-i system

Description

1   The Variable Valve Timing system is used on all models. There are two types of systems used: a single Variable Valve Timing system used on 2008 and earlier 1.8L (1ZZ-FE) engine and all 2.4L (2AZ-FE) engines, and the dual Variable Valve Timing intelligent system used on 2009 and later 1.8L (2ZR-FE and 2ZR-FAE) engine models.
2   The VVT/VVT-i system varies intake (and exhaust on 2009 and later 1.8L engines) camshaft timing that is optimized for the driving conditions by using engine oil pressure to advance or retard the controller on the front end of the camshaft.
3   The VVT system on 2008 and earlier 1.8L (1ZZ-FE) engines and the VVT-i system on 2009 and later 2.4L (2AZ-FE) engines consists of a CMP sensor, CKP sensor, camshaft timing oil control valve, Powertrain Control Module (PCM) and one controller (intake camshaft sprocket/actuator assembly). The dual VVT-i system on 2009 and later 1.8L (2ZR-FE and 2ZR-FAE) engines consists of two CMP sensors, a CKP sensor, two camshaft timing oil control valves, Powertrain Control Module (PCM) and two controllers (intake and exhaust camshaft sprocket/actuator assemblies).
4   Each controller consists of a timing rotor (for the VVT-i sensor), a housing with an impeller-type vane inside it, a lock pin and the actual timing chain sprocket for the intake camshaft. The vane is fixed on the end of the camshaft.
5   The camshaft timing oil control valve(s) are a PCM-controlled device that controls and directs the flow of oil to the advance or retard passages leading to the controller. There is one oil control valve for each camshaft. A spring-loaded spool valve inside the oil control valve directs oil pumped into the valve toward either the advance outlet or the retard outlet port, depending on the engine condition.

Component replacement

Camshaft timing oil control valve(s)
Note: *2008 and earlier 1.8L (1ZZ-FE) and 2009 and later 2.4L (2AZ-FE) engines use only one camshaft timing control valve. 2009 and later 1.8L engines use two control valves.*
6   Disconnect the cable from the negative battery terminal (see Chapter 5).
7   Remove the engine cover (see Section 4, Step 2).
8   Remove the engine harness mounting fasteners and move the harness to the side. Disconnect the electrical connector from the camshaft timing oil control valve. On 2008 and earlier 1.8L and all 2.4L engines, remove the oil control valve mounting bolt and remove the oil control valve from the cylinder head **(see illustration)**.
Note: *The oil control valves on 2009 and later 2.4L engines are located on the backside of the cylinder head.*
9   On 2009 and later 1.8L engines- remove the nuts and position aside the wiring harness, then remove the camshaft timing oil control valve mounting bolt and remove the oil control valve (intake or exhaust) from the valve cover **(see illustration)**.
10   Replace the O-ring on the oil control valve with a new O-ring.
11   Installation is the reverse of removal.

Valvematic control system - 2014 and later 2ZR-FAE engines

Description

12   The Valvematic system affects and has coordinated control of the Dual VVT-i system. Based on information received from the Valvematic shaft sensor (No. 1 crankshaft position sensor), action angle sensor and motor position sensor, the PCM monitors the Valvematic system to verify if it is operating properly. It constantly controls the variable amount of intake valve lift, intake valve action angle, and intake valve timing, as well as control of the exhaust valve timing, as needed by the engine demand to produce better engine performance and fuel economy.

5.8 The VVT oil control valve and filter are located at the front of the cylinder head (2008 and earlier models)

5.9 Camshaft timing oil control valve details - 2009 and later 1.8L (2ZR-FE and 2ZR-FAE) engine models

A Exhaust side camshaft timing oil control valve (electrical connector)
B Camshaft timing oil control valve mounting bolt
C Intake side camshaft timing oil control valve (electrical connector)
D Engine harness mounting fasteners

13   The Valvematic system consists of a continuously variable valve lift controller assembly at the actuator and Valvematic mechanism mounted next to the valve train. Along with the use of this system, a vacuum pump assembly is provided in order to provide proper brake control vacuum.

14   The continuously variable valve lift controller is mounted to the end of the camshaft housing and is attached to the control shaft. The control shaft transmits movement of the continuously variable valve lift controller assembly to the slider assembly, that contains helical spline gear and rollers. The rotation of the oscillating cam varies continuously in order to vary the amount of intake valve movement.

Removal

15   Disconnect the cable from the negative terminal of the battery (see Chapter 5).

16   Remove the air filter housing (see Chapter 4).

17   Remove the battery (see Chapter 5).

18   Disconnect all main engine harness connectors from the top, side, front and rear of the engine, labeling them as necessary. Disengage the harness retaining clips and position the harness out of the way of the Valvematic actuator (located at the left side of the cylinder head).

19   Remove the ignition coils (see Chapter 5).

20   Remove the vacuum switching valve mounting bolts, then disconnect the hoses and remove the valve from the left end of the cylinder head (see Chapter 6).

21   Remove the valve cover and gasket (see Section 4).

22   The control actuator is connected to the end of the rocker arm shaft by an actuator connector. The actuator connector slides over the end of the rocker arm shaft and the end of the continuously variable valve lift controller slides into the end of the connector. The continuously variable lift controller is held in place with a retaining pin that is locked into place using a large flat C-type clip.

23   Rotate the crankshaft clockwise by hand until the No.1 cylinder intake camshaft lobe is at 12 o'clock and the No. 3 cylinder intake lobe is at the 9 o'clock position (when viewed from the timing chain end).

24   Once in this position, rotate the crankshaft counterclockwise slightly, around 10- to 15-degrees.

25   Using a screwdriver to pry, slide the upper end of the C-clip off of the actuator connector. If you slide the entire clip off the retaining pin, it will drop out into the engine.

26   Use two flat blade screwdrivers parallel to one another to even out the force, lightly pry the actuator connector apart from the continuously variable lift controller and the camshaft carrier - just enough to create a small space between the components. The idea is to ease the load on the pin to be removed.

27   Using a magnet, pull the pin out from the actuator connector. If the magnet can't pull the pin out, fashion a piece of wire into a half moon shape, then try and push the pin up and out from the bottom to remove the pin.

Note: *If necessary, try to push the retaining pin up and out from the bottom. The C-clip must be moved back enough to allow the wire to push the pin up. Be careful not to move the C-clip all the way off so that the pin does not fall out.*

28   At this stage, it is safe to remove the connector clip completely with a screwdriver. Remove the fasteners for the continuously variable lift controller and slide the controller off the end of the cylinder head.

Caution: *Make sure the pin or the C-clip does not fall into the engine.*

29   Remove and replace the continuously variable lift controller O-ring.

Installation

Note: *The measurement from the continuously variable lift controller face to the slot of the actuator connector should be 1.36 to 1.37 inches.*

30   Install a new O-ring on the continuously

variable lift controller.

31   Rotate the crankshaft slightly clockwise to retract the valve rocker shaft.

32   Rotate the crankshaft clockwise and verify that the No.1 cylinder intake camshaft lobe is at 12 o'clock and the No. 3 cylinder intake lobe is at the 9 o'clock position (when viewed from the timing chain end).

33   Install the valve lift control actuator connector with the clip in place over the valve rocker shaft assembly.

34   Insert the continuously variable valve lift controller assembly into the cylinder head, then install the mounting bolts and tighten the bolts securely.

35   Using two screwdrivers, align the hole in the actuator connector with the hole in the continuously variable valve lift controller shaft.

36   Insert the pin into the continuously variable valve lift controller shaft and connector, making sure the C-clip is still covering the bottom of the hole, then slide the C-clip in place.

37   The remainder of installation is the reverse of removal.

6   Valve springs, retainers and seals - replacement

Note: *This Section applies to 2008 and earlier 1.8L engines and all 2.4L engines only.*

Note: *Broken valve springs and defective valve stem seals can be replaced without removing the cylinder head. Two special tools and a compressed air source are normally required to perform this operation, so read through this Section carefully. The universal shaft-type valve spring compressor required for the tight valve spring pockets of this vehicle may not be available at all tool rental yards, so check on the availability before beginning the job.*

1   Remove the valve cover (see Section 4). Refer to Section 7 and remove the timing chain, then refer to Section 8 and remove the camshafts and lifters from the cylinder head.

6.4 You'll need an air hose adapter to reach down into the spark plug tubes - they're commonly available from auto parts stores

6.8a Compress the valve spring enough to release the keepers . . .

6.8b . . . and lift them out with a magnet or needle-nose pliers

6.10 A pair of pliers will be required to remove the valve seal from the valve guide

6.15 Using a deep socket and hammer, gently tap the new seals onto the valve guide only until seated

6.17 Apply a small dab of grease to each keeper as shown here before installation - it will hold them in place on the valve stem as the spring is released

2   Remove the spark plug from the cylinder that has the defective component. If all of the valve stem seals are being replaced, all of the spark plugs should be removed.

3   Turn the crankshaft until the piston in the affected cylinder is at top dead center (TDC) on the compression stroke (see Section 3 for instructions). If you're replacing all of the valve stem seals, begin with cylinder number one and work on the valves for one cylinder at a time. Move from cylinder-to-cylinder following the firing order sequence (see this Chapter's Specifications).

4   Thread an adapter into the spark plug hole (see illustration) and connect an air hose from a compressed air source to it. Most auto parts stores can supply the air hose adapter.

Note: *Many cylinder compression gauges utilize a screw-in fitting that may work with your air hose quick-disconnect fitting.*

5   Apply compressed air to the cylinder. The valves should be held in place by the air pressure.

Warning: *If the cylinder isn't exactly at TDC, air pressure may force the piston down, causing the engine to quickly rotate. DO NOT leave a wrench on the crankshaft drive sprocket bolt or you may be injured by the tool.*

6   Stuff shop rags into the cylinder head holes around the valves to prevent parts and tools from falling into the engine.

7   Using a socket and a hammer, gently tap on the top of each valve spring retainer several times. This will break the bond between the valve keepers and the spring retainer and allow the keepers to separate from the valve spring retainer as the valve spring is compressed.

8   Use a valve spring compressor to compress the spring, then remove the keepers with small needle-nose pliers or a magnet (see illustrations).

Note: *Several different types of tools are available for compressing the valve springs with the head in place. Be sure to purchase or rent the "import type" that bolts to the top of the cylinder head. This type uses a support bar across the cylinder head for leverage as the valve spring is compressed. The lack of clearance surrounding the valve springs on these engines prohibits typical types of valve spring compressors from being used.*

9   Remove the valve spring and retainer.

Note: *If air pressure fails to retain the valve in the closed position during this operation, the valve face or seat may be damaged. If so, the cylinder head will have to be removed for repair.*

10   Remove the old valve stem seals, noting differences between the intake and exhaust seals (see illustration).

11   Wrap a rubber band or tape around the top of the valve stem so the valve won't fall

into the combustion chamber, then release the air pressure.

12   Inspect the valve stem for damage. Rotate the valve in the guide and check the end for eccentric movement, which would indicate that the valve is bent.

13   Move the valve up-and-down in the guide and make sure it doesn't bind. If the valve stem binds, either the valve is bent or the guide is damaged. In either case, the head will have to be removed for repair.

14   Reapply air pressure to the cylinder to retain the valve in the closed position, then remove the tape or rubber band from the valve stem.

15   Lubricate the valve stem with engine oil and install a new seal on the valve guide (see illustration).

16   Install the valve spring and the spring retainer in position over the valve.

17   Compress the valve spring and carefully position the keepers in the groove. Apply a small dab of grease to the inside of each keeper to hold it in place (see illustration).

18   Remove the pressure from the spring tool and make sure the keepers are seated.

19   Disconnect the air hose and remove the adapter from the spark plug hole.

20   Install the camshaft, lifters, timing chain and the valve cover by referring to the appropriate Sections.

7.7a Verify the engine is at TDC by observing the position of the camshaft sprocket marks (upper arrows) - they must be in a straight line and parallel with the top of the timing chain cover (lower arrow) (2008 and earlier models)

7.7c Location of TDC for 2009 and later 2.4L engines. The camshaft sprocket marks (lower arrows) must be aligned with the marks on the camshaft bearing caps (upper arrows)

7.7b Camshafts and crankshaft TDC timing chain mark locations (2009 and later 1.8L (2ZR-FE and 2ZR-FAE) engines)

1   *Exhaust camshaft sprocket*
2   *Intake camshaft sprocket*
3   *Exhaust camshaft sprocket timing mark*
4   *Intake camshaft sprocket timing mark*
5   *Timing chain "orange" colored link - exhaust*
6   *Timing chain "orange" colored links - intake*
7   *Index mark, not a timing mark*
8   *Crankshaft "TDC" keyway at 12 o'clock position*
9   *Crankshaft timing mark and timing chain "yellow" colored link*

21   Install the spark plugs and the ignition coils.
22   Start and run the engine, then check for oil leaks and unusual sounds coming from the valve cover area.

7   Timing chain and sprockets - removal, inspection and installation

Note: *If you're working on a 2009 and later 1.8L (2ZR-FE or 2ZR-FAE) engine, the manufacturer recommends removing the engine and transaxle assembly to perform this procedure (see Chapter 2B).*

Removal

Warning: *Wait until the engine is completely cool before beginning this procedure.*
Caution: *The timing system is complex, and severe engine damage will occur if you make any mistakes. Do not attempt this procedure*

unless you are at all unsure of your abilities, be sure to consult an expert. Double-check all your work and be sure everything is correct before you attempt to start the engine.
Note: *Special tools are required for this procedure. Read through the entire procedure and acquire the necessary tools and equipment before beginning work.*
1   Disconnect the cable from the negative battery terminal (see Chapter 5).
2   Remove the drivebelt (see Chapter 1) and the alternator (see Chapter 5).
3   Remove the windshield washer reservoir and valve cover (see Section 4).
Note: *On 2009 and later 1.8L engines, remove the O-ring gaskets from the camshaft bearing caps.*
4   With the parking brake applied and the rear wheels blocked, loosen the right front wheel lug nuts, then raise the front of the vehicle and support it securely on jackstands. Remove the right front wheel and the right splash shield from the wheelwell.

5   Drain the cooling system (see Chapter 1).
6   While the coolant is draining on 2008 and earlier models, remove the power steering pump from the engine without disconnecting the fluid lines (see Chapter 10). Tie the power steering pump to the body with a piece of wire and position it out of the way. On 2009 and later 1.8L models, remove the cowl assembly (see Chapter 11) and windshield wiper motor and linkage (see Chapter 12), if there is room to perform the procedure with the engine in-vehicle.
7   Position the number one piston at TDC on the compression stroke (see Section 3). Confirm the engine is at TDC on the compression stroke by verifying that the timing mark on the crankshaft pulley/vibration damper is aligned with the "0" mark on the timing chain cover **(see illustration 3.8)** and the camshaft sprocket marks are aligned with the marks on the camshaft front bearing caps **(see illustrations)**.
Note: *There are two sets of marks on the camshaft sprockets. The marks that align at TDC are for TDC reference only; the other two*

7.9 If an engine support fixture is not available, the engine can be supported from below using a floor jack and a block of wood

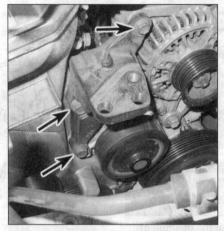

7.11 Remove the engine mount bracket bolts (2008 and earlier model shown)

7.13 Timing chain tensioner mounting nuts

marks are used to align the sprockets with the timing chain during installation.

8 Remove the crankshaft pulley/vibration damper, being careful not to rotate the engine from TDC (see Section 12). If the engine rotates off TDC during this step, reposition the engine back to TDC before proceeding.

9 Support the engine from above using an engine support fixture (available at rental yards), or from below using a floor jack. Use a wood block between the floor jack and the engine to prevent damage **(see illustration)**.

10 Remove the front exhaust pipe-to-manifold mounting bolts and the passenger's side engine mount (see Section 18).

11 Remove the drivebelt tensioner (see Chapter 1), the crankshaft position sensor (see Chapter 6), and the engine mounting bracket from the timing chain cover **(see illustration)**. Also remove the bolt securing the crankshaft position sensor wiring harness to the timing chain cover. On all 2009 and later models, remove the steel oil pan (see Section 14).

2008 and earlier 1.8L engines (1ZZ-FE)

12 Remove the water pump (see Chapter 3). Disconnect the power steering pressure switch.

13 Remove the timing chain tensioner from the rear side of the timing chain cover **(see illustration)**.

14 Remove the timing chain cover fasteners and pry the cover off the engine **(see illustrations)**.

15 Slide the crankshaft position sensor reluctor ring off the crankshaft **(see illustration)**.

16 Remove the timing chain tensioner pivot arm/chain guide **(see illustration)**.

17 Lift the timing chain off the camshaft sprockets and remove the timing chain and the crankshaft sprocket as an assembly from the engine. The crankshaft sprocket should slip off the crankshaft by hand. If not, use several flat bladed screwdrivers to evenly pry the sprocket off the crankshaft.

Note: *If you intend to reuse the timing chain,*

use white paint or chalk to make a mark indicating the front of the chain. If a used timing chain is reinstalled with the wear pattern in the opposite direction, noise and increased wear may occur.

18 Remove the stationary timing chain guide **(see illustration 7.16)**.

2009 and later 1.8L engines (2ZR-FE and 2ZR-FAE)

19 Remove the timing chain tensioner mounting nuts and tensioner from the rear side of the timing chain cover.

20 Remove the oil filter housing mounting bolts and housing from the lower front side of the cover.

21 Once the housing is off, remove the O-rings.

22 Remove the engine mounting bracket from the front of the timing chain cover. Remove the timing chain cover fasteners and carefully pry the cover off the engine from several locations.

Note: *The timing chain cover has several different size mounting bolts; take note of each*

7.14a Timing chain cover upper fasteners - this stud (A) will have to be removed with a Torx socket and tightened to 82 in-lbs during installation

7.14b Timing chain cover lower fasteners - make a note of the fastener sizes, locations and lengths as you're removing them, as they must be installed back in their original position

7.14c Pry the timing chain cover off by the casting protrusion

7.15 Slide the crankshaft position sensor reluctor ring off the crankshaft - note the "F" mark on the front (it must be facing outward upon installation)

7.16 Timing chain guide mounting details

A   Pivot bolt
B   Tensioner pivot arm/chain guide
C   Stationary chain guide mounting bolts
D   Stationary chain guide

bolt's location so they can be returned to the same locations on reassembly.

23   Once the cover is off, remove the O-rings from the crankcase.

Note: *The water pump is mounted to the timing chain cover, it is not necessary to remove the pump for the timing chain cover to be removed.*

24   Remove the top chain guide mounting bolts and guide.

25   Remove the timing chain tensioner pivot arm/chain guide and the stationary timing chain guide mounting bolts, then remove the guides from each side of the chain.

26   Place an adjustable wrench on the hex-shaped lug of the intake camshaft and turn the camshaft counterclockwise just enough to lift the timing chain off the camshaft sprockets and remove the timing chain from the engine. Then rotate the camshaft clockwise to its original position.

Note: *If you intend to reuse the timing chain, use white paint or chalk to make a mark indicating the front of the chain.If a used timing*

chain is reinstalled with the wear pattern in the opposite direction, noise and increased wear may occur.

2009 and later 2.4L engines (2AZ-FE)

27   Remove the timing chain tensioner mounting nuts and tensioner from the rear side of the timing chain cover (**see illustration**).

28   Remove the engine mounting bracket from the front of the timing chain cover, then remove the stud for the drivebelt tensioner using a Torx socket.

29   Remove the timing chain cover fasteners (**see illustrations**) and pry the cover off the engine (**see illustration 7.14c**).

Note: *The timing chain cover has several different size mounting bolts; take note of each bolt's location so they can be returned to the same locations on reassembly.*

30   Slide the crankshaft position sensor reluctor ring off the crankshaft (**see illustration 7.15**).

7.27 Timing chain tensioner mounting nuts - 2009 and later 2.4L engines

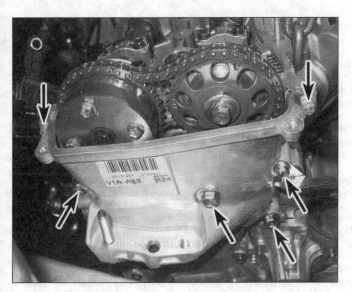

7.29a Timing chain cover upper fasteners

7.29b Timing chain cover lower fasteners

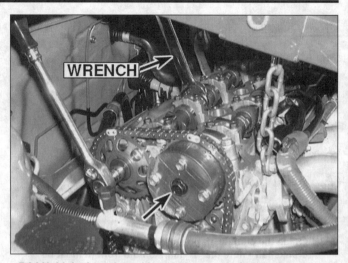

7.31 Timing chain guide mounting details
A   *Pivot bolt*
B   *Tensioner pivot arm/chain guide*
C   *Stationary chain guide mounting bolts*
D   *Stationary chain guide*
E   *Lower timing chain guide*

7.34 Hold the hex-shaped lug on the camshaft with a wrench to keep it from rotating as the sprocket bolts are loosened - when loosening the camshaft sprocket, loosen only the center bolt which secures the sprocket to the camshaft (2008 and earlier model shown, later models similar)

7.35a Wrap the chain around each of the timing sprockets and measure the diameter of the sprockets across the chain rollers - if the measurement exceeds the minimum sprocket diameter, the chain and the sprockets must be replaced

7.35b Timing chain stretch is measured by checking the length of the chain between 8 links (16 pins, 2004 and earlier; 15 pins, 2005 and later) at 3 or more places (selected randomly) around the chain - if chain stretch exceeds the specifications between any 8 links, the chain must be replaced

31   Remove the timing chain tensioner pivot arm/chain guide and the lower chain guide **(see illustration)**.

32   Lift the timing chain off the camshaft sprockets and remove the timing chain and the crankshaft sprocket as an assembly from the engine. The crankshaft sprocket should slip off the crankshaft by hand. If not, carefully pry the sprocket off the crankshaft.
Note: *If you intend to reuse the timing chain, use white paint or chalk to make a mark indicating the front of the chain.If a used timing chain is reinstalled with the wear pattern in the opposite direction, noise and increased wear may occur.*

33   Remove the stationary timing chain guide **(see illustration 7.31)**.

All models

34   To remove the camshaft sprockets (if

necessary), loosen the center bolt while holding the hex on the camshaft with a wrench **(see illustration)**. Note the identification marks on the camshaft sprockets before removal, then remove the bolt. Pull on the sprockets by hand until they slip off the dowels. If necessary, use a small puller, with the legs inserted in the relief holes, to pull the sprocket off.
Note: *These models are equipped with variable valve timing, which consists of an actuator assembly attached to the intake camshaft sprocket (and exhaust camshaft on 2009 and later 1.8L engines). When removing the intake camshaft sprocket (or exhaust camshaft sprocket on 2009 and later 1.8L engines), only loosen and remove the center bolt, which fastens the sprocket to the camshaft. Do not loosen the outer four bolts that secure the actuator to the sprocket.*

Inspection

35   Visually inspect all parts for wear and damage. Check the timing chain for loose pins, cracks, worn rollers and side plates. Check the sprockets for hook-shaped, chipped and broken teeth. Also check the timing chain for stretching and the diameter of the timing sprockets for wear with the chain assembled on the sprockets **(see illustration)**. Be sure to measure across the chain rollers when checking the sprocket diameter and to measure chain stretch at three or more places around the chain; if chain stretch exceeds the specifications between any 8 links, the chain must be replaced **(see illustration)**. Maximum chain elongation and minimum sprocket diameter (with chain) should not exceed the amount listed in this Chapter's Specifications. Replace the timing chain and sprockets as a set if the engine has high mileage or fails inspection .

7.36 Timing chain guide wear is measured from the top of the chain contact surface to the bottom of the wear grooves

7.38 Camshaft timing sprocket installation details - there should be no clearance between the sprocket and the camshaft flange (all models)

7.42 Loop the timing chain around the crankshaft sprocket and align the No.1 colored link with the mark on the crankshaft sprocket, then install the chain and crankshaft sprocket as an assembly on the engine

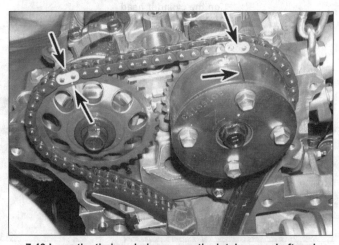

7.43 Loop the timing chain up over the intake camshaft and around the exhaust camshaft, while aligning the remaining two colored links with the marks on the camshaft sprockets

36   Check the chain guides for excessive wear (see illustration). Replace the chain guides if scoring or wear exceeds the amount listed in this Chapter's Specifications. Note that some scoring of the timing chain guide shoes is normal. If excessive wear is indicated, it will also be necessary to inspect the chain guide oil hole on the front of the oil pump for clogging (see Section 15).

Installation

Caution: Before starting the engine, carefully rotate the crankshaft by hand through at least two full revolutions (use a socket and breaker bar on the crankshaft pulley center bolt). If you feel any resistance, STOP! There is something wrong - most likely, valves are contacting the pistons. You must find the problem before proceeding.
37   Remove all traces of old sealant from the timing chain cover and the mating surfaces of the engine block and cylinder head.
38   On 2008 and earlier models and all 2.4L engines, make sure the camshafts are

positioned with the dowel pins at the top in the 12 o'clock position, then install the exhaust camshaft sprocket in the original location by aligning the dowel pin hole on the rear of the sprockets with the dowel pin on the camshaft. Apply medium-strength thread locking compound to the camshaft sprocket bolt threads and make sure the washers are in place. Hold the camshaft from turning as described in Step 47 and tighten the bolts to the torque listed in this Chapter's Specifications. Make sure the camshaft sprocket is fully seated against the camshaft flange (see illustration). Install the intake camshaft timing sprocket (see Steps 55 through 58).

2008 and earlier 1.8L engines (1ZZ-FE)

39   Rotate the camshafts as necessary to align the TDC marks on the camshaft sprockets (see illustration 7.7a).
40   If the crankshaft has been rotated off TDC during this procedure, it will be necessary to rotate the crankshaft until the keyway

is pointing straight up in the 12 o'clock position with the centerline of the cylinder bores.
41   Install the stationary timing chain guide (see illustration 7.16).
42   Loop the timing chain around the crankshaft sprocket and align the No.1 colored link with the mark on the crankshaft sprocket. Install the chain and crankshaft sprocket as an assembly on the engine (see illustration). Note: There are three colored links on the timing chain. The No.1 colored link is the link farthest away from the two colored links that are closest together.
43   Slip the timing chain into the lip of the stationary timing chain guide and over the intake camshaft sprocket, then around the exhaust camshaft sprocket, making sure to align the remaining two colored links with the marks on the camshaft sprockets (see illustration). Be sure to remove all slack from the right side of the chain when doing so. The colored links align with the two-dot mark on the exhaust sprocket and the line mark on the intake sprocket.

7.44 After the tensioner pivot arm is installed, make sure the tab (arrow) on the pivot arm can't move past the stopper on the cylinder head

7.47 Apply a bead of sealant on each side of the parting line between the cylinder head and the engine block

7.49 Raise the ratchet pawl and push the plunger inward until the hook on the tensioner body can be engaged with the pin on the plunger to lock the plunger in place

7.50 Apply a small amount of oil to the tensioner O-ring and insert the tensioner into the timing chain cover with the hook facing upward

7.52 Depress the tensioner pivot arm and disengage the hook from the plunger pin to set tension on the timing chain

44   Use one hand to remove the slack from the left side of the chain and install the timing chain tensioner pivot arm/chain guide. Tighten the pivot bolt to the torque listed in this Chapter's Specifications. After installation, make sure the tab on the pivot arm can't move past the stopper on the cylinder head (see illustration).

45   Reconfirm that the number one piston is still at TDC on the compression stroke and that the timing marks on the crankshaft and camshaft sprockets are aligned with the colored links on the chain.

46   Install the crankshaft position sensor reluctor ring with the "F" mark facing outward.

47   Apply a bead of RTV sealant to the timing chain cover sealing surfaces (see illustration). Place the timing chain cover in position on the engine and install the bolts in their original locations. Tighten the bolts evenly in several steps to the torque listed in this Chapter's Specifications (see illustrations 7.14a and 7.14b). Be sure to follow the sealant manu-

facturer's recommendations for assembly and sealant curing times.

48   Install the water pump O-ring, the water pump and the engine mount bracket all within the sealant manufacturer's specified drying times. Before installing the engine mount bracket, apply a small amount of RTV sealant to the threads of the engine mount bracket bolts.

49   Reload and lock the timing chain tensioner to its zero position as follows (see illustration).

50   Lubricate the tensioner O-ring with a small amount of oil and install the tensioner into the timing chain cover with the hook facing up (see illustration).

51   Install the crankshaft pulley/vibration damper (see Section 12).

52   Rotate the engine clockwise slightly to set the chain tension. As the engine is rotated, the hook on the tensioner body should release itself from the pin on the plunger and allow the plunger to spring out and apply tension to the timing chain. If the plunger does not spring

outward and apply tension to the timing chain, press downward on the pivot arm and release the hook with a screwdriver (see illustration).

2009 and later 1.8L engines (2ZR-FE and 2ZR-FAE)

53   Make sure the camshafts are positioned with the dowel pins at the top in the 12 o'clock position, then carefully push the camshaft timing gear onto the camshaft with the dowel pin and key groove off-center.

54   Turn the camshaft timing gear counterclockwise while pushing the gear on to the camshaft until the dowel drops in to the groove and then seat the camshaft gear to the camshaft.

Caution: Do not turn the camshaft gear clockwise at this time, it may unseat the dowel pin.

55   Observe the clearance between the sprocket and the camshaft flange (see illustration 7.38), making sure there is none.

56   Apply medium-strength thread locking compound to the camshaft sprocket bolt

7.74 Rotate the engine counterclockwise to disengage the hook from the plunger pin on the tensioner, then rotate it clockwise and confirm that the plunger has extended outward against the pivot arm/chain guide

7.70a Timing chain cover bolt identification - 2009 and later 1.8L engines

7.70b Timing chain cover bolt tightening sequence - 2009 and later 1.8L engines

threads and make sure the washers are in place.

57 Hold the camshaft from turning as described in Step 47 and tighten the bolts to the torque listed in this Chapter's Specifications.

58 On intake camshaft, check to make sure the camshaft gear can be rotated clockwise and is locked in the furthest position clockwise.

59 Temporarily install the crankshaft pulley bolt and rotate the crankshaft counterclockwise until the keyway is pointing to the 12 o'clock position.

60 Rotate the camshafts as necessary to align the TDC marks on the camshaft sprockets (see illustration 7.7b).

61 Install the stationary timing chain guide mounting bolts and guide and tighten the bolts to the torque listed in this Chapter's Specifications.

62 Align the single orange link of the timing chain with the timing mark on the exhaust camshaft gear and install the chain on the sprocket.

63 Slip the timing chain around the intake camshaft sprocket but not onto the teeth of the sprocket.

Note: There are four colored links on the timing chain. The single orange link is for the exhaust camshaft, the two orange links are for the intake camshaft and the yellow colored link (farthest away) is for the crankshaft timing gear.

64 Guide the chain into the stationary chain guide and allow the chain to rest on the crankshaft at this time.

65 Using a wrench on the lug of the intake camshaft to prevent it from turning, rotate the camshaft timing gear counterclockwise to align the timing mark on the intake camshaft gear and the chain colored links. Once the

intake camshaft gear and colored links are aligned, install the chain on to the teeth of the camshaft sprocket.

66 Again, using a wrench on the lug of the intake camshaft to prevent it from turning, slowly rotate the intake camshaft timing gear (only) clockwise, until the yellow link of the chain is aligned with the timing mark on the crankshaft sprocket at the 3 o'clock position and the keyway is pointing to the 12 o'clock position.

67 Confirm that the number one piston is still at TDC on the compression stroke and that the timing marks on the crankshaft and camshaft sprockets are aligned with the colored links on the chain (see illustration 7.7b).

68 Install the top chain guide mounting bolts and guide and tighten the bolts to the torque listed in this Chapter's Specifications.

69 Apply a bead of RTV sealant to the timing chain cover sealing surfaces. Place the timing chain cover in position on the engine and install the bolts in their original locations.

70 Tighten the bolts a little at time, in the proper sequence, to the torque listed in this Chapter's Specifications (see illustrations). Be sure to follow the sealant manufacturer's recommendations for assembly and sealant curing times.

71 Install the chain tensioner pivot arm/chain guide mounting bolt, then tighten the bolt to the torque listed in this Chapter's Specifications.

72 Reload and lock the timing chain tensioner to its zero position as follows:

a) Raise the ratchet pawl and push the plunger inward until it bottoms out (see illustration 7.49).

b) Engage the hook on the tensioner body with the pin on the tensioner plunger to lock the plunger in place.

73 Lubricate the tensioner O-ring with a small amount of oil and install the tensioner into the timing chain cover with the hook facing up (see illustration 7.50).

74 Using the crankshaft pulley/vibration damper bolt, rotate the engine counterclockwise slightly to set the chain tension (see illustration).

Note: As the engine is rotated, the hook on the tensioner body should release itself from the pin on the plunger and allow the plunger to spring out and apply tension to the timing chain. If the plunger does not spring outward and apply tension to the timing chain, press downward on the pivot arm and release the hook with a screwdriver.

75 Install the engine mounting bracket to the front of the timing chain cover and tighten the bolts in sequence to the torque listed in this Chapter's Specifications.

76 Install the crankshaft pulley/vibration damper (see Section 12) and proceed to Step 88.

2009 and later 2.4L engines (2AZ-FE)

77 Make sure the TDC marks on the camshaft sprockets are still in alignment (see illustration 7.7c).

78 If the crankshaft has been rotated off TDC during this procedure, it will be necessary to rotate the crankshaft until the keyway is pointing straight up in the 12 o'clock position with the centerline of the cylinder bores.

79 Install the stationary timing chain guide (see illustration 7.31).

7.80 Loop the timing chain around the crankshaft sprocket and align the No.1 colored link with the mark on the crankshaft sprocket. Install the chain and crankshaft sprocket as an assembly on the engine and install the lower chain guide

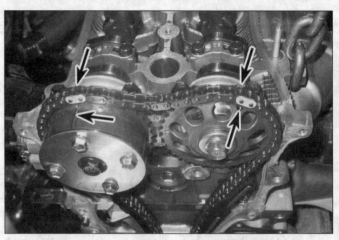

7.81 Loop the timing chain up over the exhaust camshaft and around the intake camshaft, while aligning the remaining two colored links with the marks on the camshaft sprockets

80   Loop the timing chain around the crankshaft sprocket and align the No.1 colored link with the mark on the crankshaft sprocket. Install the chain and crankshaft sprocket as an assembly on the engine, then install the lower timing chain guide **(see illustration)**.
Note: *There are three colored links on the timing chain. The No.1 colored link is the link farthest away from the two colored links that are closest together.*
81   Slip the timing chain into the lip of the stationary timing chain guide and over the exhaust camshaft sprocket, then around the intake camshaft sprocket, making sure to align the remaining two colored links with the marks on the camshaft sprockets **(see illustration)**. Remove all slack from the right side

of the chain when performing this step.
82   Use one hand to remove the slack from the left side of the chain and install the timing chain tensioner pivot arm/chain guide. Tighten the pivot bolt to the torque listed in this Chapter's Specifications. After installation, make sure the tab on the pivot arm can't move past the stopper on the cylinder head **(see illustration 7.44)**.
83   Reconfirm that the number one piston is still at TDC on the compression stroke and that the timing marks on the crankshaft and camshaft sprockets are aligned with the colored links on the chain.
84   Install the crankshaft position sensor reluctor ring with the "F" mark facing outward **(see illustration 7.15)**.

85   Apply a bead of RTV sealant to the timing chain cover sealing surfaces **(see illustration 7.47 and the accompanying illustration)**. Place the timing chain cover in position on the engine and install the bolts in their original locations.
86   Tighten the bolts evenly in several steps to the torque listed in this Chapter's Specifications. Be sure to follow the sealant manufacturer's recommendations for assembly and sealant curing times **(see illustration)**.
87   Install the timing chain tensioner. See Steps 72 through 74.

All models
Caution: *Carefully rotate the crankshaft by hand through at least two full revolutions (use a socket and breaker bar on the crankshaft pulley center bolt). If you feel any resistance, STOP! There is something wrong - most likely, valves are contacting the pistons. You must find the problem before proceeding.*
88   Rotate the engine clockwise at least two revolutions and reposition the number one piston at TDC on the compression stroke (see Section 3). Visually confirm that the timing mark on the crankshaft pulley/vibration damper is aligned with the "0" mark on the timing chain cover and the camshaft sprocket marks are aligned and parallel with the top of the timing chain cover as shown in **illustrations 7.7a, 7.7b, or 7.7c**.
89   The remainder of installation is the reverse of removal.

8   Camshafts and lifters - removal, inspection and installation

Note: *The camshafts should always be thoroughly inspected before installation and camshaft endplay should always be checked prior to camshaft removal (see Step 13).*
Note: *2014 and later 1.8L (2ZR-FAE) models require the engine to be removed and placed on a stand for the procedure - if you're work-*

7.85 Timing chain cover sealant application details - 2009 and later 2.4L models

7.86 Timing chain cover bolt tightening guide - 2009 and later 2.4L models

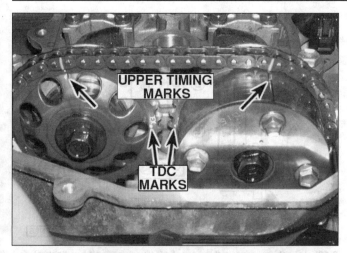

8.5 With the TDC marks aligned, apply a dab of paint to the timing chain links where they meet the upper timing marks on the camshaft sprockets (2008 and earlier 1.8L engine shown, 2.4L engine opposite)

8.8 The camshaft bearing caps are numbered and have an arrow that should face the timing chain end of the engine

ing on this engine, disregard the initial removal Steps and proceed immediately to Step 20.

Removal

1 Disconnect the cable from the negative terminal of the battery (see Chapter 5).
2 On 2009 and later 1.8L (2ZR-FE) engine models, remove cowl assembly (see Chapter 11) and the wiper motor and linkage (see Chapter 12).
3 Remove the valve cover (see Section 4).
4 Refer to Section 3 and place the engine on TDC for number 1 cylinder. Visually confirm the engine is at TDC on the compression stroke by verifying that the timing mark on the crankshaft pulley/vibration damper is aligned with the "0" mark on the timing chain cover and the camshaft sprocket TDC marks are aligned and parallel with the top of the timing chain cover **(see illustrations 3.8 and 7.7a, 7.7b or 7.7c)**.
5 With the TDC marks aligned, apply a dab of paint to the timing chain links where they meet the upper timing marks on the camshaft sprockets **(see illustration)**.
Note: *There are two sets of marks on the camshaft sprockets. The marks that align at TDC are for TDC reference only, the other two marks are used to align the sprockets with the timing chain during installation.*
6 Using a wrench at the hex portion to hold the camshaft, loosen the exhaust camshaft sprocket bolt several turns **(see illustration 7.34)**. If the camshaft sprockets have rotated during the bolt loosening process, rotate the engine clockwise until the "TDC" marks on the cam sprockets are realigned.
7 Remove the timing chain tensioner from the timing chain cover **(see illustration 7.13)** and the camshaft position sensor from the cylinder head (see Chapter 6).

2008 and earlier models and all 2.4L engine models
Caution: *Do not loosen the outer four bolts that secure the actuator to the camshaft timing gear.*

8 Verify the markings on the camshaft bearing caps. The caps should be marked from 1 to 5 with an "I" or an "E" mark on the cap indicating whether they're for the intake or exhaust camshaft **(see illustration)**.
9 Loosen the camshaft bearing caps in two or three steps, in the reverse order of the tightening sequence **(see illustrations 8.55a or 8.55b)**.
Note: *Keep the caps in order. They must go back in the same location they were removed from.*
10 Detach the bearing caps and remove the exhaust the camshaft sprocket retaining bolt. Disengage the exhaust sprocket from the camshaft and remove the exhaust camshaft from the cylinder head, then remove the intake camshaft and timing gear as an assembly.
Note: *Mark the camshaft(s) "Intake" or "Exhaust" to avoid mixing them up.*
11 After removing the sprockets and camshafts, hang the timing chain up with a piece of wire and attach it to an object on the firewall **(see illustration)**. This will prevent the timing chain from falling into the engine as the remaining steps in this procedure are performed. Also place a rag into the opening of the timing chain cover to prevent any foreign objects from falling into the engine.
Note: *The Variable Valve Timing (VVT) actuator is installed on the intake camshaft on all models (and the exhaust camshaft on 2009 and later 1.8L models).*
12 Inspect the camshafts and lifters as described below. Also inspect the camshaft sprockets for wear on the teeth. Inspect the chains for cracks or excessive wear of the rollers, and for stretching (see Section 7). If any of the components show signs of excessive wear they must be replaced.

2009 and later 1.8L (2ZR-FE) engine models
Caution: *Do not loosen the outer four bolts that secure the actuator to the camshaft timing gear.*

Note: *If the timing chain cover is not being removed, the engine can remain in the vehicle - but if the timing chain cover must be removed during this procedure the manufacturer recommends removing the engine and transaxle assembly (see Chapter 2B).*
13 Using Toyota special tool #09961-00950 or equivalent, remove the top chain guide mounting bolts and chain guide.
14 Using a wrench on the lug of the exhaust camshaft to prevent it from turning, use Toyota special tool #09249-37010 or equivalent, on the exhaust camshaft timing gear bolt and loosen the bolt.
Note: *The exhaust bolt can't be fully removed and must be removed along with the camshaft timing gear.*
15 Using a wrench on the lug of the intake camshaft, rotate the intake camshaft counterclockwise just enough to release the chain tension. Pull up on the chain, slide the exhaust camshaft gear forward then up to remove it and temporarily support the chain.

8.11 With the camshaft sprockets removed, hang the timing chain out of the way with a piece of wire and place a shop rag in the timing chain cover opening to prevent foreign objects from falling into the engine

8.16a Remove camshaft bearing cap-to-camshaft housing bolts...

8.16b ... then remove the camshaft bearing cap-to-cylinder head bolts in sequence - 2009 and later 1.8L (2ZR-FE) engine models

16   Loosen the camshaft bearing cap-to-camshaft housing bolts in sequence **(see illustration)** and remove them. Working with one bearing cap at a time, remove the three camshaft bearing cap-to-cylinder head bolts **(see illustration)** in sequence. After removing the three bearing cap-to-cylinder head bolts, lift the bearing cap off and immediately install Toyota service special bolts and spacers in the camshaft bearing bolt locations and tighten the bolts in sequence to 20 ft-lbs.
Caution: *If the service bolts are not used, oil may leak out between the camshaft housing and cylinder head.*
17   Remove the exhaust camshaft, then remove the intake camshaft with the timing gear as an assembly.
Caution: *Keep the caps in order. They must go back in the same location they were removed from.*
18   Hang the timing chain up with a piece of wire and attach it to an object on the firewall to prevent it from falling into the engine as the remaining Steps in this procedure are performed.

19   Inspect the camshafts and camshaft bearings as described below. Also inspect the camshaft sprockets for wear on the teeth. Inspect the chains for cracks or excessive wear of the rollers, and for stretching (see Section 7). If any of the components show signs of excessive wear, they must be replaced.

2014 and later 1.8L (2ZR-FAE) engine models
Note: *The camshafts and camshaft housing are replaced as an assembled unit that includes the camshaft housing, camshafts, camshaft bearing caps, valve rocker shaft and valve rocker arm lost motion damper sub-assembly. The camshafts cannot be replaced by themselves; they must be replaced as an assembly.*
Caution: *Do not loosen the outer four bolts that secure the actuator to the camshaft timing gear.*
Note: *To replace the camshafts on these models, it will be necessary to remove the engine and transaxle assembly and transfer it to an engine stand (see Chapter 2B).*

8.26 Remove the camshaft housing-to-cylinder head bolts in sequence - 2014 and later 1.8L (2ZR-FAE) engine models

20   Remove the engine and transaxle assembly and place it on an engine stand (see Chapter 2B).
21   Remove the intake manifold (see Section 9) and valve cover (see Section 4).
22   Remove the brake vacuum pump (see Chapter 9).
23   Set the engine at TDC (Section 3), then remove the automatic drivebelt tensioner (see Chapter 1) and timing chain cover and timing chain (see Section 7).
24   Using a wrench on the lug of the intake camshaft to prevent it from turning, loosen the intake camshaft timing gear bolt and remove the gear from the end of the camshaft **(see illustration 7.34)**.
25   Using a wrench on the lug of the exhaust camshaft to prevent it from turning, loosen the exhaust camshaft timing gear bolt and remove the gear from the end of the camshaft **(see illustration 7.34)**.
Caution: *Do not remove a valve rocker arm lost motion damper assembly from the camshaft housing or the shims. If a lost motion damper or shim is removed, the camshaft housing must be replaced. The lost motion damper assemblies are located between the camshaft housing mounting bolts, so be careful not to get the retaining bolts confused with the housing bolts.*
26   Loosen the camshaft housing housing mounting bolts in sequence **(see illustration)** and remove them. Using a plastic trim tool or screwdriver with the tip covered in tape, work around the edges to free the camshaft housing from the cylinder head, then lift the assembly off of the cylinder head.
27   The continuously variable valve lift controller can remain installed to the camshaft housing. If it is necessary to remove the controller, see Section 5.
28   Remove the rocker arms and lash adjusters from the cylinder head, if necessary.
29   Visually inspect the camshafts and camshaft bearings for wear. If there is a problem, replace the camshaft housing assembly. Also inspect the camshaft sprockets for wear on the

8.30 Mount a dial indicator as shown to measure camshaft endplay - with the dial zeroed, pry the camshaft forward and back and read the endplay on the dial

8.32 Measure each journal diameter with a micrometer - if any journal measures less than the specified limit, replace the camshaft

8.33 Measure the lobe heights on each camshaft - if any lobe height is less than the specified allowable minimum, replace that camshaft

teeth. Inspect the chains for cracks or excessive wear of the rollers, and for stretching (see Section 7). If any of the components show signs of excessive wear, they must be replaced.

Inspection

Note: *On 2014 and later 1.8L (2ZR-FAE) engines, the camshafts and camshaft housing are replaced as an assembled unit that includes the camshaft housing, camshafts, camshaft bearing caps, valve rocker shaft and valve rocker arm lost motion damper sub-assembly. The camshafts cannot be replaced by themselves they must be replaced as an assembly and if the camshaft housing is disassembled the entire housing must be replaced.*

Note: *The camshaft endplay must be taken with the Variable Valve Timing (VVT) actuator installed on the camshaft(s)*

30   On all models except 2ZR-FAE engines-Before the camshafts are removed from the engine, check the camshaft endplay by placing a dial indicator with the stem in line with the camshaft and touching the snout **(see illustration)**. Push the camshaft all the way to the rear and zero the dial indicator. Next, pry the camshaft to the front as far as possible and check the reading on the dial indicator. The distance it moves is the endplay. If it's greater than the Specifications listed in this Chapter, check the bearing caps for wear. If the bearing caps are worn, the cylinder head must be replaced.

31   On all models except 2ZR-FAE engines-With the camshafts removed, visually check the camshaft bearing surfaces in the cylinder head for pitting, score marks, galling and abnormal wear. If the bearing surfaces are damaged, the cylinder head may have to be replaced.

32   On all models except 2ZR-FAE engines-Measure the outside diameter of each camshaft bearing journal and record your measurements **(see illustration)**. Compare them to the journal outside diameter specified in this Chapter, then measure the inside diameter of each corresponding camshaft bearing and record the measurements. Subtract each cam journal outside diameter from its respective cam bearing bore inside diameter to

determine the oil clearance for each bearing. Compare the results to the specified journal-to-bearing clearance. If any of the measurements fall outside the standard specified wear limits in this Chapter, either the camshaft or the cylinder head, or both, must be replaced.

Note: *If precision measuring tools are not available, Plastigage may be used to determine the bearing journal oil clearance (see Chapter 2B).*

33   On all models except 2ZR-FAE engines-Using a micrometer, measure the height of each camshaft lobe **(see illustration)**. Compare your measurements with the ones listed in this Chapter's Specifications. If the height for any one lobe is less than the specified minimum, replace the camshaft.

34   On all models except 2ZR-FAE engines-Check the camshaft runout by placing the camshaft back into the cylinder head and set up a dial indicator on the center journal. Zero the dial indicator. Turn the camshaft slowly and note the dial indicator readings. Runout should not exceed 0.0012 inch. If the measured runout exceeds the specified runout, replace the camshaft.

35   Inspect each lifter for scuffing and score marks **(see illustration)**. On 2009 and later 1.8L engine models, inspect each rocker arm as well - the roller should move smoothly when spinning by hand.

Note: *On 2ZR-FAE engines, each valve lifter can be inspected in conjunction with Toyota special tool #09276-75010. Place the lifter, with the hole facing upright, into a container full of clean engine oil, then insert the special tool into the lifter. With the rod of the special tool contacting the check ball inside the lifter, depress the check ball 5 or 6 times to bleed the air. Then, once the air has been bled, remove the special tool and try to depress the plunger on the lifter with your finger. It SHOULD be very difficult to engage any movement on the lifter. If the lifter moves easily at the last part, replace it.*

36   Measure the outside diameter of each lifter **(see illustration)** and the corresponding lifter bore inside diameter. Subtract the lifter diameter from the lifter bore diameter to determine the oil clearance. Compare it to this Chapter's Specifications. If the oil clearance is excessive, a new cylinder head and/or new lifters will be required.

8.35 Wipe off the oil and inspect each lifter for wear and scuffing (2008 and earlier 1.8L and 2.4L model shown)

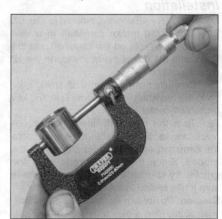

8.36 Measure the outside diameter of each lifter and the inside diameter of each lifter bore to determine the oil clearance measurement (2008 and earlier 1.8L and all 2.4L models)

8.43 Place the camshafts in the cylinder head with the No.1 cylinder lobes pointing inward at approximately a 30-degree angle

8.45a Camshaft bearing cap bolt TIGHTENING sequence - tighten the cap bolts for each camshaft in the indicated order, then tighten the front cap bolts (2008 and earlier 1.8L engine models)

8.45b Camshaft bearing cap bolts TIGHTENING sequence (2009 and later 2.4L engine models)

⬣ -Camshaft-to-cylinder head bolt
◯ -Camshaft-to-camshaft housing bolt

8.52 Camshaft bearing cap bolt TIGHTENING sequence (2009 and later 1.8L (2ZR-FE) engine models)

Installation

Note: *On 2ZR-FAE engines, proceed to Step 62.*

37   Clamp the intake camshaft in a vise using the flat spots on the camshaft, not the lobes with the dowel pin at the top in the 12 o'clock position.

38   Carefully push the camshaft timing gear on to the camshaft with the dowel pin and key groove off-center.

39   Turn the camshaft timing gear counterclockwise while pushing the gear onto the camshaft until the dowel drops in to the groove. Once the dowel drops in to the groove, try to push it in a little more to make sure it has seated to the camshaft.

Caution: *Do not turn the camshaft gear clockwise at this time; it may unseat the dowel pin.*

40   Make sure there is no clearance between the sprocket and the camshaft flange **(see illustration 7.38).**

41   Apply medium-strength thread locking compound to the intake camshaft sprocket

bolt threads, make sure the washer is in place and tighten the bolt to the torque listed in this Chapter's Specifications.

42   Rotate the timing gear assembly clockwise until it locks into place, and remove the camshaft assembly from the vise.

2008 and earlier models and all 2.4L engine models

43   Apply moly-based engine assembly lubricant to the camshaft lobes and journals and install the camshaft into the cylinder head with the No. 1 cylinder camshaft lobes pointing inward toward each other and the dowel pins facing upward **(see illustration)**. If the old camshafts are being used, make sure they're installed in the exact location from which they came.

44   Install the bearing caps and bolts and tighten them hand-tight.

45   Tighten the bearing cap bolts in several equal steps, to the torque listed in this Chap-

ter's Specifications, using the proper tightening sequence **(see illustrations)**.

46   Engage the camshaft sprocket teeth with the timing chain links so that the match marks made during removal align with the upper timing marks on the sprockets. Then position the sprockets over the dowels on the camshaft hubs and install the camshaft sprocket bolts finger-tight. At this point, the mark on the crankshaft pulley should be aligned with the "0" mark on the timing chain cover, the camshaft sprocket TDC marks should be aligned and parallel with the top of the timing chain cover, and the timing chain match marks should be aligned with the upper timing sprocket marks with all of the slack in the chain positioned towards the tensioner side of the engine **(see illustration 8.5)**.

47   Double check that the timing sprockets are returned to the proper camshaft and tighten the camshaft sprocket bolts to the torque listed in this Chapter's Specifications.

8.66 Camshaft housing bolt TIGHTENING sequence (2014 and later 1.8L (2ZR-FAE) engine models)

92037-2A-08.76 HAYNES

9.4 Label and disconnect the following components required for intake manifold removal

1 PCV hose
2 Accelerator cable
3 Air intake duct and air filter cover
4 Throttle body
5 Fuel rail and injectors

48 Install the timing chain tensioner as described in Section 7.
49 The remainder of installation is the reverse of removal.

2009 and later 1.8L (2ZR-FE) engine models

50 Apply camshaft installation lubricant to the camshaft lobes and journals. Place the exhaust camshaft, then the intake camshaft with the timing gear assembly (already installed) into the camshaft housing with both dowel pins at the 12 o'clock position.
Note: Check the rocker arms and make sure none have moved out of position.
51 Place the timing chain over the intake camshaft timing gear and align the marks made on the chain with the timing mark on the camshaft timing actuator (see illustration 8.5).
52 Working with one bearing cap at a time, remove the Toyota service special bolts and spacers and immediately install the camshaft bearing cap to the camshaft housing. Tighten the bearing cap-to-cylinder head bolts in several equal steps, using the proper tightening sequence, to the torque listed in this Chapter's Specifications. Install the bearing cap-to-camshaft housing bolts and tighten the bolts in sequence, to the torque listed in this Chapter's Specifications (see illustration).
53 Using a wrench on the lug of the intake camshaft, rotate the intake camshaft counterclockwise just enough to pull up on the chain. While holding the chain up, place the exhaust camshaft timing gear and sprocket bolt under the timing chain and align the marks made on the chain with the timing mark on the camshaft timing actuator.
54 Slide the timing chain gear down and onto the camshaft. Carefully push the camshaft timing gear on to the camshaft with the dowel pin and key groove aligned.
55 If the dowel pin will not align with the groove, hold the camshaft and slightly turn the camshaft timing gear until the dowel drops in to the groove. Once the dowel is in

the groove, push it in a little more to make sure it has seated to the camshaft.
Caution: Do not turn the camshaft gear clockwise at this time; it may unseat the dowel pin.
56 Make sure there is no clearance between the sprocket and the camshaft flange (see illustration 7.38).
57 Make sure the camshaft sprocket teeth are engaged with the timing chain links so that the match marks made during removal align with the upper timing marks on the sprockets. The mark on the crankshaft pulley should be aligned with the "0" mark on the timing chain cover, the camshaft sprocket TDC marks should be aligned, and the timing chain match marks should be aligned with the upper timing sprocket marks. All of the slack in the chain should be positioned towards the tensioner side of the engine.
58 Using Toyota special tool #09249-37010 or equivalent, tighten the camshaft gear bolt to the torque listed in this Chapter's Specifications.
59 Install the top chain guide and guide mounting bolts, and tighten the bolts to the torque listed in this Chapter's Specifications using Toyota special tool #09961-00950 or equivalent.
60 Install the chain tensioner as described in Section 7.
61 The remainder of installation is the reverse of removal.

2014 and later 1.8L (2ZR-FAE) engine models

62 The mating surfaces of the cylinder head and camshaft housing must be perfectly clean when the camshaft housing is installed.
63 Install the lifters and rocker arms into their original positions - all of them must be seated evenly.
64 Rotate the camshafts in the housings until both camshaft knock pins (sprocket alignment pins) are at approximately the 1 o'clock position. The No.1 cylinder exhaust camshaft lobe will be pointing to the 1 o'clock position

and the No.1 cylinder intake camshaft lobe will be pointing to the 7 o'clock position.
65 Apply a continuous bead (line) of Toyota Genuine Seal packing (black) or equivalent to the sealing surface of the cylinder head.
Note: Once the seal packing has been placed on the cylinder head the camshaft housing must be installed within three minutes and the bolts tightened within 10 minutes or the packing must be removed and reapplied.
66 Install the camshaft housing assembly onto the cylinder head and install the bolts. Tighten the bolts in sequence (see illustration) to the torque listed in this Chapter's Specifications.
67 Install the camshaft sprockets and timing chain (see Section 7).
68 The remainder of installation is the reverse of removal.

9 Intake manifold - removal and installation

Warning: Wait until the engine is completely cool before beginning this procedure.

Removal

1 On 2008 and earlier models and all 2.4L models, relieve the fuel system pressure (see Chapter 4).
2 Disconnect the cable from the negative terminal of the battery (see Chapter 5).

2008 and earlier 1.8L engines

3 Remove the engine cover (see Section 4), then release the two clamps and set aside the fuel-injection wiring harness. Remove the bolt securing the oil dipstick tube.
4 Remove the fuel rail and injectors as an assembly (see Chapter 4). Also remove the throttle body from the intake manifold (see Chapter 4) (see illustration).
5 Label and detach the PCV and vacuum hoses connected to the rear of the intake

9.6a Intake manifold fastener locations. . .

9.6b. . . and support bracket bolts

9.10 Detach the wiring harness retaining clips (A), then remove the bracket bolt (B) and intake manifold lower support bolt (C)

9.11 Disconnect the hoses and harness from the intake manifold (2ZR-FE model shown, 2ZR-FAE model similar)

A	Vacuum hose	D	Detach the wiring harnesses
B	Fuel vapor feed hose		(from the top, as pictured,
C	Vent hose		and bottom of the manifold)

manifold and disconnect any electrical connectors. Remove the two bolts from the alternator bracket.

6   Remove the intake manifold mounting nuts, bolts and support bracket bolts; then remove the manifold and the gasket from the engine **(see illustrations)**.

2009 and later 1.8L engines

7   Remove the engine cover (see Section 4).
8   Drain the engine coolant (see Chapter 1).
9   Remove the air cleaner assembly and throttle body (see Chapter 4). On 2014 and later 2ZR-FAE engines, disconnect the connector and remove the Manifold Absolute Pressure (MAP) sensor (see Chapter 6). Once the sensor is removed, disconnect the wiring harness clips and remove the sensor mounting bracket.
10   Detach the wiring harness from the brackets, remove the bracket mounting fastener, then remove the intake manifold lower support bolt **(see illustration)**.
11   Disconnect the fuel vapor feed hose, vacuum hose and vent hose from the intake manifold **(see illustration)**. Also detach the wiring harnesses from the top and bottom of the manifold.

12   Remove the intake manifold mounting nuts and bolts (see illustration 9.6a).
Note: *On 2014 and later 2ZR-FAE models, it may be necessary to loosen the alternator mounting bolt in order to access all of the intake manifold fasteners.*
13   Remove the intake manifold stay bracket **(see illustration)**.
14   Carefully guide the manifold and gasket out of the engine.

2009 and later 2.4L engines

15   Remove cowl assembly (see Chapter 11) and the wiper motor and linkage (see Chapter 12).
16   Remove the engine cover (see Section 4). Remove the bolt securing the oil dipstick tube.
17   Drain the engine coolant (see Chapter 1).
18   Remove the air cleaner assembly and throttle body (see Chapter 4).
19   Disconnect the main fuel line to the fuel rail (see Chapter 4).
20   Label and disconnect the coolant and vacuum hoses to the intake manifold.
21   Disconnect the electrical connector to the camshaft timing oil control valve (see

Chapter 6).
22   Remove the engine wiring harness clamp and set the harness out of the way.
23   Remove the intake manifold mounting nuts and bolts. Remove the manifold and the gasket.

Installation

24   Clean the mating surfaces of the intake manifold and the cylinder head mounting surface with a rag saturated in brake cleaner. If the gasket shows signs of leaking, have the manifold checked for warpage at an automotive machine shop and resurfaced if necessary.
25   On 2008 and earlier models, install a new gasket over the manifold studs, then position the manifold on the cylinder head and install the nuts/bolts and bracket. On 2009 and later models, press a new gasket into the grooves on the intake manifold. Install the manifold and gasket over the studs on the cylinder head then install the nuts/bolts.
26   Tighten the manifold-to-cylinder head nuts/bolts in three or four equal steps to the torque listed in this Chapter's Specifications. Work from the center out towards the ends to avoid warping the manifold. After the mani-

9.13 Remove the stay bracket, noting the orientation in which it is installed

10.3 Working below the vehicle, remove the two spring-loaded exhaust pipe bolts (A). Be careful not to damage the oxygen sensor (B)

10.5a Working from the engine compartment, disconnect and remove the oxygen sensor (A), then remove the upper heat shield mounting bolts (B) (earlier model shown)

10.5b Working from the engine compartment, detach the oxygen sensor harness from the clip (A), then remove the upper heat shield mounting bolts (B) (later model shown)

fold-to-cylinder head bolts have been tightened to the proper torque, tighten the lower bracket bolt(s).

27   The remainder of installation is the reverse of removal. Refill and check the coolant level, adding as necessary (see Chapter 1).

28   Tighten the throttle body mounting fasteners to the torque listed in Chapter 4 Specifications. Before starting the engine, check the throttle linkage for smooth operation.

29   Run the engine and check for coolant and vacuum leaks.

30   Road test the vehicle and check for proper operation of all accessories, including the cruise control system, if equipped.

10   Exhaust manifold - removal and installation

Warning: *The engine must be completely cool before beginning this procedure.*

Removal

1   Disconnect the cable from the negative terminal of the battery (see Chapter 5).

2   Raise the front of the vehicle and support it securely on jackstands.

Note: *On 2009 and later models, it may be necessary to remove the entire exhaust midsection pipe to allow for enough clearance for the manifold to be removed. Be sure to disconnect/remove the lower (downstream) oxygen sensor as necessary (see Chapter 6).*

3   Working below the vehicle, apply penetrating oil to the bolts and springs retaining the exhaust pipe to the manifold. After the bolts have soaked, remove the bolts retaining the exhaust pipe to the manifold. Separate the front exhaust pipe from the manifold, being careful not to damage the oxygen sensor **(see illustration).**

Note: *It may be necessary to remove the inner heat shield from above the right driveaxle to access one of the exhaust pipe-to-manifold*

bolts and to remove the front floor brace.

4   Unbolt the lower exhaust manifold brace and remove it from the engine.

5   Working in the engine compartment, remove the heat shield from the manifold **(see illustrations).**

6   On 2009 and later 1.8L engine models, if necessary to allow more clearance, remove the cowl assembly (see Chapter 11) and the wiper motor and linkage (see Chapter 12).

7   On 2009 and later 2.4L engine models, remove the drivebelt (see Chapter 1) and the alternator (see Chapter 5).

8   On models equipped with a driveaxle heat shield, remove the mounting nuts and shield.

9   Remove the nuts/bolts and detach the exhaust manifold and gasket.

Installation

10   Use a scraper to remove all traces of old gasket material and carbon deposits from the

11.18 Detach the ground straps (A), the ECT sensor connector (B), the coolant hoses (C) and the bracket retaining bolts (D)

11.30a Cylinder head bolt TIGHTENING sequence - All 1.8L models

manifold and cylinder head mating surfaces. If the gasket was leaking, have the manifold checked for warpage at an automotive machine shop and resurfaced if necessary.
Note: *If the manifold is being replaced with a new one, it will be necessary to remove the lower heat shield and fasten it to the new manifold.*
11   Position a new gasket over the cylinder head studs noting any directional marks or arrows on the gasket, if equipped.
12   Install the manifold and thread the mounting nuts into place.
13   Working from the center out, tighten the nuts/bolts to the torque listed in this Chapter's Specifications in three or four equal steps.
14   Reinstall the remaining parts in the reverse order of removal.
15   Run the engine and check for exhaust leaks.

11   Cylinder head - removal and installation

Warning: *The engine must be completely cool before beginning this procedure.*
Note: *If you're working on a 2009 and later model, the manufacturer recommends removing the engine and transaxle assembly to perform this procedure (see Chapter 2B).*

Removal

1   Relieve the fuel system pressure (see Chapter 4), then disconnect the cable from the negative terminal of the battery.
2   Drain the cooling system (see Chapter 1).
3   Remove the alternator (see Chapter 5).
4   Remove the valve cover (see Section 4).
5   Remove the throttle body, fuel injectors and fuel rail (see Chapter 4).
6   Remove the intake manifold (see Section 9).
7   Remove the exhaust manifold (see Section 10).

Note: *The cylinder head can be removed with the exhaust manifold attached, but remember to disconnect the oxygen sensor first.*
8   Remove the timing chain and camshaft sprockets (see Section 7).
9   On 2009 and later 2.4L models, remove the cowl assembly (see Chapter 11) and the wiper linkage (see Chapter 12).
10   On 2008 and earlier 1.8L and 2.4L models, remove the camshafts and lifters (see Section 8).
11   On 2009 and later (2ZR-FE) models, loosen the camshaft housing bearing cap bolts in two or three steps, in the reverse order of the tightening sequence **(see illustration 8.16a or 8.16b)**. On 2014 and later (2ZR-FAE) models, remove the camshaft housing assembly (see Section 8).
Note: *On 2ZR-FAE engines, the camshafts and camshaft housing are replaced as an assembled unit that includes the camshaft housing, camshafts, camshaft bearing caps, valve rocker shaft and valve rocker arm lost motion damper assembly. The camshafts cannot be replaced by themselves; they must be replaced as an assembly and if the camshaft housing is disassembled the entire housing must be replaced.*
12   Remove the bearing caps and camshafts from the camshaft housing. On 2014 and later (2ZR-FAE) models, carefully remove the camshaft housing by prying between the cylinder head and camshaft housing with a screwdriver.
13   Remove the rocker arms from the cylinder head.
Caution: *Keep the rocker arms in order; they must go back in their original positions.*
14   Remove the lifters from the cylinder head then the valve stem caps, if equipped.
Caution: *Keep the lifters and valve stem caps in order; they must go back in their original positions.*
15   Clean the camshaft housing mounting surface and the mating surface on the cylinder head.
Caution: *Be careful not to damage the cylin-*

der head and camshaft housing.
16   Inspect the camshafts, camshaft bearings, camshaft housing, rockers and lifters (see Section 8). Also inspect the camshaft sprockets for wear on the teeth. Inspect the timing chains for cracks or excessive wear of the rollers, and for stretching (see Section 7). If any of the components show signs of excessive wear, they must be replaced.
17   Refer to Section 5 and remove the variable valve timing control valve and filter.
18   Label and remove the coolant hoses, tubes and electrical connections from the cylinder head **(see illustration)**. Label the connections if necessary, to ensure correct installation.
19   Loosen the cylinder head bolts in 1/4-turn increments until they can be removed by hand. Loosen the cylinder head bolts in the reverse order of the recommended tightening sequence **(see illustration 11.32a, 11.32b or 11.32c)** to avoid warping or cracking the cylinder head.
20   Lift the cylinder head off the engine block. If it's stuck, very carefully pry up at the transaxle end beyond the gasket surface.
21   Remove any remaining external components from the cylinder head to allow for thorough cleaning and inspection.

Installation

22   The mating surfaces of the cylinder head and block must be perfectly clean when the cylinder head is installed.
23   Use a gasket scraper to remove all traces of carbon and old gasket material, then clean the mating surfaces with lacquer thinner or acetone. If there's oil on the mating surfaces when the cylinder head is installed, the gasket may not seal correctly and leaks could develop. When working on the block, stuff the cylinders with clean shop rags to keep out debris. Use a vacuum cleaner to remove material that falls into the cylinders.
24   Check the block and cylinder head mating surfaces for nicks, deep scratches and other damage. If damage is slight, it can be

11.30b Cylinder head bolt TIGHTENING sequence - 2.4L models

12.4 A puller base and several spacers can be mounted to the center hub of the pulley to keep the crankshaft from turning as the pulley retaining bolt is loosened - install the socket over the crankshaft bolt head before installing the puller, then insert the extension through the center hole of the puller

removed with a file; if it's excessive, machining may be the only alternative.

25   Use a tap of the correct size to chase the threads in the cylinder head bolt holes, then clean the holes with compressed air - make sure that nothing remains in the holes.

Warning: *Wear eye protection when using compressed air!*

26   Using a wire brush, clean the threads on each bolt to remove corrosion and restore the threads. Dirt, corrosion, sealant and damaged threads will affect torque readings. Also check the cylinder head bolts for stretching. Measure the entire length of each bolt from the underside of the head to the tip of the threads. If the length of any bolt exceeds 5.846 inches, it must be replaced.

27   Install the components that were removed from the cylinder head.

28   Position the new gasket over the dowel pins in the block. Position the gasket with the "Lot #" mark facing up and near the timing chain end of the engine.

29   Carefully set the cylinder head on the block without disturbing the gasket.

30   Install the new cylinder head bolts and tighten them finger-tight. Following the recommended sequence, tighten the bolts to the torque listed in this Chapter's Specifications **(see illustrations)**.

31   On 2009 and later models, coat the lifters with engine oil and install them into the cylinder head in the same locations from which they were removed.

32   Apply oil to the rocker arms and install them, making sure each rocker arm is seated to its lifter.

33   Install the camshaft bearings and oil control valve filter (if removed) into the camshaft housing or cylinder head.

34   Apply camshaft installation lubricant to the camshaft lobes and journals and install the camshaft into the camshaft housing or cylinder head.

Note: *On 2014 and later 2ZR-FAE engines, install the camshaft housing as an assembly with the camshafts pre-installed (see Section 8).*

35   Install the camshaft bearing caps to the camshaft housing and tighten the camshaft bearing cap-to-camshaft housing bolts in several equal steps, to the torque listed in this Chapter's Specifications, using the proper tightening sequence (see Section 8).

36   Check that the rocker arms are installed properly and have not moved.

37   Position the dowel pins facing upwards; the intake camshaft dowel pin should be at a 17-degree angle (1 o'clock position) and the exhaust pin should be straight up at the 12 o'clock position.

38   Apply a 1/4-inch wide bead of Toyota Genuine Seal Packing Black, Three Bond 1207B (or equivalent) to the camshaft housing-to-cylinder head contact surface.

Note: *The camshaft housing must be installed within three minutes, and the bolts must be tightened within 15 minutes after applying seal packing.*

39   Install the camshaft housing to the cylinder head. Install the camshaft housing-to-cylinder head mounting bolts and tighten the bolts in several equal steps, to the torque listed in this Chapter's Specifications, using the proper tightening sequence (see Section 8).

Caution: *Do not add oil or try to start the engine for at least 4 hours after installation or the seal packing will leak.*

40   The remainder of installation is the reverse of removal.

41   On 2008 and earlier models and 2.4L models, check and, if necessary, adjust the valve clearances (see Chapter 1).

42   Change the engine oil and filter (see Chapter 1).

43   Refill the cooling system (see Chapter 1), run the engine and check for leaks.

Warning: *Wait at least four hours before adding oil and coolant and starting the engine.*

12   Crankshaft pulley/vibration damper - removal and installation

1   Disconnect the cable from the negative terminal of the battery (see Chapter 5).

2   Remove the drivebelt (see Chapter 1).

3   With the parking brake applied and the shifter in Park (automatic) or in gear (manual), loosen the lug nuts from the right front wheel, then raise the front of the vehicle and support it securely on jackstands. Remove the right front wheel and the right splash shield from the wheelwell.

4   Remove the bolt from the front of the crankshaft. A breaker bar will probably be necessary, since the bolt is very tight **(see illustration)**.

5   Using a puller that bolts to the crankshaft pulley hub, remove the crankshaft pulley from the crankshaft **(see illustration)**.

Caution: *Use the proper adapter on the end of the puller screw to prevent damaging the crankshaft threads.*

Note: *Depending on the type of puller you have, it may be necessary to support the engine from above, remove the right side engine mount and lower the engine to gain sufficient clearance to use the puller.*

12.5 Reinstall the puller back onto the crankshaft pulley with the center bolt removed - using the proper adapter to prevent damaging the crankshaft threads, turn the puller screw clockwise and remove the crankshaft pulley

12.6 Align the keyway in the crankshaft pulley hub with the Woodruff key in the crankshaft

13.2 Carefully pry the old seal out of the timing chain cover - don't damage the crankshaft or timing cover in the process

6   To install the crankshaft pulley, slide the pulley onto the crankshaft as far as it will slide on, then use a vibration damper installation tool to press the pulley onto the crankshaft. Note that the slot (keyway) in the hub must be aligned with the Woodruff key in the end of the crankshaft **(see illustration)** and that the crankshaft bolt can also be used to press the crankshaft pulley into position.

7   Tighten the crankshaft bolt to the torque listed in this Chapter's Specifications.

8   The remaining installation steps are the reverse of removal.

13 Crankshaft front oil seal - replacement

1   Remove the crankshaft pulley (see Section 12).

2   Note how the seal is installed - the new one must be installed to the same depth and facing the same way. Carefully pry the oil seal out of the cover with a seal puller or a large screwdriver **(see illustration)**. Cut the lip of the seal with a utility knife to make removal easier. Be very careful not to distort the cover or scratch the crankshaft! Wrap electrical tape around the tip of the screwdriver to avoid damage to the crankshaft.

3   Apply clean engine oil or multi-purpose grease to the outer edge of the new seal, then install it in the cover with the lip (spring side) facing IN. Drive the seal into place with a seal driver or a large socket and a hammer **(see illustration)**. Make sure the seal enters the bore squarely and stop when the front face is at the proper depth.

4   Check the surface on the pulley hub that the oil seal rides on. if the surface has

been grooved from long-time contact with the seal, a press-on sleeve may be available to renew the sealing surface **(see illustration)**. This sleeve is pressed into place with a hammer and a block of wood and is commonly available at auto parts stores for various applications. Be sure to sand the contact surface on the pulley and apply the necessary glue (however stated in the sleeve manufacturer's instructions) before installing the sleeve.

5   Lubricate the pulley hub with clean engine oil and reinstall the crankshaft pulley (see Section 12).

6   Install the crankshaft pulley retaining bolt and tighten it to the torque listed in this Chapter's Specifications.

7   The remainder of installation is the reverse of removal.

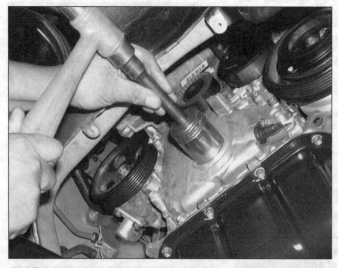

13.3 Drive the new seal into place with a large socket and hammer

13.4 If the sealing surface of the pulley hub has a wear groove from contact with the seal, repair sleeves are available at most auto parts stores

14   Oil pan - removal and installation

Removal

1   Disconnect the cable from the negative terminal of the battery.
2   Set the parking brake and block the rear wheels.
3   Raise the front of the vehicle and support it securely on jackstands.
4   Remove the two plastic splash shields under the engine, if equipped. On 2009 and earlier models (or any models where it interferes with oil pan access), support the engine from above with a hoist or engine support fixture and remove the front crossmember support (see illustration).
5   Drain the engine oil and remove the oil filter (see Chapter 1). Remove the oil dipstick.
6   Remove the bolts and detach the oil pan. If it's stuck, pry it loose very carefully with a small screwdriver or putty knife (see illustrations). Don't damage the mating surfaces of the pan and block or oil leaks could develop.

Installation

7   Use a scraper to remove all traces of old sealant from the block and oil pan. Clean the mating surfaces with a gasket scraper and rag saturated with brake cleaner.
8   Make sure the threaded bolt holes in the block are clean.
9   Check the oil pan flange for distortion, particularly around the bolt holes. Remove any nicks or burrs as necessary.
10   Inspect the oil pump pick-up tube assembly for cracks and a blocked strainer. If the pick-up was removed, clean it thoroughly and install it now, using a new gasket. Tighten the nuts/bolts to the torque listed in this Chapter's Specifications.
11   Apply a 3/16-inch wide bead of RTV sealant to the mating surface of the oil pan.
Note: Be sure to follow the sealant manufacturer's recommendations for assembly and sealant curing times.

14.4 With the engine supported from above, remove the front crossmember support (2009 and earlier models)

12   Carefully position the oil pan on the engine block and install the oil pan-to-engine block bolts loosely.
13   Working from the center out, tighten the oil pan-to-engine block bolts to the torque listed in this Chapter's Specifications in three or four steps.

14   The remainder of installation is the reverse of removal. Be sure to wait at least one hour before adding oil to allow the sealant to properly cure.
15   Run the engine and check for oil pressure and leaks.

14.6a Oil pan mounting bolts - 1ZZ-FE engine shown

14.6b Oil pan mounting bolts - 2ZR-FE engine shown (2ZR-FAE engine similar)

14.6c Pry the oil pan loose with a screwdriver or putty knife - be careful not to damage the mating surfaces of the pan and block or oil leaks may develop

15.2 Oil pump mounting bolts (2008 and earlier 1.8L model shown, 2.4L models similar)

15.4 Oil pump pressure relief valve components

A	Pressure relief valve	B	Spring
		C	Plug

15.7a Rotate the engine 90-degrees counterclockwise (from TDC) and set the crankshaft key to the left horizontal position (A), then remove the oil pump drive chain tensioner and bolt (B) (2009 and later 2.4L engine shown, 2009 and later 1.8L similar)

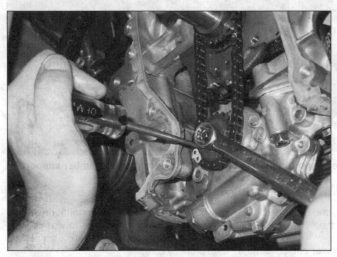

15.7b Using a screwdriver to lock the lower gear in place, loosen the retaining bolt and remove the drive chain and lower gear from the engine (2009 and later 2.4L engine shown, 2009 and later 1.8L similar)

15.8 Oil pump mounting bolts (2009 and later 2.4L engine shown, 2009 and later 1.8L similar)

15 Oil pump - removal, inspection and installation

Note: *If you're working on a 2009 and later model 1.8L engine, the manufacturer recommends removing the engine and transaxle assembly to perform this procedure (see Chapter 2B).*

Removal

2008 and earlier models

1   Remove the timing chain and the crankshaft sprocket (see Section 7).

2   Remove the oil pump mounting bolts and detach the oil pump body from the engine **(see illustration)**. You may have to pry carefully between the front of the block and the pump body with a screwdriver to remove it.

3   Use a scraper to remove all traces of sealant and old gasket material from the pump body and engine block, then clean the mating surfaces with brake system cleaner.

4   Remove the oil pressure relief valve from the pump body **(see illustration)**.

5   Remove the three screws and separate the pump cover from the body. Lift out the drive and driven rotors.

2009 and later models

6   Refer to Section 7 and remove the timing chain and crankshaft sprocket. On 2.4L engines, also remove the crankshaft position sensor plate.

7   Remove the oil pump drive chain and sprockets **(see illustrations)**. On 1.8L engine models, rotate the crankshaft clockwise 90-degrees to align the adjusting hole of the oil pump driveshaft sprocket with the

groove in the oil pump (which is at the 3 o'clock position). On 2.4L engine models, rotate the crankshaft counterclockwise 90-degrees to align the adjusting hole of oil pump driveshaft sprocket with the groove in the oil pump (which is at the 9 o'clock position).

8   Remove the oil pump mounting bolts and detach the oil pump body from the engine **(see illustration)**. You may have to pry carefully between the front of the block and the pump body with a screwdriver to remove it.

9   Use a scraper to remove all traces of sealant and old gasket material from the pump body and engine block, then clean the mating surfaces with brake system cleaner.

Inspection

10   On 2009 and later models, inspect the oil pump and chain for wear and damage. If the oil

15.10a Oil pump drive chain stretch is measured by checking the length of the chain between 8 links (15 pins) at 3 or more places (selected randomly) around the chain - if chain stretch exceeds the specifications between any 8 links, the chain must be replaced

15.10b Wrap the chain around each of the oil pump drive sprockets and measure the diameter of the sprockets across the chain rollers - if the measurement exceeds the minimum sprocket diameter, the chain and the sprockets must be replaced

15.13a Measure the driven rotor-to-body clearance with a feeler gauge

15.13b Using a straightedge and feeler gauge, measure the rotor-to-cover clearance

15.13c Measure the rotor tip clearance with a feeler gauge - install the rotors with the marks facing out, against the cover

pump shows signs of wear or you're in doubt about its condition, it is simply best to replace it. The oil pump drive chain and tensioner, however, can be inspected **(see illustrations)**. Also check the oil jet for blockage.

11   Clean all components with solvent, then inspect them for wear and damage.

12   Check the oil pressure relief valve piston sliding surface and valve spring. If either the spring or the valve is damaged, they must be replaced as a set.

13   Check the driven rotor-to-body clearance, rotor-to-cover clearance and drive rotor tip clearance with a feeler gauge **(see illustrations)** and compare the results to this Chapter's Specifications. If any clearance is excessive, replace the rotors as a set. If necessary, replace the oil pump body.

14   Check the timing chain guide oil jet for blockage **(see illustrations)**.

15.14a Check that the oil jet is free of debris (here, oil is being squirted into the port) - a blockage here will lead to an excessively worn timing chain and guides

15.14b Oil jet hole location on 2009 and later models

15.19 Place the gasket over the dowels (lower arrows) on the engine block - when installing the oil pump, align the flats in the pump rotor with the flats on the crankshaft (upper arrows)

15.27 Install the oil pump drive chain with the colored links aligned with the marks on the sprockets - 2009 and later 2.4L engine shown, other 2009 and later models similar

Installation

2008 and earlier models

15   Lubricate the drive and driven rotors with clean engine oil and place them in the pump body with the marks facing out **(see illustration 15.13c)**.
16   Pack the pump cavity with petroleum jelly and attach the pump cover. Tighten the screws to the torque listed in this Chapter's Specifications.
17   Lubricate the oil pressure relief valve piston with clean engine oil and reinstall the valve components in the pump body.
18   Place a new oil pump gasket on the engine block.
19   Position the pump assembly against the block and install the mounting bolts. Make sure that the flats on the oil pump drive rotor align with the flats on the crankshaft **(see illustration)**.
20   Tighten the bolts to the torque listed in this Chapter's Specifications in three or four steps. Follow a criss-cross pattern to avoid warping the body.
21   Install the remaining parts in the reverse order of removal.
22   Add oil if necessary, start the engine and check for oil pressure and leaks.

2009 and later models

23   Lubricate the pump cavity by pouring a small amount of clean engine oil into the inlet side of the oil pump and turning the drive gear shaft.
24   Position the oil pump and a new gasket against the block and install the mounting bolts.
25   Tighten the bolts to the torque listed in this Chapter's Specifications in several steps. Follow a criss-cross pattern to avoid warping the body.
26   On 1.8L engines, with the crankshaft key set at the 12 o'clock position and the flat on the oil pump driveshaft facing the 3 o'clock position, install the drive chain and sprockets so that the colored links on the chain align with the alignment marks on the drive gears **(see illustration 15.27)**.
Note: *The oil pump drive gear timing mark should almost be at the 3 o'clock position and the oil pump drive shaft gear timing mark should almost be at the 9 o'clock position.*
27   On 2.4L engines, place the crankshaft key in the left horizontal position and the flat on the oil pump driveshaft facing upward, install the drive chain and sprockets so that the colored links on the chain align with the alignment marks on the drive gears **(see illustration)**.
28   Tighten the lower drive sprocket retaining bolt to the torque listed in this Chapter's Specifications.
29   Install the remaining parts in the reverse order of removal.
30   Add oil to the proper level, start the engine and check for oil pressure and leaks.

16 Flywheel/driveplate - removal and installation

Note: *On 2009 through 4/2014 models, the manufacturer recommends removing the engine and transaxle assembly to perform this procedure (see Chapter 2B). On the 4/2014 and later (CVT transaxle-equipped) models, the transaxle can be removed without removing the engine - provided a special engine support bar assembly is used (special tool #09940-10020 or equivalent). If the tool is not available, the engine and transaxle must be removed as an assembly.*

Removal

1   Raise the vehicle and support it securely on jackstands, then refer to Chapter 7A or Chapter 7B and remove the transaxle.
2   Remove the pressure plate and clutch

16.3 Mark the flywheel/driveplate and the crankshaft so they can be reassembled in the same relative positions

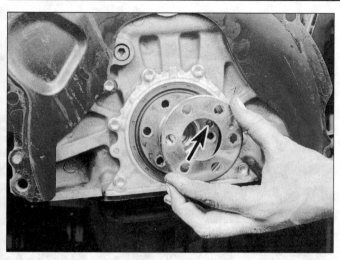

16.5 On vehicles equipped with a spacer plate, note the position of the locating pin

18.7 The preferred method to support the engine is with a support fixture like this that allows maximum working room around the engine top and bottom

disc (see Chapter 8) (manual transaxle equipped vehicles).

3   Use a center punch or paint to make alignment marks on the flywheel/driveplate and crankshaft to ensure correct alignment during reinstallation **(see illustration)**.

4   Remove the bolts that secure the flywheel/driveplate to the crankshaft. If the crankshaft turns, have an assistant wedge a screwdriver in the ring gear teeth to jam the flywheel.

5   Remove the flywheel/driveplate from the crankshaft. Since the flywheel is fairly heavy, be sure to support it while removing the last bolt. Automatic transaxle equipped vehicles may have spacers on both sides of the driveplate **(see illustration)** or a crankshaft sensor plate and spacer on the opposite side. Keep them with the drive-plate.

Warning: *The ring-gear teeth may be sharp; wear gloves to protect your hands.*

Installation

6   Clean the flywheel to remove grease and oil. Inspect the surface for cracks, rivet grooves, burned areas and score marks. Light scoring can be removed with emery cloth. Check for cracked and broken ring gear teeth. Lay the flywheel on a flat surface and use a straightedge to check for warpage.

7   Clean and inspect the mating surfaces of the flywheel/driveplate and the crankshaft. If the crankshaft rear seal is leaking, replace it before reinstalling the flywheel/driveplate (see Section 17).

8   Position the flywheel/driveplate against the crankshaft. Be sure to align the marks made during removal. Note that some engines have an alignment dowel or staggered bolt holes to ensure correct installation. Before installing the bolts, apply thread-locking compound to the threads.

9   Wedge a screwdriver in the ring gear teeth to keep the flywheel/driveplate from turning and tighten the bolts to the torque

listed in this Chapter's Specifications. Follow a criss-cross pattern and work up to the final torque in three or four steps.

10   The remainder of installation is the reverse of the removal procedure.

17   Rear main oil seal - replacement

Note: *On 2009 through 4/2014 models, the manufacturer recommends removing the engine and transaxle assembly to perform this procedure (see Chapter 2B). On the 4/2014 and later (CVT transaxle-equipped) models, the transaxle can be removed without removing the engine - provided a special engine support bar assembly is used (special tool #09940-10020 or equivalent). If the tool assembly is not available, the engine and transaxle must be removed as an assembly.*

1   Remove the transaxle (see Chapter 7A or Chapter 7B).

2   Remove the flywheel/driveplate (see Section 16).

3   Carefully pry the oil seal from the rear of the engine with a screwdriver, it may be helpful to cut the seal lip with a razor blade first to make removal of the seal easier. Be careful not to nick or scratch the crankshaft or the seal bore. Be sure to note how far it's recessed into the bore before removal so the new seal can be installed to the same depth. Thoroughly clean the seal bore in the block with a shop towel. Remove all traces of oil and dirt.

4   Lubricate the outside diameter of the seal and, using a seal installation tool, install the seal over the end of the crankshaft. Drive the new seal squarely into the seal bore and flush with the edge of the seal retainer.

5   Install the flywheel/driveplate (see Section 16).

6   Install the transaxle (see Chapter 7A or Chapter 7B).

18   Powertrain mounts - check and replacement

1   Engine mounts seldom require attention, but broken or deteriorated mounts should be replaced immediately or the added strain placed on the driveline components may cause damage or wear.

Check

Note: *During the check, the engine must be raised slightly to remove the weight from the mounts.*

2   Raise the vehicle and support it securely on jackstands, then position a jack under the engine oil pan. Place a large wood block between the jack head and the oil pan, then carefully raise the engine just enough to take the weight off the mounts. Do not position the wood block under the drain plug.

Warning: *DO NOT place any part of your body under the engine when it's supported only by a jack!*

3   Check the mounts to see if the rubber is cracked, hardened or separated from the metal casing, which would indicate the need for replacement.

4   Check for relative movement between the inner and outer portions of the mount (use a large screwdriver or pry bar to attempt to move the mounts). If movement is noted, replace the mount.

5   Check the mount fasteners to make sure they are tight.

6   Rubber preservative should be applied to the mounts to slow deterioration.

Replacement

7   Disconnect the cable from the negative terminal of the battery, then raise the vehicle and support it securely on jackstands (if not already done). The engine should be supported from above, preferably with an engine support fixture available from tool rental yards **(see illustration)**.

18.8a To remove the passenger's side mount, detach the three mount-to-body bolts, the bolt at the engine . . .

18.8b . . . and the mount bracket-to-engine mount bracket nuts (seen from below) - early models shown

18.8c Passenger's side mount details - later models

A   *Mount-to-body bolts*
B   *Mount through bolt (don't remove when installed on engine)*
C   *Mount bracket-to-engine bracket upper bolt and nut (lower mounting nut not visible - it is accessed from underneath)*

18.9a Driver's side engine mount details - early models shown

A   *Mount-to-body bolts*   B   *Through-bolt*

18.9b Driver's side engine mount details - later models shown

A   *Mount-to-body bolts*   B   *Through-bolt and nut*

18.10a Front engine mount details (early models)

A   *Mount-to-lower frame (access from below, one shown)*
B   *Through-bolt (nut indicated)*

8   To remove the right (passenger's side) engine mount, remove the three bolts securing the mount to the body, then remove the three bolts and two nuts securing the mount bracket to the engine bracket (**see illustrations**). If the vehicle is equipped with air conditioning, detach the refrigerant line bracket retaining nut and remove the mount from the engine compartment. Be sure to remove the mount bracket from the old mount and reinstall it on the new mount.

Note: *In order to access the left (driver's side) engine mount, the battery (see Chapter 5) and/or air filter housing (see Chapter 4) may need to be removed.*

9   To remove the left (driver's side) engine mount, remove the four bolts secur-

18.10b Rear engine mount details (early models)

A   Mount-to-frame crossmember   *B   Through-bolt*

18.10c Rear engine mount through bolt (later models)

No. 2 Driven Gear

No. 1 Driven Gear

Rotating Direction

MATCHMARKS

19.6 Align the matchmarks of the driven gears on the No. 1 balance shaft

18.10d Rear engine mount-to-crossmember bolts/nuts (later models)

ing the mount to the body, then remove the through-bolt securing the mount to the transaxle bracket **(see illustration)**. On manual transaxle equipped vehicles, it will be necessary to remove two bolts and an additional mount support bracket before removing the mount-to-body bolts and the mount through-bolt.

10   To remove the front and rear engine mounts, remove the bolts securing the mount to the lower frame crossmember, then remove the through-bolt securing the mount to the engine bracket **(see illustrations)**.

11   Installation is the reverse of removal. Use thread locking compound on the mount bolts/nuts and be sure to tighten them securely.

19   Engine balancer assembly - removal and installation

Note: *This procedure only applies to 2009 and later 2.4L engine models.*

Note: *It is important to note that in the following procedure, the orientation of the components and timing marks are shown with the engine inverted (as if mounted on an engine stand).*

1   Disconnect the negative battery cable

(see Chapter 5).

2   Remove the oil pan (see Section 14) and the oil pump (see Section 15).

3   Remove the balance shaft housing bolts, in the order opposite that of the tightening sequence **(see illustration 19.10)**.

4   Remove the balance shafts.

5   Remove the balance shaft bearing shells from the housing and the lower crankcase and install new ones. Lubricate the

bearing faces with engine assembly lube.

6   Turn the driven gear of balance shaft no. 1 counterclockwise until it hits its stop. Make sure the matchmarks on the no. 1 driven gear and the no. 2 driven gear are in alignment **(see illustration)**.

7   Rotate the crankshaft so the balance shaft drive gear timing mark on the crankshaft is approximately 16-degrees before the 12 o'clock position **(see illustration)**.

Approx 16°

Drive Gear

Timing Mark

19.7 The timing mark on the balance shaft drive gear must be approximately 16-degrees before the 12 o'clock position (engine shown inverted)

92009-2A-18.17 HAYNES

8   Mesh the gears of the balance shafts, aligning the matchmarks **(see illustration)**.
9   Install the balance shafts in the crank-case with the timing marks and adjusting holes aligned as shown **(see illustration)**.
10   Install the balance shaft housing and tighten the bolts, in sequence **(see illustration)**, to the torque listed in this Chapter's Specifications.

ALIGNMENT MARKS

No. 1 Balance shaft   No. 2 Balance shaft

92009-2A-18.18 HAYNES

19.8 Mesh the gears of the balance shafts with the marks in alignment

Timing Marks

Adjusting Hole   Adjusting Hole

Approx 5°   Approx 5°

Key Groove

92009-2A-18.19 HAYNES

19.9 When installed, the balance shaft markings and the key groove in the nose of the crankshaft must be positioned like this

5	8
1	4
3	2
7	6

92009-2A-18.20 HAYNES

19.10 Balance shaft housing bolt tightening sequence

Chapter 2 Part B
General engine overhaul procedures

Contents

Specifications

General

Engine type	See Chapter 2A
Displacement	
1ZZ-FE (2008 and earlier models)	1.8 liters
2ZR-FE and 2ZR-FAE (2009 and later models)	1.8 liters
2AZ-FE	2.4 liters
Bore and stroke	
1ZZ-FE (2008 and earlier models)	3.11 x 3.60 inches
2ZR-FE and 2ZR-FAE (2009 and later models)	3.17 x 3.48 inches
2AZ-FE	3.48 x 3.78 inches
Cylinder compression pressure @ 250 rpm	
1ZZ-FE (2008 and earlier models)	
Standard	189 psi or more
Minimum	145 psi
Difference between cylinders	15 psi or less
2ZR-FE and 2ZR-FAE (2009 and later models)	
Standard	199 psi or more
Minimum	157 psi
Difference between cylinders	14.2 psi or less
Difference between cylinders	29 psi or less
2AZ-FE models	
Standard	189 psi or more
Minimum	145 psi
Difference between cylinders	15 psi or less
Oil pressure (engine warm)	
1ZZ-FE (2008 and earlier models)	
At idle	4.3 psi minimum
At 3000 rpm	43 to 78 psi
2ZR-FE and 2ZR-FAE (2009 and later models)	
At idle	3.6 psi minimum
At 3000 rpm	22 to 58 psi
2AZ-FE models	
At idle	4.3 psi minimum
At 3000 rpm	22 to 44 psi

Torque specifications

Ft-lbs (unless otherwise indicated)

Note: *One foot-pound (ft-lb) of torque is equivalent to 12 inch-pounds (in-lbs) of torque. Torque values below approximately 15 ft-lbs are expressed in inch-pounds, because most foot-pound torque wrenches are not accurate at these smaller values.*

Connecting rod bearing cap nuts
   1.8L engines
      Step 1 15
      Step 2 .... Tighten an additional 90-degrees (1/4 turn)
   2.0L engine
      Step 1 28
      Step 2 .... Tighten an additional 90-degrees (1/4 turn)
   2.4L engine
      Step 1 18
      Step 2 .... Tighten an additional 90-degrees (1/4 turn)
Main bearing cap bolts
   2008 and earlier 1.8L engines
      Inner bolts 1 through 10
         Toyota models
            Step 1 33
            Step 2 .... Tighten an additional 90-degrees (1/4 turn)
         Pontiac models
            Step 1 45
            Step 2 38
            Step 3 .... Tighten an additional 90-degrees (1/4 turn)
      Outer bolts 11 through 20 .... 168 in-lbs
   2009 and later 1.8L engines
      Step 1 30
      Step 2 .... Tighten an additional 90-degrees (1/4 turn)
   2009 and later 2.4L engines
      Step 1 15
      Step 2 30
      Step 3 .... Tighten an additional 90-degrees (1/4 turn)
Lower crankcase bolts
   2009 and later 1.8L models.. 16
   2009 and later 2.4L models.. 18
Block drain plug.. 18

---

1   General information - engine overhaul

1   Included in this portion of Chapter 2B are general information and diagnostic testing procedures for determining the overall mechanical condition of your engine.

2   The information ranges from advice concerning preparation for an overhaul and the purchase of replacement parts and/or components to detailed, step-by-step procedures covering removal and installation.

3   The following Sections have been written to help you determine whether your engine needs to be overhauled and how to remove and install it once you've determined it needs to be rebuilt. For information concerning in-vehicle engine repair, see Chapter 2A.

4   The Specifications included in this Part are general in nature and include only those necessary for testing the oil pressure and checking the engine compression and assembling the crankshaft and pistons. Refer to Chapter 2A for additional engine Specifications.

5   It's not always easy to determine when, or if, an engine should be completely overhauled, because a number of factors must be considered.

6   High mileage is not necessarily an indication that an overhaul is needed, while low mileage doesn't preclude the need for an overhaul. Frequency of servicing is probably the most important consideration. An engine that's had regular and frequent oil and filter changes, as well as other required maintenance, will most likely give many thousands of miles of reliable service. Conversely, a neglected engine may require an overhaul very early in its service life.

7   Excessive oil consumption is an indication that piston rings, valve seals and/or valve guides are in need of attention. Make sure that oil leaks aren't responsible before deciding that the rings and/or guides are bad. Perform a cylinder compression check to determine the extent of the work required (see Section 3). Also check the vacuum readings under various conditions (see Section 4).

8   Check the oil pressure with a gauge installed in place of the oil pressure sending unit

1.10a An engine block being bored - an engine rebuilder will use special machinery to recondition the cylinder bores

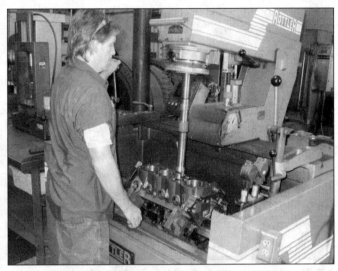

1.10b If the cylinders are bored, the machine shop will normally hone the engine on a machine like this

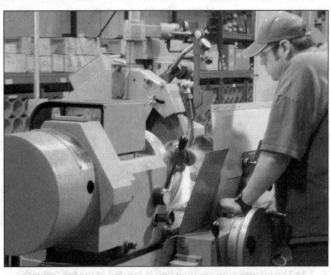

1.10c A crankshaft having a main bearing journal ground

and compare it to this Chapter's Specifications (see Section 2). If it's extremely low, the bearings and/or oil pump are probably worn out.

9   Loss of power, rough running, knocking or metallic engine noises, excessive valve train noise and high fuel consumption rates may also point to the need for an overhaul, especially if they're all present at the same time. If a complete tune-up doesn't remedy the situation, major mechanical work is the only solution.

10   An engine overhaul involves restoring the internal parts to the specifications of a new engine. During an overhaul, the piston rings are replaced and the cylinder walls are reconditioned (rebored and/or honed) **(see illustrations 1.10a and 1.10b)**. If a rebore is done by an automotive machine shop, new oversize pistons will also be installed. The main bearings, connecting rod bearings and camshaft bearings are generally replaced with new ones and, if necessary, the crankshaft may be reground to restore the journals **(see illustration 1.10c)**. Generally, the valves

are serviced as well, since they're usually in less-than-perfect condition at this point. While the engine is being overhauled, other components, such as the distributor, starter and alternator, can be rebuilt as well. The end result should be a like-new engine that will give many trouble-free miles.

Note: *Critical cooling system components such as the hoses, drivebelts, thermostat and water pump should be replaced with new parts when an engine is overhauled. The radiator should be checked carefully to ensure that it isn't clogged or leaking (see Chapter 3). If you purchase a rebuilt engine or short block, some rebuilders will not warranty their engines unless the radiator has been professionally flushed. Also, we don't recommend overhauling the oil pump - always install a new one when an engine is rebuilt.*

11   Overhauling the internal components on today's engines is a difficult and time-consuming task which requires a significant amount of specialty tools and is best left to a

professional engine rebuilder **(see illustrations 1.11a, 1.11b and 1.11c)**. A competent engine rebuilder will handle the inspection of your old parts and offer advice concerning the reconditioning or replacement of the original engine. Never purchase parts or have machine work done on other components until the block has been thoroughly inspected by a professional machine shop. As a general rule, time is the primary cost of an overhaul, especially since the vehicle may be tied up for a minimum of two weeks or more. Be aware that some engine builders only have the capability to rebuild the engine you bring them while other rebuilders have a large inventory of rebuilt exchange engines in stock. Also be aware that many machine shops could take as much as two weeks time to completely rebuild your engine depending on shop workload. Sometimes it makes more sense to simply exchange your engine for another engine that's already rebuilt to save time.

1.11a A machinist checks for a bent connecting rod, using specialized equipment

1.11b A bore gauge being used to check a cylinder bore

1.11c Uneven piston wear like this indicates a bent connecting rod

2.2a The oil pressure sending unit is located at the left (driver's) end of the cylinder head (2AZ-FE engine)

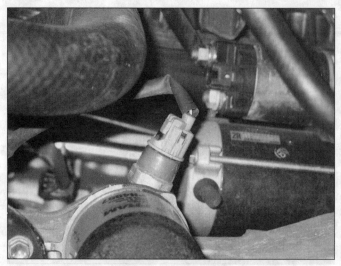

2.2b The oil-pressure sending unit is located at the front of the engine block, just above the oil filter (viewed from below) (1ZZ-FE engine)

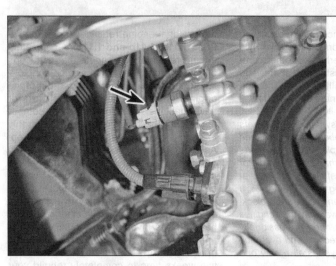

2.2c The oil-pressure sending unit is located at the front of the engine, on the rear corner of the timing chain cover (viewed from below) (2ZR-FE and 2ZR-FAE engines)

2 Oil pressure check

1   Low engine oil pressure can be a sign of an engine in need of rebuilding. A "low oil pressure" indicator (often called an "idiot light") is not a test of the oiling system. Such indicators only come on when the oil pressure is dangerously low. Even a factory oil pressure gauge in the instrument panel is only a relative indication, although much better for driver information than a warning light. A better test is with a mechanical (not electrical) oil pressure gauge.

2   Locate the oil pressure indicator sending unit:

a)   On 2AZ-FE engines, the oil pressure sending unit is located on the driver's end of the cylinder head.

b)   On 1ZZ-FE engines, the oil pressure sending unit is located just above the oil filter **(see illustration)**.

c)   On 2ZR-FE and 2ZR-FAE engines, the oil pressure sending unit is located on the timing chain cover **(see illustration)**.

3   Unscrew and remove the oil pressure sending unit and then screw in the hose for your oil pressure gauge. If necessary, install an adapter fitting. Use Teflon tape or thread sealant on the threads of the adapter and/or the fitting on the end of your gauge's hose.

4   Connect an accurate tachometer to the engine, according to the tachometer manufacturer's instructions.

5   Check the oil pressure with the engine running (normal operating temperature) at the specified engine speed, and compare it to this Chapter's Specifications. If it's extremely low, the bearings and/or oil pump are probably worn out.

3 Cylinder compression check

1   A compression check will tell you what mechanical condition the upper end of your engine (pistons, rings, valves, head gaskets) is in. Specifically, it can tell you if the compression is down due to leakage caused by worn piston rings, defective valves and seats or a blown head gasket.

Note: *The engine must be at normal operating temperature and the battery must be fully charged for this check.*

2   Begin by cleaning the area around the spark plugs before you remove them (compressed air should be used, if available). The idea is to prevent dirt from getting into the cylinders as the compression check is being done.

3   Remove all of the spark plugs from the engine (see Chapter 1).

4   Disable the fuel pump circuit by removing the circuit opening relay from the fuse/relay center in the engine compartment (see Chapter 4).

5   Install a compression gauge in the spark plug hole **(see illustration)**.

6   Have an assistant fully depress the accelerator pedal and crank the engine over at least seven compression strokes while you watch the gauge. The compression should build up quickly in a healthy engine. Low compression on the first stroke, followed by gradually increasing pressure on successive strokes, indicates worn piston rings. A low compression reading on the first stroke, which doesn't build up during successive strokes, indicates leaking valves or a blown head gasket (a cracked head could also be the cause). Deposits on the undersides of the valve heads can also cause low compression. Record the highest gauge reading obtained.

7   Repeat the procedure for the remaining cylinders and compare the results to this Chapter's Specifications.

8   Add some engine oil (about three squirts from a plunger-type oil can) to each cylinder, through the spark plug hole, and repeat the test.

9   If the compression increases after the oil is added, the piston rings are definitely worn. If the compression doesn't increase significantly, the leakage is occurring at the valves or head gasket. Leakage past the valves may be caused by burned valve seats and/or faces or warped, cracked or bent valves.

3.5 Use a compression gauge with a threaded fitting for the spark plug hole, not the type that requires hand pressure to maintain the seal - be sure to open the throttle valve as far as possible during the test

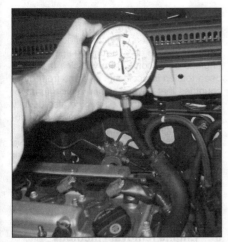

4.4 A simple vacuum gauge can be handy in diagnosing engine condition and performance

Low, steady reading

Low, fluctuating needle

Regular drops

Irregular drops

Rapid vibration

Large fluctuation

Slow fluctuation

4.6 Typical vacuum gauge readings

10   If two adjacent cylinders have equally low compression, there's a strong possibility that the head gasket between them is blown. The appearance of coolant in the combustion chambers or the crankcase would verify this condition.

11   If one cylinder is slightly lower than the others, and the engine has a slightly rough idle, a worn lobe on the camshaft could be the cause.

12   If the compression is unusually high, the combustion chambers are probably coated with carbon deposits. If that's the case, the cylinder head(s) should be removed and decarbonized.

13   If compression is way down or varies greatly between cylinders, it would be a good idea to have a leak-down test performed by an automotive repair shop. This test will pin-point exactly where the leakage is occurring and how severe it is.

4   Vacuum gauge diagnostic checks

1   A vacuum gauge provides inexpensive but valuable information about what is going on in the engine. You can check for worn rings or cylinder walls, leaking head or intake manifold gaskets, incorrect carburetor adjustments, restricted exhaust, stuck or burned valves, weak valve springs, improper ignition or valve timing and ignition problems.

2   Unfortunately, vacuum gauge readings are easy to misinterpret, so they should be used in conjunction with other tests to confirm the diagnosis.

3   Both the absolute readings and the rate of needle movement are important for accurate interpretation. Most gauges measure vacuum in inches of mercury (in-Hg). The following references to vacuum assume the diagnosis is being performed at sea level. As elevation increases (or atmospheric pressure decreases), the reading will decrease. For every 1,000 foot increase in elevation above approximately 2000 feet, the gauge readings will decrease about one inch of mercury.

4   Connect the vacuum gauge directly to the intake manifold vacuum, not to ported (throttle body) vacuum (see illustration). Be sure no hoses are left disconnected during the test or false readings will result.

5   Before you begin the test, allow the engine to warm up completely. Block the wheels and set the parking brake. With the transmission in Park, start the engine and allow it to run at normal idle speed.
Warning: *Keep your hands and the vacuum gauge clear of the fans.*

6   Read the vacuum gauge; an average, healthy engine should normally produce about 17 to 22 in-Hg with a fairly steady needle (see illustration). Refer to the following vacuum gauge readings and what they indicate about the engine's condition:

7   A low steady reading usually indicates a leaking gasket between the intake manifold and cylinder head(s) or throttle body, a leaky vacuum hose, late ignition timing or incorrect camshaft timing.

8   If the reading is three to eight inches below normal and it fluctuates at that low reading, suspect an intake manifold gasket

6.3a After tightly wrapping water-vulnerable components, use a spray cleaner on everything, with particular concentration on the greasiest areas, usually around the valve cover and lower edges of the block. If one section dries out, apply more cleaner

6.3b Depending on how dirty the engine is, let the cleaner soak in according to the directions and then hose off the grime and cleaner. Get the rinse water down into every area you can get at; then dry important components with a hair dryer or paper towels

leak at an intake port or a faulty fuel injector.

9   If the needle has regular drops of about two-to-four inches at a steady rate, the valves are probably leaking. Perform a compression check or leak-down test to confirm this.

10   An irregular drop or down-flick of the needle can be caused by a sticking valve or an ignition misfire. Perform a compression check or leak-down test and read the spark plugs.

11   A rapid vibration of about four in-Hg vibration at idle combined with exhaust smoke indicates worn valve guides. Perform a leak-down test to confirm this. If the rapid vibration occurs with an increase in engine speed, check for a leaking intake manifold gasket or head gasket, weak valve springs, burned valves or ignition misfire.

12   A slight fluctuation, say one inch up and down, may mean ignition problems. Check all the usual tune-up items and, if necessary, run the engine on an ignition analyzer.

13   If there is a large fluctuation, perform a compression or leak-down test to look for a weak or dead cylinder or a blown head gasket.

14   If the needle moves slowly through a wide range, check for a clogged PCV system, incorrect idle fuel mixture, throttle body or intake manifold gasket leaks.

15   Check for a slow return after revving the engine by quickly snapping the throttle open until the engine reaches about 2,500 rpm and let it shut. Normally the reading should drop to near zero, rise above normal idle reading (about 5 in-Hg over) and then return to the previous idle reading. If the vacuum returns slowly and doesn't peak when the throttle is snapped shut, the rings may be worn. If there is a long delay, look for a restricted exhaust system (often the muffler or catalytic converter). An easy way to check this is to temporarily disconnect the exhaust ahead of the suspected part and redo the test.

5   Engine rebuilding alternatives

1   The do-it-yourselfer is faced with a number of options when purchasing a rebuilt engine. The major considerations are cost, warranty, parts availability and the time required for the rebuilder to complete the project. The decision to replace the engine block, piston/connecting rod assemblies and crankshaft depends on the final inspection results of your engine. Only then can you make a cost effective decision whether to have your engine overhauled or simply purchase an exchange engine for your vehicle.

2   Some of the rebuilding alternatives include:

3   **Individual parts** - If the inspection procedures reveal that the engine block and most engine components are in reusable condition, purchasing individual parts and having a rebuilder rebuild your engine may be the most economical alternative. The block, crankshaft and piston/connecting rod assemblies should all be inspected carefully by a machine shop first.

4   **Short block** - A short block consists of an engine block with a crankshaft and piston/connecting rod assemblies already installed. All new bearings are incorporated and all clearances will be correct. The existing camshafts, valve train components, cylinder head and external parts can be bolted to the short block with little or no machine shop work necessary.

5   **Long block** - A long block consists of a short block plus an oil pump, oil pan, cylinder head, valve cover, camshaft and valve train components, timing sprockets and chain or gears and timing cover. All components are installed with new bearings, seals and gaskets incorporated throughout. The installation of manifolds and external parts is all that's necessary.

6   **Low mileage used engines** - Some companies now offer low mileage used engines which is a very cost effective way to get your vehicle up and running again. These engines often come from vehicles that have been totaled in accidents or come from other countries that have a higher vehicle turnover rate. A low mileage used engine also usually has a similar warranty like the newly remanufactured engines.

7   Give careful thought to which alternative is best for you and discuss the situation with local automotive machine shops, auto parts dealers and experienced rebuilders before ordering or purchasing replacement parts.

6   Engine removal - methods and precautions

1   If you've decided that an engine must be removed for overhaul or major repair work, several preliminary steps should be taken. Read all removal and installation procedures carefully prior to committing to this job. Some engines are removed by lowering to the floor and then raising the vehicle sufficiently to slide it out; this will require a vehicle hoist.

2   Locating a suitable place to work is extremely important. Adequate work space, along with storage space for the vehicle, will be needed. If a shop or garage isn't available, at the very least a flat, level, clean work surface made of concrete or asphalt is required.

3   Cleaning the engine compartment and engine before beginning the removal procedure will help keep tools clean and organized **(see illustrations)**.

4   An engine hoist or A-frame will also be necessary. Make sure the equipment is rated in excess of the combined weight of the engine and transaxle. Safety is of primary importance, considering the potential hazards

6.6a Get an engine hoist that's strong enough to easily lift your engine in and out of the engine compartment; an adapter, like the one shown here, can be used to change the angle of the engine as it's being removed or installed

6.6b Get an engine stand sturdy enough to firmly support the engine while you're working on it. Stay away from three-wheeled models; they have a tendency to tip over more easily, so get a four-wheeled unit

6.6c A clutch alignment tool is necessary if you plan to install a rebuilt engine mated to a manual transaxle

involved in lifting the engine out of the vehicle.

5   If you're a novice at engine removal, get at least one helper. One person cannot easily do all the things you need to do to lift a big heavy engine out of the engine compartment. Also helpful is to seek advice and assistance from someone who's experienced in engine removal.

6   Plan the operation ahead of time. Arrange for or obtain all of the tools and equipment you'll need prior to beginning the job (see illustrations). Some of the equipment necessary to perform engine removal and installation safely and with relative ease are (in addition to an engine hoist) a heavy duty floor jack, complete sets of wrenches and sockets as described in the front of this manual, wooden blocks, plenty of rags and cleaning solvent for mopping up spilled oil, coolant and gasoline. If the hoist must be rented, make sure that you arrange for it in advance and have everything disconnected and/or removed before bringing the hoist home. This will save you money and time.

7   Plan for the vehicle to be out of use for quite a while. A machine shop can do the work that is beyond the scope of the home mechanic. Machine shops often have a busy schedule, so before removing the engine, consult the shop for an estimate of how long it will take to rebuild or repair the components that may need work.

7   Engine - removal and installation

Warning: *The models covered by this manual are equipped with a Supplemental Restraint*

System (SRS), more commonly known as airbags. Always disable the airbag system before working in the vicinity of the impact sensors, steering column or instrument panel to avoid the possibility of accidental deployment of the airbag, which could cause personal injury (see Chapter 12).

Warning: *Gasoline is extremely flammable, so take extra precautions when you work on any part of the fuel system. Don't smoke or allow open flames or bare light bulbs near the work area, and don't work in a garage where a gas-type appliance (such as a water heater or a clothes dryer) is present. Since gasoline is carcinogenic, wear fuel-resistant gloves when there's a possibility of being exposed to fuel, and, if you spill any fuel on your skin, rinse it off immediately with soap and water. Mop up any spills immediately and do not store fuel-soaked rags where they could ignite. The fuel system is under constant pressure, so, if any fuel lines are to be disconnected, the fuel pressure in the system must be relieved first (see Chapter 4 for more information). When you perform any kind of work on the fuel system, wear safety glasses and have a Class B type fire extinguisher on hand.*

Warning: *Wait until the engine is completely cool before beginning this procedure*

Note: *Engine removal on these vehicles is a difficult job, especially for the do-it-yourself mechanic working at home. Because of the vehicle's design, the manufacturer states that the engine and transaxle have to be removed as a unit from the bottom of the vehicle, not the top. With a floor jack and jackstands, the vehicle can't be raised high enough or supported safely enough for the engine/transaxle assembly to slide out from underneath. The manufacturer recommends that removal of the engine/transaxle assembly only be performed with the use of a frame-contact type vehicle hoist.*

Note: *Keep in mind that during this procedure you'll have to adjust the height of the vehicle with the vehicle hoist to perform certain operations.*

Removal

1   Park the vehicle on a frame-contact type vehicle hoist, then engage the arms of the hoist with the jacking points of the vehicle. Raise the hoist arms until they contact the vehicle, but not so much that the wheels come off the ground.

2   Loosen the wheel lug nuts and the driveaxle/hub nuts (see Chapter 1).

3   Relieve the fuel system pressure (see Chapter 4).

4   Remove the battery and battery tray (see Chapter 5).

5   Remove the air filter housing and air intake duct (see Chapter 4).

6   Drain the engine coolant (see Chapter 1).

7   Drain the engine oil (see Chapter 1).

8   Drain the transaxle lubricant or fluid (see Chapter 1).

9   Remove the engine cooling fan. Also remove the radiator (see Chapter 3).

10 If equipped with an automatic transaxle, disconnect the fluid cooler lines from the transaxle.

11 Disconnect the fuel feed hose from the rigid line on the left (driver's) side of the engine compartment (see Chapter 4). Plug the line and fitting.

12 If equipped with cruise control, detach the cable from the throttle body, then remove the cruise control actuator.

13 Detach the heater hoses from the heater core tubes at the firewall (see Chapter 3).

14 Detach the shift cable(s) from the transaxle (see Chapter 7A or Chapter 7B).

15 If equipped with a manual transaxle, remove the clutch release cylinder (see Chapter 8).

7.17a Unplug these electrical connectors (A) from the underhood fuse/relay box, then slide the harness up and out of the slot in the side of the box (B)

7.17b Label both ends of each wire and hose before disconnecting it - do the same for vacuum hoses

16   Remove the air conditioning compressor without disconnecting the refrigerant lines (see Chapter 3). Tie the compressor out of the way.

17   Disconnect the engine wiring harness from the underhood fuse/relay box **(see illustration)**. Also label and detach any other electrical connectors/wiring harnesses and vacuum hoses between the engine and the vehicle **(see illustration)**.

18   **2008 and earlier models:** Remove the glove box door, then disconnect the electrical connectors from the PCM (see Chapter 6) and the junction block. Dislodge the grommet from the firewall and pull the harness into the engine compartment.

19   **Models with hydraulic power steering:** Using a suction gun, remove as much fluid as possible from the power steering fluid reservoir. Unscrew the nut securing the power steering gear pressure line to the right side of the engine compartment (near the strut tower), then disconnect the hose

from the line. Also, disconnect the supply (large diameter) hose from the power steering fluid reservoir.

20   Disconnect the steering column intermediate shaft from the steering gear (see Chapter 10).

21   Raise the vehicle on the hoist, then remove the front wheels. Detach the tie-rod ends from the steering knuckles (see Chapter 10).

22   Unbolt the exhaust pipe from the exhaust manifold (see Chapter 2A, Section 10).

23   Remove the driveaxle/hub nuts.

24   Unscrew the fasteners and separate the balljoints from the control arms (see Chapter 10).

25   Remove the driveaxles (see Chapter 8).

26   Disconnect the stabilizer bar links from the stabilizer bar (see Chapter 10).

27   Support the engine/transaxle assembly from above with an engine hoist. Attach the hoist chain to the lifting brackets. If no lifting brackets or hooks are present, lifting hooks

may be available from your local auto parts store or dealer parts department. If not, you will have to fasten the chains to some substantial parts of the engine - ones that are strong enough to take the weight, but in locations that will provide good balance. If you're attaching a chain to a stud on the engine, or are using a bolt passing through the chain and into a threaded hole, place a washer between the nut or bolt head and the chain and tighten the nut or bolt securely **(see illustration)**.

Warning: *Do not place any part of your body under the engine/transaxle when it's supported only by a hoist or other lifting device.*

28   Take up the slack until there is slight tension on the engine hoist. Position the chain on the hoist so it balances the engine and the transaxle level with the vehicle.

Note: *Depending on the design of the engine hoist, it may be helpful to position the hoist from the side of the vehicle, so that when the engine/transaxle assembly is lowered, it will fit between the legs of the hoist.*

7.27 This engine was equipped with one lifting hook, at the back of the cylinder head near the transaxle. At the other end of the head there was no hook, but there was a large threaded hole that we used for connecting the lifting chain

7.30 Locations of the front suspension subframe and longitudinal crossmember-to-vehicle bolts

Note: *The sling or chain must be long enough to allow the engine hoist to lower the engine/transaxle assembly to the ground, without letting the hoist arm contact the vehicle.*

29 Support the front suspension subframe with a pair of floor jacks. Recheck to be sure that there aren't any hoses or wiring harnesses between the engine, subframe and the vehicle.

30 Remove the bolts securing the front suspension subframe and the longitudinal crossmember to the vehicle **(see illustration)**.

31 Remove the through-bolt from the powertrain mount securing the transaxle to the left (driver's) side of the engine compartment, and the mount-to-engine bracket fasteners on the right-side mount (see Chapter 2A).

32 Recheck to be sure nothing is still connecting the engine or transaxle to the vehicle. Disconnect and label anything still remaining.

33 Lower the engine/transaxle/subframe assembly. Once the assembly is on the floor, disconnect the engine lifting hoist and raise the vehicle until it clears the engine/transaxle assembly.

34 Reconnect the chain or sling to support the engine and transaxle.

35 Raise the engine/transaxle assembly, remove the fasteners connecting the remaining powertrain mounts to the subframe, then move the subframe out of the way. Support the engine with blocks of wood or another floor jack, while leaving the sling or chain attached. Support the transaxle with another floor jack, preferably one with a transaxle jack head adapter. At this point the transaxle can be unbolted and removed from the engine. Be very careful to ensure that the components are supported securely so they won't topple off their supports during disconnection.

36 Reconnect the lifting chain to the engine, then raise the engine and attach it to an engine stand.

Installation

37 Installation is the reverse of removal, noting the following points:

a) *Check the powertrain mounts. If they're worn or damaged, replace them.*

b) *Attach the transaxle to the engine following the procedure described in Chapter 7A or Chapter 7B.*

c) *When installing the subframe and longitudinal crossmember, tighten the mounting bolts to the torque listed in the Chapter 10 Specifications.*

d) *Tighten the driveaxle/hub nuts to the torque listed in the Chapter 8 Specifications. Tighten all steering and suspension fasteners to the torque listed in the Chapter 10 Specifications. Tighten the wheel lug nuts to the torque listed in the Chapter 1 Specifications.*

e) *Refill the engine coolant, oil, power steering and transaxle fluids (see Chapter 1).*

f) *Run the engine and check for proper operation and leaks. Shut off the engine and recheck fluid levels.*

8 Engine overhaul - disassembly sequence

1 It's much easier to remove the external components if it's mounted on a portable engine stand. A stand can often be rented quite cheaply from an equipment rental yard. Before the engine is mounted on a stand, the flywheel/driveplate should be removed from the engine.

2 If a stand isn't available, it's possible to remove the external engine components with it blocked up on the floor. Be extra careful not to tip or drop the engine when working without a stand.

3 If you're going to obtain a rebuilt engine, all external components must come off first, to be transferred to the replacement engine. These components include:

Clutch and flywheel (models with manual transaxle)
Driveplate (models with automatic transaxle)
Ignition system components
Emissions-related components
Engine mounts and mount brackets
Fuel injection components
Intake/exhaust manifolds
Oil filter
Thermostat and housing assembly
Water pump

Note: *When removing the external components from the engine, pay close attention to details that may be helpful or important during installation. Note the installed position of gaskets, seals, spacers, pins, brackets, washers, bolts and other small items.*

4 If you're going to obtain a short block (assembled engine block, crankshaft, pistons and connecting rods), then you should remove the timing belt, cylinder head, oil pan, oil pump pick-up tube, oil pump and water pump from your engine so that you can turn in your old short block to the rebuilder as a core. See *Engine rebuilding alternatives* for additional information regarding the different possibilities to be considered.

Caution: *2009 and later models have a removable cylinder block water jacket and should not be machined.*

9 Pistons and connecting rods - removal and installation

Removal

Note: *Prior to removing the piston/connecting rod assemblies, remove the cylinder head, upper (aluminum) oil pan section and oil pan (see Chapter 2A).*

1 Use your fingernail to feel if a ridge has formed at the upper limit of ring travel (about 1/4-inch down from the top of each cylinder). If carbon deposits or cylinder wear have produced ridges, they must be completely removed with a special tool **(see illustration)**. Follow the manufacturer's instructions provided with the tool. Failure to remove the ridges before attempting to remove the piston/connecting rod assemblies may result in piston breakage.

2 After the cylinder ridges have been removed, turn the engine so the crankshaft is facing up.

3 Before the main bearing cap assembly and connecting rods are removed, check the connecting rod endplay with feeler gauges. Slide them between the first connecting rod and the crankshaft throw until the play is removed **(see illustration)**. Repeat this procedure for each connecting rod. The endplay is equal to the thickness of the feeler gauge(s). Check with an automotive machine shop for the endplay service limit. If the play exceeds the service limit, new connecting rods will be required. If new rods (or a new crankshaft) are installed, the endplay may fall under the minimum allowable clearance. If it does, the rods will have to be machined to restore it. If necessary, consult an automotive machine shop for advice.

9.1 Before you try to remove the pistons, use a ridge reamer to remove the raised material (ridge) from the top of the cylinders

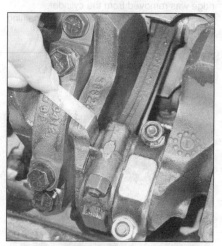

9.3 Checking the connecting rod endplay (side clearance)

9.4 If the connecting rods and caps are not marked, use a center punch or numbered impression stamps to mark the caps to the rods by cylinder number - do not confuse the markings shown here with rod numbers, these are bearing size identifications

9.13 Install the piston ring into the cylinder, then push it down into position using a piston so the ring will be square in the cylinder

9.14 With the ring square in the cylinder, measure the ring end gap with a feeler gauge

4   Check the connecting rods and caps for identification marks **(see illustration)**. If they aren't plainly marked, use a small center-punch to make the appropriate number of indentations on each rod and cap (1, 2, 3, etc., depending on the cylinder they're associated with).

5   Loosen each of the connecting rod cap bolts 1/2-turn at a time until they can be removed by hand. Remove the number one connecting rod cap and bearing insert. Don't drop the bearing insert out of the cap.

Note: *Use new bolts when reassembling the engine, but save the old ones for use when checking the bearing oil clearance.*

6   Remove the bearing insert and push the connecting rod/piston assembly out through the top of the engine. Use a wooden or plastic hammer handle to push on the upper bearing surface in the connecting rod. If resistance is felt, double-check to make sure that all of the ridge was removed from the cylinder.

7   Repeat the procedure for the remaining cylinders.

8   After removal, reassemble the connecting rod caps and bearing inserts in their respective connecting rods and install the cap bolts finger-tight.

9   Leaving the old bearing inserts in place until reassembly will help prevent the connecting rod bearing surfaces from being accidentally nicked or gouged.

10   The pistons and connecting rods are now ready for inspection and overhaul at an automotive machine shop.

Piston ring installation

11   Before installing the new piston rings, the ring end gaps must be checked. It's assumed that the piston ring side clearance has been checked and verified correct.

Note: *Pistons and rods can only be installed after the crankshaft has been installed (see Section 10).*

12   Lay out the piston/connecting rod assemblies and the new ring sets so the ring sets will be matched with the same piston and cylinder during the end gap measurement and engine assembly.

13   Insert the top (number one) ring into the

first cylinder and square it up with the cylinder walls by pushing it in with the top of the piston **(see illustration)**. The ring should be near the bottom of the cylinder, at the lower limit of ring travel.

14   To measure the end gap, slip feeler gauges between the ends of the ring until a gauge equal to the gap width is found **(see illustration)**. The feeler gauge should slide between the ring ends with a slight amount of drag. Check with an automotive machine shop for the correct end gap for your engine. If the gap is larger or smaller than specified, double-check to make sure you have the correct rings before proceeding.

15   If the gap is too small, it must be enlarged or the ring ends may come in contact with each other during engine operation, which can cause serious damage to the engine. The end gap can be increased by filing the ring ends very carefully with a fine file. Mount the file in a vise equipped with soft jaws, slip the ring over the file with the ends contacting the file face and slowly move the ring to remove material from the ends. When performing this operation, file only by pushing the ring from the outside end of the file toward the vise **(see illustration)**.

16   Excess end gap isn't critical unless it's greater than approximately 0.040-inch. Again, double-check to make sure you have the correct ring type and that you are referencing the correct section and category of specifications.

17   Repeat the procedure for each ring that will be installed in the first cylinder and for each ring in the remaining cylinders. Remember to keep rings, pistons and cylinders matched up.

18   Once the ring end gaps have been checked/corrected, the rings can be installed on the pistons.

19   The oil control ring (lowest one on the piston) is usually installed first. It's composed of three separate components. Slip the spacer/expander into the groove **(see illustration)**. If an anti-rotation tang is used,

9.15 If the ring end gap is too small, clamp a file in a vise as shown and file the piston ring ends - be sure to file the ends squarely and finish by removing all raised material or burrs with a fine stone

9.19a Installing the spacer/expander in the oil ring groove

9.19b DO NOT use a piston ring installation tool when installing the oil control side rails

9.22 Use a piston ring installation tool to install the number 2 and the number 1 (top) rings - be sure the directional mark on the piston ring(s) is facing toward the top of the piston

make sure it's inserted into the drilled hole in the ring groove. Next, install the upper side rail in the same manner **(see illustration)**. Don't use a piston ring installation tool on the oil ring side rails, as they may be damaged. Instead, place one end of the side rail into the groove between the spacer/expander and the ring land, hold it firmly in place and slide a finger around the piston while pushing the rail into the groove. Finally, install the lower side rail.

20 After the three oil ring components have been installed, check to make sure that both the upper and lower side rails can be rotated smoothly inside the ring grooves.

21 The number two (middle) ring is installed next. It's usually stamped with a mark that must face up, toward the top of the piston. Do not mix up the top and middle rings, as they have different cross-sections.

Note: *Always follow the instructions printed on the ring package or box - different manufacturers may require different approaches.*

22 Use a piston ring installation tool and make sure the identification mark is facing the top of the piston, then slip the ring into the middle groove on the piston **(see illustration)**. Don't expand the ring any more than necessary to slide it over the piston.

23 Install the number one (top) ring in the same manner. Make sure the mark is facing up. Be careful not to confuse the number one and number two rings.

24 Repeat the procedure for the remaining pistons and rings.

Installation

25 Before installing the piston/connecting rod assemblies, the cylinder walls must be perfectly clean, the top edge of each cylinder bore must be chamfered, and the crankshaft must be in place.

26 Remove the cap from the end of the number one connecting rod (refer to the marks made during removal). Remove the original bearing inserts and wipe the bearing

surfaces of the connecting rod and cap with a clean, lint-free cloth. They must be kept spotlessly clean.

Connecting rod bearing oil clearance check

27 Clean the back side of the new upper bearing insert, then lay it in place in the connecting rod. Make sure the tab on the bearing fits into the recess in the rod. Don't hammer the bearing insert into place and be very careful not to nick or gouge the bearing face. Don't lubricate the bearing at this time.

28 Clean the back side of the other bearing insert and install it in the rod cap. Again, make sure the tab on the bearing fits into the recess in the cap, and don't apply any lubricant. It's critically important that the mating surfaces of the bearing and connecting rod are perfectly clean and oil free when they're assembled.

29 Position the piston ring gaps at 90-degree intervals around the piston as shown **(see illustration)**.

30 Lubricate the piston and rings with clean engine oil and attach a piston ring compressor to the piston. Leave the skirt protruding about 1/4-inch to guide the piston into the cylinder. The rings must be compressed until they're flush with the piston.

31 Rotate the crankshaft until the number one connecting rod journal is at BDC (bottom dead center) and apply a liberal coat of engine oil to the cylinder walls.

32 With the mark (dot, arrow or letter R or L) on top of the piston facing the front (timing chain end) of the engine, gently insert the piston/connecting rod assembly into the number one cylinder bore and rest the bottom edge of the ring compressor on the engine block.

Note: *The connecting rod also has a mark on it that must face the correct direction. On all models, the marks on the connecting rods face the front (timing chain) of the engine.*

33 Tap the top edge of the ring compressor to make sure it's contacting the block around its entire circumference.

9.29 Position the piston ring end gaps as shown

92037-2A-9.30 HAYNES

9.34 Use a plastic or wooden hammer handle to push the piston into the cylinder

9.36 Place Plastigage on each connecting rod bearing journal parallel to the crankshaft centerline

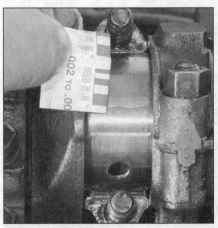

9.40 Use the scale on the Plastigage package to determine the bearing oil clearance - be sure to measure the widest part of the Plastigage and use the correct scale; it comes with both standard and metric scales

34   Gently tap on the top of the piston with the end of a wooden or plastic hammer handle **(see illustration)** while guiding the end of the connecting rod into place on the crankshaft journal. The piston rings may try to pop out of the ring compressor just before entering the cylinder bore, so keep some downward pressure on the ring compressor. Work slowly, and if any resistance is felt as the piston enters the cylinder, stop immediately. Find out what's hanging up and fix it before proceeding. Do not, for any reason, force the piston into the cylinder - you might break a ring and/or the piston.

35   Once the piston/connecting rod assembly is installed, the connecting rod bearing oil clearance must be checked before the rod cap is permanently installed.

36   Cut a piece of the appropriate size Plastigage slightly shorter than the width of the connecting rod bearing and lay it in place on the number one connecting rod journal, parallel with the journal axis **(see illustration)**.

37   Clean the connecting rod cap bearing face and install the rod cap. Make sure the mating mark on the cap is on the same side as the mark on the connecting rod.

38   Install the old rod bolts at this time, and tighten them to the torque listed in this Chapter's Specifications, working up to it in three steps. **Note:** *Use a thin-wall socket to avoid erroneous torque readings that can result if the socket is wedged between the rod cap and the bolt. If the socket tends to wedge itself between the fastener and the cap, lift up on it slightly until it no longer contacts the cap. DO NOT rotate the crankshaft at any time during this operation.*

39   Remove the fasteners and detach the rod cap, being very careful not to disturb the Plastigage. Discard the cap bolts at this time as they should not be reused.

40   Compare the width of the crushed Plastigage to the scale printed on the Plastigage envelope to obtain the oil clearance **(see illustration)**. The connecting rod oil clearance is usually about 0.001 to 0.002 inch. Consult an automotive machine shop for the clearance specified for the rod bearings on your engine.

41   If the clearance is not as specified, the bearing inserts may be the wrong size (which means different ones will be required). Before deciding that different inserts are needed, make sure that no dirt or oil was between the bearing inserts and the connecting rod or cap when the clearance was measured. Also, recheck the journal diameter. If the Plastigage was wider at one end than the other, the journal may be tapered. If the clearance still exceeds the limit specified, the bearing will have to be replaced with an undersize bearing. **Caution:** *When installing a new crankshaft always use a standard size bearing.*

Final installation

42   Carefully scrape all traces of the Plastigage material off the rod journal and/or bearing face. Be very careful not to scratch the bearing - use your fingernail or the edge of a plastic card.

43   Make sure the bearing faces are perfectly clean, then apply a uniform layer of clean moly-base grease or engine assembly lube to both of them. You'll have to push the piston into the cylinder to expose the face of the bearing insert in the connecting rod.

44   Slide the connecting rod back into place on the journal, install the rod cap, install the nuts or bolts and tighten them to the torque listed in this Chapter's Specifications. Again, work up to the torque in three steps.

45   Repeat the entire procedure for the remaining pistons/connecting rods.

46   The important points to remember are:

a) *Keep the back sides of the bearing inserts and the insides of the connecting rods and caps perfectly clean when assembling them.*

b) *Make sure you have the correct piston/rod assembly for each cylinder.*

c) *The mark on the piston must face the front (timing chain end) of the engine.*

d) *Lubricate the cylinder walls liberally with clean oil.*

e) *Lubricate the bearing faces when installing the rod caps after the oil clearance has been checked.*

47   After all the piston/connecting rod assemblies have been correctly installed, rotate the crankshaft a number of times by hand to check for any obvious binding.

48   As a final step, check the connecting rod endplay again. If it was correct before disassembly and the original crankshaft and rods were reinstalled, it should still be correct. If new rods or a new crankshaft were installed, the endplay may be inadequate. If so, the rods will have to be removed and taken to an automotive machine shop for resizing.

10   Crankshaft - removal and installation

Removal

Note: *The crankshaft can be removed only after the engine has been removed from the vehicle. It's assumed that the flywheel/driveplate, crankshaft pulley, timing chain, oil pan, lower crankcase (all 2009 and later models), oil pump body, balance shaft (2009 and later 2.4L engines), piston oil jet nozzles (all 2009 and later models), and piston/connecting rod assemblies have already been removed. The rear main oil seal retainer must be unbolted and separated from the block before proceeding with crankshaft removal.*

1   Before the crankshaft is removed, measure the endplay. Mount a dial indicator with the indicator in line with the crankshaft and touching the end of the crankshaft **(see illustration)**.

2   Pry the crankshaft all the way to the rear and zero the dial indicator. Next, pry the crankshaft to the front as far as possible and check the reading on the dial indicator. The distance traveled is the endplay. A typical crankshaft endplay will fall between 0.003 to 0.010-inch. If it's greater than that, check the crankshaft thrust sur-

10.1 Checking crankshaft endplay with a dial indicator

10.3 Checking crankshaft endplay with feeler gauges at the thrust bearing journal

faces for wear after it's removed. If no wear is evident, new main bearings should correct the endplay.

3   If a dial indicator isn't available, feeler gauges can be used. Gently pry the crankshaft all the way to the front of the engine. Slip feeler gauges between the crankshaft and the front face of the thrust bearing or washer to determine the clearance **(see illustration)**.

4   Loosen the main bearing cap bolts 1/4-turn at a time each, until they can be removed by hand. Loosen the bolts in a sequence *opposite* of the tightening sequence **(see illustration 10.19a or 10.19b)**.

5   Gently tap the main bearing cap assembly with a soft-faced hammer. Pull the main bearing cap straight up and off the cylinder block. Try not to drop the bearing inserts if they come out with the assembly. If the assembly is stuck to the engine block, pry carefully at the small slotted areas around the perimeter of the assembly (they're provided for this purpose).

6   Carefully lift the crankshaft out of the engine. It may be a good idea to have an assistant available, since the crankshaft is quite heavy and awkward to handle.

Installation

7   Crankshaft installation is the first step in engine reassembly. It's assumed at this point that the engine block and crankshaft have been cleaned, inspected and repaired or reconditioned.

8   Position the engine block with the bottom facing up.

9   If they're still in place, remove the original bearing inserts from the block and from the main bearing cap assembly.

10   Wipe the bearing surfaces of the block and main bearing cap assembly with a clean, lint-free cloth. They must be kept spotlessly clean. This is critical for determining the correct bearing oil clearance.

Main bearing oil clearance check

11   Without mixing them up, clean the back sides of the new upper main bearing inserts (with grooves and oil holes) and lay one in each main bearing saddle in the block. Each upper bearing has an oil groove and oil hole in it. The thrust bearings (washers) must be installed in the number three (center) cap. Install the thrust bearings with the oil grooves facing out. Install the thrust washers with the grooved side facing out. Install the thrust washers so that one set is located in the block and the other set is with the main bearing cap assembly. Clean the back sides of the lower main bearing inserts (without grooves) and lay them in the corresponding location in the main bearing cap assembly. Make sure the tab on the bearing insert fits into the recess in the block or main bearing cap assembly.
Caution: *The oil holes in the block must line up with the oil holes in the upper bearing inserts.*

Caution: *Do not hammer the bearing insert into place and don't nick or gouge the bearing faces. DO NOT apply any lubrication at this time.*

12   Clean the faces of the bearing inserts in the block and the crankshaft main bearing journals with a clean, lint-free cloth.

13   Check or clean the oil holes in the crankshaft, as any dirt here can go only one way - straight through the new bearings.

14   Once you're certain the crankshaft is clean, carefully lay it in position in the cylinder block.

15   Before the crankshaft can be permanently installed, the main bearing oil clearance must be checked.

16   Cut several strips of the appropriate size of Plastigage (they must be slightly shorter than the width of the main bearing journal).

17   Place one piece on each crankshaft main bearing journal, parallel with the journal axis **(see illustration)**.

18   Clean the faces of the bearing inserts in the main bearing cap assembly. Install the assembly onto the crankshaft and cylinder block. DO NOT disturb the Plastigage.

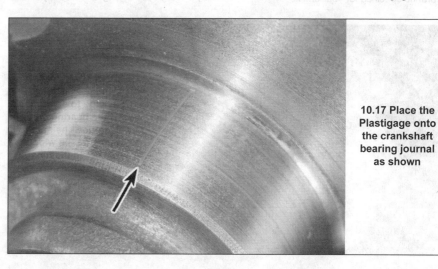

10.17 Place the Plastigage onto the crankshaft bearing journal as shown

10.19a Main bearing cap bolt tightening sequence (2008 and earlier models)

10.19b Main bearing cap bolt tightening sequence (2009 and later models)

19   Apply clean engine oil to all bolt threads prior to installation, then install all bolts finger-tight. Tighten main bearing cap assembly bolts in the sequence shown (see illustrations) progressing in two steps, to the torque listed in this Chapter's Specifications. DO NOT rotate the crankshaft at any time during this operation.

Note: *At this stage on 2008 and earlier models, it is only necessary to tighten bolts 1 through 10. Don't apply any sealant to the surfaces until final installation.*

20   Remove the bolts in the *reverse* order of the tightening sequence and carefully lift the main bearing cap assembly straight up and off the block. Do not disturb the Plastigage or rotate the crankshaft. If the main bearing cap assembly is difficult to remove, tap it gently from side-to-side with a soft-faced hammer to loosen it.

21   Compare the width of the crushed Plastigage on each journal to the scale printed on the Plastigage envelope to determine the main bearing oil clearance (see illustration). A typical main bearing oil clearance should fall between 0.0015 to 0.0023-inch. Check with an automotive machine shop for the clearance specified for your engine.

22   If the clearance is not as specified, the bearing inserts may be the wrong size (which means different ones will be required). Before deciding if different inserts are needed, make sure that no dirt or oil was between the bearing inserts and the cap assembly or block when the clearance was measured. If the Plastigage was wider at one end than the other, the crankshaft journal may be tapered. If the clearance still exceeds the limit specified, the bearing insert(s) will have to be replaced with an undersize bearing insert(s).

Caution: *When installing a new crankshaft always install a standard bearing insert set.*

23   Carefully scrape all traces of the Plastigage material off the main bearing journals and/or the bearing insert faces. Be sure to remove all residue from the oil holes. Use your fingernail or the edge of a plastic card - don't nick or scratch the bearing faces.

Final installation

24   Carefully lift the crankshaft out of the cylinder block.

25   Clean the bearing insert faces in the cylinder block, then apply a thin, uniform layer of moly-base grease or engine assembly lube to

each of the bearing surfaces. Be sure to coat the thrust faces as well as the journal face of the thrust bearing.

26   Make sure the crankshaft journals are clean, then lay the crankshaft back in place in the cylinder block.

27   Clean the bearing insert faces and apply the same lubricant to them.

28   Apply a 1/8-inch diameter bead of RTV sealant to the main bearing cap mating surface on the engine block, then place the main bearing cap assembly over the crankshaft and carefully tap it down into position on the engine block.

29   Using new bolts, apply clean engine oil to the bolt threads, wipe off any excess oil and install the bolts finger-tight.

30   On 2008 and earlier models, tighten the main bearing cap bolts in the indicated sequence (see illustration 10.19a), to 10 or 12 foot-pounds.

31   Gently tap the crankshaft back-and-forth with a soft faced mallet to seat the thrust bearing.

32   Tighten the inner main bearing cap bolts (bolts 1 through 10) in two steps in the indicated sequence (see illustration 10.19a or 10.19b) and to the torque and angle of rotation listed in this Chapter's Specifications. Then tighten the outer bolts (bolts 11 through 20) to the torque listed in this Chapter's Specifications, in sequence.

33   Recheck crankshaft endplay with a feeler gauge or a dial indicator. The endplay should be correct if the crankshaft thrust faces aren't worn or damaged and if new bearings have been installed.

34   Rotate the crankshaft a number of times by hand to check for any obvious binding. It should rotate with a running torque of 50 in-lbs or less. If the running torque is too high, correct the problem at this time.

35   Install the lower crankcase (see Section 11).

36   Install the new rear main oil seal (see Chapter 2A).

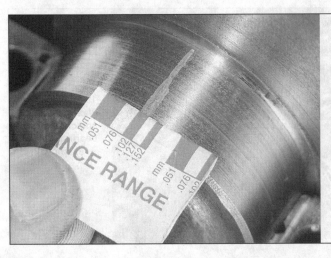

10.21 Use the scale on the Plastigage package to determine the bearing oil clearance - be sure to measure the widest part of the Plastigage and use the correct scale; it comes with both standard and metric scales

**Seal Width
2.5-3.0 mm**

11.2a Typical cylinder block-to-lower crankcase sealant
installation details (2009 and later models)

11.2b 2009 and later 1.8L engine lower crankcase bolt locations

A	5.43 inches long
B	1.38 inches long
C	2.76 inches long

11.2c 2009 and later 2.4L engine lower crankcase bolt locations

A	4.92 inches long
B	1.27 inches long

11 Engine overhaul - reassembly sequence

1   Before beginning engine reassembly, make sure you have all the necessary new parts, gaskets and seals as well as the following items on hand:

*Common hand tools
A 1/2-inch drive torque wrench
New engine oil
Gasket sealant
Thread locking compound*

2   If you obtained a short block it will be necessary to install the cylinder head, the oil pump and pick-up tube, the timing chain(s) and cover, the lower crankcase **(see illustrations)**, the front covers, the oil pan and the valve cover (see Chapter 2A).

3   In order to save time and avoid problems, the external components must be installed in the following general order:

*Thermostat and housing cover
Water pump
Intake and exhaust manifolds
Fuel injection components
Emission control components*

*Spark plugs
Ignition coils
Oil filter
Engine mounts and mount brackets
Flywheel and clutch (manual transaxle)
Driveplate (automatic transaxle)*

12 Initial start-up and break-in after overhaul

Warning: *Have a fire extinguisher handy when starting the engine for the first time.*

1   Once the engine has been installed in the vehicle, double-check the engine oil and coolant levels.

2   With the spark plugs out of the engine and the ignition system and fuel pump disabled (see Chapter 4, Section 3), crank the engine until oil pressure registers on the gauge or the light goes out.

3   Install the spark plugs, hook up the plug wires and/or ignition coils and restore the ignition system and fuel pump functions.

4   Start the engine. It may take a few moments for the fuel system to build up pressure, but the engine should start without a great deal of effort.

5   After the engine starts, it should be allowed to warm up to normal operating temperature. While the engine is warming up, make a thorough check for fuel, oil and coolant leaks.

6   Shut the engine off and recheck the engine oil and coolant levels.

7   Drive the vehicle to an area with minimum traffic, accelerate from 30 to 50 mph, then allow the vehicle to slow to 30 mph with the throttle closed. Repeat the procedure 10 or 12 times. This will load the piston rings and cause them to seat properly against the cylinder walls. Check again for oil and coolant leaks.

8   Drive the vehicle gently for the first 500 miles (no sustained high speeds) and keep a constant check on the oil level. It is not unusual for an engine to use oil during the break-in period.

9   At approximately 500 to 600 miles, change the oil and filter.

10   For the next few hundred miles, drive the vehicle normally. Do not pamper it or abuse it.

11   After 2000 miles, change the oil and filter again and consider the engine broken in.

ENGINE BEARING ANALYSIS

Debris

Babbitt bearing embedded with debris from machinings

Microscopic detail of debris

Microscopic detail of gouges

Overplated copper alloy bearing gouged by cast iron debris

Aluminum bearing embedded with glass beads

Microscopic detail of glass beads

Damaged lining caused by dirt left on the bearing back

Misassembly

Result of a lower half assembled as an upper - blocking the oil flow

Excessive oil clearance is indicated by a short contact arc

Polished and oil-stained backs are a result of a poor fit in the housing bore

Result of a wrong, reversed, or shifted cap

Overloading

Damage from excessive idling which resulted in an oil film unable to support the load imposed

Damaged upper connecting rod bearings caused by engine lugging; the lower main bearings (not shown) were similarly affected

The damage shown in these upper and lower connecting rod bearings was caused by engine operation at a higher-than-rated speed under load

Misalignment

A warped crankshaft caused this pattern of severe wear in the center, diminishing toward the ends

A poorly finished crankshaft caused the equally spaced scoring shown

A tapered housing bore caused the damage along one edge of this pair

A bent connecting rod led to the damage in the "V" pattern

Lubrication

Result of dry start: The bearings on the left, farthest from the oil pump, show more damage

Result of a low oil supply or oil starvation

Severe wear as a result of inadequate oil clearance

Corrosion

Microscopic detail of corrosion

Corrosion is an acid attack on the bearing lining generally caused by inadequate maintenance, extremely hot or cold operation, or inferior oils or fuels

Microscopic detail of cavitation

Example of cavitation - a surface erosion caused by pressure changes in the oil film

Damage from excessive thrust or insufficient axial clearance

Bearing affected by oil dilution caused by excessive blow-by or a rich mixture

COMMON ENGINE OVERHAUL TERMS

B

Backlash - The amount of play between two parts. Usually refers to how much one gear can be moved back and forth without moving the gear with which it's meshed.

Bearing Caps - The caps held in place by nuts or bolts which, in turn, hold the bearing surface. This space is for lubricating oil to enter.

Bearing clearance - The amount of space left between shaft and bearing surface. This space is for lubricating oil to enter.

Bearing crush - The additional height which is purposely manufactured into each bearing half to ensure complete contact of the bearing back with the housing bore when the engine is assembled.

Bearing knock - The noise created by movement of a part in a loose or worn bearing.

Blueprinting - Dismantling an engine and reassembling it to EXACT specifications.

Bore - An engine cylinder, or any cylindrical hole; also used to describe the process of enlarging or accurately refinishing a hole with a cutting tool, as to bore an engine cylinder. The bore size is the diameter of the hole.

Boring - Renewing the cylinders by cutting them out to a specified size. A boring bar is used to make the cut.

Bottom end - A term which refers collectively to the engine block, crankshaft, main bearings and the big ends of the connecting rods.

Break-in - The period of operation between installation of new or rebuilt parts and time in which parts are worn to the correct fit. Driving at reduced and varying speed for a specified mileage to permit parts to wear to the correct fit.

Bushing - A one-piece sleeve placed in a bore to serve as a bearing surface for shaft, piston pin, etc. Usually replaceable.

C

Camshaft - The shaft in the engine, on which a series of lobes are located for operating the valve mechanisms. The camshaft is driven by gears or sprockets and a timing chain. Usually referred to simply as the cam.

Carbon - Hard, or soft, black deposits found in combustion chamber, on plugs, under rings, on and under valve heads.

Cast iron - An alloy of iron and more than two percent carbon, used for engine blocks and heads because it's relatively inexpensive and easy to mold into complex shapes.

Chamfer - To bevel across (or a bevel on) the sharp edge of an object.

Chase - To repair damaged threads with a tap or die.

Combustion chamber - The space between the piston and the cylinder head, with the piston at top dead center, in which air-fuel mixture is burned.

Compression ratio - The relationship between cylinder volume (clearance volume) when the piston is at top dead center and cylinder volume when the piston is at bottom dead center.

Connecting rod - The rod that connects the crank on the crankshaft with the piston. Sometimes called a con rod.

Connecting rod cap - The part of the connecting rod assembly that attaches the rod to the crankpin.

Core plug - Soft metal plug used to plug the casting holes for the coolant passages in the block.

Crankcase - The lower part of the engine in which the crankshaft rotates; includes the lower section of the cylinder block and the oil pan.

Crank kit - A reground or reconditioned crankshaft and new main and connecting rod bearings.

Crankpin - The part of a crankshaft to which a connecting rod is attached.

Crankshaft - The main rotating member, or shaft, running the length of the crankcase, with offset throws to which the connecting rods are attached; changes the reciprocating motion of the pistons into rotating motion.

Cylinder sleeve - A replaceable sleeve, or liner, pressed into the cylinder block to form the cylinder bore.

D

Deburring - Removing the burrs (rough edges or areas) from a bearing.

Deglazer - A tool, rotated by an electric motor, used to remove glaze from cylinder walls so a new set of rings will seat.

E

Endplay - The amount of lengthwise movement between two parts. As applied to a crankshaft, the distance that the crankshaft can move forward and back in the cylinder block.

F

Face - A machinist's term that refers to removing metal from the end of a shaft or the face of a larger part, such as a flywheel.

Fatigue - A breakdown of material through a large number of loading and unloading cycles. The first signs are cracks followed shortly by breaks.

Feeler gauge - A thin strip of hardened steel, ground to an exact thickness, used to check clearances between parts.

Free height - The unloaded length or height of a spring.

Freeplay - The looseness in a linkage, or an assembly of parts, between the initial application of force and actual movement. Usually perceived as slop or slight delay.

Freeze plug - See Core plug.

G

Gallery - A large passage in the block that forms a reservoir for engine oil pressure.

Glaze - The very smooth, glassy finish that develops on cylinder walls while an engine is in service.

H

Heli-Coil - A rethreading device used when threads are worn or damaged. The device is installed in a retapped hole to reduce the thread size to the original size.

I

Installed height - The spring's measured length or height, as installed on the cylinder head. Installed height is measured from the spring seat to the underside of the spring retainer.

J

Journal - The surface of a rotating shaft which turns in a bearing.

K

Keeper - The split lock that holds the valve spring retainer in position on the valve stem.

Key - A small piece of metal inserted into matching grooves machined into two parts fitted together - such as a gear pressed onto a shaft - which prevents slippage between the two parts.

Knock - The heavy metallic engine sound, produced in the combustion chamber as a result of abnormal combustion - usually detonation. Knock is usually caused by a loose or worn bearing. Also referred to as detonation, pinging and spark knock. Connecting rod or main bearing knocks are created by too much oil clearance or insufficient lubrication.

L

Lands - The portions of metal between the piston ring grooves.

Lapping the valves - Grinding a valve face and its seat together with lapping compound.

Lash - The amount of free motion in a gear train, between gears, or in a mechanical assembly, that occurs before movement can begin. Usually refers to the lash in a valve train.

Lifter - The part that rides against the cam to transfer motion to the rest of the valve train.

M

Machining - The process of using a machine to remove metal from a metal part.

Main bearings - The plain, or babbit, bearings that support the crankshaft.

Main bearing caps - The cast iron caps, bolted to the bottom of the block, that support the main bearings.

O

O.D. - Outside diameter.

Oil gallery - A pipe or drilled passageway in the engine used to carry engine oil from one area to another.

Oil ring - The lower ring, or rings, of a piston; designed to prevent excessive amounts of oil from working up the cylinder walls and into the combustion chamber. Also called an oil-control ring.

Oil seal - A seal which keeps oil from leaking out of a compartment. Usually refers to a dynamic seal around a rotating shaft or other moving part.

O-ring - A type of sealing ring made of a special rubberlike material; in use, the O-ring is compressed into a groove to provide the sealing action.

Overhaul - To completely disassemble a unit, clean and inspect all parts, reassemble it with the original or new parts and make all adjustments necessary for proper operation.

P

Pilot bearing - A small bearing installed in the center of the flywheel (or the rear end of the crankshaft) to support the front end of the input shaft of the transmission.

Pip mark - A little dot or indentation which indicates the top side of a compression ring.

Piston - The cylindrical part, attached to the connecting rod, that moves up and down in the cylinder as the crankshaft rotates. When the fuel charge is fired, the piston transfers the force of the explosion to the connecting rod, then to the crankshaft.

Piston pin (or wrist pin) - The cylindrical and usually hollow steel pin that passes through the piston. The piston pin fastens the piston to the upper end of the connecting rod.

Piston ring - The split ring fitted to the groove in a piston. The ring contacts the sides of the ring groove and also rubs against the cylinder wall, thus sealing space between piston and wall. There are two types of rings: Compression rings seal the compression pressure in the combustion chamber; oil rings scrape excessive oil off the cylinder wall.

Piston ring groove - The slots or grooves cut in piston heads to hold piston rings in position.

Piston skirt - The portion of the piston below the rings and the piston pin hole.

Plastigage - A thin strip of plastic thread, available in different sizes, used for measuring clearances. For example, a strip of plastigage is laid across a bearing journal and mashed as parts are assembled. Then parts are disassembled and the width of the strip is measured to determine clearance between journal and bearing. Commonly used to measure crankshaft main-bearing and connecting rod bearing clearances.

Press-fit - A tight fit between two parts that requires pressure to force the parts together. Also referred to as drive, or force, fit.

Prussian blue - A blue pigment; in solution, useful in determining the area of contact between two surfaces. Prussian blue is commonly used to determine the width and location of the contact area between the valve face and the valve seat.

R

Race (bearing) - The inner or outer ring that provides a contact surface for balls or rollers in bearing.

Ream - To size, enlarge or smooth a hole by using a round cutting tool with fluted edges.

Ring job - The process of reconditioning the cylinders and installing new rings.

Runout - Wobble. The amount a shaft rotates out-of-true.

S

Saddle - The upper main bearing seat.

Scored - Scratched or grooved, as a cylinder wall may be scored by abrasive particles moved up and down by the piston rings.

Scuffing - A type of wear in which there's a transfer of material between parts moving against each other; shows up as pits or grooves in the mating surfaces.

Seat - The surface upon which another part rests or seats. For example, the valve seat is the matched surface upon which the valve face rests. Also used to refer to wearing into a good fit; for example, piston rings seat after a few miles of driving.

Short block - An engine block complete with crankshaft and piston and, usually, camshaft assemblies.

Static balance - The balance of an object while it's stationary.

Step - The wear on the lower portion of a ring land caused by excessive side and back-clearance. The height of the step indicates the ring's extra side clearance and the length of the step projecting from the back wall of the groove represents the ring's back clearance.

Stroke - The distance the piston moves when traveling from top dead center to bottom dead center, or from bottom dead center to top dead center.

Stud - A metal rod with threads on both ends.

T

Tang - A lip on the end of a plain bearing used to align the bearing during assembly.

Tap - To cut threads in a hole. Also refers to the fluted tool used to cut threads.

Taper - A gradual reduction in the width of a shaft or hole; in an engine cylinder, taper usually takes the form of uneven wear, more pronounced at the top than at the bottom.

Throws - The offset portions of the crankshaft to which the connecting rods are affixed.

Thrust bearing - The main bearing that has thrust faces to prevent excessive endplay, or forward and backward movement of the crankshaft.

Thrust washer - A bronze or hardened steel washer placed between two moving parts. The washer prevents longitudinal movement and provides a bearing surface for thrust surfaces of parts.

Tolerance - The amount of variation permitted from an exact size of measurement. Actual amount from smallest acceptable dimension to largest acceptable dimension.

U

Umbrella - An oil deflector placed near the valve tip to throw oil from the valve stem area.

Undercut - A machined groove below the normal surface.

Undersize bearings - Smaller diameter bearings used with re-ground crankshaft journals.

V

Valve grinding - Refacing a valve in a valve-refacing machine.

Valve train - The valve-operating mechanism of an engine; includes all components from the camshaft to the valve.

Vibration damper - A cylindrical weight attached to the front of the crankshaft to minimize torsional vibration (the twist-untwist actions of the crankshaft caused by the cylinder firing impulses). Also called a harmonic balancer.

W

Water jacket - The spaces around the cylinders, between the inner and outer shells of the cylinder block or head, through which coolant circulates.

Web - A supporting structure across a cavity.

Woodruff key - A key with a radiused backside (viewed from the side).

Notes

Chapter 3
Cooling, heating and air conditioning systems

Contents

Specifications

General

Radiator cap pressure rating	10.7 to 14.9 psi
Thermostat rating	176 to 183 degrees F
Refrigerant type..	R-134a
Refrigerant capacity..	17 ounces +/- 1 oz

Torque specifications

Ft-lbs (unless otherwise indicated)

Note: *One foot-pound (ft-lb) of torque is equivalent to 12 inch-pounds (in-lbs) of torque. Torque values below approximately 15 ft-lbs are expressed in inch-pounds, because most foot-pound torque wrenches are not accurate at these smaller values.*

Thermostat housing nuts	
2008 and earlier models	96 in-lbs
2009 and later models	
2.4L engines	80 in-lbs
1.8L engines	84 in-lbs
Water pump-to-block bolts	
1.8L engines	
2008 and earlier models	
Smaller bolt	80 in-lbs
Larger bolts	96 in-lbs
2009 and 2010 models	
Shorter bolts...	18
Longer bolts..	19
2011 and later models	
Shorter bolts...	15
Longer bolts..	19
2.4L engine	80 in-lbs
Water pump pulley bolts (2.4L engine)......................................	19

1   General Information

Warning: *Do not allow antifreeze to come in contact with your skin or painted surfaces of the vehicle. Rinse off spills immediately with plenty of water. Antifreeze is highly toxic if ingested. Never leave antifreeze lying around in an open container or in puddles on the floor; children and pets are attracted by its sweet smell and may drink it. Check with local authorities about disposing of used antifreeze. Many communities have collection centers which will see that antifreeze is disposed of safely. Never dump used antifreeze on the ground or pour it into drains.*

Engine cooling system

1   All modern vehicles employ a pressurized engine cooling system with thermostatically controlled coolant circulation. The cooling system consists of a radiator, an expansion tank or coolant reservoir, a pressure cap (located on the expansion tank or radiator), a thermostat, a cooling fan, and a water pump.

2   The water pump circulates coolant through the engine. The coolant flows around each cylinder and around the intake and exhaust ports, near the spark plug areas and in close proximity to the exhaust valve guides.

3   A thermostat controls engine coolant temperature. During warm up, the closed thermostat prevents coolant from circulating through the radiator. As the engine nears normal operating temperature, the thermostat opens and allows hot coolant to travel through the radiator, where it's cooled before returning to the engine.

Heating system

4   The heating system consists of a blower fan and heater core located in a housing under the dash, the hoses connecting the heater core to the engine cooling system and the heater/air conditioning control head on the dashboard. Hot engine coolant is circulated through the heater core. When the heater mode is activated, a flap door in the housing opens to expose the heater core to the passenger compartment through air ducts. A fan switch on the control head activates the blower motor, which forces air through the core, heating the air.

Air conditioning system

5   The air conditioning system consists of a condenser mounted in front of the radiator, an evaporator mounted adjacent to the heater core, a compressor mounted on the engine, a receiver-drier or accumulator and the plumbing connecting all of the above components.

6   A blower fan forces the warmer air of the passenger compartment through the evaporator core (sort of a radiator-in-reverse), transferring the heat from the air to the refrigerant. The liquid refrigerant boils off into low pressure vapor, taking the heat with it when it leaves the evaporator.

2.2 The cooling system pressure tester is connected in place of the pressure cap, then pumped up to pressurize the system

2   Troubleshooting

Coolant leaks

1   A coolant leak can develop anywhere in the cooling system, but the most common causes are:

a) A loose or weak hose clamp
b) A defective hose
c) A faulty pressure cap
d) A damaged radiator
e) A bad heater core
f) A faulty water pump
g) A leaking gasket at any joint that carries coolant

2   Coolant leaks aren't always easy to find. Sometimes they can only be detected when the cooling system is under pressure. Here's where a cooling system pressure tester comes in handy. After the engine has cooled completely, the tester is attached in place of the pressure cap, then pumped up to the pressure value equal to that of the pressure cap rating **(see illustration)**. Now, leaks that

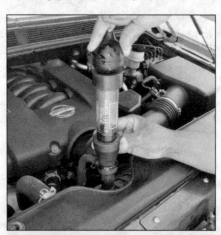

2.5b Place the tester over the cooling system filler neck and use the bulb to draw a sample into the tester

2.5a The combustion leak detector consists of a bulb, syringe and test fluid

only exist when the engine is fully warmed up will become apparent. The tester can be left connected to locate a nagging slow leak.

Coolant level drops, but no external leaks

3   If you find it necessary to keep adding coolant, but there are no external leaks, the probable causes include:

a) A blown head gasket
b) A leaking intake manifold gasket (only on engines that have coolant passages in the manifold)
c) A cracked cylinder head or cylinder block

4   Any of the above problems will also usually result in contamination of the engine oil, which will cause it to take on a milkshake-like appearance. A bad head gasket or cracked head or block can also result in engine oil contaminating the cooling system.

5   Combustion leak detectors (also known as block testers) are available at most auto parts stores. These work by detecting exhaust gases in the cooling system, which indicates a compression leak from a cylinder into the cool-

2.8 Checking the cooling system pressure cap with a cooling system pressure tester

2.10 Typical thermostat:

1	Flange	5	Valve seat
2	Piston	6	Valve
3	Jiggle valve	7	Frame
4	Main coil spring	8	Secondary coil spring

2.28 The water pump weep hole is generally located on the underside of the pump

ant. The tester consists of a large bulb-type syringe and bottle of test fluid **(see illustration)**. A measured amount of the fluid is added to the syringe. The syringe is placed over the cooling system filler neck and, with the engine running, the bulb is squeezed and a sample of the gases present in the cooling system are drawn up through the test fluid **(see illustration)**. If any combustion gases are present in the sample taken, the test fluid will change color.

6   If the test indicates combustion gas is present in the cooling system, you can be sure that the engine has a blown head gasket or a crack in the cylinder head or block, and will require disassembly to repair.

Pressure cap

Warning: *Wait until the engine is completely cool before beginning this check.*

7   The cooling system is sealed by a spring-loaded cap, which raises the boiling point of the coolant. If the cap's seal or spring are worn out, the coolant can boil and escape past the cap. With the engine completely cool, remove the cap and check the seal; if it's cracked, hardened or deteriorated in any way, replace it with a new one.

8   Even if the seal is good, the spring might not be; this can be checked with a cooling system pressure tester **(see illustration)**. If the cap can't hold a pressure within approximately 1-1/2 lbs of its rated pressure (which is marked on the cap), replace it with a new one.

9   The cap is also equipped with a vacuum relief spring. When the engine cools off, a vacuum is created in the cooling system. The vacuum relief spring allows air back into the system, which will equalize the pressure and prevent damage to the radiator (the radiator tanks could collapse if the vacuum is great enough). If, after turning the engine off and allowing it to cool down you notice any of the cooling system hoses collapsing, replace the pressure cap with a new one.

Thermostat

10   Before assuming the thermostat **(see illustration)** is responsible for a cooling system problem, check the coolant level (see Chapter 1), drivebelt tension (see Chapter 1) and temperature gauge (or light) operation.

11   If the engine takes a long time to warm up (as indicated by the temperature gauge or heater operation), the thermostat is probably stuck open. Replace the thermostat with a new one.

12   If the engine runs hot or overheats, a thorough test of the thermostat should be performed.

13   Definitive testing of the thermostat can only be made when it is removed from the vehicle. If the thermostat is stuck in the open position at room temperature, it is faulty and must be replaced.

Caution: *Do not drive the vehicle without a thermostat. The computer may stay in open loop and emissions and fuel economy will suffer.*

14   To test a thermostat, suspend the (closed) thermostat on a length of string or wire in a pot of cold water.

15   Heat the water on a stove while observing the thermostat. The thermostat should fully open before the water boils.

16   If the thermostat doesn't open and close as specified, or sticks in any position, replace it.

Cooling fan

Electric cooling fan

17   If the engine is overheating and the cooling fan is not coming on when the engine temperature rises to an excessive level, unplug the fan motor electrical connector(s) and connect the motor directly to the battery with fused jumper wires. If the fan motor doesn't come on, replace the motor.

18   If the fan motor is okay, but it isn't coming on when the engine gets hot, the cooling fan control module or the Powertrain Control Module (PCM) might be defective.

19   These control circuits are fairly complex, and checking them should be left to a qualified automotive technician.

20   Check all wiring and connections to the fan motor. Refer to the wiring diagrams at the end of Chapter 12.

21   If no obvious problems are found, the problem could be the Cylinder Head Temperature (CHT) sensor or the Powertrain Control Module (PCM). Have the cooling fan system and circuit diagnosed by a dealer service department or repair shop with the proper diagnostic equipment.

Belt-driven cooling fan

22   Disconnect the cable from the negative terminal of the battery and rock the fan back and forth by hand to check for excessive bearing play.

23   With the engine cold (and not running), turn the fan blades by hand. The fan should turn freely.

24   Visually inspect for substantial fluid leakage from the clutch assembly. If problems are noted, replace the clutch assembly.

25   With the engine completely warmed up, turn off the ignition switch and disconnect the negative battery cable from the battery. Turn the fan by hand. Some drag should be evident. If the fan turns easily, replace the fan clutch.

Water pump

26   A failure in the water pump can cause serious engine damage due to overheating.

Drivebelt-driven water pump

27   There are two ways to check the operation of the water pump while it's installed on the engine. If the pump is found to be defective, it should be replaced with a new or rebuilt unit.

28   Water pumps are equipped with weep (or vent) holes **(see illustration)**. If a failure occurs in the pump seal, coolant will leak from the hole.

29   If the water pump shaft bearings fail, there may be a howling sound at the pump while it's running. Shaft wear can be felt with the drivebelt removed if the water pump pulley is rocked up and down (with the engine off). Don't mistake drivebelt slippage, which causes a squealing sound, for water pump bearing failure.

Timing chain or timing belt-driven water pump

30 Water pumps driven by the timing chain or timing belt are located underneath the timing chain or timing belt cover.

31 Checking the water pump is limited because of where it is located. However, some basic checks can be made before deciding to remove the water pump. If the pump is found to be defective, it should be replaced with a new or rebuilt unit.

32 One sign that the water pump may be failing is that the heater (climate control) may not work well. Warm the engine to normal operating temperature, confirm that the coolant level is correct, then run the heater and check for hot air coming from the ducts.

33 Check for noises coming from the water pump area. If the water pump impeller shaft or bearings are failing, there may be a howling sound at the pump while the engine is running. **Note:** *Be careful not to mistake drivebelt noise (squealing) for water pump bearing or shaft failure.*

34 It you suspect water pump failure due to noise, wear can be confirmed by feeling for play at the pump shaft. This can be done by rocking the drive sprocket on the pump shaft up and down. To do this you will need to remove the tension on the timing chain or belt as well as access the water pump.

All water pumps

35 In rare cases or on high-mileage vehicles, another sign of water pump failure may be the presence of coolant in the engine oil. This condition will adversely affect the engine in varying degrees. **Note:** *Finding coolant in the engine oil could indicate other serious issues besides a failed water pump, such as a blown head gasket or a cracked cylinder head or block.*

36 Even a pump that exhibits no outward signs of a problem, such as noise or leakage, can still be due for replacement. Removal for close examination is the only sure way to tell. Sometimes the fins on the back of the impeller can corrode to the point that cooling efficiency is diminished significantly.

Heating system

37 Little can go wrong with a heater. If the fan motor will run at all speeds, the electrical part of the system is okay. The three basic heater problems fall into the following general categories:

a) *Not enough heat*
b) *Heat all the time*
c) *No heat*

38 If there's not enough heat, the control valve or door is stuck in a partially open position, the coolant coming from the engine isn't hot enough, or the heater core is restricted. If the coolant isn't hot enough, the thermostat in the engine cooling system is stuck open, allowing coolant to pass through the engine so rapidly that it doesn't heat up quickly enough. If the vehicle is equipped with a temperature gauge instead of a warning light,

watch to see if the engine temperature rises to the normal operating range after driving for a reasonable distance.

39 If there's heat all the time, the control valve or the door is stuck wide open.

40 If there's no heat, coolant is probably not reaching the heater core, or the heater core is plugged. The likely cause is a collapsed or plugged hose, core, or a frozen heater control valve. If the heater is the type that flows coolant all the time, the cause is a stuck door or a broken or kinked control cable.

Air conditioning system

41 If the cool air output is inadequate:

a) *Inspect the condenser coils and fins to make sure they're clear*
b) *Check the compressor clutch for slippage.*
c) *Check the blower motor for proper operation.*
d) *Inspect the blower discharge passage for obstructions.*
e) *Check the system air intake filter for clogging.*

42 If the system provides intermittent cooling air:

a) *Check the circuit breaker, blower switch and blower motor for a malfunction.*
b) *Make sure the compressor clutch isn't slipping.*
c) *Inspect the plenum door to make sure it's operating properly.*
d) *Inspect the evaporator to make sure it isn't clogged.*
e) *If the unit is icing up, it may be caused by excessive moisture in the system, incorrect super heat switch adjustment or low thermostat adjustment.*

43 If the system provides no cooling air:

a) *Inspect the compressor drivebelt. Make sure it's not loose or broken.*
b) *Make sure the compressor clutch engages. If it doesn't, check for a blown fuse.*
c) *Inspect the wire harness for broken or disconnected wires.*
d) *If the compressor clutch doesn't engage, bridge the terminals of the A/C pressure switch(es) with a jumper wire; if the clutch now engages, and the system is properly charged, the pressure switch is bad.*
e) *Make sure the blower motor is not disconnected or burned out.*
f) *Make sure the compressor isn't partially or completely seized.*
g) *Inspect the refrigerant lines for leaks.*
h) *Check the components for leaks.*
i) *Inspect the receiver-drier/accumulator or expansion valve/tube for clogged screens.*

44 If the system is noisy:

a) *Look for loose panels in the passenger compartment.*
b) *Inspect the compressor drivebelt. It may be loose or worn.*

c) *Check the compressor mounting bolts. They should be tight.*
d) *Listen carefully to the compressor. It may be worn out.*
e) *Listen to the idler pulley and bearing and the clutch. Either may be defective.*
f) *The winding in the compressor clutch coil or solenoid may be defective.*
g) *The compressor oil level may be low.*
h) *The blower motor fan bushing or the motor itself may be worn out.*
i) *If there is an excessive charge in the system, you'll hear a rumbling noise in the high pressure line, a thumping noise in the compressor, or see bubbles or cloudiness in the sight glass.*
j) *If there's a low charge in the system, you might hear hissing in the evaporator case at the expansion valve, or see bubbles or cloudiness in the sight glass.*

3 Air conditioning and heating system - check and maintenance

Air conditioning system

Warning: *The air conditioning system is under high pressure. Do not loosen any hose fittings or remove any components until after the system has been discharged. Air conditioning refrigerant should be properly discharged into an EPA-approved recovery/recycling unit at a dealer service department or an automotive air conditioning repair facility. Always wear eye protection when disconnecting air conditioning system fittings.*

Caution: *All models covered by this manual use environmentally friendly R-134a. This refrigerant (and its appropriate refrigerant oils) are not compatible with R-12 refrigerant system components and must never be mixed or the components will be damaged.*

Caution: *When replacing entire components, additional refrigerant oil should be added equal to the amount that is removed with the component being replaced. Read the can before adding any oil to the system, to make sure it is compatible with the R-134a system.*

1 The following maintenance checks should be performed on a regular basis to ensure that the air conditioning continues to operate at peak efficiency.

a) *Inspect the condition of the compressor drivebelt. If it is worn or deteriorated, replace it (see Chapter 1).*
b) *Check the drivebelt tension (see Chapter 1).*
c) *Inspect the system hoses. Look for cracks, bubbles, hardening and deterioration. Inspect the hoses and all fittings for oil bubbles or seepage. If there is any evidence of wear, damage or leakage, replace the hose(s).*
d) *Inspect the condenser fins for leaves, bugs and any other foreign material that may have embedded in the fins. Use a fin comb or compressed air to remove debris from the condenser.*
e) *Make sure the system has the correct refrigerant charge.*

3.9 Insert a thermometer in the center vent, turn on the air conditioning system and wait for it to cool down; depending on the humidity, the output air should be 35 to 40 degrees cooler than the ambient air temperature

3.11 R-134a automotive air conditioning charging kit

3.13 Location of the low-side charging port

2   It's a good idea to operate the system for about ten minutes at least once a month. This is particularly important during the winter months because long term non-use can cause hardening, and subsequent failure, of the seals. Note that using the Defrost function operates the compressor.

3   If the air conditioning system is not working properly, proceed to Step 6 and perform the general checks outlined below.

4   Because of the complexity of the air conditioning system and the special equipment necessary to service it, in-depth troubleshooting and repairs beyond checking the refrigerant charge and the compressor clutch operation are not included in this manual. However, simple checks and component replacement procedures are provided in this Chapter. For more complete information on the air conditioning system, refer to the *Haynes Automotive Heating and Air Conditioning Manual.*

5   The most common cause of poor cooling is simply a low system refrigerant charge. If a noticeable drop in system cooling ability occurs, one of the following quick checks will help you determine if the refrigerant level is low.

Checking the refrigerant charge

6   Warm the engine up to normal operating temperature.

7   Place the air conditioning temperature selector at the coldest setting and put the blower at the highest setting.

8   After the system reaches operating temperature, feel the larger pipe exiting the evaporator at the firewall. The outlet pipe should be cold (the tubing that leads back to the compressor). If the evaporator outlet pipe is warm, the system probably needs a charge.

9   Insert a thermometer in the center air

distribution duct **(see illustration)** while operating the air conditioning system at its maximum setting - the temperature of the output air should be 35 to 40 degrees F below the ambient air temperature (down to approximately 40 degrees F). If the ambient (outside) air temperature is very high, say 110 degrees F, the duct air temperature may be as high as 60 degrees F, but generally the air conditioning is 35 to 40 degrees F cooler than the ambient air.

10   Further inspection or testing of the system requires special tools and techniques and is beyond the scope of the home mechanic.

Adding refrigerant

Caution: *Make sure any refrigerant, refrigerant oil or replacement component you purchase is designated as compatible with R-134a systems.*

11   Purchase an R-134a automotive charging kit at an auto parts store **(see illustration)**. A charging kit includes a can of refrigerant, a tap valve and a short section of hose that can be attached between the tap valve and the system low side service valve.

Caution: *Never add more than one can of refrigerant to the system. If more refrigerant than that is required, the system should be evacuated and leak tested.*

12   Back off the valve handle on the charging kit and screw the kit onto the refrigerant can, making sure first that the O-ring or rubber seal inside the threaded portion of the kit is in place.

Warning: *Wear protective eyewear when dealing with pressurized refrigerant cans.*

13   Remove the dust cap from the low-side charging port and attach the hose's quick-connect fitting to the port **(see illustration)**.

Warning: *DO NOT hook the charging kit hose to the system high side! The fittings on the charging kit are designed to fit only on the low side of the system.*

14   Warm up the engine and turn on the air conditioning. Keep the charging kit hose away from the fan and other moving parts.

Note: *The charging process requires the compressor to be running. If the clutch cycles off, you can put the air conditioning switch on High and leave the car doors open to keep the clutch on and compressor working. The compressor can be kept on during the charging by removing the connector from the pressure switch and bridging it with a paper clip or jumper wire during the procedure.*

15   Turn the valve handle on the kit until the stem pierces the can, then back the handle out to release the refrigerant. You should be able to hear the rush of gas. Keep the can upright at all times, but shake it occasionally. Allow stabilization time between each addition.

Note: *The charging process will go faster if you wrap the can with a hot-water-soaked rag to keep the can from freezing up.*

16   If you have an accurate thermometer, you can place it in the center air conditioning duct inside the vehicle and keep track of the output air temperature. A charged system that is working properly should cool down to approximately 40 degrees F. If the ambient (outside) air temperature is very high, say 110 degrees F, the duct air temperature may be as high as 60 degrees F, but generally the air conditioning is 35 to 40 degrees F cooler than the ambient air.

17   When the can is empty, turn the valve handle to the closed position and release the connection from the low-side port. Reinstall the dust cap.

18   Remove the charging kit from the can and store the kit for future use with the piercing valve in the UP position, to prevent inadvertently piercing the can on the next use.

Heating systems

19   If the carpet under the heater core is damp, or if antifreeze vapor or steam is coming through the vents, the heater core is leaking. Remove it (see Section 10) and install a new unit (most radiator shops will not repair a leaking heater core).

3.24 Insert the nozzle of the disinfectant can into the return-air intake behind the glove box

4.6 Thermostat housing mounting nuts

4.7 The thermostat is installed with the spring end toward the engine, and the jiggle pin in the 12 o'clock position

20   If the air coming out of the heater vents isn't hot, the problem could stem from any of the following causes:

   a) *The thermostat is stuck open, preventing the engine coolant from warming up enough to carry heat to the heater core. Replace the thermostat (see Section 4).*

   b) *There is a blockage in the system, preventing the flow of coolant through the heater core. Feel both heater hoses at the firewall. They should be hot. If one of them is cold, there is an obstruction in one of the hoses or in the heater core, or the heater control valve is shut. Detach the hoses and back flush the heater core with a water hose. If the heater core is clear but circulation is impeded, remove the two hoses and flush them out with a water hose.*

   c) *If flushing fails to remove the blockage from the heater core, the core must be replaced (see Section 10).*

Eliminating air conditioning odors

21   Unpleasant odors that often develop in air conditioning systems are caused by the growth of a fungus, usually on the surface of the evaporator core. The warm, humid environment there is a perfect breeding ground for mildew to develop.

22   The evaporator core on most vehicles is difficult to access, and factory dealerships have a lengthy, expensive process for eliminating the fungus by opening up the evaporator case and using a powerful disinfectant and rinse on the core until the fungus is gone. You can service your own system at home, but it takes something much stronger than basic household germ-killers or deodorizers.

23   Aerosol disinfectants for automotive air conditioning systems are available in most auto parts stores, but remember when shopping for them that the most effective treatments are also the most expensive. The basic procedure for using these sprays is to start by running the system in the RECIRC mode

for ten minutes with the blower on its highest speed. Use the highest heat mode to dry out the system and keep the compressor from engaging by disconnecting the wiring connector at the compressor.

24   The disinfectant can usually comes with a long spray hose. Insert the nozzle into an intake port inside the cabin, and spray according to the manufacturer's recommendations **(see illustration)**. Try to cover the whole surface of the evaporator core, by aiming the spray up, down and sideways. Follow the manufacturer's recommendations for the length of spray and waiting time between applications.

Automatic heating and air conditioning systems

25   Some vehicles are equipped with an optional automatic climate control system. This system has its own computer that receives inputs from various sensors in the heating and air conditioning system. This computer, like the PCM, has self-diagnostic capabilities to help pinpoint problems or faults within the system. Vehicles equipped with automatic heating and air conditioning systems are very complex and

considered beyond the scope of the home mechanic. Vehicles equipped with automatic heating and air conditioning systems should be taken to dealer service department or other qualified facility for repair.

4   Thermostat - replacement

Warning: *Do not attempt to remove the radiator cap, coolant or thermostat until the engine has cooled completely.*

1   Disconnect the negative cable from the battery (see Chapter 5).

2   Drain the coolant from the radiator (see Chapter 1).

3   Disconnect the hose clamp and remove the radiator hose from the housing.

4   On 2008 and earlier 1.8L models, remove the engine drivebelt (see Chapter 1) and the alternator (see Chapter 5).

5   On 2.0L models, disconnect the electrical connector from the thermostat housing, then disconnect the coolant by-pass hose from the bottom of the thermostat housing.

6   Detach the thermostat housing from the engine **(see illustration)**. Be prepared for some

4.8 The thermostat gasket, which is actually a grooved sealing ring, fits around the edge of the thermostat

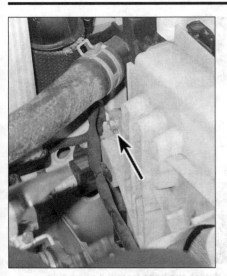

5.4a Remove the left-side mounting bolt for the fan assembly . . .

5.4b . . . and the right-side fan assembly bolt

5.5 Remove this nut to detach the fan blades from the motor

coolant to spill as the gasket seal is broken. The radiator hose can be left attached to the housing, unless the housing itself is to be replaced.

7   Remove the thermostat, noting the direction in which it was installed in the housing, and thoroughly clean the sealing surfaces **(see illustration)**.

8   Fit a new gasket onto the thermostat **(see illustration)**. Make sure it is evenly fitted all the way around.

9   Install the thermostat and housing, positioning the jiggle pin at the highest point.

10   Tighten the housing fasteners to the torque listed in this Chapter's Specifications and reinstall the remaining components in the reverse order of removal.

11   Refill the cooling system (see Chapter 1), run the engine and check for leaks and proper operation.

5   Engine cooling fan - removal and installation

Warning: *To avoid possible injury, keep clear of the fan blades, as they may start turning at any time!*

1   Disconnect the negative battery cable (see Chapter 5).

2   Disconnect the wiring connector at the fan motor.

3   Disconnect the coolant overflow hose from the top of the radiator.

2008 and earlier models

4   Unbolt the fan shroud from the radiator and lift the fan/shroud/coolant reservoir assembly from the vehicle **(see illustrations)**.

5   Hold the fan blades and remove the fan retaining nut (and spacer, if equipped) **(see illustration)**.

6   Unbolt the fan motor from the shroud **(see illustration)**.

7   Installation is the reverse of removal.

2009 and later models

Warning: *Wait until the engine is completely cool before performing this procedure.*

8   Drain the cooling system (see Chapter 1) and remove cooling fans and the radiator (see Section 6) as an assembly.

9   Remove the fan shroud mounting bolts **(see illustration)** and separate the fan assembly from the radiator.

10   Installation is the reverse of removal.

5.6 Remove the motor from the shroud

5.9 Remove the shroud mounting bolts from the bottom of the shroud

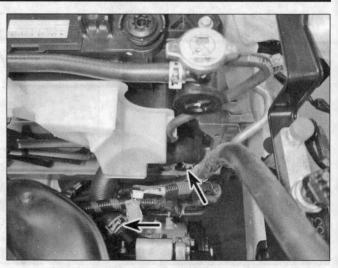

6.3a Squeeze the clamp and slide it back on the hose, then detach the hose from the left side of the radiator . . .

6.3b . . . then detach the hose from the other side (later models shown, earlier models similar)

6   Radiator and coolant reservoir - removal and installation

Warning: *Do not start this procedure until the engine is completely cool.*

Radiator

1   Disconnect the negative battery cable (see Chapter 5).
2   Drain the engine coolant (see Chapter 1).
3   Detach the the radiator hoses from the left and right sides of the radiator **(see illustration)**.
4   On 2009 through 2013 models, disconnect the reservoir hose from the radiator filler neck.
Note: *On 2009 and later non-hatchback models, the cooling fan can only be removed after*

the radiator/fan shroud assembly has been removed from the vehicle.

2008 and earlier models
5   Remove the cooling fan (see Section 5).
6   If equipped with an automatic transaxle, disconnect the cooler lines from the radiator **(see illustration)**. Place a drip pan underneath to catch the fluid and cap the fittings.
7   Remove the two upper radiator mounting brackets **(see illustration)**.
Note: *The bottom of the radiator is retained by grommeted projections that fit into holes in the body.*
8   Lift out the radiator **(see illustration)**. Be aware of dripping fluids and the sharp fins.

2009 and later models
9   Remove the battery (see Chapter 5).
10   Disconnect the electrical connector from the cooling fan ECU **(see illustration)**, then

disengage the harness retainers and move the harness out of the way. On 2014 and later models, remove the two radiator hose support bolts.
11   On 2009 through 2013 models, remove the grille and bumper cover (see Chapter 11).
12   On 2009 through 2013 models, remove the four bolts and the upper radiator support beam.
13   Unclip the ambient air temperature sensor from the bracket **(see illustration)** then move the sensor out of the way.
14   Remove the upper radiator mounting bracket bolts, brackets and rubber mounts **(see illustration 6.16)**.
15   On 2009 through 2013 models, remove the hood latch (see Chapter 11), support bracket mounting bolts and bracket. Also disconnect the horn electrical connector.
16   Disconnect the coolant bypass hose from the radiator **(see illustration)**.

6.6 Remove the automatic transaxle cooler lines and the lower radiator hose from the left side of the radiator

6.7 Remove the upper hold-down clamps (A) from each end of the radiator support - the other bolts (B) are for the air conditioning condenser

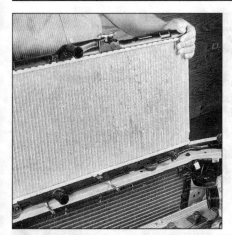

6.8 Remove the radiator carefully, and do not lose the rubber mounts - they must be in place on the bottom projections when the radiator is reinstalled

6.10 Disconnect the electrical connectors to the cooling fan motor (A) then disengage the harness retainers (B) and move the harness. On 2014 and later models, also remove the two radiator hose support bolts (C)

6.13 Disengage the ambient air sensor clip

17   Remove the upper fan shroud bolts, then disengage the upper fan shroud plastic clips and remove it **(see illustration)**.
18   Detach the two guides at the bottom of the condenser, then remove the radiator and cooling fan shroud as an assembly.
19   Remove the cooling fan shroud mounting bolts from the bottom of the radiator and separate the fan shroud from the radiator.

All models
20   With the radiator removed, it can be inspected for leaks, damage and internal blockage. If in need of repairs, have a professional radiator shop or dealer service department perform the work as special techniques are required.
21   Bugs and dirt can be cleaned from the radiator with compressed air and a soft brush. Don't bend the cooling fins as this is done.
Warning: *Wear eye protection when using compressed air.*

22   Installation is the reverse of the removal procedure. Be sure the rubber mounts are in place on the bottom of the radiator.
23   After installation, fill the cooling system with the proper mixture of antifreeze and water. Refer to Chapter 1 if necessary.
24   Start the engine and check for leaks. Allow the engine to reach normal operating temperature, indicated by both radiator hoses becoming hot. Recheck the coolant level and add more if required.
25   On automatic transmission equipped models, check and add fluid as needed.

Coolant reservoir
Note: *The coolant reservoir is an integral part of the fan shroud and can't be replaced separately from the the cooling fan shroud (see Section 5).*

7   Water pump - replacement

Warning: *Do not start this procedure until the engine is completely cool.*
1   Disconnect the cable from the negative terminal of the battery. (see Chapter 5).
2   Drain the cooling system (see Chapter 1). On 2.4L models, loosen the water pump pulley bolts then remove the drivebelt (see Chapter 1, Section 10). Unscrew the bolts and remove the pulley.
Note: *If the drivebelt doesn't prevent the pulley from turning when the loosening the bolts, use a pin spanner to hold the pulley stationary.*
3   Remove the right side splash shield.
4   On 1.8L and 2.4L models, remove the alternator (see Chapter 5).
5   On 2.4L models, remove the coolant reservoir from the radiator.
6   Detach the wiring harness and harness clamp from the water pump.

6.16 Disconnect the coolant bypass hose from the radiator neck (A), then free it from the retainers on the upper fan shroud (B). (C) are the radiator mounting bracket bolts and (D) are the upper fan shroud bolts

6.17 Upper fan shroud plastic clip locations

7.7 Water pump bolt locations (rear and lower bolts not visible in this photo) - 1.8L models shown, other models similar

9.2a Blower motor resistor location (2013 and earlier models)

7   Remove the bolts retaining the water pump to the engine block and remove the water pump **(see illustration)**. Note the length and the position of the bolts as they were originally installed before removing them.

8   Thoroughly clean all sealing surfaces, removing the O-ring from the groove in the timing chain cover.

9   Install a new O-ring in the timing chain cover and place the water pump in position. Install the bolts in their original positions and tighten them to the torque listed in this Chapter's Specifications .

10   Install the remaining parts in the reverse order of removal. Refill the cooling system (see Chapter 1), run the engine and check for leaks and proper operation.

8   Coolant temperature sensor - replacement

1   On these vehicles there is only one coolant temperature sensor - the Engine Coolant

Temperature (ECT) sensor, which provides information to the PCM for engine management and also for the temperature gauge on the instrument panel. Refer to Chapter 6 for the ECT sensor replacement procedure.

9   Blower motor - removal and installation

Warning: *These models are equipped with a Supplemental Restraint System (SRS), more commonly known as airbags. Always disable the airbag system before working in the vicinity of any airbag system component to avoid the possibility of accidental deployment of the airbag(s), which could cause personal injury (see Chapter 12).*

1   The blower unit is located in the passenger compartment under the glove box area. If the blower doesn't work, check the fuse and all connections in the circuit for looseness and corrosion. Make sure the battery is fully charged.

2   If the blower motor operates at High speed, but not at one or more of the lower speeds, check the blower motor resistor, located under the instrument panel on the passenger's side **(see illustrations)**.
Note: *On 2009 and later models, it will be necessary to remove the instrument panel under cover by releasing the three clips and letting the cover swing forward, exposing the blower motor.*

3   If the blower motor must be replaced, disconnect the wiring connector to the blower, then remove the three mounting screws and lower the blower assembly from the housing **(see illustration)**. The fan can be removed and reused on the new blower motor.

4   To remove the air conditioning amplifier, remove the acceleration pedal position (APP) sensor (see Chapter 6), then disconnect the harness clips, remove the retaining screw and slide the air conditioning amplifier out from behind the evaporator housing.

5   Installation is the reverse of removal.

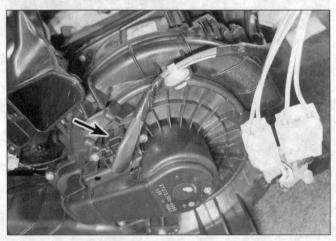

9.2b Blower motor resistor location (2014 and later models)

9.3 Disconnect the electrical connector (A) then remove the three screws (B) and lower the blower motor from the housing

10.4 Disconnect the heater hoses at the firewall

10.5 Remove the refrigerant line manifold bolt, then rotate the lock counterclockwise and disconnect the lines from the TXV valve

10   Heater core - removal and installation

Warning: *These models are equipped with a Supplemental Restraint System (SRS), more commonly known as airbags. Always disable the airbag system before working in the vicinity of any airbag system component to avoid the possibility of accidental deployment of the airbag(s), which could cause personal injury (see Chapter 12).*

Warning: *Wait until the engine is completely cool before beginning this procedure.*

Note: *This procedure requires the removal of the instrument panel, and the cross-cowl support tube and steering column. This involves disconnecting numerous electrical connectors and there is the potential for breakage of delicate plastic tabs on various components. This is a difficult job for the average home mechanic.*

1   On 2014 and later models, have the air conditioning system discharged by an automotive air conditioning technician.

Note: *On 2013 and earlier models, it's not necessary to have the refrigerant recovered because, for heater core removal, the two refrigerant connections at the firewall do not have to be disconnected. However, moving the heat/AC unit away from the firewall for heater core removal is made easier by removing the screw securing the two refrigerant lines to the right fenderwell in the engine compartment.*

2   Disconnect the negative cable from the battery (see Chapter 5).

3   Drain the cooling system (see Chapter 1).

4   Working in the engine compartment, disconnect the heater hoses at the firewall **(see illustration)**.

5   On 2014 and later models, remove the refrigerant connections at the firewall to the TXV valve **(see illustration)** then remove the nuts securing the two refrigerant lines to the firewall in the engine compartment.

Caution: *Cap the open fittings and TXV valve openings immediately to keep moisture and contamination out of the system and replace the O-ring on the lines.*

Note: *On 2014 and later models, the heater/evaporator housing cannot be pulled away from the firewall far enough to pull the heater core tubes through the firewall unless the lines to the TXV valve are disconnected.*

6   Refer to Chapter 11 and remove the center console, glove compartment, glove compartment liner, ashtray, radio (see Chapter 12) and center dash bezels.

7   Refer to Section 11 to remove the heater/air conditioning controls and the instrument panel.

8   Remove the steering column pinch-bolt at the joint near the firewall (see Chapter 10, Section 17).

Warning: *Make sure the steering column is locked. If the steering wheel turns and becomes uncentered on installation, the airbag spiral cable (clockspring) could be damaged.*

9   Major electrical harnesses are attached to the body and the cross-cowl support tube. Disconnect the main electrical connectors at either end of the instrument panel (near the kick panels), and at the center area below the instrument panel. Disconnect all harness connectors from the body side, but leave all harnesses attached to the cross-cowl tube. Use tape to tag and identify all connectors before separating them and take photos for later reference.

10   Remove all the fasteners securing the cross-cowl support tube to the cowl and the tube-to-floor brace **(see illustrations)**. When the tube is loose, you can drop the cowl tube down to the floor with the steering column still attached.

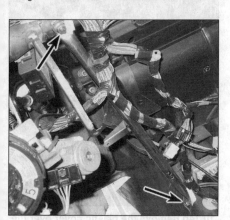

10.10a Remove the fasteners and the cowl-tube-to-floor brace(s)

10.10b The cross-cowl support tube is secured to the vehicle at each side - remove the bolts and clamp at each end (right side shown)

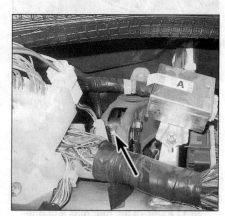

10.10c Remove this screw in the center of the cross-cowl tube

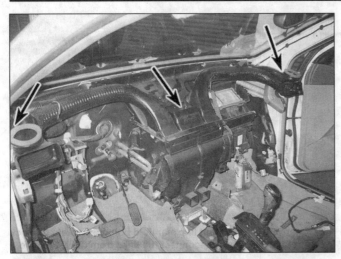

10.11 Shown with the cowl tube and steering column removed for clarity, remove the fasteners/clips and the number 1 duct

10.12 Remove the defroster duct from the top of the heat/AC housing

11   The heating/air-conditioning components are in several large plastic housings connected together and secured to the interior side of the firewall. To service the heater core, the entire assembly does not have to be removed from the vehicle, but the assembly must be unbolted and pulled out far enough for the heater core tubes to come through the firewall into the interior. Remove the number 1 air duct **(see illustration)**.

Note: *On 2009 and later models, disconnect the electrical connectors to the power steering ECU. Remove the ECU assembly mounting fasteners and the ECU for access to the top of the HVAC unit.*

12   Remove the defroster duct above the heat/air housing **(see illustration)**.

13   Remove the fasteners securing the complete HVAC housing unit to the firewall **(see illustration)**.

14   Disconnect the clips securing the tubes to the housing **(see illustrations)**.

Note: *On 2009 and later models, a second heater is used. It's an electric Quick Heater*

Assembly and is mounted with two fasteners to the HVAC assembly. Once the HVAC unit is exposed, the quick heater unit can be unbolted from the HVAC unit for replacement.

15   Pull the heater unit out away from the firewall just enough for the heater core tubes to come through the firewall all the way, then remove the heater core from the housing **(see illustration)**. On models so equipped, remove the 12 screws securing the heater core cover. Keep plenty of towels or rags on the carpeting to catch any coolant that may drip.

Caution: *Work slowly and carefully to avoid breaking any plastic components during removal. The assembly must be pulled out (toward the rear of the vehicle) far enough for the tubes to clear the brake assembly at the firewall.*

16   Installation is the reverse order of removal.

17   Refill the cooling system (see Chapter 1), reconnect the battery and run the engine. Check for leaks and proper system operation.

18   On 2014 and later models, have the air

conditioning system charged by an automotive air conditioning technician.

11   Heater and air conditioning control assembly - removal and installation

Warning: *These models are equipped with a Supplemental Restraint System (SRS), more commonly known as airbags. Always disable the airbag system before working in the vicinity of any airbag system component to avoid the possibility of accidental deployment of the airbag(s), which could cause personal injury (see Chapter 12).*

1   Disconnect the negative cable from the battery (see Chapter 5).

2   On 2013 and earlier models, pull off the center knob from the heat/AC control unit **(see illustration)**. This exposes a screw securing the top of the center trim panel, the rest of the panel is retained by clips.

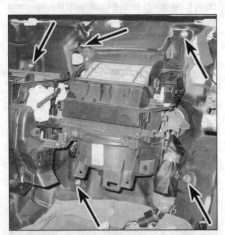

10.13 Remove the four nuts and one bolt securing the HVAC assembly to the firewall

10.14a Release this clip securing the heater core tubes to the side of the case

10.14b Remove the plastic cover over the left end of the heater core

10.15 Slide the heater core out of the left side of the housing, making sure the pipes clear obstructions on the firewall

11.2 Remove the center knob from the heat/AC control panel and remove the screw holding the trim panel

11.3 Pry the center instrument panel trim panel out, then disconnect the electrical connectors

3   Remove the center cluster trim panel (see Chapter 11). Pull the center trim panel out far enough to mark the electrical connectors, then disconnect them **(see illustration)**. On 2009 through 2014 models, disengage the clips and remove the center instrument cluster panel hole cover below the control assembly. Turn the shift lever knob counterclockwise and remove the shift lever knob, then disengage the claws and clips and remove the shifter trim cover.
4   On 2014 and later models, remove the instrument trim panels along the face of the instrument panel (see Chapter 11).
5   On 2014 and later models, use a trim tool and carefully pry the air conditioning control panel out of the instrument panel **(see illustration)**.
6   On 2013 and earlier models, pull the control unit out enough to disconnect the heater control cables from the rear of the control unit (manual A/C models). Disconnect the electrical connectors from the blower speed switch and the A/C switch **(see illustrations)**.

7   On 2014 and later models, remove the control assembly from the instrument panel and disconnect the electrical connector, then remove the control assembly trim panel mounting screws and separate the control unit from the panel **(see illustration)**.
8   Installation is the reverse of the removal procedure.
9   Run the engine and check for proper functioning of the heater (and air conditioning, if equipped).

12   Air conditioning receiver-drier - removal and installation

Warning: *The air conditioning system is under high pressure. Do not loosen any hose fittings or remove any components until the system has been discharged. Air conditioning refrigerant should be properly discharged into an EPA-approved recovery/recycling unit by a dealer service department or an automotive air conditioning repair facility. Always wear eye*

11.5 Pry the control panel out along the edges of the control panel - 2014 and later models

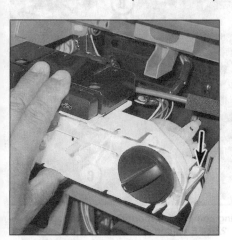

11.6a Release the control panel from two claw-clips by pulling it straight out

11.6b Behind the control panel, disconnect the electrical connectors and use a screwdriver to open the clips holding the two control cables - 2013 and earlier models

11.7 On 2014 and later non-hatchback models, disconnect the electrical connector (A) then remove the control assembly trim panel mounting screws (B)

12.3 After the system has been discharged, remove the Allen plug at the bottom of the receiver-drier

protection when disconnecting air conditioning system fittings.

Note: On 2009 and later models, the condenser must be removed for access to the receiver-drier plug (see Section 14).

1   Have the refrigerant discharged and recovered by an air conditioning technician.

2   The receiver-drier is mounted on the driver's side of the vehicle, at the end of the condenser.

3   Using an Allen wrench, remove the large plug at the bottom of the receiver-drier **(see illustration)**. Use needle-nose pliers to grip and remove the filter-drier element inside the receiver.

4   Installation is the reverse of removal. Install a new filter-drier element and lubricate the plug's O-ring with a touch of refrigerant oil.

5   Have the system evacuated, charged and leak tested by the shop that discharged it. If the receiver-drier or condenser was replaced, have them add new refrigeration oil to the system. Use only refrigerant oil compatible with R-134a refrigerant.

13   Air conditioning compressor - removal and installation

Warning: The air conditioning system is under high pressure. Do not loosen any hose fittings or remove any components until the system has been discharged. Air conditioning refrigerant should be properly discharged into an EPA-approved recovery/recycling unit by a dealer service department or an automotive air conditioning repair facility. Always wear eye protection when disconnecting air conditioning system fittings.

Caution: The receiver-drier element should be replaced whenever a new compressor is installed (see Section 12).

1   Have the refrigerant discharged by an automotive air conditioning technician.

2   Disconnect the negative cable from the battery (see Chapter 5).

3   Raise the front of the vehicle and support it securely on jackstands. Remove the engine under cover (if equipped). Remove the drivebelt from the compressor (see Chapter 1).

4   Detach the wiring connector and disconnect the refrigerant lines **(see illustrations)**.

5   Remove the bolts and nuts from the compressor.

6   Using an #8 Torx socket, remove the two studs from the compressor, then lift the compressor out of the vehicle.

7   If a new or rebuilt compressor is being installed, follow the directions supplied with the compressor regarding the proper level of oil prior to installation.

8   Installation is the reverse of removal.

Replace any O-rings with new ones specifically made for R-134a refrigerant and lubricate them with the same oil.

9   Have the system evacuated, recharged and leak tested by the shop that discharged it.

14   Air conditioning condenser - removal and installation

Removal

Warning: The air conditioning system is under high pressure. Do not loosen any hose fittings or remove any components until the system has been discharged. Air conditioning refrigerant should be properly discharged into an EPA-approved recovery/recycling unit by a dealer service department or an automotive air conditioning repair facility. Always wear eye protection when disconnecting air conditioning system fittings.

Warning: These models are equipped with a Supplemental Restraint System (SRS), more commonly known as airbags. Always disable the airbag system before working in the vicinity of any airbag system component to avoid the possibility of accidental deployment of the airbag(s), which could cause personal injury (see Chapter 12) .

Warning: Wait until the engine is completely cool before beginning this procedure.

Caution: The receiver-drier element should be replaced if the condenser is being replaced due to leakage (see Section 12).

1   Have the refrigerant discharged and recovered by an air conditioning technician.

2   Remove the radiator as described in Section 6.

3   Disconnect the condenser inlet and outlet fittings **(see illustration)**. Cap the open fittings immediately to keep moisture and contamination out of the system.

13.4a Air conditioning compressor mounting details - 1ZZ-FE engine shown

A   Electrical connector (unplugged)
B   Refrigerant line flange bolts
C   Compressor mounting bolts

13.4b Air conditioning compressor mounting details top view - 2ZR-FE engine shown

A   Compressor upper mounting nut and stud
B   Compressor upper mounting bolt
C   Refrigerant line flange bolts

13.4c Air conditioning compressor mounting details bottom view -
2ZR-FE engine shown

A   Compressor lower mounting nut and stud
B   Compressor lower mounting bolt
C   Electrical connector

14.3 Disconnect the refrigerant connections on the right
(passenger's) side of the condenser by removing the flange bolts

4   Remove the condenser mounting bolts **(see illustration 5.9)**, angle the condenser back and lift it out.

5   Install the condenser, brackets and bolts, making sure the rubber cushions fit on the mounting points properly.

6   Reconnect the refrigerant lines, using new O-rings where needed. If a new condenser has been installed, add approximately 1.5 to 2.0 fluid ounces of new, R-134a-compatible refrigerant oil.

Installation

7   Reinstall the remaining parts in the reverse order of removal.

8   Refill the cooling system (see Chapter 1).

9   Have the system evacuated, charged and leak tested by the shop that discharged it.

Notes

Chapter 4
Fuel and exhaust systems

Contents

Specifications

Fuel system
Fuel pressure
Key On, engine Off	44 to 50 psi
Engine running	44 to 50 psi
For 5 minutes after engine is turned Off	21 psi or greater
Fuel injector resistance (at 68-degrees F)	
2003 and 2004 models	13.4 to 14.2 ohms
2005 and later models	11.6 to 12.4 ohms

Torque specifications
Ft-lbs (unless otherwise indicated)

Note: *One foot-pound (ft-lb) of torque is equivalent to 12 inch-pounds (in-lbs) of torque. Torque values below approximately 15 ft-lbs are expressed in inch-pounds, because most foot-pound torque wrenches are not accurate at these smaller values.*

Fuel rail mounting bolts	
2003 and 2004 models	168 in-lbs
2005 through 2008 models	
Two forward bolts	168 in-lbs
Bolt on driver's side	80 in-lbs
2009 and later models	15
Throttle body mounting bolts/nuts	
2003 and 2004	22
2005 through 2008 models	80 in-lbs
2009 and later models	84 in-lbs
Throttle body upper bracket bolts (2003 and 2004 models with manual transaxle only)	115 in-lbs

1   General information and precautions

Fuel system warnings

Warning: *Gasoline is extremely flammable and repairing fuel system components can be dangerous. Consider your automotive repair knowledge and experience before attempting repairs which may be better suited for a professional mechanic.*

a) *Don't smoke or allow open flames or bare light bulbs near the work area*
b) *Don't work in a garage with a gas-type appliance (water heater, clothes dryer)*
c) *Use fuel-resistant gloves. If any fuel spills on your skin, wash it off immediately with soap and water*
d) *Clean up spills immediately*
e) *Do not store fuel-soaked rags where they could ignite*
f) *Prior to disconnecting any fuel line, you must relieve the fuel pressure (see Section 3)*
g) *Wear safety glasses*
h) *Have a proper fire extinguisher on hand*

Fuel system

1   The fuel system consists of a fuel tank, an electric fuel pump (located in the fuel tank), an EFI/fuel pump relay, fuel injectors, a fuel pressure regulator, an air filter assembly and a throttle body unit. All models covered by this manual are equipped with a multi port fuel injection system.

Multi port fuel injection system

2   Multi port fuel injection uses timed impulses to sequentially inject the fuel directly into the intake port of each cylinder. The injectors are controlled by the Powertrain Control Module (PCM). The PCM monitors various engine parameters and delivers the exact amount of fuel, in the correct sequence, into the intake ports. The throttle body serves only to control the amount of air passing into the system. Because each cylinder is equipped with an injector mounted immediately adjacent to the intake valve, much better control of the fuel/air mixture ratio is possible.

Fuel pump and lines

3   Fuel is delivered from the fuel tank to the fuel injection system through a metal line running along the underside of the vehicle by an electric fuel pump inside the fuel tank. The fuel pressure regulator is located in the fuel tank with the fuel pump, and excessive fuel pressure is bled-off directly into the fuel tank.
4   The fuel pump runs for a few seconds when first turning the ignition on. The fuel pump then operates as long as the engine is cranking or running and the PCM is receiving ignition reference pulses from the electronic ignition system (see Chapter 5). If there are no reference pulses, the fuel pump will shut off after 2 or 3 seconds.

2.3 The fuel pump fuse (A) is located in the engine compartment fuse box; (B) is the fuel pump relay (2013 and earlier model shown)

Exhaust system

5   The exhaust system includes an exhaust manifold, a catalytic converter, an exhaust pipe, and a muffler.
6   The catalytic converter is an emission control device added to the exhaust system to reduce pollutants. A three-way (reduction) catalyst is used to reduce hydrocarbons (HC), carbon monoxide (CO) and oxides of nitrogen (NOx). Refer to Chapter 6 for more information regarding the catalytic converter.

2   Troubleshooting

Electric fuel pump

1   The electric fuel pump is located inside the fuel tank. Sit inside the vehicle with the windows closed, turn the ignition key to On (not Start) and listen for the sound of the fuel pump as it's briefly activated. You will only hear the sound for a second or two, but that sound tells you that the pump is working. Alternatively, have an assistant listen at the fuel filler cap.
2   A fuel-cut off system is used in case of an accident. If there has been an accident, the restraint system sends a signal to the Fuel Pump Control Module (FPCM) and shuts the module off. To reset the FPCM, turn the ignition key to the Off position, then to the On position and start the engine.
Note: *This may take a few attempts.*
3   Check the fuel pump fuse (F63, 30A) and relay **(see illustration)**. On 2014 and later 2ZR-FAE engines, check the EFI Main fuse (20A) and relay. If the fuse and relay are okay, check the wiring back to the fuel pump. If the fuse, relay, wiring and inertia switch are okay, the fuel pump is probably defective. On 2014 and later 2ZR-FAE engines, a Fuel Pump Control Module (FPCM) controls the fuel pump. If the pump runs continuously with the ignition key in the On position, the Powertrain Control Module (PCM) is probably defective. Have the PCM checked by a professional mechanic.

Fuel injection system

Note: *The following procedure is based on the assumption that the fuel pump is working and the fuel pressure is adequate (see Section 4).*
4   Check all electrical connectors that are related to the system. Check the ground wire connections for tightness. Verify that the battery is fully charged (see Chapter 5, Section 2).
5   Inspect the air filter element (see Chapter 1).
6   Check all fuses related to the fuel system (see Chapter 12).
7   Check the air induction system between the throttle body and the intake manifold for air leaks. Also inspect the condition of all vacuum hoses connected to the intake manifold and to the throttle body.
8 Remove the air intake duct from the throttle body and look for dirt, carbon, varnish, or other residue in the throttle body, particularly around the throttle plate. If it's dirty, clean it with carb cleaner, a toothbrush and a clean shop towel.
9   Check to see if any trouble codes are stored in the PCM (see Chapter 6).

3   Fuel pressure relief procedure

Warning: *Gasoline is extremely flammable, so take extra precautions when you work on any part of the fuel system. Don't smoke or allow open flames or bare light bulbs near the work area, and don't work in a garage where a gas-type appliance (such as a water heater or a clothes dryer) is present. Since gasoline is carcinogenic, wear fuel-resistant gloves when there's a possibility of being exposed to fuel, and, if you spill any fuel on your skin, rinse it off immediately with soap and water. Mop up any spills immediately and do not store fuel-soaked rags where they could ignite. The fuel system is under constant pressure, so, if any fuel lines are to be disconnected, the fuel pressure in the system must be relieved first. When you perform any kind of work on the fuel system, wear safety glasses and have a Class B type fire extinguisher on hand.*

4.3a A fuel pressure testing kit like this should contain all the necessary fittings and adapters, along with the fuel pressure gauge, to test most automotive systems

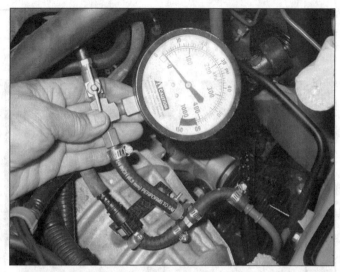

4.3b Attach the fuel pressure gauge with fuel hose and clamps between the fuel rail and the fuel feed line - turn the ignition key On and check the fuel pressure

1   Before servicing any fuel system component, you must relieve the fuel pressure to minimize the risk of fire or personal injury.
2   Remove the fuel filler cap - this will relieve any pressure built up in the tank.
3   Remove the rear seat cushion (see Chapter 11), then remove the cover and unplug the fuel pump electrical connector **(see illustrations 6.4 and 6.5a)**.
4   Attempt to start the engine - the engine will stall. Crank the engine for 3 or 4 seconds, then turn the ignition key to Off.
5   The fuel system is now depressurized.
Note: *Place a rag around the fuel line before removing any hose clamp or fitting to prevent any residual fuel from spilling onto the engine.*
6   Before working on the fuel system, disconnect the cable from the negative terminal of the battery (see Chapter 5).

4   Fuel pump/fuel pressure - check

Warning: *Gasoline is extremely flammable, so take extra precautions when you work on any part of the fuel system. See the Warning in Section 3.*

General checks
1   Check that there is adequate fuel in the fuel tank.
2   Verify the fuel pump actually runs. Have an assistant turn the ignition switch to On - you should hear a brief whirring noise (for approximately two seconds) as the pump comes on and pressurizes the system. If there is no response from the fuel pump (makes no sound) proceed to Step 9 and check the fuel pump electrical circuit. If the fuel pump runs, but a fuel system problem is suspected, continue with the fuel pump pressure check.
Note: *The fuel pump is easily heard through the gas tank filler neck.*

Fuel pump pressure check
Note: *In order to perform the fuel pressure test, you will need to obtain a fuel pressure gauge capable of measuring high fuel pressure and the proper adapter set for the specific fuel injection system.*
3   Relieve the fuel system pressure (see Section 3). Detach the fuel line from the fuel rail and where this line attaches to a steel line near the master cylinder. A simple special tool is used to separate the quick-connect fittings (see Section 5). The fuel pressure test hose temporarily replaces this factory hose **(see illustrations)**. Make sure the clamps are tight on the hoses.
4   Turn all the accessories Off and switch the ignition key On. The fuel pump should run for about two seconds; note the reading on the gauge. After the pump stops running, the pressure should hold steady. After five minutes it should not drop below the minimum listed in this Chapter's Specifications.
5   Start the engine and let it idle at normal operating temperature. The pressure should remain the same. If all the pressure readings are within the limits listed in this Chapter's Specifications, the system is operating properly.
6   If the fuel pressure is not within specifications, check the following:
   a)   *If the pressure is higher than specified, replace the fuel pressure regulator (see Section 8).*
   b)   *If the pressure is lower than specified, the fuel filter could be clogged, the fuel line from the fuel rail to the fuel tank could be restricted, the fuel injectors could be leaking, or the fuel pressure regulator and/or the fuel pump could be defective (this is probably the most likely cause). In this situation, it is recommended that both the fuel pressure*

regulator and fuel pump be replaced to prevent any future fuel pressure problems. Note: The fuel filter is part of the fuel pump assembly. Check with your local auto parts store or dealer parts department regarding parts availability.
7   Turn the engine off and monitor fuel pressure for five minutes. Fuel pressure must not drop below the value listed in this Chapter's Specifications. If the pressure is not within specifications, check the following:
   a)   *Leaking fuel pump check valve.*
   b)   *Leaking fuel pressure regulator.*
   c)   *Leaking fuel injector.*

8   After the testing is done, relieve the fuel pressure (see Section 3), remove the fuel pressure gauge and reinstall the fuel line.

Fuel pump electrical circuit check
9   If the pump does not turn on (makes no sound) with the ignition switch in the ON position, check the EFI fuse located in the engine compartment fuse center. If the fuse is blown, replace the fuse and see if the pump works. If the pump now works, check for a short in the circuit between the fuel pump relay (circuit opening relay) and the fuel pump. Also check the EFI relay and the circuit opening relay (C/OPN).
10   If the relays are good and the fuel pump does not operate, check the wiring from the underhood fuse/relay box to the fuel pump. On 2014 and later 2ZR-FAE engines, the fuel pump is controlled by the fuel pump control module.

Disconnecting Fuel Line Fittings

Two-tab type fitting; depress both tabs with your fingers, then pull the fuel line and the fitting apart

On this type of fitting, depress the two buttons on opposite sides of the fitting, then pull it off the fuel line

Threaded fuel line fitting; hold the stationary portion of the line or component (A) while loosening the tube nut (B) with a flare-nut wrench

Plastic collar-type fitting; rotate the outer part of the fitting

Metal collar quick-connect fitting; pull the end of the retainer off the fuel line and disengage the other end from the female side of the fitting . . .

. . . insert a fuel line separator tool into the female side of the fitting, push it into the fitting and pull the fuel line off the pipe

Some fittings are secured by lock tabs. Release the lock tab (A) and rotate it to the fully-opened position, squeeze the two smaller lock tabs (B) . . .

. . . then push the retainer out and pull the fuel line off the pipe

Spring-lock coupling; remove the safety cover, install a coupling release tool and close the tool around the coupling . . .

. . . push the tool into the fitting, then pull the two lines apart

Hairpin clip type fitting: push the legs of the retainer clip together, then push the clip down all the way until it stops and pull the fuel line off the pipe

5   Fuel lines and fittings - general information and disconnection

Warning: *Gasoline is extremely flammable. See* Fuel system warnings *in Section 3.*

1   Relieve the fuel pressure before servicing fuel lines or fittings (see Section 3), then disconnect the cable from the negative battery terminal (see Chapter 5) before proceeding.

2   The fuel supply line connects the fuel pump in the fuel tank to the fuel rail on the engine. The Evaporative emission (EVAP) system lines connect the fuel tank to the EVAP canister and connect the canister to the intake manifold.

3   Whenever you're working under the vehicle, be sure to inspect all fuel and evaporative emission lines for leaks, kinks, dents and other damage. Always replace a damaged fuel or EVAP line immediately.

4   If you find signs of dirt in the lines during disassembly, disconnect all lines and blow them out with compressed air. Inspect the fuel strainer on the fuel pump pick-up unit for damage and deterioration.

Steel tubing

5   It is critical that the fuel lines be replaced with lines of equivalent type and specification.

6   Some steel fuel lines have threaded fittings. When loosening these fittings, hold the stationary fitting with a wrench while turning the tube nut.

Plastic tubing

7   When replacing fuel system plastic tubing, use only original equipment replacement plastic tubing.

Caution: *When removing or installing plastic fuel line tubing, be careful not to bend or twist it too much, which can damage it. Also, plastic*

6.4 On 2003 and 2004 models and 2009 and later models, pry the fuel pump access cover off (it's secured by butyl tape). On 2005 to 2008 models, it's secured by four screws

fuel tubing is NOT heat resistant, so keep it away from excessive heat.

Flexible hoses

8   When replacing fuel system flexible hoses, use only original equipment replacements.

9   Don't route fuel hoses (or metal lines) within four inches of the exhaust system or within ten inches of the catalytic converter. Make sure that no rubber hoses are installed directly against the vehicle, particularly in places where there is any vibration. If allowed to touch some vibrating part of the vehicle, a hose can easily become chafed and it might start leaking. A good rule of thumb is to maintain a minimum of 1/4-inch clearance around a hose (or metal line) to prevent contact with the vehicle underbody.

6.5a Disconnect both of the electrical connectors

6   Fuel pump - removal and installation

Warning: *Gasoline is extremely flammable, so take extra precautions when you work on any part of the fuel system. See the Warning in Section 3.*

Fuel pump module - removal

1   Relieve the fuel system pressure (see Section 3).

2   Disconnect the cable from the negative terminal of the battery (see Chapter 5).

3   Remove the rear seat cushion (see Chapter 11).

4   Remove the fuel pump/sending unit access cover **(see illustration)**.

5   Unplug the electrical connectors **(see illustration)**, then disconnect the fuel lines **(see illustrations)**.

6.5b On 2013 and earlier models, use needle-nose pliers to release the quick-release fitting securing the vent tube

6.5c On 2014 and later models, pull out the clip and detach the vent tube

6.5d Slide out the retaining clip and remove the fuel pressure hose from the assembly

6.6 Remove the fuel pump/sending unit assembly mounting screws (2003 and 2004 models)

6.7 A tool like this will be necessary to remove and install the lock ring on 2005 and later models

6.8 Lock ring tightening marks and corresponding marks made on the body (due to the fact that the tank is recessed, the angle of this photo appears to make them look misaligned) (2014 and later models).

| 1 | Start of threads" marks | 3 | "Start of threads" rib on |
| 2 | "Fully tightened" range marks | | lock ring |

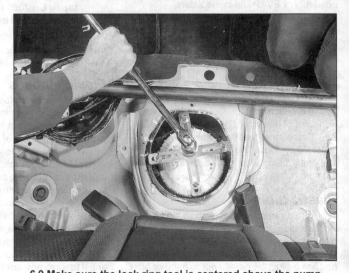

6.9 Make sure the lock ring tool is centered above the pump module and there is no play between the legs of the tool and the lock ring

6.10 Have an assistant hold down the lock ring tool while the ring is unscrewed

6   On 2003 and 2004 models, remove the fuel pump/sending unit retaining screws and remove the mounting flange **(see illustration)**.

7   On 2005 and later models, the fuel pump assembly is retained to the tank by a large screw-on lock ring. A special tool (available at most auto parts stores) is available for this purpose **(see illustration)**.

2014 and later models

8   On the fuel tank there are three marks - a "start of threads" mark and two "fully tightened" marks **(see illustration)**. These marks are used to properly tighten the lock ring on installation. Because the fuel tank is dark and these marks will be difficult to see when installing the lock ring with the lock ring tool, make corresponding marks on the vehicle for reference.

9   Assemble the lock ring removal tool on the lock ring, making sure it seats properly, then tighten the legs of the tool so there is no freeplay **(see illustration)**.

10   Have an assistant push down firmly on the lock ring tool so it doesn't slip off, then unscrew the lock ring **(see illustration)**.

Warning: *The lock ring can be very difficult to remove. In our case we had to use a knife-edge file and cut it off. If you have to resort to cutting it off, this is the only method you should use. DO NOT use a power tool such as a die grinder to remove it - fumes from the fuel tank could ignite and cause a fire and/or explosion.*

All models

11   Carefully withdraw the fuel pump/fuel level sending unit assembly from the fuel tank **(see illustration)**.

Note: *Most replacement fuel pump modules come pre-assembled as a complete unit with fuel pump, fuel pressure regulator and fuel level sending unit, and do not require individual component replacement.*

Fuel pump replacement

2004 and earlier models

12   Remove the fuel pump module as described earlier in this section.

6.11 Lift the fuel pump/sending unit assembly from the fuel tank at an angle so as not to damage the inlet screen or float arm

6.13 Exploded view of the fuel pump assembly
(2004 and earlier models)

A	Fuel filter	D	Sock (inlet) filter
B	Fuel pressure regulator	E	Fuel level sending unit
C	Fuel pump		

6.15 After removing the plastic support, carefully use a screwdriver to remove the clip securing the sock filter to the pump

6.17 Release the electrical connector at the top of the fuel pump assembly

13 The components of the fuel pump assembly are modular and all attach to the main housing (see illustration).

14 Pry the five plastic clips on the bottom of the pump module with a screwdriver and remove the plastic cover.

15 Remove the rubber cushion and fuel sock from the bottom of the fuel pump (see illustration).

16 Remove the fuel level sending unit. See Section 9.

17 Disconnect the fuel pump connector (see illustration).

18 Pry the four tabs using a screwdriver and remove the top of the fuel pump module.

19 Withdraw the pump from the filter housing.

2005 and later models

20 Remove the fuel pump module as described earlier in this section.

21 The components of the fuel pump assembly are modular and all attach to the main housing (see illustration).

6.21 Exploded view of the fuel pump (2005 and later models)

1 Fuel pump module top and fuel filter
2 Sub-tank
3 Fuel filter/pump support
4 E-clip and spring
5 Fuel level sending unit
6 Fuel pump harness
7 Fuel hose
8 Fuel pump
9 Fuel pump O-ring and spacer

6.22a To remove the fuel hose (A), release the clip at the bottom (B) . . .

6.22b . . . and move the hose out of the way (2005 and later models)

6.24 Remove the E-clip and spring

6.25 Release the clips on the sub-tank

6.26 Disconnect the fuel pump harness connector

6.27 Remove the fuel filter/pump support from the fuel filter

6.28a Disengage the fuel pump clips . . .

6.28b . . . and pull the fuel pump out of the fuel filter

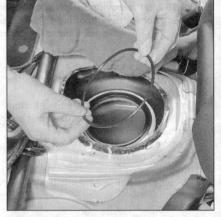

6.33 Install a new O-ring, making sure it seats properly in the tank

22 Release the clip using a screwdriver and disconnect the fuel hose at the plastic cup (sub-tank) covering the bottom of the fuel pump module **(see illustrations)**.
23 Remove the fuel level sending unit (see Section 9).
24 Remove the e-clip and spring from the rod on the fuel pump module **(see illustration)**.

25 Release the two clips for the fuel filter/pump support and remove the sub-tank from the bottom of the fuel pump module **(see illustration)**.
26 Disconnect the fuel pump harness connector from the top of the fuel pump module **(see illustration)**.
27 Use a screwdriver to remove the fuel fil-

ter/pump support from the top of the fuel filter **(see illustration)**.
28 Pry the five plastic clips on the bottom of the fuel filter/fuel pump with a screwdriver and pull out the fuel pump **(see illustrations)**.
29 Disconnect the fuel pump harness connector and remove the fuel pump.

6.39 The protrusion on the fuel pump module flange must align with the notch in the fuel tank threads (also indicated by two lines on the tank)

8.3 The fuel pressure regulator is a push-fit in the fuel pump/ sending unit assembly; make sure the old O-ring comes out with it

Reassembly (all models)

30 Inspect the strainer for contamination. If it is dirty, replace it.
31 Replace any O-rings for the fuel pump.
32 Reassemble the fuel pump/sending unit in the reverse order of disassembly.

Installation

33 Install a new fuel pump module O-ring **(see illustration)**.

2013 and earlier models

34 Install the fuel pump module in the fuel tank. On 2005 through 2013 models, make sure the protrusion on the fuel pump module flange aligns with the notch in the threaded portion of the fuel tank **(see illustration 6.39)**.
35 On 2003 and 2004 models, install the screws and tighten them securely.
36 On 2005 through 2013 models, align the "start of threads" rib on the lock ring with the "start of threads" line on the fuel tank **(see illustration 6.8)**. Tighten the lock ring two turns and align the "start of threads" rib in between the two "fully tightened" arrows on the fuel tank (also shown in illustration 6.8).
37 Connect the fuel line, vent hose and electrical connectors.
38 Cycle the ignition to pressurize the fuel system and check for fuel leaks prior to starting the engine. Also check for leaks after starting the engine.

2014 and later models

39 Install the fuel pump module in the fuel tank, making sure the protrusion on the fuel pump module flange aligns with the notch in the threaded portion of the fuel tank **(see illustration)**.
40 Align the "start of threads" rib on the lock ring with the "start of threads" line on the fuel tank and the corresponding mark that was

made on the body **(see illustration 6.8)**.
41 Install the lock ring tool onto the lock ring. Have an assistant push down on the fuel pump module while you push down on the lock ring tool, tightening the lock ring approximately 1/4 turn.
42 Quickly and firmly push down on the portion of the lock ring tool nearest the rear of the vehicle. If necessary, adjust the position of the tool. You should hear a sound or feel parts engaging with each other.
43 With your assistant still maintaining pressure on the pump module, turn the lock ring 3/4 turn until the "start of threads" rib on the lock ring lines up with the "start of threads" mark on the body.
44 Using a vernier or dial caliper, measure the distance from the top of the lock ring to the fuel tank at three locations (120-degrees apart). The difference between the measurements should be no more than 5/64-inch (2 mm). if the difference is 5/32 (4 mm) or more, remove the lock ring and start the installation process again.
45 When the lock ring initial installation is correct, proceed to tighten the lock ring until the "start of threads" rib is positioned between the two "fully tightened" arrows **(see illustration 6.8)**.
46 Connect the fuel line, vent hose and electrical connectors.

7 Fuel Pump Control Module (FPCM)- replacement

Note: *2014 and later 2ZR-FAE engines are equipped with a fuel pump control module. The fuel pump control module is located on the driver's side of the trunk, bolted to the inner quarter panel, behind the trunk trim. The FPCM is also known as the fuel pump ECU.*

1 Disconnect the cable from the negative battery terminal. See Chapter 5, Section 3.
2 Remove the spare tire cover.
3 Remove the clips and the left-side trunk trim panel to expose the Fuel Pump Control Module (FPCM).
4 Disconnect the FPCM electrical connector.
5 Remove the two bolts and the FPCM from the vehicle.
6 Installation is reverse of removal.

8 Fuel pressure regulator - removal and installation

Warning: *Gasoline is extremely flammable, so take extra precautions when you work on any part of the fuel system. See the Warning in Section 3.*
Note: *Most replacement fuel pumps modules come pre-assembled as a complete unit with fuel pump, fuel pressure regulator and fuel level sending unit, and do not require individual component replacement.*

1 Relieve the fuel system pressure (see Section 3), then disconnect the cable from the negative terminal of the battery (see Chapter 5). Remove the fuel tank cap.
2 Remove the fuel pump from the module (see Section 6).
3 Twist the fuel pressure regulator from the assembly **(see illustration)**. A small, flat-tipped screwdriver wrapped in tape may also be used to carefully pry the regulator from the housing.
4 Installation is the reverse of removal. Be sure to install a new O-ring on the fuel pressure regulator.
5 Cycle the ignition to pressurize the fuel system and check for fuel leaks prior to starting the engine. Check for leaks after starting the engine.

9.3 Disconnect the electrical connector (A) and pry the fuel-level sending unit from the clips (B) (2004 and earlier model shown)

9.4 Pry the tab (A) and slide fuel-level sending unit down from the clips (B) (2005 and later model shown)

9   Fuel level sending unit - replacement

Warning: *Gasoline is extremely flammable, so take extra precautions when you work on any part of the fuel system. See the Warning in Section 3.*

Note: *Most replacement fuel pump modules come pre-assembled as a complete unit with fuel pump, fuel pressure regulator and fuel level sending unit, and do not require individual component replacement.*

1   Remove the fuel pump/fuel level sending unit assembly from the fuel tank (see Section 6).
2   Disconnect the electrical connector from the sending unit.
3   On 2004 and earlier models, pry the sending unit from the retaining clips **(see illustration)** and separate it from the assembly.
4   On 2005 and later models, pry the retainer clip to the side and slide the sending

unit upwards and off of the module **(see illustrations)**.
5   Installation is the reverse of removal.

10   Fuel tank - removal and installation

Warning: *Gasoline is extremely flammable, so take extra precautions when you work on any part of the fuel system. See the Warning in Section 3.*

1   Remove the fuel filler cap to relieve fuel tank pressure. Relieve the fuel system pressure (see Section 3).
2   Detach the cable from the negative terminal of the battery.
3   Siphon or pump the fuel into an approved container using a siphoning kit or hand operated pump (available at most auto parts stores).
Warning: *Do not start the siphoning action by mouth!*
4   Remove the fuel pump access cover and

disconnect the fuel pump electrical connector and fuel lines from the fuel pump unit (see Section 6).
5   Raise the vehicle and support it securely on jackstands.
6   Remove the center exhaust pipe and the heat insulator from the vehicle (see Section 16).
7   Detach the parking brake cables from the underbody and position them aside.
8   Disconnect the fuel lines, the vapor return line and the fuel filler hose **(see illustration)**.
Note: *Be sure to plug the hoses to prevent leakage and contamination of the fuel system.*
9   Support the fuel tank with a floor jack. Place a sturdy plank between the jack head and the fuel tank to protect the tank. Remove the bolts from the fuel tank retaining straps **(see illustration)**.
10   Lower the tank enough to disconnect the electrical connector and ground strap from the fuel pump/fuel gauge sending unit, if you have not already done so.
11   Remove the tank from the vehicle.

10.8 Remove the clamp that retains the fuel filler hose (A) and separate the fuel hose disconnects (B) (2005 model shown)

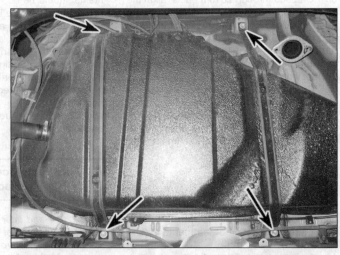

10.9 Remove the tank strap bolts (shown for clarity without supports required for tank removal) (2005 model shown)

12.4a Remove the bolts that retain the air filter housing to the engine compartment (2005 model shown)

12.4b Remove the bolts that retain the air filter housing to the engine compartment (2018 model shown)

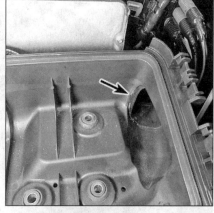

12.5 Detach the duct from the lower part of the housing (2018 model shown, others similar)

12   Installation is the reverse of removal.
13   Cycle the ignition to pressurize the fuel system and check for fuel leaks prior to starting the engine. Check for leaks after starting the engine.

11   Fuel tank cleaning and repair - general information

Note: *This pertains to steel fuel tanks only. In general, it is better to replace the fuel tank than have it repaired. Plastic fuel tanks are not repairable.*

1   Any repairs to the fuel tank or filler neck should be carried out by a professional who has experience in this critical and potentially dangerous work. Even after cleaning and flushing of the fuel system, explosive fumes can remain and ignite during repair of the tank.
2   If the fuel tank is removed from the vehicle, it should not be placed in an area where sparks or open flames could ignite the fumes coming out of the tank. Be especially careful inside garages where a gas-type appliance is located, because it could cause an explosion.

12   Air filter housing - removal and installation

1   On 2004 and earlier models, disconnect the air intake hose and breather hose from the housing cover. Disconnect the electrical connector from the intake air temperature sensor.
2   On 2005 and later models, disconnect the air intake hose from the throttle body and the breather hose from the valve cover. Disconnect the electrical connector from the mass airflow sensor.
3   Detach the clips and remove the air filter housing cover and the air filter element (see Chapter 1).
4   Remove the bolts and remove the air filter housing from the engine compartment **(see illustrations)**.
5   When removing the housing, disconnect the duct by releasing the tab **(see illustration)**.
6   Installation is the reverse of removal.

13   Accelerator cable - removal, installation and adjustment

Note: *2005 and later models do not have an accelerator cable. Instead, the throttle body has an electric motor that operates the throttle and is controlled by the PCM. See Chapter 6, Section 19.*
Note: *2004 and earlier models with cruise control have two accelerator cables - one from the accelerator pedal to the cruise control actuator and one from the cruise control actuator to the throttle body.*

Removal

1   Detach the cable from the negative terminal of the battery (see Chapter 5). On models with cruise control, remove the cover from the cruise control actuator.
2   Loosen the locknut on the threaded portion of the throttle cable at the throttle body or cruise control actuator **(see illustration)**.
3   Rotate the throttle lever or cruise control actuator and slip the throttle cable end out of the slot in the lever **(see illustrations)**.

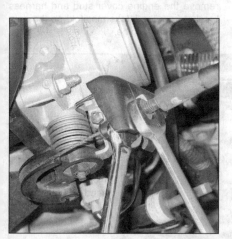

13.2 Loosen the locknuts on the accelerator cable

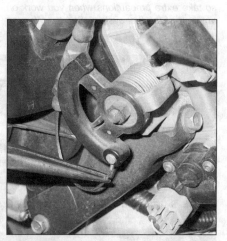

13.3a Rotate the throttle lever and remove the cable end from the slot in the throttle lever . . .

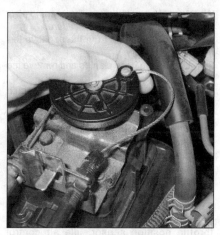

13.3b . . . or the cruise control actuator

13.4 Separate the cable from the accelerator pedal arm and slide the cable end out of the slot in the arm

14.6 Throttle-body mounting details - disconnect the electrical connectors and hoses, then remove the four mounting fasteners (2005 model shown, others similar)

4   Detach the throttle cable from the accelerator pedal **(see illustration)**. Remove the two bolts securing the cable retainer to the firewall.
5   From inside the vehicle, pull the cable through the firewall.

Installation and adjustment

6   Installation is the reverse of removal. Make sure the cable casing grommet seats properly in the firewall.
7   To adjust the cable, fully depress the accelerator pedal and check that the throttle is fully opened.
8   If not fully opened, loosen the locknuts, depress accelerator pedal and adjust the cable until the throttle is fully open.
9   Tighten the locknuts and recheck the adjustment. Make sure the throttle closes fully when the pedal is released.

14   Throttle body - removal and installation

Warning: *Wait until the engine is completely cool before beginning this procedure.*
1   Detach the cable from the negative terminal of the battery.
2   Loosen the hose clamps and remove the air intake duct.
3   On 2004 and earlier models, detach the accelerator cable from the throttle lever. Detach the throttle cable bracket and set it aside (it's not necessary to detach the throttle cable from the bracket).
4   On all models, clearly label, then detach, all vacuum and coolant hoses from the throttle body. Plug the coolant hoses to prevent coolant loss.
5   On 2004 and earlier models, disconnect the electrical connectors from the throttle position sensor, idle air control valve, manifold absolute pressure sensor and/or mass airflow sensor, as required. On 2005 and later models, disconnect the elec-

trical connector at the throttle body motor.
6   Remove the throttle body mounting bolts/nuts **(see illustration)**.
7   Detach the throttle body and gasket from the intake manifold.
8   Using a soft brush and throttle body cleaner, thoroughly clean the throttle body casting, then blow out all passages with compressed air.
Caution: *Do not clean the Throttle Position Sensor with anything. Just wipe it off carefully with a clean, soft cloth.*
9   Installation of the throttle body is the reverse of removal.
10   Tighten the throttle body mounting bolts/nuts to the torque listed in this Chapter's Specifications.
11   Check the coolant level, adding as necessary (see Chapter 3).

15   Fuel rail and injectors - removal and installation

Warning: *Gasoline is extremely flammable, so take extra precautions when you work on any part of the fuel system. See the Warning in Section 3.*

1   Relieve the fuel pressure (see Section 3) and detach the cable from the negative terminal of the battery.
2   On non-2ZR-FE and 2ZR-FAE engines, detach the PCV hose from the valve cover and remove the engine cover (over the valve cover).
3   On 2ZR-FE and 2ZR-FAE engines, remove the intake air hose and air filter housing. See Section 12.
4   Disconnect the ground wires from the valve cover, above the fuel rail and injectors.
5   On all engines, disconnect the electrical connectors from the fuel injectors. Open the wiring harness clamps and position the wiring harness aside.
6   On 2ZR-FE and 2ZR-FAE engines, remove the bolts and the wire harness brackets from the end of the cylinder head, above the transaxle.
7   On all engines, disconnect the fuel line leading to the fuel rail (see Section 5 for fuel line disconnect procedures).
8   On 2ZR-FE and 2ZR-FAE engines, remove the engine cover stud and harness bracket from the intake manifold on the driver's side of the engine.

15.10 Remove the two mounting bolts and pull up the fuel rail from the cylinder head (2005 model shown)

15.12a Remove the O-ring from the injector

15.12b Remove the grommet from the injector

9   Remove the bolt attaching the fuel rail delivery pipe clamp to the end of the cylinder head, above the transaxle.

10   On all engines, remove the fuel rail mounting bolts and carefully withdraw the fuel rail and injectors from the cylinder head **(see illustration)**.

11   Firmly pull the injectors from the fuel rail assembly.

12   Replace the O-ring and grommet on each injector **(see illustrations)**.

13   Remove the insulators in the cylinder head and replace them with new ones **(see illustration)**.

14   Lubricate the O-rings with clean engine oil and install the fuel injectors onto the fuel rail. Make sure the spacers are in place and install the fuel rail/injector assembly onto the cylinder head. Install the fuel rail mounting bolts and tighten the bolts to the torque listed in this Chapter's Specifications.

15   The remainder of installation is the reverse of removal.

16   Cycle the ignition to pressurize the fuel system and check for fuel leaks prior to starting the engine. Check for leaks after starting the engine.

16   Exhaust system servicing - general information

Warning: *Inspection and repair of exhaust system components should be done only after the system components have cooled completely.*

1   The exhaust system consists of the exhaust manifold, catalytic converter, the muffler, the tailpipe and all connecting pipes, brackets, hangers and clamps. The exhaust system is attached to the body with mounting brackets and rubber hangers **(see illustration)**. If any of these parts are damaged or deteriorated, excessive noise and vibration will be transmitted to the body.

2   Conducting regular inspections of the exhaust system will keep it safe and quiet. Look for any damaged or bent parts, open seams, holes, loose connections, excessive corrosion or other defects which could allow exhaust fumes to enter the vehicle. Deteriorated exhaust system components should not be repaired - they should be replaced with new parts.

3   If the exhaust system components are extremely corroded or rusted together, they will probably have to be cut from the exhaust system. The convenient way to accomplish this is to have a muffler repair shop remove the corroded sections with a cutting torch. If, however, you want to save money by doing it yourself and you don't have an oxy/acetylene welding outfit with a cutting torch, simply cut off the old components with a hack-saw. If you have compressed air, special pneumatic cutting chisels can also be used. If you do decide to tackle the job at home, be sure to wear eye protection to protect your eyes from metal chips and work gloves to protect your hands.

4   Here are some simple guidelines to apply when repairing the exhaust system:
   a) *Work from the back to the front when removing exhaust system components.*
   b) *Apply penetrating oil to the exhaust system component fasteners to make them easier to remove.*
   c) *Use new gaskets, hangers and clamps when installing exhaust system components.*
   d) *Apply anti-seize compound to the threads of all exhaust system fasteners during reassembly.*
   e) *Be sure to allow sufficient clearance between newly installed parts and all points on the underbody to avoid overheating the floor pan and possibly damaging the interior carpet and insulation. Pay particularly close attention to the catalytic converter and its heat shield. Warning: The catalytic converter operates at very high temperatures and takes a long time to cool. Wait until it's completely cool before attempting to remove the converter. Failure to do so could result in serious burns.*

15.13 Install new insulators in the cylinder head holes (A), and position the two spacers (B) before installing the fuel rail

16.1 Check all of the exhaust system rubber hangers for cracking, replacing them as necessary

Notes

Chapter 5
Engine electrical systems

Contents

Specifications

Charging system

Charging voltage	12.9 to 14.9 volts
Standard amperage	
All lights and accessories turned off	Less than 10 amps
Headlights (hi-beam) and heater blower motor turned on	30 amps or more

1 General information and precautions

General information

Ignition system

1   The electronic ignition system consists of the Crankshaft Position (CKP) sensor, the Camshaft Position (CMP) sensor, the Knock Sensor (KS), the Powertrain Control Module (PCM), the ignition switch, the battery, the individual ignition coils, and the spark plugs. For more information on the CKP, CMP and KS sensors, as well as the PCM, refer to Chapter 6.

Charging system

2   The charging system includes the alternator (with an integral voltage regulator), the Powertrain Control Module (PCM), the Body Control Module (BCM), a charge indicator light on the dash, the battery, a fuse or fusible link and the wiring connecting all of these

components. The charging system supplies electrical power for the ignition system, the lights, the radio, etc. The alternator is driven by a drivebelt.

3   On 2014 and later models, battery current is monitored by the battery current sensor. The sensor sends electrical current data to the ECM. The ECM can then control alternator output based on the needs of the charging system.

Starting system

4   The starting system consists of the battery, the ignition switch, the starter relay, the Powertrain Control Module (PCM), the Body Control Module (BCM), the Transmission Range (TR) switch, the starter motor and solenoid assembly, and the wiring connecting all of the components.

Precautions

5   Always observe the following precautions when working on the electrical system:

a) Be extremely careful when servicing engine electrical components. They are easily damaged if checked, connected or handled improperly.
b) Never leave the ignition switched on for long periods of time when the engine is not running.
c) Never disconnect the battery cables while the engine is running.
d) Maintain correct polarity when connecting battery cables from another vehicle during jump starting - see the Booster battery (jump) starting Section at the front of this manual.
e) Always disconnect the cable from the negative battery terminal before working on the electrical system, but read the battery disconnection procedure first (see Section 3).

6   It's also a good idea to review the safety-related information regarding the engine electrical systems located in the Safety first! Section at the front of this manual before beginning any operation included in this Chapter.

2   Troubleshooting

Ignition system

1   If a malfunction occurs in the ignition system, do not immediately assume that any particular part is causing the problem. First, check the following items:

a) *Make sure that the cable clamps at the battery terminals are clean and tight.*

b) *Test the condition of the battery (see Steps 15 through 19). If it doesn't pass all the tests, replace it.*

c) *Check the ignition coil or coil pack connections.*

d) *Check any relevant fuses in the engine compartment fuse and relay box (see Chapter 12). If they're burned, determine the cause and repair the circuit.*

Check

Warning: *Because of the high voltage generated by the ignition system, use extreme care when performing a procedure involving ignition components.*

Note: *The ignition system components on these vehicles are difficult to diagnose. In the event of ignition system failure that you can't diagnose, have the vehicle tested at a dealer service department or other qualified auto repair facility.*

Note: *You'll need a spark tester for the following test. Spark testers are available at most auto supply stores.*

2   If the engine turns over but won't start, verify that there is sufficient ignition voltage to fire the spark plugs as follows.

3   Remove a coil and install the tester between the boot at the lower end of the coil and the spark plug **(see illustration)**.

4   Crank the engine and note whether or not the tester flashes.

Caution: *Do NOT crank the engine or allow it to run for more than five seconds; running the engine for more than five seconds may set a*

2.3 Spark tester

Diagnostic Trouble Code (DTC) for a cylinder misfire.

5   If the tester flashes during cranking, the coil is delivering sufficient voltage to the spark plug to fire it. Repeat this test for each cylinder to verify that the other coils are OK.

6   If the tester doesn't flash, remove a coil from another cylinder and swap it for the one being tested. If the tester now flashes, you know that the original coil is bad. If the tester still doesn't flash, the PCM or wiring harness is probably defective. Have the PCM checked out by a dealer service department or other qualified repair shop (testing the PCM is beyond the scope of the do-it-yourselfer because it requires expensive special tools).

7   If the tester flashes during cranking but a misfire code (related to the cylinder being tested) has been stored, the spark plug could be fouled or defective.

Charging system

8   If a malfunction occurs in the charging system, do not automatically assume the alternator is causing the problem. First check

the following items:

a) *Check the drivebelt tension and condition, as described in Chapter 1, Section 10. Replace it if it's worn or deteriorated.*

b) *Make sure the alternator mounting bolts are tight.*

c) *Inspect the alternator wiring harness and the connectors at the alternator and voltage regulator. They must be in good condition, tight and have no corrosion.*

d) *Check the fusible link (if equipped) or main fuse in the underhood fuse/relay box. If it is burned, determine the cause, repair the circuit and replace the link or fuse (the vehicle will not start and/or the accessories will not work if the fusible link or main fuse is blown).*

e) *Start the engine and check the alternator for abnormal noises (a shrieking or squealing sound indicates a bad bearing).*

f) *Check the battery. Make sure it's fully charged and in good condition (one bad cell in a battery can cause overcharging by the alternator).*

2.16 To test the open circuit voltage of the battery, touch the black probe of the voltmeter to the negative terminal and the red probe to the positive terminal of the battery; a fully charged battery should be at least 12.6 volts

2.18 Connect a battery load tester to the battery and check the battery condition under load following the tool manufacturer's instructions

g) *Disconnect the battery cables (negative first, then positive). Inspect the battery posts and the cable clamps for corrosion. Clean them thoroughly if necessary (see Chapter 1, Section 9). Reconnect the cables (positive first, negative last).*

Alternator - check

9   Use a voltmeter to check the battery voltage with the engine off. It should be at least 12.6 volts **(see illustration 2.16)**.
10   Start the engine and check the battery voltage again. It should now be approximately 13.5 to 15 volts.
11   If the voltage reading is more or less than the specified charging voltage, the voltage regulator is probably defective, which will require replacement of the alternator (the voltage regulator is not replaceable separately). Remove the alternator and have it bench tested (most auto parts stores will do this for you).
12   The charging system (battery) light on the instrument cluster lights up when the ignition key is turned to On, but it should go out when the engine starts.
13   If the charging system light stays on after the engine has been started, there is a problem with the charging system. Before replacing the alternator, check the battery condition, alternator belt tension and electrical cable connections.
14   If replacing the alternator doesn't restore voltage to the specified range, have the charging system tested by a dealer service department or other qualified repair shop.

Battery - check

15   Check the battery state of charge. Visually inspect the indicator eye on the top of the battery (if equipped with one); if the indicator eye is black in color, charge the battery as described in Chapter 1, Section 9. Next perform an open circuit voltage test using a digital voltmeter.
Note: *The battery's surface charge must be removed before accurate voltage measurements can be made. Turn on the high beams for ten seconds, then turn them off and let the vehicle stand for two minutes.*
16   With the engine and all accessories Off, touch the negative probe of the voltmeter to the negative terminal of the battery and the positive probe to the positive terminal of the battery **(see illustration)**. The battery voltage should be 12.6 volts or slightly above. If the battery is less than the specified voltage, charge the battery before proceeding to the next test. Do not proceed with the battery load test unless the battery charge is correct.
17   Disconnect the negative battery cable, then the positive cable from the battery.
Note: *On some 2014 and later models, a battery current sensor is located on the negative battery cable.*
18   Perform a battery load test. An accurate check of the battery condition can only be performed with a load tester **(see illustration)**. This test evaluates the ability of the battery to operate the starter and other accessories during periods of high current draw. Connect the

load tester to the battery terminals. Load test the battery according to the tool manufacturer's instructions. This tool increases the load demand (current draw) on the battery.
19   Maintain the load on the battery for 15 seconds and observe that the battery voltage does not drop below 9.6 volts. If the battery condition is weak or defective, the tool will indicate this condition immediately.
Note: *Cold temperatures will cause the minimum voltage reading to drop slightly. Follow the chart given in the manufacturer's instructions to compensate for cold climates. Minimum load voltage for freezing temperatures (32 degrees F) should be approximately 9.1 volts.*

Starting system
The starter rotates, but the engine doesn't

20   Remove the starter (see Section 9). Check the overrunning clutch and bench test the starter to make sure the drive mechanism extends fully for proper engagement with the flywheel ring gear. If it doesn't, replace the starter.
21   Check the flywheel ring gear for missing teeth and other damage. With the ignition turned off, rotate the flywheel so you can check the entire ring gear.

The starter is noisy

22   If the solenoid is making a chattering noise, first check the battery (see Steps 15 through 19). If the battery is okay, check the cables and connections.
23   If you hear a grinding, crashing metallic sound when you turn the key to Start, check for loose starter mounting bolts. If they're tight, remove the starter and inspect the teeth on the starter pinion gear and flywheel ring gear. Look for missing or damaged teeth.
24   If the starter sounds fine when you first turn the key to Start, but then stops rotating the engine and emits a zinging sound, the problem is probably a defective starter drive that's not staying engaged with the ring gear. Replace the starter.

The starter rotates slowly

25   Check the battery (see Steps 15 through 19).
26   If the battery is okay, verify all connections (at the battery, the starter solenoid and motor) are clean, corrosion-free and tight. Make sure the cables aren't frayed or damaged.
27   Check that the starter mounting bolts are tight so it grounds properly. Also check the pinion gear and flywheel ring gear for evidence of a mechanical bind (galling, deformed gear teeth or other damage).

The starter does not rotate at all

28   Check the battery (see Steps 15 through 19).
29   If the battery is okay, verify all connections (at the battery, the starter solenoid and motor) are clean, corrosion-free and tight. Make sure the cables aren't frayed or damaged.

30   Check all of the fuses in the underhood fuse/relay box.
31   Check that the starter mounting bolts are tight so it grounds properly.
32   Check for voltage at the starter solenoid "S" terminal when the ignition key is turned to the start position. If voltage is present, replace the starter/solenoid assembly. If no voltage is present, the problem could be the starter relay, the Transmission Range (TR) switch (see Chapter 7B), or with an electrical connector somewhere in the circuit (see the wiring diagrams at the end of this manual). Also, on many modern vehicles, the Powertrain Control Module (PCM) and the Body Control Module (BCM) control the voltage signal to the starter solenoid; on such vehicles a special scan tool is required for diagnosis.

---

3   Battery - disconnection

Caution: *Always disconnect the cable from the negative battery terminal FIRST and hook it up LAST or the battery may be shorted by the tool being used to loosen the cable clamps.*
1   Some systems on the vehicle require battery power to be available at all times, either to maintain continuous operation (alarm system, power door locks, etc.), or to maintain control unit memory (radio station presets, Powertrain Control Module (PCM) and other control units). When the battery is disconnected, the power that maintains these systems is cut. So, before you disconnect the battery, please note that on a vehicle with power door locks, it's a wise precaution to remove the key from the ignition and to keep it with you, so that it does not get locked inside if the power door locks should engage accidentally when the battery is reconnected!
2   Devices known as "memory-savers" can be used to avoid some of these problems. Precise details vary according to the device used. The typical memory saver is plugged into the cigarette lighter and is connected to a spare battery. Then the vehicle battery can be disconnected from the electrical system. The memory saver will provide sufficient current to maintain audio unit security codes, PCM memory, etc., and will provide power to always hot circuits such as the clock and radio memory circuits.
Warning: *Some memory savers deliver a considerable amount of current in order to keep vehicle systems operational after the main battery is disconnected. If you're using a memory saver, make sure that the circuit concerned is actually open before servicing it.*
Warning: *If you're going to work near any of the airbag system components, the battery MUST be disconnected and a memory saver must NOT be used. If a memory saver is used, power will be supplied to the airbag, which means that it could accidentally deploy and cause serious personal injury.*
Caution: *On 2014 and later models, wait at least 90 seconds after turning the ignition switch off before disconnecting the negative battery cable.*
Note: *On some 2014 and later models, a bat-*

4.3 To remove the battery, detach the negative battery cable first (A), then the positive cable (B), then remove the hold-down clamp nut and bolt (C) and remove the hold-down clamp

4.5 Battery carrier details

1 Radiator hose bracket bolts	3 Carrier mounting bolts
2 Wiring harness clamps	

tery current sensor is located on the negative battery cable.

3   To disconnect the battery for service procedures requiring power to be cut from the vehicle, loosen the cable clamp nut and disconnect the cable from the negative battery terminal. Isolate the cable end to prevent it from coming into accidental contact with the battery terminal.

4   Battery, battery tray and carrier - removal and installation

Warning: *Hydrogen gas is produced by the battery, so keep open flames and lighted cigarettes away from it at all times. Always wear eye protection when working around a battery. Rinse off spilled electrolyte immediately with large amounts of water.*
Caution: *On 2014 and later models, wait at least 90 seconds after turning the ignition switch off before disconnecting the negative battery cable.*
Note: *On some 2014 and later models, a battery current sensor is located on the negative battery cable.*
1   Disconnect the cable from the negative battery terminal (see Section 3).
2   Disconnect the positive battery cable.
3   Remove the battery hold-down clamp **(see illustration)**.
4   Remove the battery and place it on a workbench.
Note: *Battery handling tools are available at most auto parts stores for a reasonable price. They make it easier to remove and carry the battery.*
5   While the battery is removed, inspect the tray, retainer brackets and related fasteners for corrosion or damage. If it's necessary to remove the carrier, remove the bolts and detach the radiator hose bracket, free the wiring harness clamps from the rear edge of the carrier, then remove the carrier mounting

bolts **(see illustration)**.
Note: *If corrosion is evident, remove the battery tray and use a baking soda/water solution to clean the corroded area to prevent further oxidation. Repaint the area as necessary using rust resistant paint.*
6   Clean and service the battery and cables (see Chapter 1).
7   If you are replacing the battery, make sure you purchase one that is identical to yours, with the same dimensions, amperage rating, cold cranking amps rating, etc. Make sure it is fully charged prior to installation in the vehicle.
8   Installation is the reverse of removal. Connect the positive cable first and the negative cable last.
9   After connecting the cables to the battery, apply a light coating of battery terminal corrosion inhibitor to the connections to help prevent corrosion.

5   Battery current sensor - replacement

Caution: *On 2014 and later models, wait at least 90 seconds after turning the ignition switch off before disconnecting the negative battery cable.*
Note: *Some 2014 and later models are equipped with a battery current sensor to assist with generator output by monitoring battery current at the negative (-) battery terminal. The battery current sensor is located at the negative battery cable terminal at the battery. The battery current sensor may also be referred to as the generator control ECU.*
1   Remove the nut and negative battery cable from the sensor.
2   Disconnect the electrical connector from the sensor.
3   Unscrew the nut and detach the sensor from the negative battery cable.
4   Installation is reverse of removal.

6   Battery cables - replacement

Caution: *On 2014 and later models, wait at least 90 seconds after turning the ignition switch off before disconnecting the negative battery cable.*
Note: *On some 2014 and later models, a battery current sensor is located on the negative battery cable.*
1   Periodically inspect the entire length of each battery cable for damage, cracked or burned insulation and corrosion. Poor battery cable connections can cause starting problems and decreased engine performance.
2   Check the cable-to-terminal connections at the ends of the cables for cracks, loose wire strands and corrosion. The presence of white, fluffy deposits under the insulation at the cable terminal connection is a sign that the cable is corroded and should be replaced. Check the terminals for distortion, missing mounting bolts and corrosion.
3   When removing the cables, always disconnect the negative cable first and hook it up last or the battery may be shorted by the tool used to loosen the cable clamps. Even if only the positive cable is being replaced, be sure to disconnect the negative cable from the battery first (see Section 6 for further information regarding battery cable removal).
4   Disconnect the old cables from the battery, then trace each of them to their opposite ends and detach them from the starter solenoid and ground terminals. Note the routing of each cable to ensure correct installation.
5   If you are replacing either or both of the old cables, take them with you when buying new cables. It is vitally important that you replace the cables with identical parts. Cables have characteristics that make them easy to identify: positive cables are usually red, larger in cross-section and have a larger diameter battery post clamp; ground cables are usu-

7.3 Disconnect the electrical connector (A) and remove the mounting bolt (B), then pull the coil out of the valve cover with a twisting motion

8.4 Disconnect the electrical connections from the alternator (2005 model shown, others similar)

ally black, smaller in cross-section and have a slightly smaller diameter clamp for the negative post.

6   Clean the threads of the solenoid or ground connection with a wire brush to remove rust and corrosion. Apply a light coat of battery terminal corrosion inhibitor or petroleum jelly to the threads to prevent future corrosion.

7   Attach the cable to the solenoid or ground connection and tighten the mounting nut/bolt securely.

8   Before connecting a new cable to the battery, make sure that it reaches the battery post without having to be stretched.

9   Connect the positive cable first, followed by the negative cable.

7   Ignition coils - replacement

Note: *Toyota does not publish primary or secondary resistance specifications for the ignition coils units used on these models. The only way to check them is to substitute a known good unit. But this option isn't feasible for a home mechanic because you can't return electrical components to a parts department once you have purchased them. If you have already eliminated all other possible causes of an ignition malfunction, a defective ignition coil/igniter unit is the likely cause of the problem, but the only way to verify this is to substitute a known good unit.*

1   Remove the engine cover.
2   Disconnect the cable from the negative battery terminal (see Section 3).
3   Disconnect the electrical connector(s) from the coil(s), then remove the mounting bolt(s) **(see illustration)**.
4   Carefully withdraw the coil from the cylinder head.
5   Installation is the reverse of removal.

8   Alternator - removal and installation

1   Disconnect the cable from the negative battery terminal (see Section 3).
2   Remove the engine cover.
3   Remove the drivebelt (see Chapter 1, Section 10).
4   Disconnect the electrical connectors from the alternator **(see illustration)**.
5   Remove the alternator mounting bolts **(see illustration)**. Disconnect any wire harnesses from the alternator bracket.
6   Remove the alternator from the engine.
7   If you are replacing the alternator, take the old alternator with you when purchasing a replacement unit. Make sure that the new/rebuilt unit is identical to the old alternator. Look at the terminals - they should be the same in number, size and locations as the terminals on the old alternator. Finally, look at the identification markings - they will be stamped in the housing or printed on a tag or plaque affixed to the housing. Make sure that these numbers are the same on both alternators.

8   Some new/rebuilt alternators do not have a pulley installed, so you may have to switch the pulley from the old unit to the new/rebuilt one. When buying an alternator, find out the shop's policy regarding installation of pulleys - some shops will perform this service free of charge.
9   Installation is the reverse of removal.
10   After the alternator is installed, install the drivebelt and adjust the tension (see Chapter 1, Section 10).
11   Check the charging voltage to verify proper operation of the alternator (see Section 2).

9   Starter motor - removal and installation

1   Disconnect the cable from the negative battery terminal (see Section 3). Raise the vehicle and support it securely on jackstands.
2   On 2008 and earlier models and 2014 and later models, remove the splash shield from under the engine.

8.5 Alternator mounting bolts (2005 model shown, others similar)

9.7a Disconnect the electrical connector . . .

9.7b . . . then flip up the cover, remove the nut and detach the starter cable. B is the starter lower mounting bolt (2ZR-FE engine)

3   On 2009 through 2013 2AZ-FE models, remove the air filter housing (see Chapter 4, Section 12).

4   On 2009 through 2013 2AZ-FE models, remove the battery and the battery tray (see Section 4).

5   On 2009 through 2016 models with automatic transaxles, remove the bolt and retainer securing the oil cooler tubes from the bracket.

6   On models where it would interfere, remove the transaxle fluid dipstick tube bracket bolt and pull the dipstick tube from the transaxle.

Note: *The O-ring at the bottom of the dipstick tube should be replaced.*

7   On all models, disconnect the electrical connector from the starter solenoid, then remove the nut and disconnect the

battery cable from the solenoid, too **(see illustrations)**.

8   Remove the starter motor mounting bolts and remove the starter.

Note: *The starter mounting bolts are installed in opposite directions.*

9   Installation is the reverse of removal.

Chapter 6
Emissions and engine control systems

Contents

Specifications

Torque specifications

Ft-lbs (unless otherwise indicated)

Note: *One foot-pound (ft-lb) of torque is equivalent to 12 inch-pounds (in-lbs) of torque. Torque values below approximately 15 ft-lbs are expressed in inch-pounds, because most foot-pound torque wrenches are not accurate at these smaller values.*

Knock sensor bolt...15

1   General information

1   To prevent pollution of the atmosphere from incompletely burned and evaporating gases, and to maintain good driveability and fuel economy, a number of emission control systems are incorporated. They include the:

Catalytic converter

2   A catalytic converter is an emission control device in the exhaust system that reduces certain pollutants in the exhaust gas stream. There are two types of converters: oxidation converters and reduction converters.

3   Oxidation converters contain a monolithic substrate (a ceramic honeycomb) coated with the semi-precious metals platinum and palladium. An oxidation catalyst reduces unburned hydrocarbons (HC) and carbon monoxide (CO) by adding oxygen to the exhaust stream as it passes through the substrate, which, in the presence of high temperature and the catalyst materials, converts the HC and CO to water vapor (H_2O) and carbon dioxide (CO_2).

4   Reduction converters contain a monolithic substrate coated with platinum and rhodium. A reduction catalyst reduces oxides of nitrogen (NOx) by removing oxygen, which in the presence of high temperature and the catalyst material produces nitrogen (N) and carbon dioxide (CO_2).

5   Catalytic converters that combine both types of catalysts in one assembly are known as three-way catalysts or TWCs. A TWC can reduce all three pollutants.

Evaporative Emissions Control (EVAP) system

6   The Evaporative Emissions Control (EVAP) system prevents fuel system vapors (which contain unburned hydrocarbons) from escaping into the atmosphere. On warm days, vapors trapped inside the fuel tank expand until the pressure reaches a certain threshold. Then the fuel vapors are routed from the fuel tank through the fuel vapor vent valve and the fuel vapor control valve to the EVAP canister, where they're stored temporarily until the next time the vehicle is operated. When the conditions are right (engine warmed up, vehicle up to speed, moderate or heavy load on the engine, etc.) the PCM opens the canister purge valve, which allows fuel vapors to be drawn from the canister into the intake manifold. Once in the intake manifold, the fuel vapors mix with incoming air before being drawn through the intake ports into the combustion chambers where they're burned up with the rest of the air/fuel mixture. The EVAP system is complex and virtually impossible to troubleshoot without the right tools and training.

Powertrain Control Module (PCM)

7   The Powertrain Control Module (PCM) is the brain of the engine management system. It also controls a wide variety of other vehicle systems. In order to program the new PCM, a technician equipped with the proper scan tool needs the vehicle as well as the new PCM. If you're planning to replace the PCM with a new one, there is no point in trying to do so at home because you won't be able to program it yourself.

Positive Crankcase Ventilation (PCV) system

8   The Positive Crankcase Ventilation (PCV) system reduces hydrocarbon emissions by scavenging crankcase vapors, which are rich in unburned hydrocarbons. A PCV valve or orifice regulates the flow of gases into the intake manifold in proportion to the amount of intake vacuum available.

9   The PCV system generally consists of the fresh air inlet hose, the PCV valve or orifice and the crankcase ventilation hose (or PCV hose). The fresh air inlet hose connects the air intake duct to a pipe on the valve cover. The crankcase ventilation hose (or PCV hose) connects the PCV valve or orifice in the valve cover or crankcase vent oil separator to the intake manifold.

Vehicle Emission Control Information (VECI) label

10   An emission control label is attached to the vehicle under the hood or in the engine compartment. The label identifies important emission controls the vehicle is equipped with **(see illustration)**.

Vacuum hose routing diagram label

11   The vacuum hose routing diagram label provides a schematic of the routing of the vacuum hoses for the emission controls **(see illustration)**.
Note: *Not all models have a vacuum hose routing diagram.*

Variable Valve Timing (VVT) system

12   The VVT system controls intake valve timing (2008 and earlier models) or intake and exhaust valve timing (2009 and later models) to increase engine torque in the low and mid-speed range and to increase horsepower in the high-speed range. The VVT system consists of the PCM-controlled Oil Control Valve(s) (OCV), mounted on top of the cylinder head, and the VVT actuator(s), which is mounted on the front end of the camshaft(s). The PCM-controlled OCV varies the oil pressure in the VVT actuator(s), which continually varies the timing of the camshaft(s).

1.10 Example of a VECI label

1.11 Example of a vacuum hose routing diagram label

Information Sensors

Accelerator Pedal Position (APP) sensor - as you press the accelerator pedal, the APP sensor alters its voltage signal to the PCM in proportion to the angle of the pedal, and the PCM commands a motor inside the throttle body to open or close the throttle plate accordingly

Camshaft Position (CMP) sensor - produces a signal that the PCM uses to identify the number 1 cylinder and to time the firing sequence of the fuel injectors

Crankshaft Position (CKP) sensor - produces a signal that the PCM uses to calculate engine speed and crankshaft position, which enables it to synchronize ignition timing with fuel injector timing, and to detect misfires

Engine Coolant Temperature (ECT) sensor - a thermistor (temperature-sensitive variable resistor) that sends a voltage signal to the PCM, which uses this data to determine the temperature of the engine coolant

Fuel tank pressure sensor - measures the fuel tank pressure and controls fuel tank pressure by signaling the EVAP system to purge the fuel tank vapors when the pressure becomes excessive

Intake Air Temperature (IAT) sensor - monitors the temperature of the air entering the engine and sends a signal to the PCM to determine injector pulse-width (the duration of each injector's on-time) and to adjust spark timing (to prevent spark knock)

Knock sensor - a piezoelectric crystal that oscillates in proportion to engine vibration which produces a voltage output that is monitored by the PCM. This retards the ignition timing when the oscillation exceeds a certain threshold

Manifold Absolute Pressure (MAP) sensor - monitors the pressure or vacuum inside the intake manifold. The PCM uses this data to determine engine load so that it can alter the ignition advance and fuel enrichment

Mass Air Flow (MAF) sensor - measures the amount of intake air drawn into the engine. It uses a hot-wire sensing element to measure the amount of air entering the engine

Oxygen sensors - generates a small variable voltage signal in proportion to the difference between the oxygen content in the exhaust stream and the oxygen content in the ambient air. The PCM uses this information to maintain the proper air/fuel ratio. A second oxygen sensor monitors the efficiency of the catalytic converter

Throttle Position (TP) sensor - a potentiometer that generates a voltage signal that varies in relation to the opening angle of the throttle plate inside the throttle body. Works with the PCM and other sensors to calculate injector pulse width (the duration of each injector's on-time)

Photos courtesy of Wells Manufacturing, except APP and MAF sensors.

2   On Board Diagnosis (OBD) system

General description

1   All models are equipped with the second generation OBD-II system. This system consists of an on-board computer known as the Powertrain Control Module (PCM), and information sensors, which monitor various functions of the engine and send data to the PCM. This system incorporates a series of diagnostic monitors that detect and identify fuel injection and emissions control system faults and store the information in the computer memory. This system also tests sensors and output actuators, diagnoses drive cycles, freezes data and clears codes.

2   The PCM is the brain of the electronically controlled fuel and emissions system. It receives data from a number of sensors and other electronic components (switches, relays, etc.). Based on the information it receives, the PCM generates output signals to control various relays, solenoids (fuel injectors) and other actuators. The PCM is specifically calibrated to optimize the emissions, fuel economy and driveability of the vehicle.

3   It isn't a good idea to attempt diagnosis or replacement of the PCM or emission control components at home while the vehicle is under warranty. Because of a Federally mandated warranty which covers the emissions system components and because any owner-induced damage to the PCM, the sensors and/or the control devices may void this warranty, take the vehicle to a dealer service department if the PCM or a system component malfunctions.

Scan tool information

4   Because extracting the Diagnostic Trouble Codes (DTCs) from an engine management system is now the first step in troubleshooting many computer-controlled systems and components, a code reader, at the very least, will be required **(see illustration)**. More powerful scan tools can also perform many of

2.4a Simple code readers are an economical way to extract trouble codes when the CHECK ENGINE light comes on

the diagnostics once associated with expensive factory scan tools **(see illustration)**. If you're planning to obtain a generic scan tool for your vehicle, make sure that it's compatible with OBD-II systems. If you don't plan to purchase a code reader or scan tool and don't have access to one, you can have the codes extracted by a dealer service department or an independent repair shop.
Note: *Some auto parts stores even provide this service.*

3   Obtaining and clearing Diagnostic Trouble Codes (DTCs)

1   All models covered by this manual are equipped with on-board diagnostics. When the PCM recognizes a malfunction in a monitored emission or engine control system, component or circuit, it turns on the Malfunction Indicator Light (MIL) on the dash. The PCM will continue to display the MIL until the problem is fixed and the Diagnostic Trouble Code (DTC) is cleared from the PCM's memory. You'll need a scan tool to access any DTCs stored in the PCM.

2   Before outputting any DTCs stored in the PCM, thoroughly inspect ALL electrical con-

nectors and hoses. Make sure that all electrical connections are tight, clean and free of corrosion. And make sure that all hoses are correctly connected, fit tightly and are in good condition (no cracks or tears).

Accessing the DTCs

3   The Diagnostic Trouble Codes (DTCs) can only be accessed with a code reader or scan tool. Professional scan tools are expensive, but relatively inexpensive generic code readers or scan tools **(see illustrations 2.4a and 2.4b)** are available at most auto parts stores. Simply plug the connector of the scan tool into the diagnostic connector **(see illustration)**. Then follow the instructions included with the scan tool to extract the DTCs.

4   Once you have outputted all of the stored DTCs, look them up on the accompanying DTC chart.

5   After troubleshooting the source of each DTC, make any necessary repairs or replace the defective component(s).

Clearing the DTCs

6   Clear the DTCs with the code reader or scan tool in accordance with the instructions provided by the tool's manufacturer.

2.4b Hand-held scan tools like these can extract computer codes and also perform diagnostics

3.3 The Data Link Connector (DLC) is located below the steering column

Diagnostic Trouble Codes

Trouble code	Code identification
P0010	Camshaft position "A" actuator circuit (bank 1)
P0011	Camshaft position "A" - timing over-advanced or system performance (bank 1)
P0012	Camshaft position "A" - timing over-retarded (bank 1)
P0013	Camshaft position "B" actuator circuit open (bank 1)
P0014	Camshaft position "B" - timing over-advanced or system performance (bank 1)
P0015	Camshaft position "B" - timing over-retarded (bank 1)
P0016	Crankshaft position - camshaft position correlation (bank 1 sensor B)
P0017	Crankshaft position - camshaft position correlation (bank 1 sensor B)
P0031	Oxygen (A/F) sensor heater control circuit low (bank 1 sensor 1)
P0032	Oxygen (A/F) sensor heater control circuit high (bank 1 sensor 1)
P0037	Oxygen sensor heater control circuit low (bank 1 sensor 2)
P0038	Oxygen sensor heater control circuit high (bank 1 sensor 2)
P0100	Mass airflow sensor or circuit fault
P0101	Mass airflow sensor range or performance problem
P0102	Mass or volume air flow circuit low input
P0103	Mass or volume air flow circuit high input
P0110 - P0113	Intake air temperature sensor or circuit fault
P0115 - P0118	Engine coolant temperature sensor or circuit fault
P011B	Engine coolant temperature (ECT), intake air temperature (IAT) correlation
P0120 - P0123	Throttle position sensor or circuit fault
P0125	Insufficient coolant temperature for closed loop; O2 sensor heater malfunction
P0128	Thermostat malfunction
P0130	Pre-converter O2 sensor or circuit fault
P0133	Pre-converter O2 sensor circuit slow response fault
P0135	Pre-converter O2 sensor heater fault
P0136 - P0139, P013A	Post-converter O2 sensor or circuit fault
P0141	Post-converter Oxygen sensor heater or circuit fault
P014C	A/F Sensor Slow Response - Rich to Lean Bank 1 Sensor 1
P014D	A/F Sensor Slow Response - Lean to Rich Bank 1 Sensor 1
P015A	A/F Sensor Delayed Response - Rich to Lean Bank 1 Sensor 1

Diagnostic Trouble Codes (continued)

Trouble code	Code identification
P015B	A/F Sensor Delayed Response - Lean to Rich Bank 1 Sensor 1
P0171	Fuel injection system lean
P0172	Fuel injection system rich
P0220 - P0223	Throttle pedal position sensor or switch "B" circuit fault
P0300	Multiple cylinder misfire detected
P0301	Cylinder no. 1 misfire detected
P0302	Cylinder no. 2 misfire detected
P0303	Cylinder no. 3 misfire detected
P0304	Cylinder no. 4 misfire detected
P0325 - P0328	Knock sensor or circuit fault
P0335 - P0339	Crankshaft position sensor or circuit fault
P0340 - P0341	Camshaft position sensor or circuit fault
P0342	Camshaft position sensor "A" circuit low input (bank 1 or single sensor)
P0343	Camshaft position sensor "A" circuit high input (bank 1 or single sensor)
P0351	Ignition coil "A" primary or secondary circuit fault
P0352	Ignition coil "B" primary or secondary circuit fault
P0353	Ignition coil "C" primary or secondary circuit fault
P0354	Ignition coil "D" primary or secondary circuit fault
P0365	Camshaft position sensor "B" circuit (bank 1)
P0367	Camshaft position sensor "B" circuit low input (bank 1)
P0368	Camshaft position sensor "B" circuit high input (bank 1)
P0420	Catalytic converter system fault
P043E	EVAP system reference orifice clog up
P043F	EVAP system reference orifice high flow
P0440	EVAP system malfunction
P0441	EVAP system incorrect purge flow detected
P0443	EVAP system purge control valve circuit fault
P0450	EVAP system pressure sensor or circuit fault
P0451	EVAP system pressure sensor range or performance problem
P0452	EVAP pressure sensor or switch low input

Trouble code	Code identification
P0453	EVAP system pressure sensor or switch high input
P0455	EVAP system leak detected (gross leak)
P0456	EVAP system leak detected (very small leak)
P0500	Vehicle speed sensor or circuit fault
P0504	Brake switch "A" or "B" correlation
P0505	Idle air control valve or circuit fault
P050A	Cold start idle air control system performance
P0560	System voltage
P0601	Internal control memory check sum error
P0604	Random access memory (ram)
P0606	ECM/PCM processor fault
P0607	Control module performance
P060A	ICM monitoring processor performance
P060D	ICM accelerator pedal position performance
P060E	ICM throttle position performance
P0617	Starter relay circuit high
P062F	Internal Control Module EEPROM Error
P0630	VIN not programmed or mismatch - ECM/PCM
P0657	Actuator supply voltage circuit fault or open
P0705	Automatic transmission range sensor circuit failure
P0710	Automatic transaxle fluid temperature sensor or circuit fault
P0711	Automatic transaxle fluid temperature sensor range performance or circuit fault
P0724	Brake switch "B" circuit high
P0741	Automatic transmission, torque converter clutch solenoid problem
P0750 - P0751	Automatic transaxle shift solenoid A stuck open or closed
P0753	Automatic transaxle shift solenoid A circuit fault
P0755 - P0756	Automatic transaxle shift solenoid B stuck open or closed
P0765	Automatic transaxle shift solenoid D stuck open or closed
P0850	Park/Neutral switch input circuit fault
P0973 - P0974	Automatic transaxle shift solenoid A control circuit
P0976 - P0977	Automatic transaxle shift solenoid B control circuit

Diagnostic Trouble Codes (continued)

Trouble code	Code identification
P1300	Ignition system malfunction (#1 coil/igniter circuit fault)
P1305	Ignition system malfunction (#2 coil/igniter circuit fault)
P1310	Ignition system malfunction (#3 coil/igniter circuit fault)
P1315	Ignition system malfunction (#4 coil/igniter circuit fault)
P1335	Crankshaft position sensor or circuit fault
P1346	VVT (variable valve timing) sensor circuit fault
P1349	VVT (variable valve timing) system malfunction
P1520	Brake light signal malfunction
P1600	ECM battery supply malfunction
P1603	Engine Stall History
P1604	Startability Malfunction
P1605	Rough Idling
P1607	Cruise control input processor
P1656	OCV (oil control valve) circuit malfunction
P1780	Park/Neutral position switch or circuit fault
P2102	Throttle actuator control motor circuit low
P2103	Throttle actuator control motor circuit high
P2111	Throttle actuator control system - stuck open
P2112	Throttle actuator control system - stuck closed
P2118	Throttle actuator control motor current range or performance
P2119	Throttle actuator control throttle body range or performance
P2120 - P2123	Throttle or pedal position sensor or switch "D" circuit fault
P2125 - P2128	Throttle or pedal position sensor or switch "E" circuit fault
P2135	Throttle or pedal position sensor or switch "A" or "B" voltage correlation
P2138	Throttle or pedal position sensor or switch "D" or "E" voltage correlation
P2195	Oxygen (A/F) sensor signal stuck lean (bank 1 sensor 1)
P2196	Oxygen (A/F) sensor signal stuck rich (bank 1 sensor 1)
P2237	Oxygen (A/F) sensor pumping current circuit or open (bank 1 sensor 1)
P2238	Oxygen (A/F) sensor pumping current circuit low (bank 1 sensor 1)
P2239	Oxygen (A/F) sensor pumping current circuit high (bank 1 sensor 1)

Trouble code	Code identification
P2252	Oxygen (A/F) sensor reference ground circuit low (bank 1 sensor 1)
P2253	Oxygen (A/F) sensor reference ground circuit high (bank 1 sensor 1)
P2401	EVAP leak detection pump stuck off
P2402	EVAP leak detection pump stuck on
P2419	EVAP pressure switching valve stuck on
P2420	EVAP switching valve control circuit high
P2610	ECM/PCM internal engine off timer performance
P2716	Automatic transaxle, pressure control solenoid D
P2769	Automatic transaxle, DSL solenoid circuit low
P2770	Automatic transaxle, DSL solenoid circuit high
P2A00	A/F sensor circuit slow response (bank 1 sensor 1)

4   Powertrain Control Module (PCM) - removal and installation

Warning: *The models covered by this manual are equipped with a Supplemental Restraint systems (SRS), more commonly known as airbags. Always disable the airbag system before working in the vicinity of any airbag system components to avoid the possibility of accidental deployment of the airbag, which could cause personal injury (see Chapter 12).*

Caution: *To avoid electrostatic discharge damage to the PCM, handle the PCM only by its case. Do not touch the electrical terminals during removal and installation. If available, ground yourself to the vehicle with an anti-static ground strap, available at computer supply stores.*

Note: *When replacing the PCM it is recommended to be performed by a qualified repair facility. Newer vehicles require a scan tool that can read information from the old PCM and program that information into the new PCM - referred to as the "initialization procedure". Failure to do so may result in a no start condition or other issues. This procedure is for removal and installation purposes only.*

2008 and earlier models

1   The PCM is located inside the passenger compartment under the glove box **(see illustration)**.
2   Disconnect the cable from the negative battery terminal (see Chapter 5).
3   Remove the glove box (see Chapter 11).

4   Use a trim tool to pry up the two clips securing the plastic cover over the PCM.
5   Unplug the electrical connectors from the PCM.
Caution: *The ignition switch must be turned Off when pulling out or plugging in the electrical connectors to prevent damage to the PCM.*
6 Remove the two mounting screws, accessing them from the glove box area.
7   Release the two claw-clips and carefully remove the PCM.
Caution: *Avoid any static electricity damage to the computer by grounding yourself to the body before touching the PCM and using a special anti-static pad to store the PCM on once it is removed.*

8   Installation is the reverse of removal.

2009 and later models

9   The Powertrain Control Module (PCM) is located in the engine compartment, mounted to a bracket near the air filter housing.
10   Disconnect the cable from the negative battery terminal (see Chapter 5).
11   Remove the engine cover.
12   Remove the air filter cover and intake duct (see Chapter 1).
13   Remove the air filter housing bracket mounting bolts and bracket.
Caution: *The ignition switch must be turned OFF when pulling out or plugging in the electrical connectors to prevent damage to the PCM.*

4.1 PCM mounting location under the glove box (there are two push-fasteners securing the cover) (2008 and earlier models)

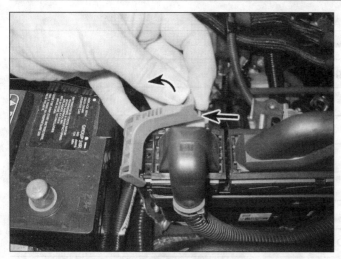

4.14a Push in the PCM connector lever locks and lift the connector lever

4.14b PCM mounting details (2009 and later models)
1   *PCM Connectors*
2   *PCM bracket-to-body mounting fasteners*
3   *Harness bracket*

14   To release the PCM connectors, push in the lever locks at the end of each lever, then pull the levers up **(see illustrations)**, then detach the connectors from the PCM.

15   Remove the air filter housing bracket fasteners, then the PCM bracket-to-body fasteners **(see illustration 4.16b)**.

16   Carefully remove the PCM and bracket. **Caution:** *Avoid any static electricity damage to the computer by grounding yourself to the body before touching the PCM and using a special anti-static pad to store the PCM on once it is removed.*

17   Remove the bracket-to-PCM mounting bolts and separate the bracket from the PCM.

18   Installation is the reverse of removal.

5   Throttle Position Sensor (TPS) and throttle control motor - replacement

1   The Throttle Position Sensor (TPS) on 2003 and 2004 models is attached to the firewall side of the throttle body **(see illustration)**. Problems with the TPS and/or motor can cause intermittent bursts of fuel from the injectors and an unstable idle because the PCM thinks the throttle is moving. The PCM is constantly comparing the driver's input from the accelerator pedal position sensor to the actual throttle position at the throttle body. A problem with the TPS circuits will set a diagnostic trouble code (see Section 3).

2   Disconnect the negative battery cable (see Chapter 5).

3   Disconnect the electrical connector at the TPS and remove the two mounting screws.

4   Installation is the reverse of removal.

5   On 2005 and later models, the throttle body is operated by an electric throttle control motor instead of a cable. One these models, the TPS is part of throttle motor assembly and cannot be replaced separately. If there are problems with the throttle control motor or the TPS, the complete throttle body must be replaced (see Chapter 4).

6   Mass Airflow (MAF) sensor - replacement

1   The Mass Airflow (MAF) sensor is located on the air filter housing. The MAF system circuit consists of a platinum hot wire, a thermistor and a control circuit inside a plastic housing. The sensor uses a hot-wire sensing element to measure the molecular mass (weight) of air entering the engine. As the throttle opens, increasing volume of air passes over the hot wire, which cools the wire. The MAF sensor circuit is designed to maintain the hot wire at a constant preset temperature by controlling the current flow through the hot wire. So, as the wire cools, the PCM increases the flow of current through the hot wire in order to maintain the wire at a constant temperature. The output voltage signal of the MAF sensor varies in accordance with this current flow. This voltage signal is measured by the PCM, which converts this signal into a digital waveform, calculates the fuel injector pulse width (duration) and turns

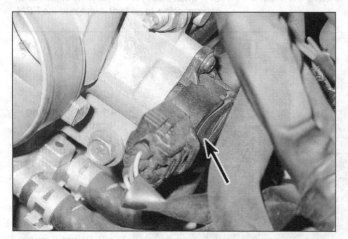

5.1 The TPS is mounted on the firewall-side of the throttle body (2003 and 2004 models)

6.3 The MAF sensor is located on the air filter housing (intake tube removed for clarity) - note the two mounting screws (A) and the electrical connector (B) (2005 model shown, others similar)

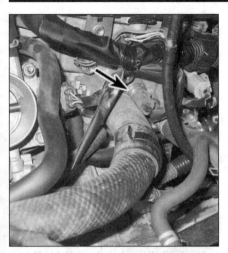

8.7 Location of the Engine Coolant Temperature sensor (2005 model shown)

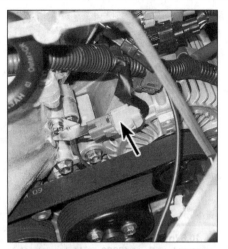

9.6 Crankshaft Position sensor with attached harness connector location shown (2005 model shown)

9.7a On 2008 and earlier models, the CKP sensor is mounted on the front side of the timing chain cover

9.7b On 2009 and later models, the Crankshaft Position sensor is mounted on the back side of the timing chain cover

the injectors on and off accordingly. A problem in the MAF sensor circuit will set a diagnostic trouble code (see Section 3). The Intake Air Temperature (IAT) sensor is part of the MAF and measures the incoming air temperature for the engine.

2   Make sure the ignition key is in the Off position.

3   Disconnect the electrical connector from the MAF sensor **(see illustration)**.

4   Remove the two sensor retaining screws and remove the MAF sensor and O-ring from the air filter housing.

5   Installation is the reverse of removal. Be sure to install a new O-ring between the MAF sensor and the filter housing.

7   Intake air temperature (IAT) sensor - replacement

1   The Intake Air Temperature (IAT) sensor is part of the Mass Airflow (MAF) sensor and replaced as one unit. See Section 6.

8   Engine Coolant Temperature (ECT) sensor - replacement

Warning: *Wait until the engine has cooled completely before performing either procedure.*

Caution: *When replacing the ECT, it is recommended to be performed by a qualified repair facility. Newer vehicles require a scan tool to perform after repair procedures - referred to as the "initialization procedure." Failure to do so may result in a no start condition or other issues.*

Caution: *Handle the coolant sensor with care. Damage to this sensor will affect the operation of the entire fuel injection system.*

1   *The ECT is located on the end of the cylinder head, above the transaxle.*

2   The engine coolant temperature (ECT)

sensor is a thermistor (a resistor which varies the value of its resistance in accordance with temperature changes). The change in the resistance values will directly affect the voltage signal from the sensor to the PCM. As the sensor temperature DECREASES, the resistance values will INCREASE. As the sensor temperature INCREASES, the resistance values will DECREASE. A problem in the ECT sensor circuit will set a diagnostic trouble code.

3   Make sure the ignition key is in the OFF position.

4   Drain approximately one gallon from the cooling system (see Chapter 1).

5   Remove components as necessary to access the sensor.

6   Disconnect the ECT sensor electrical connector.

7   Carefully unscrew the sensor **(see illustration)**.

8   Install a new seal for the ECT sensor.

9   Installation is the reverse of removal.

9   Crankshaft Position (CKP) sensor - inspection and replacement

1   The crankshaft position sensor (CKP) determines the timing for the fuel injection and ignition on each cylinder. The crankshaft sensor is mounted on the timing chain cover next to the crankshaft pulley. A problem in the crankshaft sensor circuit will set a diagnostic trouble code (see Section 3).

Inspection

2004 and earlier models

2   When cold - 14F to 122F (-10C to 50C) resistance across the CKP terminals should be 985 to 1600 ohms. When hot - 122F to 222F (50C to 100C) resistance across the CKP terminals should be 1265 to 1890 ohms.

2005 and later models

3   When cold - 14F to 122F (-10C to 50C) resistance across the CKP terminals should be 1630 to 2740 ohms. When hot - 122F to 222F (50C to 100C) resistance across the CKP terminals should be 2065 to 3225 ohms.

Replacement

Caution: *Handle the CKP sensor with care. Damage to this sensor will affect the operation of the entire fuel injection system.*

4   Loosen the right front wheel lug nuts. Disconnect the cable from the negative battery terminal (see Chapter 5).

5   Raise the front of the vehicle and support it securely on jackstands. Remove the wheel and the inner fender shield (see Chapter 10).

6   Disconnect the CKP sensor connector **(see illustration)**.

7   Remove the bolt and detach the sensor **(see illustrations)**. Some models have two bolts; one secures the sensor, the other is close by and secures the harness.

10.1 The CMP sensor is retained by one bolt to the cylinder head (connector removed for clarity) (2008 and earlier model shown)

10.8 Intake (A) and exhaust (B) CMP sensor locations (2009 and later models)

11.2a The upstream oxygen sensor (A) is located in the exhaust manifold - B is the sensor harness connector

11.2b Location of the downstream oxygen sensor

11.4 Locating the downstream O2 sensor connector inside of the vehicle (2018 model shown)

11.6 Use a slotted socket to remove the oxygen sensors

8   On models with a harness attached to the CKP, at the upper part of the timing chain cover, disconnect the harness connector and remove the harness and sensor.

9   Installation is the reverse of removal. Be sure to use a new O-ring on the sensor, lightly coated with engine oil.

10 Camshaft Position (CMP) sensor - replacement

2008 and earlier 1ZZ-FE and 2ZZ-GE engines and 2009 and later 2AZ-FE engines

1   The camshaft position sensor determines the position of the cylinder for sequential fuel injection signals to each cylinder. On 2008 and earlier 1ZZ-FE and 2ZZ-GE engines, the camshaft sensor is mounted on the cylinder head near the intake runner for cylinder no. 4 **(see illustration)**. On 2009 and later 2AZ-FE engines, the camshaft sensor

is mounted on the end of the cylinder head above the transaxle. A problem in the camshaft sensor circuit will set a diagnostic trouble code (see Section 3).

2   Make sure the ignition key is in the Off position.

3   Remove the engine cover (see Chapter 2A, Section 4).

4   Disconnect the harness connector, remove the mounting bolt and remove the camshaft sensor from the cylinder head.

5   Installation is the reverse of removal. Use a new O-ring, lightly coated with engine oil.

2009 and later 2ZR-FE and 2014 and later 2ZR-FAE engines

6   Disconnect the cable from the negative battery terminal (see Chapter 5).

7   Remove the engine cover.

8   The sensors are mounted on the top of the valve cover **(see illustration)**.

9   Disconnect the harness electrical connector.

10   Remove the mounting bolt(s) and remove the camshaft sensor(s) from the valve cover.

11   Installation is the reverse of removal.

11 Oxygen sensor and air/fuel sensor - general information and replacement

General information

1   All vehicles covered by this manual have On-Board Diagnostics II (OBD-II) engine management systems, which means that they have the ability to verify the accuracy of the basic feedback loop between the oxygen sensor and the PCM. They accomplish this by using an oxygen sensor or air/fuel sensor ahead of the catalytic converter and an oxygen sensor behind the catalytic converter. By sampling the exhaust gas before and after the catalytic converter, the PCM can determine the efficiency of the converter and can even predict when it will fail.

12.6 The knock sensor is attached with a bolt (or nut and stud) to the side of the block below the intake manifold

13.3 The VSS is located on top of the transaxle (viewed here looking straight down on the transaxle in the engine compartment)

2   The primary (upstream) oxygen sensor (bank 1, sensor 1) is located in the exhaust manifold and the secondary (downstream) oxygen sensor (bank 1, sensor 2) is located behind the catalytic converter **(see illustrations)**. The upstream oxygen sensor is also refered to as the air/fuel ratio sensor.

3   Special care must be taken whenever a sensor is serviced.

a) *Oxygen sensors and air/fuel sensors have a permanently attached pigtail and electrical connector, which should not be removed from the sensor. Damage or removal of the pigtail or electrical connector can adversely affect operation of the sensor.*

b) *Grease, dirt and other contaminants should be kept away from the electrical connector and the louvered end of the sensor.*

c) *Do not use cleaning solvents of any kind on an oxygen sensor or air/fuel ratio sensor.*

d) *Do not drop or roughly handle an oxygen sensor or air/fuel ratio sensor.*

e) *The silicone boot must be installed in the correct position to prevent the boot from being melted and to allow the sensor to operate properly.*

Replacement

Note: *Because it is installed in the exhaust manifold or pipe, which contracts when cool, the oxygen sensor may be very difficult to loosen when the engine is cold. Rather than risk damage to the sensor (assuming you are planning to reuse it in another manifold or pipe), start and run the engine for a minute or two, then shut it off. Be careful not to burn yourself during the following procedure.*

4   If you're replacing the downstream sensor, raise the vehicle and secure it on jackstands. Follow the oxygen sensor harness through the floor pan, then unplug the electrical connector inside the vehicle behind

the driver's side of the center console **(see illustration)**.

5   The upstream sensor can be replaced without raising the vehicle. Follow the harness from the sensor (mounted in the exhaust manifold) to the electrical connector, then unplug the connector.

6   Unscrew the sensor from the exhaust manifold or exhaust pipe **(see illustration)**.

Note: *The best tool for removing an oxygen sensor is a special slotted socket, especially if you're planning to reuse a sensor. If you don't have this tool, and you plan to reuse the sensor, be extremely careful when unscrewing the sensor.*

7   Apply anti-seize compound to the threads of the sensor to facilitate future removal. The threads of new sensors should already be coated with this compound, but if you're planning to reuse an old sensor, recoat the threads. Install the sensor and tighten it securely.

Caution: *Do not get anti-seize compound on the sensor tip or it could be ruined.*

8   Reconnect the electrical connector of the pigtail lead to the main wiring harness.

9   Lower the vehicle (if it was raised), test drive the car and verify that no trouble codes have been set.

12   Knock sensor - replacement

Warning: *Wait for the engine to cool completely before performing this procedure.*

1   The knock control system is designed to reduce spark knock during periods of heavy detonation. This allows the engine to use optimal spark advance to improve driveability. The knock sensor detects abnormal vibration in the engine and produces a voltage output that increases with the severity of the knock. The voltage signal is monitored by the PCM, which retards ignition timing until the detonation ceases. The knock sensor is located on the back-

side of the engine block, directly below the cylinder head (facing toward the rear of the engine compartment).

2   On all 2008 and earlier models and 2013 and earlier 2AZ-FE (2.4L) models, relieve the fuel system pressure (see Chapter 4, Section 3). On all models, disconnect the cable from the negative terminal of the battery.

3   Clamp off the coolant hoses to the throttle body (see Chapter 3).

4   Remove the intake manifold (see Chapter 2A).

5   Disconnect the electrical connector.

6   Remove the bolt or nut and knock sensor **(see illustration)**.

7   Install the knock sensor and tighten the bolt or nut to the torque in this Chapter's Specifications. Don't overtighten or damage/improper operation may occur.

8   The remainder of installation is reverse of removal.

9   Check the coolant level (see Chapter 3) and check for leaks.

13   Vehicle Speed Sensor (VSS)/Transaxle Speed Sensors - replacement

Four-speed automatic transaxle

1   Remove the air filter housing (see Chapter 4).

2   Remove the battery and battery tray (see Chapter 5).

2008 and earlier models

3   Disconnect the electrical connector from the VSS **(see illustration)**.

4   Remove the hold-down bolt and pull the VSS from the transaxle.

5   Installation is the reverse of removal. Be sure to install a new O-ring if the old sensor is installed.

13.15 Location of the input shaft speed sensor, viewed from the front with the radiator removed (CVT transaxle)

13.18 Location of the output shaft speed sensor

2009 and later models

Input shaft speed sensor

Note: *The input shaft speed sensor is located on the front side of the transaxle case.*

6   Remove the transaxle fluid dipstick tube.

7   Disconnect the electrical connector from the sensor.

8   Remove the hold-down bolt and pull the sensor from the transaxle.

9   Installation is the reverse of removal. Be sure to install a new O-ring if the old sensor is installed.

Output shaft speed sensor

Note: *The output shaft speed sensor is located on the back of the transaxle, above where the right driveaxle is inserted.*

10   Disconnect the electrical connector from the sensor.

11   Remove the hold-down bolt and pull the sensor from the transaxle.

12   Installation is the reverse of removal. Be sure to install a new O-ring if the old sensor is installed.

CVT transaxle

13   Loosen the left front wheel lug nuts, then raise the front of the vehicle and support it securely on jackstands. Remove the wheel.

14   Remove the left engine under-cover from the wheelwell.

Input shaft speed sensor

Note: *The input shaft speed sensor is located on the front side of the transaxle case, near the transaxle fluid cooler.*

15   Disconnect the electrical connector from the sensor **(see illustration)**.

16   Remove the hold-down bolt and pull the sensor from the transaxle.

17   Installation is the reverse of removal. Be sure to install a new O-ring if the old sensor is installed.

Output shaft speed sensor

Note: *The output shaft speed sensor is located on the left side of the transaxle case, near the top.*

18   Disconnect the electrical connector from the sensor **(see illustration)**.

19   Remove the hold-down bolt and pull the sensor from the transaxle.

20   Installation is the reverse of removal. Be sure to install a new O-ring if the old sensor is installed.

14   Positive Crankcase Ventilation (PCV) system

1   The Positive Crankcase Ventilation (PCV) system reduces hydrocarbon emissions by scavenging crankcase vapors. It does this by circulating fresh air from the air cleaner through the crankcase, where it mixes with blow-by gases and is then rerouted through a PCV valve to the intake manifold **(see illustrations)**.

2   The main components of the PCV system are the PCV valve and the vacuum hose connecting the valve to the intake manifold. On 2008 and earlier 1ZZ-FE and 2ZZ-GE engines and 2009 and later 2AZ-FE engines, the PCV valve is located on the valve cover. On 2009 and later 2ZR-FE and 2014 and later 2ZR-FAE engines, the PCV valve is located on the front of the engine, and requires the intake manifold to be removed to accessed and serviced. See Chapter 2A, Section 9.

3   To maintain idle quality, the PCV valve restricts the flow when the intake manifold vacuum is high. If abnormal operating conditions (such as piston ring problems) arise, the system is designed to allow excessive amounts of blow-by gases to flow back through the crankcase vent tube into the air cleaner to be consumed by normal combustion.

4   Checking and replacement of the PCV valve is covered in Chapter 1.

14.1a PCV valve location at the valve cover (2005 model shown)

14.1b PCV valve location at the oil separator (2018 model shown with intake manifold removed)

15.1 The EVAP canister is located above the rear crossmember, near the fuel tank (2018 model shown)

15.6 The purge valve is mounted in the engine compartment (2018 model shown)

15 Evaporative emissions control (EVAP) system

General description

1 The fuel evaporative emissions control (EVAP) system absorbs fuel vapors and, during engine operation, releases them into the engine intake where they mix with the incoming air-fuel mixture. The charcoal canister is mounted behind the fuel tank under the vehicle **(see illustration)**.

2 When the engine is not operating, fuel vapors are transferred from the fuel tank, throttle body and intake manifold to the charcoal canister where they are stored. When the engine is running, the fuel vapors are purged from the canister by the purge control valve. The gasses are consumed in the normal combustion process. The electronic purge control valve is directly controlled by the PCM.

3 The fuel filler cap is fitted with a two-way valve as a safety device. The valve vents fuel vapors to the atmosphere if the EVAP system fails.

4 The EVAP system also incorporates a vapor pressure sensor. This sensor detects abnormal vapor pressure in the system. The vapor pressure sensor is mounted in the fuel pump/sending unit assembly on top of the fuel tank.

5 After the engine has been running and warmed up to a pre-set temperature, the vacuum switching valve (VSV) opens. The vacuum switching valve (purge control valve) allows intake manifold vacuum to draw the fuel vapors from the canister to the intake manifold, where they are mixed with intake air before being burned with the air/fuel mixture inside the combustion chambers.

6 The fuel tank vapor pressure sensor monitors changes in pressure inside the tank and, when the pressure exceeds a preset threshold, opens a vacuum switching valve (VSV) **(see illustration)**, which allows a purge port in the canister to admit fuel tank vapors into the canister. Some models have three vacuum switching valves, two in the engine

compartment and one on the charcoal canister. Also on 2005 and later models, there is a timer in the PCM that operates the leak detection pump to check for fuel vapor leakage five hours after the vehicle has been turned off. The leak detection pump is mounted to the charcoal canister.

Replacement

Charcoal canister

7 Disconnect the cable from the negative battery terminal (see Chapter 5).

8 Raise the rear of the vehicle and support it securely on jackstands.

9 Unplug all electrical connectors and clearly label and disconnect the vent hoses to the charcoal canister, remove the bolts and separate the canister from the underside of the vehicle **(see illustration)**. For information on disconnecting the vent hoses with quick-disconnect fittings, see Chapter 4, Section 5.

10 Remove the leak detection pump and check the canister for foreign material. Turn the canister upside down and check again for foreign material. Replace the canister if any is found.

11 Installation is the reverse of removal.

Leak detection pump

12 Remove the charcoal canister from the vehicle.

13 Clean the area around the leak detection pump to prevent contamination of the canister.

14 On 2005 through 2013 models, remove the bolts securing the pump to the canister and remove the pump.

15 On 2014 and later models, release the two clips and use a small, flat-bladed screwdriver, to push the pump out of the canister **(see illustration 15.9)**.

16 Installation is the reverse of removal. Ensure the pump is fully seated into the canister.

16 Catalytic converters

Note: *Because of a Federally mandated extended warranty which covers emissions-related components such as the catalytic converter, check with a dealer service department before replacing the converter at your own expense.*

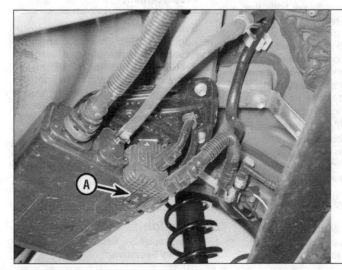

15.9 Disconnect the EVAP canister hoses and electrical connector. Two tabs (A) secure the leak detection pump the the canister (2018 model shown)

16.6 Remove the two spring-loaded bolts at the front of the catalytic converter

18.4 Identifying the oil control valves (2018 2AZ-FE model shown)

General description

1   The catalytic converter is an emission control device added to the exhaust system to reduce pollutants from the exhaust gas stream. There are two types of converters. The conventional oxidation catalyst reduces the levels of hydrocarbon (HC) and carbon monoxide (CO). The three-way catalyst lowers the levels of oxides of nitrogen (NOx) as well as hydrocarbons (HC) and carbon monoxide (CO). These models are equipped only with three-way catalytic converters.

Check

2   The test equipment for a catalytic converter is expensive and highly sophisticated. If you suspect that the converter on your vehicle is malfunctioning, take it to a dealer or authorized emissions inspection facility for diagnosis and repair.
3   Whenever the vehicle is raised for servicing of underbody components, check the converter for leaks, corrosion, dents and other damage. Check the welds/flange bolts that attach the front and rear ends of the converter to the exhaust system. If damage is discovered, the converter should be replaced.
4   Although catalytic converters don't break too often, they can become plugged. The easiest way to check for a restricted converter is to use a vacuum gauge to diagnose the effect of a blocked exhaust on intake vacuum.

   a) Connect a vacuum gauge to an intake manifold vacuum source.
   b) Warm the engine to operating temperature, place the transaxle in Park (automatic) or Neutral (manual) and apply the parking brake.
   c) Note and record the vacuum reading at idle.
   d) Quickly open the throttle to near full throttle and release it shut. Note and record the vacuum reading.

   e) Perform the test three more times, recording the reading after each test.
   f) If the reading after the fourth test is more than one in-Hg lower than the reading recorded at idle, the exhaust system may be restricted (the catalytic converter could be plugged or an exhaust pipe or muffler could be restricted).

Replacement

5   Be sure to spray the nuts on the exhaust flange studs before removing them from the front of the catalytic converter.
6   Remove the nuts and separate the catalytic converter from the exhaust manifold **(see illustration)**. The rear of the converter is welded to the exhaust pipe and must be cut off for replacement. A new converter must be welded in.
7   Installation is the reverse of removal. Install new gaskets where required.

17   Transmission Range (TR) sensor - replacement

1   Even though the Society of Automotive Engineers (SAE) has recommended since 1996 that all manufacturers refer to the Park/Neutral Position (PNP) switch as the Transmission Range (TR) sensor, Toyota continues to refer to the TR sensor as the PNP switch. To avoid confusion, we have therefore included the TR sensor/PNP switch in Chapter 7B.

18   Variable Valve Timing-intelligent system - description and component replacement

Description

1   See Chapter 2A, Section 5 for a description of the VVT-i system.

Camshaft timing oil control valve(s) replacement

Note: On 2008 and earlier 1ZZ-FE and 2ZZ-GE engines, the one oil control valve is located on the cylinder head, near the No. 1 intake runner. On 2009 and later 2AZ-FE engines, the one oil control valve is located on the back side of the valve cover, near the front of the engine. On 2009 and later 2ZR-FE and 2014 and later 2ZR-FAE engines, the two oil control valves are located on top of the valve cover, at the right end (passenger's side) of the valve cover.
2   Disconnect the cable from the negative battery terminal (see Chapter 5).
3   Remove the engine cover(s).
4   Remove the engine harness mounting fasteners and move the harness to the side. Disconnect the electrical connector(s) from the camshaft timing oil control valve(s) **(see illustration)**.
5   Remove the camshaft timing oil control valve mounting bolt(s) and remove the oil control valve(s) from the engine **(see illustration)**.
6   Installation is the reverse of removal.

19   Accelerator Pedal Position (APP) sensor - replacement

Note: The APP sensor and the accelerator pedal are removed as a single assembly
1   Disconnect the cable from the negative battery terminal (see Chapter 5).
2   On 2014 and later models, remove the dash panel below the steering column. See Chapter 11, Sections 20 and 21.
3   On all models, working under the dash, disconnect the APP sensor electrical connector **(see illustration)**.
4   Remove the accelerator pedal/APP sensor assembly mounting bolts and sensor assembly.

19.3 Typical Accelerator Pedal Position (APP) sensor details (2005 model shown)

A   APP sensor   B   Electrical connector   C   Mounting fasteners

5   Installation is the reverse of removal. Be sure to tighten the accelerator pedal assembly mounting bolts securely.

20 Manifold Absolute Pressure (MAP) sensor - removal and installation

Note: *This procedure applies to 2014 and later models with the 2ZR-FAE engine only.*
Note: *The MAP sensor is located on a bracket above the intake manifold.*
1   Remove the engine cover by pulling it straight up and off its ballstuds.
2   Disconnect the electrical connector and vacuum hose from the MAP sensor.
3   Remove the mounting bolt and detach the sensor from its bracket.
4   Installation is the reverse of the removal procedure, making sure that the protrusion on the bracket engages with the hole on the sensor.

Notes

Chapter 7 Part A
Manual transaxle

Contents

Specifications

Torque specifications
Ft-lbs (unless otherwise indicated)

Note: *One foot-pound (ft-lb) of torque is equivalent to 12 inch-pounds (in-lbs) of torque. Torque values below approximately 15 ft-lbs are expressed in inch-pounds, because most foot-pound torque wrenches are not accurate at these smaller values.*

Back-up light switch	30
Park/Neutral Position switch	30
Drain and fill plugs	
5-speed	29
6-Speed	33
Exhaust manifold brace	31
Floor pan brace nuts	
2008 and earlier	22
2009 and later	12
Shift lever mounting bolts	108 in-lbs
Subframe crossmember - 2008 and earlier models **(see illustration 5.22)**	
Bolt A	116
Bolt B	83
Bolts/nuts C	38
Balljoint bolts/nuts D	66
Transaxle-to-engine bolts **(see illustration 5.32)**	
2008 and earlier models (C50, C59, E351 and MK5)	
Bolt A	47
Bolt B	35
Bolt C	17
2009 and later models (C59, EC60, EC65)	24
Mount bracket bolts	
2008 and earlier models	47
2009 and later models	
Front bracket	47
Rear bracket	33
Left-side bracket	38

1 General information

1   The vehicles covered by this manual are equipped with either a 5-speed manual, 6-speed manual, a four-speed automatic transaxle or a Continuously Variable Transaxle (CVT). The 5-speed manual transaxles used in these models are named the C50, C59, E351, and MK5. The 6-speed manual transaxle used in these models are named the EC60 and EC65. Information on the manual transaxle is included in this Part of Chapter 7. Service procedures for the automatic transaxle are contained in Chapter 7B.

2   The manual transaxle is a compact, two-piece, lightweight aluminum alloy housing containing both the transmission and differential assemblies.

3   Because of the complexity, unavailability of replacement parts and special tools necessary, internal repair procedures for the manual transaxle are not recommended for the home mechanic. The bulk of information in this Chapter is devoted to removal and installation procedures.

2 Shift and select cables - replacement

2008 and earlier models

1   Disconnect the cable from the negative terminal of the battery.

2   Remove the center floor console (see Chapter 11).

3   Remove the large clips and disconnect the cable ends at the shifter mechanism.

4   Pull back the carpeting and remove the three bolts securing the airbag ECU to the floor and set the ECU aside.

5   Remove the plastic shield at the lower-left of the heating/air conditioning unit. Remove the nuts securing the shift cable plate and grommet to the floor.

6   Remove the large clips that secure the cable ends to the transaxle, then separate the cables from the cable bracket on the transaxle.

7   Under the vehicle, remove the two nuts securing the cable bracket to the floor, then pull

5.1 The backup light switch is threaded into the top of the transaxle case

7.15 Support the engine with an engine support fixture (these are available at most tool rental yards and some auto parts stores)

the cables/grommet through the floor and out.

8   Installation is the reverse of the removal procedure. Ensure the air bag light does not illuminate after repairs.

2009 and later models

Replacement

9   Unscrew the shift lever knob from the shift lever.

10   Remove the center console and center trim panels (see Chapter 11, Section 22).

11   Carefully pry the shift and select cable ends from the ballstuds.

12   Using a small screwdriver, pry the stop open, but not off of the control cable.

13   Rotate each of the cable housing lock nuts 180-degrees, then hold the nut in this position and disconnect the cable(s) from the bracket.

Caution: *If the lock nut is rotated more than 180-degrees, the housing will be damaged and the cable will need to be replaced.*

14   To gain access to the transaxle end of the cable, remove the battery, battery tray and carrier (see Chapter 5).

15   Remove the air filter housing (see Chapter 4).

16   Remove the wire clips that attach the cable ends to the transaxle and separate the cables from the transaxle.

17   Remove the front portion of the exhaust pipe (see Chapter 4).

18   Remove the floor heat shield mounting screws and remove the heat shield from under the vehicle.

19   Remove the cable bracket retaining nut and cable assembly nuts, and remove the cable assembly from under the vehicle.

20 Installation is the reverse of removal.

21   Adjust the select cable (see Steps 22 through 27).

Adjustment

22   If not previously done, remove the center console and disconnect the shift cable from the ballstud of the shifter. See Chapter 11, Section 22.

23   Place the transaxle in the neutral position.

Note: *Some models have a latch that locks the transaxle shift lever in position for the purpose of adjusting the cable.*

24   Place the shift lever in the neutral position.

25   Push in the two tabs at the top and bottom of the select cable lock piece. Similar to the procedure in Chapter 7B Section 3.

26   While holding the select cable lock piece in this position, push the two lugs on each side of the lock piece inwards and upwards, then pull out the lock piece.

27   With the lock piece extending out, install the select cable onto the ballstud of the shifter, then press the lock into place.

28   Installation is the reverse of removal.

---

3   Shift knob - replacement

1   Unscrew the knob to remove.

2   To install, screw the knob back on.

---

4   Shift lever - removal and installation

1   Remove the center console (see Chapter 11).

2   Remove the shift and select cable retainers and disconnect both cables from the shift lever (see Section 2).

3   Release the wiring harness clamps and detach the harness from the shift lever assembly.

4   Remove the retaining bolts and detach the shift lever assembly from the floor.

5   Installation is the reverse of removal.

---

5   Back-up light switch - check and replacement

1   The backup light switch is mounted on the transaxle **(see illustration)**. With the igni-

tion key in the On position, place the shift lever in Reverse. The back-up lights should come on.

a) *If the lights don't come on, check the ignition switch, the GAUGE fuse, the bulbs and the wire harness (see Chapter 12).*

b) *If the lights remain on all the time, even when the shift lever is not in REVERSE, the switch is most likely defective.*

c) *If only one light comes on, but not the other, check the bulb for that light and check the harness.*

2   To check the operation of the back-up light switch itself, disconnect the electrical connector and unscrew the switch from the top of the transaxle, then use an ohmmeter to verify that there's continuity when the plunger is depressed, and no continuity when the plunger is released.

3   If the switch doesn't operate as described, replace it. Disconnect the electrical connector from the switch and unscrew it from the case.

4   Test the new switch before installation by depressing the plunger with an ohmmeter connected across the switch terminals. There should be continuity only when the plunger is depressed.

5   Install the new switch and tighten it securely.

---

6   Park/neutral switch - replacement

Note: *2017 and later EC65 6-speed transaxles are equipped with a neutral position switch located on the rear of the transaxle case, below the shift lever assembly. This switch may also be referred to as a park/neutral position switch.*

1   Loosen the left-front wheel lug nuts, then raise the front of the vehicle and support it securely on jackstands. Remove the wheel.

2   Locate the switch and disconnect the electrical connector.

7.22 Remove the front suspension subframe bolts (with an overhead support for the engine and a floor jack under the transaxle) - refer to the letter designations for torque specs when installing fasteners for the subframe (A and B), engine mount crossmember (C) and the lower control arm balljoint bolts (D)

3   Using a deep socket, unsrew the switch from the transaxle case.

4   To test the switch, use a digital volt-ohm meter (DVOM) set to measure resistance (ohms). Connect the leads to the terminal of the switch and the switch body. Press and release the switch plunger. If the switch is OK, the readings on the DVOM should alternate between continuity and no continuity.

5   If the switch is to be reused, discard the gasket and install a new one.

6   Installation is reverse of removal. Tighten it securely.

7   Manual transaxle - removal and installation

2008 and earlier models
Removal

1   Place protective covers on the fenders and cowl and remove the hood (see Chapter 11).

2   Relieve the fuel system pressure (see Chapter 4).

3   Disconnect the negative cable from the battery (see Chapter 5) and drain the transaxle lubricant (see Chapter 1).

4   If the vehicle is equipped with cruise control, unplug the electrical connector for the actuator and remove the actuator (see Chapter 12).

5   Remove the battery and the battery tray (see Chapter 5).

6   Remove the air intake duct and the air filter housing (see Chapter 4).

7   Release the residual fuel pressure in the tank by removing the gas cap, then disconnect the fuel lines connecting the engine to the chassis (see Chapter 4). Plug or cap all open fittings.

8   Remove the starter (see Chapter 5).

9   Disconnect the ground cable from the transaxle.

10   Disconnect the clutch release cylinder mounting bolts from the transaxle but do NOT disconnect the hydraulic line. Remove the two mounting bolts from the clutch line bracket.

11   Clearly label, then disconnect all vacuum lines, coolant and emissions hoses, wiring harness connectors (VSS and back-up light switch) and ground straps.

12   Masking tape and/or a touch-up paint applicator work well for marking items. Take instant photos or sketch the locations of components and brackets.

13   Disconnect the shift and select cables (see Section 2).

14   Remove the exhaust manifold brace.

15   Loosen but do NOT remove the front wheel lug nuts. Also loosen the driveaxle/hub nuts (see Chapter 8). Secure the engine using an engine support fixture **(see illustration)**. Raise the front of the vehicle and support it securely on jackstands, then remove the front wheels.

Warning: *Be sure the engine/transaxle is securely supported by the support fixture. If it is not securely supported, it could fall during the removal procedure, causing injury or death.*

16   Detach the exhaust pipe from the manifold and separate the front exhaust pipe from the rear portion of the exhaust system (see Chapter). Remove the floorpan brace to allow the exhaust to drop out of the way.

17   Remove the splash shields.

18   Remove the driveaxles (see Chapter 8).

19   Disconnect the two power steering fluid lines from the steering gear. Also detach the tie-rod ends from the steering knuckles (see Chapter 10).

20   Disconnect the stabilizer bar links from the stabilizer bar (see Chapter 10).

21   Remove the bolts from the engine/transaxle mounts to the subframe (see Chapter 2A, Section 18).

22   Remove the subframe mounting bolts from the chassis, using a floor jack to lower the subframe **(see illustration)**. Be sure to note the size and location of each fastener to insure correct reassembly.

Note: *The transaxle should be supported by a floor jack immediately after the subframe is removed from the vehicle. The transaxle will tilt slightly but should remain steady if the engine is properly secured with the engine support fixture.*

23   Support the transaxle with a floor jack, preferably a floor jack with a transmission adapter head. Safety chains will help steady the transaxle on the jack.

24   Remove the transaxle-to-engine bolts.
25   Recheck to be sure nothing is connecting the engine to the vehicle or to the transaxle. Disconnect and label anything still remaining.
26   Slowly lower the transaxle assembly out of the vehicle. Keep the transaxle level as you're separating it from the engine to prevent damage to the input shaft. It may be necessary to pry the mounts away from the frame brackets.
Caution: *Do not depress the clutch pedal while the transaxle is removed from the vehicle.*
Warning: *Do not place any part of your body under the transaxle as it's being removed.*
27   Move the transaxle assembly away from the vehicle and carefully place the transaxle assembly on the floor onto wood blocks. Leave enough room for a floor jack underneath the transaxle.
28   The clutch components can now be inspected (see Chapter 8). In most cases, new clutch components should be routinely installed whenever the transaxle is removed.
29   Check the engine and transaxle mounts and the transaxle shock absorber. If any of these components are worn or damaged, replace them.

Installation

30   If removed, install the clutch components (see Chapter 8). Apply a thin film of high temperature grease to the input shaft splines and the surface of the input shaft bearing retainer.
31   With the transaxle secured to the jack as on removal, raise it into position and then carefully slide it forward, engaging the input shaft with the clutch splines. Do not use excessive force to install the transaxle - if the input shaft does not slide into place, readjust the angle of the transaxle so it is level and/or turn the input shaft so the splines engage properly with the clutch.
Caution: *Do NOT use transaxle-to-engine bolts to force the engine and transaxle into alignment. Doing so could crack or damage major components. If you experience difficulties, have an assistant help you line up the dowel pins on the block with the transaxle. Some wiggling of the engine and/or the transaxle will probably be necessary to secure proper alignment of the two.*
32   Install the transaxle-to-engine bolts and the engine-to-transaxle bolt. Tighten the bolts to the torque listed in this Chapter's Specifications **(see illustration)**.
33   Install the right engine mount, the front engine mount, the left transaxle mount and the rear engine mount. Tighten all mounting bolts and nuts securely.
34   Install the remaining components in the reverse order of removal. When installing the subframe, use a rod of the same diameter as the four subframe to-chassis bolts to align each side until that side's bolts can be inserted one at a time. Do not tighten any of the bolts until all have been installed finger-tight, then tighten them to the torque listed in this Chapter's Specifications.

7.32 Refer to these letter designations for torque specs on the transaxle-to-engine bolts (2008 and earlier models)

Front of vehicle

92036-7a-5.25 HAYNES

35   Install the wheels and lug nuts, then lower the vehicle. Tighten the lug nuts to the torque listed in the Chapter 1 Specifications. Tighten the driveaxle/hub nuts to the torque listed in the Chapter 8 Specifications.
36   Refill the transaxle with the proper lubricant (see Chapter 1).
37   Road test the vehicle to check for proper transaxle operation and check for leakage.
38   Have the wheel alignment checked and, if necessary, adjusted.

2009 and later models

Removal

39   Set the front wheels to point straight ahead and secure the steering wheel so it does not turn. Remove the front wheels.
40   Remove the battery and the battery tray (see Chapter 5, Section 4).
41   Remove the air filter housing (see Chapter 4, Section 12).
42   Remove the wiper motor (see Chapter 12, Section 12).
43   Remove the wiper cowl panels (see Chapter 11, Section 25).
44   Disconnect the shift cables from the transaxle (see Section 2).
45   Remove the Powertrain Control Module (PCM) (see Chapter 6, Section 4).
46   Disconnect the transaxle harness and connectors from the transaxle assembly. Disconnect any ground cables attached to the transaxle.
47   Disconnect the clutch hose from the clutch line and remove the clip attaching the hose to the bracket.
48   Working inside of the vehicle, remove the center console panel on the driver's side, near the accelerator pedal assembly (see Chapter #), then disconnect the rear oxygen sensor electrical connector from the opening on the side of the center console (see Chapter 6, Section 11).
49   Loosen the front wheel lug nuts and the driveaxle/hub nuts, then raise the front of the vehicle and support it securely on jackstands. Remove the wheels.

50   Remove the under-vehicle splash shield.
51   Remove the vehicle brace below the exhaust at the center of the vehicle.
52   Working under the vehicle, disconnect the harness clip and carefully pull the grommet from the floor. Pull the rear oxygen sensor connector through the opening in the floor.
53   Remove the bolts at the front and rear of the exhaust pipe, disconnect the exhaust hangers, and remove the exhaust pipe from the vehicle. Use care not to damage the oxygen sensor.
54   Drain the transaxle lubricant (see Chapter 1, Section 27), then remove the driveaxles (see Chapter 8, Section 9).
55   Secure the engine using an engine support fixture that is installed above the engine compartment **(see illustration 7.15)**.
56   Disconnect the steering shaft from the steering steering gear (see Chapter 10, Section 17).
57   Remove the front subframe (see Chapter 10).
58   Remove the center transaxle mount support brace.
59   Remove the through-bolts from the front and rear transaxle mounts and remove the mounts from the vehicle (see Chapter 2A, Section 18).
60   Remove the flywheel inspection cover.
61   Remove the starter (see Chapter 5, Section 9).
62   Remove the left transaxle mount through-bolt and remove the chassis side of the mount from the vehicle (see Chapter 2A, Section 18).
63   Support the transaxle with a floor jack, preferably a floor jack with a transmission adapter head. Safety chains will help steady the transaxle on the jack.
64   Remove the transaxle-to-engine bolts.
65   Recheck to be sure nothing is connecting the engine to the vehicle or to the transaxle. Disconnect and label anything still remaining.
66   Slide the transaxle out of the engine and slowly lower the transaxle out of the vehicle. Keep the transaxle level as you're separating

it from the engine to prevent damage to the input shaft.

Caution: *Do not depress the clutch pedal while the transaxle is removed from the vehicle.*

Warning: *Do not place any part of your body under the transaxle as it's being removed.*

67   Move the transaxle assembly away from the vehicle and carefully place it on the floor onto wood blocks. Leave enough room for a floor jack underneath the transaxle.

68   The clutch components can now be inspected (see Chapter 8, Section 3). In most cases, new clutch components should be routinely installed whenever the transaxle is removed.

69   Replace the clutch release cylinder at this time if necessary (see Chapter 8, Section 6).

70   Check the engine and transaxle mounts. If any of these components are worn or damaged, replace them.

71   If the transaxle is to be replaced, transfer any components over to the new transaxle from the old one.

Installation

72   Apply a thin film of high temperature grease to the input shaft splines and the surface of the input shaft bearing retainer.

73   With the transaxle secured to the jack as on removal, raise it into position and then carefully slide it forward, engaging the input shaft with the clutch splines. Do not use excessive force to install the transaxle - if the input shaft does not slide into place, readjust the angle of the transaxle so it is level and/or turn the input shaft so the splines engage properly with the clutch.

Caution: *Do NOT use transaxle-to-engine bolts to force the engine and transaxle into alignment. Doing so could crack or damage*

major components. If you experience difficulties, have an assistant help you line up the dowel pins on the block with the transaxle. Some wiggling of the engine and/or the transaxle will probably be necessary to secure proper alignment of the two.

74   The remainder of the installation is reverse of removal, noting the following points:

a) *Tighten all fasteners to the torque listed in this Chapter's Specifications.*

b) *Bleed the clutch hydraulic system (see Chapter 8, Section 7).*

c) *Refill the transaxle with the proper lubricant (see Chapter 1).*

d) *Adjust the shift cable (see Section 2).*

e) *Road test the vehicle to check for proper transaxle operation and check for leakage.*

f) *Have the wheel alignment checked and, if necessary, adjusted.*

8   Manual transaxle overhaul - general information

1   Overhauling a manual transaxle is a difficult job for the do-it-yourselfer. It involves the disassembly and reassembly of many small parts. Numerous clearances must be precisely measured and, if necessary, changed with select-fit spacers and snap-rings. As a result, if transaxle problems arise, it can be removed and installed by a competent do-it-yourselfer, but overhaul should be left to a transmission repair shop. Rebuilt transaxles may be available - check with your dealer parts department and auto parts stores. At any rate, the time and money involved in an overhaul is almost sure to exceed the cost of a rebuilt unit.

2   Nevertheless, it's not impossible for an inexperienced mechanic to rebuild a transaxle if the special tools are available and the job is done in a deliberate step-by-step manner so nothing is overlooked.

3   The tools necessary for an overhaul include internal and external snap-ring pliers, a bearing puller, a slide hammer, a set of pin punches, a dial indicator and possibly a hydraulic press. In addition, a large, sturdy workbench and a vise or transaxle stand will be required.

4   During disassembly of the transaxle, make careful notes of how each component was removed, where it fits in relation to other components and what holds it in place. Noting how they are installed when you remove the components will make it much easier to get the transaxle back together correctly.

5   Before taking the transaxle apart for repair, it will help if you have some idea what area of the transaxle is malfunctioning. Certain problems can be closely tied to specific areas in the transaxle, which can make component examination and replacement easier. Refer to the *Troubleshooting* section at the front of this manual for information regarding possible sources of trouble.

9   Manual transaxle mounts - inspection and replacement

1   Checking the condition of and replacing the transaxle mounts is covered in Chapter 2A, Section 18.

Warning: *When replacing any of the mounts, be sure to properly support the drivetrain using a jack or suitable engine support tool to prevent injury or damage to components.*

Notes

Chapter 7 Part B
Automatic transaxle

Contents

Specifications

Torque specifications   Ft-lbs (unless otherwise indicated)

Note: *One foot-pound (ft-lb) of torque is equivalent to 12 inch-pounds (in-lbs) of torque. Torque values below approximately 15 ft-lbs are expressed in inch-pounds, because most foot-pound torque wrenches are not accurate at these smaller values.*

Drain plug	See Chapter 1
Fluid pressure sensor (CVT transaxle)	15
Subframe crossmember	See Chapter 10

Transaxle-to-engine bolts **(see illustrations 7.21a and 7.21b)**

2008 and earlier models

Bolt A	47
Bolt B	34
Bolt C	17

2009 and later models

Bolt A	47
Bolt B	34
Bolt C	34
Bolt D	32

Torque converter-to-driveplate bolts

2008 and earlier models	20
2009 and later models	30

1   General information

1   Information on the automatic transaxle is included in this Part of Chapter 7. Service procedures for the manual transaxle are contained in Chapter 7A. Automatic transaxles available in these models are as follows:

a) *Four-speed: A245E, A246e, U240E, U241E, U341E*
b) *Five-speed: U250E*
c) *CVTi: K313*

2   Due to the complexity of the automatic transaxles covered in this manual and to the specialized equipment necessary to perform most service operations, this Chapter contains only those procedures related to general diagnosis, routine maintenance, adjustment and removal and installation.

3   If the transaxle requires major repair work, it should be left to a dealer service department or an automotive or transmission shop. You can, however, remove and install the transaxle yourself and save the expense, even if a transmission shop does

the repair work (but be sure a proper diagnosis has been made before removing the transaxle).

2   Diagnosis - general

1   Automatic transaxle malfunctions may be caused by five general conditions:

a) *Poor engine performance*
b) *Improper adjustments*
c) *Hydraulic malfunctions*
d) *Mechanical malfunctions*
e) *Malfunctions in the computer or its signal network*

2   Diagnosis of these problems should always begin with a check of the easily repaired items: fluid level and condition (see Chapter) and shift cable adjustment. Next, perform a road test to determine if the problem has been corrected or if more diagnosis is necessary. If the problem persists after the preliminary tests and corrections are completed, additional diagnosis should be done by a dealer service department or

transmission shop. Refer to the *Trouble-shooting* section at the front of this manual for information on symptoms of transaxle problems.

Preliminary checks

3   Drive the vehicle to warm the transaxle to normal operating temperature.

4   Check the fluid level as described in Chapter 1.

a) *If the fluid level is unusually low, add enough fluid to bring the level within the designated area of the dipstick, then check for external leaks (see below).*
b) *If the fluid is foaming, drain it and refill the transaxle, then check for coolant in the fluid, or a high fluid level.*

5   Check for any stored Diagnostic Trouble Codes (DTCs) (see Chapter 6).

Note: *If the engine is malfunctioning, do not proceed with the preliminary checks until it has been repaired and runs normally.*

6   Inspect the shift cable (see Section 3). Make sure that it's properly adjusted and that it operates smoothly.

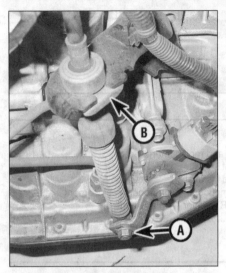

3.3 Before adjusting the shift cable, loosen the nut (A) that connects the shift cable to the manual lever on the transaxle - B is the clip securing the cable to the bracket on the transaxle (2008 and earlier models)

3.4 To adjust the shift cable, push the manual lever all the way DOWN, return it two clicks to the Neutral position, place the shift lever inside the vehicle at the Neutral position and tighten the swivel nut (2008 and earlier models)

3.10 Detach the shift cable from the ballstud

Fluid leak diagnosis

7   Most fluid leaks are easy to locate visually. Repair usually consists of replacing a seal or gasket. If a leak is difficult to find, the following procedure may help.

8   Identify the fluid. Make sure it's transmission fluid and not engine oil or brake fluid (most automatic transmission fluid is a deep red color).

9   Try to pinpoint the source of the leak. Drive the vehicle several miles, then park it over a large sheet of cardboard. After a minute or two, you should be able to locate the leak by determining the source of the fluid dripping onto the cardboard.

10   Make a careful visual inspection of the suspected component and the area immediately around it. Pay particular attention to gasket mating surfaces. A mirror is often helpful for finding leaks in areas that are hard to see.

11   If the leak still cannot be found, clean the suspected area thoroughly with a degreaser or solvent, then dry it.

12   Drive the vehicle for several miles at normal operating temperature and varying speeds. After driving the vehicle, visually inspect the suspected component again.

13   Once the leak has been located, the cause must be determined before it can be properly repaired. If a gasket is replaced but the sealing flange is bent, the new gasket will not stop the leak. The bent flange must be straightened.

14   Before attempting to repair a leak, check to make sure that the following conditions are corrected or they may cause another leak.

Note: *Some of the following conditions cannot be fixed without highly specialized tools and expertise. Such problems must be referred to a transmission shop or a dealer service department.*

Gasket leaks

15   Check the pan periodically. Make sure the bolts are tight, no bolts are missing, the gasket is in good condition and the pan is flat (dents in the pan may indicate damage to the valve body inside).

16   If the pan gasket is leaking, the fluid level or the fluid pressure may be too high, the vent may be plugged, the pan bolts may be too tight, the pan sealing flange may be warped, the sealing surface of the transaxle housing may be damaged, the gasket may be damaged or the transaxle casting may be cracked or porous. If sealant instead of gasket material has been used to form a seal between the pan and the transaxle housing, it may be the wrong sealant.

Seal leaks

17   If a transaxle seal is leaking, the fluid level or pressure may be too high, the vent may be plugged, the seal bore may be damaged, the seal itself may be damaged or improperly fitted, the surface of the shaft protruding through the seal may be damaged or a loose bearing may be causing excessive shaft movement.

18   Make sure the dipstick tube seal is in good condition and the tube is properly seated. Periodically check the area around the vehicle speed sensor for leakage. If fluid is evident, check the O-ring for damage.

Case leaks

19   If the case itself appears to be leaking, the casting is porous and will have to be repaired or replaced.

20   Make sure the oil cooler hose fittings are tight and in good condition.

Fluid comes out vent pipe or fill tube

21   If this condition occurs, the transaxle is overfilled, there is coolant in the fluid, the case is porous, the dipstick is incorrect, the vent is plugged or the drain-back holes are plugged.

3   Shift cable - adjustment and replacement

Warning: *The models covered by this manual are equipped with a Supplemental Restraint System (SRS), more commonly known as airbags. Always disable the airbag system before working in the vicinity of the impact sensors, steering column or instrument panel to avoid the possibility of accidental deployment of the airbag, which could cause personal injury (see Chapter 12).*

Adjustment

2008 and earlier models

1   When the shift lever inside the vehicle is moved from the Neutral position to other positions, it should move smoothly and accurately to each position and the shift indicator should indicate the correct gear position.

2   If the indicator isn't aligned with the correct position, adjust the shift cable as follows:

3   Loosen the nut on the manual shift lever at the transaxle **(see illustration)**.

4   Move the manual lever down into Park (counterclockwise), then return it (clockwise) two notches to the Neutral position **(see illustration)**.

5   Move the shift lever inside the vehicle to the Neutral position.

6   While holding the lever with a slight force toward the Reverse position, tighten the swivel nut securely.

7   Check the operation of the transaxle in each shift lever position (try to start the engine in each gear - the starter should operate in the Park and Neutral positions only).

3.11 To remove the shift cable from the bracket

1   Pull up the cable lock
2   Rotate the collar 180 degrees counter-clockwise

3.12 Pull the lock piece out toward the driver's side (shown attached to the ballstud for reference only)

3.20 Remove the three bolts at the airbag ECU (two are shown here) and set the unit aside - the shift cable is under the ECU (2008 and earlier models)

2009 and later models

8   Place the shift lever in the neutral position.

9   Remove the center console and center trim panels (see Chapter 11).

10   Carefully pry the control cable end from the shift lever ballstud (see illustration).

11   Pull upwards on the cable lock and rotate the collar to the rear of the lock 180-degrees counterclockwise. Hold in that position and remove the cable from the bracket (see illustration).

12   Push in the two tabs at the top and bottom of the control cable lock piece. While holding the control cable lock piece in this position, push the two lugs on each side of the lock piece inwards and upwards, then pull out the lock piece (see illustration).

13   Rotate the collar again 180-degrees counterclockwise (the spring is at the bottom of the collar). Hold in this position and press the cable lock until it clicks two times.

14   Install the shift cable into the bracket. The collar will lock the cable into place when installed. Verify the spring is at the top of the collar and press the cable lock down.

15   Install the control cable onto the shift lever ballstud, and press the lock into place.

16   Verify proper shift cable and lever operation.

Replacement

2008 and earlier models

17   Remove the battery and battery tray (see Chapter 5, Section 4).

18   Disconnect the cable from the manual lever and remove the large C-clip cable

retainer from the bracket above the manual lever (see illustration 3.3).

19   Remove the floor console, then pull back the carpeting at the front of the floor tunnel (see Chapter 11, Section 22).

20   Remove the bolts securing the airbag ECU to the floor and set it aside (see illustration).

21   Remove the bolts from the cable housing retainer on the floor inside the vehicle (see illustration).

22   Pry off the cable ends from the shift housing and disconnect the cable eye from the shifter (see illustration).

23   Pull the cable and grommet through the floor pan.

24   Installation is the reverse of removal.

25   Adjust the cable (see Adjustment in this section).

3.21 To detach the cable boot seal from the floor under the heater housing, remove the mounting bolts (2008 and earlier models)

3.22 To detach the shift cables from the shift lever assembly, twist the flange (A) to release its clips, then remove the clips and pry the cable eye (B) from the shifter arm (2008 and earlier models)

6.6 Remove the manual shift lever retaining nut (A), disconnect the electrical connector (B), and remove the mounting bolts (C) (2005 model shown; others similar)

6.10 Detach the manual lever, then loosen the switch retaining bolts (A) - the flat on the shaft (B) and the pointer (C) should align with the neutral line on the switch (D) when installing the switch (2005 model shown; others similar)

2009 and later models

26   Remove the center console to expose the shift lever and the location where the shift cable runs through the floor. See Chapter 11, Section 22.

27   Place the shift lever in Neutral (N).

28   Pry the shift cable from the shift lever assembly **(see illustration 3.10)**.

29   Pull upwards on the cable lock and rotate the collar to the rear of the lock 180-degrees counterclockwise and remove the cable from the bracket **(see illustration 3.11)**.

30   Remove the air filter housing to access the shift cable at the transaxle (see Chapter 4, Section 12).

31   On 2014 and later models, remove the battery and battery tray (see Chapter 5, Section 4).

32   On all models, remove the nut attaching the shift cable to the transaxle shift lever.

33   Remove the clip and the shift cable from the bracket on the transaxle.

34   Raise the vehicle and support it securely on jackstands.

35   Remove the engine under-cover.

36   Remove the front portion of the exhaust system. Disconnect the oxygen sensor connectors prior to removing to prevent damage to the sensors or harness (see Chapter 6, Section 11).

37   Remove the heat shield from the tunnel.

38   Remove the nut and the cable bracket from the engine mount.

39   Remove the two nuts attaching the cable grommet to the body and pull the cable out though the bottom of the vehicle.

40   Installation is reverse of removal.

41   Adjust the cable (see *Adjustment* in this section).

4   Shift knob - replacement

Warning: *The models covered by this manual are equipped with a Supplemental Restraint*

System (SRS), more commonly known as airbags. Always disable the airbag system before working in the vicinity of the impact sensors, steering column or instrument panel to avoid the possibility of accidental deployment of the airbag, which could cause personal injury (see Chapter 12).

2007 and earlier models

1   Remove the center console (see Chapter 11).

2   Locate the 4-pin connector at the driver's rear of the shift lever assembly.

3   Disengage the terminal lock on the connector and pull out pins No. 2 and 4.

4   Remove the two screws on the front of the shift knob base.

5   Pull the shift knob up and carefully pull the wire and connector out with it.

6   Pull down on the shift knob lower cover to remove from the shift knob.

7   Use a screwdriver to carefully pry out the transmission control switch on the shift knob. **Caution:** *Use care as when the transmission control switch is removed; the shift knob button and spring may fly out.*

8   Installation is reverse of removal.

9   Ensure the pins are in the proper locations on the connector and the terminal lock is engaged.

2008 and later models

10   On CVT models, carefully detach the shift boot from the bottom of the shift knob.

11   On all models, unscrew the knob to remove.

12   To install, screw the knob back on.

5   Shift lever - removal and installation

Warning: *The models covered by this manual are equipped with a Supplemental Restraint System (SRS), more commonly known as*

airbags. *Always disable the airbag system before working in the vicinity of the impact sensors, steering column or instrument panel to avoid the possibility of accidental deployment of the airbag, which could cause personal injury (see Chapter 12).*

1   Remove the center console (see Chapter 11, Section 22).

2   Remove the shift knob (see Section 4).

3   Pry the shift cable end from the shift lever assembly **(see illustration 3.10)**.

4   On 2008 and earlier models, press inwards on the shift cable retainers and remove from the bracket.

5   On 2009 and later models, pull upwards on the cable lock and rotate the collar to the rear of the lock 180-degrees counterclockwise and remove the cable from the bracket **(see illustration 3.11)**.

6   On 2008 and earlier models, pry the shift interlock cable from the shift lever assembly. Press inwards on the shift interlock cable retainers and remove from the bracket.

7   On all models, disconnect the electrical connectors and harness clips from the shift lever assembly.

8   Remove the four bolts and remove the shift lever from the vehicle.

9   Installation is reverse of removal.

10   Adjust the shift cable and verify proper operation (see Section 3).

6   Transmission Range (TR) sensor - replacement and adjustment

1   The Transmission Range sensor is also referred to as the Park/Neutral Position switch. The transmission range sensor incorporates the Park/Neutral function as well as the back-up light switch and inputs transmission gear position information to the PCM. The Park/Neutral function of the switch prevents the engine from starting in any gear other than Park or Neutral. If

7.3 Locating the fluid pressure sender on CVT models (2018 model shown)

8.3 Disconnect the shift lock cable at the shifter end - squeeze the clip (A), then pry the cable eye off the stud (B)

8.4 Use a screwdriver to release the clip securing the cable at the top of the ignition lock cylinder housing on the steering column

the engine starts with the shift lever in any position other than Park or Neutral, adjust the switch. The transmission position switch is also an information sensor for the Electronic Controlled Transaxle (ECT) Powertrain Control Module (PCM). When the shift lever is placed in position, the Park/Neutral position switch sends a voltage signal to the PCM.

Replacement

2   On 2008 and earlier models, remove the battery and battery tray (see Chapter 5, Section 4).
3   On 2009 through 2013 models, remove the driver's side engine under cover.
4   On 2014 and later models, remove air filter housing, the battery and the battery tray (see Chapter 4, Section 12 and Chapter 5, Section 4).
5   On all models, disconnect the electrical connector.
6   Remove the manual lever retaining nut and its lock plate (see illustration).
Note: If equipped, bend the tabs flat on the lock plate before removing it.
7   Disconnect the electrical connector from the switch.
8   Remove the retaining bolts and the switch (see illustration 6.6).
9   Installation is the reverse of removal. Be sure to adjust the switch.

Adjustment

10   Loosen the switch retaining bolts and rotate the switch until the flat on the shaft and the neutral basic line on the switch are aligned (see illustration). Hold the switch in this position and tighten the bolts.
Note: The pointer on the sheetmetal lock plate will indicate the alignment of the flat on the shaft with the neutral line on the body of the switch.
11   Refer to Section 3 for the cable adjustment procedure.

7   Fluid pressure sensor - replacement

Note: CVT model transaxles are equipped with a fluid pressure sensor located on the side of the transaxle case.
1   Loosen the left-front wheel lug nuts, then raise the front of the vehicle and support it securely on jackstands. Remove the wheel.
2   Remove the Left-side engine under cover to access the side of the transaxle.
3   Locate the fluid pressure sensor and disconnect the electrical connector (see illustration).
4   Unscrew the sensor from the transaxle case.
5   Installation is reverse of removal. Be sure to use a new O-ring and lubricate it with clean CVT fluid. Tighten the sensor to the torque listed in this Chapter's Specifications.

8   Shift lock system - description and component replacement

Warning: The models covered by this manual are equipped with a Supplemental Restraint System (SRS), more commonly known as airbags. Always disable the airbag system before working in the vicinity of the impact sensors, steering column or instrument panel to avoid the possibility of accidental deployment of the airbag, which could cause personal injury (see Chapter 12).
Note: 2008 and earlier models are equipped with a cable operated shift interlock system.

Description

1   The shift lock system prevents the shift lever from being shifted out of Park until the brake pedal is applied. The system consists of the brake light switch, a key interlock cable, a shift lock override button, a shift lock solenoid, and a shift lock control computer.

Component replacement

2   Remove the center console (see Chapter 11).
3   To disconnect the cable, push in the locking tab and separate the cable end (see illustration).
4   Remove the steering column covers (see Chapter 11, Section 21). Where the cable mounts at the steering column, disconnect the clip and detach the cable from the lock cylinder housing (see illustration).
Note: Whenever this end of the cable is connected or disconnected, the ignition switch must be in the ACC position.
5   The shift lock control computer is located at the bottom of the shift lever base on the right side (see illustration). Disconnect the electrical connector and unclip the shift-lock computer from the shifter assembly.
6   Installation is the reverse of removal.

8.5 Shift lock system computer location

9.4 Carefully pry out the old driveaxle seal with a prybar, screwdriver or a special seal removal tool; make sure you don't gouge or nick the surface of the seal bore

9.6 Drive in the new driveaxle seal with a large socket or a special seal installer

9   Oil seal replacement

1   Fluid leaks frequently occur due to wear of the driveaxle oil seals and/or the vehicle speed sensor/transmission speed sensor(s) O-ring(s). Replacement of these seals/O-rings is relatively easy, since the repairs can be performed without removing the transaxle from the vehicle.

Driveaxle seals

2   The driveaxle oil seals are located in either side of the transaxle, where the driveaxle shaft is splined into the differential. If leakage at the seal is suspected, raise the vehicle and support it securely on jackstands. If the seal is leaking, fluid will be found on the side of the transaxle.
3   Remove the driveaxle assembly (see Chapter 8).
4   Using a screwdriver or prybar, carefully pry the oil seal out of the transaxle bore **(see illustration)**.
5   If the oil seal cannot be removed with a screwdriver or prybar, a special oil seal removal tool (available at auto parts stores) will be required.
6   Using a seal driver (preferably) or a large deep socket as a drift, install the new oil seal. Drive it into the bore squarely and make sure that it is completely seated **(see illustration)**. Lubricate the lip of the new seal with multi-purpose grease.
7   Install the driveaxle assembly (see Chapter 8). Be careful not to damage the lip of the new seal.

Speed sensor

8   The vehicle speed sensor/transmission speed sensor(s) is/are located on the case of the transaxle. Look for lubricant around the sensor housing to determine if an O-ring is leaking.
9   Disconnect the electrical connector from

the vehicle or transmission speed sensor and remove it from the transaxle (see Chapter 6).
10   Remove the O-ring or gasket from the sensor.
11   Install a new O-ring or gasket, as applicable, and reinstall the sensor. Tighten the hold-down bolt securely.

10   Automatic transaxle - removal and installation

Note: *This procedure applies to 2008 and earlier models and 2014 and later models only. On 2009 through 2013 models, the manufacturer recommends removing the engine and transaxle as an assembly (see Chapter 2A).*

2008 and earlier models

Removal

1   Place protective covers on the fenders and cowl and remove the hood (see Chapter 11).
2   Relieve the fuel system pressure (see Chapter 4), and drain the transaxle fluid (see Chapter 1).
3   Remove the battery and the battery tray (see Chapter 5).
4   Remove the air filter housing (see Chapter 4).
5   Remove the fluid cooler hoses from the rigid lines at the transaxle. Be sure to position a pan below the line connections to catch any residual fluid. From the fluid cooler lines, remove the bolts and bracket securing the transmission fluid filler pipe to the cooler lines, then pull the filler tube from the transmission case.
6   Disconnect the transmission range sensor electrical connector (see Section 6).
7   Disconnect the electrical connector(s) from the Vehicle Speed Sensor (VSS) or transaxle speed sensors (see Chapter 6, Section 13).

8   Clearly label, then disconnect all vacuum lines, hoses, wiring harness connectors and ground straps. Masking tape and/or a touch-up paint applicator works well for marking items. Take instant photos or sketch the locations of components and brackets.
9   Disconnect the shift cable from the transaxle (see Section 3).
10   Loosen but do NOT remove the front wheel lug nuts. Also loosen the driveaxle/hub nuts (see Chapter 8). Secure the engine using an engine support fixture **(see illustration)**. Raise the vehicle and support it securely on jackstands, then remove the front wheels.
Warning: *Be sure the engine/transaxle is securely supported by the support fixture. If it is not securely supported, it could fall during the removal procedure, causing injury or death.*
11   Remove the under-vehicle splash shields.
12   Remove the starter (see Chapter 5).
13   Detach the exhaust pipe from the manifold (see Chapter 4). Remove the floor pan brace under the car and drop the exhaust system out of the way.
14   Disconnect the two power steering fluid lines from the steering gear. Also separate the tie-rod ends from the steering knuckles (see Chapter 10).
15   Disconnect the stabilizer bar links from the bar (see Chapter 10).
16   Remove the stabilizer bar bracket bolts (see Chapter 10).
17   Remove the bolts from the engine/transaxle mounts to the subframe (see Chapter 2A, Section 18).
18   Remove the subframe mounting bolts from the chassis, using a floor jack to lower the subframe. Be sure to note the size and location of each nut and bolt to insure correct reassembly.
19   Support the transaxle with an approved transaxle jack and safety chains. Floor jacks are often not stable enough to support and lower the transaxle from the vehicle.
Note: *The transaxle should be supported immediately after the subframe is removed*

10.10 Support the engine with an engine support fixture (these are available at most tool rental yards and some auto parts stores)

10.20 Remove the torque converter-to-driveplate bolts - rotate the engine by hand to gain access to successive bolts - also seen clearly here are the lower transaxle-to-engine bolts

from the vehicle. The transaxle will tilt slightly but should remain steady if the engine is properly secured with the engine compartment brace.

20   Remove the access cover in the bellhousing and rotate the engine until all of the six converter-to-driveplate bolts can be removed **(see illustration)**. Have an assistant keep the engine from turning by using a socket and breaker bar on the crankshaft pulley bolt.

21   Remove the transaxle-to-engine bolts **(see illustrations)**.

22   Recheck to be sure nothing is connecting the engine to the vehicle or to the transaxle. Disconnect and label anything still remaining.

23   Slowly lower the transaxle assembly out of the vehicle. Keep the transaxle level as you're separating it from the engine to prevent damage to the input shaft.

Caution: *Do not allow the transaxle to tilt for-*

ward very much (toward the engine) or the converter may slide out.

Warning: *Do not place any part of your body under the transaxle assembly when it's being removed.*

24   Check the engine and transaxle mounts and the transaxle shock absorber. If any of these components are worn or damaged, replace them.

Installation

25   If removed, install the torque converter on the transaxle input shaft. Make sure the converter hub splines are properly engaged with the splines on the transaxle input shaft.

26   With the transaxle secured to the jack as on removal, and with an assistant holding the torque converter in place, raise the transaxle into position and turn the converter to align the bolt holes in the converter with the bolt holes in the driveplate. Install the converter-to-driveplate bolts, starting with

the green bolt. Do not use excessive force to install the transaxle - if something binds and the transaxle won't mate with the engine, alter the angle of the transaxle slightly until it does mate.

Note: *Install all of the bolts before tightening any of them.*

27   Install the transaxle-to-engine bolts. Tighten the bolts to the torque listed in this Chapter's Specifications **(see illustration 10.21a or 10.21b)**.

Caution: *Do NOT use transaxle-to-engine bolts to force the engine and transaxle into alignment. Doing so could crack or damage major components. If you experience difficulties, have an assistant help you line up the dowel pins on the block with the transaxle. Some wiggling of the engine and/or the transaxle will probably be necessary to secure proper alignment of the two.*

28   Install the right engine mount, the front engine mount, the left transaxle mount and

Front of vehicle

92036-7a-5.25 HAYNES

10.21a Transaxle-to-engine mounting bolts (2008 and earlier models)

Front of vehicle

92009-7A-5.16 HAYNES

10.21b Transaxle-to-engine mounting bolts (2009 and later models)

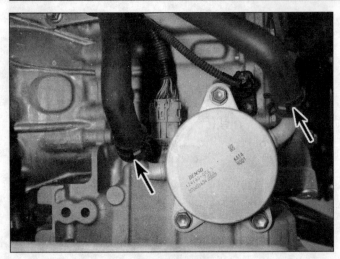

10.45 Disconnect the oil cooler coolant hoses on CVT models
(2018 model shown)

10.59 Pull off the inspection cover, then remove the torque
converter-to-driveplate bolts - rotate the engine by hand
to gain access to successive bolts

the rear engine mount. Tighten all mounting bolts and nuts securely.

29   Reinstall the remaining components in the reverse order of removal. When installing the subframe, use a rod of the same diameter as the four subframe-to-chassis bolts to align each side until that side's bolts can be inserted and started. Do not tighten any of the four bolts until all have been installed finger-tight, then tighten to the torque listed in this Chapter's Specifications **(see illustration 5.22 in Chapter 7A)**.

30   Remove the jack and support fixture and lower the vehicle. Tighten the wheel lug nuts to the torque listed in the Chapter 1 Specifications.

31   Add the specified amount of new transaxle fluid (see Chapter 1).

32   Connect the negative battery cable. Road test the vehicle to check for proper transmission operation and check for leakage.

33   Recheck the fluid level.

34   It is recommended to have the vehicle aligned since the front suspension was removed. **Note:** *Since this an electronically-controlled transaxle, the manufacturer recommends that when a transaxle has been replaced, you should take the vehicle to a dealer or other service facility with a scan tool to perform a "reset memory" procedure for optimum transmission performance.*

2009 through 2013 models

35   On 2009 through 2013 models, the manufacturer recommends removing the engine and transaxle as an assembly (see Chapter 2B, Section 7).

2014 and later models

Removal

36   Set the front wheels pointing straight and secure the steering wheel so it cannot rotate.

37   Disconnect the cable from the negative battery terminal (see Chapter 5, Section 3).

38   Remove the wiper motor (see Chapter 12, Section 12) and cowl (see Chapter 11, Section 25).

39   Remove the under-vehicle splash shields.

40   Remove the engine cover and the air filter housing (see Chapter 4, Section 12).

41   Remove the battery and battery tray (see Chapter 5, Section 4).

42   Disconnect the shift cable at the transaxle shift lever and cable housing bracket (see Section 3).

43   Remove the bolt and disconnect the ground cable at the transaxle case and detach from the transaxle mount.

44   Disengage the clamp and detach the vent hose from the bracket. On CVT models, disconnect and remove the hose from the transaxle.

45   On CVT models, disconnect the coolant hoses from the transaxle oil cooler **(see illustration)**.

46   Working inside of the vehicle, remove the center console panel on the driver's side, near the accelerator pedal assembly (see Chapter 11).

47   From inside of the vehicle, disconnect the rear O2 sensor electrical connector from the opening on the side of the center console **(see illustration 11.2** in Chapter 6).

48   Loosen the front wheel lug nuts and driveaxle/hub nuts, then raise the front of the vehicle and support it securely on jackstands. Remove the wheels.

49   Remove the under-vehicle splash shields.

50   Working under the vehicle, remove the clips and the left vehicle undercover from the fenderwell.

51   Disconnect the transaxle harness retainers and connectors at the speed sensor, park/neutral switch and transaxle case.

52   Drain the coolant and the transaxle fluid (see Chapter 1, Section 26).

53   Remove the brace below the exhaust at

the center of the vehicle.

54   Working under the vehicle, disconnect the harness clip and carefully pull the grommet from the floor. Pull the rear O2 sensor connector through the opening in the floor.

55   Remove the bolts at the front and rear of the exhaust pipe, disconnect the exhaust hangers, and remove the exhaust pipe from the vehicle. Use care not to damage the O2 sensor.

56   Remove the left and right driveaxles (see Chapter 8, Section 9).

57   Remove the starter (see Chapter 5, Section 9).

58   Remove the driveplate inspection cover.

59   Remove the driveplate-to-torque converter bolts. Use the tool to rotate the engine to remove the next bolt **(see illustration)**.

60   On non-CVT models, disconnect the transaxle cooler hoses from the fittings at the transaxle case.

61   Remove the bolt and the bracket securing the transaxle cooler lines.

62   Remove the transaxle dipstick tube bracket bolt, and pull the dipstick tube straight up and out. Inspect the O-ring and replace as necessary.

63   On all models, secure the engine using an engine support fixture **(see illustration 10.12)**. **Warning:** *Be sure the engine/transaxle is securely supported by the support fixture. If it is not securely supported, it could fall during the removal procedure, causing injury or death.*

64   Disconnect the steering column shaft from the steering gear (see Chapter 10, Section 17).

65   Remove the center transaxle mount support brace and front and rear engine mounts **(see illustration)**.

66   Remove the subframe (see Chapter 10, Section 21).

67   Remove the left transaxle mount through-bolt and remove the chassis side of the mount from the vehicle **(see illustration)**.

10.65 Identifying the center transaxle mount support brace (2018 model shown)

10.67 Remove the through-bolt from the transaxle mount

68 Support the transaxle with a floor jack, preferably a floor jack with a transmission adapter head. Safety chains will help steady the transaxle on the jack.

69 Remove the transaxle-to-engine bolts.

70 Recheck to be sure nothing is connecting the engine to the vehicle or to the transaxle. Disconnect and label anything still remaining.

71 Slowly lower the transaxle assembly out of the vehicle. Keep the transaxle level as you're separating it from the engine to prevent damage to the input shaft. It may be necessary to pry the mounts away from the frame brackets.

Caution: *Do not allow the transaxle to tilt forward very much (toward the engine) or the converter may slide out.*

Warning: *Do not place any part of your body under the transaxle assembly when it's being removed.*

72 Check the engine and transaxle mounts. Replace if damaged.

Installation

73 If removed, install the torque converter on the transaxle input shaft. Make sure the converter hub splines are properly engaged with the splines on the transaxle input shaft.

74 Install the transaxle in the reverse of the removal procedure.

75 Tighten all fasteners to the torque values listed in this Chapter's Specifications.

76 Add the specified amount of new transaxle fluid (see Chapter 1, Section 26).

77 Adjust the shift cable (see Section 3).

78 Connect the negative battery cable. Road test the vehicle to check for proper transmission operation and check for leakage.

79 Recheck the fluid level.

80 It is recommended to have the vehicle aligned since the front suspension subframe was removed.

Note: *Since this an electronically-controlled transaxle, the manufacturer recommends that when a transaxle has been replaced, you should take the vehicle to a dealer or other service facility with a scan tool to perform a "reset memory" procedure for optimum transmission performance.*

11 Electronic control system

Trouble codes

1 The electronic control system for the transaxle has some self-diagnostic capabilities. If certain kinds of system malfunctions occur, the PCM stores the appropriate diagnostic trouble code in its memory and the CHECK ENGINE indicator light illuminates to inform the driver. The diagnostic trouble codes can only be extracted from the PCM using a scan tool that can be linked to the On Board Diagnostic (OBD II) computer via the 16-pin diagnostic link. Codes are listed below for reference (refer to Chapter 6, Section 3 for additional information).

Trouble code	Code identification
P0500	Vehicle speed sensor or circuit failure
P0705	Transmission range sensor circuit malfunction
P0710	Transmission fluid temperature sensor "A" Circuit
P0711	Transmission fluid temperature sensor, range or performance fault
P0712	Transmission fluid temperature sensor "A" Circuit (low) input
P0713	Transmission fluid temperature sensor "A" Circuit (high) input
P0715	Input/turbine speed sensor circuit malfunction
P0717	Turbine speed sensor circuit No Signal
P0724	Brake switch "B" circuit High

Trouble code	Code identification
P0741	Torque converter clutch solenoid performance malfunction
P0746	Pressure control solenoid "A" performance malfunction
P0748	Pressure control solenoid "A" electrical malfunction
P0750 - P0751	Shift solenoid "A" performance (Shift Solenoid Valve S1)
P0756	Shift solenoid "B" performance (Shift Solenoid Valve S2)
P0766	Shift solenoid "D" performance malfunction
P0771	Shift solenoid "E" performance malfunction
P0776	Pressure control solenoid "B" performance malfunction
P0778	Pressure control solenoid "B" electrical malfunction
P0787	Shift/timing solenoid low (Shift Solenoid Valve ST)
P0788	Shift/timing solenoid high (Shift Solenoid Valve ST)
P0791	Intermediate shaft speed sensor "A" circuit malfunction
P0793	Intermediate shaft speed sensor "A" circuit malfunction
P0796	Pressure control solenoid "C" performance malfunction
P0798	Pressure control solenoid "C" electrical malfunction
P0850	Park/Neutral function performance
P0973	Shift solenoid "A" control circuit low (Shift Solenoid Valve S1)
P0974	Shift solenoid "A" control circuit high (Shift Solenoid Valve S1)
P0976	Shift solenoid "B" control circuit low (Shift Solenoid Valve S2)
P0977	Shift solenoid "B" control circuit high (Shift Solenoid Valve S2)
P0982	Shift solenoid "D" control circuit (low) problem
P0983	Shift solenoid "D" control circuit (high) problem
P0985	Shift solenoid "E" control circuit (low) problem
P0986	Shift solenoid "E" control circuit (high) problem
P2714	Pressure control solenoid "D" performance malfunction
P2716	Pressure control solenoid "D" electrical malfunction
P2757	Torque converter clutch pressure control solenoid performance (Shift Solenoid Valve SLU)
P2759	Torque converter clutch pressure control solenoid control circuit electrical (Shift Solenoid Valve SLU)
P2769	Torque converter clutch solenoid, circuit (low) problem
P2770	Torque converter clutch solenoid, circuit (high) problem

Other Electronic Control System checks

Preliminary checks

2   Check the fluid level and condition. If the fluid smells burned, replace it (see Chapter 1).

3   Check for fluid leaks (see Section 2).

4   Check and, if necessary, adjust the shift cable (see Section 3).

5   Check and, if necessary, adjust the Transmission Range sensor (see Section 6).

O/D OFF indicator light check

6   Turn the ignition switch to On.

7   Verify that the O/D Off indicator light comes on when the O/D main switch is in the Off (up) position, and goes out when the O/D main switch is pushed to the On position.

8   If the O/D Off indicator light does not light up, or remains on all the time, have the circuit checked out by a dealer service department or other qualified repair shop.

12 Automatic transaxle mounts - inspection and replacement

1   Checking the condition of and replacing the automatic transaxle mounts is similar to checking and replacing the engine mounts (see Chapter 2A, Section 18).

Warning: *When replacing any of the mounts, be sure to properly support the drivetrain using a jack or suitable engine support tool to prevent injury or damage to components.*

Notes

Chapter 8
Clutch and driveaxles

Contents

Specifications

Clutch
Fluid type .... See Chapter 1
Pedal freeplay .... See Chapter 1

Torque specifications
Note: *One foot-pound (ft-lb) of torque is equivalent to 12 inch-pounds (in-lbs) of torque. Torque values below approximately 15 ft-lbs are expressed in inch-pounds, since most foot-pound torque wrenches are not accurate at these smaller values.*

Ft-lbs (unless otherwise indicated)
Clutch master cylinder mounting nuts .... 108 in-lbs
Clutch pressure plate-to-flywheel bolts .... 168 in-lbs
Clutch release cylinder mounting bolts
  2013 and earlier models .... 108 in-lbs
  2014 and later models 17
Clutch release cylinder line fitting .... 132 in-lbs

Driveaxle
Driveaxle/hub nut 159
Wheel lug nuts .... See Chapter 1

1 General information

1 The information in this Chapter deals with the components from the rear of the engine to the front wheels, except for the transaxle, which is dealt with in Chapter 7A and Chapter 7B. For the purposes of this Chapter, these components are grouped into two categories: clutch and driveaxles.

2 Since nearly all the procedures covered in this Chapter involve working under the vehicle, make sure it's securely supported on sturdy jackstands or a hoist where the vehicle can be easily raised and lowered.

2   Clutch - description and check

1   All vehicles with a manual transaxle use a single dry plate, diaphragm spring type clutch **(see illustration)**. The clutch disc has a splined hub that allows it to slide along the splines of the transaxle input shaft. The clutch and pressure plate are held in contact by spring pressure exerted by the diaphragm in the pressure plate.

2   The clutch release system is operated by hydraulic pressure. On 2013 and earlier models, the hydraulic release system consists of the clutch pedal, a master cylinder and fluid reservoir, the hydraulic line, a release cylinder which actuates the clutch release lever and the clutch release (or throw-out) bearing. On 2014 and later models, the hydraulic release system consists of the clutch pedal, a master cylinder and fluid reservoir, the hydraulic line, and a concentric release cylinder which includes the clutch release (or throw-out) bearing.

3   When pressure is applied to the clutch pedal to release the clutch, hydraulic pressure is exerted against the outer end of the clutch release lever and/or release bearing. As the lever pivots, the shaft fingers push against the release bearing. The bearing pushes against the fingers of the diaphragm spring of the pressure plate assembly, which in turn releases the clutch plate.

4   Terminology can be a problem regarding the clutch components because common names have in some cases changed from that used by the manufacturer. For example, the driven plate is also called the clutch plate or disc, the pressure plate assembly is sometimes referred to as the clutch cover, the clutch release bearing is sometimes called a throw-out bearing, and the release cylinder is sometimes called the operating or slave cylinder.

5   Other than replacing components that have obvious damage, some preliminary checks should be performed to diagnose a clutch system failure.

 a) *The first check should be of the fluid level in the clutch master cylinder (see Chapter 1). If the fluid level is low, add fluid as necessary and inspect the hydraulic clutch system for leaks. If the master cylinder reservoir has run dry, bleed the system (see Section 7) and retest the clutch operation.*

 b) *To check "clutch spin down time," run the engine at normal idle speed with the transaxle in Neutral (clutch pedal up - engaged). Disengage the clutch (pedal down), wait several seconds and shift the transaxle into Reverse. No grinding noise should be heard. A grinding noise would most likely indicate a problem in the pressure plate or the clutch disc.*

 c) *To check for complete clutch release, run the engine (with the parking brake applied to prevent movement) and hold the clutch pedal approximately 1/2-inch from the floor. Shift the transaxle between 1st gear and Reverse several times. If the shift is not smooth, com-*

2.1 Typical clutch disc

1   **Lining** - *this will wear down in use*

2   **Springs or dampers** - *check for cracking and deformation*

3   **Splined hub** - *the splines must not be worn and should slide smoothly on the transaxle input shaft splines*

4   **Rivets** - *these secure the lining and will damage the flywheel or pressure plate if allowed to contact the surfaces*

ponent failure is indicated. Check the release cylinder pushrod travel. With the clutch pedal depressed completely the release cylinder pushrod should extend substantially. If it doesn't, check the fluid level in the clutch master cylinder.

 d) *Visually inspect the clutch pedal bushing at the top of the clutch pedal to make sure there is no sticking or excessive wear.*

 e) *On 2013 and earlier models, under the vehicle, check that the clutch release lever is solidly mounted on the ball stud.*

3   Clutch components - removal, inspection and installation

Warning: *Dust produced by clutch wear and deposited on clutch components is hazardous to your health. DO NOT blow it out with compressed air and DO NOT inhale it. DO NOT use gasoline or petroleum based solvents to remove the dust. Brake system cleaner should be used to flush the dust into a drain pan. After the clutch components are wiped clean with a rag, dispose of the contaminated rags and cleaner in a labeled, covered container.*

Removal

1   Access to the clutch components is normally accomplished by removing the transaxle, leaving the engine in the vehicle. If, of course, the engine is being removed for major overhaul, then the opportunity should always be taken to check the clutch for wear and replace worn components as necessary. However, the relatively low cost of the clutch components compared to the time and labor involved in gaining access to them warrants their

3.6 Mark the relationship of the pressure plate to the flywheel (in case you're going to reuse the same pressure plate)

replacement any time the engine or transaxle is removed, unless they are new or in near-perfect condition. The following procedures assume that the engine will stay in place.

2   On 2013 and earlier models, remove the release cylinder (see Section 6). Hang it out of the way with a piece of wire - it isn't necessary to disconnect the hose.

3   Remove the transaxle from the vehicle (see Chapter 7A). Support the engine while the transaxle is out. Preferably, an engine hoist or support fixture should be used to support it from above. However, if a jack is used underneath the engine, make sure a piece of wood is used between the jack and oil pan to spread the load.

Caution: *The pick-up for the oil pump is very close to the bottom of the oil pan. If the pan is bent or distorted in any way, engine oil starvation could occur.*

4   The release fork and/or release bearing can remain attached to the transaxle for the time being.

5   To support the clutch disc during removal, install a clutch alignment tool through the clutch disc hub.

6   Carefully inspect the flywheel and pressure plate for indexing marks. The marks are usually an X, an O or a white letter. If they cannot be found, scribe marks yourself so the pressure plate and the flywheel will be in the same alignment during installation **(see illustration)**.

7   Slowly loosen the pressure plate-to-flywheel bolts. Work in a diagonal pattern and loosen each bolt a little at a time until all spring pressure is relieved. Then hold the pressure plate securely and completely remove the bolts, followed by the pressure plate and clutch disc.

Inspection

8   Ordinarily, when a problem occurs in the clutch, it can be attributed to wear of the clutch driven plate assembly (clutch disc). However, all components should be inspected at this time.

3.10 Examine the clutch disc for evidence of excessive wear, such as smeared friction material, loose rivets, worn hub splines and distorted damper cushions or springs

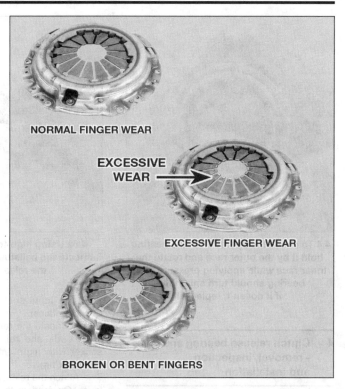

NORMAL FINGER WEAR

EXCESSIVE WEAR

EXCESSIVE FINGER WEAR

BROKEN OR BENT FINGERS

3.12a Replace the pressure plate if excessive wear or damage are noted

3.12b Examine the pressure plate friction surface for score marks, cracks and evidence of overheating (blue spots)

3.14 Center the clutch disc in the pressure plate with a clutch alignment tool

9   Inspect the flywheel for cracks, heat checking, score marks and other damage. If the imperfections are slight, a machine shop can resurface it to make it flat and smooth. Refer to Chapter 2A for the flywheel removal procedure.

10   Inspect the lining on the clutch disc. There should be at least 1/32-inch of lining above the rivet heads **(see illustration 2.1)**. Check for loose rivets, distortion, cracks, broken springs and other obvious damage **(see illustration)**. As mentioned above, ordinarily the clutch disc is replaced as a matter of course, so if in doubt about the condition, replace it with a new one.

11   The release bearing should be replaced along with the clutch disc (see Section 6).

12   Check the machined surface and the diaphragm spring fingers of the pressure plate **(see illustrations)**. If the surface is grooved or otherwise damaged, replace the pressure plate assembly. Also check for obvious damage, distortion, cracking, etc. Light glazing can be removed with emery cloth or sandpaper. If a new pressure plate is indicated, new or factory rebuilt units are available.

Installation

13   Before installation, carefully wipe the flywheel and pressure plate machined surfaces

clean. It's important that no oil or grease is on these surfaces or the lining of the clutch disc. Handle these parts only with clean hands.

14   Position the clutch disc and pressure plate with the clutch held in place with an alignment tool **(see illustration)**. Make sure it's installed properly (most replacement clutch plates will be marked "flywheel side" or something similar - if not marked, install the clutch disc with the damper springs or cushion toward the transaxle).

15   Tighten the pressure plate-to-flywheel bolts only finger-tight, working around the pressure plate.

16   Center the clutch disc by ensuring the alignment tool is through the splined hub and into the recess in the crankshaft. Wiggle the

tool up, down or side-to-side as needed to bottom the tool. Tighten the pressure plate-to-flywheel bolts a little at a time, working in a criss-cross pattern to prevent distortion of the cover. After all of the bolts are snug, tighten them to the torque listed in this Chapter's Specifications. Remove the alignment tool.

17   Using high-temperature grease, lubricate the inner groove of the release bearing (see Section 4). Also place grease on the release lever contact areas and the transaxle input-shaft bearing retainer.

18   Install the clutch release bearing (see Section 4).

19   Install the transaxle, release cylinder and all components removed previously, tightening all fasteners to the proper torque specifications.

4.4 To check the operation of the bearing, hold it by the outer race and rotate the inner race while applying pressure - the bearing should turn smoothly - if it doesn't, replace it

4.6a Using high-temperature grease, lubricate the ballstud socket in the back of the release lever . . .

4.6b . . . the lever ends and the depression for the cylinder pushrod

4   Clutch release bearing and lever - removal, inspection and installation

Warning: *Dust produced by clutch wear and deposited on clutch components is hazardous to your health. DO NOT blow it out with compressed air and DO NOT inhale it. DO NOT use gasoline or petroleum-based solvents to remove the dust. Brake system cleaner should be used to flush it into a drain pan. After the clutch components are wiped clean with a rag, dispose of the contaminated rags and cleaner in a labeled, covered container.*

Note: *The following procedure applies to 2013 and earlier models. On 2014 and later models, the clutch release bearing is part of the clutch release cylinder and serviced as one unit. See Section 6.*

Removal

1   Disconnect the negative cable from the battery (see Chapter 5).
2   Remove the transaxle (see Chapter 7A).
3   Remove the clutch release lever from the ballstud by pulling on the retention spring, then remove the bearing and the lever.

Inspection

4   Hold the bearing by the outer race and rotate the inner race while applying pressure **(see illustration)**. If the bearing doesn't turn smoothly or if it's noisy, replace the bearing/hub assembly with a new one. Wipe the bearing with a clean rag and inspect it for damage, wear and cracks. Don't immerse the bearing in solvent - it's sealed for life and to do so would ruin it. Also check the release lever for cracks and bends.

Installation

5   Fill the inner groove of the release bearing with high-temperature grease. Also apply a light coat of the same grease to the

transaxle input shaft splines and the front bearing retainer.
6   Lubricate the release lever ball socket, lever ends and release cylinder pushrod socket with high-temperature grease **(see illustrations)**.
7   Attach the release bearing to the release lever. On models that use a retaining clip, make sure it engages properly with the lever.
8   Slide the release bearing onto the transaxle input shaft front bearing retainer while passing the end of the release lever through the opening in the clutch housing. Push the clutch release lever onto the ball stud until it's firmly seated.
9   Apply a light coat of high-temperature grease to the face of the release bearing where it contacts the pressure plate diaphragm fingers.
10   The remainder of installation is the reverse of the removal procedure.

5   Clutch master cylinder - removal and installation

Removal

1 Disconnect the negative cable from the battery.

2   On 2008 and earlier models, remove the brake master cylinder and power brake booster Chapter 9. On 2014 and later models, remove the power brake booster (see Chapter 9, Section 12).
3   Disconnect the hydraulic line at the clutch master cylinder. If available, use a flare-nut wrench on the fitting, to protect the fitting from being rounded off. Have rags handy as some fluid will be lost as the line is removed.
Caution: *Don't allow brake fluid to come into contact with paint, as it will damage the finish.*
4   Remove the driver's side knee bolster (see Chapter 11). Under the dashboard, disconnect the pushrod from the top of the clutch pedal. It's held in place with a clevis pin. To remove the clevis pin, remove the clip **(see illustration)**.
5   From under the dash, remove the nuts which attach the master cylinder to the firewall. Remove the master cylinder, again being careful not to spill any of the fluid.

Installation

6   Position the master cylinder on the firewall, installing the mounting nuts finger-tight.
7   Connect the hydraulic line to the master cylinder, moving the cylinder slightly as

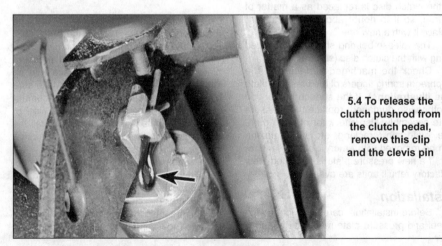

5.4 To release the clutch pushrod from the clutch pedal, remove this clip and the clevis pin

necessary to thread the fitting properly into the bore. Don't cross-thread the fitting as it's installed.

8   Tighten the mounting nuts and the hydraulic line fitting securely.

9 Connect the pushrod to the clutch pedal.

10   Install the power brake booster and master cylinder if removed (see Chapter 9). Connect the clutch fluid feed line to the brake fluid reservoir.

11   Fill the brake fluid reservoir with the proper brake fluid (see Chapter 1) and bleed the clutch system (see Section 7) and the brake system (see Chapter 9).

12   Check the clutch pedal height and free-play (see Chapter 1).

6   Clutch release cylinder - removal and installation

2013 and earlier models

Removal

1   Disconnect the negative cable from the battery (see Chapter 5).

2   Raise the vehicle and support it securely on jackstands.

3   Disconnect the hydraulic line at the release cylinder. If available, use a flare-nut wrench on the fitting, which will prevent the fitting from being rounded off **(see illustration)**. Have a small can and rags handy, as some fluid will be spilled as the line is removed.

4   Remove the release cylinder mounting bolts.

5   Remove the release cylinder.

Installation

6   Install the release cylinder on the clutch housing. Make sure the pushrod is seated in the release fork pocket.

7   Connect the hydraulic line to the release cylinder. Tighten the connection securely.

8   Fill the brake master cylinder with the proper brake fluid (see Chapter 1).

9   Bleed the system (see Section 7).

10   Lower the vehicle and connect the negative battery cable.

2014 and later models

Removal

11   Remove the transaxle. See Chapter 7A, Section 7.

12   Disconnect the clutch hydraulic lines from the bleeder union on the transaxle assembly.

13   Remove the two bolts and remove the bleeder union from the transaxle.

14   Remove the rubber boot from the transaxle where the hydraulic line enters to the clutch release cylinder.

15   Remove the three bolts and remove the clutch release cylinder from the transaxle input shaft.

Installation

16   Transfer over the hydraulic line to the

6.3 Use a flare-nut wrench when disconnecting the hydraulic line fitting (left) to prevent rounding off the corners of the tubing nut, then remove the mounting bolts (typical installation)

new clutch release cylinder if necessary.

17   Installation is reverse of removal. Tighten all hydraulic fittings securely.

18   Bleed the clutch hydraulic system (see Section 7).

19   Verify proper operation.

7   Clutch hydraulic system - bleeding

1   The hydraulic system should be bled of all air whenever any part of the system has been removed or if the fluid level has been allowed to fall so low that air has been drawn into the master cylinder. The procedure is similar to bleeding a brake system.

2   Fill the brake master cylinder with new brake fluid of the proper type (see Chapter 1).

3 Raise the vehicle and place it securely on jackstands to gain access to the release cylinder, which is located on the left side of the clutch housing.

Caution: *Do not re-use any of the fluid coming from the system during the bleeding operation or use fluid which has been inside an open container for an extended period of time.*

4   Locate the bleeder valve on the clutch release cylinder (right above the fitting for the hydraulic fluid line) or on the bleeder junction block. Remove the dust cap that fits over the bleeder valve and push a length of clear tubing over the valve. Place the other end of the hose into a clear container with about two inches of brake fluid in it. The hose end must be submerged in the fluid.

5   Have an assistant depress the clutch pedal and hold it. Open the bleeder valve on the release cylinder, allowing fluid to flow through the hose. Close the bleeder valve when fluid stops flowing from the hose. Once closed, have your assistant release the pedal.

6   Continue this process until all air is evacuated from the system, indicated by a full, solid stream of fluid being ejected from the bleeder valve each time and no air bubbles in the hose or container. Keep a close watch on the fluid level inside the clutch master cylinder reservoir; if the level drops too low, air will be

sucked back into the system and the process will have to be started all over again.

7   Install the dust cap and lower the vehicle. Check carefully for proper operation before placing the vehicle in normal service.

8   Clutch start switch - check and replacement

1   Check the pedal height, pedal freeplay and pushrod play (see Chapter 1).

2   Verify that the engine will not start when the clutch pedal is released.

3   Verify that the engine will start when the clutch pedal is depressed all the way.

4   The clutch start switch is located on a bracket forward of the clutch pedal (under the dash).

5   If the switch fails either of the tests, replace it. This is accomplished by removing the nut nearest the plunger end of the switch and unscrewing the switch. Disconnect the wire harness. Installation is the reverse of removal.

6   To adjust the clutch start switch, depress the clutch pedal completely and turn the switch in or out to achieve the spacing of the original switch.

7   Verify that the switch operates properly by performing Steps 2 and 3 again.

9   Driveaxle - removal and installation

Caution: *The manufacturer states that a new driveaxle/hub nut must be installed whenever it is removed.*

Removal

1   Disconnect the cable from the negative terminal of the battery (see Chapter 5).

2   Set the parking brake.

3   Loosen the front wheel lug nuts, raise the vehicle and support it securely on jackstands. Remove the wheel.

9.4 Using a hammer and punch, unstake the driveaxle/hub nut

9.5 Use a large prybar to immobilize the hub while loosening the driveaxle/hub nut

9.6 Using a brass punch, strike the end of the driveaxle sharply with a hammer; when it breaks free, it will move noticeably

4   Unstake the driveaxle/hub nut **(see illustration)**.

5   Remove the driveaxle/hub nut. To prevent the hub from turning, wedge a prybar between two of the wheel studs and allow the prybar to rest against the ground or the floor pan of the vehicle **(see illustration)**.

6   To loosen the driveaxle from the hub splines, tap the end of the driveaxle with a soft-faced hammer or a hammer and a brass punch **(see illustration)**.
Note: *Don't attempt to push the end of the driveaxle through the hub yet. Applying force to the end of the driveaxle, beyond just breaking it loose from the hub, can damage the driveaxle or transaxle. Avoid damaging the speed sensor and sensor rotor when separating the driveaxle from the hub.*

7   If the driveaxle is stuck in the hub splines and won't move, it may be necessary to remove the brake disc (see Chapter 9) and push it from the hub with a two-jaw puller after the lower ball joint is disconnected.

8   Remove the engine splash shields. Place a drain pan underneath the transaxle to catch any lubricant that may spill out when the driveaxle is removed.

9   Detach the ABS sensor and if necessary, the brake line from the strut bracket so they are not damaged.

10   Remove the nut and disconnect the tie rod from the steering knuckle.

11   Disconnect the stabilizer bar link at the stabilizer bar or strut assembly (if necessary to allow the lower control arm to be lowered independently of the opposite control arm for balljoint separation).

12   Remove the nuts and bolt securing the balljoint to the control arm, then pry the control arm down to separate the components (see Chapter 10).

13   Pull out and rotate the steering knuckle and detach the driveaxle from the hub.
Caution: *Don't let the driveaxle hang by the inner CV joint after the outer end has been detached from the steering knuckle, as the inner joint could become damaged. Support the outer end of the driveaxle with a piece of wire, if necessary.*

14   Carefully pry the inner CV joint out of the transaxle **(see illustrations)**. On some manual transaxle models, the case protector next to the right side CV joint may need to be removed to allow removal of the CV joint.

15   If necessary, refer to Chapter 7B for the driveaxle oil seal replacement procedure.

Installation

16   Installation is the reverse of the removal procedure, but with the following additional points:

a) *If the same driveaxle is to be reused, it is recommended to replace the snap ring on the inner axle splines.*
b) *Push the driveaxle sharply in to seat the retaining ring on the inner CV joint in the groove in the differential side gear.*
c) *Tighten the new driveaxle/hub nut to the torque listed in this Chapter's Specifications, then stake the collar of the nut into the groove in the driveaxle.*
d) *Tighten the tie rod ends, balljoints and stabilizer bar links to the torque listed in the Chapter 10 Specifications.*
e) *Tighten the lug nuts to the torque listed in the Chapter 1 Specifications.*
f) *Check the transaxle lubricant and add, if necessary, to bring it to the proper level (see Chapter 1).*

9.14a To separate the inner end of the driveaxle from the transaxle, pry on the CV joint housing like this with a large screwdriver or prybar - you may need to give the prybar a sharp rap with a brass hammer . . .

9.14b . . . or use a slide hammer to pop the driveaxle out of the transaxle

Chapter 9
Brakes

Contents

Specifications

General

Brake fluid type	See Chapter 1
Brake pedal height	
2008 and earlier models	
Manual transmission models	5.311 to 5.703 inches
Automatic transmission models	5.353 to 5.547 inches
2009 through 2013 models	5.57 to 5.96 inches
2014 and later models	5.83 to 6.22 inches
Brake pedal freeplay	3/64 to 1/4 inch
Power brake booster pushrod-to-master cylinder piston clearance	0.0 inch
Brake light switch plunger protrusion (from threaded portion of switch)	1/32 to 3/32 inch

Disc brakes

Brake pad minimum thickness	See Chapter 1
Disc minimum thickness	Cast into disc
Disc runout limit	
Front	0.002 inch
Rear	0.006 inch
Parking brake shoe minimum thickness	1/32 inch

Drum brakes

Brake shoe minimum lining thickness	See Chapter 1
Drum inside diameter (maximum)	Cast into drum

Torque specifications

Ft-lbs (unless otherwise indicated)

Note: *One foot-pound (ft-lb) of torque is equivalent to 12 inch-pounds (in-lbs) of torque. Torque values below approximately 15 ft-lbs are expressed in inch-pounds, since most foot-pound torque wrenches are not accurate at these smaller values.*

Caliper mounting bolts	
Front	25
Rear	26
Caliper torque plate bolts	
Front	79
Rear	46
Brake hose-to-caliper banjo bolt	21
Wheel cylinder mounting bolt	87 in-lbs
Master cylinder-to-brake booster nuts	108 in-lbs
Power brake booster mounting nuts	108 in-lbs
Vacuum pump mounting bolts (2ZR-FAE engine only)	15
Wheel lug nuts	See Chapter 1

1 General Information

1   The vehicles covered by this manual are equipped with hydraulically operated front and rear brake systems. The front brakes are disc type and the rear brakes are disc or drum type. Both the front and rear brakes are self adjusting. The disc brakes automatically compensate for pad wear, while the drum brakes incorporate an adjustment mechanism that is activated as the parking brake is applied.

Hydraulic system

2   The hydraulic system consists of two separate circuits. The master cylinder has separate reservoirs for the two circuits, and, in the event of a leak or failure in one hydraulic circuit, the other circuit will remain operative. A dual proportioning valve on the firewall provides brake balance between front and rear brakes.

Power brake booster

3   The power brake booster, utilizing engine manifold vacuum and atmospheric pressure to provide assistance to the hydraulically operated brakes, is mounted on the firewall in the engine compartment.

Parking brake

4   The parking brake operates the rear brakes only, through cable actuation. It's activated by a lever mounted in the center console.

Service

5   After completing any operation involving disassembly of any part of the brake system, always test drive the vehicle to check for proper braking performance before resuming normal driving. When testing the brakes, perform the tests on a clean, dry, flat surface. Conditions other than these can lead to inaccurate test results.
6   Test the brakes at various speeds with both light and heavy pedal pressure. The vehicle should stop evenly without pulling to one side or the other. Avoid locking the brakes, because this slides the tires and diminishes braking efficiency and control of the vehicle.
7   Tires, vehicle load and wheel alignment are factors which also affect braking performance.

Precautions

8   There are some general cautions and warnings involving the brake system on this vehicle:

a) Use only brake fluid conforming to DOT 3 specifications.
b) The brake pads and linings contain fibers that are hazardous to your health if inhaled. Whenever you work on brake system components, clean all parts with brake system cleaner. Do not allow the fine dust to become airborne. Also, wear an approved filtering mask.
c) Safety should be paramount whenever any servicing of the brake components is performed. Do not use parts or fasteners that are not in perfect condition, and be sure that all clearances and torque specifications are adhered to. If you are at all unsure about a certain procedure, seek professional advice. Upon completion of any brake system work, test the brakes carefully in a controlled area before putting the vehicle into normal service. If a problem is suspected in the brake system, don't drive the vehicle until it's fixed.
d) Used brake fluid is considered a hazardous waste and it must be disposed of in accordance with federal, state and local laws. DO NOT pour it down the sink, into septic tanks or storm drains, or on the ground. Clean up any spilled brake fluid immediately and then wash the area with large amounts of water. This is especially true for any finished or painted surfaces.

2 Troubleshooting

PROBABLE CAUSE	CORRECTIVE ACTION

No brakes - pedal travels to floor

PROBABLE CAUSE	CORRECTIVE ACTION
1 Low fluid level 2 Air in system	1 and 2 Low fluid level and air in the system are symptoms of another problem a leak somewhere in the hydraulic system. Locate and repair the leak
3 Defective seals in master cylinder	3 Replace master cylinder
4 Fluid overheated and vaporized due to heavy braking	4 Bleed hydraulic system (temporary fix). Replace brake fluid (proper fix)

Brake pedal slowly travels to floor under braking or at a stop

PROBABLE CAUSE	CORRECTIVE ACTION
1 Defective seals in master cylinder	1 Replace master cylinder
2 Leak in a hose, line, caliper or wheel cylinder	2 Locate and repair leak
3 Air in hydraulic system	3 Bleed the system, inspect system for a leak

Brake pedal feels spongy when depressed

PROBABLE CAUSE	CORRECTIVE ACTION
1 Air in hydraulic system	1 Bleed the system, inspect system for a leak
2 Master cylinder or power booster loose	2 Tighten fasteners
3 Brake fluid overheated (beginning to boil)	3 Bleed the system (temporary fix). Replace the brake fluid (proper fix)
4 Deteriorated brake hoses (ballooning under pressure)	4 Inspect hoses, replace as necessary (it's a good idea to replace all of them if one hose shows signs of deterioration)

PROBABLE CAUSE   **CORRECTIVE ACTION**

Brake pedal feels hard when depressed and/or excessive effort required to stop vehicle

Probable Cause	Corrective Action
1 Power booster faulty	1 Replace booster
2 Engine not producing sufficient vacuum, or hose to booster clogged, collapsed or cracked	2 Check vacuum to booster with a vacuum gauge. Replace hose if cracked or clogged, repair engine if vacuum is extremely low
3 Brake linings contaminated by grease or brake fluid	3 Locate and repair source of contamination, replace brake pads or shoes
4 Brake linings glazed	4 Replace brake pads or shoes, check discs and drums for glazing, service as necessary
5 Caliper piston(s) or wheel cylinder(s) binding or frozen	5 Replace calipers or wheel cylinders
6 Brakes wet	6 Apply pedal to boil-off water (this should only be a momentary problem)
7 Kinked, clogged or internally split brake hose or line	7 Inspect lines and hoses, replace as necessary

Excessive brake pedal travel (but will pump up)

Probable Cause	Corrective Action
1 Drum brakes out of adjustment	1 Adjust brakes
2 Air in hydraulic system	2 Bleed system, inspect system for a leak

Excessive brake pedal travel (but will not pump up)

Probable Cause	Corrective Action
1 Master cylinder pushrod misadjusted	1 Adjust pushrod
2 Master cylinder seals defective	2 Replace master cylinder
3 Brake linings worn out	3 Inspect brakes, replace pads and/or shoes
4 Hydraulic system leak	4 Locate and repair leak

Brake pedal doesn't return

Probable Cause	Corrective Action
1 Brake pedal binding	1 Inspect pivot bushing and pushrod, repair or lubricate
2 Defective master cylinder	2 Replace master cylinder

Brake pedal pulsates during brake application

Probable Cause	Corrective Action
1 Brake drums out-of-round	1 Have drums machined by an automotive machine shop
2 Excessive brake disc runout or disc surfaces out-of-parallel	2 Have discs machined by an automotive machine shop
3 Loose or worn wheel bearings	3 Adjust or replace wheel bearings
4 Loose lug nuts	4 Tighten lug nuts

Brakes slow to release

Probable Cause	Corrective Action
1 Malfunctioning power booster	1 Replace booster
2 Pedal linkage binding	2 Inspect pedal pivot bushing and pushrod, repair/lubricate
3 Malfunctioning proportioning valve	3 Replace proportioning valve
4 Sticking caliper or wheel cylinder	4 Repair or replace calipers or wheel cylinders
5 Kinked or internally split brake hose	5 Locate and replace faulty brake hose

Brakes grab (one or more wheels)

Probable Cause	Corrective Action
1 Grease or brake fluid on brake lining	1 Locate and repair cause of contamination, replace lining
2 Brake lining glazed	2 Replace lining, deglaze disc or drum

Troubleshooting (continued)

PROBABLE CAUSE	CORRECTIVE ACTION

Vehicle pulls to one side during braking

1 Grease or brake fluid on brake lining	1 Locate and repair cause of contamination, replace lining
2 Brake lining glazed	2 Deglaze or replace lining, deglaze disc or drum
3 Restricted brake line or hose	3 Repair line or replace hose
4 Tire pressures incorrect	4 Adjust tire pressures
5 Caliper or wheel cylinder sticking	5 Repair or replace calipers or wheel cylinders
6 Wheels out of alignment	6 Have wheels aligned
7 Weak suspension spring	7 Replace springs
8 Weak or broken shock absorber	8 Replace shock absorbers

Brakes drag (indicated by sluggish engine performance or wheels being very hot after driving)

1 Brake pedal pushrod incorrectly adjusted	1 Adjust pushrod
2 Master cylinder pushrod (between booster and master cylinder)	2 Adjust pushrod incorrectly adjusted
3 Obstructed compensating port in master cylinder	3 Replace master cylinder
4 Master cylinder piston seized in bore	4 Replace master cylinder
5 Contaminated fluid causing swollen seals throughout system	5 Flush system, replace all hydraulic components
6 Clogged brake lines or internally split brake hose(s)	6 Flush hydraulic system, replace defective hose(s)
7 Sticking caliper(s) or wheel cylinder(s)	7 Replace calipers or wheel cylinders
8 Parking brake not releasing	8 Inspect parking brake linkage and parking brake mechanism, repair as required
9 Improper shoe-to-drum clearance	9 Adjust brake shoes
10 Faulty proportioning valve	10 Replace proportioning valve

Brakes fade (due to excessive heat)

1 Brake linings excessively worn or glazed	1 Deglaze or replace brake pads and/or shoes
2 Excessive use of brakes	2 Downshift into a lower gear, maintain a constant slower speed (going down hills)
3 Vehicle overloaded	3 Reduce load
4 Brake drums or discs worn too thin	4 Measure drum diameter and disc thickness, replace drums or discs as required
5 Contaminated brake fluid	5 Flush system, replace fluid
6 Brakes drag	6 Repair cause of dragging brakes
7 Driver resting left foot on brake pedal	7 Don't ride the brakes

Brakes noisy (high-pitched squeal)

1 Glazed lining	1 Deglaze or replace lining
2 Contaminated lining (brake fluid, grease, etc.)	2 Repair source of contamination, replace linings
3 Weak or broken brake shoe hold-down or return spring	3 Replace springs
4 Rivets securing lining to shoe or backing plate loose	4 Replace shoes or pads
5 Excessive dust buildup on brake linings	5 Wash brakes off with brake system cleaner
6 Brake drums worn too thin	6 Measure diameter of drums, replace if necessary
7 Wear indicator on disc brake pads contacting disc	7 Replace brake pads
8 Anti-squeal shims missing or installed improperly	8 Install shims correctly

PROBABLE CAUSE	CORRECTIVE ACTION

Brakes noisy (scraping sound)

1 Brake pads or shoes worn out; rivets, backing plate or brake	1 Replace linings, have discs and/or drums machined (or replace) shoe metal contacting disc or drum

Brakes chatter

1 Worn brake lining	1 Inspect brakes, replace shoes or pads as necessary
2 Glazed or scored discs or drums	2 Deglaze discs or drums with sandpaper (if glazing is severe, machining will be required)
3 Drums or discs heat checked	3 Check discs and/or drums for hard spots, heat checking, etc. Have discs/drums machined or replace them
4 Disc runout or drum out-of-round excessive	4 Measure disc runout and/or drum out-of-round, have discs or drums machined or replace them
5 Loose or worn wheel bearings	5 Adjust or replace wheel bearings
6 Loose or bent brake backing plate (drum brakes)	6 Tighten or replace backing plate
7 Grooves worn in discs or drums	7 Have discs or drums machined, if within limits (if not, replace them)
8 Brake linings contaminated (brake fluid, grease, etc.)	8 Locate and repair source of contamination, replace pads or shoes
9 Excessive dust buildup on linings	9 Wash brakes with brake system cleaner
10 Surface finish on discs or drums too rough after machining	10 Have discs or drums properly machined (especially on vehicles with sliding calipers)
11 Brake pads or shoes glazed	11 Deglaze or replace brake pads or shoes

Brake pads or shoes click

1 Shoe support pads on brake backing plate grooved or	1 Replace brake backing plate excessively worn
2 Brake pads loose in caliper	2 Loose pad retainers or anti-rattle clips
3 Also see items listed under Brakes chatter	

Brakes make groaning noise at end of stop

1 Brake pads and/or shoes worn out	1 Replace pads and/or shoes
2 Brake linings contaminated (brake fluid, grease, etc.)	2 Locate and repair cause of contamination, replace brake pads or shoes
3 Brake linings glazed	3 Deglaze or replace brake pads or shoes
4 Excessive dust buildup on linings	4 Wash brakes with brake system cleaner
5 Scored or heat-checked discs or drums	5 Inspect discs/drums, have machined if within limits (if not, replace discs or drums)
6 Broken or missing brake shoe attaching hardware	6 Inspect drum brakes, replace missing hardware

Rear brakes lock up under light brake application

1 Tire pressures too high	1 Adjust tire pressures
2 Tires excessively worn	2 Replace tires
3 Defective proportioning valve	3 Replace proportioning valve

Brake warning light on instrument panel comes on (or stays on)

1 Low fluid level in master cylinder reservoir (reservoirs with fluid level sensor)	1 Add fluid, inspect system for leak, check the thickness of the brake pads and shoes
2 Failure in one half of the hydraulic system	2 Inspect hydraulic system for a leak
3 Piston in pressure differential warning valve not centered	3 Center piston by bleeding one circuit or the other (close bleeder valve as soon as the light goes out)

Troubleshooting (continued)

PROBABLE CAUSE	CORRECTIVE ACTION

Brake warning light on instrument panel comes on (or stays on) (continued)

4 Defective pressure differential valve or warning switch	4 Replace valve or switch
5 Air in the hydraulic system	5 Bleed the system, check for leaks
6 Brake pads worn out (vehicles with electric wear sensors - small probes that fit into the brake pads and ground out on the disc when the pads get thin)	6 Replace brake pads (and sensors)

Brakes do not self adjust

Disc brakes

1 Defective caliper piston seals	1 Replace calipers. Also, possible contaminated fluid causing soft or swollen seals (flush system and fill with new fluid if in doubt)
2 Corroded caliper piston(s)	2 Same as above

Drum brakes

1 Adjuster screw frozen	1 Remove adjuster, disassemble, clean and lubricate with high-temperature grease
2 Adjuster lever does not contact star wheel or is binding	2 Inspect drum brakes, assemble correctly or clean or replace parts as required
3 Adjusters mixed up (installed on wrong wheels after brake job)	3 Reassemble correctly
4 Adjuster cable broken or installed incorrectly (cable-type adjusters)	4 Install new cable or assemble correctly

Rapid brake lining wear

1 Driver resting left foot on brake pedal	1 Don't ride the brakes
2 Surface finish on discs or drums too rough	2 Have discs or drums properly machined
3 Also see Brakes drag	

3 Anti-lock Brake System (ABS) - general information

1 The Anti-lock Brake System (ABS) is designed to maintain vehicle steerabilty, directional stability and optimum deceleration under severe braking conditions and on most road surfaces. It does so by monitoring the rotational speed of each wheel and controlling the brake line pressure to each wheel during braking. This prevents the wheel from locking up. The ABS system is primarily designed to prevent wheel lockup during heavy braking, but the information provided by the wheel speed sensors of the ABS system is shared with an optional system that uses the data to control vehicle handling. Electronic Brake-force Distribution (EBD) varies the front-to-rear and side-to-side braking balance under different vehicle loads.

Components

Actuator assembly

2 The actuator assembly is mounted in the right front corner of the engine compart-ment (behind the headlight housing), and consists of the master cylinder, an electric hydraulic pump and four solenoid valves **(see illustration)**.
Note: *The actuator assembly for ABS brakes and ABS with EBD are similar, but the configu-ration of actuator and ECU differ.*

a) *The electric pump provides hydraulic pressure to charge the reservoirs in the actuator, which supplies pressure to the braking system. The pump and reservoirs are housed in the actuator assembly.*
b) *The solenoid valves modulate brake line pressure during ABS operation. The body contains four valves - one for each wheel.*

Speed sensors

3 These sensors are located at each wheel and generate small electrical pulsations when the toothed sensor rings are turning, sending a signal to the electronic controller indicating wheel rotational speed.
4 The front speed sensors are mounted to the front steering knuckle in close relationship to the toothed sensor rings, which are integral with the front driveaxle outer CV joints **(see illustration)**.
5 The rear wheel sensors are integral with the rear hub and bearing assemblies.

ABS computer

6 The ABS computer is mounted with the actuator and is the "brain" for the ABS system. The function of the computer is to accept and process information received from the wheel speed sensors to control the hydraulic line pressure, avoiding wheel lock up. The com-puter also constantly monitors the system, even under normal driving conditions, to find faults within the system.

Diagnosis and repair

7 If a problem develops within the system, an "ABS" light will glow on the dashboard. If the dashboard warning light comes on and stays on while the vehicle is in operation, the ABS system requires attention. Here are few simple checks you can perform:

a) *Check the brake fluid level in the master cylinder reservoir.*

3.2 The ABS actuator assembly is located behind the right headlight housing

3.4 The speed sensor is mounted to the steering knuckle with a single bolt

4.5 Before removing the front caliper, be sure to depress the piston into its bore in the caliper with a large C-clamp to make room for the new pads

b) Check that all electrical connectors are securely connected.
c) Check all the applicable fuses.

8   If the above preliminary checks do not rectify the problem, the vehicle should be diagnosed and repaired by a dealer service department or other qualified repair shop.

Wheel speed sensor - removal and installation

Front

9   Disconnect the negative battery cable from the battery.
10   Loosen the front wheel lug nuts, then raise the front of the vehicle and support it securely on jackstands. Remove the wheel.
11   Loosen the inner fender splash shield enough to expose the wire harness and connection to the speed sensor.
12   Disconnect the speed sensor harness and remove the hold-down bolts that secure the harness to the vehicle.
13   Remove the mounting bolt and withdraw the speed sensor from the steering knuckle.
14   Installation is the reverse of removal.
Note: Before installing the speed sensor - Clean the area completely and apply a very light coating of lubrication to the speed sensor

O ring. Use a slight twisting motion to fully seat and align the speed sensor into the steering knuckle. Tighten the bolt to the torque listed in this Chapter's Specifications.

Rear

The rear speed sensor is a part of the rear hub and bearing assembly; it t is not serviced separately. See Chapter 10, Section 11 for the hub and bearing replacement procedure.

4   Disc brake pads - replacement

Warning: Disc brake pads must be replaced on both front wheels at the same time - never replace the pads on only one wheel. Also, the dust created by the brake system is harmful to your health. Never blow it out with compressed air and don't inhale any of it. An approved filtering mask should be worn when working on the brakes. Do not, under any circumstances, use petroleum-based solvents to clean brake parts. Use brake system cleaner only!
Note: The manufacturer recommends replacing the pad shims and wear-indicators whenever the pads are replaced.
1   Remove the cap from the brake fluid reservoir.

2   Loosen the wheel lug nuts, raise the front or rear of the vehicle and support it securely on jackstands. Block the wheels at the opposite end.
3   Remove the wheels. Work on one brake assembly at a time, using the assembled brake for reference if necessary.
4   Inspect the brake disc carefully as outlined in Section 6. If machining is necessary, follow the information in that Section to remove the disc, at which time the pads can be removed as well.

Front brake pads

5   Push the piston back into its bore to provide room for the new brake pads. A C-clamp can be used to accomplish this (see illustration). As the piston is depressed to the bottom of the caliper bore, the fluid in the master cylinder will rise. Make sure that it doesn't overflow. If necessary, siphon off some of the fluid.
6   Follow the accompanying photos, beginning with illustration 4.6a. Be sure to stay in order and read the caption under each illustration, then proceed to Step 12.

4.6a Always wash the brakes with brake cleaner before disassembling anything

4.6b You can either remove the caliper by removing both of the bolts indicated by the upper and lower arrows (the center arrow points to the brake hose banjo bolt, which shouldn't be unscrewed unless the caliper is being completely removed from the vehicle), or you can remove the lower bolt . . .

4.6c . . . and swing the caliper up and out of the way. But, you can remove the caliper . . .

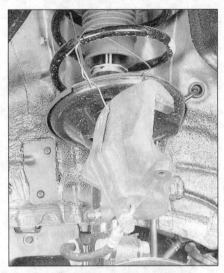

4.6d . . . and hang it from the strut coil spring with a piece of wire if it makes the job easier for you; do not allow the caliper to hang by the flexible brake hose

4.6e Remove the outer shim . . .

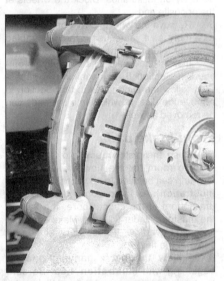

4.6f . . . and the inner shim from the outer brake pad

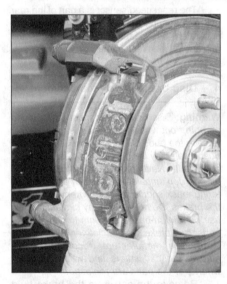

4.6g Remove the outer brake pad

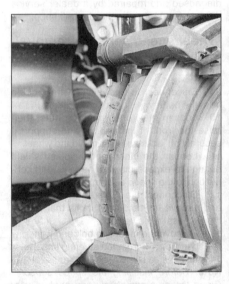

4.6h Remove the outer shim . . .

4.6i . . . and the inner shim from the inner brake pad

4.6j Remove the inner brake pad

4.6k Remove the upper and lower pad support plates; inspect them for damage and replace as necessary (the supports should "snap" into place in the torque plate; if they're weak or distorted, they should be replaced)

4.6l If equipped, pry the wear indicator off the old inner brake pad and transfer it to the new inner pad (if the wear indicator is worn or bent, replace it)

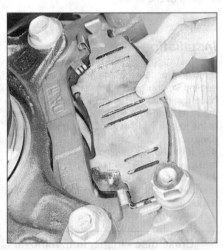

4.6m Install the upper and lower pad support plates, the new inner brake pad and the shims; make sure the ears on the pad are properly engaged with the pad support plates as shown

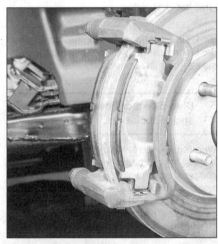

4.6n Install the outer pad and the shims, engaging the pad with the support plates

4.6o Pull out the upper and lower sliding pins and clean them off (if either rubber boot is damaged, replace it) . . .

4.6p . . . apply a light coat of high-temperature grease to the pins and to any areas where the pad will come in contact, including the shims, then install them

4.6q Install the caliper and tighten the caliper bolts to the torque listed in this Chapter's Specifications

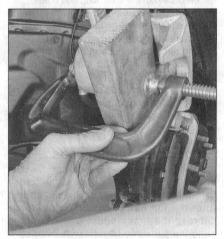

4.6r If you have difficulty installing the caliper over the new pads, use a C-clamp with a flat piece of wood to bottom the piston in its bore, then try again - it should now slip over the pads

4.9 A pair of needle-nose pliers will work just fine (in most cases) if you can't find a retracting tool. Turn the piston to retract it into the caliper until it is flush with the face of the caliper piston bore. Make sure the piston is positioned so that one of the notches in the piston face will engage with the projection on the brake pad backing plate

5.2a Using a piece of rubber hose of the appropriate size, plug the brake line banjo fitting to prevent brake fluid from leaking out and to prevent dirt and moisture from contaminating the fluid in the hose

Rear brake pads

7   Wash the caliper and disc with brake system cleaner (see illustration 4.6a). Remove the caliper mounting bolts, then lift off the caliper. Support the caliper with a length of wire - don't let it hang by the brake hose (see illustration 4.6d).

8   Follow illustrations 4.6e through 4.6q to replace the pads.

9   Using a caliper piston retracting tool (or needle-nose pliers), rotate the piston to retract it to make room for the new pads (see illustration). On the left side caliper, turn the piston counterclockwise; on the right side caliper, turn the piston clockwise. Once the piston has bottomed in the bore, turn it back the other way far enough to position one of the notches in the piston face point straight up towards the center of the caliper frame (90-degrees from the centerline of the mounting bolt holes).
Warning: *Do NOT use a C-clamp to push the caliper piston inward.*

10   Install the caliper over the brake pads, making sure the projection on the inner pad engages with the slot in the caliper piston face.

11   Install the caliper mounting bolts and tighten them to the torque listed in this Chapter's Specifications, then proceed to the next Step.

Front or rear brake pads

12   When reinstalling the caliper, be sure to tighten the mounting bolts to the torque listed in this Chapter's Specifications. After the job has been completed, firmly depress the brake pedal a few times to bring the pads into contact with the disc. If you replaced the pads on the rear brakes, operate the parking brake several times, too. Check the level of the brake fluid, adding some if necessary. Tighten the wheel lug nuts to the torque listed in the Chap-

ter 1 Specifications. Check the operation of the brakes carefully before placing the vehicle into normal service.

---

5   Disc brake caliper - removal and installation

Warning: *Dust created by the brake system is harmful to your health. Never blow it out with compressed air and don't inhale any of it. An approved filtering mask should be worn when working on the brakes. Do not, under any circumstances, use petroleum-based solvents to clean brake parts. Use brake system cleaner only!*
Note: *Always replace the calipers in pairs - never replace just one of them.*

Removal

1   Loosen the wheel lug nuts, raise the vehicle and support it securely on jackstands. Remove the wheels.

2   Remove the brake hose banjo bolt and disconnect the hose from the caliper (see illustration 4.6b). Plug the hose to keep contaminants out of the brake system and to prevent losing any more brake fluid than is necessary (see illustration). If you are removing the rear brake caliper on a 2009 or later model, loosen the parking brake cable adjustment from inside the vehicle (see Section 13), then remove the bolt holding the parking brake cable clamp to the control arm. Detach the cable end from the lever on the caliper.
Note: *If you're just removing the caliper for access to other components, don't disconnect the hose.*

3   Remove the caliper mounting bolts (see illustration 4.6b).

4   Remove the caliper. If necessary, remove the caliper torque plate (see illustration 6.2).

Installation

5   Install the caliper by reversing the removal procedure. Remember to install new sealing washers on either side of the brake hose banjo fitting. Tighten the caliper mounting bolts (and torque plate bolts, if removed) to the torque listed in this Chapter's Specifications.

6   If the hose was disconnected, bleed the brake system (see Section 11).

7   Install the wheels and lug nuts. Lower the vehicle and tighten the lug nuts to the torque listed in the Chapter 1 Specifications.

---

6   Brake disc - inspection, removal and installation

Inspection

1   Loosen the wheel lug nuts, raise the vehicle and support it securely on jackstands. Remove the wheel and install the lug nuts to hold the disc in place.

2   Remove the brake caliper as outlined in Section 5. It isn't necessary to disconnect the brake hose. After removing the caliper bolts, suspend the caliper out of the way with a piece of wire (see illustration 4.6d). Remove the torque plate mounting bolts and detach the torque plate (see illustration).

3   Visually inspect the disc surface for score marks and other damage. Light scratches and shallow grooves are normal after use and may not always be detrimental to brake operation, but deep scoring requires disc removal and refinishing by an automotive machine shop. Be sure to check both sides of the disc (see illustration). If pulsating has been noticed during application of the brakes, suspect disc runout.

4   To check disc runout, place a dial indicator at a point about 1/2-inch from the outer

6.2 To remove the caliper torque plate from the steering knuckle, remove these two bolts

6.3 The brake pads on this vehicle were obviously neglected, as they wore down completely and cut deep grooves into the disc - wear this severe means the disc must be replaced

6.4a Use a dial indicator to check disc runout; if the reading exceeds the maximum allowable runout limit, the disc will have to be machined or replaced

edge of the disc (see illustration). Set the indicator to zero and turn the disc. The indicator reading should not exceed the specified allowable runout limit. If it does, the disc should be refinished by an automotive machine shop.

Note: *The discs should be resurfaced regardless of the dial indicator reading, as this will impart a smooth finish and ensure a perfectly flat surface, eliminating any brake pedal pulsation or other undesirable symptoms related to questionable discs. At the very least, if you elect not to have the discs resurfaced, remove the glaze from the surface with sandpaper or emery cloth using a swirling motion* (see illustration).

5   It's absolutely critical that the disc not be machined to a thickness under the specified minimum allowable thickness. The minimum (or discard) thickness is cast into the inside of the disc (see illustration). The disc thickness can be checked with a micrometer (see illustration).

Removal

6   Remove the lug nuts that were put on to hold the disc in place and slide the disc from the hub.

Installation

7   Place the disc in position over the threaded studs.

8   Install the torque plate, tightening the bolts to the torque listed in this Chapter's Specifications.

9   Install the caliper, tightening the bolts to the torque listed in this Chapter's Specifications. Bleeding won't be necessary unless the brake hose was disconnected from the caliper.

10   Install the wheel and lug nuts. Lower the vehicle and tighten the lug nuts to the torque listed in the Chapter 1 Specifications. Depress the brake pedal a few times to bring the brake pads into contact with the disc. Check the operation of the brakes carefully before driving the vehicle.

6.4b Using a swirling motion, remove the glaze from the disc surface with sandpaper or emery cloth

6.5a The minimum wear dimension is cast into the back side of the disc (typical)

6.5b Use a micrometer to measure disc thickness

7 Drum brake shoes - replacement

Warning: *Drum brake shoes must be replaced on both wheels at the same time - never replace the shoes on only one wheel. Also, the dust created by the brake system is harmful to your health. Never blow it out with compressed air and don't inhale any of it. An approved filtering mask should be worn when working on the brakes. Do not, under any circumstances, use petroleum-based solvents to clean brake parts. Use brake system cleaner only!*

Caution: *Whenever the brake shoes are replaced, the return and hold-down springs should also be replaced. Due to the continuous heating/cooling cycle the springs are subjected*

to, they lose tension over a period of time and may allow the shoes to drag on the drum and wear at a much faster rate than normal.

1   Loosen the wheel lug nuts, raise the rear of the vehicle and support it securely on jackstands. Block the front wheels to keep the vehicle from rolling.
2   Release the parking brake.
3   Remove the wheel.
Note: *All four rear brake shoes must be replaced at the same time, but to avoid mixing up parts, work on the brake assembly for only one side at a time.*

NUMMI/TMMC-made brake

4   Follow the accompanying illustrations

for the brake shoe replacement procedure **(see illustrations 7.4a through 7.4y)**. Be sure to stay in order and read the caption under each illustration.

Note: *If the brake drum cannot be easily removed, make sure the parking brake is completely released. If the drum still cannot be pulled off, the brake shoes will have to be retracted. This is done by first removing the plug from the backing plate. With the plug removed, push the lever off the adjuster star wheel with a narrow screwdriver while turning the adjuster wheel with another screwdriver, moving the shoes away from the drum. The drum should now come off.*

7.4a Mark the relationship of the drum to the hub to insure that the dynamic balance is unaltered

7.4b Before removing anything, clean the brake assembly with brake cleaner and allow it to dry (position a drain pan under the brake to catch the fluid and residue); DO NOT USE COMPRESSED AIR TO BLOW OFF BRAKE DUST!

7.4c This is the complete rear brake assembly, refer to this photo during your disassembly/assembly procedure (NUMMI/TMMC-manufactured brake)

7.4d Unhook the return spring from the adjuster lever

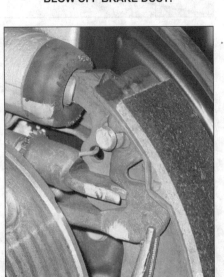

7.4e Remove the brake adjuster lever from the stud at the top of the rear shoe

7.4f Remove the lower spring between the primary and secondary shoes

7.4g Depress the hold-down spring and turn the retainer 90-degrees, then release it; a pair of pliers will work, but a special hold-down spring removal tool makes the job easier (these inexpensive tools are available at most auto parts stores)

7.4h Pull the front shoe away from the adjuster mechanism and the wheel cylinder while holding the adjuster mechanism back - twist the shoe until the spring end comes free of the shoe

7.4i With the front shoe removed, disconnect the other end of the upper return spring and remove it

7.4j Remove the hold-down spring from the rear shoe

7.4k Remove the rear shoe and adjuster assembly from the backing plate, then use pliers to remove the clip holding the parking brake lever to the stud on the rear shoe

7.4l Remove the parking brake lever from the rear shoe

7.4m Assemble the parking brake lever to the new rear shoe and crimp the C-washer closed with a pair of pliers (always use a new C-washer)

7.4n These points of shoe contact on the backing plate should receive a small dab of high-temperature grease before installing the new shoes

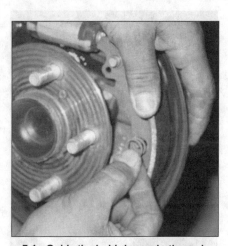

7.4o Guide the hold-down pin through while positioning the rear shoe

7.4p Secure the rear shoe with the hold-down
cup/spring/outer cup over the pin

7.4q Lubricate the moving parts of the adjuster screw with a light
coat of high-temperature grease; the screw portion of the adjuster
will need to be threaded in further than before to allow the
drum to fit over the new shoes

7.4r Install the adjuster assembly on the
rear shoe (make sure the end fits properly
into the slot in the shoe)

7.4s Hook the spring into the hole
in the rear shoe

7.4t Hold the front end of the spring with
pliers while guiding it through
the front shoe

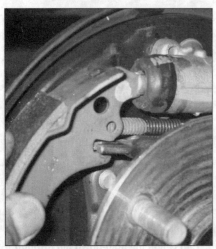

7.4u Align the top of the front shoe with
the adjuster and the slot in the piston
on the wheel cylinder

7.4v Wiggle the shoe to make sure it's
seated properly against the backing plate,
then secure it with the hold-down spring

7.4w Install the lever for the
automatic adjuster

7.4x Install the upper spring and connect it to the adjuster lever

7.4y Install the lower spring between the two shoes

TMC-made brake

5   Follow the accompanying illustrations for the brake shoe replacement procedure **(see illustrations 7.5a through 7.5x)**. Be sure to stay in order and read the caption under each illustration.

Note: *If the brake drum cannot be easily removed, make sure the parking brake is completely released. If the drum still cannot be pulled off, the brake shoes will have to be retracted. This is done by first removing the plug from the backing plate. With* *the plug removed, push the lever off the adjuster star wheel with a narrow screwdriver while turning the adjuster wheel with another screwdriver, moving the shoes away from the drum. The drum should now come off.*

7.5a The TMC rear brake system is very similar but different than the NUMMI/TMMC brake system. For that reason, we've added a complete break down of the disassembly and assembly procedures. The main difference is the upper return spring and adjuster. Use this photo as a guide for your brake repair

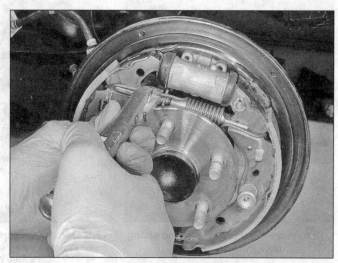

7.5b Using a pair of locking pliers, unhook the upper spring from the brake shoe

7.5c Depress the hold-down spring and turn the retainer 90-degrees, then release it and remove the upper retainer, spring and lower retainer

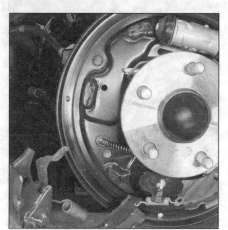

7.5d Remove the leading shoe and disconnect the lower spring

7.5e Remove the hold-down retainer and spring from the trailing shoe, then remove the trailing shoe and adjuster assembly

7.5f Unhook the upper spring from the trailing shoe and detach the adjuster from the shoe

7.5g Slide the spring back on the parking brake cable and hold it there with a pair of locking pliers, then detach the cable from the parking brake lever

7.5h It's not a bad idea to lay all the parts out and examine them not only for wear but to be sure you've got all the parts and check that any of the small components haven't suddenly come up missing

7.5i Remove the adjuster lever and spring from the leading shoe

7.5j Transfer the parking brake lever to the new trailing shoe and install a new C-clip . . .

7.5k . . . then secure the clip by squeezing its ends together

7.5l Unscrew the threaded portion of the adjuster . . .

7.5m . . . then remove the spring. Clean the adjuster components with brake system cleaner

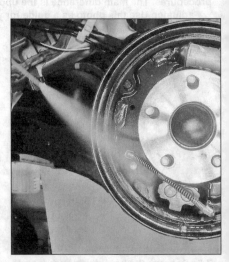

7.5n Before reassembly, thoroughly clean the backing plate area

7.5o Use a high-temp lubricant that is specifically made for brakes on any of the surfaces where the shoe will be in contact with the backing plate

7.5p Lubricate the adjuster threaded area as well

7.5q Hold the end of the parking brake cable with locking pliers, then slide the spring back on the cable and hold it in place with another pair of locking pliers . . .

7.5r . . . then place the cable into the hooked part of the parking brake lever and release the locking pliers

7.5s Install the adjuster and spring to the trailing shoe and slide them into place

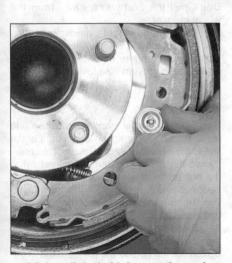

7.5t Install the hold-down spring and retainers to secure the trailing shoe

7.5u To install the leading shoe, hook the lower spring into both shoes and place the shoe against the backing plate

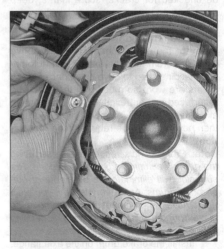

7.5v Install the hold-down spring and retainers

7.5x Use two screwdrivers, one to hold the adjuster lever off of the star wheel, while using the other one to rotate the adjuster star wheel. Keep trying the drum for fit. Once it can slide on, the automatic adjusters will then make the final adjustment for you

7.5w Hook the upper spring to the leading shoe

7.6 The maximum drum diameter is cast into the inside of the rear drums (typical)

8.4 To remove the wheel cylinder, unscrew the hydraulic line-to-wheel cylinder threaded fitting (1), then remove the mounting bolt (2)

All models

6   Before reinstalling the drum, it should be checked for cracks, score marks, deep scratches and hard spots, which will appear as small discolored areas. If the hard spots cannot be removed with fine emery cloth or if any of the other conditions listed above exist, the drum must be taken to an automotive machine shop to have it resurfaced. If the drums are worn so much that they can't be resurfaced without exceeding the maximum allowable diameter (stamped into the drum), then new ones will be required **(see illustration)**.

Note: *Professionals recommend resurfacing the drums each time a brake job is done. Resurfacing will eliminate the possibility of out-of-round drums. At the very least, if you elect not to have the drums resurfaced, remove the glaze from the surface with emery cloth using a swirling motion.*

7   Install the brake drum on the axle flange.
8   Install the wheel and lug nuts, then lower the vehicle. Tighten the lug nuts to the torque listed in Chapter 1 Specifications.

9   Make a number of forward and reverse stops and operate the parking brake to adjust the brakes until satisfactory pedal action is obtained.
10   Check the operation of the brakes carefully in an isolated area before driving the vehicle in traffic.

8   Wheel cylinder - removal and installation

Note: *Never replace only one wheel cylinder - always replace both of them at the same time.*

Removal

1   Raise the rear of the vehicle and support it securely on jackstands. Block the front wheels to keep the vehicle from rolling.
2   Remove the brake shoe assembly (see Section 7).
3   Remove all dirt and foreign material from around the wheel cylinder.
4   Disconnect the brake line with a flare-nut wrench, if available **(see illustration)**.

Don't pull the brake line away from the wheel cylinder.
5   Remove the wheel cylinder mounting bolt and detach the wheel cylinder from the brake backing plate. Immediately plug the brake line to prevent fluid loss and contamination.

Installation

6   Place the wheel cylinder in position and install the bolt finger-tight. Connect the brake line to the cylinder, being careful not to cross-thread the fitting. Tighten the wheel cylinder bolt to the torque listed in this Chapter's Specifications.
7   Tighten the brake line fitting securely and install the brake shoes and drum.
8   Bleed the brakes (see Section 11). Install the wheel and lug nuts. Lower the vehicle and tighten the lug nuts to the torque listed in Chapter 1 Specifications.
9   Check the operation of the brakes carefully before driving the vehicle.

9.1 Master cylinder installation details

A   Electrical connector
B   Brake line fittings
C   Mounting nut (right shown)

9.10 The best way to bleed air from the master cylinder before installing it on the vehicle is with a pair of bleed tubes (typical master cylinder)

9   Master cylinder - removal and installation

Warning: *On 2009 and later models, do not drop or hit the master cylinder. If the master cylinder is dropped, it may not be reused.*
Caution: *The master cylinder is piston protrudes past the master cylinder body. Hold the master cylinder by the body, not the piston, or the master cylinder could be damaged.*
Note: *Before beginning this procedure, pump the brake pedal several times (until the pedal gets hard) to deplete the vacuum inside the power brake booster.*

Removal

1   Remove the cover from the air filter housing. Unplug the electrical connector for the brake fluid level warning switch **(see illustration)**. On 2009 and later models, remove the windshield wiper arms, linkage, wiper motor (see Chapter 12) and the upper and lower cowl (see Chapter 11).
2   Remove as much fluid as possible from the reservoir with a syringe. If the vehicle is equipped with a manual transaxle, clamp off the fluid feed hose to the clutch master cylinder, then detach the hose from the brake fluid reservoir.
3   Place rags under the fittings and prepare caps or plastic bags to cover the ends of the lines once they're disconnected.
Caution: *Brake fluid will damage paint. Cover all body parts and be careful not to spill fluid during this procedure.*
4   Loosen the fittings at the ends of the brake lines where they enter the master cylinder. To prevent rounding off the flats, use a flare-nut wrench, which wraps around the fitting hex.
5   Pull the brake lines away from the master cylinder and plug the ends to prevent contamination.
6   Remove the nuts attaching the master cylinder to the power booster **(see illustration 9.1)**. Pull the master cylinder off the studs to remove it. Again, be careful not to spill the fluid as this is done.

Installation

Note: *On 2009 and later models, when installing the master cylinder, remove the piston and port protective caps. Apply only the grease supplied to the piston and brake booster.*
Note: *On 2009 and later models, If the piston gets dirty, clean it with a rag or cloth and apply lithium soap based glycol grease, evenly, around the sliding portion of the piston.*
Warning: *Do not use any other type of grease.*
7   On 2008 and earlier models, bench bleed the new master cylinder before installing it. On 2009 and later models, the master cylinder must be bled in the vehicle.
8   On 2008 and earlier models, it is recommended that the master cylinder be mounted in a vise, with the jaws of the vise clamping on the mounting flange.
9   On 2009 and later models, install the reservoir cover, then install the master cylinder over the studs on the power brake booster and tighten the attaching nuts only finger-tight at this time.
Caution: *Keep the master cylinder level or piston end up as much as possible to prevent the piston from falling out.*
10   Attach a pair of master cylinder bleeder tubes to the outlet ports of the master cylinder **(see illustration)**.
11   Fill the reservoir with brake fluid of the recommended type (see Chapter 1).
12   On 2008 and earlier models, use a Phillips screwdriver to slowly push the piston into the master cylinder. On 2009 and later models, have an assistant slowly push the brake pedal down inside the vehicle. Air will be expelled from the pressure chambers and into the reservoir. Because the tubes are submerged in fluid, air can't be drawn back into the master cylinder when you release the pedal.
Caution: *Have plenty of rags on hand to catch the fluid - brake fluid will ruin painted surfaces.*
13   Repeat the procedure until no more air bubbles are present.
14   On 2008 and earlier models, remove the bleed tubes, one at a time, and install plugs in the open ports to prevent fluid leakage and air from entering. If installing a new master cylinder, adjust the booster push-rod length (see Section 12). Also install a new O-ring on the master cylinder body.

15   On 2008 and earlier models, install the master cylinder on the power brake booster in the same manner as Step 9.
16   Thread the brake line fittings into the master cylinder. Since the master cylinder is finger-tight, the nuts can be easily loosened and moved slightly in order for the fittings to thread in easily. Do not strip the threads as the fittings are tightened.
17   Fully tighten the mounting nuts, then tighten the brake line fittings.
18   Fill the master cylinder reservoir with fluid, then bleed the master cylinder and the brake system as described in Section 11. To bleed the cylinder on the vehicle, have an assistant depress the brake pedal slowly and then hold the pedal to the floor. Loosen the fitting nut to allow air and fluid to escape **(see illustration)**. Repeat this procedure on both fittings until the fluid is clear of air bubbles.
Caution: *Have plenty of rags on hand to catch the fluid - brake fluid will ruin painted surfaces.*
19   Test the operation of the brake system carefully before placing the vehicle into normal service.
Warning: *Do not operate the vehicle if you are in doubt about the effectiveness of the brake system.*

9.18 Have an assistant depress the brake pedal and hold it down, then loosen the fitting nut, allowing the air and fluid to escape; repeat this procedure on both fittings until the fluid is clear of air bubbles

10.3 Unscrew the brake line threaded fitting with a flare-nut wrench to protect the fitting corners from being rounded off

10.4 Remove the brake hose-to-brake line U-clip (A) with a pair of pliers - B is the brake hose bracket bolt on the strut

10 Brake hoses and lines - inspection and replacement

Inspection

1   About every six months, with the vehicle raised and supported securely on jackstands, the rubber hoses which connect the steel brake lines with the front and rear brake assemblies should be inspected for cracks, chafing of the outer cover, leaks, blisters and other damage. These are important and vulnerable parts of the brake system and inspection should be complete. A light and mirror will be helpful for a thorough check. If a hose exhibits any of the above conditions, replace it with a new one.

Replacement

Front brake hose

2   Loosen the wheel lug nuts, raise the vehicle and support it securely on jackstands. Remove the wheel.
3   At the frame bracket, unscrew the brake line fitting from the hose (see illustration). Use a flare-nut wrench to prevent rounding off the corners.
4   Remove the U-clip from the female fitting at the bracket with a pair of pliers (see illustration), then pass the hose through the bracket.
5   At the caliper end of the hose, remove the banjo fitting bolt (see illustration 3.6b), then separate the hose from the caliper. Note that there are two copper sealing washers on either side of the fitting - they should be replaced with new ones during installation.
6   Remove the U-clip from the strut bracket, then feed the hose through the bracket.
7   To install the hose, pass the caliper fitting end through the strut bracket, then connect the fitting to the caliper with the banjo bolt and copper washers. Make sure the locating lug on the fitting is engaged with the hole in the caliper, then tighten the bolt to the torque listed in this Chapter's Specifications.

8   Push the metal support into the strut bracket and install the U-clip. Make sure the hose isn't twisted between the caliper and the strut bracket.
9   Route the hose into the frame bracket, again making sure it isn't twisted, then connect the brake line fitting, starting the threads by hand. Install the clip and E-ring, if equipped, then tighten the fitting securely.
10   Bleed the caliper (see Section 11).
11   Install the wheel and lug nuts, lower the vehicle and tighten the lug nuts to the torque listed in the Chapter 1 Specifications.

Rear brake hose

12   Perform Steps 2, 3 and 4 above, then repeat Steps 3 and 4 at the other end of the hose. Be sure to bleed the wheel cylinder (see Section 11).

Metal brake lines

13   When replacing brake lines, be sure to use the correct parts. Don't use copper tubing for any brake system components. Purchase genuine steel brake lines from a dealer or auto parts store.
14   Prefabricated brake line, with the tube ends already flared and fittings installed, is available at auto parts stores and dealer parts departments.
15   When installing the new line, make sure it's securely supported in the brackets and has plenty of clearance between moving or hot components.
16   After installation, check the master cylinder fluid level and add fluid as necessary. Bleed the brake system (see Section 11) and test the brakes carefully before driving the vehicle in traffic.

11 Brake hydraulic system - bleeding

Warning: *Wear eye protection when bleeding the brake system. If the fluid comes in contact with your eyes, immediately rinse them with water and seek medical attention.*

Note: *Bleeding the hydraulic system is necessary to remove any air that manages to find its way into the system when it's been opened during removal and installation of a hose, line, caliper or master cylinder.*

1   You'll probably have to bleed the system at all four brakes if air has entered it due to low fluid level, or if the brake lines have been disconnected at the master cylinder.
2   If a brake line was disconnected only at a wheel, then only that caliper or wheel cylinder must be bled.
3   If a brake line is disconnected at a fitting located between the master cylinder and any of the brakes, that part of the system served by the disconnected line must be bled.
4   Remove any residual vacuum from the brake power booster by applying the brake several times with the engine off.
5   Remove the master cylinder reservoir cover and fill the reservoir with brake fluid. Reinstall the cover.
6   Have an assistant on hand, as well as a supply of new brake fluid, a clear container partially filled with clean brake fluid, a length of tubing to fit over the bleeder valve and a wrench to open and close the bleeder valve.
Note: *Check the fluid level often during the bleeding operation and add fluid as necessary to prevent the fluid level from falling low enough to allow air bubbles into the master cylinder.*
7   Beginning at the right rear wheel, loosen the bleeder valve slightly, then tighten it to a point where it's snug but can still be loosened quickly and easily.
8   Place one end of the tubing over the bleeder valve and submerge the other end in brake fluid in the container (see illustration).
9   Have the assistant depress the brake pedal slowly, then hold the pedal down firmly.
10   While the pedal is held down, open the bleeder valve just enough to allow a flow of fluid to leave the valve. Watch for air bubbles to exit the submerged end of the tube. When the fluid flow slows after a couple of seconds, close the valve and have your assistant release the pedal.

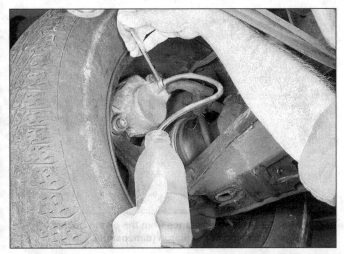

11.8 When bleeding the brakes, a hose is connected to the bleeder valve at the caliper or wheel cylinder and then submerged in brake fluid. Air will be seen as bubbles in the tube and container. All air must be expelled before moving to the next wheel

12.11 To disconnect the power brake booster pushrod from the brake pedal, remove the retaining clip and clevis pin (center); to detach the booster from the firewall, remove the four mounting nuts (three seen here)

11   Repeat Steps 9 and 10 until no more air is seen leaving the tube, then tighten the bleeder valve and proceed to the left rear wheel, the right front wheel and the left front wheel, in that order, and perform the same procedure. Be sure to check the fluid in the master cylinder reservoir frequently.

12   Never use old brake fluid. It contains moisture that will deteriorate the brake system components.

13   Refill the master cylinder with fluid at the end of the operation.

14   Check the operation of the brakes. The pedal should feel solid when depressed, with no sponginess. If necessary, repeat the entire process.

Warning: *Do not operate the vehicle if you're in doubt about the effectiveness of the brake system.*

12   Power brake booster - check, removal and installation

Operating check

1   Depress the brake pedal several times with the engine off and make sure there's no change in the pedal reserve distance.

2   Depress the pedal and start the engine. If the pedal goes down slightly, operation is normal.

Airtightness check

3   Start the engine and turn it off after one or two minutes. Depress the brake pedal slowly several times. If the pedal depresses less each time, the booster is airtight.

4   Depress the brake pedal while the engine is running, then stop the engine with the pedal depressed. If there's no change in the pedal reserve travel after holding the pedal for 30 seconds, the booster is airtight.

Removal

5   Power brake booster units shouldn't be disassembled. They require special tools not normally found in most automotive repair stations or shops. They're fairly complex and, because of their critical relationship to brake performance, should be replaced with a new or rebuilt one.

6   Remove the air filter housing (see Chapter 4).

7   Remove the brake master cylinder (see Section 9).

8   In the engine compartment, disconnect the vacuum hose from the booster.

9   On models with cruise control, remove the cruise control actuator and bracket.

10   Unclip and/or detach any brake lines around the booster, as necessary, to allow the booster to be removed without damaging the lines.

11   Using a flashlight, locate the clevis which connects the booster pushrod to the top of the brake pedal. Remove the clevis pin retaining clip with pliers and pull out the pin **(see illustration)**.

12   Remove the four nuts and washers holding the brake booster to the firewall (you may need a light to see them). Slide the booster straight out from the firewall until the studs clear the holes.

Installation

13   Installation procedures are basically the reverse of removal. Tighten the clevis locknut securely and the booster mounting nuts to the torque listed in this Chapter's Specifications.

14   If a new power brake booster unit is being installed, check the pushrod clearance in the following Steps **(see illustration)**.

Note: *If a new genuine Toyota power brake booster is being installed, it is likely that the pushrod is pre-adjusted to achieve the correct clearance.*

12.14a Measure the distance from the master cylinder mounting surface to the top of the booster pushrod (dimension A)

1)   *Measure the distance from the face of the booster to the tip of the pushrod. Write down this measurement(see illustration). This is dimension A.*

2)   *Measure the distance from the mounting flange to the end of the piston (see illustration). Write down this measurement. This is dimension B.*

3)   *Measure the distance from the piston pocket (inside the master cylinder) to the end of the piston (see illustration). Write down this measurement. This is dimension C.*

4)   *Subtract measurement C from measurement B, then subtract measurement A from the difference between C and B. This is the pushrod clearance.*

5)   *Compare your calculated pushrod clearance to the pushrod clearance listed in this Chapter's Specifications. If necessary, adjust the pushrod length to achieve the correct clearance (see illustration).*

12.14b Measure the distance from the mounting flange to the end of the piston (dimension B)

12.14c Measure the distance from the piston pocket to the end of the piston (dimension C)

12.14d To adjust the length of the booster pushrod, have an assistant press the brake pedal down and hold it. This moves the front booster pushrod out of the booster for access. Hold the stationary portion of the pushrod (A) with pliers and turn the adjusting screw (B) in or out. Note: Remember to release the brake pedal fully while checking the clearance after each adjustment and don't apply any grease to the pushrod until after the clearance has been achieved

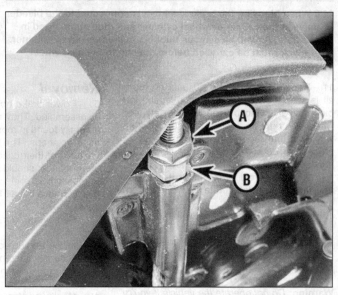

13.3 Loosen the locknut (A), then turn the adjusting nut (B) until the desired handle travel is obtained

15   After the final installation of the master cylinder and brake lines, the system must be bled (see Section 11) and the brake pedal height and freeplay must be checked (see Section 14).

16   Carefully test the operation of the brakes before placing the vehicle in normal operation.

13   Parking brake - adjustment

1   The parking brake lever, when properly adjusted, should travel six to nine clicks when a moderate pulling force is applied. If it travels less than six clicks, there's a chance the parking brake might not be releasing completely and might be dragging on the drum or disc. If the lever can be pulled up more than nine clicks, the parking brake may not hold adequately on an incline, allowing the car to roll.

2   To gain access to the parking brake cable adjuster, remove the center console (see Chapter 11).

3   Loosen the locknut (the upper nut) while holding the adjusting nut (lower nut) with a wrench **(see illustration)**. Tighten the adjusting nut until the desired travel is attained. Tighten the locknut.

4   Install the console.

14   Brake pedal - adjustment

Pedal height

1   The height of the brake pedal is the distance the pedal sits off the floor **(see illustration)**. If the pedal height is not within Specifications, it must be adjusted.

2   Loosen the locknut on the brake light switch and unscrew the switch until it doesn't contact the pedal arm. Before measuring the brake pedal height, make sure the pedal is in the fully-returned position. Measure the pedal height and, if necessary, adjust it by loosening the locknut on the pedal pushrod and turning the pushrod to achieve the proper height.

When the proper height has been obtained, tighten the locknut securely.

3   Adjust the brake light switch (see Section 15).

Pedal freeplay

4   The freeplay is the pedal slack, or the distance the pedal can be depressed before it begins to have any effect on the brake system. Before checking brake pedal freeplay, depress the brake pedal several times (with the engine off).

5   If the pedal freeplay is not within the specified range, check the adjustment of the brake light switch (see Section 15).

6   If the brake light switch is properly adjusted, troubleshoot the brake system for the cause of excessive freeplay (suspect either air in the hydraulic system [see Section 11], excessive clearance between the booster pushrod and the master cylinder piston [see Section 12]), or excessive clearance between the rear brake shoes and the brake drums.

92037-9-13.1 HAYNES

14.1 Brake pedal adjusting details

A *Pedal height adjusting point*
B *Brake light switch locknut*
C *Pedal height measurement point*
D *Freeplay measurement point*

Brake pedal reserve distance

7   With the parking brake released and the engine running, depress the pedal with normal braking effort and have an assistant measure the distance from the center of the pedal pad to the floor. If the distance is less than specified, troubleshoot the brake system (see Step 6).

15   Brake light switch - check, removal, installation and adjustment

Check

1   The brake light switch is located on the brake pedal bracket. You'll need to remove the trim panel beneath the steering column to get to the switch and connector.
2   With the brake pedal in the fully released position, the switch opens the brake light circuit. When the brake pedal is depressed, the switch closes the circuit and sends current to the brake lights.
3   If the brake lights are inoperative, check the fuse and the bulbs (see Chapter 12).
4   If the fuse and bulbs are okay, verify that voltage is available at the switch.
5   If there's no voltage to the switch, search for an open circuit condition between the fuse block and the switch. If there is voltage to the switch, close the switch (depress the brake pedal) and verify that there's voltage on the other side of the switch.
6   If there's no voltage on the other side of the switch, replace the switch. If there is voltage but the brake lights still don't work, look for an open circuit condition between the switch and the brake lights.

15.7 The brake light switch (A) is located at the top of the brake pedal - (B) is the adjusting locknut

Note: *There is always the remote possibility that all of the brake light bulbs are burned out, but this is not very likely.*

Removal and installation

2008 and earlier models

7   The brake light switch **(see illustration)** is located on a bracket at the top of the brake pedal.
8   Disconnect the wiring harness at the brake light switch.
9   Loosen the locknut and unscrew the switch from the pedal bracket.
10   Installation is the reverse of removal.

2009 and later models

11   Disconnect the electrical connector from the brake light switch.
12   Rotate the switch counterclockwise 90-degrees, so that it unlocks from its holder, then pull it directly out of the holder **(see illustration)**.
13   To install the switch, insert it into its holder and push it in until the switch body contacts the rubber stop on the brake pedal bracket. Hold the brake pedal up while placing the switch in position. Rotate the switch 90-degrees clockwise (1/4 turn) to lock it into place. It will achieve the proper clearance (0.020 to 0.102 inch) to the rubber stop automatically.
Caution: *Do not press in on the switch while turning it.*
14   Plug the electrical connector into the switch.
15   Confirm that the brake lights work properly before placing the vehicle into normal service.

Adjustment

16   Check and, if necessary, adjust brake pedal height (see Section 14).
17   Loosen the switch locknut, adjust the switch so that the distance the plunger protrudes **(see illustration)** is within the range listed in this Chapter's Specifications. (If you're unable to measure this distance, adjust the plunger so that it lightly contacts the pedal stop.) Tighten the locknut.

15.12 The plastic mounting bracket doesn't come with the replacement switch (in most cases), rotate the switch to remove it from the bracket

92008-9-15.6 HAYNES

15.17 To adjust the brake light switch, loosen the locknut and rotate the switch until the plunger distance (dimension A) is within the range listed in this Chapter's Specifications, then tighten the locknut

18   Plug the electrical connector into the switch and reconnect the battery. Make sure the brake lights come on when the brake pedal is depressed and go off when the pedal is released. If not, repeat the adjustment procedure until the brake lights function properly.
Note: *On the older models with the threaded type brake switch. If you find the brake lights are staying on after the car is shut off. Before assuming it is the brake light switch that has failed, check the rubber stopper that the brake switch plunger rests against. Toyota (and may other manufacturers) use a soft rubber stopper to cushion the brake switch plunger. This eliminates any harsh tapping sounds when the brake pedal is released. In a lot of cases the rubber stopper has deteriorated and fallen out, (Check the floor board area for any small fragments of rubber) leaving a hole where the brake switch plunger will pass through. Replacement stoppers are available at most parts stores, usually in a small assortment pack with the most popular sizes.*

16   Parking brake shoes (2008 and earlier rear disc brake models) - removal and installation

Warning: *Dust created by the brake system is hazardous to your health. Never blow it out with compressed air and don't inhale any of it. An approved filtering mask should be worn when working on the brakes. Do not, under any circumstances, use petroleum-based solvents to clean brake parts. Use brake system cleaner only!*

Warning: *Parking brake shoes must be replaced on both wheels at the same time - never replace the shoes on only one wheel.*

1   Remove the rear brake discs (see Section 6).

2   Measure the thickness of the lining material on the shoes. If the lining has worn down to 1.0 mm or less, replace the shoes.

3   Inspect the drum portion of the disc for scoring, grooves or cracks due to heat. If any of these conditions exist or there is significant wear to the drum, the disc must be replaced.

4   Wash off the brake parts with brake system cleaner.

5   Remove the parking brake shoes upper return springs **(see illustrations)**.

6   Remove the lower return spring and adjuster assembly **(see illustrations)**.

7   Remove the front shoe hold-down clip and pin **(see illustration)**. Remove the shoe.

8   Remove the strut and spring **(see illustration)**.

9   Remove the rear shoe **(see illustration)** and disconnect it from the parking brake shoe lever.

10   Apply a thin coat of high temperature brake grease to the shoe contact points on the backing plate.

11   Lubricate the adjuster with high temperature brake grease **(see illustration)**.

12   Apply a very small amount of high temperature brake grease to the contact point of the new rear shoe and parking brake lever. Attach the parking brake lever to the rear shoe.

16.5a Remove the front parking brake shoe upper return spring from the anchor and unhook it from the shoe

16.5b Remove the rear parking brake shoe upper return spring from the anchor and unhook it from the shoe

16.6a Remove the lower return spring. . .

16.6b. . . and the adjuster assembly

13   Install the rear shoe clip, shoe pin and shoe.

14   Install the front shoe clip, pin and shoe.

15   Install the strut and spring **(see illustration)**.

16   Install the adjuster and lower return spring **(see illustrations)**.

17   Install the upper return springs **(see illustrations)**.

18   Install the brake disc and use two lug

16.7 Remove the front shoe hold-down clip, pin and shoe

16.8 Remove the strut and spring

16.9 Remove the rear shoe hold-down clip, pin and shoe

16.11 Lubricate these areas of the adjuster with high-temperature brake grease

16.15 Spread the upper part of the shoes and install the strut and spring

16.16a Install the adjuster. . .

16.16b. . . and the lower return spring

nuts with washers (for spacing) to hold the disc securely against the hub.

19 With the hole in the disc and hub flange aligned with the star-wheel adjuster, you can adjust the parking brake shoe-to-drum clearance with a screwdriver by turn-ing the star-wheel adjuster up to contract the shoes, or down to expand the shoes

20 Install the brake caliper (see Section 5). Be sure to tighten the bolts to the torque values listed in this Chapter's Spec-ifications.

21 Install the wheels, then lower the vehi-cle. Tighten the wheel lug nuts to the torque listed in the Chapter 1 Specifications.

22 Check the parking brake for proper oper-ation and adjust it again if necessary.

16.17a Install the rear shoe upper return spring. . .

16.17b. . . and the front shoe upper return spring

17   Vacuum pump - removal and installation

Note: *This procedure applies to 2ZR-FAE models only.*

1   Disconnect the cable from the negative terminal of the battery (see Chapter 5).

2   Remove the engine cover by pulling it straight up to disengage its grommets from their corresponding ballstuds.

3   Unbolt the wiring harness bracket from the left end (driver's side) of the cylinder head. Reposition the harness out of the way.

4   Squeeze the hose clamp and slide it up the hose, then detach the vacuum hose from the pump.

5   Remove the three pump mounting bolts and pull the pump from its mounting hole.

6   Install new O-rings to the pump shaft and housing.

Note: *Lubricate the O-rings with clean engine oil before installation.*

7   Apply a film of clean engine oil to the pump bore in the cylinder head, then install the pump, making sure the drive tangs on the pump engage with the slot in the camshaft.

8   Install the bolts and tighten them evenly, a little at a time, to the torque listed in this Chapter's Specifications.

9   The remainder of installation is the reverse of removal.

Chapter 10
Suspension and steering systems

Contents

Specifications

Torque specifications

Ft-lbs (unless otherwise indicated)

Note: *One foot-pound (ft-lb) of torque is equivalent to 12 inch-pounds (in-lbs) of torque. Torque values below approximately 15 ft-lbs are expressed in inch-pounds, since most foot-pound torque wrenches are not accurate at these smaller values.*

Front suspension
Balljoints
Balljoint-to-control arm bolt/nuts ... 66
Balljoint-to-steering knuckle nut
1.8L engine models ... 76
2.4L engine models ... 91
Control arm-to-cross member
Corolla models
2009 and earlier ... 101
2010 through 2013
Front bolt ... 101
Rear bolt ... 107
2014 and later
Front bolt ... 101
Rear bolt ... 93
Matrix models
2011 and earlier ... 101
2012 and later
Front bolt ... 101
Rear bolt ... 93
Vibe models ... 101
Stabilizer bar
Bracket-to-cross member bolts
2008 and earlier models ... 168 in-lbs
2009 and later models ... 18
Link nuts ... 55
Struts
Strut-to-steering knuckle bolts/nuts
2008 and earlier models ... 113
2009 and later models ... 177
Strut upper mounting nuts
2008 and earlier models ... 29
2009 and later models ... 37
Damper shaft nut ... 35
Subframe/crossmember **(see illustration 4.6)**
Bolt A ... 116
Bolt B ... 83
Bolts/nuts C ... 38
Bolt 1 (if equipped)** ... 64

**Some models may be equipped with a larger bolt (labeled as "1" in the illustration) than the nearby surrounding bolts - if this is the case, be sure to tighten this bolt to the correct alternative torque specification. If the bolt is the same size as the surrounding bolts, tighten it to specification "C".

Torque specifications (continued)

Note: *One foot-pound (ft-lb) of torque is equivalent to 12 inch-pounds (in-lbs) of torque. Torque values below approximately 15 ft-lbs are expressed in inch-pounds, since most foot-pound torque wrenches are not accurate at these smaller values.*

Ft-lbs (unless otherwise indicated)

Rear suspension

Axle beam pivot bolts
2008 and earlier models	66
2009 to 2013 models	63
2014 and later models	122

Hub and bearing assembly-to-rear axle beam bolts
2008 and earlier models	45
2009 and later models	74

Stabilizer bar-to-rear axle beam bolts/nuts
2008 and earlier models	144
2009 and later models	184

Shock absorber/coil spring assembly
Lower mounting nut	59
Upper mounting nuts/bolt	59

Damper shaft nut
2008 and earlier models	41
2009 and later models	29

Steering

Airbag module Torx screws	78 in-lbs
Steering gear-to-crossmember bolts	43
Steering wheel nut	37
Tie-rod end-to-steering knuckle nut	36
Tie-rod end locknuts	55
U joint-to-pinion shaft pinch bolt	26
Power steering pressure line fitting-to-pump	30
Power steering pump mounting bolts	27
Pressure lines to steering gear	108 in-lbs

Steering column mounting fasteners
2008 and earlier models (w/o electric power steering)	15
2009 to 2012 models (with electric power steering) - bolt/nuts	18

2013 and later models (with electric power steering)
Bolt	27
Nuts	18

1   General information

Front suspension

1   The front suspension **(see illustration)** is a MacPherson strut design. The upper end of each strut/coil spring assembly is attached to the vehicle's body strut support. The lower end of the strut assembly is connected to the upper end of the steering knuckle. The steering knuckle is attached to a balljoint mounted on the outer end of the suspension control arm. A stabilizer bar reduces body roll.

Rear suspension

2   The rear suspension **(see illustration)** utilizes shock absorber/coil spring assemblies. The upper end of each assembly is attached to the vehicle body. The lower ends are attached to a beam axle. The axle has two integral forward arms located to the chassis by bolts through pivot bushings.

Steering

3   The rack-and-pinion steering gear is located behind the engine/transaxle assembly on the front suspension crossmember and actuates the tie-rods, which are attached to the steering knuckles. The inner ends of the tie-rods are protected by rubber boots, which should be inspected periodically for secure attachment, tears and leaking lubricant.

4   On 2008 and earlier models, the power assist system consists of a belt-driven pump and associated lines and hoses. The fluid level in the power steering pump reservoir should be checked periodically (see Chapter 1). On 2009 and later models, an electric motor on the steering column provides power assist.

5   The steering wheel operates the steering shaft, which actuates the steering gear through universal joints. Looseness in the steering can be caused by wear in the steering shaft universal joints, the steering gear, the tie-rod ends and loose retaining bolts.

Precautions

6   Frequently, when working on the suspension or steering system components, you may come across fasteners that seem impossible to loosen. These fasteners on the underside of the vehicle are continually subjected to water, road grime, mud, etc., and can become rusted or "frozen," making them extremely difficult to remove. In order to unscrew these stubborn fasteners without damaging them (or other components), be sure to use lots of penetrating oil and allow it to soak in for a while. Using a wire brush to clean exposed threads will also ease removal of the nut or bolt and prevent damage to the threads. Sometimes a sharp blow with a hammer and punch will break the bond between a nut and bolt threads, but care must be taken to pre- vent the punch from slipping off the fastener and ruining the threads. Heating the stuck fastener and surrounding area with a torch sometimes helps too, but isn't recommended because of the obvious dangers associated with fire. Long breaker bars and extension, or "cheater," pipes will increase leverage, but never use an extension pipe on a ratchet - the ratcheting mechanism could be damaged. Sometimes tightening the nut or bolt first will help to break it loose. Fasteners that require drastic measures to remove should always be replaced with new ones.

7   Since most of the procedures dealt with in this Chapter involve jacking up the vehicle and working underneath it, a good pair of jackstands will be needed. A hydraulic floor jack is the preferred type of jack to lift the vehicle, and it can also be used to support certain components during various operations.

Warning: *Never, under any circumstances, rely on a jack to support the vehicle while working on it. Whenever any of the suspension or steering fasteners are loosened or removed they must be inspected and, if necessary, replaced with new ones of the same part number or of original equipment quality and design. Torque specifications must be followed for proper re- assembly and component retention. Never attempt to heat or straighten any suspension or steering components. Instead, replace any bent or damaged part with a new one.*

1.1 Front suspension and steering components

1	Stabilizer bar	3	Balljoint
2	Control arm	4	Strut/coil spring assembly

5	Support brace
6	Suspension crossmember

1.2 Typical rear suspension components

1	Rear axle beam	3	Shock absorber/coil spring assembly
2	Rear axle beam pivots	4	Rear stabilizer bar (inside axle beam)

2   Strut assembly (front) - removal, inspection and installation

Removal

Note: *On 2009 and later models, it is necessary to remove the windshield wiper motor and link assembly to perform this procedure (see Chapter 12).*

1   Loosen the wheel lug nuts, raise the vehicle and support it securely on jackstands. Remove the wheel.

2   Unbolt the brake hose bracket from the strut. If the vehicle is equipped with ABS, detach the speed sensor wiring harness from the strut by removing the clamp bracket bolt **(see illustrations)**. Refer to Section 4 and disconnect the stabilizer bar link from the strut.

Note: *Always reattach all the hold-down fasteners back into place to avoid any wire harness damage.*

3   Mark the relationship of the strut to the steering knuckle. Remove the strut-to-knuckle nuts **(see illustration)** and knock the bolts out with a hammer and punch.

Note: *Also mark the positions of the bolts, as special camber adjusting bolts may have been fitted at some point.*

4   Separate the strut from the steering knuckle. Be careful not to overextend the inner CV joint. Also, don't let the steering knuckle fall outward and strain the brake hose.

5   Support the strut and spring assembly (an assistant would be helpful here) and remove the three strut-to-body nuts **(see illustration)**. Remove the assembly out from the fenderwell.

Inspection

6   Check the strut body for leaking fluid, dents, cracks and other obvious damage that would warrant repair or replacement.

7   Check the coil spring for chips or cracks in the spring coating (this will cause premature spring failure due to corrosion). Inspect the spring seat for cuts, hardness and general deterioration.

8   If any undesirable conditions exist, proceed to the strut disassembly procedure (see Section 3).

Installation

9   Guide the strut assembly up into the fenderwell and insert the upper mounting studs through the holes in the body. Once the studs protrude, install the nuts so the strut won't fall back through. This is most easily accomplished with the help of an assistant, as the strut is quite heavy and awkward.

10 Slide the steering knuckle into the strut flange and insert the two bolts. Install the nuts, align the previously made match-marks and tighten them to the torque listed in this Chapter's Specifications.

11 Connect the brake hose bracket to the strut and tighten the bolt securely. If the vehicle is equipped with ABS, install the speed sensor wiring harness bracket.

12 Install the wheel and lug nuts, then lower the vehicle and tighten the lug nuts to the

2.2a Remove the bolt that secures the brake line to the strut . . .

2.2b . . . then detach the line from the bracket

2.2c To remove this type of speed sensor fastener, pinch the two sides together

2.2d Use a flat trim tool to release the plastic retainer

2.3 To detach the strut assembly from the steering knuckle, remove the two nuts, then knock out the bolts with a hammer and punch - note marks of bolt/strut relationship

2.5 To detach the upper end of the strut assembly from the body, remove the upper mounting nuts

3.3 Install the spring compressor according to the tool manufacturer's instructions and compress the spring until all pressure is relieved from the upper spring seat

3.4 Remove the damper shaft nut - if the upper spring seat turns while loosening the nut, immobilize it with a chain wrench or strap wrench

3.5 Lift the suspension support off the damper shaft

torque listed in the Chapter 1 Specifications.
13   Tighten the upper mounting nuts to the torque listed in this Chapter's Specifications.
14   Drive the vehicle to an alignment shop to have the front-end alignment checked, and if necessary, adjusted.

3   Strut or shock absorber/coil spring assembly - replacement

1   If the struts or coil springs exhibit the tell-tale signs of wear (leaking fluid, loss of damping capability, chipped, sagging or cracked coil springs) explore all options before beginning any work. The strut/shock absorber assemblies are not serviceable and must be replaced if a problem develops. However, strut assemblies complete with springs may be available on an exchange basis, which eliminates much time and work. Whichever route you choose to take, check on the cost and availability of parts before disassembling your vehicle.

Warning: *Disassembling a strut is potentially dangerous and utmost attention must be directed to the job, or serious injury may result. Use only a high-quality spring compressor and carefully follow the manufacturer's instructions furnished with the tool. After removing the coil spring from the strut assembly, set it aside in a safe, isolated area.*

Disassembly

2   Remove the strut assembly following the procedure described in Section 2 (front) or if you're working on a rear shock absorber/coil spring assembly, Section 10. Mount the assembly in a vise. Line the vise jaws with wood or rags to prevent damage to the unit and don't tighten the vise excessively.
3   Following the tool manufacturer's instructions, install the spring compressor (which can be obtained at most auto parts stores or equipment yards on a daily rental basis) on the spring and compress it sufficiently to relieve all pressure from the upper spring seat **(see illustration)**. This can be verified by wiggling the spring.

4   Mark the positions of the upper and lower spring seats and suspension support to each other. Loosen the damper shaft nut with a socket **(see illustration)**.
5   Remove the nut and suspension support **(see illustration)**. Inspect the bearing in the suspension support for smooth operation. If it doesn't turn smoothly, replace the suspension support. Check the rubber portion of the suspension support for cracking and general deterioration. If there is any separation of the rubber, replace it.
6   Lift the spring seat and upper insulator from the damper shaft **(see illustration)**. Check the rubber spring seat for cracking and hardness, replacing it if necessary.
7   Carefully lift the compressed spring from the assembly **(see illustration)** and set it in a safe place.
Warning: *Never place your head near the end of the spring!*
8   Slide the rubber bumper off the damper shaft.
9   Check the lower insulator (if equipped) for wear, cracking and hardness and replace it if necessary.

3.6 Remove the spring seat from the damper shaft

3.7 Remove the compressed spring assembly - keep the ends of the spring pointed away from your body

3.11 When installing the spring, make sure the end fits into the recessed portion of the lower seat

3.12 The flats on the damper shaft must match up with the flats in the spring seat

Reassembly

10   If the lower insulator is being replaced, set it into position with the dropped portion seated in the lowest part of the seat. Extend the damper rod to its full length and install the rubber bumper.

11   Carefully place the coil spring onto the lower insulator, with the end of the spring resting in the lowest part of the insulator (**see illustration**).

12   Install the upper insulator and spring seat, making sure that the flats in the hole in the seat match up with the flats on the damper shaft (**see illustration**).

13   Install the dust seal and suspension support to the damper shaft. Make sure all of the marks made in Step 4 are in alignment.

14   Install a new nut and tighten it to the torque listed in this Chapter's Specifications.
Warning: *The manufacturer states that a new damper shaft nut must be installed.*

15   Install the strut assembly following the procedure outlined in Section 2 (front), or the rear shock absorber/coil spring as described in Section 10.

---

4   Stabilizer bar and bushings (front) - removal and installation

Note: *This is a difficult procedure for the novice mechanic, since the engine/transaxle must be supported from above with an engine support fixture or hoist, while the front suspension crossmember is unbolted and lowered.*

Removal

1   Loosen the front wheel lug nuts. Raise the front of the vehicle and support it securely on jackstands. Apply the parking brake and block the rear wheels to keep the vehicle from rolling off the stands. Remove the front wheels.

4.2 If you're removing the stabilizer bar, detach the bar from the link by removing the lower nut; if you're removing the strut, remove the upper nut and detach the link from the strut

2   Detach the stabilizer bar link from the bar (**see illustration**). If the ballstud turns with the nut, use an Allen wrench to hold the stud.

3   Remove the steering shaft pinch bolt (see Section 17).

4   Support the engine/transaxle assembly from above with an engine hoist or support fixture (**see illustration 17.3**).

5   Remove the mounting bolts from the engine/transaxle mounts to the crossmember. Refer to Chapter 2A for engine and transaxle mount replacement procedures.

6   Remove the subframe/crossmember mounting bolts from the chassis, using a floor jack to lower the crossmember enough to access the stabilizer bar clamps (**see illustration**). Be sure to note exactly the size and location of each nut and bolt to insure correct reassembly.
Note: *The transaxle should be supported by a floor jack immediately after the subframe is removed from the vehicle. The transaxle will tilt slightly but should remain steady if the engine is properly secured with the engine compartment brace.*
Caution: *There are two types of subframe/ crossmembers: TMC manufacture and non-TMC manufacture, and the mounting bolt torque values are different depending on which type your vehicle has. On non-TMC subframes, the bolt indicated by the "1" in illustration 4.6 is larger than the other "C" bolts.*

7   Unbolt the stabilizer bar bushing clamps and remove the stabilizer bar (**see illustration**).

8   While the stabilizer bar is off the vehicle, slide off the retainer bushings and inspect them. If they're cracked, worn or deteriorated, replace them. It's also a good idea to inspect the stabilizer bar link. To check it, flip the balljoint stud side-to-side five or six times, then install the nut. Using an inch-pound torque

4.6 Remove the front suspension subframe bolts with an overhead support for the engine/transaxle and a floor jack under the subframe - refer to the letter designations for torque specs when installing fasteners for the subframe (A and B), engine mount crossmember (C) and the lower control arm balljoint bolts (D)

wrench, turn the nut continuously one turn every two to four seconds and note the torque reading on the fifth turn. It should be about 0.4 to 8.7 in-lbs. If it isn't, replace the link.
9   Clean the bushing area of the stabi-

lizer bar with a stiff wire brush to remove any rust or dirt.

Installation
10   Lubricate the inside and outside of

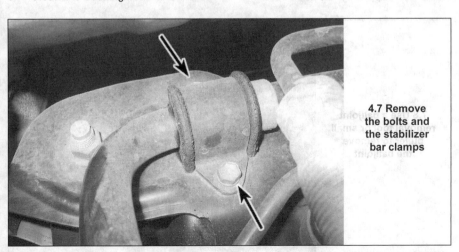

4.7 Remove the bolts and the stabilizer bar clamps

the new bushing with vegetable oil (used in cooking) to simplify reassembly.
Caution: *Don't use petroleum or mineral-based lubricants or brake fluid - they will lead to deterioration of the bushings.*
11   Installation is the reverse of removal. Tighten all fasteners to the torque values listed in this Chapter's Specifications.
Note: *When installing the subframe, use a rod of the same diameter as the four subframe to-chassis bolts to align each side until that side's bolts can be inserted one at a time. Do not tighten any of the four bolts until all have been installed finger-tight, then tighten to the Specifications in this Chapter.*
12   Install the wheel and lug nuts, lower the vehicle and tighten the lug nuts to the torque listed in the Chapter 1 Specifications.
13   It's a good idea to have the front wheel alignment checked, and if necessary, adjusted after this job has been performed.

5.2a To detach the control arm from the steering knuckle balljoint, remove this bolt and these two nuts . . .

5.2b . . . and pry the control arm and balljoint apart with a large prybar or screwdriver

6.3 Separate the balljoint from the steering knuckle with a picklefork-type balljoint separator

5   Control arm - removal, inspection and installation

Removal

1   Loosen the wheel lug nuts on the side to be dismantled, raise the front of the vehicle, support it securely on jackstands and remove the wheel.
2   Remove the bolt and two nuts holding the control arm to the steering knuckle. Use a prybar to disconnect the control arm from the steering knuckle **(see illustrations)**.
3   Refer to Section 4 and unbolt and lower the front suspension crossmember with a floor jack.
4   Remove the control arm front pivot bolt.
5   Remove the rear bushing bolt.
6   Remove the control arm.

Inspection

7   Check the control arm for distortion and the bushings for wear, replacing parts as necessary. Do not attempt to straighten a bent control arm.

Installation

8   Installation is the reverse of removal. Tighten all of the fasteners to the torque values listed in this Chapter's Specifications, but don't tighten the front pivot bolt until the outer end of the control arm has been raised with a floor jack to simulate normal ride height.
Note: *When installing the subframe, use a rod of the same diameter as the four subframe-to-chassis bolts to align each side until that side's bolts can be inserted one at a time. Do not tighten any of the four bolts until all have been installed finger-tight, then tighten them to the torque listed in this Chapter's Specifications.*
9   Install the wheel and lug nuts, lower the vehicle and tighten the lug nuts to the torque listed in the Chapter 1 Specifications.
10   It's a good idea to have the front wheel alignment checked, and if necessary, adjusted after this job has been performed.

6   Balljoint - replacement

1   Loosen the wheel lug nuts, raise the vehicle and support it securely on jackstands. Remove the wheel.
2   Remove the cotter pin from the balljoint stud and loosen the nut (but don't remove it yet).
3   Separate the balljoint from the steering knuckle with a picklefork-type balljoint separator **(see illustration)**. Remove the balljoint stud nut. The clearance between the balljoint stud and the CV joint is very tight. To remove the stud nut, you'll have to alternately back off the nut a turn or two, pull down the stud, turn the nut another turn or two, etc., until the nut is off.
4   Remove the bolt and nuts securing the balljoint to the control arm, then separate the balljoint from the control arm with a prybar **(see illustrations 5.2a and 5.2b)**.
5   To install the balljoint, insert the balljoint stud through the hole in the steering knuckle and install the nut, but don't tighten it yet. Don't push the balljoint stud all the way up into and through the hole; instead, thread the nut onto the stud as soon as the stud protrudes through the hole, then turn the nut to draw the stud up through the hole.

6   Attach the balljoint to the control arm and install the bolt and nuts, tightening them to the torque listed in this Chapter's Specifications.
7   Tighten the balljoint stud nut to the torque listed in this Chapter's Specifications and install a new cotter pin. If the cotter pin hole doesn't line up with the slots on the nut, tighten the nut additionally until it does line up - don't loosen the nut to insert the cotter pin.
8   Install the wheel and lug nuts. Lower the vehicle and tighten the lug nuts to the torque listed in the Chapter 1 Specifications.

7   Steering knuckle and hub - removal and installation

Warning: *Dust created by the brake system is harmful to your health. Never blow it out with compressed air and don't inhale any of it. Do not, under any circumstances, use petroleum-based solvents to clean brake parts. Use brake system cleaner only.*

Removal

1   Loosen the wheel lug nuts, raise the vehicle and support it securely on jackstands, then remove the wheel.

7.8 Use a balljoint removal tool or small puller to remove the balljoint

9.2 To detach the rear stabilizer bar (A) from the axle beam, remove the bolts/nuts (B, right side shown)

10.4 Inside the trunk, remove the two nuts (A) securing the upper part of the shock absorber - the bolt (B) is removed from below

10.6 To detach the rear shock absorber from the axle beam, remove the nut and washer, then pull the shock off the stud

2   Remove the brake caliper (don't disconnect the hose) and the brake disc (see Chapter 9), and disconnect the brake hose from the strut. Hang the caliper from the coil spring with a piece of wire - don't let it hang by the brake hose.
3   If the vehicle is equipped with ABS, disconnect and remove the wheel speed sensor.
4   Mark the relationship of the strut to the steering knuckle **(see illustration 2.3)**. Loosen, but don't remove the strut-to-steering knuckle nuts and bolts (see Section 2).
5   Separate the tie-rod end from the steering knuckle arm (see Section 15).
6   Remove the balljoint-to-lower arm bolt and nuts **(see illustrations 5.2a and 5.2b)**.
7   Remove the driveaxle/hub nut and push the driveaxle from the hub as described in Chapter 8. Support the end of the driveaxle with a piece of wire.
8   Since the axle is out in this case, you can use a balljoint removal tool **(see illustration)** or a small puller to remove the balljoint from the steering knuckle.
Note: *If you're removing the steering knuckle to replace the hub bearings, and the balljoint is in good condition, the balljoint can remain attached.*
9   The strut-to-knuckle bolts can now be removed.
10   Carefully separate the steering knuckle from the strut.

Installation
11   Guide the knuckle and hub assembly into position, inserting the driveaxle into the hub.
12   Push the knuckle into the strut flange and install the bolts and nuts, but don't tighten them yet.
13   If you removed the balljoint from the old knuckle, and are planning to use it with the new knuckle, connect the balljoint to the knuckle and tighten the balljoint stud nut to the torque listed in this Chapter's Specifications. Install a new cotter pin.
14   Attach the balljoint to the control arm, but don't tighten the bolt and nuts yet.

15   Attach the tie-rod to the steering knuckle arm (see Section 15). Tighten the strut bolt nuts, the balljoint-to-control arm bolt and nuts and the tie-rod nut to the torque listed in this Chapter's Specifications.
16   Place the brake disc on the hub and install the caliper as outlined in Chapter 9.
17   Install the driveaxle/hub nut and tighten it to the torque listed in the Chapter 8 Specifications.
18   Install the wheel and lug nuts. Lower the vehicle and tighten the lug nuts to the torque listed in the Chapter 1 Specifications.
19   Have the front-end alignment checked and, if necessary, adjusted.

8   Hub and bearing assembly (front) - removal and installation

1   Due to the special tools and expertise required to press the hub and bearing from the steering knuckle, this job should be left to a professional shop. However, the steering knuckle and hub may be removed and the assembly taken to an automotive machine shop or other qualified repair facility equipped with the necessary tools. See Section 7 for the steering knuckle and hub removal procedure.

9   Stabilizer bar and bushings (rear) - removal and installation

1   Loosen the rear wheel lug nuts. Raise the rear of the vehicle and place it securely on jackstands.
2   Remove the stabilizer bar-to-axle beam bolts/nuts **(see illustration)**.
3   The stabilizer bar is mounted inside the open back of the U-channel axle beam. Once the bolts are removed, you may have to use a prybar to remove the stabilizer bar from the axle beam.
4   Installation is the reverse of the removal procedure. When reinstalling the bar to the

axle beam, look for a distinctive mark on the top of the bar at one side. When properly installed, this mark will face Up and be on the left side of the axle beam.
5   Tighten the bolts/nuts to the torque listed in this Chapter's Spcecifications.

10   Shock absorber/coil spring assembly (rear) - removal, inspection and installation

Note: *Shock absorber/coil spring assemblies should only be replaced in pairs.*

Removal
1   Open the trunk.
2   Refer to Chapter 11 and remove the left and right inner trim panels at the sides of the trunk compartment, and the floor trim panel ahead of the spare tire well.
3   Raise the rear of the vehicle and support it securely on jackstands. Support the axle beam with a floor jack, nearest the shock absorber being removed.
4   From inside the trunk remove the two nuts at the upper mount **(see illustration)**.
Note: *The shock absorber is still secured by one bolt, which is accessed from below.*
5   From below, remove the bolt securing the upper part of the shock absorber to the body.
6   Remove the shock absorber lower mounting nut and washer **(see illustration)**.
7   Remove the shock absorber assembly. It may be necessary to lower the floor jack far enough to disengage the upper mount before pulling the shock off the lower mounting stud.

Inspection
8   Follow the inspection procedures described in Section 2. If you determine that the shock absorber assembly must be disassembled for replacement of the shock body or the coil spring, refer to Section 3.

11.3 Remove the four bolts that attach the hub and bearing assembly to the rear axle beam

12.7 On each side, remove the bolt and nut securing the axle beam to the body (right side shown)

Installation

9   Maneuver the assembly up into the fenderwell and install the lower mount onto the stud and guide the upper mounting studs into the holes in the body. Install the bolt from below, tightening it to the torque listed in this Chapter's Specifications.
10   Install the lower washer and nut. Raise the axle beam with the floor jack to simulate normal ride height, then tighten the nut to the torque listed in this Chapter's Specifications.
11   Install the two upper mounting nuts and tighten them to the torque listed in this Chapter's Specifications.
12   Install the spare tire and the trim panels in the trunk.

11   Hub and bearing assembly (rear) - removal and installation

Warning: *Dust created by the brake system is harmful to your health. Never blow it out with compressed air and don't inhale any of it. Do not, under any circumstances, use petroleum-based solvents to clean brake parts. Use brake system cleaner only.*

Removal

1   Loosen the wheel lug nuts, raise the vehicle and support it securely on jackstands. Remove the wheel.
2   Remove the brake disc or drum (see Chapter 9). On models with ABS, disconnect the wheel sensor.
3   Remove the four hub-to-axle beam bolts, accessed from behind the brake backing plate **(see illustration)**.
4   If applicable, disconnect the speed sensor electrical harness connection and remove the hold down bolts securing the harness to the vehicle.
5   Remove the hub and bearing assembly from its seat, maneuvering it out through the brake assembly.

6   If the hub exhibits looseness or excessive runout, the hub and bearing assembly must be replaced as a unit.

Installation

7   Position the hub and bearing assembly on the axle carrier and align the holes in the backing plate. After all four bolts have been installed, tighten them to the torque listed in this Chapter's Specifications.
8   Install the brake drum (and ABS sensor if equipped) and the wheel. Lower the vehicle and tighten the lug nuts to the torque listed in the Chapter 1 Specifications.

12   Rear axle beam - removal and installation

Warning: *Dust created by the brake system is harmful to your health. Never blow it out with compressed air and don't inhale any of it. Do not, under any circumstances, use petroleum-based solvents to clean brake parts. Use brake system cleaner only.*

Removal

1   Loosen the rear wheel lug nuts, raise the vehicle and support it on jackstands. Block the front wheels and remove the rear wheels.
2   On models with ABS, disconnect the sensors and unbolt the ABS wire harness on each side from the axle beam.
3   Remove the rear stabilizer bar (see Section 9).
4   Remove the rear hub and bearing assembly on each side (see Section 11).
5   Detach the backing plate and rear brake assembly and brake lines from the axle beam. It isn't necessary to disassemble the brake shoe assembly or disconnect the parking brake cable from the backing plate. Suspend the backing plate and brake assembly from the coil spring with a piece of wire. Be careful not to kink the brake line.

6   Support the axle beam with a floor jack, then disconnect the shock absorbers from the studs on the axle beam (see Section 10).
7   Lower the axle beam down, then remove the two bolts/nuts through the pivot bushings and remove the axle beam **(see illustration)**.

Installation

8   Inspect the axle beam bushings for cracks, deformation and signs of wear. If either is worn out, take the beam to a dealer service department or other repair shop to have the old ones pressed out and new ones pressed in.
Note: *Only replace the bushings as a pair.*
9   Push the axle beam up to the vehicle until the bolts can be inserted into the front bushings and body. Install the nuts, but do not tighten yet.
10   Raise the axle beam and push the bottom of the shock absorbers onto the axle beam studs and secure with the washers and nuts.
11   Raise the axle beam to simulate normal ride height, then tighten the bushing bolts/nuts and the shock absorber lower mounting nuts to the torque listed in this Chapter's Specifications.
12   The remainder of the installation is the reverse of the removal procedure. Install the wheel and lug nuts. Lower the vehicle and tighten the lug nuts to the torque listed in the Chapter 1 Specifications.

13   Steering system - general information

1   All models are equipped with rack-and-pinion steering. The steering gear operates the steering knuckles via tie-rods. The inner ends of the tie-rods are protected by rubber boots that should be inspected periodically for secure attachment, tears and leaking lubricant.

14.2 Back out the Torx screws until the airbag module is free, but don't try to remove the screw from the screw case. Just back them out until they contact the screw case (left side shown)

14.3a Remove the small side cover from around the cruise control stalk . . .

14.3b . . . then dislodge the torsion spring underneath that retains the airbag

2   On 2008 and earlier models, the power assist system consists of a belt-driven pump and associated lines and hoses. The fluid level in the power steering pump reservoir should be checked periodically (see Chapter 1).

3   On 2009 and later models, an electronic power steering system is used, consisting of a non-serviceable electro-mechanical motor incorporated into the steering column, an ECM, a torque sensor and an angle rotation sensor.

4   The steering wheel operates the steering shaft, which actuates the steering gear through universal joints. Looseness in the steering can be caused by wear in the steering shaft universal joints, the steering gear, the tie-rod ends, or loose retaining bolts.

14.3c The other two torsion springs are accessed through holes in the steering wheel

14.3d Airbag removed, location of the retention springs shown

14   Steering wheel - removal and installation

Warning: *These models are equipped with airbags. Always disable the airbag system before working in the vicinity of any airbag system component to avoid the possibility of accidental deployment of the airbag(s), which could cause personal injury (see Chapter 12).*

Removal

1   Turn the ignition key to Off, then disconnect the cable from the negative terminal of the battery (see Chapter 5). Wait at least two minutes before proceeding.

2   **2013 and earlier models:** Turn the steering wheel so the wheels are pointing straight ahead, then loosen the Torx screws that attach the airbag module to the steering wheel **(see illustration)**. Loosen each screw until the groove in the circumference of the screw catches on the screw case.

Note: *On 2009 through 2013 models, use a small screwdriver to pry off the plastic cover from each side of the steering wheel to remove the Torx screws.*

3   **2014 and later models:** Pry off the side

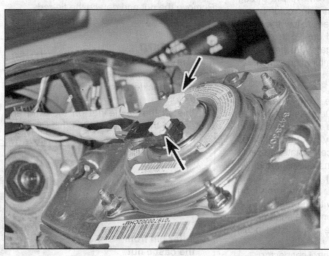

14.4 Lift the airbag module straight out from the steering wheel, then disconnect the electrical connectors at the back of the module

cover from around the cruise control stalk, then use a Torx TH30 driver to dislodge the torsion springs from their posts. There are three torsion springs: left side, right side, and bottom **(see illustrations)**.

4   Pull the airbag module off the steering wheel and disconnect the module electrical connectors **(see illustration)**. To disconnect

the connectors, use a small screwdriver to pry up the locks (center part), then disconnect the connectors. Set the airbag module in a safe, isolated area.

Warning: *Carry the airbag module with the trim side facing away from you, and set the airbag module down with the trim side facing up. Don't place anything on top of the airbag module.*

14.6 Mark the relationship of the steering wheel to the shaft before removing the wheel

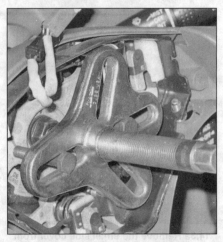

14.7 If the steering wheel is difficult to remove from the shaft, use a steering wheel puller to remove it

14.9 After properly centering the spiral cable as described in the text, make sure the pointers are aligned. On 2013 and earlier models the arrows are at 6 o'clock. On 2014 and later models, the window (left arrow) will appear yellow when properly centered

5   Unplug the electrical connector for the cruise control (if equipped).

6   Mark the relationship of the steering shaft to the hub (if marks don't already exist or don't line up) to simplify installation and ensure steering wheel alignment, then remove the steering wheel retaining nut **(see illustration)**.

7   Use a puller to disconnect the steering wheel from the shaft **(see illustration)**.

Warning: *Do not hammer on the shaft or the puller in an attempt to loosen the wheel from the shaft. Also, don't allow the steering shaft to turn with the steering wheel removed. If the shaft turns, the airbag spiral cable will become uncentered, which may cause the wire inside to break when the vehicle is returned to service.*

8   If it is necessary to remove the airbag spiral cable, remove the steering column covers (see Chapter 11). Then, follow the spiral cable wiring harness and unplug the electrical connector, then disengage the three claws and detach it from the combination switch.

Installation

9   Make sure that the front wheels are pointing straight ahead. Depress the lock tab or hub of the spiral cable and turn the spiral cable counterclockwise by hand until it stops (don't apply too much force). Rotate the cable clockwise about 2-1/2 turns and align the two pointers **(see illustration)**.

10   To install the wheel, align the mark on the steering wheel hub with the mark on the shaft and slip the wheel onto the shaft. Install the nut and tighten it to the torque listed in this Chapter's Specifications.

11   Plug in the cruise control connector.

12   Plug in the electrical connectors for the airbag module and press down the locking tab.

13   Make sure the airbag module electrical connector is positioned correctly and that the wires don't interfere with anything, then install the airbag module and tighten the retaining screws to the torque listed in this Chapter's Specifications.

14   Connect the negative battery cable.

15   Tie-rod ends - removal and installation

Removal

1   Loosen the wheel lug nuts. Raise the front of the vehicle, support it securely on jackstands, block the rear wheels and set the parking brake. Remove the front wheel.

2   Remove the cotter pin **(see illustration)** and loosen the nut on the tie-rod end stud.

3   Hold the tie-rod with a pair of locking pliers or wrench and loosen the jam nut enough to mark the position of the tie-rod end in relation to the threads **(see illustrations)**.

4   Disconnect the tie-rod from the steering knuckle arm with a puller **(see illustration)**. Remove the nut and detach the tie-rod.

5   Unscrew the tie-rod end from the tie-rod.

Installation

6   Thread the tie-rod end on to the marked position and insert the tie-rod stud into the steering knuckle arm. Tighten the jam nut securely.

7   Install the castle nut on the stud and tighten it to the torque listed in this Chapter's

Specifications. Install a new cotter pin. If the hole for the cotter pin doesn't line up with one of the slots in the nut, turn the nut an additional amount until it does.

8   Install the wheel and lug nuts. Lower the vehicle and tighten the lug nuts to the torque listed in the Chapter 1 Specifications.

9   Have the alignment checked and, if necessary, adjusted.

16   Steering gear boots - replacement

1   Loosen the lug nuts, raise the vehicle and support it securely on jackstands. Remove the wheel.

2   Remove the tie-rod end and jam nut (see Section 15).

3   Remove the outer steering gear boot clamp with a pair of pliers **(see illustration)**. Cut off the inner boot clamp with a pair of diagonal cutters **(see illustration)**. Slide off the boot.

15.2 Remove the cotter pin from the castle nut and loosen - but don't remove - the nut

15.3a Loosen the jam nut . . .

15.3b . . . then mark the position of the tie-rod end in relation to the threads

15.4 Disconnect the tie-rod from the steering knuckle arm with a puller

4   Before installing the new boot, wrap the threads and serrations on the end of the steering rod with a layer of tape so the small end of the new boot isn't damaged.
5   Slide the new boot into position on the steering gear until it seats in the groove in the steering rod and install new clamps.
6   Remove the tape and install the tie-rod end (see Section 15).
7   Install the wheel and lug nuts. Lower the vehicle and tighten the lug nuts to the torque listed in the Chapter 1 Specifications.

17   Steering gear - removal and installation

Warning: *These models are equipped with airbags. Always disable the airbag system-before working in the vicinity of any airbag system component to avoid the possibility of accidental deployment of the airbag(s), which could cause personal injury (see Chapter 12) .*
1   Disconnect the cable from the negative terminal of the battery.
2   Remove the steering wheel (see Section 14).
Note: *This will prevent the spiral cable from being damaged in the event the steering gear is not centered when it is installed.*

16.3a The outer ends of the steering gear boots are secured by spring-type clamps; they're easily released with a pair of pliers

16.3b The inner ends of the steering gear boots are retained by boot clamps, which must be cut off and discarded

3   Support the engine from above with an engine support fixture **(see illustration)**. This tool can be obtained at most equipment rental yards.
4   Loosen the front wheel lug nuts, raise the front of the vehicle and support it securely on jackstands. Apply the parking brake and remove the wheels. Remove the

engine under covers.
5   On 2008 and earlier models, place a drain pan under the steering gear. Detach the power steering pressure and return lines **(see illustration)** and cap the ends to prevent excessive fluid loss and contamination. Also unbolt the line clamp from the top of the steering gear.

17.3 Support the engine from above with an engine support fixture

17.5 Disconnect the power steering line fittings

17.6a Pull back the carpeting at the bottom of the steering column and remove the universal joint cover

17.6b Mark the relationship of the universal joint to the steering gear input shaft, loosen the upper U-joint pinch bolt (A), then remove the lower bolt (B) and detach the joint from the steering gear input shaft

6   Remove the universal joint cover **(see illustration)**. Mark the relationship of the lower universal joint to the steering gear input shaft and remove the lower intermediate shaft pinch-bolt **(see illustration)**. Loosen the upper universal joint bolt, then slide the joint up and disconnect it from the steering gear input shaft.
7   Separate the tie-rod ends from the steering knuckle arms (see Section 15). Separate the stabilizer bar links from the bar (see Section 4).
8   Disconnect the balljoints from the control arms **(see illustrations 5.2a and 5.2b)**.
9   Remove the front section of the exhaust pipe. Unbolt the suspension crossmember and lower it along with the control arms **(see illustration 4.6)**.
10   Remove the bolts securing the steering gear to the crossmember.
11   Installation is the reverse of removal, noting the following points:

a)   *Tighten all steering and suspension fasteners to the torque listed in this Chapter's Specifications.*
b)   *Install the wheels and lug nuts. Lower the vehicle and tighten the lug nuts to the torque listed in the Chapter 1 Specifications.*

c)   *Set the front wheels in the straight-ahead position, then center the spiral cable and install the steering wheel and airbag module (see Section 14).*
d)   *On 2009 and earlier models, fill the power steering fluid reservoir with the recommended fluid (see Chapter 1). Bleed the steering system (see Section 19).*

---

18   Power steering pump - removal and installation

Note: *This procedure applies to 2008 and earlier models only - 2009 and later models have electrically assisted power steering*

Removal

1   Disconnect the cable from the negative battery terminal (see Chapter 5).
2   Using a large syringe or suction gun, suck as much fluid out of the power steering fluid reservoir as possible. Place a drain pan under the vehicle to catch any fluid that spills out when the hoses are disconnected.

18.4 Power steering pump mounting details

A   *Power steering pressure switch connector*
B   *Pressure line fitting*

3   Remove the drivebelt (see Chapter 1). Loosen the right front wheel lug nuts, raise the front of the vehicle and support it securely on jackstands. Remove the wheel and the right side engine under cover.
4   Unplug the electrical connector from the power steering fluid pressure switch **(see illustration)**.
5   Unscrew the pressure line-to-pump fitting, using a flare-nut wrench, if available, to avoid rounding-off the corners of the fitting.
6   Loosen the hose clamp and detach the return hose from the pump.
7   Remove the two mounting nuts and detach the power steering pump from the engine.
Note: *The pump-to-mounting bracket nuts are accessible through the holes in the pump pulley, using a short extension and socket.*

Installation

8   Installation is the reverse of removal. Be sure to tighten the mounting bolts/nuts and the pressure line fitting to the torque listed in this Chapter's Specifications.
9   Install the engine under cover, wheel and lug nuts. Lower the vehicle and tighten the lug nuts to the torque listed in the Chapter 1 Specifications.
10   Install the drivebelt (see Chapter 1).
11   Top up the fluid level in the reservoir (see Chapter 1) and bleed the system (see Section 19).

---

19   Power steering system - bleeding

Note: *This procedure applies to 2008 and earlier models only. 2009 and later models have electrically assisted power steering.*
1   Following any operation in which the power steering fluid lines have been disconnected, the power steering system must be bled to remove all air and obtain proper steering performance.
2   With the front wheels in the straight ahead position, check the power steering fluid level and, if low, add fluid until it reaches the Cold mark on the reservoir.
3   Start the engine and allow it to run at fast idle. Recheck the fluid level and add more if necessary to reach the Cold mark.
4   Bleed the system by turning the wheels from side to side, without hitting the stops. This will work the air out of the system. Keep the reservoir full of fluid as this is done.
5   When the air is worked out of the system, return the wheels to the straight-ahead position and leave the vehicle running for several more minutes before shutting it off.
6   Road test the vehicle to be sure the steering system is functioning normally and noise free.
7   Recheck the fluid level to be sure it is up to the Hot mark on the reservoir while the engine is at normal operating temperature. Add fluid if necessary (see Chapter 1).

20.3 Use a press tool to push the stud out of the flange

1   Hub flange   3   Press tool
2   Lug nut on stud

20.4 Install a spacer and a lug nut on the stud, then tighten the nut to draw the stud into place

1   Hub flange   2   Spacer

20 Wheel studs - replacement

Note: *This procedure applies to both the front and rear wheel studs.*

1   Loosen the wheel lug nuts, raise the vehicle and support it securely on jackstands. Remove the wheel.

2   Remove the brake disc or drum (see Chapter 9).

3   Install a lug nut part way onto the stud being replaced. Push the stud out of the hub flange with a press tool **(see illustration)**.

4   Insert the new stud into the hub flange from the back side and install some flat washers and a lug nut on the stud **(see illustration)**.

5   Tighten the lug nut until the stud is seated in the flange.

6   Reinstall the brake drum or disc. Install the wheel and lug nuts. Lower the vehicle and tighten the lug nuts to the torque listed in the Chapter 1 Specifications.

21 Crossmember/subframe (front) - removal and installation

1   See Section 4 for this procedure.

22 Wheels and tires - general information

1   All vehicles covered by this manual are equipped with metric-sized steel belted radial tires **(see illustration)**. Use of other size or type of tires may affect the ride and handling of the vehicle. Don't mix different types of tires, such as radials and bias belted on the same vehicle, as handling may be seriously affected. It's recommended that tires be replaced in pairs on the same axle, but if only one tire is being replaced, be sure it's the same size, structure and tread design as the other.

METRIC TIRE SIZES
P 185 / 80 R 13

TIRE TYPE
P-PASSENGER
T-TEMPORARY
C-COMMERCIAL

ASPECT RATIO
(SECTION HEIGHT)
──────────────
(SECTION WIDTH)
70
75
80

RIM DIAMETER
(INCHES)
13
14
15

SECTION WIDTH
(MILLIMETERS)
185
195
205
ETC

CONSTRUCTION TYPE
R-RADIAL
B-BIAS - BELTED
D-DIAGONAL (BIAS)

SECTION
WIDTH

SECTION
HEIGHT

22.1 Metric tire size code

2   Because tire pressure has a substantial effect on handling and wear, the pressure on all tires should be checked at least once a month or before any extended trips (see Chapter 1).

3   Wheels must be replaced if they are bent, dented, leak air, have elongated bolt holes, are heavily rusted, out of vertical symmetry or if the lug nuts won't stay tight. Wheel repairs that use welding or peening are not recommended.

4   Tire and wheel balance is important in the overall handling, braking and performance of the vehicle. Unbalanced wheels can adversely affect handling and ride characteristics as well as tire life. Whenever a tire is installed on a wheel, the tire and wheel should be balanced by a shop with the proper equipment.

23   Wheel alignment - general information

1   A wheel alignment refers to the adjustments made to the wheels so they are in proper angular relationship to the suspension and the ground. Wheels that are out of proper alignment not only affect vehicle control, but also increase tire wear. The alignment angles normally measured are camber, caster and toe-in **(see illustration)**. Toe-in and camber are the only adjustable angles on the front. Caster should be measured to check for bent or worn suspension parts. Camber and toe-in should be measured on the rear to check for a bent rear axle.

2   Getting the proper wheel alignment is a very exacting process, one in which complicated and expensive machines are necessary to perform the job properly. Because of this, you should have a technician with the proper equipment perform these tasks. We will, however, use this space to give you a basic idea of what is involved with a wheel alignment so you can better understand the process and deal intelligently with the shop that does the work.

3   Toe-in is the turning in of the wheels. The purpose of a toe specification is to ensure parallel rolling of the wheels. In a vehicle with zero toe-in, the distance between the front edges of the wheels will be the same as the distance between the rear edges of the wheels. The actual amount of toe-in is normally only a fraction of an inch. On the front end, toe-in is controlled by the tie-rod end position on the tie-rod. On the rear end, it's not adjustable. Incorrect toe-in will cause the tires to wear improperly by making them scrub against the road surface.

4   Camber is the tilting of the wheels from vertical when viewed from one end of the vehicle. When the wheels tilt out at the top, the camber is said to be positive (+). When the wheels tilt in at the top the camber is negative (-). The amount of tilt is measured in degrees from vertical and this measurement is called the camber angle. This angle affects the amount of tire tread which contacts the road and compensates for changes in the

23.1 Camber, caster and toe-in angles

suspension geometry when the vehicle is cornering or traveling over an undulating surface. On the front end, camber is adjusted by altering the position of the steering knuckle in the strut flange. If camber can't be adjusted within the specified range, special adjuster bolts, which replace the standard strut-to-knuckle bolts, are available. On the rear end, camber is not adjustable.

5   Caster is the tilting of the front steering axis from the vertical. A tilt toward the rear is positive caster and a tilt toward the front is negative caster. Caster is not adjustable on these vehicles

24   Tire Pressure Monitoring System (TPMS)

1   The TPMS or Tire Pressure Monitoring System has been on every passenger car since 2008. The system is designed to help monitor the air pressure in the tires and warn you if the pressure drops by more than 10 percent. When a tire's air pressure drops below the preset amount, a warning light on the instrument panel lights up.

2   Each wheel (including the spare) has a specially designed valve stem with a small transmitter attached to it. This signal is sent back to the vehicle's TPMS monitor ECU. The ECU constantly updates and verifies the air pressure against its internal data that is stored in the ECU memory. Not only does it monitor the tire pressure, but it also keeps track of the tires (actually the sensors) locations.

3   Any time a sensor is replaced, the ECU is replaced, the tires are rotated, new tires are installed or the rims are changed, the TPMS will need to be reset.

4   Each sensor has a unique serial ID number to it, and the ECU has to learn these numbers in order to locate the actual tire. This is why when a new sensor is installed, the TPMS ECU will need to be informed of these new serial ID numbers. This will require the use of a scanner capable of registering the serial ID numbers into the ECU memory.

5   For regular maintenance, such as tire rotation, and air pressure adjustment, Toyota uses a TPMS reset button located in the driver's area to initialize any changes to the already registered information.

TPMS Reset button locations

6   **2008 and earlier models** - To the left of the steering wheel on the center of the dash.

7   **2009 through 2013 models** - Lower right corner of the driver's area (about where your right knee would be).

8   **2014 and later models** - In the lower right corner of the center display (just above the center console).

Reset procedure -
Initialization procedure

Note: *This procedure is for after performing a tire rotation or tire pressure adjustments. This is NOT for replacing tire sensors or the TPMS ECU. That will require registering those particular ID numbers into the software with a scanner.*

Note: *In most instances, an initialization is not necessary for the typical seasonal tire pressure adjustment. Just fill the tire with the appropriate amount of air pressure listed on the yellow and black sticker in the driver's door jam area. The system will recognize the air pressure change on its own.*

9   Turn the ignition to the On position.

10   Hold the TPMS reset button in for three seconds. The TPMS monitor symbol on the dash will blink three times, indicating you are in the initialization mode.

Note: *This can take up to two or three minutes to complete.*

11   If the system fails to receive all four tires and the spare tire's data, a code will be stored (usually after you have gained a speed greater than 25 mph.

12   To verify the initialization has completed correctly, have the vehicle connected to a scanner to read the actual tire pressures and locations.

25 Steering column - removal and installation

Warning: *These models are equipped with airbags. Always disable the airbag system before working in the vicinity of any airbag system component to avoid the possibility of accidental deployment of the airbag(s), which could cause personal injury (see Chapter 12).*

Note: *To remove the steering column it is not necessary to disconnect all the components from the column. However, you may find it easier to remove some components beforehand.*

1   Park the vehicle on a flat and level surface. Apply the parking brake, set the front wheels straight ahead, then disconnect the cable from the negative terminal of the battery (see Chapter 5).

2   Remove the lower knee bolster trim from under the steering column (see Chapter 11).

3   Remove the steering column covers (see Chapter 11).

4   **Floor shift (automatic) equipped vehicles:** Disconnect the shift interlock cable from the steering column by inserting the key and turning it to the ACC position. Then, push in on the retaining clip claw and withdraw the cable from the ignition switch housing.

5   Disconnect the electrical connections to the wiper switch, headlamp switch, airbag spiral cable (clockspring), brake light switch and security transponder connections.

Note: *If needed, now is a good time to remove the various switches and the steering wheel. Follow the steps provided in the appropriate sections of this manual.*

6   Lift carpet area at the bottom of the steering shaft to expose the fasteners to the silencer cover for the steering column (see Section 17).

7   Remove the fasteners to the silencer cover and pull it up far enough to expose the steering column intermediate shaft.

8   Match mark the intermediate shaft and coupler for re-installation purposes, then remove the bolt securing the intermediate shaft to the column.

9   If equipped - remove the sub reinforcement bar (two bolts, one on each side) to gain access to the steering column mounting bolts and to give you more room to maneuver the column out of the car.

10   If equipped - remove the air duct section below the steering column. (This is the ducting section that directs air to the driver's foot area.) The air duct is held in place with two claw like clips. Slide the duct off and reuse the clips when reinstalling.

11   **2ZR-FE models - (Electric steering models):** Disconnect the steering ECU har-

25.11 Remove the harness connections from the ECU. Leave the ECU in place. (Shown with entire dash removed for clarity)

ness from the steering ECU **(see illustration)**. Be sure to detach the harness hold down clamps from the steering column.

12   **2013 and later models:** Remove the brake pedal support bracket.

13   **2009 and earlier models:** Remove the three bolts securing the steering column to the dash support.

14   **2010 and later models:** Remove the two nuts and single bolt securing the steering column to the dash support **(see illustrations)**.

15   Carefully guide the steering column out of the instrument panel.

Note: *If exchanging the column for a replacement one, be sure to transfer all the original components over to the replacement column.*

Note: *Some components may require drilling out the reinforcement brackets break-away security bolts. Be sure to secure the steering column shaft in a vise and carefully drill out the shear-head bolts. The original bolts cannot be reused.*

16   Installation is the reverse of removal.

25.14a Remove these nuts from the column

25.14b The single bolt is a through-bolt securing the bottom end of the column

Notes

Chapter 11
Body

Contents

1 General Information

Warning: *The models covered by this manual are equipped with Supplemental Restraint Systems (SRS), more commonly known as airbags. Always disable the airbag system before working in the vicinity of any airbag system components to avoid the possibility of accidental deployment of the airbags, which could cause personal injury (see Chapter 12).*

1   Certain body components are particularly vulnerable to accident damage and can be unbolted and repaired or replaced. Among these parts are the hood, doors, tailgate, liftgate, bumpers and front fenders.

2   Only general body maintenance practices and body panel repair procedures within the scope of the do-it-yourselfer are included in this Chapter.

2 Body - maintenance

1   The condition of your vehicle's body is very important, because the resale value depends a great deal on it. It's much more difficult to repair a neglected or damaged body than it is to repair mechanical components. The hidden areas of the body, such as the wheel wells, the frame and the engine compartment, are equally important, although they don't require as frequent attention as the rest of the body.

2   Once a year, or every 12,000 miles, it's a good idea to have the underside of the body steam cleaned. All traces of dirt and oil will be removed and the area can then be inspected carefully for rust, damaged brake lines, frayed electrical wires, damaged cables and other problems. The front suspension components should be greased after completion of this job.

3   At the same time, clean the engine and

the engine compartment with a steam cleaner or water soluble degreaser.

4   The wheel wells should be given close attention, since undercoating can peel away and stones and dirt thrown up by the tires can cause the paint to chip and flake, allowing rust to set in. If rust is found, clean down to the bare metal and apply an anti-rust paint.

5   The body should be washed about once a week. Wet the vehicle thoroughly to soften the dirt, then wash it down with a soft sponge and plenty of clean soapy water. If the surplus dirt is not washed off very carefully, it can wear down the paint.

6   Spots of tar or asphalt thrown up from the road should be removed with a cloth soaked in solvent.

7   Once every six months, wax the body and chrome trim. If a chrome cleaner is used to remove rust from any of the vehicle's plated parts, remember that the cleaner also removes part of the chrome, so use it sparingly.

3.1a Make sure the damaged area is perfectly clean and rust free. If the touch-up kit has a wire brush, use it to clean the scratch or chip. Or use fine steel wool wrapped around the end of a pencil. Clean the scratched or chipped surface only, not the good paint surrounding it. Rinse the area with water and allow it to dry thoroughly

3.1b Thoroughly mix the paint, then apply a small amount with the touch-up kit brush or a very fine artist's brush. Brush in one direction as you fill the scratch area. Do not build up the paint higher than the surrounding paint

3.1c If the vehicle has a two-coat finish, apply the clear coat after the color coat has dried

3.1d Wait a few days for the paint to dry thoroughly, then rub out the repainted area with a polishing compound to blend the new paint with the surrounding area. When you're happy with your work, wash and polish the area

3   Body repair - minor damage

Repairing of minor paint scratches

1   No matter how hard you try to keep your vehicle looking like new, it will inevitably be scratched, chipped or dented at some point. If the metal is actually dented, seek the advice of a professional. But you can fix minor scratches and chips yourself (see illustrations). Buy a touch-up paint kit from a dealer service department or an auto parts store. To ensure that you get the right color, you'll need to have the specific make, model and year of your vehicle and, ideally, the paint code, which is located on a special metal plate under the hood or in the door jamb.

Plastic body panels

2   The following repair procedures are for minor scratches and gouges. Repair of more serious damage should be left to a dealer service department or qualified auto body shop. Below is a list of the equipment and materials necessary to perform the following repair procedures on plastic body panels.

Wax, grease and silicone removing solvent
Cloth-backed body tape
Sanding discs
Drill motor with three-inch disc holder
Hand sanding block
Rubber squeegees
Sandpaper
Non-porous mixing palette
Wood paddle or putty knife
Wood paddle or putty knife
Curved-tooth body file
Flexible parts repair material

Flexible panels (bumper trim)

3   Remove the damaged panel, if necessary or desirable. In most cases, repairs can be carried out with the panel installed.
4   Clean the area(s) to be repaired with a wax, grease and silicone removing solvent applied with a water-dampened cloth.
5   If the damage is structural, that is, if it extends through the panel, clean the backside of the panel area to be repaired as well. Wipe dry.
6   Sand the rear surface about 1-1/2 inches beyond the break.
7   Cut two pieces of fiberglass cloth large enough to overlap the break by about 1-1/2 inches. Cut only to the required length.
8   Mix the adhesive from the repair kit according to the instructions included with the kit, and apply a layer of the mixture approximately 1/8-inch thick on the backside of the panel. Overlap the break by at least 1-1/2 inches.
9   Apply one piece of fiberglass cloth to the adhesive and cover the cloth with additional adhesive. Apply a second piece of fiberglass cloth to the adhesive and immediately cover the cloth with additional adhesive in sufficient quantity to fill the weave.

10 Allow the repair to cure for 20 to 30 minutes at 60-degrees to 80-degrees F.

11 If necessary, trim the excess repair material at the edge.

12 Remove all of the paint film over and around the area(s) to be repaired. The repair material should not overlap the painted surface.

13 With a drill motor and a sanding disc (or a rotary file), cut a "V" along the break line approximately 1/2-inch wide. Remove all dust and loose particles from the repair area.

14 Mix and apply the repair material. Apply a light coat first over the damaged area; then continue applying material until it reaches a level slightly higher than the surrounding finish.

15 Cure the mixture for 20 to 30 minute at 60-degrees to 80-degrees F.

16 Roughly establish the contour of the area being repaired with a body file. If low areas or pits remain, mix and apply additional adhesive.

17 Block sand the damaged area with sandpaper to establish the actual contour of the surrounding surface.

18 If desired, the repaired area can be temporarily protected with several light coats of primer. Because of the special paints and techniques required for flexible body panels, it is recommended that the vehicle be taken to a paint shop for completion of the body repair.

Steel body panels

Repairing simple dents

19 When repairing dents, the first job is to pull the dent out until the affected area is as close as possible to its original shape. There is no point in trying to restore the original shape completely as the metal in the damaged area will have stretched on impact and cannot be restored to its original contours. It is better to bring the level of the dent up to a point that is about 1/8-inch below the level of the surrounding metal. In cases where the dent is very shallow, it is not worth trying to pull it out at all.

20 If the backside of the dent is accessible, it can be hammered out gently from behind using a soft-face hammer. While doing this, hold a block of wood firmly against the opposite side of the metal to absorb the hammer blows and prevent the metal from being stretched.

21 If the dent is in a section of the body which has double layers, or some other factor makes it inaccessible from behind, a different technique is required. Drill several small holes through the metal inside the damaged area, particularly in the deeper sections. Screw long, self-tapping screws into the holes just enough for them to get a good grip in the metal. Now pulling on the protruding heads of the screws with locking pliers can pull out the dent.

22 The next stage of repair is the removal of paint from the damaged area and from an inch or so of the surrounding metal. This

is easily done with a wire brush or sanding disk in a drill motor, although it can be done just as effectively by hand with sandpaper. To complete the preparation for filling, score the surface of the bare metal with a screwdriver or the tang of a file or drill small holes in the affected area. This will provide a good grip for the filler material. To complete the repair, see the Section on filling and painting.

Repair of rust holes or gashes

23 Remove all paint from the affected area and from an inch or so of the surrounding metal using a sanding disk or wire brush mounted in a drill motor. If these are not available, a few sheets of sandpaper will do the job just as effectively.

24 With the paint removed, you will be able to determine the severity of the corrosion and decide whether to replace the whole panel, if possible, or repair the affected area. New body panels are not as expensive as most people think and it is often quicker to install a new panel than to repair large areas of rust.

25 Remove all trim pieces from the affected area except those which will act as a guide to the original shape of the damaged body, such as headlight shells, etc. Using metal snips or a hacksaw blade, remove all loose metal and any other metal that is badly affected by rust. Hammer the edges of the hole in to create a slight depression for the filler material.

26 Wire-brush the affected area to remove the powdery rust from the surface of the metal. If the back of the rusted area is accessible, treat it with rust inhibiting paint.

27 Before filling is done, block the hole in some way. This can be done with sheet metal riveted or screwed into place, or by stuffing the hole with wire mesh.

28 Once the hole is blocked off, the affected area can be filled and painted. See the following subsection on filling and painting.

Filling and painting

29 Many types of body fillers are available, but generally speaking, body repair kits which contain filler paste and a tube of resin hardener are best for this type of repair work. A wide, flexible plastic or nylon applicator will be necessary for imparting a smooth and contoured finish to the surface of the filler material. Mix up a small amount of filler on a clean piece of wood or cardboard (use the hardener sparingly). Follow the manufacturer's instructions on the package, otherwise the filler will set incorrectly.

30 Using the applicator, apply the filler paste to the prepared area. Draw the applicator across the surface of the filler to achieve the desired contour and to level the filler surface. As soon as a contour that approximates the original one is achieved, stop working the paste. If you continue, the paste will begin to stick to the applicator. Continue to add thin layers of paste at 20-minute intervals until the level of the filler is just above the surrounding metal.

31 Once the filler has hardened, the excess can be removed with a body file. From then

on, progressively finer grades of sandpaper should be used, starting with a 180-grit paper and finishing with 600-grit wet-or-dry paper. Always wrap the sandpaper around a flat rubber or wooden block, otherwise the surface of the filler will not be completely flat. During the sanding of the filler surface, the wet-or-dry paper should be periodically rinsed in water. This will ensure that a very smooth finish is produced in the final stage.

32 At this point, the repair area should be surrounded by a ring of bare metal, which in turn should be encircled by the finely feathered edge of good paint. Rinse the repair area with clean water until all of the dust produced by the sanding operation is gone.

33 Spray the entire area with a light coat of primer. This will reveal any imperfections in the surface of the filler. Repair the imperfections with fresh filler paste or glaze filler and once more smooth the surface with sandpaper. Repeat this spray-and-repair procedure until you are satisfied that the surface of the filler and the feathered edge of the paint are perfect. Rinse the area with clean water and allow it to dry completely.

34 The repair area is now ready for painting. Spray painting must be carried out in a warm, dry, windless and dust free atmosphere. These conditions can be created if you have access to a large indoor work area, but if you are forced to work in the open, you will have to pick the day very carefully. If you are working indoors, dousing the floor in the work area with water will help settle the dust that would otherwise be in the air. If the repair area is confined to one body panel, mask off the surrounding panels. This will help minimize the effects of a slight mismatch in paint color. Trim pieces such as chrome strips, door handles, etc., will also need to be masked off or removed. Use masking tape and several thickness of newspaper for the masking operations.

35 Before spraying, shake the paint can thoroughly, then spray a test area until the spray painting technique is mastered. Cover the repair area with a thick coat of primer. The thickness should be built up using several thin layers of primer rather than one thick one. Using 600-grit wet-or-dry sandpaper, rub down the surface of the primer until it is very smooth. While doing this, the work area should be thoroughly rinsed with water and the wet-or-dry sandpaper periodically rinsed as well. Allow the primer to dry before spraying additional coats.

36 Spray on the top coat, again building up the thickness by using several thin layers of paint. Begin spraying in the center of the repair area and then, using a circular motion, work out until the whole repair area and about two inches of the surrounding original paint is covered. Remove all masking material 10 to 15 minutes after spraying on the final coat of paint. Allow the new paint at least two weeks to harden, then use a very fine rubbing compound to blend the edges of the new paint into the existing paint. Finally, apply a coat of wax

These photos illustrate a method of repairing simple dents. They are intended to supplement *Body repair - minor damage* in this Chapter and should not be used as the sole instructions for body repair on these vehicles.

1 If you can't access the backside of the body panel to hammer out the dent, pull it out with a slide-hammer-type dent puller. In the deepest portion of the dent or along the crease line, drill or punch hole(s) at least one inch apart . . .

2 . . . then screw the slide-hammer into the hole and operate it. Tap with a hammer near the edge of the dent to help 'pop' the metal back to its original shape. When you're finished, the dent area should be close to its original contour and about 1/8-inch below the surface of the surrounding metal

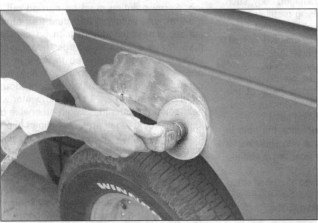

3 Using coarse-grit sandpaper, remove the paint down to the bare metal. Hand sanding works fine, but the disc sander shown here makes the job faster. Use finer (about 320-grit) sandpaper to feather-edge the paint at least one inch around the dent area

4 When the paint is removed, touch will probably be more helpful than sight for telling if the metal is straight. Hammer down the high spots or raise the low spots as necessary. Clean the repair area with wax/silicone remover

5 Following label instructions, mix up a batch of plastic filler and hardener. The ratio of filler to hardener is critical, and, if you mix it incorrectly, it will either not cure properly or cure too quickly (you won't have time to file and sand it into shape)

6 Working quickly so the filler doesn't harden, use a plastic applicator to press the body filler firmly into the metal, assuring it bonds completely. Work the filler until it matches the original contour and is slightly above the surrounding metal

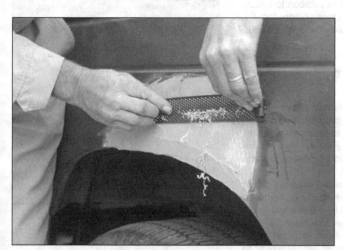

7 Let the filler harden until you can just dent it with your fingernail. Use a body file or Surform tool (shown here) to rough-shape the filler

8 Use coarse-grit sandpaper and a sanding board or block to work the filler down until it's smooth and even. Work down to finer grits of sandpaper - always using a board or block - ending up with 360 or 400 grit

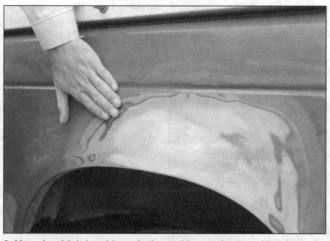

9 You shouldn't be able to feel any ridge at the transition from the filler to the bare metal or from the bare metal to the old paint. As soon as the repair is flat and uniform, remove the dust and mask off the adjacent panels or trim pieces

10 Apply several layers of primer to the area. Don't spray the primer on too heavy, so it sags or runs, and make sure each coat is dry before you spray on the next one. A professional-type spray gun is being used here, but aerosol spray primer is available inexpensively from auto parts stores

11 The primer will help reveal imperfections or scratches. Fill these with glazing compound. Follow the label instructions and sand it with 360 or 400-grit sandpaper until it's smooth. Repeat the glazing, sanding and respraying until the primer reveals a perfectly smooth surface

12 Finish sand the primer with very fine sandpaper (400 or 600-grit) to remove the primer overspray. Clean the area with water and allow it to dry. Use a tack rag to remove any dust, then apply the finish coat. Don't attempt to rub out or wax the repair area until the paint has dried completely (at least two weeks)

4   Body repair - major damage

1   Major damage must be repaired by an auto body shop specifically equipped to perform body and frame repairs. These shops have the specialized equipment required to do the job properly.
2   If the damage is extensive, the frame must be checked for proper alignment or the vehicle's handling characteristics may be adversely affected and other components may wear at an accelerated rate.
3   Due to the fact that all of the major body components (hood, fenders, etc.) are separate and replaceable units, any seriously damaged components should be replaced rather than repaired. Sometimes the components can be found in a wrecking yard that specializes in used vehicle components, often at considerable savings over the cost of new parts.

5   Fastener and trim removal

1   There is a variety of plastic fasteners used to hold trim panels, splash shields and other parts in place in addition to typical screws, nuts and bolts. Once you are familiar with them, they can usually be removed without too much difficulty.
2   The proper tools and approach can prevent added time and expense to a project by minimizing the number of broken fasteners and/or parts.
3   The following illustration shows various types of fasteners that are typically used on most vehicles and how to remove and install them (see illustration). Replacement fasteners are commonly found at most auto parts stores, if necessary.
4   Trim panels are typically made of plastic and their flexibility can help during removal. The key to their removal is to use a tool to pry the panel near its retainers to release it without damaging surrounding areas or breaking-off any retainers. The retainers will usually snap out of their designated slot or hole after force is applied to them. Stiff plastic tools designed for prying on trim panels are available at most auto parts stores **(see illustration)**. Tools that are tapered and wrapped in protective tape, such as a screwdriver or small pry tool, are also very effective when used with care.

5.4 These small plastic pry tools are ideal for prying off trim panels

6   Upholstery, carpets and vinyl trim - maintenance

Upholstery and carpets

1   Every three months remove the floormats and clean the interior of the vehicle (more frequently if necessary). Use a stiff whiskbroom to brush the carpeting and loosen dirt and dust, then vacuum the upholstery and carpets thor-

Fasteners

This tool is designed to remove special fasteners. A small pry tool used for removing nails will also work well in place of this tool

A Phillips head screwdriver can be used to release the center portion, but light pressure must be used because the plastic is easily damaged. Once the center is up, the fastener can easily be pried from its hole

Here is a view with the center portion fully released. Install the fastener as shown, then press the center in to set it

This fastener is used for exterior panels and shields. The center portion must be pried up to release the fastener. Install the fastener with the center up, then press the center in to set it

This type of fastener is used commonly for interior panels. Use a small blunt tool to press the small pin at the center in to release it . . .

. . . the pin will stay with the fastener in the released position

Reset the fastener for installation by moving the pin out. Install the fastener, then press the pin flush with the fastener to set it

This fastener is used for exterior and interior panels. It has no moving parts. Simply pry the fastener from its hole like the claw of a hammer removes a nail. Without a tool that can get under the top of the fastener, it can be very difficult to remove

oughly, especially along seams and crevices.

2   Dirt and stains can be removed from carpeting with basic household or automotive carpet shampoos available in spray cans. Follow the directions and vacuum again, then use a stiff brush to bring back the "nap" of the carpet.

3   Most interiors have cloth or vinyl upholstery, either of which can be cleaned and maintained with a number of material-specific cleaners or shampoos available in auto supply stores. Follow the directions on the product for usage, and always spot-test any upholstery cleaner on an inconspicuous area (bottom edge of a backseat cushion) to ensure that it doesn't cause a color shift in the material.

4   After cleaning, vinyl upholstery should be treated with a protectant.

Note: *Make sure the protectant container indicates the product can be used on seats - some products may make a seat too slippery.*

Caution: *Do not use protectant on vinyl-covered steering wheels.*

5   Leather upholstery requires special care. It should be cleaned regularly with saddle-soap or leather cleaner. Never use alcohol, gasoline, nail polish remover or thinner to clean leather upholstery.

6   After cleaning, regularly treat leather upholstery with a leather conditioner, rubbed in with a soft cotton cloth. Never use car wax on leather upholstery.

7   In areas where the interior of the vehicle is subject to bright sunlight, cover leather seating areas of the seats with a sheet if the vehicle is to be left out for any length of time.

Vinyl trim

8   Don't clean vinyl trim with detergents, caustic soap or petroleum-based cleaners. Plain soap and water works just fine, with a soft brush to clean dirt that may be ingrained. Wash the vinyl as frequently as the rest of the vehicle.

9   After cleaning, application of a high-quality rubber and vinyl protectant will help prevent oxidation and cracks. The protectant can also be applied to weather-stripping, vacuum lines and rubber hoses, which often fail as a result of chemical degradation, and to the tires.

7   Hinges and locks - maintenance

1   Once every 3000 miles, or every three months, the hinges and latch assemblies on the doors, hood and trunk should be given a few drops of light oil or lock lubricant. The door latch strikers should also be lubricated with a thin coat of grease to reduce wear and ensure free movement. Lubricate the door and trunk locks with spray-on graphite lubricant.

8   Windshield and fixed glass - replacement

1   Replacement of the windshield and fixed glass requires the use of special fast-setting adhesive/caulk materials and some specialized tools. It is recommended that these operations be left to a dealer or a shop specializing in glass work.

9   Hood - removal, installation and adjustment

Note: *The hood is heavy and somewhat awkward to remove and install - at least two people should perform this procedure.*

Removal and installation

1   Make marks around the hinge plate to ensure proper alignment during installation (see illustrations). Also disconnect the windshield washer line before removing the hood.

2   Use blankets or pads to cover the cowl area of the body and fenders. This will protect the body and paint as the hood is lifted off.

3   Disconnect any cables or wires that will interfere with removal. On some models, it may be necessary to remove the lower hood insulation retaining pins and peel the insulation back enough to disconnect the windshield washer hoses.

4   Have an assistant support one side of the hood while you support the other. Simultaneously remove the hinge-to-hood bolts.

5   Lift off the hood.

6   Installation is the reverse of removal.

Adjustment

Note: *On 2009 and later models, centering bolts are used to mount the hood and hood latch. The hood and hood latch cannot be adjusted with the centering bolts in place. Replace the centering bolts with standard bolts and washers when making adjustments.*

7   Fore-and-aft and side-to-side adjustment of the hood is done by moving the hinge plate slot after loosening the bolts.

8   Scribe a line around the entire hinge plate so you can judge the amount of movement **(see illustration 9.1a)**

9   Loosen the bolts or nuts and move the hood into correct alignment. Move it only a little at a time. Tighten the hinge bolts and carefully lower the hood to check the position.

10   If necessary after installation, the entire hood latch assembly can be adjusted up-and-down as well as from side-to-side on the radiator support so the hood closes securely, flush with the fenders. To make the adjustment, scribe a line around the hood latch mounting bolts to provide a reference point, then loosen them and reposition the latch assembly, as necessary **(see illustration)**. Following adjustment, retighten the mounting bolts.

9.1a Before removing the hood, make marks around the hinge plate . . .

9.1b . . . and disconnect the windshield washer line as well

9.10 Loosen the hood latch bolts, move the latch and retighten bolts, then close the hood to check the fit - repeat the procedure until the hood is flush with the fenders

9.11 Adjust the hood height by screwing the hood bumpers in-or-out

10.2 Remove the plastic retainers and the trunk lid trim panel

10.3a Draw a mark around the bolt heads to help with lid realignment on installation (early model shown)

10.3b Draw a mark around the bolt heads to help with lid realignment on installation (later model shown)

10.8a Loosen the bolts, then adjust the striker position (early model shown)

11   Finally, adjust the hood bumpers on the radiator support so the hood, when closed, is flush with the fenders **(see illustration)**.

12   The hood latch assembly, as well as the hinges, should be periodically lubricated with white, lithium-base grease to prevent binding and wear.

10   Trunk lid/liftgate - removal, installation and adjustment

Corolla models (trunk lid)

Note: *On 2009 and later models, centering bolts are used to mount the trunk and trunk latch. The trunk and trunk latch cannot be adjusted with the centering bolts in place. Replace the centering bolts with standard bolts and washers if adjustment is necessary.*

Trunk lid - removal and installation

1   Open the trunk lid and cover the edges of the trunk compartment with pads or cloths to protect the painted surfaces when the lid is removed.

2   Open the trunk lid and remove the trunk lid trim cover **(see illustrations)**. Follow the wiring harness into the trunk lid, mark and dis-

connect all electrical connectors, then pull the harness out of the lid.

3   Make alignment marks around the hinge mounting bolts **(see illustrations)**.

4   While an assistant supports the lid, remove the lid-to-hinge bolts on both sides and lift it off.

5   Installation is the reverse of removal.

Note: *When reinstalling the trunk lid, align the lid-to-hinge bolts with the marks made during removal.*

Adjustment

6   After installation, close the lid and make sure it's in proper alignment with the surrounding panels.

7   Forward-and-backward and side-to-side adjustments are made by loosening the hinge-to-lid bolts and gently moving the lid into correct alignment.

8   To adjust the lid so it is flush with the body when closed, loosen the mounting bolts and move the lock and striker **(see illustrations)**.

10.8b Remove the trunk panel fasteners . . .

10.8c . . . then loosen the bolts and adjust the striker position (later model shown)

10.9 Loosen the latch mounting bolts and move it slightly to align with the striker

10.11a Carefully pry up the lower liftgate trim panel

10.11b Remove the upper liftgate trim panel

10.12a Use a plastic trim tool to pry out the upper quarter trim panel

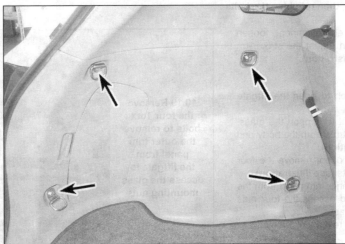

10.12b Remove the lower quarter trim panel by removing the four screws, then prying around the edge to release the clips

9   To adjust the trunk latch, loosen the mounting bolts. By loosening the bolts you'll be able to align the latch to the striker **(see illustration)**.

Matrix/Vibe models (liftgate)
Liftgate - removal and installation
10   Open the liftgate and cover the edges of

the trunk compartment with pads or cloths to protect the painted surfaces when the liftgate is removed.
11   Open the liftgate and remove the liftgate trim covers **(see illustrations)**.
12   With the upper and lower left-rear quarter trim panel removed, disconnect the electrical connectors leading to the liftgate **(see illustrations)**.

13   With an assistant to support the liftgate, remove the support struts from the liftgate **(see illustration)**.
14   Draw a mark around the bolt heads and hinges to help with lid realignment on installation, then remove the hinge bolts **(see illustration)**.
15   Installation is the reverse of removal.

10.12c Disconnect the electrical connectors for the liftgate, then work the connector through the liftgate grommet

10.13 Use a small screwdriver to release the clip securing the support strut to the liftgate, then disconnect it from the ball-stud

10.14 Remove the hinge-to-liftgate bolts

10.16 Loosen the bolts to adjust the striker position, then retighten the bolts

10.18 Liftgate glass support strut

16   If the liftgate needs alignment, loosen the striker bolts, then adjust the striker-to-latch position **(see illustration)**.

Liftgate glass
17   Release the latch to open the liftgate glass.
18   With an assistant to support the glass, remove the support struts from the body and the glass **(see illustration)**.
19   With the liftgate open, remove the four large-headed Torx bolts **(see illustration)**.
20   Remove the exterior trim panel from the top of the liftgate and access the four nuts securing the liftgate glass.
21   Installation is the reverse of removal.

10.19 Remove the four Torx bolts to remove the outer trim panel from the liftgate to access the glass mounting nuts

11   Door trim panel - removal and installation (and window regulator initialization)

Warning: *These models are equipped with airbags. Always disable the airbag system before working in the vicinity of any airbag system component to avoid the possibility of accidental deployment of the airbag(s), which could cause personal injury (see Chapter 12).*

1   Disconnect the cable from the negative terminal of the battery (see Chapter 5).

Corolla models

2008 and earlier models
2   On manual window regulator equipped models, remove the window crank by work-

ing a cloth back-and-forth behind the handle to dislodge the retaining clip **(see illustrations)**. A special tool is available for this purpose but it's not essential. With the retainer removed, pull off the handle. On power window models, pry out the switch assembly, unplug the electrical connector and remove it **(see illustration)**.

11.2a Work a cloth up behind the regulator handle and move it back-and-forth . . .

11.2b . . . until the retaining clip is pushed up so you can remove it

11.2c Pry up on the power window switch and disconnect the electrical connector

11.5a Pry the armrest up with a screwdriver or trim tool . . .

11.5b . . . and remove the door panel screws

11.6 Use a trim panel removal tool to detach the trim panel retaining clips, then pull the door trim up and out to remove it

3   Remove the outside mirror trim cover (see Section 16).
4   On 2008 and earlier models, remove the screw in the inside handle trim.
5   Pry up the armrest panel with a trim tool and remove the two door panel screws under the armrest (see illustrations).
6   Insert a wide putty knife, a thin screwdriver or a special trim panel removal tool

between the trim panel and door to disengage the retaining clips. Work around the outer edge until the panel is free (see illustration).
7   Once all of the clips are disengaged, detach the trim panel, unplug any electrical connectors and remove the trim panel from the vehicle by gently pulling it up and out.
8   For access to the inner door remove the

plastic watershield. Peel back the plastic cover, taking care not to tear it (see illustration). Remove the plastic grommets, if necessary.

2009 to 2013 models

Note: If the vehicle you're working on is equipped with manual windows, refer to Step 1 for the removal of the window crank
9   Using a trim tool, pry out the interior handle trim panel and remove the exposed screw.
10   Pry up the window control switch assembly and disconnect the electrical connector. On models with manual windows, remove the grab handle/tray panel.
11   On the inside of the grab handle, pry up the small cover and remove the exposed screw.
12   Using a sturdy trim tool, pry between the trim panel and door to disengage the retaining clips - work around the outer edge until the panel is free (see illustration 11.6).
13   Lift up the door panel to disengage it from the upper seal, then disconnect the cables from the door handle (see illustration 11.15h).
14   Peel back the watershield to gain access to the interior components (see illustration 11.8).

11.8 If the plastic watershield is peeled off carefully it can be reused

11.15a Use a flat trim tool to pry off the grab handle trim

11.15b With the flat trim tool, pry off the arm rest trim

11.15c Pry up the window control switch assembly and disconnect the electrical connector from the bottom

11.15d Pry off the door sail trim panel . . .

11.15e . . . and disconnect the speaker electrical connector, if equipped

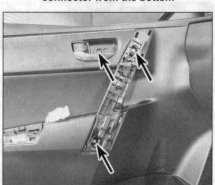

11.15f Use a small flat screwdriver to expose the hidden screw inside the interior door handle, then remove the screw as well as the two other screws hidden by the grab handle trim

2014 and later models

15 For the removal of the door panel on these models, refer to **illustrations 11.15a through 11.15i** mentioned below, following the captions beneath each photo.

Matrix/Vibe models
Removal

16 Disconnect the cable from the negative terminal of the battery (see Chapter 5).

17 On manual window regulator equipped models, refer to Step 1 of this Section.
18 On power window models, pry out the switch assembly, unplug the electrical connector and remove it **(see illustration)**.

11.15g Using a sturdy trim tool, pry between the trim panel and door to disengage the retaining clips - work around the outer edge until the panel is free

11.15h With all the pressure clips released, lift up the panel slightly to disconnect it along the top edge. Then, disconnect the cables from the inside handle.

A   *Pull the cable housing straight out of the bracket*
B   *Detach the cable ball end from the handle mechanism*

11.15i Before peeling back the plastic watershield, disconnect the side airbag impact sensor (A) and the speaker connector (B). Then, carefully peel the watershield back without tearing it - use a razor blade to assist in cutting the butyl tape, if necessary.

11.18 Pry up on the power window switch and disconnect the electrical connector

11.20 Lift the tab to access the screw in the inside door handle trim

11.21 Remove the screw and the door pull cup

11.24 Remove the fasteners securing the inside door handle

Note: *On 2009 and later models, once the power window switch assembly is removed, remove the panel mounting screws.*

19   Remove the outside mirror trim cover (see Section 16).

20   On 2008 and earlier models, remove the screw in the inside handle trim **(see illustration)**. On 2009 and later models, carefully pry the inside trim panel out using a trim tool.

21   On 2008 and earlier models, remove the door panel screw securing the door pull cup, then remove the cup **(see illustration)**.

22   Insert a wide putty knife, a thin screwdriver or a trim panel removal tool between the trim panel and door to disengage the eight retaining clips. Work around the outer edge until the panel is free **(see illustration 11.15g)**.

23   Once all of the clips are disengaged, detach the trim panel, unplug any electrical connectors and remove the trim panel from the vehicle by gently pulling it up and out.

24   If you are removing the plastic watershield, remove the inside door handle **(see illustration)**.

25   For access to components in the door, peel back the watershield, taking care not to tear it. Remove the plastic grommets, if necessary.

Installation

26   To install the trim panel, first press the watershield back into place. If necessary,

add more sealant to hold it in place.

27   Prior to installation of the door panel, be sure to reinstall any clips in the panel which may have come out during the removal procedure and stayed in the door.

28   Plug in any electrical connectors and place the panel in position. Press it into place until the clips are seated. The remainder of installation is the reverse of removal.

Window regulator initialization

Note: *Any time certain components within the door are replaced (such as the window glass or regulator), you will need to initialize the window motor auto features. By factory standards, there are two initialization procedures - each one pertaining to the job that has been performed.*

Note: *This procedure is written for 2014 and later models, but is similar enough for 2013 and earlier models.*

After window regulator/motor has been replaced or a regulator malfunction is detected

29   Reconnect the battery (if you haven't already) and turn the key to the On position, engine Off.

30   With the window in the closed position, push the window switch all the way down - hold the switch down for a little over

one second after the window has been fully opened.

31   With the window in the open position, pull the window switch all the way up - hold the switch up for a little over one second after the window has been fully closed.

32   Initialization is complete.

After window glass has been replaced (but regulator is being reused)

33   Reconnect the battery (if you haven't already) and turn the key to the On position, engine Off.

34   Raise the window to the complete closed position. If the window stops halfway up, release the switch and try again.

35   Hold the switch in the up position for 6 seconds or more after the window glass has completely closed.

36   Lower the window to its complete open position and hold the switch in this position for a least 1 second after the window has opened.

37   Release the switch, then repress the switch in the down position and hold it for at least four seconds.

38   Close the window completely and hold the switch in the up position for at least one second after the window has closed.

39   Initialization is complete.

12.2 Use two jackstands padded with rags
(to protect the paint) to support the
door during the removal and
installation procedures

12.3 Remove the bolt and
detach the stop strut

12.4a Mark the position of each hinge to
the door, then remove the hinge bolts
(early model shown)

12 Door - removal, installation and adjustment

Warning: *These models are equipped with airbags. Always disable the airbag system before working in the vicinity of any airbag system component to avoid the possibility of accidental deployment of the airbag(s), which could cause personal injury (see Chapter 12).*

Removal and installation

1   Remove the door trim panel (see Section 11). Disconnect any electrical connectors and push them through the door opening so they won't interfere with removal.
Note: *If a jack or jackstand is used, place a rag between it and the door to protect the door's paint.*
2   Position a jack or jackstands under the door or have an assistant on hand to support the door when the hinge bolts are removed **(see illustration).**
3   Remove the door stop strut bolt **(see illustration).**
4   Draw a mark around the hinges to aid in alignment, then remove the hinge-to-door bolts and carefully detach the door **(see illustrations).** To access the door hinge bolts on later models, the fenderwell splash shield and inner fender insulator will need to be removed (see Section 27).
5   Installation is the reverse of removal.

Adjustment

Note: *On 2009 and later models, centering bolts are used to mount the door hinge. The hinge cannot be adjusted with the centering bolts in place. Replace the centering bolts with standard bolts and washers when making adjustments.*
6   Following installation, make sure the door is aligned properly. Adjust it if necessary as follows:

a) *Up-and-down and forward-and-backward adjustments are made by loosening the hinge-to-body bolts (see illustrations 12.4a or 12.4b) and moving the door, as*

12.4b On later models, working from inside
the fenderwell, mark the position of each
hinge to the door, then remove the hinge
bolts (entire fender removed for clarity)

necessary. A special offset tool may be required to reach some of the bolts.
b) *In-and-out and up-and-down adjustments are made by loosening the door side hinge bolts and moving the door, as necessary. A special offset tool may be required to reach some of the bolts.*
c) *The door lock striker can also be adjusted both up-and-down and sideways to provide a positive engagement with the locking mechanism. This is done by loosening the screws and moving the striker, as necessary (see illustration).*

13 Door latch, lock cylinder and handles (and trunk lid/liftgate latch) - removal and installation

Warning: *These models are equipped with airbags. Always disable the airbag system before working in the vicinity of any airbag*

12.6 Adjust the door lock striker by
loosening the mounting screws and
gently tapping the striker in
the desired direction

system component to avoid the possibility of accidental deployment of the airbag(s), which could cause personal injury (see Chapter 12).
1   Remove the door trim panel and the plastic watershield (see Section 11). Make sure the window is rolled up all the way. On models equipped with a door panel brace, remove the fasteners and brace **(see illustration).**

Door latch

2   Reach inside the door and disconnect the control rods from the latch **(see illustration).**
3   Remove the latch retaining screws from the end of the door **(see illustrations).**
4   Remove the door latch assembly and if equipped, the door lock solenoid.
5   Installation is the reverse of removal.

Lock cylinder and outside handle

Note: *On some models, it may not be necessary to disconnect the control rods from the lock cylinder/outside handle*

13.1 If equipped, remove the fasteners securing the door panel brace

13.2 Disconnect the latch control rods by disengaging (rotating out) the plastic piece, then pulling the rod out - (one shown)

13.3a Remove the latch screws from the end of the door (A), then, if equipped, disconnect the electrical connector (B) and remove the window track mounting bolt (C)

13.3b Disengage the window track from the rubber, then pull it out of the door to allow room for the removal of the latch

13.7 Remove the plastic cover and loosen the outside handle/lock cylinder retention screw

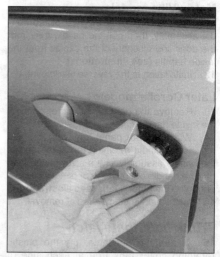

13.8a With the retaining bolt removed, slide the lock cylinder out of the door, then . . .

6   Working through the access hole in the door, disconnect the control rods from the lock cylinder and outside handle.

7   Loosen the screw with a Torx bit and pull the lock cover and lock cylinder from the outside of the door **(see illustration)**.

8   Use a screwdriver to pry off the cover, then loosen the lock cylinder retaining bolt and remove the lock cylinder from the door **(see illustration)**. With the lock cylinder removed, the outside handle can slide toward the edge of the door to be disengaged, then removed by pulling it out of the door **(see illustration)**.

9   If the outside handle bracket (mounted to inside of the door) needs replacement, make sure the control rod(s) are disconnected, then remove the bracket retaining screws from the inside of the door.

10   Installation is the reverse of removal.

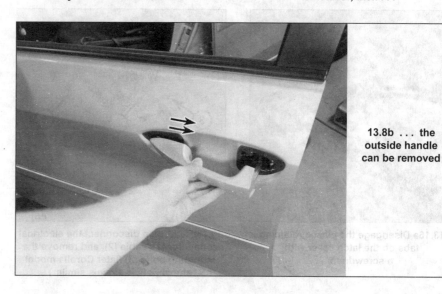

13.8b . . . the outside handle can be removed

13.11a Release the clip securing the inside handle assembly to the door . . .

13.11b . . . detach the control cables with a small screwdriver, then lift the cable eyes out of the handle assembly

13.14 Depress the retaining tab at the end of the handle assembly with a screwdriver, then pull the handle out of the door panel (A) while disengaging the other tabs (B)

Inside handle

Early Corolla models and Matrix/Vibe models

11   Pry the clip out at the rear of the handle assembly, then pull the handle free from the door and disconnect the cables from the inside handle (see illustrations).
12   Installation is the reverse of removal.

Later Corolla models

13   Remove the door panel and disconnect the inside handle cables (see Section 11).
14   With the door panel removed, depress the inside handle retaining tab at the end of the handle assembly with a screwdriver, then pull the handle out of the door panel while disengaging the other 3 tabs (see illustration).
15   Installation is the reverse of removal.

Trunk lid/liftgate latch

16   To remove the latch, pry the plastic retaining cover tabs free at each side (if equipped) (see illustration), then disconnect the electrical connector and cable. Remove

the mounting bolts and latch from the trunk lid or liftgate (see illustration). On some models, there may be a control rod that also needs to be disconnected, similar to the type shown in illustration 13.2.
17   Installation is the reverse of removal.

14   Door window glass and regulator - removal and installation

Warning: *These models are equipped with airbags. Always disable the airbag system before working in the vicinity of any airbag system component to avoid the possibility of accidental deployment of the airbag(s), which could cause personal injury (see Chapter 12).*

Window glass - removal and installation

1   Remove the door trim panel and the plastic watershield (see Section 11).
Note: *On some models, the door access plate is retained by rivets which must be drilled out*

2   Lower the window glass (reconnecting the battery and window control switch, if necessary). Remove the door access plate from the door frame (see illustration).
3   If necessary, carefully pry the inner weatherstrip out of the door window opening. This will allow more clearance for the window to be rotated and removed through the window frame.
4   Place a rag(s) inside the door panel to help prevent scratching the glass, then remove the two glass mounting bolts (see illustration).
5   Remove the glass by pulling it up and guiding it carefully out of the window frame, rotating it as necessary.
6   Installation is the reverse of the removal procedure.

Window Regulator - removal and installation

7   Follow the steps listed for the window glass removal (see Section 14).

13.16a Disengage the plastic retaining tabs on the latch cover with a screwdriver . . .

13.16b . . . then disconnect the electrical connector (1), cable (2), and remove the mounting bolts (3) (later Corolla model shown, other models similar)

14.2 Remove the screws (or rivets) and this plate for access to one of the glass mounting bolts

14.4 Location of glass mounting bolts

14.8 Disconnect the regulator electrical connector (1), remove the mounting bolts (2), but only loosen the last regulator bolt (3) (later model shown, earlier models similar)

8   Disconnect the electrical connector, then locate the bolts that secure the regulator assembly to the door and remove them **(see illustration)**. Take note of the single bolt that should only be loosened and NOT removed - this will prevent the regulator assembly from falling downward.
9   Guide the assembly out of the door opening.
10   With assembly removed, remove the bolts that secure the motor to the regulator **(see illustration)**.
11   Installation is the reverse of removal.

14.10 Motor-to-regulator mounting bolt locations (later model shown, earlier models similar)

15   Bumper covers - removal and installation

Warning: *The models covered by this manual are equipped with a Supplemental Restraint System (SRS), more commonly known as airbags. Always disable the airbag system before working in the vicinity of any airbag system component to avoid the possibility of accidental deployment of the airbag, which could cause personal injury (see Chapter 12).*

Note: *Don't try to forcefully remove the bumper cover - wait until all fasteners have been located and removed.*

Front bumper

1   Apply the parking brake, raise the vehicle and support it securely on jackstands.
2   Disconnect the negative battery cable (see Chapter 5), then wait two minutes before proceeding any further. On models equipped with fog lights, disconnect the electrical con-

nectors at the fog lights on the back of the bumper fascia.

Corolla models (earlier trim)
Note: *Use a small screwdriver to pop the center button up on the plastic fasteners, but do not try to remove the center buttons. They stay in the ferrules.*
3   Detach the screws and/or pushpins securing the top, bottom, and sides of the bumper cover **(see illustrations)**.

15.3a Remove the fasteners and the inner fenderwell liner

15.3b From below (shown without engine splash panels) remove the screws and plastic pins securing the bumper cover

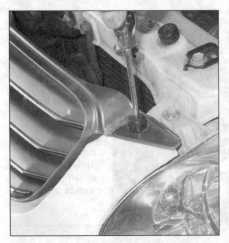

15.3c Remove the two screws (one shown) at either side of the grille - these screws also secure the bumper cover

15.4a Remove the bumper cover lower fasteners

15.4b Remove the pushpin fastener (A), then turn the fastener (B) 90-degrees with a screwdriver and pry it out

15.4c Disconnect the electrical connector (A), then disengage the tab (B) and slide it out slightly

15.4d Remove the bumper cover upper fasteners

Corolla models (later trim)

4   Detach the screws and/or pushpins securing the top, bottom, and sides of the bumper cover (see illustrations).

Matrix/Vibe models

5   Detach the screws and/or pushpins securing the top, bottom, and sides of the bumper cover (see illustrations).

All models

6   Disengage the bumper cover from the plastic retainers at each side near the headlight housing (see illustration), then remove the bumper cover from the vehicle, making sure nothing else is connected. An assistant's help may be necessary at this stage.

7   If the bumper beam itself is to be replaced, remove the fasteners and pull the beam off its mounts (see illustrations).

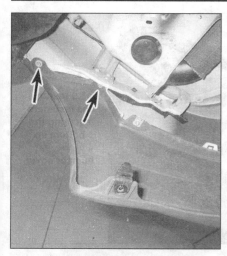

15.5a Remove the lower engine splash
shield to access these two front bumper
cover bolts on each side

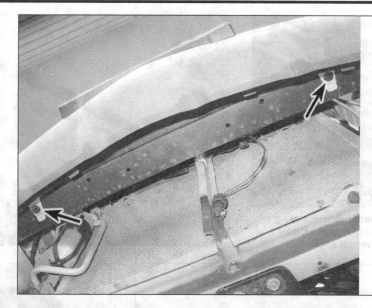

15.5b From
below, remove
the fasteners
securing
the bumper
cover

15.5c Remove the fasteners at each side of the grille -
these screws also secure the bumper cover (2008 and
earlier models shown, later models similar)

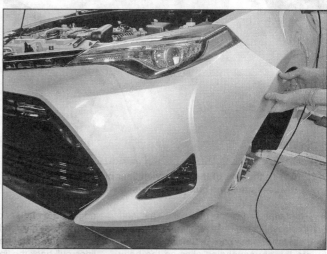

15.6 Disengage the bumper cover from the retainers at each
side of the headlight housing (later Corolla model shown,
other models similar)

15.7a Remove the bumper impact foam
piece - reuse it when installing the
bumper cover assembly

15.7b Front bumper beam mounting nuts (accessed through holes)

15.7c The bumper side mounting bolt locations (if equipped, later Corolla model shown)

15.9 Remove the fasteners securing the bottom lip of the rear bumper cover

15.10 With the rear of the fenderwell liner pulled back, you can access the one bumper cover screw on each side

15.11a Pry out the plastic fasteners and remove the left and right side trim panels in the trunk

8   Installation for the bumper beam and bumper cover is the reverse of removal. Make sure the tabs on the back of the bumper cover fit into the corresponding clips on the body before attaching the bolts and screws. An assistant would be helpful at this point.

Rear bumper

Early Corolla models

9   Working under the vehicle, detach the plastic clips and screws securing the lower

edge of the bumper cover (see illustration).
10   In the rear fenderwells, remove the fasteners securing the rear of the fenderwell liner, pull back the liner and remove the screw securing the front edge of the bumper cover to the fenderwell (see illustration).
11   Remove the fasteners securing the bumper cover in each corner inside the trunk, and those behind the rear trunk trim panel (see illustrations). To access these fasteners, pull up the trunk mat, then use a trim tool to release the clips securing the

15.11b With a socket and extension remove the rear bumper cover mounting nuts through the body holes (three of the four are seen here)

rear trunk trim panel and the left and right rear corner panels.
12   Installation is the reverse of removal.

Later Corolla models

13   At each side, remove the upper screw and pushpin fasteners at the rear of the fenderwell area (see illustration).
14   Remove the bumper cover lower fasteners (see illustration).
15   With the trunk open, remove the upper fasteners (see illustration).
16   Disconnect any electrical connectors from the inside of the bumper cover. Once all the fasteners have been removed, pull out on the sides of the bumper cover to disengage it from the body (similar to illustration 15.6), then remove the bumper cover from the vehicle. An assistant's help may be necessary.
17   Installation is the reverse of removal.

Matrix/Vibe models

18   Working under the vehicle, detach the plastic clips and screws securing the lower edge of the bumper cover (see illustration).
19   In the rear fenderwells, remove the fasteners securing the splash panel, then remove the bolt securing the front edge of the bumper cover to the fender (see illustrations).

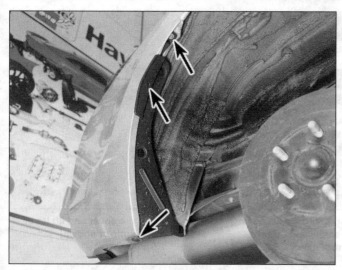

15.13 Rear bumper cover fenderwell fasteners
(remove from each side)

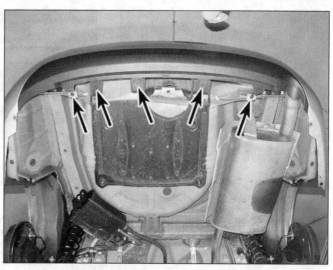

15.14 Rear bumper cover lower fasteners

15.15 Rear bumper cover upper fasteners

15.18 Remove the fasteners securing the bottom lip of
the rear bumper cover

15.19a Remove the fasteners securing the splash panel to the
rear fender liner and bumper cover

15.19b With the panel removed, remove the bumper cover bolt
in each rear fenderwell

15.20 In the liftgate opening, remove the one upper screw on each side

16.1a On manually operated side view mirrors, remove the screw and detach the mirror control handle

16.1b Detach the cover and lift it out (power mirror shown)

20   With the liftgate open, remove the fasteners securing the bumper cover in each corner **(see illustration)**. To access these fasteners, pull up the trunk mat, then use a trim tool to release the clips securing the rear trunk trim panel and the left and right rear corner panels.

21   Installation is the reverse of removal.

16   Mirrors - removal and installation

Outside mirror

1   On manually operated mirrors, remove the control handle **(see illustration)**. On all models, detach the mirror cover by using a small screwdriver to pry the retainers free from the door **(see illustration)**. On later models, disconnect the tweeter speaker electrical connector **(see illustration 11.15e)**.

2   Remove the retaining nuts and detach the mirror **(see illustration)**. On power mirrors, unplug the electrical connector **(see illustration)**.

3   Installation is the reverse of removal.

Inside mirror

Note: *There are different types of inside mirrors used on various models throughout the years covered in this manual. Each one is slightly different in the way they are attached.*
Note: *The different types can be identified by their mounting and attachment points. A TMC-manufactured type will have a cap over the attachment point, the TMMC/NUMMI manufactured type will have a single Torx head screw attachment point with no cover cap over the screw, while the E/C (Electrochromic with compass) will have a cover to disconnect an electrical connector as well as a single Torx head screw.*

4   Remove the protective cover (if equipped) by releasing the various claw-like attachment points and sliding the cover off.

5   **TMC type** - Press the two winged clips inward and slide the mirror off of the mounting bracket.

16.2a Remove the nuts securing the outside mirror to the door - on some models, the nuts also secure a small speaker

16.2b On vehicles equipped with power side view mirrors, unplug the electrical connector

16.7a Disconnect the electrical connector . . .

16.7b . . . then remove the Torx screw and slide the mirror off the bracket

16.8a Pry the inner cover off with a flat trim tool

16.8b Pry the forward recognition cover off with a flat trim tool

16.8c Loosen the single Torx screw, then slide the mirror off of the bracket

17.1a Slide the seat rearward and remove the trim covers, then remove the front mounting bolts

17.1b Slide the seat forward and remove the two covers over the tracks . . .

17.1c . . . then remove the seat mounting bolts

6   **TMMC/NUMMI type** - Rotate the mirror up enough to reach the Torx screw. Loosen the screw, then slide the mirror off of the mounting bracket.

7   **E/C type or Matrix/Vibe model type** - Remove the covers (if equipped), disconnect the electrical connection, then remove the Torx screw and slide the mirror off of the bracket **(see illustrations)**.

8   **Models with Toyota safety sense/forward recognition system** - Follow the photos for removal of the inside mirror **(see illustrations)**.

9   Installation is the reverse of removal.

Caution: *Do not over tighten the mirror screw. It should be snug to prevent rattling, but not so tight that you would risk breaking the glass.*

Compass calibration (later models with front facing camera)

Note: *Because each vehicle and its location will have a slightly different magnetic signature, the compass may need to be recalibrated. These next steps will guide you through the process to restore the accuracy of the compass.*

10   Find a large open/unobstructed area with no large metal buildings or structures within a 300 foot radius.

11   Then, begin the calibration by holding the compass button (the "auto" or "power" button on the rearview mirror, depending on the model) in for about 12 seconds. The compass will start to search for the correct compass direction by displaying the various compass positions in the digital display.

12   Drive the vehicle in a clockwise circle at a speed of 5 mph or less.

13   After one to three continuous circles, the corrected direction should be displayed in the mirror, which will be your indication that the procedure has completed. A "C" will be displayed if the calibration was not successful.

17   Seats - removal and installation

Warning: *These models are equipped with airbags. Always disable the airbag system before working in the vicinity of any airbag system component to avoid the possibility of accidental deployment of the airbag(s), which could cause personal injury (see Chapter 12).*
Note: *Disconnect the cable from the negative terminal of the battery (see Chapter 5). If your model is equipped with power seats and it is necessary to connect the battery cable to move the seat, disconnect the battery cable once the seat is at its final position and wait at least 2 minutes before proceeding any further.*

Front seats

1   Pry off the seat bolt covers, if equipped, then remove the retaining bolts. Unplug any electrical connectors and guide the seat out of the vehicle **(see illustrations)**.

2   Installation is the reverse of removal.

Rear seats

Corolla models and 2009 and later Matrix/Vibe models

3   Lift the front of the cushion up, then pull it out toward the front of the vehicle **(see illustration)**.

17.3 Pull up on the seat bottom to release the one clip at each side

17.5 On split-back models, pull the release cables for each half of the seatback (early model shown)

17.6 If your model is equipped with a seat cushion retaining bolt, it will need to be removed before the rear seat cushion can be removed

17.7a With the split seat-backs folded down, pull back the carpet and remove this trim piece (early models)

17.7b Remove the mounting bolts securing the seat-backs to the floor - center bolts shown

17.7c On later models, you'll need to remove this bolt at each end, too

7   Remove the bolts in the middle (and on later models, the ends, too) securing the seat-back assembly to the floor **(see illustrations)**. Lift each section up and out to disengage its pins from the brackets at each end on early models.
8   Installation is the reverse of removal.

2008 and earlier Matrix/Vibe models

9   Pull the seatback release levers and lay the seat back(s) down.
10   Twist the quarter-turn fasteners counterclockwise and remove the flat panel **(see illustration)**.
11   Remove the four bolts and the black-plastic panel **(see illustration)**.
12   Remove the bolts and brackets securing the tray **(see illustrations)**.
13   Remove the two bolts securing the center hinge plate of the seat, then pull up the seatback for access to the center seat belt mounting bolt **(see illustration)**.
14   Remove the bolts along the front edge of the seat bottom **(see illustration)**.
15   With the help of an assistant, remove the seat.
16   Installation is the reverse of removal.

4   On models with a one-piece seatback, remove the seat back retaining bolts at the floor, then lift up on the back to release the seat back from the body.
5   On models with a split-back rear seat, open the trunk and release the two seatback

cables, allowing the seatbacks to fold down **(see illustration)**. On later models, pull the seat back release knobs, located next to the headrests.
6   Some models may have a seat cushion retaining bolt **(see illustration)**. Peel back the trim cover from the trunk side to check and see if there is one present.

17.10 Twist the quarter-turn fasteners and lift off this panel

17.11 Remove the fasteners and the black tray

17.12a Remove the bolts and brackets

17.12b Remove the black plastic tray

18 Instrument cluster bezel - removal and installation

Warning: *These models are equipped with airbags. Always disable the airbag system before working in the vicinity of any airbag system component to avoid the possibility of accidental deployment of the airbag(s), which could cause personal injury (see Chapter 12).*

1   Disconnect the cable from the negative battery terminal (see Chapter 5). Tilt the steering column to its lowest position.

Corolla models

2008 and earlier

2   Remove the one pushpin at the top of the bezel, then detach the bezel clips at the lower edges by prying with a screwdriver to release the clips **(see illustrations)**.
3   Installation is the reverse of the removal procedure.

2009 and later

4   Pry out and remove the hazard switch/ radio trim bezel (see Section 20).
5   Using a trim tool, remove the access trim panel, then carefully pry out the cluster bezel and remove it **(see illustrations)**.
6   Installation is the reverse of the removal procedure.

17.13 Unbolt the center seatback hinge bolts (A), then lift the seat to access the seatbelt bolt (B)

17.14 Remove the four front bolts to the seat bottom and remove the rear seat assembly

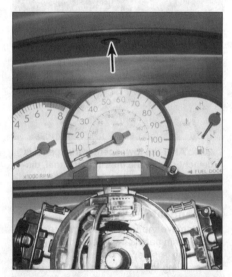

18.2a Remove the one pushpin fastener at the center-top of the instrument bezel

18.2b Pop the center out of the pushpin, then remove it from the bezel (2008 and earlier models)

18.5a Using a flat trim tool, pry the outer trim piece from the side of the bezel . . .

18.5b . . . then work your way around the bezel making sure that all the fasteners have been disengaged (steering wheel and column shrouds removed for clarity)

18.7 Carefully pry the bezel from the instrument panel until the clips come free

19.1 Remove the damper screw at the right side of the glove box (2008 and earlier model shown)

20.3 Pull off this knob for access to the panel screw behind it

20.4a Use a trim tool to release the clips holding the lower trim panel and pull it out

20.4b After the lower center trim panel is detached from the instrument panel, disconnect the electrical connectors at the back

20.7 Remove the four bolts at the bottom of the upper trim panel - the other fasteners are clips

Matrix/Vibe models

2008 and earlier

7   Carefully pry the bezel from the instrument panel **(see illustration)**.
8   Grasp the bezel securely and remove it.
9   Installation is the reverse of the removal procedure.

2009 and later

10   Remove the upper center trim and driver's side trim panels (see Section 20).
11   Using a screwdriver with the tip taped with masking tape, and starting at the bottom of the bezel, carefully pry the outer edges of the bezel away from the instrument panel until the clips are released. Take care not to scratch the surrounding trim on the instrument panel.
12   Installation is the reverse of removal. Make sure the clips are engaged properly before pushing the bezel firmly into place.

19   Glove box - removal and installation

Warning: *These models are equipped with airbags. Always disable the airbag system before working in the vicinity of any airbag system component to avoid the possibility of accidental deployment of the airbag(s), which could cause personal injury (see Chapter 12).*
1   Open the glove box and remove the screw at the lower right corner **(see illustration)**. On later models, squeeze the tabs (in place of the screw) to disengage the damper.

2   Squeeze the sides of the glove box toward the center enough to clear the stoppers on each side. Remove the glove box from the lower hinge.
3   Installation is the reverse of removal.

20   Center trim panels - removal and installation

Warning: *These models are equipped with airbags. Always disable the airbag system before working in the vicinity of any airbag system component to avoid the possibility of accidental deployment of the airbag(s), which could cause personal injury (see Chapter 12).*
1   Disconnect the cable from the negative battery terminal (see Chapter 5).

Corolla models
2008 and earlier

Lower trim panel

2   Refer to Section 22 and remove the shift bezel panel at the front of the floor console.
3   Remove the center knob from the heating/air conditioning control panel, then

20.8 Pull the upper panel out far enough to disconnect the electrical connectors and the antenna cable

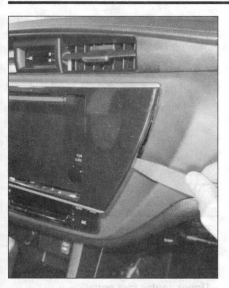

20.13a Using a trim tool, pry out and
around the radio trim panel to release
all the retaining clips . . .

20.13b . . . then disconnect the panel
electrical connectors

20.16a Pry off the end cap with
a trim tool . . .

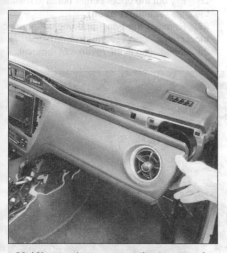

20.16b . . . then, pry out the two panels
together, releasing all the clips along
both panels and being careful not
to crack the plastic . . .

20.16c . . . once removed, the panels can be separated if necessary (A).
If desired, the vent can now also be removed (B).

remove the screw behind it **(see illustration)**.
4   Using a small screwdriver, detach the
retaining clips at each corner, then remove
the panel and unplug the electrical connectors
(see illustrations).
5   Installation is the reverse of removal.

Upper trim panel
6   Remove the lower trim panel.
7   Remove the screws at the bottom of the
panel, then pry the panel from its clips with a
trim tool or taped screwdriver **(see illustration)**.
8   Pull the upper trim panel out and unplug
the electrical connectors and antenna cable
from the radio **(see illustration)**.
9   Installation is the reverse of removal.

2009 through 2013
10   Using a trim tool, pry out and remove

the center bordering trim panels, starting
with the lower border trim panels on each
side (they extend past the shifter), then
remove the upper border panels on each
side (in line with the radio and vents). The
upper border panels will need to be pried
out at the top first, then worked down
towards the bottom.
11   Pry out and remove the center vent
assembly using a trim tool. This will now give
you access to further components such as the
a/c control assembly (see Chapter 3), radio
(Chapter 12), etc.
12   Installation is the reverse of removal.

2014 and later

Radio and hazard flasher trim panel
13   Pry out along the radio trim panel

circumference to release all the retaining
clips, then disconnect the electrical connectors and remove the panel **(see illustrations)**.
14   Installation is the reverse of removal.

**A/C control assembly and
clock trim panel(s)**
15   Remove the radio/hazard flasher trim
panel.
16   Pry out and remove the a/c control and
clock trim panels, which can be removed
together and separated later, if necessary
(see illustrations).
17   Installation is the reverse of removal.

Cigarette lighter and USB panel
18   Remove the previously mentioned trim
paneling.

20.19a Pry the panel out at each end . . .

20.19b . . . then disconnect the connectors and remove the panel

20.21 Pull off this knob for access to the panel screw behind it

19   Pry out the panel and disconnect the electrical connectors **(see illustrations)**.
20   Installation is the reverse of removal.

Matrix/Vibe models

2008 and earlier

Lower center trim panel
21   Remove the center knob from the heating/air conditioning control panel, then remove the screw behind it **(see illustration)**.
22   Pry out the switches in the panel and pull them out enough to disconnect the electrical connectors behind them **(see illustration)**.
23   Detach the retaining clips at each corner, then remove the panel and unplug the electrical connectors at the back of the panel **(see illustration)**.

24   Installation is the reverse of removal.

Upper center trim panel
25   Refer to the previous Steps and remove the lower center trim panel.
26   Pry out the upper center panel to release the clips **(see illustration)**.
27   Remove the panel and unplug the electrical connectors **(see illustration)**.
28   Installation is the reverse of removal.

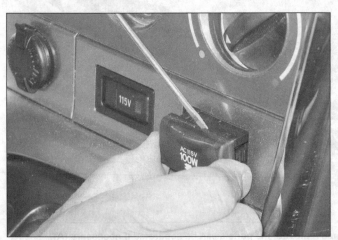

20.22 Use a small screwdriver to pry out the switches, then disconnect the electrical connectors

20.23 Carefully pry up the panel to release the clips holding the lower trim panel

20.26 Carefully pry out the upper panel

20.27 Pull the upper panel out far enough to disconnect the electrical connectors

21.2 Remove the lower column cover screws (early model shown)

21.13 Remove the column cover front face screws

2009 and later

Upper center trim panel

29   Remove the steering column covers (see Section 21).
30   Using a trim removal tool with the tip taped with masking tape, and starting at the bottom of the panel, carefully pry the outer edges of the panel away from the instrument panel until the claw type clips are released. Take care not to scratch the surrounding instrument panel.
31   With the clips released, lift the bottom of the panel up then out. **Note:** *There is a hook at the top of the panel, if the panel is pulled straight out the hook may be damaged.*
32   Installation is the reverse of the removal procedure. Make sure the clips are engaged properly before pushing the bezel firmly into place.

Lower center trim panel

33   Unscrew the shift knob from the shifter.
34   Using a trim removal tool, starting at the center edge of the panel, and carefully pry the outer edges of the panel away from the center console until the claw type clips are released.
35   With the clips released, separate the panel from the center console and the lower section of the instrument panel.
36   Installation is the reverse of the removal procedure. Make sure the clips are engaged properly before pushing the panel firmly into place.

Driver's side upper trim panel

37   Release the claw tabs. Starting at the bottom of the panel and working from left to right, use a trim removal tool to carefully pry the outer edges of the panel away from the instrument panel until the clips are released. Take care not to scratch the instrument panel.
38   Pull the panel back and disconnect the electrical connector for the power mirror switch and remove the panel.
39   Installation is the reverse of removal. Make sure the clips are engaged properly before pushing the panel firmly into place.

Driver's side lower trim panel

40   Release the claw tabs. Starting at the

sides of the panel and working from left to right, Use trim removal tool to carefully pry the outer edges of the panel away from the instrument panel until the clips are released. Take care not to scratch the instrument panel.
41   Pull the panel back and disconnect the electrical connectors for the switches and remove the panel.
42   Installation is the reverse of the removal procedure. Make sure the clips are engaged properly before pushing the panel firmly into place.

21   Steering column covers - removal and installation

Warning: *These models are equipped with airbags. Always disable the airbag system before working in the vicinity of any airbag system component to avoid the possibility of accidental deployment of the airbag(s), which could cause personal injury (see Chapter 12).*
1   Disconnect the cable from the negative battery terminal (Chapter 5).
Note: *2008 and earlier models have three screws in the lower cover (two mounted horizontally and one mounted vertically). It will be necessary to rotate the steering wheel in order to access the forward facing (horizontally mounted) screws on the lower cover. 2009 through 2013 models do not have retaining screws - only clips holding the covers in place. 2014 and later models have only the horizontally mounted screws securing the covers, plus retaining clips.*

2008 and earlier models

2   Remove the screws securing the lower steering column cover **(see illustration)**.
3   Separate the cover halves and detach them from the steering column.
4   Disconnect any electrical connections, if necessary, and remove the covers.
5   Installation is the reverse of removal.

2009 through 2013 models

6   Remove the steering wheel (see Chapter 10).

21.14 With the screws removed, carefully pry the cover halves apart while avoiding breaking any clips

7   Push the left and right sides of the lower steering column cover inward and downward - this should disengage the side retaining clips.
8   Reach your hand into the steering column tilt lever opening and disengage the inside clip.
9   Using a small screwdriver, disengage the clips on the front face of the column covers, allowing the lower cover to be separated and removed.
10   Disengage the front face clips, then the hidden center clip and remove the upper column cover.
11   Installation is the reverse of removal.

2014 and later models

12   Remove the steering wheel (see Chapter 10).
13   Remove the upper and lower column cover retaining screws **(see illustration)**.
14   Using a trim tool, carefully pry the upper cover upward to disengage the clips on the front and sides **(see illustration)**.
15   Release the clips for the lower column cover and carefully guide it off the column.
16   Installation is the reverse of removal.

22.2a Remove the retaining bolts in the console storage box (early Corolla models)

22.2b Remove the center console retaining bolts (Vibe model shown, Matrix similar)

22   Center console - removal and installation

Warning: *These models are equipped with airbags. Always disable the airbag system before working in the vicinity of any airbag system component to avoid the possibility of accidental deployment of the airbag(s), which could cause personal injury (see Chapter 12).*

2013 and earlier Corolla, 2009 and later Matrix, and all Vibe models

Note: *On 2008 and earlier Corolla models, it is necessary to remove the lower center trim panel (see Section 20) prior to removing the console.*

1   Disconnect the cable from the negative battery terminal (see Chapter 5).
2   Lift up the console armrest, remove the mat and remove the retaining bolts from the storage compartment. On Vibe models, also

22.3a Carefully pry up the shift bezel to release the clips . . .

remove the retaining bolts at the front of the console, then remove the console **(see illustrations)**.
3   Using a plastic trim tool, detach the shift bezel, then disconnect the 12-volt power

source connector **(see illustrations)**.
4   Remove the four screws, disconnect the electrical connector and remove the floor console **(see illustration)**.
5   Installation is the reverse of removal.

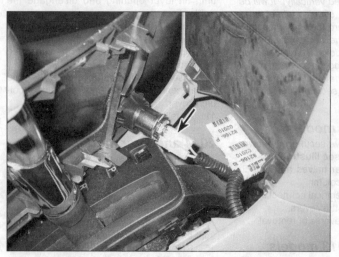

22.3b . . . then pull up the bezel and disconnect the electrical connector

22.4 Remove the four screws securing the front portion of the console to the floor, then disconnect the electrical connector

22.7a At each side, pull the side panels free from their retaining clips

22.7b Use a flat trim tool to lift the shifter bezel trim from the console. On manual transmissions, unscrew the shifter knob, then release the shifter boot by prying the retaining clips loose

22.7c Pry the cup holder panel off of the center console . . .

2014 and later Corolla models

6   Disconnect the cable from the negative battery terminal (see Chapter 5).
7   For the removal of the center console, follow the illustrations and their captions mentioned below, in sequence **(see illustrations)**.
8   Lift the center console up far enough to disconnect any additional electrical connections, then remove the console.
9   Installation is the reverse of removal.

2008 and earlier Matrix models

10   Disconnect the cable from the negative battery terminal (see Chapter 5).
11   Remove the lower center trim panel (see Section 20).
12   Remove the center console lower storage bin by opening it and pulling it upward.
13   Remove the various upper screws, then remove the lower screw(s) that are exposed by the removed storage bin.
14   Remove the console by sliding it rearward.
15   Installation is the reverse of removal.

22.7d . . . then disconnect any electrical connectors from underneath

22.7e Free the retaining clip from the shifter housing panel . . .

22.7f . . . then remove the trim panel from around the shifter housing (if equipped with an auto transmission, you will need to be shifted into Neutral to allow for removal space)

22.7g Remove the felt bottom trim from the storage compartment to gain access to the fasteners

22.7h Remove the screws securing the front of the center console

23.3a Typical passenger's side airbag module electrical connector

23.3b On later models, the arrangement is similar - disconnect the connector (A), release the wiring harness clips (B) and remove the bolt (C)

23   Instrument panel - removal and installation

Warning: *These models are equipped with airbags. Always disable the airbag system before working in the vicinity of any airbag system component to avoid the possibility of accidental deployment of the airbag(s), which could cause personal injury (see Chapter 12).*
Note: *This procedure requires the removal of the instrument panel, the cross-cowl support beam and steering column. This involves disconnecting numerous electrical connectors - there is also the potential for breakage of delicate plastic tabs on various components. Label all connections, where necessary. This is a difficult job for the home mechanic - if in doubt, consult a professional.*

Instrument panel
All models

1   Disconnect the cable from the nega-tive battery terminal (see Chapter 5).
2   Remove the driver's airbag module and the steering wheel (see Chapter 10).
3   Remove the glove box assembly (see Section 19), disconnect the passenger's air-bag module electrical connector **(see illus-trations)**. The electrical connectors used in the airbag system are a twin-lock design; use the proper method for disconnecting these connectors or damage to the connector may occur (see Chapter 12).
4   Remove the instrument cluster bezel (see Section 18) and remove the instrument cluster (see Chapter 12).
5   Remove the center trim panels (see Section 20), the heater and air conditioning control panel (see Chapter 3) and the radio (see Chapter 12).
6   Remove the steering column covers (see Section 21).
7   Remove the center console (see Sec-tion 22).
8   Remove the front door scuff plates

and the kick panels from both sides **(see illustrations)**.

Earlier Corolla and Matrix/Vibe models

9   Pry out the left and right air vents in the upper instrument panel.
10   Use a trim tool to remove the left and right trim pieces along the inside of the wind-shield pillars **(see illustration)**. Cover the entire length of the curtain shield airbag with a protective cover as soon as the front pillar trim is removed.
11   Remove the fasteners and release the clips, then remove the upper instrument panel **(see illustrations)**. Be sure to disconnect any electrical connectors attached behind the upper instrument panel.
12   On the left side of the lower instru-ment panel, disconnect and remove the release handle for the hood **(see illus-tration)**. Also, separate the diagnostic

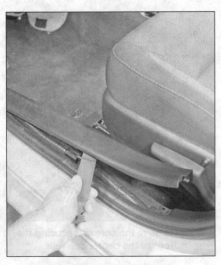

23.8a Pry up the scuff plate from the door sill . . .

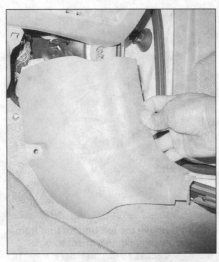

23.8b . . . then remove the plastic screw and the kick panel at both sides

23.10 Carefully pry off the windshield pillar trim panels

23.11a Indicated here are the clips (A), screws (B) and the one mounting bolt (C) for removal of the upper instrument panel (early Corolla model shown)

23.11b Indicated here are the screws (A, larger arrow indicates one screw under the passenger airbag), clips (B) and the claw tabs (C) for removal of the upper instrument panel (Matrix/Vibe model shown)

connector under the left edge of the instrument panel.

13 Pry up the plastic pins securing the vent ducts at the center and each side of the lower instrument panel (**see illustration**).

14 Remove the fasteners and remove the lower instrument panel (**see illustration**). Do not force the panel off, make sure you have found all the fasteners first. Make notes and use plastic bags to keep track of which fasteners go where.

15 The remainder of installation is the reverse of removal.

Cowl reinforcement beam

16 If the cowl reinforcement beam must be removed for a service procedure, follow the previous Steps, then proceed to disconnect all components fastened to the reinforcement beam (**see illustration**).

23.12 Pry down on the clip with a screwdriver (or trim tool, as shown) then slide the hood release handle assembly off of the panel

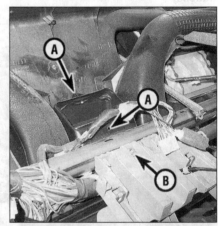

23.13 Remove the pins (A) securing the left, right and center (shown) ducts - also remove the center bolt (B) securing the lower instrument panel to the reinforcement tube

23.14 Location of lower instrument panel screws (A) and pins (B) (typical installation - some model's screw/pin locations may vary)

23.16 Go along the width of the beam, disconnecting electrical components bolted to the beam and harnesses attached with pins

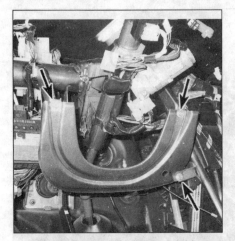

23.17a Remove the bolts and this reinforcement plate below the steering column

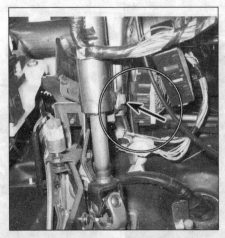

23.17b Remove the lower steering column mounting bolt . . .

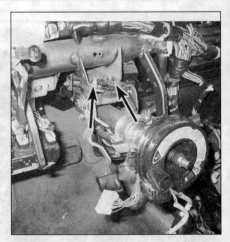

23.17c . . . and the two upper mounting bolts (upper captive nuts indicated, bolt heads are below bracket)

17   Disconnect the electrical connectors at the steering column and remove the bolts securing the column to the beam **(see illustrations)**.

18   At the left and right sides of the beam, remove the bolts holding braces from the tube to other components, then remove the two bolts holding the beam into the body

saddles at either end **(see illustration)**. Remove the beam from the vehicle.
19   Installation is the reverse of removal.

23.18 At the right side of the beam, disconnect the brace to the blower housing (A), the two end mounting bolts (B), and the bottom screw (C). Then move to the left side and detach the braces and mounting bolts

23.20 Pry out the left air vent in the upper instrument panel

23.21a Pry off the small cover . . .

23.21b . . . remove the screw . . .

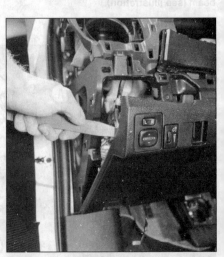

23.21c . . . the pry out the interior fuse box panel and disconnect the electrical connectors

23.22a Remove the upper bolts through the column opening . . .

23.22b . . . then remove the lower bolts . . .

23.22c . . . pull out the knee bolster airbag and disconnect the electrical connector by prying up the center tab with a small screwdriver, then pulling off the connector

Later Corolla models

20   Pry out the left air vent in the upper instrument panel **(see illustration)**.

21   Remove the interior fuse box cover **(see illustrations)**.

22   Remove the screws and the driver's side lower insulator panel, then remove the knee bolster airbag **(see illustrations)**.

23   Use a trim tool to pry off and remove the left and right trim pieces along the inside of the windshield pillars (see illustrations). There is a plastic retaining stop that will need to be rotated with needle nose pliers until the tab can pass through the slot in the trim piece.

24   Remove the clock from the upper instrument panel **(see illustrations)**.

23.23a Pry out the A-pillar trim panel . . .

23.23b . . . then disconnect the retaining stop tab from the trim panel - it will need to be rotated and aligned with the slot

23.23c Lift out the trim panel from the dash - when installing, make sure these tabs align with the slots in the dash

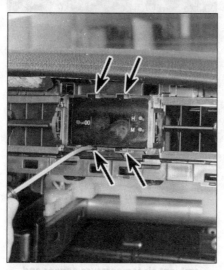

23.24a Release the tabs with a screwdriver and push the clock into the dash . . .

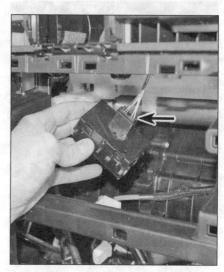

23.24b . . . then disconnect the clock electrical connector

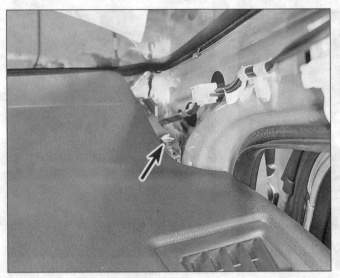

23.25a Upper instrument panel - upper-right pushpin fastener

23.25b Upper instrument panel - upper-left pushpin fastener and lower-left screw fastener

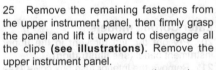

23.25c Pull up on the upper instrument panel to disengage the clips along the front

25   Remove the remaining fasteners from the upper instrument panel, then firmly grasp the panel and lift it upward to disengage all the clips **(see illustrations)**. Remove the upper instrument panel.

26   Remove the trim cover, then release the ambient air temperature sensor from the lower dash **(see illustrations)**. Also remove the small trim panel on the opposite side of the steering column.

27   Release the hood release lever assembly from the lower panel **(see illustration 23.12)**.

28   Remove the fasteners, disengage any remaining wiring harness clips from underneath the panel, then remove the lower instrument panel **(see illustrations)**.

29   Installation is the reverse of removal.

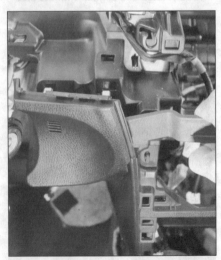

23.26a Pry off the trim panel . . .

23.26b . . . then release the tabs for the ambient air temperature sensor and push it into the dash

23.28a Lower instrument panel right side fastener locations

23.28b Lower instrument panel left side fastener locations

23.31 Release the tabs and swing out the levers, disconnecting the electrical connectors (1), then remove the mounting bolts (2) and ground wire screw (3) for the interior junction block assembly

Cowl reinforcement beam

30   Remove the steering column (see Chapter 10).

Note: *There may be more electrical connections and wiring harness clips to be disconnected than what is pictured, so use caution not to forcefully remove the junction block.*

31   Disconnect the connectors, remove the mounting bolts and remove the interior fuse box/junction block assembly **(see illustration)**. Also disconnect the skid control buzzer electrical connector (the small blue box in top-right of illustration).

32   Disconnect the electrical connector and remove the driver support module, then remove the lower air duct **(see illustration)**.

33   Remove the dash brace, then release the tabs and remove the center air vent hub **(see illustration)**.

34   Disconnect these electrical connectors from below the HVAC assembly **(see illustration)**.

23.32 Remove the driver support module by disconnecting the electrical connector and removing the mounting bolt (1), then remove the lower air duct (2)

23.33 Remove the bolts (1) and dash brace, then pry and release the retaining tabs to remove the center air vent hub (2)

23.34 Disconnect these electrical connectors

23.35a Disconnect the connector and remove the central gateway module (1), remove the various wiring harness clips and bolts (2) and remove the cowl beam mounting bolts (3)

23.35b Disconnect the connector and remove the power steering module (1), and remove the various wiring harness clips and bolts (2)

23.35c Remove the wiring harness bolts (1) and remove the cowl beam mounting bolts (2)

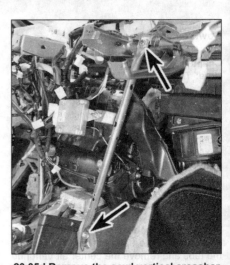

23.35d Remove the cowl vertical crossbar bolts and crossbar from each side

35   Disconnect the connector and remove the bolt for the central gateway module, disconnect and remove the power steering module, then disconnect the various wiring harness clips and connectors from the cowl beam. Remove the cowl reinforcement beam bolts and lift off the beam **(see illustrations)**.
36   Installation is the reverse of removal.

24   Radiator grille - removal and installation

Warning: *These models are equipped with airbags. Always disable the airbag system before working in the vicinity of any airbag system component to avoid the possibility of accidental deployment of the airbag(s), which could cause personal injury (see Chapter 12).*

Corolla models

1   Remove three fasteners along the top of the grille **(see illustration)**.
2   Pull the top of the grille out for access and disengage the lower retaining clips with a screwdriver.
3   Installation is the reverse of removal.

Vibe/Matrix models

4   Remove the front bumper cover (see Section 15).

23.35e Remove the cowl-to-HVAC assembly attachment bolts

24.1 Along the top of the grille, remove the screws at each side and the pushpin at the center, then disengage the clips along the bottom and pull the grille forward and out (early model shown, later models similar)

24.5 Release the clips at the rear of the bumper cover to remove the grille panels (2008 and earlier models shown, later models similar)

25.2a Remove the pushpins (A) from each side of the cowl panel - Some models might also require you to remove the weatherstripping (B)

25.2b The center of this type of pushpin should be pushed down, then the entire pushpin pulled out

5   At the rear of the bumper cover, release the clips securing the left and right grille panels (see illustration).

6   Installation is the reverse of removal.

25 Cowl louver panels - removal and installation

Upper cowl panel

Note: This procedure is shown on a later model Corolla, but the procedure for all earlier models is similar.

Note: On models with two-piece cowl panels, remove the right side panel first, then the left.

1   Mark the position of the windshield wiper blades on the windshield with a wax marking pen or tape, then remove the wiper arms (see Chapter 12).

2   Remove the pushpin clips securing the upper cowl panel to the vehicle (see illustration).

3   On models that apply, remove the plastic end caps from each side (see illustrations).

25.3a Use a screwdriver to pry up the end caps at each side . . .

25.3b . . . then remove the caps

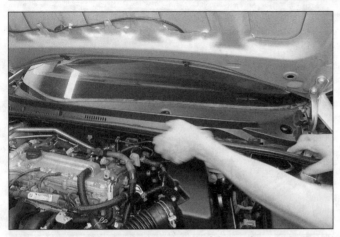

25.4 Carefully guide the cowl panel out of the engine compartment

**25.7 Lower cowl mounting bolts
(later model shown, earlier models similar)**

4   Disconnect the windshield washer hose(s), if necessary, and detach the cowl louver panel(s) from the vehicle **(see illustration)**. Note that there are also clips underneath the panel closest to the windshield. Installation is the reverse of removal. Make sure to align the wiper blades with the marks made during removal.

Lower cowl panel

5   Remove the upper cowl panel and windshield wiper motor (see Chapter 12).
6   On models that apply, remove the water guard plate clamp and slightly bend the plate to the left.
7   Remove the lower cowl mounting fasteners **(see illustration)** and remove the cowl from the vehicle.
8   Installation is the reverse of removal.

26 Seat belts - check

1   Check the seat belts, buckles, latch plates and guide loops for any obvious damage or signs of wear.
2   Make sure the seat belt reminder light comes on when the key is turned on.
3   The seat belts are designed to lock up during a sudden stop or impact, yet allow free movement during normal driving. The retractors should hold the belt against your chest while driving and rewind the belt when the buckle is unlatched.
4   If any of the above checks reveal problems with the seat-belt system, replace parts as necessary.

27 Fender (front) - removal and installation

Warning: *The models covered by this manual are equipped with a Supplemental Restraint System (SRS), more commonly known as airbags. Always disable the airbag system before working in the vicinity of any airbag system component to avoid the possibility of accidental deployment of the airbag, which could cause personal injury (see Chapter 12).*

Corolla models

Note: *This procedure is photographed on a later model Corolla - the removal and installation steps are similar for earlier Corolla models*
1   Raise the vehicle, support it securely on jackstands and remove the front wheel for the fender being replaced.
2   Remove the front bumper cover (see Section 15), headlight housing (see Chapter 12) and cowl louver paneling (see Section 25).
3   Remove the fenderwell splash shield **(see illustration)**.
4   Remove the frontmost fender bolt from the headlight housing opening **(see illustration)**.

27.3 Remove the various fenderwell splash shield fasteners (later model shown)

A   *Twist fastener - turn 90-degrees and pull it out (when installing, push straight in without turning 90-degrees)*
B   *Inner-tab fastener - insert screwdriver or punch inside the fastener*
       hole to release inner tabs, then pull it out
C   *Retaining bolts*
D   *Pushpin fastener - pry out the center tab, then pull out the fastener*

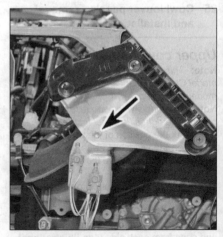

27.4 Fender bolt location (frontmost bolt)

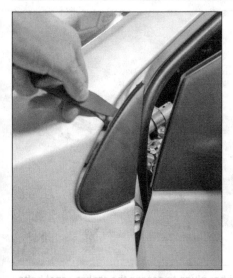

27.5a Pry off the cover with a trim tool . . .

27.5b . . . then remove the two rear door sill bolts

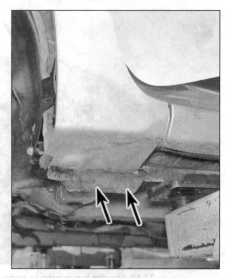

27.6 Fender rocker panel bolts

5   Open the door, then pry off the cover from the body and remove the fender door sill bolts **(see illustrations)**.
6   Remove the fender rocker panel bolts **(see illustration)**. There may be a thick rubber-like coating on these bolts, which may require them to be turned with extra force. Be careful not to round the bolt heads.
Note: *When removing the plastic panel clip fasteners from inside the fenderwell, it may be easiest to remove them from the other side with the door open, by pinching the retaining tabs with needle nose pliers. This method may also prevent breakage of the clips.*
7   Working inside the fenderwell, remove the plastic panel and the inside fender bolt **(see illustrations)**.
8   With the cowl panel removed, peel back the rubber sealing strip to access the uppermost fender bolt **(see illustration)**.
9   Remove the engine compartment fender bolts **(see illustration)**.

27.7a Remove the plastic fasteners (A) and disengage the rubber grommet (B) . . .

27.7b . . . remove the panel . . .

27.7c . . . then remove the inside fender mounting bolt

27.8 Peel back the rubber and remove the uppermost bolt

27.9 Engine compartment fender bolts

27.10 Fender inner rubber support piece

27.17 Remove the rubber plugs to access the rocker panel bolts

10   When removing the fender, take note of the inner rubber piece and the orientation in which it is installed **(see illustration)**.

11   Lift off the fender. It's a good idea to have an assistant support the fender while it's being moved away from the vehicle to prevent dam-

age to the surrounding body panels. Be careful not to distort the fender while removing it.

12   Installation is the reverse of removal. Check the alignment of the fender to the hood and front edge of the door before final tightening of the fender fasteners.

Matrix/Vibe models

13   Raise the vehicle, support it securely on jackstands and remove the front wheel for the fender being replaced.

14   Remove the headlight housing (see Chapter 12).

15   Detach the inner fenderwell screws and clips, then remove the inner fenderwell liner **(similar to illustration 27.3)**.

16   Remove the front bumper cover (see Section 15).

17   The lower rocker panel must be removed for access to the lower fender-to-body bolt. Remove the rubber plugs covering the rocker panel bolts, then remove the bolts and the rocker panel **(see illustration)**.

27.18a Carefully pry off the fender flare

27.18b Location of the clips on the fender flare

27.19 Remove the lower fender bolt at the rocker area

27.20 Remove the fender-to-body bolts in the door opening (one shown)

27.21 After removal of the front bumper cover and headlight, remove these two bolts in the front of the fender

18   Use a plastic trim tool to remove the front fender flare panel (see illustrations).
19   Remove the lower fender bolt revealed by removal of the fender flare (see illustration).
20   Open the front door, and remove the two fender-to-body bolts and the one bolt inside the fenderwell (see illustration).
21   Under the headlight housing area, remove the two fender fasteners (see illustration).
22   Remove the cowl louver panel and the rubber hood sealing strip along the top of the fender (see Section 25), then remove the two upper fender-to-body mounting bolts (see illustration).
23   Lift off the fender. It's a good idea to have an assistant support the fender while it's being moved away from the vehicle to prevent damage to the surrounding body panels. Be careful not to distort the fender while removing it.
24   Installation is the reverse of removal. Check the alignment of the fender to the hood and front edge of the door before final tightening of the fender fasteners.

27.22 Remove the two fender-to-body upper bolts

Notes

Chapter 12
Chassis electrical system

Contents

1 General information

1 The electrical system is a 12-volt, negative ground type. Power for the lights and all electrical accessories is supplied by a lead/acid-type battery, which is charged by the alternator.

2 This Chapter covers repair and service procedures for the various electrical components not associated with the engine. Information on the battery, alternator and starter motor can be found in Chapter 5.

3 It should be noted that when portions of the electrical system are serviced, the cable should be disconnected from the negative battery terminal to prevent electrical shorts and/or fires.

2 Electrical troubleshooting - general information

1 A typical electrical circuit consists of an electrical component, any switches, relays, motors, fuses, fusible links or circuit breakers related to that component and the wiring and connectors that link the component to both the battery and the chassis. To help you pinpoint an electrical circuit problem, wiring diagrams are included at the end of this Chapter.

2 Before tackling any troublesome electrical circuit, first study the appropriate wiring diagrams to get a complete understanding of what makes up that individual circuit. Trouble spots, for instance, can often be narrowed down by noting if other components related to the circuit are operating properly. If several components or circuits fail at one time, chances are the problem is in a fuse or ground connection, because several circuits are often routed through the same fuse and ground connections.

3 Electrical problems usually stem from simple causes, such as loose or corroded connections, a blown fuse, a melted fusible link or a failed relay. Visually inspect the condition of all fuses, wires and connections in a problem circuit before troubleshooting the circuit.

4 If test equipment and instruments are going to be utilized, use the diagrams to plan ahead of time where you will make the necessary connections in order to accurately pinpoint the trouble spot.

2.5a The most useful tool for electrical troubleshooting is a digital multimeter that can check volts, amps, and test continuity

2.5b A test light is a very handy tool for checking voltage

5   The basic tools needed for electrical troubleshooting include a circuit tester or voltmeter (a 12-volt bulb with a set of test leads can also be used), a continuity tester, which includes a bulb, battery and set of test leads, and a jumper wire, preferably with a circuit breaker incorporated, which can be used to bypass electrical components **(see illustrations)**. Before attempting to locate a problem with test instruments, use the wiring diagram(s) to decide where to make the connections.

Voltage checks

6   Voltage checks should be performed if a circuit is not functioning properly. Connect one lead of a circuit tester to either the negative battery terminal or a known good ground. Connect the other lead to a connector in the circuit being tested, preferably nearest to the battery or fuse **(see illustration)**. If the bulb of the tester lights, voltage is present, which means that the part of the circuit between the connector and the battery is problem free. Continue checking the rest of the circuit in the same fashion. When you reach a point at which no voltage is present, the problem lies between that point and the last test point with voltage. Most of the time the problem can be traced to a loose connection.

Note: *Keep in mind that some circuits receive voltage only when the ignition key is in the Accessory or Run position.*

Finding a short

7   One method of finding shorts in a circuit is to remove the fuse and connect a test light or voltmeter in place of the fuse terminals. There should be no voltage present in the circuit. Move the wiring harness from side-to-side while watching the test light. If the bulb goes on, there is a short to ground somewhere in that area, probably where the insulation has rubbed through. The same test can be performed on each component in the circuit, even a switch.

Ground check

8   Perform a ground test to check whether a component is properly grounded. Disconnect the battery and connect one lead of a continuity tester or multimeter (set to the ohms scale), to a known good ground. Connect the other lead to the wire or ground connection being tested. If the resistance is low (less than 5 ohms), the ground is good. If the bulb on a self-powered test light does not go on, the ground is not good.

Continuity check

9   A continuity check is done to determine if there are any breaks in a circuit - if it is passing electricity properly. With the circuit off (no power in the circuit), a self-powered continuity tester or multimeter can be used to check the circuit. Connect the test leads to both ends of the circuit (or to the power end and a good ground), and if the test light comes on the circuit is passing current properly **(see illustration)**. If the resistance is low (less than 5 ohms), there is continuity; if the reading is 10,000 ohms or higher, there is a break somewhere in the circuit. The same procedure can be used to test a switch, by connecting the continuity tester to the switch terminals. With the switch turned On, the test light should come on (or low resistance should be indicated on a meter).

Finding an open circuit

10   When diagnosing for possible open circuits, it is often difficult to locate them by sight because the connectors hide oxidation or terminal misalignment. Merely wiggling a connector on a sensor or in the wiring harness may correct the open circuit condition. Remember this when an open circuit is indicated when troubleshooting a circuit. Intermittent problems may also be caused by oxidized or loose connections.

11   Electrical troubleshooting is simple if you keep in mind that all electrical circuits are basically electricity running from the battery, through the wires, switches, relays, fuses and fusible links to each electrical component (light bulb, motor, etc.) and to ground, from which it is passed back to the battery. Any electrical problem is an interruption in the flow of electricity to and from the battery.

3   Fuses and fusible links - general information

Fuses

1   The electrical circuits of the vehicle are protected by a combination of fuses, circuit

2.6 In use, a basic test light's lead is clipped to a known good ground, then the pointed probe can test connectors, wires or electrical sockets - if the bulb lights, the part being tested has battery voltage

2.9 With a multimeter set to the ohms scale, resistance can be checked across two terminals - when checking for continuity, a low reading indicates continuity, a high reading indicates lack of continuity

3.1a The interior fuse box is tucked up under the instrument panel, to the left of the steering column - it's fairly difficult to reach

3.1b The main engine compartment fuse/relay box is located near the left strut tower

breakers and fusible links. The fuse blocks are located under the instrument panel and in the engine compartment **(see illustrations)**.
2   Each of the fuses is designed to protect a specific circuit, and the various circuits are identified on the fuse panel cover.
3   Miniaturized fuses are employed in the fuse blocks. These compact fuses, with blade terminal design, allow fingertip removal and replacement. If an electrical component fails, always check the fuse first. The best way to check a fuse is with a test light. Check for power at the exposed terminal tips of each fuse. If power is present on one side of the fuse but not the other, the fuse is blown. A blown fuse can also be confirmed by visually inspecting it **(see illustration)**.
4   Be sure to replace blown fuses with the correct type. Fuses of different ratings are physically interchangeable, but only fuses of the proper rating should be used. Replacing a fuse with one of a higher or lower value than specified is not recommended. Each electrical circuit needs a specific amount of protection. The amperage value of each fuse is molded into the fuse body.
5   If the replacement fuse immediately fails, don't replace it again until the cause of the problem is isolated and corrected. In most

cases, this will be a short circuit in the wiring caused by a broken or deteriorated wire.

Fusible links

6   Some circuits are protected by fusible links. The links are used in circuits which are not ordinarily fused, such as the ignition circuit, or which carry high current.
7   Cartridge type fusible links are located in the engine compartment fuse box and are similar to a large fuse. After disconnecting the negative battery cable, simply unplug and replace it with a fusible link of the same amperage.
8   A wire-type fusible link, installed in the harness between the battery and the fuse/relay blocks, protects the entire chassis electrical system. It's located near the positive battery terminal. If the fusible link melts, the cause of the short must first be repaired, then the fusible link must be replaced with a fusible link of the same gauge. Never substitute a regular wire for a fusible link.
9   To replace a wire-type fusible link, disconnect the cable from the negative terminal of the battery, cut the damaged link out and solder a new one in its place. Cover the exposed wires with shrink-wrap tubing or plenty of electrical tape.

4   Circuit breakers - general information

1   Circuit breakers protect certain circuits, such as the power windows or heated seats. Depending on the vehicle's accessories, there may be one or two circuit breakers, located in the fuse/relay box in the engine compartment **(see illustration 3.1b)**.
2   Because the circuit breakers reset automatically, an electrical overload in a circuit-breaker-protected system will cause the circuit to fail momentarily, then come back on. If the circuit does not come back on, check it immediately.
3   For a basic check, pull the circuit breaker up out of its socket on the fuse panel, but just far enough to probe with a voltmeter. The breaker should still contact the sockets.
4   With the voltmeter negative lead on a good chassis ground, touch each end prong of the circuit breaker with the positive meter probe. There should be battery voltage at each end. If there is battery voltage only at one end, the circuit breaker must be replaced.
5   Some circuit breakers must be reset manually.

5   Relays - general information and testing

General information

1   Several electrical circuits in the vehicle use relays to transmit the electrical signal to the component. Relays use a low-current circuit (the control circuit) to open and close a high-current circuit (the power circuit). If the relay is defective, that component will not operate properly. Most relays are mounted in the engine compartment fuse/relay box, with some specialized relays located above the interior fuse box in the dash **(see illustrations 3.1a and 3.1b)**. If a faulty relay is suspected, it can be removed and tested using the procedure below or by a dealer service department or a repair shop. Defective relays must be replaced as a unit.

3.3 When a fuse blows, the element between the terminals melts

BAD   GOOD

Relay with internal resistor

Relay with internal diode

24053-12-5.2a HAYNES

5.2a Typical ISO relay designs, terminal numbering and circuit connections

5.2b Most relays are marked on the outside to easily identify the control circuits and the power circuits (four-terminal type shown)

Testing

2   Most of the relays used in these vehicles are of a type often called "ISO" relays, which refers to the International Standards Organization. The terminals of ISO relays are numbered to indicate their usual circuit connections and functions. There are two basic layouts of terminals on the relays used in these vehicles (see illustrations).

3   Refer to the wiring diagram for the circuit to determine the proper connections for the relay you're testing. If you can't determine the correct connection from the wiring diagrams, however, you may be able to determine the test connections from the information that follows.

4   Two of the terminals are the relay control circuit and connect to the relay coil. The other relay terminals are the power circuit. When the relay is energized, the coil creates a magnetic field that closes the larger contacts of the power circuit to provide power to the circuit loads.

5   Terminals 85 and 86 are normally the control circuit. If the relay contains a diode, terminal 86 must be connected to battery positive (B+) voltage and terminal 85 to ground. If the relay contains a resistor, terminals 85 and 86 can be connected in either direction with respect to B+ and ground.

6   Terminal 30 is normally connected to the battery voltage (B+) source for the circuit loads. Terminal 87 is connected to the circuit leading to the component being powered. If the relay has several alternate

terminals for load or ground connections, they usually are numbered 87A, 87B, 87C, and so on.

7   Use an ohmmeter to check continuity through the relay control coil.

  a) *Connect the meter according to the polarity shown in illustration 5.2a for one check; then reverse the ohmmeter leads and check continuity in the other direction.*

  b) *If the relay contains a resistor, resistance will be indicated on the meter, and should be the same value with the ohmmeter in either direction.*

  c) *If the relay contains a diode, resistance should be higher with the ohmmeter in the forward polarity direction than with the meter leads reversed.*

  d) *If the ohmmeter shows infinite resistance in both directions, replace the relay.*

8   Remove the relay from the vehicle and use the ohmmeter to check for continuity between the relay power circuit terminals. There should be no continuity between terminal 30 and 87 with the relay de-energized.

9   Connect a fused jumper wire to terminal 86 and the positive battery terminal. Connect another jumper wire between terminal 85 and ground. When the connections are made, the relay should click.

10   With the jumper wires connected, check for continuity between the power circuit terminals. Now, there should be continuity between terminals 30 and 87.

11   If the relay fails any of the above tests, replace it.

6   Electrical connectors - general information

1   Most electrical connections on these vehicles are made with multiwire plastic connectors. The mating halves of many connectors are secured with locking clips molded into the plastic connector shells. The mating halves of some large connectors, such as some of those under the instrument panel, are held together by a bolt through the center of the connector.

2   To separate a connector with locking clips, use a small screwdriver to pry the clips apart carefully, then separate the connector halves. Pull only on the shell, never pull on the wiring harness, as you may damage the individual wires and terminals inside the connectors. Look at the connector closely before trying to separate the halves. Often the locking clips are engaged in a way that is not immediately clear. Additionally, many connectors have more than one set of clips.

3   Each pair of connector terminals has a male half and a female half. When you look at the end view of a connector in a diagram, be sure to understand whether the view shows the harness side or the component side of the connector. Connector halves are mirror images of each other, and a terminal shown on the right side end-view of one half will be on the left side end-view of the other half.

4   It is often necessary to take circuit voltage measurements with a connector connected. Whenever possible, carefully insert a small straight pin (not your meter probe) into the rear of the connector shell to contact the terminal inside, then clip your meter lead to the pin. This kind of connection is called "backprobing." When inserting a test probe into a terminal, be careful not to distort the terminal opening. Doing so can lead to a poor connection and corrosion at that terminal later. Using the small straight pin instead of a meter probe results in less chance of deforming the terminal connector.

Electrical connectors

Most electrical connectors have a single release tab that you depress to release the connector

Some electrical connectors have a retaining tab which must be pried up to free the connector

Some connectors have two release tabs that you must squeeze to release the connector

Some connectors use wire retainers that you squeeze to release the connector

Critical connectors often employ a sliding lock (1) that you must pull out before you can depress the release tab (2)

Here's another sliding-lock style connector, with the lock (1) and the release tab (2) on the side of the connector

On some connectors the lock (1) must be pulled out to the side and removed before you can lift the release tab (2)

Some critical connectors, like the multi-pin connectors at the Powertrain Control Module employ pivoting locks that must be flipped open

---

7   Turn signal and hazard flasher - check and replacement

Warning: *The models covered by this manual are equipped with a Supplemental Restraint System (SRS), more commonly known as airbags. Always disable the airbag system before working in the vicinity of any airbag system components to avoid the possibility of accidental deployment of the airbags, which could cause personal injury (see Section 27).*
Note: *This procedure applies to 2013 and earlier models only.*

1   The turn signal and hazard flasher is a single combination unit, located on the interior fuse/relay box **(see illustration)**.

7.1 Turn signal flasher unit (2008 and earlier shown) - on 2009 to 2013 models, the flasher unit is in the same area but on the far right side of the fuse/relay box

8.6 Release the switch retaining claw with a plastic tool (steering wheel removed for clarity, but it isn't necessary to remove the steering wheel for switch removal)

8.10 Disconnect the headlight/turn signal and washer/wiper switch electrical connectors

8.11a Lift the locking claw and slide the assembly off of the steering column

8.11b Switch assembly removed from the steering column

A Airbag spiral cable (clockspring)   C Wiper/washer switch
B Lighting switch

2   When the flasher unit is functioning properly, an audible click can be heard during its operation. If the turn signals fail on one side or the other and the flasher unit does not make its characteristic clicking sound, or if a bulb on one side of the vehicle flashes much faster than normal but the bulb at the other end of the vehicle (on the same side) doesn't light at all, a faulty turn signal bulb may be indicated.

3   If both turn signals fail to blink, the problem may be due to a blown fuse, a faulty flasher unit, a defective switch or a loose or open connection. If a quick check of the fuse box indicates that the turn signal fuse has blown, check the wiring for a short before installing a new fuse.

4   Locate the turn signal flasher:
2008 and earlier models - The flasher relay is on the left hand side of the fuse/relay box.
2009 through 2013 models - The flasher relay is on the right side of the fuse/relay box.
2014 and later models - The flashing of the

turn signals and hazard flashers are accomplished through the combination meter (instrument cluster). There is NO serviceable flasher unit.

5   Pull the turn signal flasher from the fuse/relay box. Make sure that the replacement unit is identical to the original. Compare the old one to the new one before installing it.

6   Installation is the reverse of removal.

8   Steering column switches and steering wheel switch assembly - replacement

Steering column switches
Warning: *The models covered by this manual are equipped with a Supplemental Restraint System (SRS), more commonly known as airbags. Always disable the airbag system before working in the vicinity of any airbag system components to avoid the possibility of*

accidental deployment of the airbag(s), which could cause personal injury (see Section 27).
1   Disconnect the cable from the negative terminal of the battery (see Chapter 5).
2   Remove the steering column covers (see Chapter 11).
3   The steering column switches on these models are two separate switch units connected to a central plastic housing. The windshield wiper/washer switch can be replaced separately, but the headlight/turn signal switch is replaced along with the switch housing.

Windshield wiper/washer switch
4   Remove the steering column covers (see Chapter 11).
5   Disconnect the electrical connectors from the switch.
6   Depress the claw in the switch, then pull the switch from the steering column (**see illustration**).
Note: *Excessive force may break the claw.*
7   Installation is the reverse of removal.

8.12 The spiral cable is retained to the switch housing with three locking claws

8.15a Press out the wire harness fastener by squeezing the tabs inward and pushing the wire fastener out of the steering wheel

8.15b Turn the wheel over, and pull the harness up and out of the way

8.15c With a flat trim tool, start working your way around the wheel, releasing the pressure clips

8.15d With the switch assembly removed, you have access to the cruise control switch, which is retained by two screws

8.15e If there are any cracks or warped sections, or one of the switches doesn't work, replace the assembly

Headlight/turn signal switch

8   Park the vehicle with the wheels pointing straight ahead, then remove the steering wheel (see Chapter 10, Section 14).

9   Remove the steering column covers (see Chapter 11, Section 21). place a piece of tape across the airbag spiral cable (clockspring) and across its the sides of the spiral cable housing to prevent it from turning when it's removed.

10   Disconnect the electrical connectors from the windshield wiper/washer switch and the headlight/turn signal switch **(see illustration)**.

11   Lift up the retaining claw to release the switch housing from the steering column **(see illustrations)**.

12   To separate the spiral cable from the switch housing, pry up the three locking claws and detach it from the housing **(see illustration)**.

13   Installation is the reverse of removal. **Warning:** *Be sure to center the spiral cable before installing the steering wheel (see Chapter 10, Section 14).*

Steering wheel switch assembly and cruise control switch

Warning: *The models covered by this manual are equipped with a Supplemental Restraint System (SRS), more commonly known as airbags. Always disable the airbag system before working in the vicinity of any airbag system components to avoid the possibility of accidental deployment of the airbag(s), which could cause personal injury (see Section 27).*

14   Remove the steering wheel (see Chapter 11).

15   Follow the photo sequence for disassembly **(see illustrations)**.

16   To install the switch assembly, reverse the removal sequence.

9   Ignition switch (key and tumbler type) and start button (Smart Key models)

Warning: *The models covered by this manual are equipped with a Supplemental Restraint System (SRS), more commonly known as airbags. Always disable the airbag system before working in the vicinity of any airbag system components to avoid the possibility of accidental deployment of the airbag(s), which could cause personal injury (see Section 27).*

1   Disconnect the cable from the negative terminal of the battery (see Chapter 5).

9.3 Disconnect the electrical connectors at the bottom of the ignition switch housing

9.4 Unscrew the retaining screws to remove the electrical portion of the ignition switch

9.8 With the lock cylinder in the ACC position, depress the retaining pin with a small screwdriver, then pull the cylinder straight out

Ignition switch

2   Remove the steering column covers (see Chapter 11).
3   Unplug the ignition switch wiring harness connectors (see illustration).
4   Remove the switch retaining screws **(see illustration)** then pull the switch from the lock cylinder housing.
5   Installation is reverse of the removal.

Lock cylinder

6   On models equipped with the engine immobilizer system, gently pry off the plastic shroud around the key-lock cylinder and disconnect the electrical connector. Lift the shroud edge from the locating tab only enough to slip the shroud off. The shroud houses the amplifier for the special transponder keys. Pry lightly to remove the illumination ring, then remove the unlock arming switch.
7   Insert the key and turn it to the ACC position.
8   Use a small screwdriver or punch to depress the lock cylinder retaining pin, then withdraw the key cylinder **(see illustration)**.

9   To install the lock cylinder, depress the retaining pin and guide the lock cylinder into the housing until the retaining pin extends itself back into the locating hole in the housing.
10   The remainder of the installation is the reverse of removal.

Smart Key start button

Note: *Today's advanced electronics using a start button don't have the same problems as a conventional ignition switch using a key. There are virtually no moving parts to wear out or a tumbler that wears down. The electrical signal to the start button is very low (5 volts in most cases) which means the common problems found with conventional ignition systems such as a drop in voltage or melted connections rarely, if ever, happen. So the chances of a start button being the cause of a no-start condition are very slim. But, in the case that there is a failure, the following procedures will explain how to replace the start button.*

11   Remove the instrument panel trim and instrument cluster bezel (see Chapter 11).

12   Remove the start button trim bezel by pulling outward away from the dash.
13   From the back of the start button, squeeze inward the tabs holding the button into the mounting hole.
14   Slide the button out of the hole far enough to reach the electrical connection. Disconnect the electrical connection.
15   Installation is the reverse of removal.

10   Instrument panel switches - replacement

Warning: *The models covered by this manual are equipped with a Supplemental Restraint System (SRS), more commonly known as airbags. Always disable the airbag system before working in the vicinity of any airbag system components to avoid the possibility of accidental deployment of the airbag(s), which could cause personal injury (see Section 27).*

10.5 Use a trim tool to pry the dimmer/mirror switch panel from the left side of the dash

10.6 Disconnect the electrical connector and release the two clips securing the light control switch - mirror switch removal is similar

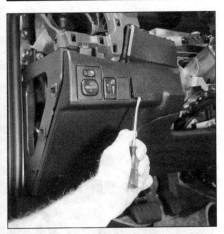

10.9a Pry out the trim cover . . .

10.9b . . . then remove the screw

10.9c Starting from any corner edge, pry the pressure clips free with a flat trim tool

Hazard warning switch

1   Disconnect the negative battery cable (see Chapter 5).
2   Carefully remove the center cluster finish panel (see Chapter 11) from the instrument panel and pull the assembly out until you can disconnect the electrical connector at the rear of the switch.
3   Use two screwdrivers to depress the switch retaining tangs, then remove the switch cluster from the panel.
4   Installation is the reverse of the removal procedure.

Power mirror control switch and instrument panel dimmer switch

2013 and earlier models

5   Carefully pry the panel from the dash with a trim tool (see illustration).
6   Disconnect the electrical connector and remove the switches (see illustration).
7   Installation is the reverse of the removal procedure.

2014 and later models

8   Remove the instrument panel trim that is overlapping the lower dash edge panel

10.9d Turn the trim panel over to disconnect the electrical connections. The actual switches are held in with plastic tabs. Press the tabs inward to remove the switch

(see Chapter 11).
9   The accompanying photos will guide you through the removal process (see illustrations).

Defogger switch

10   The rear window defogger switch is located in the heating and air conditioning control panel.
11   Refer to Chapter 3, Section 11 and remove the control panel, then pull the assembly out until you can disconnect the

electrical connector at the rear of the switch. Depress the tab and remove the switch from the bezel.
12   Installation is the reverse of the removal procedure.

Clock

13   Remove the dash trim panels from around the clock (see Chapter 11). To remove the clock, see the accompanying illustrations.

10.13a The clock is held in with plastic tabs. A little wiggle while pulling on the clock body will release it

10.13b One electrical connection needs to be disconnected

10.14a With the console trim removed, a flat trim tool will release the pressure clips holding the cigarette lighter and USB port bracket in place

10.14b The electrical connections can be disconnected with the assembly flipped over

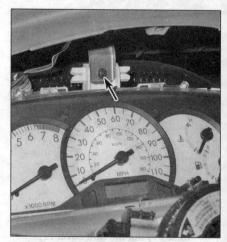

11.3 Remove this screw at the top of the instrument cluster (2008 and earlier models; 2009 through 2013 models have two screws) . . .

Cigarette lighter and USB port

14　Remove the trim from the center console area (see Chapter 11). To remove the cigarette lighter and USB port **see the accompanying illustrations.**

11　Instrument cluster - removal and installation

Warning: *The models covered by this manual are equipped with a Supplemental Restraint System (SRS), more commonly known as airbags. Always disable the airbag system before working in the vicinity of any airbag system component to avoid the possibility of accidental deployment of the airbag(s), which could cause personal injury (see Section 27).*

1　Disconnect the negative battery cable (see Chapter 5). On models with a tilt steering column, place it in the lowest position.
2　Remove the instrument cluster bezel (see Chapter 11).

2013 and earlier models

3　Remove the cluster mounting screw(s) at the top **(see illustration)**.
4　Pry at the two bottom clips to release them, then pull the cluster out **(see illustration)**.

2014 and later models

5　Remove the two screws from the bottom of the cluster **(see illustration)**, then disengage the upper retaining clips by pulling cluster from the instrument panel.

All models

6　Disconnect the electrical connector(s) **(see illustrations)**.
7　Guide the instrument cluster out from between the instrument panel and steering wheel, being careful not to scratch the steering column cover.
8　Installation is the reverse of removal.

12　Wiper system - check and component replacement

Wiper motor circuit check

Note: *Refer to the wiring diagrams for wire colors and locations in the following checks. When checking for voltage, probe a grounded 12-volt test light to each terminal at a connector until it lights; this verifies voltage (power) at the terminal. If the following checks fail to locate the problem, have the system diagnosed by a dealer service department or other properly equipped repair facility.*

1　If the wipers work slowly, make sure the battery is in good condition and has a strong charge (see Chapter 5). If the battery is in good condition, remove the wiper motor (see below) and operate the wiper arms by hand. Check for binding linkage and pivots. Lubricate or repair the linkage or pivots as necessary. Reinstall the wiper motor. If the

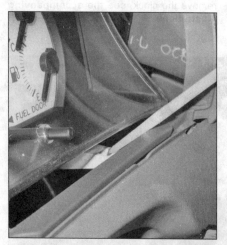

11.4 . . . then release the clips and pull the cluster out at the bottom

11.5 Instrument cluster retaining screws (2014 and later models, steering wheel removed for clarity)

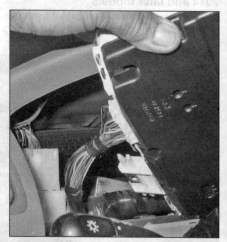

11.6a Disconnect the electrical connector(s) at the back of the cluster. Earlier models have one connector . . .

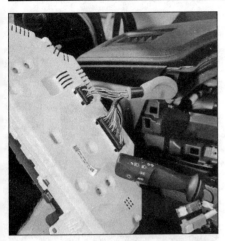

11.6b . . . while later models have
two connectors

12.7a Lift the end cap to access the wiper
arm nut, remove the nut, then make a
reference mark before removing the arm

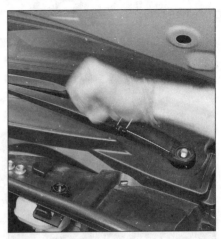

12.7b To release the arm from the spindle,
strike downward on the arm lever like this.
It will pop the connection loose

wipers still operate slowly, check for loose or
corroded connections, especially the ground
connection. If all connections look OK,
replace the motor.

2   If the wipers fail to operate when activated, check the fuse in the driver's side
interior fuse panel. If the fuse is OK, connect
a jumper wire between the wiper motor's
ground terminal and ground, then retest. If
the motor works now, repair the ground connection. If the motor still doesn't work, turn the
wiper switch to the HI position and check for
voltage at the motor.
Note: *The cowl cover will have to be removed
(see Chapter 11) to access the electrical connector.*

3   If there's voltage at the connector,
remove the motor and check it off the vehicle
with fused jumper wires from the battery. If the
motor now works, check for binding linkage
(see Step 1). If the motor still doesn't work,
replace it. If there's no voltage to the motor,
check for voltage at the wiper control relays. If
there's voltage at the wiper control relays and
no voltage at the wiper motor, have the switch
tested. If the switch is OK, the wiper control

relay is probably bad. See Section 5 for relay
testing.

4   If the interval (delay) function is inoperative, check the continuity of all the wiring
between the switch and wiper control module.
Note: *Wiper switch replacement is covered in
the Section 8.*

5   If the wipers stop at the position they're
in when the switch is turned off (fail to park),
check for voltage at the park feed wire of the
wiper motor connector when the wiper switch
is Off but the ignition is On. If no voltage is
present, check for an open circuit between
the wiper motor and the fuse panel.

Component replacement

Windshield wiper motor

6   Disconnect the negative cable from the
battery (see Chapter 5).

7   Remove the covers over the wiper arm
mounting nuts. Remove the nuts, mark the
relationship of the arms to the spindles, then
pry up the wiper arms **(see illustrations)**.

8   Remove the cowl louver panels (see
Chapter 11).

9   Release the harness retaining clips,
remove the windshield wiper motor/linkage
assembly mounting bolts, then disconnect the
wiper motor electrical connector and remove
the assembly **(see illustrations)**.

12.9a Release the harness retaining clips

12.9b Location of the wiper linkage
mounting bolts - 2008 and earlier models

12.9c Location of the wiper linkage
mounting bolts - 2009 and later models

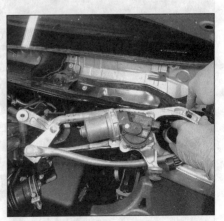

12.9d With the linkage and motor
assembly upside down you can easily
disconnect the wire harness connection

12.11 Pry the link from the motor arm (A), then remove the wiper motor mounting bolts (B)

12.13 Remove the liftgate wiper arm nut

12.14 Remove the liftgate wiper assembly cover

10   **2008 and earlier models** - Slide the assembly toward the passenger's side to detach the rubber pin near the motor from the cowl sheetmetal, then lift the windshield wiper motor assembly from the cowl area.

11   Pry the linkage from the motor arm, remove the wiper motor mounting bolts and separate the motor from the frame **(see illustration)**.

12   Installation is the reverse of removal.

Liftgate wiper motor

13   Remove the wiper arm nut and the wiper arm **(see illustration)**.

14   With the liftgate open, use a trim tool to pry off the cover over the wiper assembly trim panel from the liftgate **(see illustration)**.

15   Disconnect and unbolt the electrical junction from the wiper assembly and lay it aside **(see illustration)**.

16   Remove the wiper assembly mounting bolts and remove the assembly **(see illustration)**.

17   Installation is the reverse of removal.

Washer fluid reservoir/pump

18   The washer fluid reservoir is located in the lower right front corner of the engine compartment. Access is from underneath **(see illustrations)**. Remove the inner fender splash shield (see Chapter 11).

---

13   Radio and speakers - removal and installation

Warning: *The models covered by this manual are equipped with a Supplemental Restraint System (SRS), more commonly known as airbags. Always disable the airbag system before working in the vicinity of any airbag system components to avoid the possibility of accidental deployment of the airbag(s), which could cause personal injury (see Section 27).*

1   Disconnect the negative battery cable (see Chapter 5).

Radio

2008 and earlier Corolla models

2   The air conditioning control panel must be removed before the radio mounting screws can be accessed (see Chapter 3, Section 11).

3   Remove the retaining screws and pull the radio panel outward to access the backside, then disconnect the electrical connectors and the antenna lead. Release the clips and separate the radio from the panel **(see illustration)**.

4   Installation is the reverse of removal.

2009 and later Corolla and all Matrix/Vibe models

5   Remove the center trim panel from the instrument panel (see Chapter 11).

6   Remove the four mounting bolts, then pull out the radio and bracket and disconnect the electrical connectors **(see illustrations)**.

7   Installation is the reverse of removal.

12.15 Disconnect the electrical connector (A), then remove the bolts (B) and the electrical junction (C)

12.16 Remove the three mounting bolts and the wiper assembly (the left bolt here is beneath the electrical junction)

12.18a Washer fluid reservoir mounting bolts (two of three shown) and upper push-fastener that retains the filler neck (bumper cover removed for clarity)

12.18b From the bottom, you can gain access to replace the washer pump (A) or the level sensor (B). One more mounting bolt is also accessible from this position (C). The pump or fluid level sensor is removed by twisting and pulling it out of its grommet

Door speakers

8   Remove the door trim panel (see Chapter 11). All models have speakers in both front and rear doors. Rear door speakers are mounted similarly to the front door speakers.
9   Remove the speaker mounting rivets (see illustration). Disconnect the electrical connector and remove the speaker from the vehicle.
10   Installation is the reverse of removal.

Tweeters

11   In addition to the standard door and rear speakers, some models are equipped with small tweeters for improved high-range sound.
12   The tweeters are mounted in the front of the doors under the mirror cover, or sail panel. Refer to Chapter 11 and remove the outside mirror covers.

13.3 The radio comes out with this panel and two vents - release the clips top and bottom to remove the radio from the vent panel

13.6a Remove the four bolts . . .

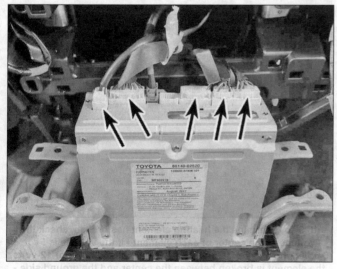

13.6b . . . then pull the unit out and disconnect the electrical connectors (Corolla shown, Matrix/Vibe similar)

13.9 Drill out the rivets securing the door speaker, then pull the speaker out and disconnect the electrical connector

13   On earlier models, remove the tweeter mounting nuts and disconnect the electrical connector (see illustration).

14   On later models, pry the tweeter from the retaining claws on the back of the trim panel (see illustration).

15   Installation is the reverse of removal.

14 Antenna - replacement

1   Some vehicles covered by this manual are equipped with a mast-type antenna attached to the rear of the roof.

2   If the antenna mast is damaged, it can be removed by turning it counterclockwise. Wrap the antenna with tape for a good grip and it can be removed by hand or pliers.

3   On other models, the antenna is mounted at the center rear of the roof, but does not have a mast.

4   On some later models, there is no external antenna at all - the antenna is a grid incorporated into the rear window glass.

5   The antenna cable runs from the radio up through the passenger's side windshield pillar under the headliner and is joined with a connector at the rear of the roof.

6   It's a difficult job for the home mechanic to remove all the panels and the headliner for access to the cables or replacement of the antenna mast base. This procedure is best left to a qualified shop.

15 Rear window defogger - check and repair

1   The rear window defogger consists of a number of horizontal elements baked onto the glass surface. If the defogger isn't working, first check the defogger relay and fuse in the interior fuse/relay box.

2   Small breaks in the element can be repaired without removing the rear window.

13.13 The tweeters are the small speakers located behind the outside mirror mounting nut covers. On earlier models they're secured by two of the mirror mounting nuts

13.14 On later models, the tweeter is mounted on the back of the sail trim panel and secured by retaining claws

Check

3   Turn the ignition switch and defogger system switches to the On position. Using a voltmeter, place the positive probe against the defogger grid positive terminal and the negative probe against the ground terminal. If battery voltage is not indicated, check the defogger switch and related wiring. If voltage is indicated, but all or part of the defogger doesn't heat, proceed with the following tests.

4   When measuring voltage during the next two tests, wrap a piece of aluminum foil around the tip of the voltmeter positive probe and press the foil against the heating element with your finger (see illustration). Place the negative probe on the defogger grid ground terminal.

5   Check the voltage at the center of each heating element (see illustration). If the voltage is 5- or 6-volts, the element is okay (there is no break). If the voltage is 0-volts, the element is broken between the center

of the element and the positive end. If the voltage is 10- to 12-volts the element is broken between the center of the element and ground. Check each heating element.

6   Connect the negative lead to a good body ground. The reading should stay the same. If it doesn't, the ground connection is bad.

7   To find the break, place the voltmeter negative probe against the defogger ground terminal. Place the voltmeter positive probe with the foil strip against the heating element at the positive terminal end and slide it toward the negative terminal end. The point at which the voltmeter deflects from several volts to zero is the point at which the heating element is broken (see illustration).

Repair

8   Repair the break in the element using a repair kit specifically recommended for this purpose, available at most auto parts stores. Included in this kit is plastic conductive epoxy.

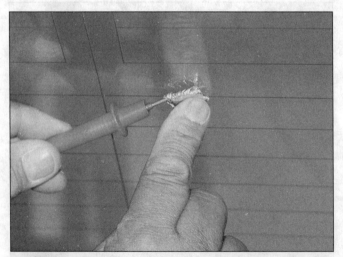

15.4 When measuring the voltage at the rear window defogger grid, wrap a piece of aluminum foil around the positive probe of the voltmeter and press the foil against the wire with your finger

15.5 To determine if a heating element has broken, check the voltage at the center of each element - if the voltage is 5- or 6-volts, the element is unbroken - if the voltage is 10- or 12-volts, the element is broken between the center and the ground side - if there is no voltage, the element is broken between the center and the positive side

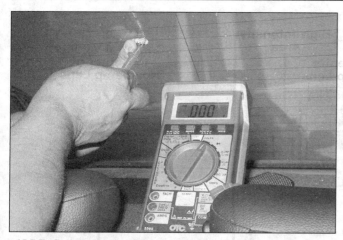

15.7 To find the break, place the voltmeter negative lead against the defogger ground terminal, place the voltmeter positive lead with the foil strip against the heating element at the positive terminal end and slide it toward the negative terminal end - the point at which the voltmeter reading changes abruptly is the point at which the element is broken

15.13 To use a defogger repair kit, apply masking tape to the inside of the window at the damaged area, then brush on the special conductive coating

9   Prior to repairing a break, turn off the system and allow it to cool off for a few minutes.

10   Lightly buff the element area with fine steel wool, then clean it thoroughly with rubbing alcohol.

11   Use masking tape to mask off the area being repaired.

12   Thoroughly mix the epoxy, following the instructions provided with the repair kit.

13   Apply the epoxy material to the slit in the masking tape, overlapping the undamaged area about 3/4-inch on either end **(see illustration)**.

14   Allow the repair to cure for 24 hours before removing the tape and using the system.

16   Headlight bulb - replacement

Headlights with halogen bulbs

Corolla models

Warning: *Halogen gas filled bulbs are under pressure and may shatter if the surface is scratched or the bulb is dropped. Wear eye protection and handle the bulbs carefully, grasping only the base whenever possible. Do not touch the surface of the bulb with your fingers because the oil from your skin could cause it to overheat and fail prematurely. If you do touch the bulb surface, clean it with rubbing alcohol.*

1   Open the hood. Reach behind the headlight assembly and unplug the electrical connector, depressing the clip on the harness connector **(see illustration)**. To access the left-side headlight bulbs, remove the battery (see Chapter 5), then remove the pushpin securing the air intake duct and set the duct aside.

16.1 Location of the two headlight bulbs (A) and the aiming screw (B) (2008 and earlier shown)

Note: *On some models, it's easier to take the front three screws out of the inner fender, then peel back the inner fender to reach the bulb.*

2   Grasp the bulb holder securely and rotate it counterclockwise to remove it from the housing **(see illustration)**.

3   Pull straight out on the bulb to remove from it from the bulb holder. Without touching the glass with your bare fingers, insert the new bulb assembly into the headlight housing.

4   Plug in the electrical connector.

Matrix/Vibe models

5   Open the hood. Reach behind the headlight assembly and unplug the electrical connector **(see illustration)**.

Note: *If you're removing the left-side headlight, remove the fresh air intake duct.*

16.2 Disconnect the electrical connector, then twist the bulb holder counterclockwise and pull the holder out (2008 and earlier shown)

16.5 Disconnect the headlight bulb electrical connector, then remove the rubber ring

16.6 Release the spring clip to remove the headlight bulb holder

6   Release the spring clip to remove the bulb holder **(see illustration)**.

7   Pull straight out on the bulb to remove from it from the bulb holder. Without touching the glass with your bare fingers, use a clean lint-free cloth to hold the bulb during installation. Insert the bulb assembly into the headlight housing.

8   Installation is the reverse of removal.

LED headlights

9   Some 2013 and later models have LED headlights. LED lights require no maintenance and last longer than conventional headlamp systems. The bulbs cannot be replaced, because the entire headlamp assembly is the bulb. Go to Section 18 for headlight housing removal and installation.

17   Headlights - adjustment

Note: *The headlights must be aimed correctly. If adjusted incorrectly they could blind the driver of an oncoming vehicle and cause a serious accident or seriously reduce your ability to see the road. The headlights should be checked for proper aim every 12 months and any time a new headlight is installed or front-end bodywork is performed. It should be emphasized that the following procedure is only an interim step, which will provide temporary adjustment until the headlights can be adjusted by a properly equipped shop.*

1   The vertical adjustment screws are located behind each headlight housing **(see illustration 16.1)**. (There are no horizontal adjustment screws.)

2   There are several methods for adjusting the headlights. The simplest method requires masking tape, a blank wall and a level floor.

3   Position masking tape vertically on the wall in reference to the vehicle centerline and the centerlines of both headlights **(see illustration)**.

4   Position a horizontal tape line in reference to the centerline of all the headlights.

5   Adjustment should be made with the vehicle parked 25 feet from the wall, sitting

17.3 Headlight adjustment details

level, the gas tank half-full and no heavy load in the vehicle.

Note: *It might be easier to position the tape on the wall with the vehicle parked only a few inches away.*

6   Starting with the low beam adjustment, position the high intensity zone so it is two inches below the horizontal line. Adjustment is made by turning the adjusting screw clockwise to raise the beam and counterclockwise to lower the beam.

7   With the high beams on, the high intensity zone should be vertically centered with the exact center just below the horizontal line.

Note: *It might not be possible to position the headlight aim exactly for both high and low beams. If a compromise must be made, keep in mind that the low beams are the most used and have the greatest effect on safety.*

8   Have the headlights adjusted by a dealer service department or service station at the earliest opportunity.

18   Headlight housing - replacement

Warning: *Some models are equipped with halogen gas-filled headlight bulbs that are under pressure and may shatter if the surface is damaged or the bulb is dropped. Wear eye pro-*

tection and handle the bulbs carefully, grasping only the base whenever possible. Do not touch the surface of the bulb with your fingers because the oil from your skin could cause it to overheat and fail prematurely. If you do touch the bulb surface, clean it with rubbing alcohol.

Note: *Headlight housings are expensive to replace, but on most models repair kits are available at Toyota dealerships that can save a headlight housing that has broken mounting tabs.*

1   Remove the front bumper cover (see Chapter 11).

2   Remove the retaining bolts, detach the housing and withdraw it from the vehicle **(see illustrations)**.

3   Installation is the reverse of removal. Be sure to check headlight adjustment (see Section 17).

19   Horn - check and replacement

Warning: *The models covered by this manual are equipped with a Supplemental Restraint System (SRS), more commonly known as airbags. Always disable the airbag system before working in the vicinity of any airbag system components to avoid the possibility of accidental deployment of the airbag(s), which could cause personal injury (see Section 27).*

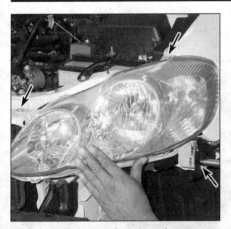

18.2a Headlight housing mounting screws - 2009 and earlier models

18.2b On 2010 and later models the appearance is different, but the headlight housing mounting screw locations are basically the same

18.2c On 2014 and later models, insert a screwdriver between the housing and the support bracket and pry down to disengage the retainer, then slide the housing forward

18.2d Release the harness hold-down clips once you've turned it upside down

18.2e Disconnect the electrical connectors

Check

Note: *Check the fuses before beginning electrical diagnosis.*

1   Disconnect the electrical connector from the horn.

2   To test the horn, connect battery voltage to the horn terminal with a jumper wire. If the horn doesn't sound, replace it.

3   If the horn does sound, check for voltage at the terminal when the horn button is depressed. If there's voltage at the terminal, check for a bad ground at the horn.

4   If there's no voltage at the horn, check the relay (see Section 5).

5   If the relay is OK, check for voltage to the relay power and control circuits. If either of the circuits is not receiving voltage, inspect the wiring between the relay and the fuse panel.

6   If both relay circuits are receiving voltage, depress the horn button and check the circuit from the relay to the horn button for continuity to ground. If there's no continuity, check the circuit for an open. If there's no open circuit, replace the horn button.

7   If there's continuity to ground through the horn button, check for an open or short in the circuit from the relay to the horn.

Replacement

8   To access the horn, open the hood. The horn is located in front of the radiator.

9   To replace the horn, disconnect the electrical connector and remove the bracket bolt **(see illustration)**.

10   Installation is the reverse of removal.

19.9 Location of the horn mounting bolt (A) and electrical connector (B)

Bulb removal

To remove many modern exterior bulbs from their holders, simply pull them out

On bulbs with a cylindrical base ("bayonet" bulbs), the socket is spring-loaded; a pair of small posts on the side of the base hold the bulb in place against spring pressure. To remove this type of bulb, push it into the holder, rotate it 1/4-turn counterclockwise, then pull it out

If a bayonet bulb has dual filaments, the posts are staggered, so the bulb can only be installed one way

To remove most overhead interior light bulbs, simply unclip them

20   Bulb replacement

Front park/turn signal lights

1   The park/turn signal lights and side marker lights are all are part of the headlight housing. These bulbs are accessible from behind the headlight housing (in place), although with some difficulty. If you have trouble, refer to Section 18 and remove the headlight housing for access to these bulbs.

2   Rotate the bulb holder counterclockwise and pull the bulb out **(see illustration)**. Remove the bulb from the holder. On some models, the side marker light is a separate unit mounted in the front fender. On these models, access to the bulb is from underneath the fender.

3   Installation is the reverse of removal.

Rear taillight/brake light/turn signal/side marker/backup lights

Corolla models

4   The taillight/brake/turn signal bulbs can be accessed by removing access panels in the trunk interior **(see illustrations)**.

5   Rotate the bulb holders counterclockwise and pull the bulbs out to remove them. Remove the bulb from the holder.

6   The backup lights in the trunk lid are accessible only after opening a cover on the inside of the trunk lid, using a screwdriver to release it **(see illustration)**. Twist the bulb holder counterclockwise to remove it.

7   Installation is the reverse of removal.

Matrix/Vibe models

8   The taillight/brake/turn signal bulbs can be accessed by removing access panels in the cargo area **(see illustration)**.

9   Rotate the bulb holders counterclockwise and pull the bulbs out to remove them. Remove the bulb from the holder.

10   Installation is the reverse of removal.

Center high-mounted stop light

Corolla models

11   Open the trunk and crawl in enough to see the underside of the rear package shelf. Reach the bulb through the opening under the CHMSL housing **(see illustration)**.

12   Twist the bulb holder counterclockwise to remove it, then pull the bulb straight out of the holder.

13   Installation is the reverse of removal.

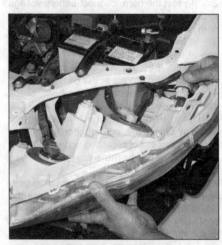

20.2 Rotate the bulb holder counterclockwise to remove the park/turn/marker bulb from the headlight housing

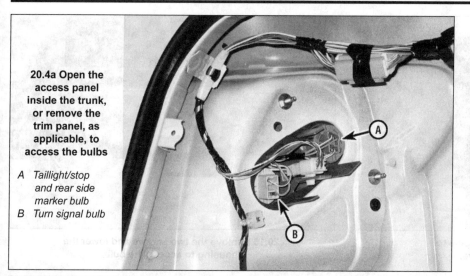

20.4a Open the access panel inside the trunk, or remove the trim panel, as applicable, to access the bulbs

A   Taillight/stop and rear side marker bulb
B   Turn signal bulb

20.4b To make bulb removal easier on later models, use a flat trim tool and move the wire harness out of the way

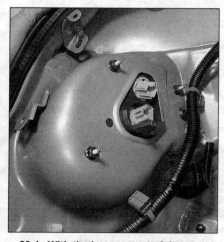

20.4c With the harness out of the way, disconnect the electrical connection to the bulb socket. Twist the bulb socket a quarter turn counterclockwise to remove the socket from the housing

20.4d The bulb pulls straight out of the socket

20.6 Swing open this hinged cover on the trunk lid to access the backup light bulb

20.8 Open the panel inside the cargo area to access the bulbs

1   Taillight/stop and rear side marker bulb
2   Turn signal bulb

20.11 Rotate the bulb holder and remove it from the high-mounted brake light assembly

20.14 Remove the two pushpins to remove the CHMSL cover

20.15 Remove the two screws and lower the housing to access the bulb

20.16 Disconnect the electrical connector (A), then twist and remove the bulb holder (B)

20.19 Twist the bulb holders counterclockwise to remove them from the back of the instrument cluster

Matrix/Vibe models

14   Open the liftgate and remove the two pushpins securing the bottom cover of the CHMSL **(see illustration)**.
15   Remove the two screws and lower the bulb housing **(see illustration)**.
16   Twist the bulb holder counterclockwise to remove it, then pull the bulb straight out of the holder **(see illustration)**.
17   Installation is the reverse of removal.

Instrument cluster lights

Note: *This only applies to early models. Later models have LED lighting elements for instrument cluster illumination.*

18   To gain access to the instrument cluster illumination bulbs, the instrument cluster will have to be removed (see Section 11). The bulbs can then be removed and replaced from the rear of the cluster.
19   Rotate the bulb holder counterclockwise to remove it **(see illustration)**.
20   Installation is the reverse of removal.

20.22a Carefully pry off the dome light lens using a flat-bladed screwdriver, (early model fixture shown) then remove the bulb.

20.22b To remove the bulb on the front overhead dome light fixture, start by prying the lens cover off

20.22c With the cover off, pull the
bulb out of the fixture

20.22d The center overhead bulb
replacement starts by prying
off the lens cover

20.22e With the cover off, the bulb can
be replaced. Always replace with the
same type of bulb

20.24a Use a flat trim tool to pry the
outside edge away from the headliner,
then slide the fixture outward to
unhook it from the other end

Interior lights

21   Pry the lens off the interior light housing.
22   Detach the bulb from the terminals **(see**

20.30 Depress the tab and disconnect the
license plate light electrical connector

20.24b Pull the bulb from the fixture,
replace the bulb, then reinstall the
fixture in the reverse manner
that you took it out

illustration). It may be necessary to pry the bulb out - if this is the case, pry only on the ends of the bulb (otherwise the glass may shatter).
23   Installation is the reverse of removal.

Visor light

24   To replace the visor light bulb, the entire housing must be removed from the headliner (see illustrations).

License plate light
Corolla

25   Open the trunk and remove the trunk lid trim panel.

2013 and earlier models

26   On 2008 and earlier models, remove the trunk lid lock cylinder by disconnecting the rods and removing the two mounting bolts.
27   Release the four clips inside the trunk lid and remove the outside trim panel.
28   On the outside, push the license light bezel to the left to compress the clip, then withdraw the bezel and bulb holder.
29   Installation is the reverse of removal.

2014 and later models

30   Disconnect the electrical connector from the light housing **(see illustration)**.
31   Depress the retaining tang and remove the light housing from the trunk lid **(see illustration)**.
32   Pull the bulb straight out of the housing.
33   Installation is the reverse of removal.

20.31 License plate light housing retaining tang

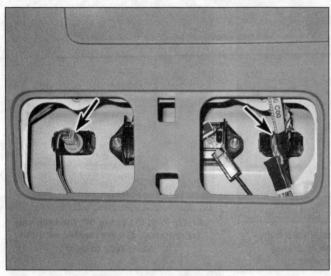

20.34 Remove the panel in the liftgate to access the license plate lights

20.35 Twist the bulb holder counterclockwise to remove it, then change the bulb

Matrix/Vibe

34   Use a plastic trim tool or taped screwdriver to remove the access cover in the interior side of the liftgate **(see illustration)**.

35   Remove the bulb holder(s) and replace the bulb(s) **(see illustration)**.

36   Installation is the reverse of removal.

Fog light

37   Raise the vehicle and support it securely on jackstands.

38   Remove the splash shield.

39   Twist the bulb holder from the housing and replace the bulb.

40   Installation is the reverse of removal.

21   Electric side view mirrors - description

1   Most electric rear view mirrors use two motors to move the glass; one for up and down adjustments and one for left-right adjustments.

2   The control switch has a selector portion that sends voltage to the left or right side mirror. With the ignition On but the engine Off, roll down the windows and operate the mirror control switch through all functions (left-right and up-down) for both the left and right side mirrors.

3   Listen carefully for the sound of the electric motors running in the mirrors.

4   If the motors can be heard but the mirror glass doesn't move, there's a problem with the drive mechanism inside the mirror.

5   If the mirrors do not operate and no sound comes from the mirrors, check the fuses.

6   If the fuse is OK, remove the mirror control switch from the dashboard. Have the switch continuity checked by a dealership service department or other qualified automobile repair facility.

7   If the mirror still doesn't work, remove the mirror and check the wires at the mirror for voltage.

8   If there's not voltage in each switch position, check the circuit between the mirror and control switch for opens and shorts.

9   If there's voltage, remove the mirror and test it off the vehicle with jumper wires. Replace the mirror if it fails this test.

22   Cruise control system - description

1   On 2003 and 2004 models the accelerator pedal is linked to the throttle body with a pair of cables; one running to the cruise control actuator and another running from the actuator to the throttle body. 2005 and later models utilize an electric motor to operate the throttle body, and wiring between the accelerator pedal and the throttle body. The ECM communicates between them. Listed below are some general procedures that may be used to locate common problems.

2   With the ignition switch turned to the On position, turn the cruise control main switch On. The Cruise light on the instrument panel should light up, and turn off when you turn the cruise control main switch back to Off.

3   Check the fuses (see Section 3).

4   If the check in Step 2 is abnormal, further diagnosis requires a scan tool to read diagnostic trouble codes for the cruise control system. For more information on diagnostic code retrieval, see Chapter 6.

5   The cruise control system uses inputs from the Vehicle Speed Sensor (VSS). Refer to Chapter 6 for more information on the VSS.

6   Test-drive the vehicle to determine if the cruise control is now working. If it isn't, take it to a dealer service department or an

automotive electrical specialist for further diagnosis.

23   Power window system - description

1   The power window system operates electric motors, mounted in the doors, which lower and raise the windows. The system consists of the control switches, relays, the motors, regulators, glass mechanisms and associated wiring.

2   The power windows can be lowered and raised from the master control switch by the driver or by remote switches located at the individual windows. Each window has a separate motor that is reversible. The position of the control switch determines the polarity and therefore the direction of operation.

3   The circuit is protected by a fuse and a circuit breaker. Each motor is also equipped with an internal circuit breaker; this prevents one stuck window from disabling the whole system.

4   The power window system will only operate when the ignition switch is On. In addition, many models have a window lockout switch at the master control switch that, when activated, disables the switches at the rear windows and, sometimes, the switch at the passenger's window also. Always check these items before troubleshooting a window problem.

5   These procedures are general in nature, so if you can't find the problem using them, take the vehicle to a dealer service department or other properly equipped repair facility.

6   If the power windows won't operate, always check the fuse and circuit breaker first.

7   If only the rear windows are inoperative, or if the windows only operate from the mas-

ter control switch, check the rear window lock-out switch for continuity in the unlocked position. Replace it if it doesn't have continuity.

8   Check the wiring between the switches and fuse panel for continuity. Repair the wiring, if necessary.

9   If only one window is inoperative from the master control switch, try the other control switch at the window.

Note: *This doesn't apply to the driver's door window.*

10 If the same window works from one switch, but not the other, check the switch for continuity. Have the switch checked at a dealer service department or other qualified automobile repair facility.

11 If the switch tests OK, check for a short or open in the circuit between the affected switch and the window motor.

12 If one window is inoperative from both switches, remove the trim panel from the affected door and check for voltage at the switch and at the motor while the switch is operated.

13 If voltage is reaching the motor, disconnect the glass from the regulator (see 11). Move the window up and down by hand while checking for binding and damage. Also check for binding and damage to the regulator. If the regulator is not damaged and the window moves up and down smoothly, replace the motor. If there's binding or damage, lubricate, repair or replace parts, as necessary.

14 If voltage isn't reaching the motor, check the wiring in the circuit for continuity between the switches and motors. You'll need to consult the wiring diagram for the vehicle. If the circuit is equipped with a relay, check that the relay is grounded properly and receiving voltage.

15 Test the windows after you are done to confirm proper repairs.

24 Power door lock system - description

1   A power door lock system operates the door lock actuators mounted in each door. The system consists of the switches, actuators, a control unit and associated wiring. Diagnosis can usually be limited to simple checks of the wiring connections and actuators for minor faults that can be easily repaired.

2   Power door lock systems are operated by bi-directional solenoids located in the doors. The lock switches have two operating positions: Lock and Unlock. When activated, the switch sends a ground signal to the door lock control unit to lock or unlock the doors. Depending on which way the switch is activated, the control unit reverses polarity to the solenoids, allowing the two sides of the circuit to be used alternately as the feed (positive) and ground side.

3   Some vehicles may have an anti-theft system incorporated into the power locks. If you are unable to locate the trouble using

the following general Steps, consult a dealer service department or other qualified repair shop.

4   Always check the circuit protection first. Some vehicles use a combination of circuit breakers and fuses.

5   Operate the door lock switches in both directions (Lock and Unlock) with the engine off. Listen for the click of the solenoids operating.

6   Test the switches for continuity. Remove the switches and have them checked by a dealer service department or other qualified automobile repair facility.

7   Check the wiring between the switches, control unit and solenoids for continuity. Repair the wiring if there's no continuity.

8   Check for a bad ground at the switches or the control unit.

9   If all but one lock solenoids operate, remove the trim panel from the affected door (see Chapter 11) and check for voltage at the solenoid while the lock switch is operated. One of the wires should have voltage in the Lock position; the other should have voltage in the Unlock position.

10 If the inoperative solenoid is receiving voltage, replace the solenoid.

11 If the inoperative solenoid isn't receiving voltage, check the relay for an open or short in the wire between the lock solenoid and the control unit.

Note: *It's common for wires to break in the portion of the harness between the body and door (opening and closing the door fatigues and eventually breaks the wires).*

25 Power sunroof - description

1   The power sunroof or sliding roof system consists of the control switch, the module, the roof motor and the glass and track mechanism. The sunroof switch is located in a panel in the headliner, above the rear-view mirror. If there is a problem with sunroof operation, first check the 30-amp "Power" and 10-amp "Gauge" fuses in the instrument panel fuse/relay box. If the fuse is OK, check the P/W relay, also in the instrument panel fuse/relay box, as this relay supplies power to the sunroof relay which is located in the module behind the sunroof control switch bezel.

26 Daytime Running Lights (DRL) - general information

1   The Daytime Running Lights (DRL) system illuminates the headlights whenever the engine is running. The only exception is with the engine running and the parking brake engaged. Once the parking brake is released, the lights will remain on as long as the ignition switch is on, even if the parking brake is later applied.

2   The DRL system supplies reduced

power to the headlights so they won't be too bright for daytime use, while prolonging headlight life.

27 Airbag system - general information

1   All models are equipped with a Supplemental Restraint System (SRS), more commonly known as an airbag. This system is designed to protect the driver, and the front seat passenger, from serious injury in the event of a head-on or frontal collision. It consists of two impact sensors behind the front bumper, an airbag module in the center of the steering wheel and the right side of the instrument panel and a sensing/diagnostic module mounted in the center of the vehicle, ahead of the floor console. Additionally, some models are equipped with side impact airbags and side curtain airbags.

Airbag module
Driver's side

2   The airbag inflator module contains a housing incorporating the cushion (airbag) and inflator unit, mounted in the center of the steering wheel The inflator assembly is mounted on the back of the housing over a hole through which gas is expelled, inflating the bag almost instantaneously when an electrical signal is sent from the system. A spiral cable assembly (also known as the clockspring) on the steering column under the steering wheel carries this signal to the module.

3   This spiral cable assembly can transmit an electrical signal regardless of steering wheel position. The igniter in the airbag converts the electrical signal to heat and ignites the powder, which inflates the bag.

Passenger's side

4   The airbag is mounted above the glove compartment and designated by the letters SRS (Supplemental Restraint System). It consists of an inflator containing an igniter, a bag assembly, a reaction housing and a trim cover.

5   The airbag is considerably larger than the steering wheel-mounted unit and is supported by the steel reaction housing. The trim cover is textured and painted to match the instrument panel and has a molded seam that splits when the bag inflates.

Side impact airbags

6   Extra protection is provided on some models with the addition of optional side-impact airbags. These are smaller devices located in the seat backs on the side toward the exterior of the vehicle. The impact sensors for the side-impact airbags are located at the bottom of the door pillars in the body, in the bottom of the driver's and passenger's seats, or in the driver's and passenger's doors.

27.7 Side curtain air bags offer a great deal of protection to the occupants. Use caution when removing these A pillar trim sections. They are the side curtain bags on some models. (Note the air bag information stamped into the A pillar trim.) You'll have to disconnect the leads before they can be completely removed from the car

27.8a The diagnostic module is located under the center console area just in front of the shifter

27.8b The impact sensors have a single bolt attaching them to the chassis, always with a yellow connector

Side curtain airbags

7   Extra side-impact protection is provided on some models with the addition of optional side-curtain airbags (in addition to the side-impact airbags in the seatbacks on some models). These are long airbags that, in the event of a side impact, come out of the headliner or A pillar of the windshield at each side of the car and come down between the side windows, windshield and the seats **(see illustration)**. They are designed to protect the heads of both front seat and rear seat passengers.

Diagnostic module and impact sensors

8   The sensing and diagnostic module supplies the current to the airbag system in the event of a collision, even if battery power is cut off. It checks this system every time the vehicle is started, causing the "AIR BAG" light to go on then off, if the system is operating properly. If there is a fault in the system, the light will go on and stay on, flash, or the dash will make a beeping sound. If this happens, the vehicle should be taken to your dealer immediately for service **(see**

illustration). Impact sensors are mounted under the front bumper rail (early models) or on the radiator support uprights (later models) **(see illustration)**. They detect the impact and send the data to the diagnostic module on a high speed communication line.

Disarming the system and other precautions

Warning: *Failure to follow these precautions could result in accidental deployment of the airbag and personal injury.*

9   Whenever working in the vicinity of the steering wheel, steering column or any of the other SRS system components, the system must be disarmed. To disarm the system:

 a) *Point the wheels straight ahead and turn the key to the Lock position.*

 b) *Disconnect the cable from the negative battery terminal. Make sure the cable is positioned so that it cannot come into contact with the battery terminal.*

 c) *Wait at least two minutes for the back-up power supply to be depleted.*

10   Whenever handling an airbag module, always keep the airbag opening (the trim

side) pointed away from your body. Never place the airbag module on a bench of other surface with the airbag opening facing the surface. Always place the airbag module in a safe location with the upholstered side of the airbag facing up.

11   Never measure the resistance of any SRS component. An ohmmeter has a built-in battery supply that could accidentally deploy the airbag.

12   Never use electrical welding equipment on a vehicle equipped with an airbag without first disconnecting the yellow airbag connector, located under the steering column near the combination switch connector (driver's airbag) and behind the glove box (passenger's airbag).

13   Never dispose of a live airbag module. Return it to a dealer service department or other qualified repair shop for safe deployment and disposal.

Component removal and installation

Driver's side airbag module and spiral cable

14   Refer to Chapter 11 - *Steering wheel - removal and installation*, for the driver's side airbag module and spiral cable removal and installation procedures.

Passenger's side airbag module

15   Disarm the airbag system as described previously in this Section. Under the right side of the instrument panel, disconnect the yellow connectors for the passenger's airbag.

16   Remove the glove box (see Chapter 11). The airbag is bolted to the underside of the instrument panel. Remove the fasteners and detach the airbag module from the instrument panel **(see illustrations)**. Be sure to heed the precautions outlined previously in this Section.

17   Installation is the reverse of the removal procedure. Tighten the airbag module mounting fasteners to 15 ft-lbs (20 Nm).

27.16a Remove the bolt and two nuts to remove the passenger's airbag from behind the instrument panel

27.16b A slightly different view of the passenger's air bag. Do not disconnect the air bag connectors at this point (arrows), use the large yellow connector instead

28 Key fob battery replacement and programming

Without Smart Key system

1 Using a flat tip screwdriver (a jeweler's size works best) pry the transmitter housing cover apart **(see illustration)**.
Caution: *Do not force the covers apart. They should gently pop apart.*
2 The battery (or batteries) is/are inside the sub-assembly module. Use a thin coin to pry the sub-assembly apart to gain access to the battery **(see illustrations)**.
3 Remove the old battery.
4 Install the replacement battery(ies) with the positive (+) side of the battery facing upward.
5 Re-install the sub-assembly back onto the transmitter housing and snap the case halves back together.

With Smart Key

6 Remove the mechanical key.
7 Insert a small screwdriver into the slot

and pry the housings apart.
8 Gently remove the battery. Battery number CR2032.
9 Install the replacement battery with the positive (+) markings facing upwards.
10 Snap the case halves together and insert the metal key.

Programming a key fob (to add a key fob)

Note: *During this procedure, if the door locks cycle twice, this could indicate a problem with the transmitter or the procedure. In that case, repeat the steps over again and verify that you have the correct and a properly working transmitter.*
11 Start by removing the key from the ignition.
12 The driver's door must be open and unlocked. All other doors should be closed.
13 Within five seconds of removing the ignition key, insert the key in the ignition and remove it twice.
14 Within another 40 seconds close and open the driver's door twice again and

insert the key into the ignition cylinder. This time, leave the key in the ignition and close the driver's door. Now, turn the key to On position.
Warning: *Do not turn the key to crank or start the vehicle.*
15 Turn the key back to the Off position and remove the key.
16 Within three seconds, the power door locks should lock and unlock automatically indicating that you have successfully entered the programming mode.
17 You have 40 seconds to simultaneously press the lock and unlock buttons on the remote that you are trying to program. Hold them for 1.5 seconds, then press and hold the lock button for two seconds.
18 Within three seconds, the power door locks should lock and unlock once automatically, indicating that you have successfully programmed the new remote.
19 To program additional remotes, repeat the steps holding the lock buttons on the next remote.
20 Opening the driver's door will exit the programming mode.

28.1 Gently pry the halves apart

28.2a Earlier models have two batteries . . .

28.2b . . . while later models only have one

29 Wiring diagrams - general information

1   Since it isn't possible to include all wiring diagrams for every year covered by this manual, the following diagrams are those that are typical and most commonly needed.

2   Prior to troubleshooting any circuits, check the fuse and circuit breakers (if equipped) to make sure they're in good condition. Make sure the battery is properly charged and check the cable connections (see Chapter 1).

3   When checking a circuit, make sure that all connectors are clean, with no broken or loose terminals. When unplugging a connector, do not pull on the wires. Pull only on the connector housings themselves.

Wiring Diagrams List

1. Starting and charging systems - 2008 and earlier models
2. Exterior lighting system - 2008 and earlier models (1 of 2)
3. Exterior lighting system - 2008 and earlier models (2 of 2)
4. Interior lighting system - 2008 and earlier models
5. Instrument cluster warning system - 2008 and earlier models
6. Air conditioning and engine cooling systems - 2008 and earlier models
7. Power window system - 2008 and earlier models
8. Power door lock system - 2008 and earlier models
9. Audio system - 2008 and earlier models
10. Windshield wiper and washer system - 2008 and earlier models
11. Cruise control - 2008 and earlier models (1 of 2)
12. Cruise control - 2008 and earlier models (2 of 2)
13. Fuses and relays - 2008 and earlier models (1 of 3)
14. Fuses and relays - 2008 and earlier models (2 of 3)
15. Fuses and relays - 2008 and earlier models (3 of 3)
16. Starting and charging systems - 2009 through 2013 models
17. Heating and air conditioning systems - 2009 through 2013 models
18. Seat heating and engine cooling fan systems - 2009 through 2013 models
19. Power window system - 2009 through 2013 models
20. Power door lock system (without Smart Key) - 2009 through 2013 models
21. Power door lock system (with Smart Key) - 2009 through 2013 models
22. Windshield wiper and washer systems - 2009 through 2013 models
23. Exterior lighting system - 2009 through 2013 models
24. Interior lighting system - 2009 through 2013 models
25. Audio system - 2009 through 2013 models
26. Fuel pump system - 2009 through 2013 models
27. Fuses and relays - 2009 through 2013 models (1 of 5)
28. Fuses and relays - 2009 through 2013 models (2 of 5)
29. Fuses and relays - 2009 through 2013 models (3 of 5)
30. Fuses and relays - 2009 through 2013 models (4 of 5)
31. Fuses and relays - 2009 through 2013 models (5 of 5)
32. Starting and charging systems - 2014 and later models
33. Heating and air conditioning systems - 2014 and later models
34. Seat heating and engine cooling fan systems - 2014 and later models
35. Power window system - 2014 and later models
36. Power door lock system - 2014 and later models
37. Windshield wiper and washer systems - 2014 and later models
38. Exterior lighting system - 2014 and later models
39. Interior lighting system - 2014 and later models
40. Audio system - 2014 and later models
41. Fuel pump system - 2014 and later models
42. Fuses and relays - 2014 and later models (1 of 6)
43. Fuses and relays - 2014 and later models (2 of 6)
44. Fuses and relays - 2014 and later models (3 of 6)
45. Fuses and relays - 2014 and later models (4 of 6)
46. Fuses and relays - 2014 and later models (5 of 6)
47. Fuses and relays - 2014 and later models (6 of 6)

1. Starting and charging systems - 2008 and earlier models

2. Exterior lighting system - 2008 and earlier models (1 of 2)

4. Interior lighting system - 2008 and earlier models

5. Instrument cluster warning system - 2008 and earlier models

6. Air conditioning and engine cooling systems - 2008 and earlier models

7. Power window system - 2008 and earlier models

8. Power door lock system - 2008 and earlier models

9. Audio system - 2008 and earlier models

10. Windshield wiper and washer system - 2008 and earlier models

11. Cruise control - 2008 and earlier models (1 of 2)

12. Cruise control - 2008 and earlier models (2 of 2)

FUSE AND RELAY IN ENGINE COMPARTMENT

FUSE/RELAY	VALUE	DESCRIPTION	OEM NAME
1	15 A	Cruise control, Electronically Controlled Transmission, Engine Control	EFI2
2	10 A	Headlight	HEAD RH LWR
3	10 A	Headlight	HEAD LH LWR
4	-	Not used	-
5	40 A	Combination Meter, Headlight, Security system, Wireless Door Lock Control	HEAD MAIN
6	5 A	Charging	ALT-S
7	20 A	Cruise Control, Electronically Controlled Transmission, Engine Control	EFI
8	10 A	Turn Signal and Hazard Warning Light	HAZARD
9	10 A	Horn, Security system, Wireless Door Lock Control	HORN
10	15 A	ABS, Audio System, Clock, Combination Meter, Cruise Control, Electronically Controlled Transmission, Engine Control, Headlight, Illumination, Interior Light, Key Reminder, Light Reminder, Seat Belt Warning, SRS, TRAC, Security system, ESP, Wireless Door Lock Control	DOME
11	30 A	ABS	MAIN
12	30 A	Audio System	AMP
13	10 A	Cruise Control, Electronically Controlled Transmission, Engine Control	ETCS
14	100 A	ABS, Charging, Engine Immobiliser System, Illumination, Taillight, ESP	ALT
15	-	Not used	-
16	-	Not used	-
17	-	Not used	-
18	10 A	Headlight, Combination Meter	HEAD RH UPR
19	10 A	Headlight	HEAD LH UPR
20	50 A	(40 A also used)	ABS 2
21	30 A	Radiator Fan	RDI FAN
22	30 A	ABS, ESP	ABS 1
23	15 A	Fog Light	FOG
24	-	Not used	-
R1	-	HEAD relay	HEAD RELAY
R2	-	M/G CLT relay	M/G CLT RELAY
R3	-	DIMMER relay	DIMMER RELAY
R4	-	EFI relay	EFI RELAY
R5	-	FOG relay	FOG RELAY
R6	-	HORN relay	HORN RELAY
R7	-	FAN 2 relay	FAN 2 RELAY
R8	-	FAN 1 relay	FAN 1 RELAY

FUSE AND RELAY BOX IN PASSENGER COMPARTMENT FRONT

FUSE/RELAY	VALUE	DESCRIPTION	OEM NAME
1	40 A	Air Conditioning, Heater	HEATER
2	40 A	Engine Control, Rear Window Defogger	DEFOG
3	30 A	Moon Roof, Power Window	POWER
4	10 A	Air Conditioning	A/C
5	10 A	Engine Control	M-HTR/DEF-UP
6	15 A	ABS, Charging, Combination Meter, Cruise Control, Electronically Controlled Transmission, Engine Control, Engine Immobiliser System, Ignition, Seat Belt Warning, SRS, Starting, ESP	AM2
7	-	Not used	-
8	15 A	Wiper and Washer	WASHER
9	25 A	Wiper and Washer	WIPER
10	10 A	ABS, Radiator Fan, Shift Lock, Tire Pressure Warning System, ESP	ECU-IG
11	10 A	ABS, Air Conditioning, Automatic Glare-Resistant EC Mirror, Back-Up Light, Charging, Combination Meter, Compass, Cruise Control, Door Lock Control Electronically Controlled Transmission, Engine Control, Fog Light, Headlight, Heater, Illumination, Interior Light, Key Reminder, Light Reminder, Moon Roof, Power Window, Rear Window Defogger, Seat Belt Warning, SRS, Tire Pressure Warning System, ESP, Turn Signal and Hazard Warning Light, Wireless Door Lock Control	GAUGE
12	-	Not used	-
13	-	Not used	-
14	15 A	Audio, Cigarette Lighter, Clock, Power Outlet, Remote Control Mirror	CIG
15	-	Not used	-
16	25 A	No information is available	AM1
17	10 A	ABS, Engine Immobiliser System, Fog Light, Headlight, Seat Belt Warning, SRS, ESP	ECU-B
18	7.5 A	Engine Control	OBD
19	25 A	Door Lock Control, Interior Light, Wireless Door Lock Control	DOOR
20	15 A	Power Outlet	P/POINT
21	15 A	Clock, Engine Control, Headlight, Illumination, Key Reminder, Light Reminder, Taillight	TAIL
22	15 A	ABS, Cruise Control, Electronically Controlled Transmission, Engine Control, Shift Lock, Stop Light, ESP	STOP
23	-	Not used	-

14. Fuses and relays - 2008 and earlier models (2 of 3)

FUSE AND RELAY BOX IN PASSENGER COMPARTMENT BACK

FUSE/RELAY	VALUE	DESCRIPTION	OEM NAME
R1		ST relay	ST RELAY
R2	-	Def relay	DEF RELAY
R3	-	C/OPN relay	C/OPN RELAY
R4	-	P/W relay	P/W RELAY
R5	-	Ig 1 relay	IG1 RELAY

15. Fuses and relays - 2008 and earlier models (3 of 3)

16. Starting and charging systems - 2009 through 2013 models

*1 Charging
*2 Starting
*3 With smart key
*4 Without smart key
*5 Engine code: 2ZR-FE
*6 Engine code: 2AZ-FE

17. Heating and air conditioning systems - 2009 through 2013 models

18. Seat heating and engine cooling fan systems - 2009 through 2013 models

*1 Heated seat
*2 Cooling fan
*3 Engine code: 2ZR-FE
*4 Engine code: 2ZR-FAE

19. Power window system - 2009 through 2013 models

20. Power door lock system (without Smart Key) - 2009 through 2013 models

*1 With smart key system.
*2 Without smart key system
*3 With power window
*4 Without power window

WIRE COLOR CODE INDEX
BE - BEIGE
BK - BLACK
BN - BROWN
BU - BLUE
DG - DARK GREEN
DB - DARK BLUE
GN - GREEN
GY - GREY
LA - LAVENDER
LB - LIGHT BLUE
LG - LIGHT GREEN
OG - ORANGE
PK - PINK
RD - RED
VT - VIOLET
WH - WHITE
YE - YELLOW

21. Power door lock system (with Smart Key) - 2009 through 2013 models

WIRE COLOR CODE INDEX

BE	BE - BEIGE
BK	BK - BLACK
BN	BN - BROWN
BU	BU - BLUE
DG	DG - DARK GREEN
DB	DB - DARK BLUE
GN	GN - GREEN
GY	GY - GREY
LA	LA - LAVENDER
LB	LB - LIGHT BLUE
LG	LG - LIGHT GREEN
OG	OG - ORANGE
PK	PK - PINK
RD	RD - RED
VT	VT - VIOLET
WH	WH - WHITE
YE	YE - YELLOW

22. Windshield wiper and washer systems - 2009 through 2013 models

23. Exterior lighting system - 2009 through 2013 models

*1 With auto air conditioning
*2 With rear spoiler
*3 Without rear spoiler

24. Interior lighting system - 2009 through 2013 models

*1 With smart key system
*2 Without smart key system
*3 With sliding roof
*4 Without sliding roof

25. Audio system - 2009 through 2013 models

*1 With display
*2 Without display
*3 With 6 speaker
*4 With 4 speaker
*5 Without USB
*6 With steering pad switch
*7 With USB and Microphone
*8 With sliding roof
*9 Without sliding roof
*10 With extension module
*11 Without extension module

WIRE COLOR CODE INDEX

BE	BE - BEIGE
BK	BK - BLACK
BN	BN - BROWN
BU	BU - BLUE
DG	DG - DARK GREEN
DB	DB - DARK BLUE
GN	GN - GREEN
GY	GY - GREY
LA	LA - LAVENDER
LB	LB - LIGHT BLUE
LG	LG - LIGHT GREEN
OG	OG - ORANGE
PK	PK - PINK
RD	RD - RED
VT	VT - VIOLET
WH	WH - WHITE
YE	YE - YELLOW

26. Fuel pump system - 2009 through 2013 models

FUSE AND RELAY IN ENGINE COMPARTMENT

FUSE/RELAY	VALUE	DESCRIPTION	OEM NAME
1	10 A	Headlight	H-LP LH LO
2	10 A	Headlight	H-LP RH LO
3	10 A	Headlight	H-LP LH HI
4	10 A	Headlight	H-LP RH HI
5	10 A	Cruise Control, Electronically Controlled Transmission and A/T Indicator, Engine Control	EFI 1
6	10 A	Engine Control	EFI 2
7	-	Not used	-
8	20 A	Engine Immobiliser System, Smart Key System, Starting, Steering Lock, Wireless Door Lock Control	STRG LOCK
9	30 A	Engine Immobiliser System, Ignition, Smart Key System, Starting, Steering Lock, Wireless Door Lock Control	AM2
10	7.5 A	Door Lock Control, Engine Control, Engine Immobiliser System, Ignition, Interior Light, Light Reminder, Power Window, Sliding Roof, Smart Key System, Starting, Steering Lock, Wireless Door Lock Control	AM2 2
11	7.5 A	Charging	ALT-S
12	10 A	Turn Signal and Hazard Warning Light	TURN-HAZ
13	10 A	Cruise Control, Electronically Controlled Transmission and A/T Indicator, Engine Control	ETCS
14	10 A	Engine Immobiliser System, Interior Light, Smart Key System, Starting, Steering Lock, Theft Deterrent, Wireless Door Lock Control	DOME
15	15 A	Audio System, Navigation System	RAD 1
16	10 A	ABS, Audio System, Automatic Air Conditioning, Charging, Clock, Combination Meter, Cruise Control, Door Lock Control, Electronically Controlled Transmission and A/T Indicator, Engine Control, Engine Immobiliser System, EPS, Headlight, Illumination, Interior Light, Key Reminder, Light Reminder, Navigation System, Power Window, Seat Belt Warning, Sliding Roof, Smart Key System, SRS, Starting, Steering Lock, Taillight, Theft Deterrent, Tire Pressure Warning System, ESP, Wireless Door Lock Control	ECU-B
17	-	Not used	-
18	10 A	Automatic Air Conditioning, Engine Immobiliser System, Manual Air Conditioning, Smart Key System, Steering Lock, Wireless Door Lock Control	ECU-B2

27. Fuses and relays - 2009 through 2013 models (1 of 5)

19	7.5 A	Engine Control, Ignition	IG2 2
20	-	Not used	-
21	-	Not used	-
22	-	Not used	-
23	-	Not used	-
24	-	Not used	-
25	30 A	Automatic Air Conditioning, Manual Air Conditioning	HTR SUB 1
26	-	Not used	-
27	30 A	Automatic Air Conditioning, Manual Air Conditioning	HTR SUB 3
28	-	Not used	-
29	-	Not used	-
30	-	Not used	-
31	-	Not used	-
32	-	Not used	-
33	50 A	Automatic Air Conditioning, Manual Air Conditioning	HTR
34	50 A	ABS, ESP	ABS 1
35	30 A	ABS, ESP	ABS 3
36	40 A	Cooling Fan	RDI FAN
37	30 A	Cooling Fan	CDS FAN
38	-	Not used	-
39	-	Not used	-
40	-	Not used	-
41	-	Not used	-
42	50 A	Automatic Air Conditioning, Engine Immobiliser System, Front Fog Light, Headlight, Manual Air Conditioning, Smart Key System, Steering Lock, Theft Deterrent, Wireless Door Lock Control	H-LP MAIN
43	50 A	No information is available	P/I
44	-	Not used	-
45	-	Not used	-
46	-	Not used	-
47	60 A	EPS	EPS
48	120 A	Charging, Engine Control, Engine Immobiliser System, Front Fog Light, Illumination, Light Reminder, Power Window, Sliding Roof, Starting, Steering Lock, Taillight, Theft Deterrent	ALT
R1	-	Fan 1 relay	FAN 1 RELAY
R2	-	Fan 3 relay	FAN 3 RELAY
R3	-	Fan 2 relay	FAN 2 RELAY
R4	-	Heater 1 relay	HTR SUB 1 RELAY
R5	-	Heater 3 relay	HTR SUB 3 RELAY
R6	-	Dimmer relay	DIMMER RELAY
R7	-	Headlamp relay	H-LP RELAY

28. Fuses and relays - 2009 through 2013 models (2 of 5)

FUSE IN ENGINE COMPARTMENT UNIT B

FUSE/RELAY	VALUE	DESCRIPTION	OEM NAME
1	15 A	Engine Control, Engine Immobiliser System, Ignition, Smart Key System, Starting, Steering Lock, Wireless Door Lock Control	IG2
2	10 A	Engine Immobiliser System, Horn, Smart Key System, Steering Lock, Theft Deterrent, Wireless Door Lock Control	HORN
3	20 A	Cruise Control, Electronically Controlled Transmission and A/T Indicator, Engine Control	EFI MAIN
4	-	Not used	-

FUSE BOX IN PASSENGER COMPARTMENT

FUSE	VALUE	DESCRIPTION	OEM NAME
1	7.5 A	Engine Control, Shift Lock, Starting	AM1
2	15 A	Front Fog Light	FR FOG
3	-	Not used	-
4	25 A	Engine Immobiliser System, Smart Key System, Starting, Steering Lock, Wireless Door Lock Control	ACC-B
5	25 A	Door Lock Control, Engine Immobiliser System, Interior Light, Key Reminder, Light Reminder, Power Window, Sliding Roof, Smart Key System, Starting, Steering Lock, Theft Deterrent, Wireless Door Lock Control	DOOR
6	-	Not used	-
7	10 A	ABS, Cruise Control, Electronically Controlled Transmission and A/T Indicator, Engine Control, Engine Immobiliser System, Shift Lock, Smart Key System, Starting, Steering Lock, Stop Light, ESP, Wireless Door Lock Control	STOP
8	7.5 A	Data Link Connector	OBD

29. Fuses and relays - 2009 through 2013 models (3 of 5)

9	10 A	ABS, Audio System, Automatic Air Conditioning, Manual Air Conditioning , Automatic Glare-Resistant EC Mirror with Compass, Back-Up Light, Charging, Cruise Control, Door Lock Control, Electronically Controlled Transmission and A/T Indicator, Engine Control, Mirror Heater, Navigation System, Rear Window Defogger, Seat Belt Warning, SRS, ESP, Turn Signal and Hazard Warning Light	ECU-IG NO.2
10	10 A	ABS, Cooling Fan, Cruise Control, Door Lock Control, Electronically Controlled Transmission and A/T Indicator, EPS, Headlight, Interior Light, Key Reminder, Light Reminder, Power Window, Shift Lock, Sliding Roof, Smart Key System, Starting, Steering Lock, Theft Deterrent, Tire Pressure Warning System, ESP, Wireless Door Lock Control	ECU-IG NO.1
11	15 A	Front Wiper and Washer	WASHER
12	-	Not used	-
13	25 A	Front Wiper and Washer	WIPER
14	10 A	Automatic Air, Manual Air Conditioning, Mirror Heater, Rear Window Defogger	HTR-IG
15	15 A	Seat Heater	SEAT HTR
16	7.5 A	ABS, Audio System, Automatic Air Conditioning, Charging, Combination Meter, Cruise Control, Electronically Controlled Transmission and A/T Indicator, Engine Control, Engine Immobiliser System, EPS, Illumination, Key Reminder, Light Reminder, Navigation System, Seat Belt Warning, Sliding Roof, Smart Key System, SRS, Starting, Steering Lock, Taillight, Tire Pressure Warning System, ESP, Wireless Door Lock Control	METER
17	7.5 A	Cruise Control, Electronically Controlled Transmission and A/T Indicator, Engine Control, Engine Immobiliser System, Seat Belt Warning, Seat Belt Warning, Smart Key System, SRS, Starting, Steering Lock, Wireless Door Lock Control	IGN
18	-	Not used	-
19	-	Not used	-
20	-	Not used	-
21	10 A	Engine Control, Mirror Heater, Rear Window Defogger	MIR HTR
22	-	Not used	-
23	7.5 A	Audio System, Clock, Door Lock Control, Engine Immobiliser System, Interior Light, Key Reminder, Navigation System, Power Window, Remote Control Mirror, Sliding Roof, Smart Key System, Starting, Steering Lock, Theft Deterrent, Wireless Door Lock Control	ACC
24	15 A	Cigarette Lighter, Power Outlet	CIG
25	20 A	Sliding Roof	SUNROOF
26	20 A	Power Window	RR DOOR
27	20 A	Power Window	RL DOOR
28	20 A	Power Window, Sliding Roof	FR DOOR
29	-	Not used	-
30	7.5 A	Illumination, Taillight	PANEL
31	10 A	Engine Control, Front Fog Light, Illumination, Light Reminder, Taillight	TAIL

30. Fuses and relays - 2009 through 2013 models (4 of 5)

RELAY BOX IN PASSENGER COMPARTMENT

RELAY	VALUE	DESCRIPTION	OEM NAME
R1	-	Ignition relay 1	IG1 RELAY
R2	-	Heater relay	HTR RELAY
R3	-	Flasher relay	FLASHER RELAY

WIRE COLOR CODE INDEX

BE - BE - BEIGE
BK - BK - BLACK
BN - BN - BROWN
BU - BU - BLUE
DG - DG - DARK GREEN
DB - DB - DARK BLUE
GN - GN - GREEN
GY - GY - GREY
LA - LA - LAVENDER
LB - LB - LIGHT BLUE
LG - LG - LIGHT GREEN
OG - OG - ORANGE
PK - PK - PINK
RD - RD - RED
VT - VT - VIOLET
WH - WH - WHITE
YE - YE - YELLOW

32. Starting and charging systems - 2014 and later models

*1 Charging
*2 Starting
*3 From August 2016
*4 Automatic transmission
*5 Engine code: 2ZR-FE
*6 Engine code: 2ZR-FAE
*7 With Colour display
*8 Without Colour display
*9 Manual transmission

33. Heating and air conditioning systems - 2014 and later models

*1 Up to July 2016
*2 From August 2016
*3 Engine code: 2GR-FAE
*4 Engine code: 2ZR-FE
*5 With ECO switch

34. Seat heating and engine cooling fan systems - 2014 and later models

*1 Heated seat
*2 Cooling fan
*3 Up to July 2016
*4 From August 2016
*5 Version 1
*6 Version 2

35. Power window system - 2014 and later models

*1 Up to July 2016
*2 From August 2016

36. Power door lock system - 2014 and later models

*1 With Tyre pressure warning system
*2 Without Tyre pressure warning system
*3 With wireless door lock control
*4 Without wireless door lock control

37. Windshield wiper and washer systems - 2014 and later models

38. Exterior lighting system - 2014 and later models

*1 Up to July 2016
*2 From August 2016
*3 With dynamic radar
*4 With automatic light
*5 Without dynamic radar
*6 Without LED park light
*7 Without LED park light
*8 With Colour display
*9 Without Colour display

39. Interior lighting system - 2014 and later models

*1 With sliding roof
*2 Without sliding roof
*3 Up to July 2016
*4 From August 2016
*5 From August 2017
*6 With wireless door lock control
*7 With smart key system and theft deterrent

40. Audio system - 2014 and later models

*1 Radio and display
*2 Navigation
*3 Radio
*4 With 6 speaker
*5 With 4 speaker
*6 Up to July 2016
*7 From August 2016
*8 With stereo component tuner assembly
*9 With sliding roof
*10 Without sliding roof

41. Fuel pump system - 2014 and later models

*1 Engine code: 2ZR-FE
*2 Engine code: 2ZR-FAE

FUSE AND RELAY IN ENGINE COMPARTMENT

FUSE/RELAY	VALUE	DESCRIPTION	OEM NAME
1	7.5 A	ABS, Audio System, Automatic Air Conditioning, Automatic Glare-Resistant EC Mirror, Charging, Combination Meter, Cruise Control, CVT and Shift Indicator, Electronically Controlled Transmission and A/T Indicator, Engine Control, EPS, Garage Door Opener, Headlight, Illumination, Immobiliser System, Key Reminder, Light Reminder, Multiplex Communication System, Navigation System, PTC Heater, Rear View Monitor System, Seat Belt Warning, Sliding Roof, Smart Key System, SRS, Starting, Steering Lock, Taillight, Theft Deterrent, Tire Pressure Warning System, ESP, Turn Signal and Hazard Warning Light, Wireless Door Lock Control	ECU-B NO.2
2	-	Not used	-
3	7.5 A	Cruise Control, CVT and Shift Indicator, Electronically Controlled Transmission and A/T Indicator, Engine Control, Immobiliser System, Smart Key System, Starting, Steering Lock, Wireless Door Lock Control	AM2
4	30 A	Power Source	D/C CUT
5	10 A	Horn, Immobiliser System, Smart Key System, Starting, Steering Lock, Theft Deterrent, Wireless Door Lock Control	HORN
6	30 A	Immobiliser System, Smart Key System, Starting, Steering Lock, Wireless Door Lock Control	ST
7	5 A	Charging	ICS
8	10 A	Cruise Control, CVT and Shift Indicator, Electronically Controlled Transmission and A/T Indicator, Engine Control	ETCS
9	10 A	Combination Meter, Immobiliser System, Smart Key System, Starting, Steering Lock, Theft Deterrent, Turn Signal and Hazard Warning Light, Wireless Door Lock Control	TURN AND HAZ
10	15 A	Cruise Control, CVT and Shift Indicator, Electronically Controlled Transmission and A/T Indicator, Engine Control, Ignition, Immobiliser System, Smart Key System, Starting, Steering Lock, Wireless Door Lock Control	IG2
11	15 A	Cruise Control, CVT and Shift Indicator, Engine Control, Ignition	INJ
12	20 A	Immobiliser System, Smart Key System, Starting, Steering Lock,	STRG LOCK

42. Fuses and relays - 2014 and later models (1 of 6)

		Wireless Door Lock Control	
13	20 A	Cruise Control, CVT and Shift Indicator, Electronically Controlled Transmission and A/T Indicator, Engine Control	EFI-MAIN
14	30 A	Cruise Control, CVT and Shift Indicator, Engine Control	VLVMATIC
15	40 A	Automatic Light Control, Headlight, Immobiliser System, Light Auto Turn Off System, Smart Key System, Starting, Steering Lock, Theft Deterrent, Wireless Door Lock Control	H-LP MAIN
16	80 A	EPS	EPS
17	10 A	ABS, Automatic Light Control, Clock, Combination Meter, Door Lock Control, Front Fog Light, Headlight, Illumination, Immobiliser System, Interior Light, Key Reminder, Light Auto Turn Off System, Light Reminder, Power Window, Seat Belt Warning, Sliding Roof, Smart Key System, SRS, Starting, Steering Lock, Taillight, Theft Deterrent, Tire Pressure Warning System, ESP, Wireless Door Lock Control	ECU-B
18	10 A	Immobiliser System, Interior Light, Smart Key System, Starting, Steering Lock, Theft Deterrent, Wireless Door Lock Control	DOME
19	20 A	Audio System, Navigation System, Rear View Monitor System	RADIO
20	20 A	Front Fog Light (10 A also used)	FOG FR/DEICER
21	10 A	Immobiliser System, Smart Key System, Starting, Steering Lock, Theft Deterrent, Wireless Door Lock Control	S-HORN
22	10 A	Headlight	DRL
23	30 A	Cooling Fan	RDI
24	30 A	ABS, ESP	ABS NO.2
25	50 A	Cruise Control, CVT and Shift Indicator, Electronically Controlled Transmission and A/T Indicator, Engine Control, Mirror Heater, Rear Window Defogger	DEF
26	50 A	ABS, ESP	ABS NO.1
27	50 A	Automatic Air Conditioning, Manual Air Conditioning, PTC Heater	HTR
28	120 A	Automatic Light Control, Charging, Cruise Control, CVT and Shift Indicator, Electronically Controlled Transmission and A/T Indicator, Engine Control, Front Fog Light, Headlight, Illumination, Immobiliser System, Light Auto Turn Off System, Light Reminder, Power Window, Smart Key System, Starting, Steering Lock, Taillight, Theft Deterrent, Wireless Door Lock Control	ALT
29	10 A	Cooling Fan, Cruise Control, CVT and Shift Indicator, Electronically Controlled Transmission and A/T Indicator, Engine Control	EFI NO.1
30	10 A	Cruise Control, CVT and Shift Indicator, Electronically Controlled Transmission and A/T Indicator, Engine Control	EFI NO.2
31	5 A	Charging	WIP-S
32	10 A	Cruise Control, CVT and Shift Indicator, Electronically Controlled Transmission and A/T Indicator, Engine Control, Mirror Heater, Rear Window Defogger	MIR HTR
33	10 A	Headlight	H-LP RH-LO
34	10 A	Headlight	H-LP LH-LO
35	10 A	Headlight	H-LP RH-HI
36	10 A	Headlight	H-LP LH-HI
37	-	Not used	-
38	-	Not used	-
39	-	Not used	-
40	-	Not used	-
41	-	Not used	-
42	-	Not used	-
43	-	Not used	-

44	-	Not used	-
45	-	Not used	-
46	30 A	Automatic Air Conditioning, Manual Air Conditioning, PTC Heater	HTR SUB NO.3
47	30 A	Automatic Air Conditioning, Manual Air Conditioning, PTC Heater	HTR SUB NO.1
R1	-	Horn relay	HORN RELAY
R2	-	Dimmer relay (From August 2016)	DIM RELAY
R3	-	Injector relay	IGT/INJ RELAY
R4	-	Back-up lamp relay	BKUP LP RELAY
R5	-	Starter relay	ST NO.1 RELAY
R6	-	Main relay	EFI-MAIN RELAY
R7	-	Fan relay 1	FAN NO.1 RELAY
R8	-	Ignition relay	IG2 RELAY
R9	-	Headlamp relay	H-LP RELAY
R10	-	Compressor relay	MGC RELAY
R11	-	Horn relay	S-HORN RELAY
R12	-	Relay	DEF RELAY
R13	-	PTC heater relay 3	PTC NO.3 RELAY
R14	-	PTC heater relay 1	PTC NO.1 RELAY

RELAY IN ENGINE COMPARTMENT

UP TO JULY 2016

FUSE/RELAY	VALUE	DESCRIPTION	OEM NAME
R1	-	Dimmer relay	DIM RELAY

FROM AUGUST 2016

FUSE/RELAY	VALUE	DESCRIPTION	OEM NAME
R1	-	Daylight relay	DRL RELAY
R2	-	Stop lamp relay	STP LP RELAY

FUSE BOX IN PASSENGER COMPARTMENT 1

FUSE	VALUE	DESCRIPTION	OEM NAME
1	-	Not used	-
2	10 A	ABS, Charging, Cruise Control, CVT and Shift Indicator, Electronically Controlled Transmission and A/T Indicator, Engine Control, Immobiliser System, Shift Lock, Smart Key System, Starting, Steering Lock, Stop Light, ESP, Wireless Door Lock Control	STOP
3	7.5 A	Data Link Connector	OBD
4	-	Not used	-
5	20 A	Sliding Roof	S/ROOF
6	15 A	Steering heater	STRG HTR
7	25 A	Door Lock Control, Immobiliser System, Smart Key System, Starting, Steering Lock, Wireless Door Lock Control	D/L-ALT
8	5 A	Power Source	AM1
9	10 A	Immobiliser System, Smart Key System, Starting, Steering Lock, Wireless Door Lock Control	D/L BACK
10	20 A	Power Window	DOOR F/R
11	20 A	Power Window	DOOR R/R
12	20 A	Power Window	DOOR R/L
13	15 A	Front Wiper and Washer	WASHER
14	-	Not used	-
15	-	Not used	-
16	25 A	Charging, Front Wiper and Washer	WIPER
17	15 A	Power Outlet	P/OUTLET
18	7.5 A	ABS, Audio System, Automatic Light Control, Back-Up Light, Charging, Clock, Combination Meter, Cruise Control, CVT and Shift Indicator, Door Lock Control, Electronically Controlled Transmission and A/T Indicator, Engine Control, Front Fog Light, Headlight, Illumination, Immobiliser System, Interior Light, Key Reminder, Light Auto Turn Off System, Light Reminder, CAN, Navigation System, Power Window, Rear View Monitor System, Remote Control Mirror, Seat Belt Warning, Sliding Roof, Smart Key System, SRS, Starting, Steering Lock, Taillight, Theft Deterrent, Tire Pressure Warning System, ESP, Wireless Door Lock Control	ACC
19	5 A	Shift Lock	SFT LOCK
20	10 A	Cruise Control, CVT and Shift Indicator, Electronically Controlled Transmission and A/T Indicator, Engine Control, Front Fog Light, Headlight, Illumination, Taillight	TAIL
21	5 A	Illumination, Taillight	PANEL

22	10 A	Automatic Air Conditioning, Cruise Control, CVT and Shift Indicator, Electronically Controlled Transmission and A/T Indicator, Engine Control, Manual Air Conditioning, Mirror Heater, PTC Heater, PTC Heater, Rear Window Defogger	HTR-IG
23	10 A	ABS, Audio System, Back-Up Light, Charging, Combination Meter, Cruise Control, Cruise Control, CVT and Shift Indicator, Door Lock Control, Electronically Controlled Transmission and A/T Indicator, Engine Control, Navigation System, Rear View Monitor System, Seat Belt Warning, ESP	ECU-IG NO.2
24	5 A	EPS	ECU-IG NO.4
25	7.5 A	ABS, Automatic Light Control, Combination Meter, Door Lock Control, Front Fog Light, Headlight, Illumination, Immobiliser System, Interior Light, Key Reminder, Light Auto Turn Off System, Light Reminder, Power Window, Seat Belt Warning, Sliding Roof, Smart Key System, SRS, Starting, Steering Lock, Taillight, Theft Deterrent, Tire Pressure Warning System, ESP, Wireless Door Lock Control	ECU-IG NO.1
26	7.5 A	ABS, Audio System, Automatic Glare-Resistant EC Mirror, Cruise Control, Cruise Control, CVT and Shift Indicator, Electronically Controlled Transmission and A/T Indicator, Engine Control, Garage Door Opener, CAN, Navigation System, Rear View Monitor System, Seat Belt Warning, Shift Lock Sliding Roof, SRS, Stop Light, Tire Pressure Warning System, ESP	ECU-IG NO.3
27	7.5 A	Cruise Control, CVT and Shift Indicator, Electronically Controlled Transmission and A/T Indicator, Engine Control, Immobiliser System, CAN, Smart Key System, Starting, Steering Lock, Wireless Door Lock Control	IGN
28	10 A	Seat Belt Warning, SRS	A/B
29	5 A	ABS, Audio System, Automatic Air Conditioning, Charging, Combination Meter, Cruise Control, CVT and Shift Indicator, Electronically Controlled Transmission and A/T Indicator, Engine Control, EPS, Headlight, Illumination, Immobiliser System, Key Reminder, Light Reminder, Navigation System, PTC Heater, Rear View Monitor System, Seat Belt Warning, Sliding Roof, Smart Key System, SRS, Starting, Steering Lock, Taillight, Theft Deterrent, Tire Pressure Warning System, ESP, Turn Signal and Hazard Warning Light, Wireless Door Lock Control	METER
30	15 A	Seat Heater	S/HTR F/R
31	15 A	Seat Heater	S/HTR F/L
32	-	Not used	-

FUSE BOX IN PASSENGER COMPARTMENT 1

FUSE	VALUE	DESCRIPTION	OEM NAME
1	30 A	Power Seat	P/SEAT F/L
2	-	Not used	-
3	-	Not used	-
4	30 A	Power Window	POWER

Notes

Index

Notes

Haynes Automotive Manuals

NOTE: If you do not see a listing for your vehicle, please visit our website haynes.com for the latest product information.

ACURA
- **12020 Integra** '86 thru '89 **& Legend** '86 thru '90
- **12021 Integra** '90 thru '93 **& Legend** '91 thru '95
- **Integra** '94 thru '00 - *see HONDA Civic (42025)*
- **MDX** '01 thru '07 - *see HONDA Pilot (42037)*
- **12050 Acura TL** all models '99 thru '08

AMC
- **Jeep CJ** - *see JEEP (50020)*
- **14020 Mid-size models** '70 thru '83
- **14025 (Renault) Alliance & Encore** '83 thru '87

AUDI
- **15020 4000** all models '80 thru '87
- **15025 5000** all models '77 thru '83
- **15026 5000** all models '84 thru '88
- **Audi A4** '96 thru '01 - *see VW Passat (96023)*
- **15030 Audi A4** '02 thru '08

AUSTIN-HEALEY
- **Sprite** - *see MG Midget (66015)*

BMW
- **18020 3/5 Series** '82 thru '92
- **18021 3-Series** incl. Z3 models '92 thru '98
- **18022 3-Series** incl. Z4 models '99 thru '05
- **18023 3-Series** '06 thru '10
- **18025 320i** all 4 cyl models '75 thru '83
- **18050 1500 thru 2002** except Turbo '59 thru '77

BUICK
- **19010 Buick Century** '97 thru '05
- **Century** (front-wheel drive) - *see GM (38005)*
- **19020 Buick, Oldsmobile & Pontiac Full-size** **(Front-wheel drive)** '85 thru '05
  Buick Electra, LeSabre and Park Avenue; Oldsmobile Delta 88 Royale, Ninety Eight and Regency; Pontiac Bonneville
- **19025 Buick, Oldsmobile & Pontiac Full-size** **(Rear wheel drive)** '70 thru '90
  Buick Estate, Electra, LeSabre, Limited, Oldsmobile Custom Cruiser, Delta 88, Ninety-eight, Pontiac Bonneville, Catalina, Grandville, Parisienne
- **19030 Mid-size Regal & Century** all rear-drive models with V6, V8 and Turbo '74 thru '87
  Regal - *see GENERAL MOTORS (38010)*
  Riviera - *see GENERAL MOTORS (38030)*
  Roadmaster - *see CHEVROLET (24046)*
  Skyhawk - *see GENERAL MOTORS (38015)*
  Skylark - *see GM (38020, 38025)*
  Somerset - *see GENERAL MOTORS (38025)*

CADILLAC
- **21015 CTS & CTS-V** '03 thru '12
- **21030 Cadillac Rear Wheel Drive** '70 thru '93
  Cimarron - *see GENERAL MOTORS (38015)*
  DeVille - *see GM (38031 & 38032)*
  Eldorado - *see GM (38030 & 38031)*
  Fleetwood - *see GM (38031)*
  Seville - *see GM (38030, 38031 & 38032)*

CHEVROLET
- **10305 Chevrolet Engine Overhaul Manual**
- **24010 Astro & GMC Safari Mini-vans** '85 thru '05
- **24015 Camaro V8** all models '70 thru '81
- **24016 Camaro** all models '82 thru '92
- **24017 Camaro & Firebird** '93 thru '02
  Cavalier - *see GENERAL MOTORS (38016)*
  Celebrity - *see GENERAL MOTORS (38005)*
- **24020 Chevelle, Malibu & El Camino** '69 thru '87
- **24024 Chevette & Pontiac T1000** '76 thru '87
  Citation - *see GENERAL MOTORS (38020)*
- **24027 Colorado & GMC Canyon** '04 thru '10
- **24032 Corsica/Beretta** all models '87 thru '96
- **24040 Corvette** all V8 models '68 thru '82
- **24041 Corvette** all models '84 thru '96
- **24045 Full-size Sedans** Caprice, Impala, Biscayne, Bel Air & Wagons '69 thru '90
- **24046 Impala SS & Caprice and Buick Roadmaster** '91 thru '96
  Impala '00 thru '05 - *see LUMINA (24048)*
- **24047 Impala & Monte Carlo** all models '06 thru '11
  Lumina '90 thru '94 - *see GM (38010)*
- **24048 Lumina & Monte Carlo** '95 thru '05
  Lumina APV - *see GM (38035)*
- **24050 Luv Pick-up** all 2WD & 4WD '72 thru '82
  Malibu '97 thru '00 - *see GM (38026)*
- **24055 Monte Carlo** all models '70 thru '88
  Monte Carlo '95 thru '01 - *see LUMINA (24048)*
- **24059 Nova** all V8 models '69 thru '79
- **24060 Nova and Geo Prizm** '85 thru '92
- **24064 Pick-ups** '67 thru '87 - Chevrolet & GMC
- **24065 Pick-ups** '88 thru '98 - Chevrolet & GMC

- **24066 Pick-ups** '99 thru '06 - Chevrolet & GMC
- **24067 Chevrolet Silverado & GMC Sierra** '07 thru '12
- **24070 S-10 & S-15 Pick-ups** '82 thru '93, Blazer & Jimmy '83 thru '94,
- **24071 S-10 & Sonoma Pick-ups** '94 thru '04, including Blazer, Jimmy & Hombre
- **24072 Chevrolet TrailBlazer, GMC Envoy & Oldsmobile Bravada** '02 thru '09
- **24075 Sprint** '85 thru '88 **& Geo Metro** '89 thru '01
- **24080 Vans** - Chevrolet & GMC '68 thru '96
- **24081 Chevrolet Express & GMC Savana** Full-size Vans '96 thru '10

CHRYSLER
- **10310 Chrysler Engine Overhaul Manual**
- **25015 Chrysler Cirrus, Dodge Stratus, Plymouth Breeze** '95 thru '00
- **25020 Full-size Front-Wheel Drive** '88 thru '93
  K-Cars - *see DODGE Aries (30008)*
  Laser - *see DODGE Daytona (30030)*
- **25025 Chrysler LHS, Concorde, New Yorker, Dodge Intrepid, Eagle Vision**, '93 thru '97
- **25026 Chrysler LHS, Concorde, 300M, Dodge Intrepid**, '98 thru '04
- **25027 Chrysler 300, Dodge Charger & Magnum** '05 thru '09
- **25030 Chrysler & Plymouth Mid-size** front wheel drive '82 thru '95
  Rear-wheel Drive - *see Dodge (30050)*
- **25035 PT Cruiser** all models '01 thru '10
- **25040 Chrysler Sebring** '95 thru '06, **Dodge** Stratus '01 thru '06, **Dodge** Avenger '95 thru '00

DATSUN
- **28005 200SX** all models '80 thru '83
- **28007 B-210** all models '73 thru '78
- **28009 210** all models '79 thru '82
- **28012 240Z, 260Z & 280Z** Coupe '70 thru '78
- **28014 280ZX** Coupe & 2+2 '79 thru '83
  300ZX - *see NISSAN (72010)*
- **28018 510 & PL521 Pick-up** '68 thru '73
- **28020 510** all models '78 thru '81
- **28022 620 Series Pick-up** all models '73 thru '79
  720 Series Pick-up - *see NISSAN (72030)*
- **28025 810/Maxima** all gasoline models '77 thru '84

DODGE
- **400 & 600** - *see CHRYSLER (25030)*
- **30008 Aries & Plymouth Reliant** '81 thru '89
- **30010 Caravan & Plymouth Voyager** '84 thru '95
- **30011 Caravan & Plymouth Voyager** '96 thru '02
- **30012 Challenger/Plymouth Saporro** '78 thru '83
- **30013 Caravan, Chrysler Voyager, Town & Country** '03 thru '07
- **30016 Colt & Plymouth Champ** '78 thru '87
- **30020 Dakota Pick-ups** all models '87 thru '96
- **30021 Durango** '98 & '99, **Dakota** '97 thru '99
- **30022 Durango** '00 thru '03 **Dakota** '00 thru '04
- **30023 Durango** '04 thru '09, **Dakota** '05 thru '11
- **30025 Dart, Demon, Plymouth Barracuda, Duster & Valiant** 6 cyl models '67 thru '76
- **30030 Daytona & Chrysler Laser** '84 thru '89
  Intrepid - *see CHRYSLER (25025, 25026)*
- **30034 Neon** all models '95 thru '99
- **30035 Omni & Plymouth Horizon** '78 thru '90
- **30036 Dodge and Plymouth Neon** '00 thru '05
- **30040 Pick-ups** all full-size models '74 thru '93
- **30041 Pick-ups** all full-size models '94 thru '01
- **30042 Pick-ups** full-size models '02 thru '08
- **30045 Ram 50/D50 Pick-ups & Raider and Plymouth Arrow Pick-ups** '79 thru '93
- **30050 Dodge/Plymouth/Chrysler RWD** '71 thru '89
- **30055 Shadow & Plymouth Sundance** '87 thru '94
- **30060 Spirit & Plymouth Acclaim** '89 thru '95
- **30065 Vans** - Dodge & Plymouth '71 thru '03

EAGLE
- **Talon** - *see MITSUBISHI (68030, 68031)*
- **Vision** - *see CHRYSLER (25025)*

FIAT
- **34010 124 Sport Coupe & Spider** '68 thru '78
- **34025 X1/9** all models '74 thru '80

FORD
- **10320 Ford Engine Overhaul Manual**
- **10355 Ford Automatic Transmission Overhaul**
- **11500 Mustang** '64-1/2 thru '70 Restoration Guide
- **36004 Aerostar Mini-vans** all models '86 thru '97
- **36006 Contour & Mercury Mystique** '95 thru '00
- **36008 Courier Pick-up** all models '72 thru '82
- **36012 Crown Victoria & Mercury Grand Marquis** '88 thru '10
- **36016 Escort/Mercury Lynx** all models '81 thru '90
- **36020 Escort/Mercury Tracer** '91 thru '02

- **36022 Escape & Mazda Tribute** '01 thru '11
- **36024 Explorer & Mazda Navajo** '91 thru '01
- **36025 Explorer/Mercury Mountaineer** '02 thru '10
- **36028 Fairmont & Mercury Zephyr** '78 thru '83
- **36030 Festiva & Aspire** '88 thru '97
- **36032 Fiesta** all models '77 thru '80
- **36034 Focus** all models '00 thru '11
- **36036 Ford & Mercury Full-size** '75 thru '87
- **36044 Ford & Mercury Mid-size** '75 thru '86
- **36045 Fusion & Mercury Milan** '06 thru '10
- **36048 Mustang V8** all models '64-1/2 thru '73
- **36049 Mustang II** 4 cyl, V6 & V8 models '74 thru '78
- **36050 Mustang & Mercury Capri** '79 thru '93
- **36051 Mustang** all models '94 thru '04
- **36052 Mustang** '05 thru '10
- **36054 Pick-ups & Bronco** '73 thru '79
- **36058 Pick-ups & Bronco** '80 thru '96
- **36059 F-150 & Expedition** '97 thru '09, **F-250** '97 thru '99 **& Lincoln Navigator** '98 thru '09
- **36060 Super Duty Pick-ups, Excursion** '99 thru '10
- **36061 F-150 full-size** '04 thru '10
- **36062 Pinto & Mercury Bobcat** '75 thru '80
- **36066 Probe** all models '89 thru '92
  Probe '93 thru '97 - *see MAZDA 626 (61042)*
- **36070 Ranger/Bronco II** gasoline models '83 thru '92
- **36071 Ranger** '93 thru '10 **& Mazda Pick-ups** '94 thru '09
- **36074 Taurus & Mercury Sable** '86 thru '95
- **36075 Taurus & Mercury Sable** '96 thru '05
- **36078 Tempo & Mercury Topaz** '84 thru '94
- **36082 Thunderbird/Mercury Cougar** '83 thru '88
- **36086 Thunderbird/Mercury Cougar** '89 thru '97
- **36090 Vans** all V8 Econoline models '69 thru '91
- **36094 Vans** full size '92 thru '10
- **36097 Windstar Mini-van** '95 thru '07

GENERAL MOTORS
- **10360 GM Automatic Transmission Overhaul**
- **38005 Buick Century, Chevrolet Celebrity, Oldsmobile Cutlass Ciera & Pontiac 6000** all models '82 thru '96
- **38010 Buick Regal, Chevrolet Lumina, Oldsmobile Cutlass Supreme & Pontiac Grand Prix** (FWD) '88 thru '07
- **38015 Buick Skyhawk, Cadillac Cimarron, Chevrolet Cavalier, Oldsmobile Firenza & Pontiac J-2000 & Sunbird** '82 thru '94
- **38016 Chevrolet Cavalier & Pontiac Sunfire** '95 thru '05
- **38017 Chevrolet Cobalt & Pontiac G5** '05 thru '11
- **38020 Buick Skylark, Chevrolet Citation, Olds Omega, Pontiac Phoenix** '80 thru '85
- **38025 Buick Skylark & Somerset, Oldsmobile Achieva & Calais and Pontiac Grand Am** all models '85 thru '98
- **38026 Chevrolet Malibu, Olds Alero & Cutlass, Pontiac Grand Am** '97 thru '03
- **38027 Chevrolet Malibu** '04 thru '10
- **38030 Cadillac Eldorado, Seville, Oldsmobile Toronado, Buick Riviera** '71 thru '85
- **38031 Cadillac Eldorado & Seville, DeVille, Fleetwood & Olds Toronado, Buick Riviera** '86 thru '93
- **38032 Cadillac DeVille** '94 thru '05 **& Seville** '92 thru '04 **Cadillac DTS** '06 thru '10
- **38035 Chevrolet Lumina APV, Olds Silhouette & Pontiac Trans Sport** all models '90 thru '96
- **38036 Chevrolet Venture, Olds Silhouette, Pontiac Trans Sport & Montana** '97 thru '05
  General Motors Full-size Rear-wheel Drive - *see BUICK (19025)*
- **38040 Chevrolet Equinox** '05 thru '09 **Pontiac Torrent** '06 thru '09
- **38070 Chevrolet HHR** '06 thru '11

GEO
- **Metro** - *see CHEVROLET Sprint (24075)*
- **Prizm** - '85 thru '92 see CHEVY (24060), '93 thru '02 see TOYOTA Corolla (92036)
- **40030 Storm** all models '90 thru '93
  Tracker - *see SUZUKI Samurai (90010)*

GMC
- **Vans & Pick-ups** - *see CHEVROLET*

HONDA
- **42010 Accord CVCC** all models '76 thru '83
- **42011 Accord** all models '84 thru '89
- **42012 Accord** all models '90 thru '93
- **42013 Accord** all models '94 thru '97
- **42014 Accord** all models '98 thru '02
- **42015 Accord** '03 thru '07
- **42020 Civic 1200** all models '73 thru '79
- **42021 Civic 1300 & 1500 CVCC** '80 thru '83
- **42022 Civic 1500 CVCC** all models '75 thru '79

(Continued on other side)

Haynes North America, Inc., 859 Lawrence Drive, Newbury Park, CA 91320-1514 • (805) 498-6703 • www.haynes.com

Haynes Automotive Manuals (continued)

NOTE: If you do not see a listing for your vehicle, please visit our website *haynes.com* for the latest product information.

42023 Civic all models '84 thru '91
42024 Civic & del Sol '92 thru '95
42025 Civic '96 thru '00, CR-V '97 thru '01, Acura Integra '94 thru '00
42026 Civic '01 thru '10, CR-V '02 thru '09
42035 Odyssey all models '99 thru '10 Passport - see ISUZU Rodeo (47017)
42037 Honda Pilot '03 thru '07, Acura MDX '01 thru '07
42040 Prelude CVCC all models '79 thru '89

HYUNDAI
43010 Elantra all models '96 thru '10
43015 Excel & Accent all models '86 thru '09
43050 Santa Fe all models '01 thru '06
43055 Sonata all models '99 thru '08

INFINITI
G35 '03 thru '08 - see NISSAN 350Z (72011)

ISUZU
Hombre - see CHEVROLET S-10 (24071)
47017 Rodeo, Amigo & Honda Passport '89 thru '02
47020 Trooper & Pick-up '81 thru '93

JAGUAR
49010 XJ6 all 6 cyl models '68 thru '86
49011 XJ6 all models '88 thru '94
49015 XJ12 & XJS all 12 cyl models '72 thru '85

JEEP
50010 Cherokee, Comanche & Wagoneer Limited all models '84 thru '01
50020 CJ all models '49 thru '86
50025 Grand Cherokee all models '93 thru '04
50026 Grand Cherokee '05 thru '09
50029 Grand Wagoneer & Pick-up '72 thru '91 Grand Wagoneer '84 thru '91, Cherokee & Wagoneer '72 thru '83, Pick-up '72 thru '88
50030 Wrangler all models '87 thru '11
50035 Liberty '02 thru '07

KIA
54050 Optima '01 thru '10
54070 Sephia '94 thru '01, Spectra '00 thru '09, Sportage '05 thru '10

LEXUS
ES 300/330 - see TOYOTA Camry (92007) (92008)
RX 330 - see TOYOTA Highlander (92095)

LINCOLN
Navigator - see FORD Pick-up (36059)
59010 Rear-Wheel Drive all models '70 thru '10

MAZDA
61010 GLC Hatchback (rear-wheel drive) '77 thru '83
61011 GLC (front-wheel drive) '81 thru '85
61012 Mazda3 '04 thru '11
61015 323 & Protogé '90 thru '03
61016 MX-5 Miata '90 thru '09
61020 MPV all models '89 thru '98 Navajo - see Ford Explorer (36024)
61030 Pick-ups '72 thru '93 Pick-ups '94 thru '00 - see Ford Ranger (36071)
61035 RX-7 all models '79 thru '85
61036 RX-7 all models '86 thru '91
61040 626 (rear-wheel drive) all models '79 thru '82
61041 626/MX-6 (front-wheel drive) '83 thru '92
61042 626, MX-6/Ford Probe '93 thru '02
61043 Mazda6 '03 thru '11

MERCEDES-BENZ
63012 123 Series Diesel '76 thru '85
63015 190 Series four-cyl gas models, '84 thru '88
63020 230/250/280 6 cyl sohc models '68 thru '72
63025 280 123 Series gasoline models '77 thru '81
63030 350 & 450 all models '71 thru '80
63040 C-Class: C230/C240/C280/C320/C350 '01 thru '07

MERCURY
64200 Villager & Nissan Quest '93 thru '01 All other titles, see FORD Listing.

MG
66010 MGB Roadster & GT Coupe '62 thru '80
66015 MG Midget, Austin Healey Sprite '58 thru '80

MINI
67020 Mini '02 thru '11

MITSUBISHI
68020 Cordia, Tredia, Galant, Precis & Mirage '83 thru '93
68030 Eclipse, Eagle Talon & Ply. Laser '90 thru '94
68031 Eclipse '95 thru '05, Eagle Talon '95 thru '98
68035 Galant '94 thru '12
68040 Pick-up '83 thru '96 & Montero '83 thru '93

NISSAN
72010 300ZX all models including Turbo '84 thru '89
72011 350Z & Infiniti G35 all models '03 thru '08
72015 Altima all models '93 thru '06
72016 Altima '07 thru '10
72020 Maxima all models '85 thru '92
72021 Maxima all models '93 thru '04
72025 Murano '03 thru '10
72030 Pick-ups '80 thru '97 Pathfinder '87 thru '95
72031 Frontier Pick-up, Xterra, Pathfinder '96 thru '04
72032 Frontier & Xterra '05 thru '11
72040 Pulsar all models '83 thru '86 Quest - see MERCURY Villager (64200)
72050 Sentra all models '82 thru '94
72051 Sentra & 200SX all models '95 thru '06
72060 Stanza all models '82 thru '90
72070 Titan pick-ups '04 thru '10 Armada '05 thru '10

OLDSMOBILE
73015 Cutlass V6 & V8 gas models '74 thru '88 For other OLDSMOBILE titles, see BUICK, CHEVROLET or GENERAL MOTORS listing.

PLYMOUTH
For PLYMOUTH titles, see DODGE listing.

PONTIAC
79008 Fiero all models '84 thru '88
79018 Firebird V8 models except Turbo '70 thru '81
79019 Firebird all models '82 thru '92
79025 G6 all models '05 thru '09
79040 Mid-size Rear-wheel Drive '70 thru '87 Vibe '03 thru '11 - see TOYOTA Matrix (92060) For other PONTIAC titles, see BUICK, CHEVROLET or GENERAL MOTORS listing.

PORSCHE
80020 911 except Turbo & Carrera 4 '65 thru '89
80025 914 all 4 cyl models '69 thru '76
80030 924 all models including Turbo '76 thru '82
80035 944 all models including Turbo '83 thru '89

RENAULT
Alliance & Encore - see AMC (14020)

SAAB
84010 900 all models including Turbo '79 thru '88

SATURN
87010 Saturn all S-series models '91 thru '02
87011 Saturn Ion '03 thru '07
87020 Saturn all L-series models '00 thru '04
87040 Saturn VUE '02 thru '07

SUBARU
89002 1100, 1300, 1400 & 1600 '71 thru '79
89003 1600 & 1800 2WD & 4WD '80 thru '94
89100 Legacy all models '90 thru '99
89101 Legacy & Forester '00 thru '06

SUZUKI
90010 Samurai/Sidekick & Geo Tracker '86 thru '01

TOYOTA
92005 Camry all models '83 thru '91
92006 Camry all models '92 thru '96
92007 Camry, Avalon, Solara, Lexus ES 300 '97 thru '01
92008 Toyota Camry, Avalon and Solara and Lexus ES 300/330 all models '02 thru '06
92009 Camry '07 thru '11
92015 Celica Rear Wheel Drive '71 thru '85
92020 Celica Front Wheel Drive '86 thru '99
92025 Celica Supra all models '79 thru '92
92030 Corolla all models '75 thru '79
92032 Corolla all rear wheel drive models '80 thru '87
92035 Corolla all front wheel drive models '84 thru '92
92036 Corolla & Geo Prizm '93 thru '02
92037 Corolla models '03 thru '11
92040 Corolla Tercel all models '80 thru '82
92045 Corona all models '74 thru '82
92050 Cressida all models '78 thru '82
92055 Land Cruiser FJ40, 43, 45, 55 '68 thru '82
92056 Land Cruiser FJ60, 62, 80, FZJ80 '80 thru '96
92060 Matrix & Pontiac Vibe '03 thru '11
92065 MR2 all models '85 thru '87
92070 Pick-up all models '69 thru '78
92075 Pick-up all models '79 thru '95
92076 Tacoma, 4Runner, & T100 '93 thru '04
92077 Tacoma all models '05 thru '09
92078 Tundra '00 thru '06 & Sequoia '01 thru '07
92079 4Runner all models '03 thru '09
92080 Previa all models '91 thru '95
92081 Prius all models '01 thru '08
92082 RAV4 all models '96 thru '10
92085 Tercel all models '87 thru '94
92090 Sienna all models '98 thru '09
92095 Highlander & Lexus RX-330 '99 thru '07

TRIUMPH
94007 Spitfire all models '62 thru '81
94010 TR7 all models '75 thru '81

VW
96008 Beetle & Karmann Ghia '54 thru '79
96009 New Beetle '98 thru '11
96016 Rabbit, Jetta, Scirocco & Pick-up gas models '75 thru '92 & Convertible '80 thru '92
96017 Golf, GTI & Jetta '93 thru '98, Cabrio '95 thru '02
96018 Golf, GTI, Jetta '99 thru '05
96019 Jetta, Rabbit, GTI & Golf '05 thru '11
96020 Rabbit, Jetta & Pick-up diesel '77 thru '84
96023 Passat '98 thru '05, Audi A4 '96 thru '01
96030 Transporter 1600 all models '68 thru '79
96035 Transporter 1700, 1800 & 2000 '72 thru '79
96040 Type 3 1500 & 1600 all models '63 thru '73
96045 Vanagon all air-cooled models '80 thru '83

VOLVO
97010 120, 130 Series & 1800 Sports '61 thru '73
97015 140 Series all models '66 thru '74
97020 240 Series all models '76 thru '93
97040 740 & 760 Series all models '82 thru '88
97050 850 Series all models '93 thru '97

TECHBOOK MANUALS
10205 Automotive Computer Codes
10206 OBD-II & Electronic Engine Management
10210 Automotive Emissions Control Manual
10215 Fuel Injection Manual '78 thru '85
10220 Fuel Injection Manual '86 thru '99
10225 Holley Carburetor Manual
10230 Rochester Carburetor Manual
10240 Weber/Zenith/Stromberg/SU Carburetors
10305 Chevrolet Engine Overhaul Manual
10310 Chrysler Engine Overhaul Manual
10320 Ford Engine Overhaul Manual
10330 GM and Ford Diesel Engine Repair Manual
10333 Engine Performance Manual
10340 Small Engine Repair Manual, 5 HP & Less
10341 Small Engine Repair Manual, 5.5 - 20 HP
10345 Suspension, Steering & Driveline Manual
10355 Ford Automatic Transmission Overhaul
10360 GM Automatic Transmission Overhaul
10405 Automotive Body Repair & Painting
10410 Automotive Brake Manual
10411 Automotive Anti-lock Brake (ABS) Systems
10415 Automotive Detailing Manual
10420 Automotive Electrical Manual
10425 Automotive Heating & Air Conditioning
10430 Automotive Reference Manual & Dictionary
10435 Automotive Tools Manual
10440 Used Car Buying Guide
10445 Welding Manual
10450 ATV Basics
10452 Scooters 50cc to 250cc

SPANISH MANUALS
98903 Reparación de Carrocería & Pintura
98904 Manual de Carburador Modelos Holley & Rochester
98905 Códigos Automotrices de la Computadora
98906 OBD-II & Sistemas de Control Electrónico del Motor
98910 Frenos Automotriz
98913 Electricidad Automotriz
98915 Inyección de Combustible '86 al '99
99040 Chevrolet & GMC Camionetas '67 al '87
99041 Chevrolet & GMC Camionetas '88 al '98
99042 Chevrolet & GMC Camionetas Cerradas '68 al '95
99043 Chevrolet/GMC Camionetas '94 al '04
99048 Chevrolet/GMC Camionetas '99 al '06
99055 Dodge Caravan & Plymouth Voyager '84 al '95
99075 Ford Camionetas y Bronco '80 al '94
99076 Ford F-150 '97 al '09
99077 Ford Camionetas Cerradas '69 al '91
99088 Ford Modelos de Tamaño Mediano '75 al '86
99089 Ford Camionetas Ranger '93 al '10
99091 Ford Taurus & Mercury Sable '86 al '95
99095 GM Modelos de Tamaño Grande '70 al '90
99100 GM Modelos de Tamaño Mediano '70 al '88
99106 Jeep Cherokee, Wagoneer & Comanche '84 al '00
99110 Nissan Camioneta '80 al '96, Pathfinder '87 al '95
99118 Nissan Sentra '82 al '94
99125 Toyota Camionetas y 4Runner '79 al '95

Over 100 Haynes motorcycle manuals also available

5/22

Haynes North America, Inc., 859 Lawrence Drive, Newbury Park, CA 91320-1514 • (805) 498-6703 • www.haynes.com